THE ROUTLEDGE INTERNATIONAL HANDBOOK OF CRIMINAL RESPONSIBILITY

Presenting cutting-edge research and scholarship, this extensive volume covers everything from abstract theorising about the meanings of responsibility and how we blame, to analysing criminal law and justice responses, and factors that impact individual responsibility.

Inviting exchanges across a burgeoning critical scholarship on criminal responsibility, this Handbook showcases the diverse range of methodologies applied to the field, including sociopolitical approaches, critical historical methods, criminological and sociological perspectives, and interdisciplinary studies bridging law and the mind sciences. Spanning global networks of established and emerging scholars of responsibility for crime, this book explores how we relate to one another as human beings under the spotlight of the criminal law. In doing so, it is hoped that the collection not only does justice to the vibrant landscape of criminal responsibility studies, but inspires new directions and future synergies in this compelling field.

The Routledge International Handbook of Criminal Responsibility will appeal to scholars and students of criminal law, criminal justice, criminology, sociology, psychology, neuroscience, philosophy, and socio-legal studies, as well as practitioners and policymakers working in related fields.

Thomas Crofts is a Professor in the School of Law and in the Department of Social and Behavioural Sciences at City University Hong Kong, and an Adjunct Professor at Northumbria University, Queensland University of Technology, and the University of Sydney. His research in comparative criminal law and criminal justice focuses on criminalisation and criminal responsibility, particularly in relation to young people, gender, and sexuality.

Louise Kennefick is Senior Lecturer in Criminal Law at the University of Glasgow. She researches across the fields of criminal law theory and criminal justice. Her monograph, *The Boundaries of Blame: Towards a Universal Partial Defence for the Criminal Law*, is forthcoming.

Arlie Loughnan is Professor of Criminal Law and Criminal Law Theory at the University of Sydney. Her interests range across criminal law, legal theory, and legal history. She is the author of *Self, Others and the State: Relations of Criminal Responsibility* (2020) and *Manifest Madness: Mental Incapacity in Criminal Law* (2012).

ROUTLEDGE INTERNATIONAL HANDBOOKS

THE ROUTLEDGE INTERNATIONAL HANDBOOK OF VALUATION AND SOCIETY
Edited by Anne K. Krüger, Thorsten Peetz, and Hilmar Schäfer

THE ROUTLEDGE HANDBOOK ON MEANINGFUL STAKEHOLDER ENGAGEMENT
Edited by Karin Buhmann, Alberto Fonseca, Nathan Andrews and Giuseppe Amatulli

ROUTLEDGE INTERNATIONAL HANDBOOK OF COMPLEXITY ECONOMICS
Edited by Ping Chen, Wolfram Elsner and Andreas Pyka

THE ROUTLEDGE INTERNATIONAL HANDBOOK OF PUBLIC ADMINISTRATION AND DIGITAL GOVERNANCE
Edited by Sarah Giest and Ian Roberge

ROUTLEDGE INTERNATIONAL HANDBOOK OF CRITICAL POLICING STUDIES
Edited by Nicole L. Asquith, Jess Rodgers, James Clover, Gary Cordner, Angela Dwyer and Rishweena Ahmed

THE ROUTLEDGE INTERNATIONAL HANDBOOK OF SOCIAL WORK AND DISASTER PRACTICE
Edited by Carole Adamson, Margaret Alston, Bindi Bennett, Jennifer Boddy, Heather Boetto, Louise Harms, and Raewyn Tudor

THE ROUTLEDGE INTERNATIONAL HANDBOOK OF CRIMINAL RESPONSIBILITY
Edited by Thomas Crofts, Louise Kennefick, and Arlie Loughnan

THE ROUTLEDGE INTERNATIONAL HANDBOOK OF CRIMINAL RESPONSIBILITY

Edited by Thomas Crofts, Louise Kennefick, and Arlie Loughnan

LONDON AND NEW YORK

Designed cover image: Getty Images

First published 2025
by Routledge
4 Park Square, Milton Park, Abingdon, Oxon OX14 4RN

and by Routledge
605 Third Avenue, New York, NY 10158

Routledge is an imprint of the Taylor & Francis Group, an informa business

© 2025 selection and editorial matter, Thomas Crofts, Louise Kennefick, and Arlie Loughnan; individual chapters, the contributors

The right of Thomas Crofts, Louise Kennefick, and Arlie Loughnan to be identified as the authors of the editorial material, and of the authors for their individual chapters, has been asserted in accordance with sections 77 and 78 of the Copyright, Designs and Patents Act 1988.

All rights reserved. No part of this book may be reprinted or reproduced or utilised in any form or by any electronic, mechanical, or other means, now known or hereafter invented, including photocopying and recording, or in any information storage or retrieval system, without permission in writing from the publishers.

Trademark notice: Product or corporate names may be trademarks or registered trademarks, and are used only for identification and explanation without intent to infringe.

British Library Cataloguing-in-Publication Data
A catalogue record for this book is available from the British Library

Library of Congress Cataloging-in-Publication Data
Names: Crofts, Thomas (Wayne Thomas), editor. | Kennefick, Louise, editor. | Loughnan, Arlie, editor.
Title: The Routledge international handbook on criminal responsibility / edited by Thomas Crofts, Louise Kennefick, and Arlie Loughnan.
Description: Abingdon, Oxon [UK] ; New York, NY : Routledge, 2025. | Series: Routledge international handbooks | Includes bibliographical references and index.
Identifiers: LCCN 2024030069 (print) | LCCN 2024030070 (ebook) | ISBN 9781032284439 (hbk) | ISBN 9781032285313 (pbk) | ISBN 9781003297260 (ebk)
Subjects: LCSH: Criminal liability (International law)
Classification: LCC KZ7094 .R68 2025 (print) | LCC KZ7094 (ebook) | DDC 345/.04–dc23/eng/20241022
LC record available at https://lccn.loc.gov/2024030069
LC ebook record available at https://lccn.loc.gov/2024030070

ISBN: 9781032284439 (hbk)
ISBN: 9781032285313 (pbk)
ISBN: 9781003297260 (ebk)

DOI: 10.4324/9781003297260

Typeset in Galliard
by Newgen Publishing UK

CONTENTS

Contributors   *ix*
Foreword   *xiv*

Introduction   1
Thomas Crofts, Louise Kennefick, and Arlie Loughnan

PART I
Foundations of criminal responsibility   11

1 Cultures of responsibility and blaming   13
 Henrique Carvalho

2 Context matters: An argument for a socio-contextual model of criminal responsibility   26
 Federica Coppola

3 The reciprocity of criminal responsibility   37
 Antony Duff

4 Criminal responsibility, civilisation, and empire   47
 Catherine L Evans

5 Criminal responsibility attribution as a step on the road to desistance? Exploring theoretical intersections   59
 Louise Kennefick

Contents

6 Responsibility and "blameworthiness" in criminal law 82
   Claes Lernestedt & Matt Matravers

7 Criminal responsibility, mental disorder, and behavioural neuroscience 93
   Stephen J Morse

8 Criminal responsibility in the Italian colonies: The eritrean case (Nineteenth–Twentieth Centuries) 111
   Emilia Musumeci

9 On dispositional–relational responsibility: from punishment to reconciliation 123
   Alan Norrie and Amanda Wilson

10 From casuistry to the general part: the conception of criminal responsibility from the *ius commune* to the penal codes (Twelfth–Nineteenth Centuries) 138
   Michele Pifferi

PART II
Doctrines and principles of criminal responsibility 153

11 Law, emotions, and "reactive defences" 155
   Grant Barclay

12 Recklessness and negligence in the criminal law 169
   Marcia Baron

13 The denial/defence and offence/defence distinction: Rehabilitating gardner to answer the incorporationist challenge 181
   David Campbell

14 The criminal law of triage: a rights-based approach to justificatory defences 193
   Ivó Coca-Vila

15 Responsibility over crime and tort 206
   Matthew Dyson

16	Criminal responsibility for market misconduct *Lindsay Farmer*	219
17	Elements of blameworthiness in the law of homicide: harmfulness, wrongness, and culpability *Stuart P Green*	232
18	Criminal insanity and mental disorder: Reconsidering the relation *Linda Gröning*	246
19	Comparing criminal and civil responsibility: contextualising claims to distinctiveness *Chloë Kennedy*	258
20	Criminal responsibility under changing knowledge conditions *Arlie Loughnan*	272
21	Forms of duress as defence and mitigation *Martin Wasik*	289

PART III
Domains of criminal responsibility — 305

22	Corporate accountability for international crimes: Towards an international enforcement mechanism *Evelyne Owiye Asaala*	307
23	Disclosure of childhood criminal records in england and wales: Imposing enduring criminal responsibility for childhood behaviours *Raymond Arthur*	319
24	Stuck in time: The minimum age of criminal responsibility in England and wales *Tim Bateman*	332
25	Corporate criminal ir/responsibility *Penny Crofts*	343
26	Rethinking the age of criminal responsibility *Thomas Crofts*	360

Contents

27 Neurotechnology and the insanity defence 376
   Allan McCay

28 Criminal capacity and the age of criminal responsibility:
   Dissecting the assumptions underlying a single chronological age 392
   Claire McDiarmid

29 Organisational culture, industry norms, and corporate wrongdoing:
   A new integrated theory of crime prevention 406
   Joe McGrath

30 Ecocide, ecojustice, and criminal responsibility in international law 423
   Liana Georgieva Minkova

31 Criminal responsibility in children 440
   Anthony Pillay

Index 453

CONTRIBUTORS

Raymond Arthur is a Professor of Law at the Northumbria University in the UK and is a Fellow of the Academy of Social Sciences. He specialises in researching children's right to self-determination in justice settings and developing a deeper understanding of the experiences of vulnerable young people of navigating legal processes and systems.

Evelyne Owiye Asaala is a Senior Lecturer of Law at the University of Nairobi, Kenya. She holds a PhD from the University of Witwatersrand, a Master of Laws Degree in Human Rights and Democratization in Africa from the University of Pretoria and a Bachelor of Laws Degree from the University of Nairobi. Evelyne has published and consulted widely in the area of criminal law, international criminal law, and transitional justice. Her publications can be accessed online.

Grant Barclay is an Early Career Fellow in Evidence and Criminal at the University of Edinburgh, in Scotland. He holds degrees from Edinburgh and Glasgow and has previously worked at the Scottish Law Commission. His research is primarily focused on interdisciplinary approaches to criminal responsibility and liability, particularly in the context of substantive defences and their intersection with vulnerable defendants, and the historical contextualisation of criminal law concepts.

Marcia Baron is the James H. Rudy Professor of Philosophy at Indiana University in the USA. She writes on an array of topics in moral philosophy and the philosophy of criminal law. Publications include "*The Ticking Bomb Hypothetical*", "*The Mens Rea and Moral Status of Manipulation*", "*Rape, Seduction, Shame, and Culpability in Tess of the d'Urbervilles*", "*Shame and Shamelessness*", "*Negligence, Mens Rea, and What We Want the Element of Mens Rea to Provide*". She is currently trying to complete a book, *Self-Defense, Reason, and the Law*.

Tim Bateman was Reader in Youth Justice at the University of Bedfordshire, until his retirement in 2022. He has a background in youth justice policy and has extensive experience of social work with children in trouble. Tim was co-editor of the *Safer Communities* journal, News Editor for the *Youth Justice* journal and, for many years, Chair of the National Association for Youth Justice.

David Campbell participated as an Associate Research Fellow in the ERC funded Roots of Responsibility project lead by Prof John Hyman. During this time, he also held a stipendiary lectureship with Lady Margaret Hall, at the University of Oxford. In 2023, he was elected to permanent Tutorial Fellowship at Lady Margaret Hall.

Henrique Carvalho is Reader in Law and Co-Director of the Centre for Critical Legal Studies at the School of Law, University of Warwick. His main research interests are in criminalisation, punishment, justice, and cultural, social, and political theory. He is the author of *The Preventive Turn in Criminal Law* (2017) and (with Anastasia Chamberlen) *Questioning Punishment* (Routledge 2024).

Ivó Coca-Vila is Tenure-Track Professor at the Law Faculty of Pompeu Fabra University (Barcelona) and Senior Researcher at the Max Planck Institute for the Study of Crime, Security, and Law (Freiburg). His main research interests are criminalisation, justificatory defences, and corporate crime.

Federica Coppola is Assistant Professor of Law at IE University Law School in Madrid. Upon pursuing her PhD at the European University Institute, she was Robert A. Burt Presidential Scholar in Society and Neuroscience at Columbia University in New York and Senior Researcher at the Max Planck Institute for the Study of Crime, Security, and Law. Her research primarily focuses on penal theory, criminal constitutional law, criminal law and social justice, and neurolaw.

Penny Crofts is a Professor at the Faculty of Law, University of Technology Sydney. Penny's current research focus includes legal models of blameworthiness, law and horror, and corporate criminal responsibility. Recent publications include (with Honni van Rijswijk) *Technology: New Trajectories in Law* (Routledge 2022) and *Evil Corporations: Law, Culpability and Regulation* (Routledge 2025).

Thomas Crofts is a Professor in the School of Law and in the Department of Social and Behavioural Sciences at City University Hong Kong, and an Adjunct Professor at Northumbria University, Queensland University of Technology, and the University of Sydney. His research in comparative criminal law and criminal justice focuses on criminalisation and criminal responsibility, particularly in relation to young people, gender, and sexuality.

Before he retired, **Antony Duff** taught in the Department of Philosophy at the University of Stirling and in the University of Minnesota Law School. He works in the philosophy of criminal law – on criminalisation, the structures of criminal responsibility, the criminal process, and criminal punishment.

After a PhD in Cambridge on the comparative legal history of the relationship between civil and criminal law, **Matthew Dyson** was a Fellow and Director of Studies at Jesus College, Cambridge, and then Trinity College, Cambridge, before moving to Corpus Christi College,

Oxford, in 2016. He became a full professor in 2021. He is also President of the European Society for Comparative Legal History.

Catherine L Evans is Associate Professor at the Centre for Criminology and Sociolegal Studies at the University of Toronto. She is the author of *Unsound Empire: Civilization and Madness in Late-Victorian Law* (2021). Her research interests include the histories of forensic medicine, empire, and criminal law, especially insanity and arson.

Lindsay Farmer is Professor of Law at the University of Glasgow. He is the author, most recently, of *Making the Modern Criminal Law. Criminalisation and Civil Order* (2016).

Stuart P Green teaches criminal law and procedure at Rutgers Law School in New Jersey. His books include *Criminalizing Sex: A Unified Liberal Theory* (2020); *Thirteen Ways to Steal a Bicycle: Theft Law in the Information Age* (2012); and *Lying, Cheating, and Stealing: A Moral Theory of White Collar Crime* (2007). Among his current projects is a monograph on the law and theory of homicide.

Linda Gröning is a professor at the Faculty of Law in Bergen, where she leads the research group on Criminal Justice & Mental Health. She is also employed as a researcher at the Competence Center for Security, Forensic and Prison Psychiatry (SIFER west). Gröning became a Juris Doctor in Lund in 2008, and since then has concentrated her research on issues of criminal responsibility and punishment. Gröning became Chair of the Norwegian Criminal Law Commission in 2019.

Chloë Kennedy is Senior Lecturer in Criminal Law at the University of Edinburgh School of Law. She has published in the areas of criminal law, legal history, legal theory, and law and gender. She is co-editor of two books – *Scottish Feminist Judgments: (Re)Creating Law from the Outside In* (2019) and *Leading Works in Criminal Law* (Routledge 2023). Her forthcoming monograph, *Inducing Intimacy: Deception, Consent and the Law*, is the product of an Arts and Humanities Research Council fellowship.

Louise Kennefick is Senior Lecturer in Criminal Law at the University of Glasgow. She researches across the fields of criminal law theory and criminal justice. Her monograph, *The Boundaries of Blame: Towards a Universal Partial Defence for the Criminal Law*, is forthcoming with Cambridge University Press.

Claes Lernestedt is Professor of Criminal Law at Stockholm University, Sweden. His latest publications in English include *What is Wrong with Human Trafficking?* (2019) (ed with R Haverkamp & E Herlin-Karnell), and *The Criminal Law's Person* (2022) (ed with M Matravers).

Arlie Loughnan is Professor of Criminal Law and Criminal Law Theory at the University of Sydney. Her interests range across criminal law, legal theory, and legal history. She is the author of *Self, Others and the State: Relations of Criminal Responsibility* (2020) and *Manifest Madness: Mental Incapacity in Criminal Law* (2012).

Contributors

Matt Matravers is Professor of Law and Director of the Morrell Centre for Legal and Political Philosophy at the University of York. He is the author of two monographs, *Justice and Punishment* (2000), and *Responsibility and Justice* (2007), and of numerous papers in legal and political philosophy. In addition, he has edited seven volumes the latest of which, *The Criminal Law's Person* (2022), is co-edited with Claes Lernestedt.

Allan McCay is Codirector of The Sydney Institute of Criminology and an Academic Fellow at the University of Sydney Law School. His published books include *Free Will and the Law: New Perspectives* and *Neurointerventions and the Law: Regulating Human Mental Capacity*. He was commissioned by the Law Society of England and Wales to write the report "Neurotechnology, Law and the Legal Profession".

Claire McDiarmid joined the University of Glasgow on 1 October 2023 as Head of the School of Law and Professor of Criminal Law and Children's Rights. She has particular research interests in criminal law generally and in the way in which law and legal systems respond to children who offend. She has published extensively in these areas, especially in relation to the child's criminal capacity.

Joe McGrath is an Irish Research Council Scholar, a Fulbright Scholar, and an Assistant Professor of Law at the Sutherland School of Law at University College Dublin, where he also serves as Vice Principal for Equality, Diversity and Inclusion of the College of Social Sciences and Law. His research interests relate to corporate and white-collar crime, corporate governance, financial regulation, and organisational culture.

Liana Georgieva Minkova is a postdoctoral research fellow at the University of Cambridge, Newnham College, and a fellow at the Lauterpacht Centre for International Law. She will be joining the Department of POLIS, University of Cambridge as a Teaching Associate in International Organisation in 2024. She is the author of *Responsibility on Trial* (2023).

Stephen J Morse is Ferdinand Wakeman Hubbell Professor of Law and Professor of Psychology and Law in Psychiatry at the University of Pennsylvania. His most recent book is *An Advanced Introduction to Criminal Law* (2023).

Emilia Musumeci is Associate Professor of Legal History at the University of Teramo in Italy, where she teaches Introduction to Legal History and History of Criminal Law and Criminology. Recently, she achieved the National Scientific qualification (ASN) as Full Professor. She has written extensively on many aspects of the history of criminal law.

Alan Norrie is Professor of Law at the University of Warwick. He is author of a number of books including *Crime, Reason and History* (2014) and is completing a monograph entitled *Criminal Justice and Moral Psychology: Violation, Punishment, Abolition*.

Michele Pifferi is Professor of Legal History at the University of Ferrara, Law Department, and Humboldt Fellow. His main research interests focus on the history of criminal law and criminology and the history of migration law.

Contributors

Anthony Pillay, PhD is an Associate Professor and Principal Clinical Psychologist in the Department of Behavioural Medicine at the Nelson Mandela School of Medicine, University of KwaZulu-Natal, South Africa. He was the Editor-in-Chief of the South African Journal of Psychology and is a Past President of the Psychological Society of South Africa. His research areas include forensic psychology, women and children's mental health, and social justice issues.

Martin Wasik is a retired academic and practising lawyer, who was Professor of Law at Manchester University and Keele University. He sat as a Crown Court Recorder for 15 years and was the first chairman of the Sentencing Advisory Panel. He was appointed CBE for services to criminal justice in 2008.

Amanda Wilson is an Associate Professor of Law at the University of Warwick and Director of the Law School's Criminal Justice Centre. Her current monograph project, *Restoring Restorative Justice*, pursues an ethically real-institutionally critical account of restorative justice through moral psychology.

FOREWORD

It gives me great pleasure to open this Handbook. Its editors have put together a collection which is remarkable in both its quality and its range. In this brief Foreword, I will try to capture what makes the Handbook such a distinctive and important contribution to criminal law scholarship.

On the face of it, a large volume tackling criminal responsibility requires some justification: it is, after all, a topic extensively written about in virtually every country enjoying a vibrant tradition of criminal law scholarship. In the common law world, the conceptual contours, underlying rationale, doctrinal form and practical upshot of the responsibility component of criminal liability have arguably constituted the backbone of criminal law theory at least since the publication of Glanville Williams' *Criminal Law: The General Part* in 1953. And yet, as the editors persuasively argue in their fine introduction, many elements of the work so far are incomplete or unsatisfactory.

This is due in part to the rather parsimonious engagement between criminal law scholars and theorists and psychologists, criminologists, historians, neuroscientists, which has left the field with, among other things, an implicit model of mind and action arguably out of kilter with what we now know about human being; and an often decontextualised, ahistorical picture of criminal law. It is also due to the – in part resultant – difficulties faced by criminal law in accommodating the position of non-human or non-standard subjects: corporations and children, to take two rather different examples that receive attention in this collection. Further tensions surface in the law's struggles to articulate, rationalise, and stabilise some key distinctions around which it operates: the boundaries between responsibility in civil and criminal liability; those between offence and defence; and between capacity and responsibility. Neither sentencing nor evidential issues have ever been fully articulated with doctrines of responsibility. Last but not least, these difficulties stand to complicate the task of deciding whether, and how, newly emerging harms and wrongs, notably climate-related harms, should be accommodated in criminal law. A renewed scholarly emphasis in recent years on criminalisation, and on theorising the special part of criminal law, has begun to fill some of the gaps. But the upshot of this literature for criminal responsibility remains to be fully articulated: and responsibility requirements – understood, in the editors' terms, as evaluations grounded in

Foreword

distinctive institutional practices – sit at the heart of any adequate explanatory or normative theory of criminalisation.

These among many other issues are tackled in this collection, which features many of the world's best-known and most innovative criminal law scholars. The collection includes contributions relating to a very wide range of jurisdictions, several of them poorly represented in scholarship in English to date. The echoes of history, notably those of Empire, are shown to be etched onto the conceptual framework of criminal responsibility which we have inherited; the dense cultural meanings borne by criminal law are unearthed and examined; criminal law's role in the constitution of state authority and of relations among political subjects are scrutinised; and the lived reality of criminal law for those subjects is kept in view alongside its existence as a system of rules and principles. The collection accordingly makes a significant contribution to both criminal law theory and socio-legal, contextual studies of criminal law. I trust that it will reach a wide and appreciative audience.

Nicola Lacey
London School of Economics, May 2024

INTRODUCTION

Thomas Crofts, Louise Kennefick, and Arlie Loughnan

Criminal law and justice systems across the world are tasked with crafting and enforcing the rules and mechanisms by which the state ascribes responsibility. The evaluations and practices of responsibility for crime have a profound impact on the subject who is charged and condemned, and on the society to which they belong. The construct at the core of these evaluations and practices – criminal responsibility – forms the subject matter of this collection.

The topic of criminal responsibility has received renewed intellectual attention in recent decades, owing to a burgeoning critical scholarship across criminal law theory, criminology and criminal justice studies, and law and mind sciences. Key trends include new perspectives on state responsibility; the responsibility of corporations; responsibility for environmental harms; shared and collective responsibility; the role of defences in light of existing and emergent knowledge of human psychology and action; the implications of advances in neurotechnology; changing understandings of maturity and the age of criminal responsibility, and; the concept of personhood in the criminal law and its place in relation to the state. In addition, in criminal law practice, given long-standing recognition of the association between adverse circumstances, such as deprivation, addiction, and developmental immaturity, and criminal behaviour, criminal justice agencies are seeking to respond to these associations in a way that continues to fulfil core penal purposes like rehabilitation and desistance from crime. Yet, despite this established knowledge base and progressive penal policy trend evident in numerous countries, the doctrines and practices of criminal responsibility across jurisdictions continue to be based on a now dated, highly conservative, and abstracted understanding of human psychology and action. How do we bridge this gap between the lived reality of those coming before the criminal law and the rules and principles that ascribe criminal responsibility? This question is more urgent than ever.

Notwithstanding the intellectual interest and vigour, and the urgency of these issues as a matter of practice, literature offering a comprehensive overview of the field of criminal responsibility is rare. Scholarly investigations of criminal responsibility tend to come in single-authored, monograph form, and concentrate on the topic from one particular methodology (typically, legal-philosophical approaches).[1] Other contributions focus on one aspect of criminal responsibility, such as the responsibility of children.[2] In recent years, critical scholars have begun to apply a critical historical lens to examine how criminal responsibility in its social, historical, and institutional context.[3] Edited collections on criminal responsibility tend towards a philosophical approach, and often consider the question of responsibility together with issues pertaining to criminalisation and punishment.[4] These important contributions sit alongside an established scholarship relating to the impact of psychological and neuroscientific findings on legal concepts and practices.[5] These titles are thematically relevant to the Handbook, but do not capture the perspectives of the multiple disciplines that have considered criminal responsibility at a global scale. Even at a more interdisciplinary level, while there are some collections that bring together the work of legal scholars and political psychologists, they are of a more general nature and do not focus on criminal responsibility specifically.[6]

The *Routledge International Handbook on Criminal Responsibility* responds to a pressing need to capture and consolidate the important contributions emerging at this exciting time in criminal responsibility discourses. The Handbook is the first comprehensive collection to present an in-depth account of the research and scholarship representing the broad and vibrant landscape of criminal responsibility studies across the globe in the fields of legal theory, history, philosophy, psychology, neuroscience, criminology, and sociology. The collection analyses pressing themes in the literature, including the following: the nature of state responsibility; the scope of criminal excuses; core issues surrounding the age of criminal responsibility across jurisdictions; notions of corporate responsibility; responsibility for environmental crimes; the relationship between criminal law and neuroscience; and the role of behavioural sciences in evaluating responsibility for crime. In addition, it invites exchanges across a growing critical scholarship on criminal responsibility, showcasing the diverse range of methodologies applied to the field, including socio-political approaches, critical historical methods, criminological and sociological perspectives, and interdisciplinary studies bridging law and mind sciences.

The chapters are arranged thematically into three parts. Part I (Foundations) presents fresh insights into enduring landscapes relating to ideas, histories, and cultures of criminal responsibility. Part II (Doctrine and Principles) takes a mechanistic turn and considers principles and doctrines of responsibility both within and in relation to the criminal law. Finally, Part III (Domains) surveys key sites where questions of responsibility are at the forefront of long-standing, existing, and emerging discourses.

Overview of the collection

Part I – Foundations of criminal responsibility

This section begins with **Henrique Carvalho**'s presentation of a cultural analysis of criminal responsibility. Carvalho notes that, within the modern social imaginary, the criminal law is intimately related to ideas of individual responsibility and justice. This chapter deploys insights from cultural theory to suggest that, beyond the patterns of responsibility reflected in the structure of criminal liability, criminal culpability is also underpinned by cultural patterns of blaming, material and symbolic articulations built around culturally constructed dangers to the security of civil order. Carvalho explores a tension in the law of intention and murder in the UK, related to shifts in the law of joint enterprise, to illustrate the dynamic relationship between responsibility and blaming in the criminal law.

Introduction

In her chapter, **Federica Coppola** engages with a different methodological tradition to argue for the adoption of a socio-contextual model of criminal responsibility. Acknowledging the empirical evidence about the many social adversities that lie at the core of much criminal offending, Coppola emphasises the need for a "situated" view of criminal behaviour and argues that socio-contextual factors should be included as a criterion for adjudication. To this aim, the chapter focuses on the voluntarist model of criminal responsibility and suggests an expansive interpretation of the component of "fair opportunity to do otherwise" to also include social and environmental factors of criminal conduct, including the social background and living environment, as well as structural factors that may have played a contributing role in the aetiology of offending. The chapter subsequently examines the potential implications of this rethought theoretical model of criminal responsibility for legal doctrine and sentencing, suggesting it may result in more just and equitable criminal justice.

Antony Duff's chapter concerns the idea of responsibility – understood as accountability – as being both relational (responsibility *to* some person or body who has the authority to call you to account) and reciprocal (in that if we call you to answer to us, we must be ready to answer to you). Thinking about responsibility in this way can help us to understand why the criminal prosecution and punishment of those who have suffered serious social injustice is problematic: the political community can retain the standing to call such offenders to criminal account only if it is ready to answer to them for the injustices they have suffered at its hands or through its neglect.

In her chapter, **Catherine L Evans** offers a historical account of nineteenth-century debates over the limits and definition of criminal responsibility in the context of the British Empire. Evans argues that Victorian understandings of "civilization" inflected medical and legal controversies over the nature of the mind and legal responses to violence in Britain and the wider British world. By knitting together the legal histories of pluralism and insanity, Evans draws out the political stakes of criminal responsibility during a period of imperial legal consolidation and Anglicisation. Evans suggests that criminal responsibility was more than just a legal or even a medical quandary – it was also a site for the elaboration of what she calls "psychological subjecthood".

In chapter 5, **Louise Kennefick** considers the idea of characterising criminal responsibility attribution as part of the desistance process. Though scholarship relating to the two areas rarely overlaps, the chapter argues that there are reasons to look more closely at their theoretical intersection. For criminal responsibility scholarship, this exercise may lend force to existing arguments that seek to destabilise the rational agency paradigm underpinning state blame, in addition to foregrounding the conceptual mechanisms and significance of blame in securing and maintaining social cohesion. For desistance theory, attending to criminal responsibility attribution has the potential to bolster calls for desistance as an overarching criminal justice paradigm and broader social movement.

In their chapter, **Claes Lernestedt** and **Matt Matravers** examine the concept of blameworthiness. They note that it is often assumed that blameworthiness is a crucial component, and sometimes even a necessary condition, for society to hold someone criminally responsible for what they did, but, despite this, the concept is sometimes used without its being subject to a thorough discussion or even a clear definition. Lernstedt and Matravers suggest that there appear to be a wide range of uses, ranging from superficial assessments to (attempts at) profound characterisations, from evaluations solely of the action to those of the individual's character, and from measuring against rigid, impersonal standards to considering the individual's unique traits. In their chapter, they map the landscape of the use of the concept and discuss how it should (and should not) be used if it is to have a useful role.

Stephen J Morse's chapter explores how mental disorder and the findings of the new behavioural neuroscience fuelled by imaging studies both pose challenges to the evaluation of criminal responsibility. Mental disorder, including intellectual disability, is a familiar problem, but nonetheless continues to put pressure on the law's concept of responsible agency. The new neuroscience, in contrast, has motivated quite radical challenges to the concept of criminal responsibility itself in addition to claims that it might help guide criminal law policy and individual case adjudication. The chapter clarifies the issues both types of challenges present and offers a normatively attractive set of proposals for making progress.

In chapter 8, **Emilia Musumeci** investigates the influence of the positivist school of criminal law in the evaluation of mental capacity in the Italian colonies, with a specific focus on Eritrea. The chapter shows how this area, as well as the wider colonial situation, was a privileged ground for developing new models of punishment between the nineteenth and twentieth centuries. Musumeci argues that even though it is overly simplistic to see the authoritarian traces of criminal justice in Eritrea merely as a distortion of the positivist thesis, acknowledging that Italian colonialism itself is a complex phenomenon, it is nevertheless true that many principles of the positivist school were adopted and used by colonialists for their own ends.

In their chapter, **Alan Norrie** and **Amanda Wilson** develop a critical account of criminal responsibility. They propose what they call a dispositional–relational conception of responsibility, which involves a structural (intra- and inter-psychic) understanding of what a person did in the light of their past and present and with an eye to the future: why they did it, how they feel about having done it, and how they might on reflection respond and change. Grounded in moral psychology, they argue that dispositional–relational responsibility accounts for the individual in the social and the social in the individual. This move opens the way for a practical shift from blame and punishment to approaches based on restoration and reconciliation.

Michele Pifferi's chapter considers the origins and development of the notion of criminal responsibility in late medieval legal sources and its modern shift from a casuistic to a principled conception, linked to the formation and institutionalisation of the modern state since the sixteenth century. Highlighting the significance of the discovery of the criminal man in the 1870s, Pifferi unearths the challenge posed by criminal anthropology and criminological positivism to the idea of criminal responsibility, and their contribution to reshaping the liberal notion of criminal intent.

Part II – Doctrine and principles of criminal responsibility

In chapter 11, **Grant Barclay** explores how contemporary scholarship has identified an important role for emotions in criminal culpability, one that challenges the traditional voluntarist understanding and perhaps compatibilism more generally. In particular, this chapter examines the role of emotions in connecting the criminal law doctrines of duress, necessity, and self-defence, understood as a sub-category of substantive criminal law defences known as "reactive defences". By drawing out the normative features which these defences share, Barclay argues that a focus on the previously underappreciated emotive content of self-defence can help to answer difficult doctrinal questions relating to duress and necessity.

Introduction

Delving into key principles of *mens rea*, **Marcia Baron**'s chapter on recklessness and negligence addresses enduring disagreements on whether negligence should suffice for criminal liability. With a focus on the US, Baron probes the meaning of these concepts through an examination of the Model Penal Code definitions, bringing out features that tend to be overlooked in discussions of negligence and recklessness. She articulates and resolves an unclarity in the MPC definition of "recklessness", and then draws out some implications for the debate over whether negligence suffices for criminal liability.

Turning to structural concerns, **David Campbell**'s chapter considers controversial distinctions relating to criminal responsibility, in terms of the denial/defence and the offence/defence divide. Drawing on the work of John Gardner and Joseph Raz, Campbell advances a "novel(ish)" theory of defences that identifies a difference of kind between offences and defences, offering an answer to the question posed by sceptics of the distinction.

Staying in the realm of defences, **Ivó Coca-Vila** examines the allocation of scarce medical resources (triage) in pandemic situations where these circumstances may, at least *prima facie*, involve killing. Coca-Vila questions under what conditions are doctors' conduct in "life-or-death" decisions justified. Coca-Vila defends a rights-based reading of the system of justificatory defences in criminal law, which aims not to maximise scarce medical resources, but to find a solution that respects the rights of all subjects involved. In this chapter, Coca-Vila proposes that in situations of *ex ante* triage, doctors will not commit homicide regardless of which patients they treat, and that *ex ante* preventive triage and *ex post* triage constitute forms of killing that deserve to be punished.

Matthew Dyson's chapter considers the concept of responsibility across crime and tort, highlighting points of substantive unity and difference as well as procedural interaction. The contribution explores how configurations of "responsibility" are given different explanatory force across the two areas, but the doctrinal outcome is the same: liability, the obligation to satisfy the law's demand. On the way, the chapter examines how responsibility entwines, divides, and interacts across criminal law and tort law, concluding that though some demarcation exists in substance, the two remain connected by procedure.

In his chapter on responsibility for market misconduct, **Lindsay Farmer** explores the affinity between the rational calculating economic subject (*homo economicus*) and the responsible subject of criminal law. As Farmer posits, according to this affinity, one might expect that it would be relatively easy to establish liability for market misconduct where the calculating actor and responsible subject come together. However, the question of establishing fault for forms of market misconduct is beset by both theoretical and practical problems. This leads Farmer to identify tension between the idea of the rational entrepreneurial subject and the capacity of criminal law to attribute responsibility for any particular outcome. His chapter explores some of these issues, asking how the criminal law can make individuals or organisations responsible for market misconduct.

Stuart P Green's chapter examines the central role played by the concept of blameworthiness in the retributive theory of criminal law. Through an exploration of the question "what exactly makes conduct blameworthy?", Green develops a systematic framework that identifies a collection of basic "elements" to which the concept of blameworthiness can be reduced: *harmfulness*, *wrongness*, and *culpability*. Focusing on the law of homicide, his argument draws out the wide variety of factors, involving a range of possible mental states and justifying or excusing conditions that determine the extent that an individual ought to be considered blameworthy.

Linda Gröning explores the legal doctrine of criminal insanity and how this doctrine is associated with disorder. Following the paradigm in Anglo-American law, the insanity law of most countries requires both that a defendant suffered from a mental disorder, and that this disorder influenced the commission of the crime. Norwegian law challenges this paradigm as it identifies insanity exclusively with mental disorder, disregarding how it influenced the crime. Gröning's chapter outlines an alternative account of this association, presenting two key arguments and challenges to current rules and practices: first, that the insanity doctrine should not involve any causal or functional requirement that a mental disorder influenced the crime, and second that the association between insanity and mental disorder should not hinge upon psychiatric diagnoses. This alternative approach requires lawyers to engage more closely with mental health research, which casts light on constructs such as delusions and the relation between symptom severity and functional impairments.

Contextualising criminal responsibility in the wider legal order, and comparing it with civil responsibility, **Chloë Kennedy** examines some of the purportedly distinctive features of criminal responsibility. Using examples from the law of sexual wrongs, the chapter outlines some key points of contention that arise in the case of congruent wrongs (i.e. civil and criminal wrongs that overlap or are identical) and incongruent wrongs (i.e. civil wrongs with no corresponding criminal wrong and vice versa), mapping these across three areas: the substantive basis for responsibility, the process governing the attribution of responsibility, and the aims and effects of these two forms of responsibility. The chapter argues that across each of these areas there is a tension between the desire to demarcate the boundary between civil and criminal responsibility clearly, and the desire (or at least tendency) to blur this boundary in practice.

In her chapter, **Arlie Loughnan** analyses the relevance of the changing knowledge conditions – the epistemic setting of the criminal law – for criminal responsibility. She suggests that changing knowledge conditions challenge (or have the potential to challenge) three key dichotomies which structure the criminal responsibility inquiry: offence and defence, perpetrator and victim, and responsibility and non-responsibility. These dichotomies reflect the law's normative commitments to a particular idea of the legal subject and liberal political precepts. Because changing knowledge conditions affect the legitimacy of criminal responsibility practices and decision-making in criminal law more broadly, Loughnan suggests that new approaches are needed to future-proof criminal law.

In his chapter, **Martin Wasik** considers the relationship of duress by threats and duress of circumstances (a restricted form of the necessity defence) to criminal responsibility. In the UK, in 2015, a further defence was added to the mix, but limited to defendants who have committed an offence as a consequence of their being a victim of human trafficking, modern slavery, or exploitation. All three defences are tightly circumscribed in law. This chapter considers these old and new forms of duress, both in terms of the ascription of criminal responsibility and, since such defences often fail at trial, their likely impact upon sentencing outcome in terms of mitigation. In the context of the modern slavery defence, Wasik argues that such circumstances are closer to loss of capacity than duress, demonstrating the range of juristic techniques deployed to facilitate forms of necessity in English law.

Part III – Domains of criminal responsibility

Part III begins with **Evelyne Owiye Asaala** exploring corporate accountability for international crimes. She identifies two major impediments to imposing corporate accountability

Introduction

for atrocities: the overreaching economic and political influence of corporations and the absence of binding substantive international norms to guide the development. Economic and political influence by corporations is often exerted to undermine corporate accountability initiatives including the adoption of binding international obligations. The overall objective of Asaala's contribution is to evoke a debate around these controversial issues and suggest solutions that favour the establishment of an enforcement mechanisms for corporate accountability for international crimes.

Raymond Arthur's chapter turns attention to the criminal responsibility of children and asks whether the disclosure of the criminal records of children in England and Wales imposes enduring criminal responsibility for childhood behaviours. Adopting Hollingsworth's theory of foundational rights, he critically explores the need for a closer alignment between the regulation of the disclosure of childhood criminal records with its emphasis on imposing enduring criminal responsibility for childhood offending, international children's rights instruments, and the Youth Justice Board's commitment to the development of a youth justice system in England and Wales that is "Child First".

Staying with the theme of the criminal responsibility of children and the "Child First" vision, **Tim Bateman** asks whether the minimum age of criminal responsibility in England and Wales is stuck in time. The "Child First" vision for youth justice, which promotes the best interests of the child and aspires to minimise criminalisation, has been associated with a reformulation of responses to youth crime and a dramatic reduction in the number of children subject to formal youth justice processes. Despite this, Bateman finds a steadfast refusal by the government to countenance increasing the age of criminal responsibility. He explores this paradox and concludes that defence of the current threshold of criminal liability is evidence that "Child First" has failed to counter a discourse which responsibilises children who offend differently from those who do not come to the attention of youth justice agencies.

Returning to the theme of corporate criminal responsibility **Penny Crofts** examines why, despite long-standing recognition of the large-scale harms inflicted by corporations and large organisations, criminal prosecutions of corporations are rare, and successful prosecutions even rarer. She explores the obstacles militating against prosecution and examines the various methods adopted to criminalise corporations. She finds that underlying these various approaches to corporate ir/responsibility is a philosophical question of blameworthiness – can corporations be sufficiently culpable to justify the imposition of criminal law? Crofts considers these approaches to corporations as criminal legal subjects through the lens of philosophies of wickedness.

The varied understandings of, and approaches to, criminal responsibility in relation to children are explored in **Thomas Crofts**'s chapter. He finds that these differences are often not clearly acknowledged or articulated but they fundamentally shape debates about the minimum age level of criminal responsibility. In unravelling these differences his chapter allows for a better understanding of the implications that these conceptualisations have for arguments about how the law does and should deal with children who transgress the criminal law. The chapter concludes by recommending how the law ought to address the criminal responsibility of children.

Writing in a field that has seen extraordinary advances in recent years, **Allan McCay** investigates how developments in neurotechnology present challenges to the criminal law's responsibility practices. McCay focusses on criminal responsibility in the context of the defence of insanity as set out in the common law's *M'Naghten* test and in a statutory implementation of something approximating it in the law of New South Wales, Australia. His chapter is a piece of anticipatory legal scholarship that aims to stimulate debate amongst criminal law scholars and theorists about a challenge to law and concepts of criminal responsibility that is likely to become increasingly significant as neurotechnology becomes integrated into more people's lives.

Claire McDiarmid's chapter dissects the assumptions underlying the setting of a single chronological age of criminal responsibility. She examines the complexity of the concept of criminal capacity, which underlies setting the age of criminal responsibility, and makes a proposal for the content of the bundle of understandings which it comprises. She then considers the limitations of using a single chronological age to signify the acquisition of capacity by all and possible legal responses to those who, in fact, acquire it earlier or later. Children's rights are considered throughout. Overall, McDiarmid sets out the difficulty both of imputing criminal responsibility to children and doing so by age and concludes that an age of criminal responsibility is essential but not sufficient in this context.

Joe McGrath's chapter takes a different approach to corporate criminal responsibility by shifting attention away from the more traditional question of how we punish corporate offenders to the issue of how further offending by corporations can be prevented. McGrath employs an innovative, cross-disciplinary approach, drawing on regulatory theory (meta-regulation), behavioural science (groups as moral anchors), and criminological theory (stakes in conformity), to explore how certain type of controls, attachments, and group dynamics, can inform individual decision-making processes and generate more ethical actions. Accordingly, he does not seek to outline how we punish "bad" companies, or ask why good actors do bad things, but to ask how we can help to promote positive workplace practices that prevent corporate crimes.

Criminal responsibility for wrongs to the environment is the topic of **Liana Georgieva Minkova**'s chapter. Her chapter, first, situates the efforts to criminalise ecocide within the political and normative context of international criminal law. This includes analysing the degree earlier definitions of ecocide conform to both state expectations and the principled foundations of international criminal law. Second, her chapter contributes to the critical scholarship discussing the implications of pursuing socio-ecological justice through international criminal law by exploring the question whether individual criminal responsibility could be an effective tool for delivering ecojustice.

The collection concludes with **Anthony Pillay**'s exploration of some of the global issues affecting criminal responsibility in children. He discusses the international variation in the minimum age of criminal capacity, the rebuttable presumption of *doli incapax*, the challenges in assessing criminal capacity, and the relevant neurodevelopment research pertaining to adolescent cognitive and conative capacities. Pillay draws on some examples from the law in South Africa, but reviews the issues within the global context, noting concerns at the policy and practice levels, with some recommendations. The need for collaboration between legal and child development experts is raised, with the aim of securing a just, rights-based approach to dealing with children in conflict with the law.

Spanning global networks of established and emergent scholarship in criminal responsibility, the *Routledge International Handbook on Criminal Responsibility* explores how we relate to one another as human beings under the spotlight of the criminal law. The collection combines theoretical insights into the internal legal and moral dilemmas underpinning

Introduction

ascription of responsibility for crime, with wider, political, historical, and scientific enquiry into the dynamics of blame that both engage with and transcend criminal law doctrine. In doing so, it is hoped that the collection not only does justice to the broad and vibrant landscape of criminal responsibility studies, but inspires new directions and future synergies in this compelling field.

Notes

1. See e.g. V Tadros, *Criminal Responsibility* (Oxford University Press: Oxford, 2005).
2. See e.g. T Crofts, *Criminal Responsibility of Children and Young People* (Ashgate: Surrey, 2002); D Cipriani, *Children's Rights and the Minimum Age of Criminal Responsibility* (Routledge: London, 2009); E Scott & L Steinberg, *Rethinking Juvenile Justice* (Harvard University Press: Cambridge MA, 2008); G Yaffe, *The Age of Culpability* (Oxford University Press: Oxford, 2018).
3. See e.g. E Kelly, *The Limits of Blame: Rethinking Punishment and Responsibility* (Harvard University Press: Cambridge MA, 2020); L Farmer, *Making Modern Criminal Law* (Oxford University Press: Oxford 2016); N Lacey, *In Search of Criminal Responsibility: Ideas, Interests and Institutions* (Oxford University Press: Oxford, 2016); A Loughnan, *Self, Others and the State: Relations of Criminal Responsibility* (Cambridge University Press: Cambridge, 2019).
4. See e.g. A Duff (ed) *Philosophy and the Criminal Law* (Cambridge University Press: Cambridge, 1998).
5. See e.g. MS Moore, *Law and Psychiatry: Rethinking the Relationship* (Cambridge University Press: Cambridge, 1984) as well as titles from the *Oxford Series in Neuroscience, Law and Philosophy*, in particular, N Vincent (ed), *Neuroscience and Legal Responsibility* (Oxford University Press: Oxford, 2013).
6. See e.g. J Hanson & J Jost, *Ideology, Psychology and Law* (Oxford University Press: Oxford, 2012).

PART I

Foundations of Criminal Responsibility

1
CULTURES OF RESPONSIBILITY AND BLAMING

Henrique Carvalho

Introduction

The notion of criminal responsibility is one of the main corollaries of modern, liberal criminal law, grounded on principles of individual freedom and autonomy and serving as the main basis for individual justice.[1] This idea sits at the core of the legitimatory and explanatory frameworks of criminal law, operating in two important dimensions. First, it "accords individuals the status of autonomous moral agents who, because they have axiomatic freedom of choice, can fairly be held accountable and punishable for the rational choices of wrongdoing that they make".[2] Second, it upholds that individuals should *only* be held liable for those criminal offences for which they can be deemed responsible, therefore requiring the state to prove that responsibility has been established. Thus understood, criminal responsibility functions as both a condition and a limitation of the criminal law: it explains and, in so doing, legitimates the imposition of criminal liability, but only to the extent allowed by its scope. The relevance and contours of responsibility have been extensively discussed in legal scholarship, with a wide variety of accounts and perspectives.[3] However, these debates are almost universally underpinned by a strong common sense around the assumptions that individuals can be held responsible for crimes which they commit; that this responsibility reflects a notion of individual autonomy and agency; and that the criminal law has (or can develop) the means to determine the extent of that responsibility. This consensus finds expression not only in academic scholarship and doctrine, but also in the rules of criminal liability, particularly in the *mens rea* categories grounding culpability. The category of intention, in particular, is said to epitomise the dominant contemporary conception of criminal responsibility, based on ideas of individual capacity and choice.[4]

This chapter aims to call this common sense around criminal responsibility into question, by proposing a cultural reading of its material and symbolic underpinnings. One of the main grounds for the legitimacy of criminal legal rules and decisions lies in the idea that imputations of culpability follow strict logics and procedures, aimed at respecting individual responsibility and guaranteeing fairness. Against this, this chapter argues that a cultural reading of criminal responsibility reveals that it is significantly attached to culturally conditioned patterns of blaming—indeed, it suggests that tensions and contradictions in legal theory and practice

DOI: 10.4324/9781003297260-3

can be made more fully intelligible through an awareness and exploration of these patterns. To pursue this argument, the chapter develops a conceptual framework grounded on an engagement with the work of cultural theorists, such as Antonio Gramsci, Stuart Hall, Mary Douglas, and Raymond Williams.

The chapter starts by restating the broader project of which it is a part,[5] which is to develop a cultural theory of criminalisation by advancing a conceptual framework grounded on the application of "culture" as the basis for an analytical methodology of studying the criminal law. The aim of this framework is to conceptualise the criminal law as a cultural apparatus, embedded in cultural structures and processes that are part of the broader (re)production of meanings, identities, and affects in society. For this purpose, the chapter deploys a Gramscian conception of hegemony further developed in the work of scholars, such as Stuart Hall, that sees the cultural field as dynamic and conflictual, in which dominant and emerging perspectives struggle for and against the control of common sense.[6]

Once this broader framework is established, the chapter turns to a more focused discussion of responsibility in criminal law. It examines how the dominant logic of criminal responsibility maintains the "cultural mode"[7] of separation between the individual and the social, privileging the former over the latter in formal, superficial terms, and how critical approaches to criminal responsibility reveal that the opposite is in fact the case. These critiques expose how notions of responsibility in criminal law are contingent and abstract, a product of social, historical, and political arrangements rather than a reflection of concrete individuality and agency; furthermore, they shatter illusions about a unitary, coherent conception of criminal responsibility, instead exposing a complex and hybrid environment. The work of Nicola Lacey, in particular, explores how the contemporary framework of criminal responsibility espouses four distinct patterns of responsibility–attribution, which both reflect and respond to needs of legitimation and coordination by the criminal law.[8] I build on this insight regarding patterns of responsibility to suggest that there is a further patterned structure underpinning criminal culpability, concerning culturally produced *patterns of blaming*.

The chapter then develops the notion of patterns of blaming through an engagement with cultural theory, particularly the work of Mary Douglas and Raymond Williams. From Douglas, it takes the idea that blaming is moralised and politicised, and that it is central to the social reproduction of notions of identity, belonging, community, and boundaries.[9] It then links these insights to Williams' elaboration of the notion of structures of feeling,[10] and suggests that these patterns of blaming are symbolic structures which engender affectively loaded "common senses" around culpability, which significantly condition practices of responsibility–attribution in criminal law. These symbolic structures are grounded on culturally constructed "danger formations", images which constitute and regulate perceptions about what kinds of conduct, harm, and subjectivity ought to be considered more (or less) dangerous to the security of civil order.

The final section illustrates the influence of patterns of blaming on the framework of criminal culpability by discussing tensions and variations in the law of intention and murder. It suggests that these tensions can be seen to reflect and reveal specific danger formations underpinning responsibility–attribution, alluding to structures of feeling around issues, such as racialisation, marginalisation, and urban violence, as exemplified in the case of joint enterprise.

Criminal law as a cultural apparatus

Williams famously stated that "culture is one of the two or three most complicated words in the English language".[11] He describes "three broad active categories of usage"—culture as "a general process of intellectual, spiritual or aesthetic development"; as "a particular way of life, whether of a people, period, a group, or humanity in general"; and as "the works and practices of intellectual and especially artistic activity".[12] Furthermore, the breadth of the term is illustrated by how, depending on its usage, culture tends to sometimes emphasise "*material* production" (for instance, in anthropological scholarship), and sometimes "*signifying* or *symbolic* systems" (as, he indicates, is usual in history and cultural studies).[13] But rather than promoting indeterminacy or pressing the need for selecting or privileging one usage over others, Williams proposes that "it is the range and overlap of meanings that is significant."[14] This is because this range and overlap present culture as an invaluable analytical concept, as it serves to highlight and recognise the relationality and interconnectedness between different aspects of human activity and organisation—between values, affects and habits, structural and institutional social arrangements, and intellectual and creative practices and modes of analysis, both in their material and symbolic manifestations.

To examine the criminal law as a cultural apparatus, then, requires us to see it as embedded within these broader meanings and processes of meaning-making. For this purpose, it is useful to link this examination to a concept of significant currency both in cultural theory and in socio-legal studies, that of hegemony. Having its main roots in the work of Antonio Gramsci, this conception of hegemony refers to the idea of "predominance by consent",[15] in which the state and ruling groups maintain power and exercise leadership by means of a dominant or "common" worldview, which is maintained primarily via cultural processes and institutions. In other words, political power and authority rely on its ideological apparatus having a hegemonic character—that is, on it appearing intelligible, acceptable, and ideally "natural" and desirable. For Stuart Hall, following Gramsci, this ideological dimension of power and authority has two elements. The first is a "philosophy", a "conception of the [social] world" that gives it formal coherence.[16] However, the values and ideas contained within this "official...imposition of the legitimate vision of the social world"[17] only become effective when they "enter into, modify, and transform the practical, everyday consciousness" of the population; Gramsci called this second element "common sense".[18] Common sense is thus the implicit aspect of this ideological dimension of power and authority, which gives it a "feeling of obviousness and necessity".[19]

It is interesting to note that, while the majority of intellectual work and debate appears to focus on the philosophy, that is, on formal conceptions and visions of the social world, and while common sense appears as the "already-formed and 'taken for granted' terrain" of cultural production, it is in reality "disjointed", it is "fragmentary and contradictory",[20] and it is the main stage of ideological contestation. This is because, as Williams proposed, the social realm is home to competing perspectives and distinct ways of life, some of which are longstanding and many others which are constantly emerging; that some appear natural and even necessary, while others are seen as strange, noxious, and threatening, is primarily the reflection—and the purpose—of hegemony. But we should not mistake the outward appearance of a phenomenon with the phenomenon itself. Thus, it is imperative to resist a simplistic conception of hegemony, which tends to see it as "a model of a static, dominant ideology unproblematically suffused throughout a society", and to instead conceive it "as an inherently unstable process of constantly shifting equilibria".[21] Hegemony is perhaps best conceptualised as a site of struggle for the dominance of common sense, so that complex and often disparate social conditions can be naturalised and legitimised—while others are marginalised, discredited, and excluded—under the appearance of a common vision of the social world.

Therefore, while we may "tend to experience the particular 'realities' of our cultural world as fixed and unalterable, no more than simple reflections of the way the world is",[22] this impression is grounded on "an articulation of different processes or 'modes of production', that constitutes a set of relations, articulating different, often paradoxical 'modes' that are governed by an overarching, dominant outlook or 'formation' or 'structure'".[23] In other words, a dominant outlook contains and conceals a complex array of different, contradictory structural factors and relations that need to be somehow reconciled and harmonised by the state's ideological apparatus if it hopes to remain hegemonic. The key to understanding the criminal law as a cultural apparatus performing a cultural function arguably lies in examining how it relates to specific hegemonic outlooks and the role it performs in their articulation.

The hegemonic outlook of criminal responsibility

There is little doubt that the idea of criminal responsibility presented at the beginning of this chapter is hegemonic; however, as seen in the previous section, it is necessary to further scrutinise what it means to say that this idea is hegemonic. The dominant, liberal conception of criminal responsibility, grounded on the primacy of the free and autonomous individual as "the primary focus of concern in the moral assessment of any particular set of political arrangements",[24] is often presented as unitary and static. However, a cultural understanding suggests that this superficial constancy is the result of active work to manage and stabilise a much more complicated and conflictive reality. Indeed, a significant body of critical legal scholarship has explored and exposed how the criminal law and criminal responsibility are shaped and defined by historical, institutional, structural, and ideological factors, which are both reflected and obscured by the law; as such, criminal responsibility is contingent and mired with tensions and contradictions.[25]

This critical approach has significant implications to how we should understand the hegemonic position of criminal responsibility. For instance, it suggests that, in being part of an ideological framework linked to specific socio-political arrangements, criminal responsibility is inherently abstract, and thus unable to fully capture the complexity of concrete individuality; the abstract individualism grounding criminal responsibility leads the law to perennially preserve antinomies, unresolvable conflicts, which tend to destabilise legal concepts and arrangements.[26] This implies that, in order to preserve the hegemony of criminal responsibility, the law has to constantly work through its antinomies, incorporating variations and exceptions to its rules under a veneer of coherence and integrity.

One of the most sophisticated illustrations of this working through which happens in the framework of criminal responsibility can be seen in Nicola Lacey's work. Demystifying the notion that responsibility is a unitary and universalistic concept, Lacey has compellingly argued that it is best understood as a complex, fluid, and hybrid environment, where different conceptions coexist and dynamically interact within the framework of criminal liability. In the latest iteration of her study, Lacey identifies four distinct patterns of responsibility–attribution in the modern criminal law. Lacey argues that three of these patterns or conceptions of responsibility, those of capacity, character, and outcome, have a longer history, while a fourth one, linked to assessments of risk, was more recently developed, as a reflection of the recent preventive turn in criminal law.[27]

Capacity constitutes "the dominant way of thinking about responsibility in contemporary British and American criminal law doctrine",[28] being most closely aligned with ideas of individual rationality and choice at the core of the "orthodox subjectivism" of liberal modernity,[29] as well as dominant psychological notions of subjective agency. It reflects the understanding of individuals as responsible subjects, upholding a presumption of responsibility which is only exceptionally negated by special circumstances (such as a very young age, specific kinds of mental illness, etc.). Simultaneously, it establishes that responsibility is only attributable when an individual's capacity has been exercised in an unhindered manner, such as in circumstances of advertent conduct, a view that supports a minimalist conception of criminal responsibilisation. In doctrinal terms, this form of responsibility is best expressed through subjective categories of *mens rea*, such as intention and recklessness.

While capacity is the current dominant conception of criminal responsibility, Lacey shows how it only represents part of its complex tapestry. Especially historically, although the normative ideas that inform it have been influential at least since the work of the Enlightenment reformers, capacity did not become fully embedded into criminal law doctrine and practice until the mid-twentieth century.[30] In contrast, character appeared as the prevalent form of responsibility–attribution throughout the eighteenth and nineteenth centuries. While capacity highlights matters of cognition and volition, character focuses on an evaluation of the individual's conduct, usually by contrasting it to that "of an idealised conception of an agent of good character".[31] As such, character attributes responsibility through a judgment that an individual has failed to attain a standard expected of them. Although no longer dominant in the sense of being the primary way in which responsibility for crime is explained and justified, this pattern is still amply manifested in contemporary criminal law, especially in the many standards of "reasonableness" that abound in offences and defences.

In these cases, Lacey argues that character appears in a more "cautious" form, in which the implied evaluation is primarily directed at the individual's conduct. However, character can also appear in a more extreme version, an "overall-character principle" which "holds that the attribution of criminal responsibility is founded in a judgment that the defendant's conduct is evidence of a wrongful, bad, disapproved character trait".[32] This inference is at odds with dominant ideas of responsible agency, as it suggests that culpability arose not from the individual making a "bad choice", but from them being a "bad person". Nevertheless, Lacey holds that this overall-character principle can be seen in many contemporary offences, such as preventive offences or status offences more generally.[33] In fact, one of the main findings of Lacey's analysis of patterns of criminal responsibility is the identification of an impulse in criminal law to move from cautious to more extreme conceptions of character, which "surfaces at key points in the history of English criminal justice" and "has large practical and normative implications for the extent to which criminal law exhibits an inclusionary versus an exclusionary temper."[34] The contemporary moment would be one such key point, where an overall-character principle appears more prominent, besides also giving rise to a new form of responsibility–attribution based on risk. This new pattern of responsibility–attribution is closely associated with character and outcome but has a more distinctive preventive focus, assuming a future-oriented form and thereby grounding new forms of culpability such as pre-inchoate offences and the rapidly proliferating gamut of hybrid preventive measures.[35]

From this perspective, what first appears as a largely stable and common-sensical framework for understanding responsibility for crime is revealed as a fluid and multifaceted environment in which different conceptions coexist and dynamically interact. Lacey highlights how the hybridity of criminal responsibility results from its role in legitimating and coordinating different interests, ideas, and institutions in society, naturalising their sense of validity and coherence and, in so doing, presenting the criminal law itself as a legitimate and ordered institution.[36] This last point resonates with a relatively recent strand of legal scholarship that sees criminal law primarily as a political institution. The main elaboration of this perspective can be found in Lindsay Farmer's institutional account of criminal law, which builds on Neil MacCormick's work to posit criminal law's main function as that of securing civil order. According to MacCormick, "an effective and properly functioning system of criminal law and criminal justice is essential for the relative security of mutual expectations which is a condition of the civility of civil society. Criminal law becomes fully intelligible only from this perspective."[37] Three primary insights can be taken from this postulate. First, that the criminal law is "an integral component of society's basic structure",[38] and therefore has a constitutive role to play in social arrangements. Second, that this role is what allows us to make sense of what the criminal law is and what it does, to make it intelligible. And third, that this role is primarily about securing mutual expectations to preserve "the civility of civil society".

The idea of civility at the core of civil order suggests a specific notion of social order based on "a particular configuration of selfhood, violence, and law produced by the modernizing process".[39] It is thus inherently tied to a modern social imaginary that sees civil society as peaceful and civilised, and as having equality and mutual respect as base values. This idea is thus both descriptive, in that it locates civil order within a particular history and context, and normative, in that it invests civil order with an aura of validity and desirability. But, just like hegemony, it must be acknowledged that civil order is also complex, fluid, and fragmented. As Farmer stated, "there is no single or simple concept of civil order which it is the aim of the criminal law to secure or produce".[40] Rather, this order is very much a reflection of civil society, where disparate values and interests are constantly interacting and often competing. Furthermore, unlike the political imaginary of the state where every individual is a citizen endowed with equal rights, civil society is replete with substantial inequalities and structural violence, so that it is home to radically different experiences and perceptions of social reality. Particularly in late modernity, the fragmented and structurally violent character of civil society also means that social experience is pervaded by ontological insecurity and anxiety.[41] The social arrangements underpinning civil order are thus home to significant tensions and contradictions, many of which betray the values and ideals situated at the core of the notion of civility. The apparent unity and coherence of civil order, and the sense of civic identity and belonging it fosters, are largely the product of the dominant ideological apparatus preserved by the state, in its effort to maintain its hold on common sense.

This discussion highlights how the superficial coherence and integrity of criminal responsibility not only conceals and represses a multifaceted framework, but that it also actively necessitates this complexity to preserve its hegemonic position. Criminal responsibility needs to be patterned to reflect the "messiness" of civil society, at the same time as it needs to actively incorporate and naturalise this complexity to preserve a sense of legitimacy and to secure dominant social conditions. A cultural analysis feeds into these insights from critical criminal law theory, emphasising the need to uncover, de-naturalise, and challenge what legal discourse and practice takes for granted, what it does not say or what it presents as unproblematic. This is particularly important to understand how criminal responsibility can preserve its hegemonic status despite its significant shifts and variations. To do so, it is arguably necessary to move beyond the structure of criminal liability and offences, into an analysis of underlying structures of feeling and their manifestation in patterns of blaming.

From patterns of responsibility to patterns of blaming

To a significant extent, practices of responsibility–attribution rely on the assumption that the evaluations of culpability embedded in them are fair and objective. The law is replete with measures, instruments, and procedures that are both grounded in this assumption and meant to reinforce it, from principles like the presumption of innocence and the need for a fair trial to the rules of evidence, the training and authority of judges, and the protective and sanctified character of jury deliberations. The belief in the validity of legal attributions of responsibility and the techniques utilised to reinforce such validity are largely reflective of a broader hegemonic conception in contemporary thought and societies, which is that "modern" evaluations of risk and blame are grounded on objective criteria, guided by sophisticated methods and epistemologies which give it significant accuracy and reliability. Legal rationality, as Weber indicated long ago,[42] is one of the primary, if not the primary, articulations of this hegemonic position, legitimising forms of political authority and engendering regimes of truth. Criminal responsibility in a sense goes even further, as it conjoins this legal form of rationality with (also dominant) medicalised and psychologised ideas around agency, capacity, volition, and so on.

A critique of this hegemonic common sense around legal responsibility–attribution arguably requires a cultural examination of the specific articulations and ideological formations underpinning the criminal law. Here, our endeavour can benefit from an engagement with Mary Douglas's discussion of conceptions of danger and patterns of blaming in contemporary societies and its inversion of the traditional anthropological gaze. Douglas spent a significant portion of her earlier work scrutinising how issues of danger, blame, pollution, and taboo had a socio-political function in "primitive" societies.[43] There was, in this work, already a hint that these ideas carried contemporary relevance. This insight was crystallised and developed in the essays collected in *Risk and Blame*,[44] in which the starting point was to challenge the presumption that there was a fundamental difference between "modern" and "primitive" blaming practices. This idea assumes that, while "primitive" societies had a politicised and moralised conception of danger, where "bad things" were always interpreted to have a charged meaning—for instance, the collapse of someone's house was seen as the result of an envious neighbour's curse, or the consequence of a moral failure on the part of one of the residents—in "modern" societies, ideas of danger had a logical, scientific basis, and therefore blaming for harmful consequences was "real" and objective. Against this, Douglas argued that modern conceptions of danger are just as moralised and politicised.

For Douglas, dangers are predominantly cultural: they are socially and politically constructed and play a prominent role in "the making of community consensus".[45] In other words, our perceptions and evaluations of what and who is dangerous are significantly conditioned by our social imaginary and its underlying conception of order. Danger is thus "defined to protect the public good and the incidence of blame is a by-product of arrangements for persuading fellow members to contribute to it."[46] This notion that danger is defined in relation to the public good and to the needs and values of the community finds resonance in criminal law doctrine and scholarship, from the idea that crimes are "public wrongs" that concern the community as a whole,[47] to the importance given to considerations of welfare as a central principle of the criminalisation.[48] But the proposition that the social character of danger conditions the incidence of blame presents a substantial challenge to the possibility of what Douglas calls "real blaming"—that is, "objective" blaming such as that assumed by criminal culpability. Rather, it implies that our blaming practices tend to follow specific patterns, related to our cultural perceptions with regards to danger and dangerousness. These perceptions, shaped and conditioned by symbolic and material structures and representations, ground assumptions and sensibilities that strongly suggest what and who is to blame for specific dangers and harms, in accordance with cultural expectations.

In my previous work,[49] I discussed how criminalisation in many areas can be seen to revolve around "danger formations", which culturally shape perceptions and sensibilities, channelling hostility towards specific groups identified as dangerous in order to legitimise and naturalise—in Farmer's terms, to "secure"—structures of inequality and oppression.[50] These danger formations can often find expression in formal structures and rules of criminal liability; for instance, terrorism offences can be traced back to notions of dangerousness surrounding the terrorist threat,[51] which are reflected in how responsibility for these offences are shaped around patterns of risk and follow the overall-character principle.[52] However, these danger formations also influence the law in more subtle ways, which are not easily trackable by focusing only on patterns of responsibility–attribution. To understand how they operate, it is necessary to move beyond the surface of the "form" or, as Hall would call it, the "philosophy" of criminal liability, to reach into its underpinning common sense—the produced cultural formations that influence blaming.[53]

To better understand how danger formations operate, it is helpful to engage with Raymond Williams's conception of structures of feeling. For Williams, a structure of feeling "is as firm and definite as 'structure' suggests, yet it operates in the most delicate and least tangible parts of our activity".[54] Likewise, a danger formation "has a solid structure which can be traced to ostensive material and symbolic processes; and yet its effect is subtle, that of a common sense 'feeling' of what/who is dangerous and criminal which is rarely scrutinised".[55] As such, a danger formation is often unacknowledged, at least as a basis for culpability and blaming; for this reason, it can coexist with dominant ideas about the reliability of practices of responsibility–attribution without disturbing them. To examine a danger formation, then, it is necessary to actively look for moments and circumstances in which its "taken for granted" character falters and its cultural content becomes apparent. Then, it becomes possible to observe not only the formation underpinning the "dominant social character" of a field, but also its "omissions and consequences, as lived".[56]

As a structure of feeling, then, a danger formation reveals itself more clearly in the gap and the tensions between "public ideals" and the concrete social reality which they strive to regulate—in Williams's words, "the conflict between the ethic and the experience".[57] This approach thus has a primary focus on the dynamics of suppression involved in criminalisation, tracing and exposing what it takes for granted, what it leaves out, what it does not say or address, and what it tries to prevent from emerging, as well as the consequences of such dynamics. Williams highlighted that this conflict is most apparent in moments of social change, during which there are ruptures and disturbances in the dominant social character before a new (or renewed) common sense becomes established. Further, the way these changes are reflected in criminalisation can affect the formal structure of criminal liability, but they can also consist of more subtle variations, of changes of tone, impulse, and restraint—changes of *presence* which nevertheless "exert palpable pressures and set effective limits on experience and on action".[58]

Criminalisation is significantly conditioned by structures of feeling which permeate its practical consciousness, in ways which can often appear idiosyncratic—instances of bias, procedural unfairness, reflections of power imbalances in a specific case—but which are revealed, upon analysis, as emergent social formations, which can be traced to specific patterns of blaming. Thus, although on the surface specific rules of criminal liability may appear general in application and "neutral" in language, in practice we can observe changes of presence which effect significant variations pointing to socially structured, even if formally undefined, patterns of criminalisation and blaming. These patterns are often linked to more structured—fixed—social conditions, such as histories and processes of racialisation, misogyny, socio-economic inequalities and so on; but it would be a mistake to suggest that these structural conditions are simply being passively reproduced in criminal culpability. Rather, criminal culpability exists within a multifaceted, multilayered, patterned ideological framework—in which we can identify intersections and specific dynamics, such as hierarchies, dependencies, and tensions. As such, patterns of blaming are themselves multifaceted, usually articulating together multiple ideological structures in a relation which is mediated by contemporary moral and political sensibilities. These sensibilities not only significantly structure the relation and composition of specific patterns, but also their expression—the pressures and limitations which they exert are primarily about the circulation and naturalisation of ways of feeling—about arranging and facilitating certain moral[59] and affective[60] economies.

Patterns of blaming in intention and murder

To illustrate these points, it is useful to go back to a study I made regarding the law of joint enterprise in England and Wales.[61] My aim was to investigate how this area is influenced by a pattern of blaming which primarily targets young, racialised, and marginalised men from deprived urban areas by constructing their identities as gang members, and therefore allowing them to be held culpable for serious crimes even in circumstances in which they only had a very tenuous relation to the crime; for instance, by being present at the scene, being an acquaintance of other people involved, or appearing with them in a rap or drill music video. This targeting was facilitated by a special legal doctrine, "parasitic accessorial liability" or "PAL". While this is an old doctrine, from the 1980s onwards, it became predominantly used in the criminalisation of gang violence. PAL allowed liability to be established for any offence, but mostly murder, on the basis that the defendant was part of a joint enterprise, during or because of which another offence had been committed, and the defendant foresaw that there was a real possibility that such an offence could be committed. Formally, this doctrine was of general application, potentially used in any instance in which a crime arose out of previous criminal activity or association; but, in substance, it became wrapped around what I called a danger formation centred on the image of the gang as a serious social threat, and on racialised and marginalised urban youth as paradigmatic gang members. I could thus identify a pattern of blaming in this regard, given that this danger formation was primarily a structure of feeling, rather than a structured formation defined and embedded into legal doctrine and ideology.

What really made this area of law a focus of interest to me was the fact that this doctrine was consistently and increasingly criticised in legal academic and professional circles, as well as in political and media discourse in recent times, until it was abolished by a Supreme Court decision, *R v Jogee*,[62] in 2016. The decision attracted significant interest and was hailed (at least initially) as a significant corrective turn in criminal law, restoring established principles of criminal liability. However, there were already signs in the decision itself that although the law was formally being changed, the underpinning danger formation was likely to persist, something which—unfortunately—proved to be accurate: joint enterprise cases continue to be identified, treated, and resolved in much the same way as before, despite the significant legal change suggested by the decision.[63] In my analysis, the decision was necessitated by an increasing challenge to the danger formation centred around gang violence raised by emerging structures of feeling (for instance, around social and racial injustice), which in turn threatened to undermine the hegemony of the dominant ideology of criminal responsibility. The decision sought primarily to safeguard this dominant ideology, by formally abolishing the doctrine and restating the validity of broader principles of individual responsibility and justice. However, it also simultaneously resisted any implication that this might substantially change criminalisation in this area, and even that the formal error identified in the law would imply that the way the previous—erroneous—law had been applied was similarly problematic.

From the perspective of patterns of responsibility, it can be said that the older doctrine of PAL was a manifestation of character, as although it focused on the subjective category of foresight, it effectively suggested an evaluation of the defendant's character based on their participation in a joint enterprise.[64] When *Jogee* abolished PAL, such crimes became governed by the general rules of accomplice liability, which require an intention to assist or encourage the commission of the substantive offence to be established. In this sense, one of the main critiques of joint enterprise—that it essentially allowed individuals to be convicted of murder on the basis of a lower threshold of culpability—was resolved, as now intention—the kind of *mens rea* required for murder—was also required for establishing liability in these cases. However, as it was made clear in the judgment in *Jogee* and in decisions and reports succeeding it, this formal change made no substantive impact in the fairness of previous decisions nor in how similar cases were conducted and decided after the decision. This is because while the pattern of responsibility may have formally changed, the pattern of blaming underpinning this area of criminalisation was effectively re-articulated, thus allowing a common sense regarding the danger of gang-related violence to continue to drive perceptions of culpability in these cases. If anything, such re-articulation created new conditions for its circulation which are potentially more resistant against competing structures of feeling—for instance, by making it harder to claim that the law is being explicitly discriminatory, as there no longer is an explicit doctrine facilitating that area of criminalisation.

Conclusion

Critical approaches to criminal responsibility have urged us to resist the allure of dominant conceptions of responsibility–attribution, and to see criminal culpability for what it is: a complex, multifaceted, and hybrid environment, full of tensions and contradictions, and significantly influenced by issues of ideology, power, and structural violence. This chapter has sought to contribute to this critical endeavour by adding a more specifically cultural dimension, which places a nuanced conception of hegemony and the inherently politicised and moralised character of our practices of blaming at its core.

Notes

1. See A Ashworth & J Horder, *Principles of Criminal Law* (Oxford University Press: Oxford, 7th edn, 2013); H Carvalho, *The Preventive Turn in Criminal Law* (Oxford University Press: Oxford, 2017).
2. I Dennis, "The Critical Condition of Criminal Law", *Current Legal Problems*, vol. 50, no. 1 (1997), p.213 at p.237.
3. For a few notable examples, see HLA Hart, *Punishment and Responsibility: Essays in the Philosophy of Law* (Oxford University Press: Oxford, 1968); V Tadros, *Criminal Responsibility* (Oxford University Press: Oxford, 2005); RA Duff, *Answering for Crime: Responsibility and Liability in the Criminal Law* (Hart Publishing: Oxford, 2009).
4. N Lacey, *In Search of Criminal Responsibility: Ideas, Interests, and Institutions* (Oxford University Press: Oxford, 2016); see also Dennis, "Critical"; RA Duff, *Intention, Agency and Criminal Liability* (Blackwell: London, 1990).
5. H Carvalho, "Dangerous Patterns: Joint Enterprise and the Culture of Criminal Law", *Social and Legal Studies*, vol. 32, no. 3 (2023), p.335.
6. See S Hall, *Essential Essays* (Duke University Press: Durham, 2019), vols I and II.
7. R Williams, *Marxism and Literature* (Oxford University Press: Oxford, 1977), p.128.
8. For a synthesis of over 16 years of work on these matters, see Lacey, *Search*.
9. M Douglas, *Risk and Blame* (Routledge: London, 1992).
10. See Williams, *Marxism*; R Williams, *The Long Revolution* (Parthian Books: Cardigan, 2013).
11. R Williams, *Keywords: A Vocabulary of Culture and Society* (Fontana Press: London, 1988), p.87.
12. Williams, *Keywords*, p.90.
13. Williams, *Keywords*, p.90.
14. Williams, *Keywords*, p.91.
15. Q Hoare & GN Smith, *Selections from the Prison Notebooks of Antonio Gramsci* (Lawrence & Wishart: London, 2005).
16. Hall, *Essential*, vol II, p.43.
17. P Bourdieu, *Language and Symbolic Power* (Harvard University Press: Cambridge, 1991), p.239.
18. Hall, *Essential*, vol II, p.43.
19. Bourdieu, *Language*, p.131.
20. Hall, *Essential*, vol II, p.44.
21. Hall, *Essential*, vol I, p.104.
22. K Crehan, "Gramsci's concept of common sense: A useful concept for anthropologists?", *Journal of Modern Italian Studies*, vol. 16, no. 2 (2011), p.273 at p.277.
23. Hall, *Essential*, vol I, p.172.
24. N Lacey, *State Punishment* (New York: Routledge, 1988), p.144.
25. See A Norrie, *Crime, Reason and History* (Cambridge University Press: Cambridge, 2013); Lacey, *Search*; L Farmer, *Making the Modern Criminal Law: Criminalization and Civil Order* (Oxford University Press: Oxford, 2016); P Ramsay, "The Responsible Subject as Citizen", *Modern Law Review*, vol. 69, no. 1 (2006), p.29; A Loughnan, *Self, Others and the State* (Cambridge University Press, Cambridge: 2020).
26. Norrie, *Crime*.
27. Lacey, *Search*, p.26.
28. N Lacey, "Space, Time and Function: Intersecting Principles of Responsibility Across the Terrain of Criminal Justice", *Criminal Law and Philosophy*, vol. 1 (2007), p.233 at p.236.
29. Dennis, "Critical", p.237.
30. Lacey, *Search*, p.33.
31. Horder, "Criminal", p.207.
32. N Lacey, "Character, Capacity, Outcome", in MD Dubber & L Farmer (eds) *Modern Histories of Crime and Punishment* (Stanford University Press: Redwood, 2007) at p.29.
33. See Lacey, *Search*.

34 Lacey, *Search*, pp.36–37.
35 Lacey, *Search*, pp. 46–48. See also Carvalho, *Preventive*.
36 See Lacey, *Search*.
37 MacCormick cited in L Farmer, "Civil order, markets, and the intelligibility of the criminal law", *University of Toronto Law Journal*, vol. 70, no. 1 (2020), p.123.
38 V Chiao, "What Is the criminal law for?", *Law and Philosophy*, vol. 35, no. 2 (2016), p.137 at p.139.
39 Farmer, *Making*, p.55.
40 Farmer, *Making*, p.63.
41 For a detailed discussion of the contrast between state and civil society and its importance to criminal law theory, see Carvalho, *Preventive*.
42 M Weber, *Economy and Society* (Harvard University Press: Cambridge MA, 2019 [1922]).
43 See M Douglas, *Purity and Danger* (Routledge: London, 1966).
44 Douglas, *Risk*.
45 Douglas, *Risk*, p.21.
46 Douglas, *Risk*, p.19.
47 See RA Duff, *The Realm of Criminal Law* (Oxford University Press: Oxford, 2018).
48 See Ashworth and Horder, *Principles*.
49 Carvalho, "Dangerous".
50 Farmer, *Making*, p. 29.
51 Carvalho, *Preventive*.
52 Lacey, *Search*.
53 Hall, *Essential*, vol II, p.43.
54 Williams, *Long*, p.69.
55 Carvalho, "Dangerous", p.343.
56 Williams, *Long*, p.85.
57 Williams, *Long*, p.87.
58 Williams, *Marxism*, p.132.
59 D Fassin, "Moral Economies Revisited", *Annales, Histoire, Sciences Sociales*, vol. 64, no. 6 (2009), p.1237.
60 S Ahmed, *The Cultural Politics of Emotion* (Edinburgh University Press: Edinburgh, 2004).
61 Carvalho, "Dangerous".
62 *R v Jogee* [2016] UKSC 8.
63 See Carvalho, "Dangerous".
64 See Carvalho, "Dangerous".

References
Books and book chapters

Ahmed S, *The Cultural Politics of Emotion* (Edinburgh University Press: Edinburgh, 2004).
Ashworth A & Horder J, *Principles of Criminal Law* (Oxford University Press: Oxford, 7th edn, 2013).
Bourdieu P, *Language and Symbolic Power* (Harvard University Press: Cambridge, 1991).
Carvalho H, *The Preventive Turn in Criminal Law* (Oxford University Press: Oxford, 2017).
Douglas M, *Purity and Danger* (Routledge: London, 1966).
Douglas M, *Risk and Blame: Essays in Cultural Theory* (Routledge: London, 1992).
Duff RA, *Answering for Crime: Responsibility and Liability in the Criminal Law* (Hart Publishing: Oxford, 2009).
Duff RA, *Intention, Agency and Criminal Liability: Philosophy of Action and the Criminal Law* (Blackwell: London, 1990).
Duff RA, *The Realm of Criminal Law* (Oxford University Press: Oxford, 2018).
Farmer L, *Making the Modern Criminal Law: Criminalization and Civil Order* (Oxford University Press: Oxford, 2016).
Hall S, *Essential Essays* (Duke University Press: Durham NC, 2019), vols I & II.
Hart HLA, *Punishment and Responsibility: Essays in the Philosophy of Law* (Oxford University Press: Oxford, 1968).

Hoare Q & Smith GN, *Selections from the Prison Notebooks of Antonio Gramsci* (Lawrence & Wishart: London, 2005).

Lacey N, "Character, Capacity, Outcome", in Dubber MD & Farmer L (eds), *Modern Histories of Crime and Punishment* (Stanford University Press: Redwood, 2007).

Lacey N, *In Search of Criminal Responsibility: Ideas, Interests, and Institutions* (Oxford University Press: Oxford, 2016).

Lacey N, *State Punishment* (New York: Routledge, 1988).

Loughnan A, *Self, Others and the State* (Cambridge University Press: Cambridge, 2020).

Norrie A, *Crime, Reason and History* (Cambridge University Press: Cambridge, 2013).

Tadros V, *Criminal Responsibility* (Oxford University Press: Oxford, 2005).

Weber M, *Economy and Society* (Harvard University Press: Cambridge, 2019).

Williams R, *Keywords: A Vocabulary of Culture and Society* (Fontana Press: London, 1988).

Williams R, *Marxism and Literature* (Oxford University Press: Oxford, 1977).

Williams R, *The Long Revolution* (Parthian Books: Cardigan, 2013).

Journal articles

Carvalho H, "Dangerous Patterns: Joint Enterprise and the Culture of Criminal Law", *Social and Legal Studies*, vol. 32, no. 3 (2023), pp.335–355.

Chiao V, "What Is the Criminal Law For?", *Law and Philosophy*, vol. 35, no. 2 (2016), pp.137–163.

Crehan K, "Gramsci's Concept of Common Sense: A Useful Concept for Anthropologists?", *Journal of Modern Italian Studies*, vol. 16, no. 2 (2011), pp.273–287.

Dennis I, "The Critical Condition of Criminal Law", *Current Legal Problems*, vol. 50, no. 1 (1997), pp.213–249.

Farmer L, "Civil Order, Markets, and the Intelligibility of the Criminal Law", *University of Toronto Law Journal*, vol. 70, no. 1 (2020), pp.123–140.

Fassin D, "Moral Economies Revisited", *Annales, Histoire, Sciences Sociales*, vol. 64, no. 6 (2009), pp.1237–1266.

Lacey N, "Space, Time and Function: Intersecting Principles of Responsibility Across the Terrain of Criminal Justice", *Criminal Law and Philosophy*, vol. 1 (2007), pp.233–250.

Ramsay P, "The Responsible Subject as Citizen", *Modern Law Review*, vol. 69, no. 1 (2006), pp.29–58.

2
CONTEXT MATTERS

An Argument for a Socio-Contextual Model of Criminal Responsibility

Federica Coppola

Introduction

Scholarly efforts to bring social justice matters to the forefront of criminal law have intensified. The increasing recognition of the social injustices[1] that plague the reality of criminal justice across legal systems is raising calls for paradigm shifts that give more prominence to the structural factors of crime through the implementation of socially informed approaches to offending behaviour. Such proposals emphasise the clash between criminal law *as it ought to be* and criminal law *as it is*, including the social, economic, and political contingencies that influence its concrete application in real-life criminal justice. Hence, a recurring discussion in contemporary criminal law scholarship is on whether—and to what extent—criminal law can (and should) plausibly incorporate such contingencies into its notions and practices, or whether such law would be better off in its dogmatic and normative dimensions.

Among others, one area of controversy concerns the "place" of the social aspects of crime in the notion of criminal responsibility. For many, criminal responsibility is the least suited venue for accommodating the social factors of criminal offence. The reasons are manifold, spanning from the irrelevance of social influences on human behaviour and agency, to the fact that giving weight to such influences, however criminogenic, in criminal adjudication may risk frustrating the criminal law's commitment to its prescribed goals of individual blame, punishment, and respect for the dignity of crime perpetrators. By contrast, other scholars underscore the improved fairness of a criminal law system that values and addresses the adverse social[2] and environmental[3] factors that lie at the core of much criminal offending. To these scholars, an acknowledgment of the social factors of crime in criminal adjudication may be a critical avenue for addressing the disproportionate and uneven criminalisation of the most socially disadvantaged, consequently decreasing punitiveness, promoting greater safety, and reducing inequality.

Against this backdrop, this chapter merges these two strands of the debate with modern empirical insights into the influence of socio-contextual factors on individual choices and behaviours and proposes several arguments for the adoption of a socio-contextual model of criminal responsibility. The proposed model draws upon the idea that criminal choices should not be adjudicated in isolation but in the context of the social environment of individuals, including both the immediate context in which they operate, and their living background. Of course, the proposed model does not dismiss the current structure of criminal responsibility. More simply, the model "situates" its structural components in the framework of broader socio-contextual contingencies that may bear a meaningful influence on criminal decision-making.

Furthermore, the chapter examines the selected potential implications of such a rethought theoretical model of criminal responsibility for legal doctrine and sentencing. The latter analysis emphasises that a model of criminal responsibility that gives normative weight to socio-contextual factors would be capable of enhancing the accuracy of culpability ascriptions and can lead to sentencing determinations that better fulfil the retributivist and utilitarian goals of punishment.

Current state of criminal responsibility

Criminal responsibility is definitionally rooted in the common-sense-based idea of crime as a "concurrence of an evil-meaning mind [and] an evil-doing hand".[4] Such an idea builds upon the culture of individualism that has historically characterised the development of Western criminal law, in which the notions of blame and punishment are nearly exclusively focused on the individual's guilty act committed with a guilty state of mind. By operating through such an individualistic lens, the doctrine of criminal responsibility essentialises and allocates the source of criminal conduct "inside" the individual and their choice to commit a criminal act, to the large neglect of socio-contextual influences. Accordingly, so long as blaming practices are directed at targeting an individual's choice to do wrong, the criminal law is severely limited in potentially accommodating the social aspects of crime.

The individualistic conception of criminal responsibility is a key vehicle for the criminal law to fulfil its universal commitment to respecting the dignity of crime perpetrators as autonomous and rational beings.[5] Rationality and autonomy constitute the fundamental features of the criminal law's person and the touchstones of the (dominant) voluntarist model of criminal responsibility. With HLA Hart as its major proponent,[6] voluntarism structures criminal responsibility along three main components: choice, mental capacity (or normative competence), and a fair opportunity to do otherwise. Hence, the scope of criminal responsibility is narrowed down to encompassing the individual's choice to do wrong, having adequately engaged their cognitive and volitional capacities, and being free from immediate and exceptional external pressures.

In its traditional outlook, the voluntarist model overlooks more longitudinal socio-contextual influences on behaviour, such as an individual's upbringing, living environment, social background, and personal life experiences. Embracing a compatibilist[7] view of human agency, the model posits that these factors are secondary to the question of responsibility on the grounds that human action is governed by reason and people are provided with critical thinking skills to master situational pressures. Accordingly, a person is responsible for their actions, even if such actions were caused by forces beyond the person's control. In other words, the fact that factors outside a person's control influence their actions is *compatible* with the idea that *the person* is the ultimate causer of their actions. Thus, a person is culpable (i.e. responsible) for the actions that *they* cause, even if external factors contribute to the production of such actions. From this perspective, even if criminal law acknowledged that certain socio-environmental circumstances do influence and, in a sense, cause human behaviour, it would still presuppose that humans have a margin of freedom that allows them to act in a non-compelled manner. Thus, an acknowledgment that external, socio-environmental factors impact behaviour is compatible with the assumption that the individual is nonetheless able to effectuate autonomous and rational choices and is responsible for them.

From a doctrinal standpoint and consistent with the theoretical one, the limited relevance of the socio-contextual factors of the offence is self-evident in positive law, in which no express socio-environmental doctrine exists and extant doctrines are structurally unsuited to accommodate the broader socio-contextual factors of crime. In actual practice, the social conditions or backgrounds of perpetrators may have evidentiary value insofar as they can offer insight into facts that are determinative of the existence of other defences. Nevertheless, the evidentiary value of socio-environmental factors is mostly indirect and altogether secondary in assessing criminal responsibility.[8]

Scholarly criticism of this narrow model of criminal responsibility, including its reluctance to give due consideration to the socio-contextual contingencies of criminal conduct, has powerfully resonated over the years. One scholarly prong[9] has advanced an internal, philosophical critique emphasising the gross implausibility of assuming that socio-contextual influences are not determining factors in an individual's choice to do wrong. Another scholarly prong[10] has offered an external, political critique, highlighting that the deemed irrelevance of the socio-contextual factors of crime for questions of criminal responsibility is a mask for conservative political aims, using criminal law as a tool for keeping social adversities, such as poverty, institutional abuses, and structural racism further at the margins. This critique draws upon the objectively uneven application of criminal law to citizens with different social backgrounds and the fact that the categories of persons who are disproportionately subjected to mechanisms of blame, conviction, and punishment across legal systems are the least socially advantaged. As a result, the critique goes, the criminal law's indifference to the social dimension of crime frustrates its proclaimed goals of justice, equality, and dignity and provides another latent mechanism of social exclusion and marginalisation.

Science of social contextualism

The drawbacks of the criminal law's individualism become even more evident under the lens of the solid body of empirical data about the inescapable influence of social contexts on human conduct. Empirical research unanimously suggests that socio-contextual factors are among the major determinants of human behaviour.[11] This perspective, known as *social contextualism*,[12] posits that the specific meaning or appropriateness of a given conduct is shaped by the relevant context in which it occurs. In other words, the reason why people appraise and respond to salient social cues with specific behavioural reactions depends on a variety of social-contextual factors. The latter not only encompass the immediate context that the individual operates in or interacts with at a given time, but also extend more broadly to more constant and longitudinal factors, such as family, peers, neighbourhood, cultural factors, and life experiences.[13] Accordingly, the quality of these types of factors largely influences a person's thoughts, feelings, and behavioural outcomes both in the short and long run—for the better or for the worse.[14]

Exposure to negative social environments is consistently considered to carry worsening criminogenic effects. Causal chains are admittedly complex; however, the wide consensus[15] is that the continued and unbuffered exposure to unhealthy social contexts and experiences of personal and social traumas (e.g. lack of economic resources or opportunities, or chronic exposure to violence) exposes individuals to a heightened risk of harmful psychological and behavioural patterns and negatively affects prosociality. In addition to background adversities, even ongoing contexts such as living environments, settings, and circumstances influence and drive behavioural responses throughout one's life. Importantly, although some situational forces (i.e. provocations) may trigger immediate behavioural reactions, other factors such as chronic or repeated exposure to abuse, violence, structural racism, and socioeconomic deprivation can generate (or exacerbate) traumas and impact behaviour in a manner that is more gradual and cumulative.[16]

Neurobiologically, these factors generate an overwhelming amount of toxic stress,[17] which in turn affects a variety of brain pathways that govern self-regulation, empathetic responding, perception and responsiveness to social cues, and other psychological functions that act as protective factors against harmful conduct, including criminal conduct. Accordingly, being exposed to toxic environments and situations can have lingering effects on the individual's neurobiology and result in problematic behaviours even in the long run.

Importantly, in harmful situations of social adversity, impacted individuals usually keep their rational mental capacities substantially intact; that is, they do not develop any mental impairment. *However,* the ways in which these people interpret and respond to social cues are contingent on the pathological contexts and experiences with which they interact. Therefore, the continued presence in harmful and criminogenic situations can act as a situational trigger for law-breaking conduct and barriers to desistance, often as a means of adaptation and survival to cope with or respond to the adversities emanating from such contexts, especially when institutional support is lacking or unhelpful and motivation to engage with the law is largely reduced.

Situating criminal responsibility: an argument for a socio-contextual model

The scientific insights summarised above add an important layer of support to scholarly positions advocating for attributing relevance to the socio-environmental factors of crime. Of course, nothing in science suggests that criminal behaviour is not the product of people's choices, reasons, and capacities. Rather, science indicates that such choices, reasons, and capacities are to be viewed in the context of the situation in which they transpire, including the immediate circumstances and broader socio-environmental contingencies that bear on the life of the relevant individual.

Remarkably, empirical research reveals that in contexts of persistent social adversity, criminal conduct may emerge as a rational mechanism of adaptation through which an individual copes with or responds to the situational demands emanating from such contexts. Accordingly, people who commit crimes under the influence of and in connection with such circumstances are to be viewed as rational agents who adapt to abnormal contexts in which the range of genuine choices is substantially limited by adverse socio-environmental dynamics. As has been observed, "the social context provides the material conditions within which the individual acts, and the individual's reasoning power serves to mediate between herself, her subjective agency and her social context."[18] On the one hand, individuals are provided with the capacity to critically think of and respond to situational demands through their choices and practical reasoning skills. On the other hand, contexts principally influence individual's minds and behaviours, including their practical reasoning, emotional needs, and reactions to adaptively cope with situational demands. From this perspective, we should conceive of rationality and autonomy as notions that are tied to circumstances and social contexts.

A rethinking of the ideas of autonomy and rationality through broader, contextualised lenses may lay the groundwork for the criteria of criminal responsibility that embrace a *situated* understanding of the individual's choice to engage in criminal wrongdoing—one in which the locus of criminal responsibility goes beyond the traditional focus on individual capacities or mental states and expands to the context of the individual's social environment. Tellingly, such an expansion implies neither the rejection nor the abandonment of the traditional voluntarist choice/capacity/opportunity structure of responsibility. Less ambitiously, it implies a broadening of the scope of these structural components to also encompass socio-contextual factors.[19]

Of particular importance in this case is the component of *fair opportunity to do otherwise*. As previously illustrated, the fair opportunity to do otherwise definitionally refers to the absence of unfair situational constraints that place individuals under such pressure that they cannot genuinely choose to behave differently. This situational pressure is normally restricted to the circumstances actually existing at the moment of the commission of the offence. Doctrinally, this scenario is typical of the excuse of duress,[20] whereby the individual acts criminally under an extreme threat of serious harm. In cases of duress, the individual has (at least metaphorically) no choice but to give in to the threat and act wrongfully.

A person acting under duress presumably behaves under strong stress, however transient or episodic, triggered by the fear that something unpleasant might happen if they do not engage in illegal conduct. In such cases, the individual remains a rational subject who acts upon a rational assessment of the circumstances. When thethreat is absent, the individual would not engage in illegal conduct. The same logic applies to an individual who is subject to constant and serious situational pressures and chooses to engage in illegal conduct to cope with or survive them. When such situations are severely harmful, individuals may resort to crime because their range of genuine choices is substantially limited by objective situational pressures of hardship. A key question consequently arises: *Why should transient stress due to episodic pressure receive practical and normative relevance in determining criminal responsibility as opposed to the chronic, inescapable systemic stress faced by people who live in seriously adverse conditions?*

As I illustrated in the previous section, there are cases where a person may suffer a series of situational pressures (often with traumatising effects) that present lingering effects both in the short and long run. The adverse impact of such chronically adverse socio-environmental circumstances on the individual derives from the choice-limiting effects of such circumstances. In addition, research suggests that these choice-limiting effects precisely constitute objective situational pressures toward illegal conduct. *Prima facie*, one might argue that people who engage in illegal conduct that links with their social situation still retain the practical reasoning skills that allow them to comply with the law and do otherwise. Viewed through a different lens, though, one might argue that many of these people who engage in illegal conduct that links with their social situation have diminished situational control because they are subject to constant situational pressures that impact and condition their behaviour.

Richard Lippke has advanced a similar argument for socially deprived perpetrators by drawing upon the notion of "chronic temptations".[21] For Lippke, the persistent and significant struggles that people inhabiting severe social deprivation constantly face, establish a "perverse incentive structure" that chronically tempts even individuals with well-developed self-control to yield in criminal offending. Under his account, people living in poverty are required to over-exercise their capacity for self-control and resist situational pressures to commit criminal offences, such that such capacity at some point inevitably depletes.

Consider as an example the crime of child neglect committed by parents living in chronic conditions of severe poverty, especially when institutional help is lacking. The literature[22] is quite consistent in saying that socio-economic deprivation can create the difficulty of parenting effectively, including a failure to respond to a child's emotional needs. *Prima facie*, we are indeed tempted to hold that the reason for such illegal conduct is the parents' conscious disregard for their children. However, if we broaden our lens to include the context of deprivation, then what we will see is not the neglectful parents but their deprived situation and the effects of such a situation on their behaviour.

As Lippke also holds, an undeniable fact is that the perverse incentive structure of poverty does not put such overwhelming pressure on people at the level that constitutes duress. However, when these situations occur, a key question concerns whether we as a society are in the position of expecting and demanding that individuals in such circumstances refrain from wrongdoing and act in conformity with the law. Perhaps, the most suitable answer to this question is "*not entirely*". If a person's opportunities and options have been compromised and limited by their exposure to toxic environments and life experiences—all forces the person did not choose and over which they have little or no control—then life-altering contexts may gain practical and normative significance in terms of diminished fair opportunity to do otherwise and, as a result, diminished blameworthiness.[23]

This consideration brings me to the meaning of *fairness*. As has been observed, HLA Hart's conception of fairness[24] hinges upon "a conception of society in which people live together sharing the same values and being subject to rules of conduct that work to everyone's advantage".[25] This conception appears too far off base in the case of individuals who live in adverse social conditions. Although even the least advantaged members of society may be believed to enjoy some benefits from living under the law, including a certain degree of personal protection, these people cannot be said to enjoy the benefits of social cooperation, which are distributed under the law's protection. From this perspective, the claim that each person in society is given a fair opportunity to choose between "keeping the law or paying the penalty"[26] is questionable. A truly fair criminal legal system should acknowledge the objective inequalities that affect people who live in a determinate set of substandard and depriving circumstances and recognise that these people have objectively fewer opportunities to comply with the law.[27]

Corollaries

Legal doctrine

A socio-contextual model of criminal responsibility that broadens the boundaries of adjudication to include the social and environmental factors of criminal conduct may have repercussions on the doctrinal level. One potential repercussion, which I have thoroughly analysed elsewhere,[28] includes the provision of a generic *situational* partial excuse (SPE) defence to become available for cases in which crime is triggered by conditions of severe social hardship that unfairly condition the defendant's choice to conform to the law. Consistent with the theoretical socio-contextual model of responsibility, the focus of this defence is not strictly the defendant's mind but the adverse context of hardship and its limiting impact on the defendant's choice to do otherwise. Accordingly, SPE qualifies as a coercion-based defence that embraces the same rationales of the excuse of duress—that is, coercion and reasonableness—but with some modification to encompass broader and more longitudinal situational pressures, including the social and material adversities that characterise the defendant's living environment. Furthermore, as the situational pressure emanating from social hardships is less "pressing" than the one that emerges from a condition of extreme coercion or threat as is in the case of duress, then responsibility is merely diminished but not entirely excluded.

Procedurally, this partial excuse can qualify as an affirmative defence that burdens the defendant to demonstrate by a preponderance of evidence of convincing quality (documental, testimonial, or both) that a direct link exists between a given situation of social hardship, a diminished opportunity to behave lawfully under the circumstances in view of their context, the state of mind of the defendant in view of the social hardship, and the offence committed. Subjectively, an SPE defendant would also have to prove their lack of culpability for the situation of social hardship, including whether they non-culpably failed to escape the situation of social hardship that led to the crime. For instance, the defendant would need to prove that they affirmatively sought but failed to receive adequate social and institutional support to address the adverse social situation that led to the commission of the offense due to a lack of public resources, inefficiency of public services, or criminogenic criminal policies.

SPE recognises that not all individuals confronted with social hardships engage in criminal conduct; thus, the defence entails a case-by-case assessment, whereby the fact-finder would have to adjudicate the defendant's motivation to engage in wrongdoing through the lens of the defendant's context. Importantly, the defence demands that the crime be judged from the viewpoint of the concrete individual affected by the pressing circumstances, with the ultimate assessment being whether the defendant's wrongful behaviour constitutes a reasonable response to the context of adversity in which they, through no fault of their own, were at the time of the crime.

Sentencing

In addition to legal doctrine, a socio-contextual model of criminal responsibility would also lead to a systematic consideration of the individual's circumstances and background in sentencing determinations. The focus of the latter would expand to give greater weight to the structural factors that contributed to the relevant conduct. Thus, sentencing would more systematically consider an individual's socio-economic status, family dynamics, trauma history, and even broader contextual elements such as state-created inequalities that may have played a contributory role in the aetiology of the offence. The latter aspects translate into a more profound consideration of individuals' past and ongoing socio-environmental backgrounds and lived experience that present meaningful links with the offence, as well as of the protective social factors that may act as *qualitative* benchmarks for identifying the most optimal sentencing options for the relevant individual in view of their social conditions.

Consideration of these factors at the sentencing stage may have twofold relevance, including both retributive/backward-looking and utilitarian/forward-looking perspectives. From a backward-looking perspective, socio-contextual factors of crime assume relevance under the principles of deserts and proportionality. In fact, sentencing determinations would imply a more comprehensive and individualised assessment of the circumstances surrounding the criminal choice and possibly result in sanctions that are better proportionate to the actual degree of the defendant's culpability by balancing the socio-contextual factors that played a role in the commission of the offence.[29]

Even more important than meeting backward-looking goals, a serious consideration of the socio-contextual factors of crime at sentencing would have significant forward-looking implications, particularly under the goal of social rehabilitation.[30] Consistent with the tenets of social rehabilitation, a socio-contextual model of responsibility fundamentally entails a normative acknowledgment of the structural contingencies on the aetiology of criminal offending, including the adversities that the defendant may have suffered prior to offending.[31] Such an acknowledgment is critical for incentivising sentencing authorities to more thoroughly apprehend the impacts of these factors on the defendants' behaviour and be prompted to identify sentencing options that are creative and efficient and that, while addressing the social factors of crime, create opportunities for crime desistance and minimise the risk of further adversity and re-traumatisation.

Finally, a socio-contextual model of criminal responsibility might also provide a tangible, normative avenue for recognising the state's contributory role to the creation or maintenance of the social hardships underpinning the criminal offence within the sentencing process—provided that such contribution is convincingly demonstrated by the facts of the case. Such an outcome resonates with Manikis's proposal[32] for the provision of a complimentary sentencing framework that allows for a separate assessment of state's blame and harms in addition to the individual's (reduced) culpability. Manikis's framework adopts a relational and communicative approach to acknowledge the state's responsibility in the genesis of (much) criminal offending, including via the creation or maintenance of criminogenic social harms and inequalities that especially affect the most marginalised groups. Hypothesising the complimentary recognition of state responsibility, sentencing determinations would not only address the defendant's individual and social needs but would also "engage the state through actions that seek to minimize or partially redress the harms"[33] it either created or maintained.

Conclusion

This chapter has focused on empirical and normative insights to assign normative weight to the socio-contextual factors of crime within the notion of criminal responsibility. As emphasised, the resulting model does not revolutionise the extant canons of adjudication; however, it rearticulates their boundaries by broadening the lens of adjudication from the individual to their social environment to accommodate the structural factors that may have meaningfully affected an individual's choice to break the law. Although the proposed model keeps the tenets of criminal responsibility fundamentally unaltered, it may lead to adjudication and sentencing outcomes that pay closer attention to the role of the individual's social background in the genesis of the offence and seek to also address social factors to offer meaningful opportunities for positive change.

Altogether, a socio-contextual model of criminal responsibility is doctrinally plausible and empirically sound, and it promotes a narrative that invites a more nuanced understanding of the complexities surrounding criminal choices, including an acceptance of the inescapable social dimension of human conduct. More importantly, such a model may be critical for delivering more equitable justice and reducing the risk of either perpetuating or aggravating social disadvantage. Whether the latter goals should be attained ultimately rests on the question of whether the functions of criminal law should remain solely or mostly framed in terms of blame, punishment, and protection, or whether such functions should more broadly be framed as also encompassing positive reform, actual second chances, equality, and social inclusion. The latter are certainly compatible with careful and respectful attempts to understand and adjudicate the role of the social context in offending behaviours.

Notes

1. See, e.g. N Lacey, "Criminal Justice and Social Injustice", *LSE Working Paper*, No 84 (2022), available at: https://eprints.lse.ac.uk/116949/1/Lacey_criminal_justice.pdf.
2. As understood in this chapter, social factors include socioeconomic status, family background, peer influence, cultural norms, access to education, employment opportunities, and social support systems, structural racism, and institutional abuses.
3. As understood in this chapter, environmental factors encompass the physical and situational context in which criminal behaviour occurs, such as neighbourhood dynamics, availability of drugs, presence of firearms, and community disorganization, all of which can contribute to an individual's exposure to criminal opportunities.
4. *Morissette v. the United States*, 342 U.S. 246, 352 (1952).
5. See F Coppola, *The Emotional Brain and the Guilty Mind: Novel Paradigms of Culpability and Punishment* (Hart Publishing: Oxford, 2021), Ch.1.
6. See HLA Hart, *Punishment and Responsibility: Essays in the Philosophy of Law* (Oxford University Press: Oxford, 1968).
7. See, e.g. SJ Morse, "Determinism and the Death of Folk Psychology: Two Challenges to Responsibility from Neuroscience", *Minnesota Journal of Law Science & Technology*, vol. 9, no.1 (2008), p.1.
8. While socio-environmental factors are not essential to responsibility ascriptions, they *may* gain circumstantial weight in sentencing to modulate penalty determinations. Considering the generalised discretion afforded to sentencers, there is not a consistent scheme through which such factors are evaluated across legal systems.
9. E.g. M Fondacaro, "Toward an Ecological Jurisprudence Rooted in Concepts of Justice and Empirical Research", *UMCK Law Review*, vol. 69 (2000-2001), p.179; A Norrie, "The Limits of Justice: Finding Fault in the Criminal Law", *The Modern Law Review*, vol. 59, no. 4 (1996), p.540; N Lacey, "Socializing the Subject of Criminal Law? Criminal Responsibility and the Purposes of Criminalization", *Marquette Law Review*, vol. 99, no. 3 (2016), p.541.
10. E.g. A Kaye, "The Secret Politics of Compatibilist Criminal Law", *Kansas Law Review*, vol. 55 (2007), p.365; A Ristroph, "How (Not) To Think like a Punisher", *Florida Law Review*, vol. 61 (2009), p.727.
11. See, e.g. C Haney et al, "Interpersonal Dynamics in A Simulated Prison", *Journal of Criminology and Penology*, vol. 1, no. 1 (1973), p.69; U Bronfenbrenner, *The Ecology of Human Development* (Harvard University Press: Cambridge, MA, 1979); J Bowlby et al, "An Interview with John Bowlby on the Origins and Reception of His Work", *Free Associations*, vol. 6 (1986), p.36.
12. See generally C Haney, *Criminality in Context: The Psychological Foundations of Criminal Justice Reform* (American Psychological Association: Washington DC, 2020).
13. Haney, *Criminality*.
14. Haney, *Criminality*.
15. For a review, see Haney, *Criminality*.
16. Haney, *Criminality*.
17. G Evans et al., "Stressing Out the Poor: Chronic Physiological Stress and the Income Achievement Gap", *Pathways*, Winter (2011), p.16; JD Bremmer, "Traumatic Stress: Effects on the Brain", *Dialogues in Clinical Neuroscience*, vol. 8, no. 4 (2006), p.449.
18. A Norrie, "Practical Reasoning and Criminal Responsibility: A Jurisprudential Approach", in D Cornish & R Clarke (eds), *The Reasoning Criminal: Rational Choice Perspectives on Offending* (Transaction Publishers: New Brunswick NJ, 2014), p.217.
19. For instance, David Brink and Dana Nelkin have advanced a modified version of the voluntarist model that "brings together" the mental and situational components of human behaviour. Although their scholarship rejects situationist challenges to criminal responsibility, Brink and

Nelkin acknowledge that "how much and what sorts of capacity one needs depend on situational features." They further recognise that the influence of situational pressures on individual behaviour depends on the baseline level of normative competence, which varies across individuals. Altogether, the requisite levels of normative competence and situational control are not invariant, but they need to be contextualised. What Brink and Nelkin exactly mean by "context" is unclear, as they do not provide any explanation of it. However, it is not implausible to think that their idea of "context" may include broad circumstantial variables. See generally D Brink & D Nelkin, "Fairness and the Architecture of Responsibility", in D Shoemaker (ed), *Oxford Studies in Agency and Responsibility* (Oxford University Press: New York, 2013), vol I, p.284.
20 See e.g. DV Gomez, "Duress and the Antcolony's Ethic: Reflections on the Foundations of the Defense and Its Limits", *New Criminal Law Review*, vol. 11, no. 4 (2008), p.615.
21 R Lippke, "Social Deprivation as Tempting Fate", *Criminal Law & Philosophy*, vol. 5, no. 3 (2011), p.277.
22 See, e.g. R Rebbe et al, "The Association of Race, Ethnicity, and Poverty with Child Maltreatment Reporting", *Pediatrics*, no. 150 (2022), e2021053346.
23 See also Lippke, "Social Deprivation" (reaching the same conclusion).
24 Hart, *Punishment*, pp.22–23.
25 G Mousourakis, "Character, Choice, and Criminal Responsibility", *Le Cahiers Du Droit*, vol. 39, no. 1 (1998), p.71.
26 Hart, *Punishment*, pp.22–23.
27 See also A Duff, "Blame, Moral Standing, and the Legitimacy of Criminal Trial", *Ratio*, vol. 23, no. 2 (2010), p.123; M Tonry, "Can Desert be Just in an Unjust World?", in AP Simester, A du Bois-Pedain & U Neumann (eds), *Liberal Criminal Theory: Essays for Andreas von Hirsch* (Hart Publishing: Portland, 2014), p.141.
28 F Coppola, "Bringing Social (In)Justice to the Fore of Substantive Criminal Law A Proposal for a *Situational* Partial Excuse ('SPE')", *unpublished* (on file with author).
29 Cf. e.g. A Ashworth, *Sentencing and Criminal Justice* (Cambridge University Press: Cambridge, 6th edn, 2015), p.159.
30 See generally F Coppola & A Martufi (eds), *Social Rehabilitation and Criminal Justice* (Routledge: Oxford, forthcoming).
31 See F Coppola & A Martufi, "Introduction: What is *Social* Rehabilitation?", in Coppola & Martufi, *Social Rehabilitation*.
32 M Manikis, "Recognising State Blame in Sentencing: A Communicative and Relational Framework", *Cambridge Law Journal*, vol. 81, no. 2 (2022), p.294.
33 Manikis, "Recognising State Blaming", p.320.

References

Books and book chapters

Ashworth A, *Sentencing and Criminal Justice* (Cambridge University Press: Cambridge, 6th edn, 2015).
Brink D & Nelkin D, "Fairness and the Architecture of Responsibility", in Shoemaker D (ed), *Oxford Studies in Agency and Responsibility* (Oxford University Press: New York, 2013), vol I.
Bronfenbrenner U, *The Ecology of Human Development* (Harvard University Press: Cambridge MA, 1979).
Coppola F & Martufi A (eds), *Social Rehabilitation and Criminal Justice* (Routledge: London, 2023).
Coppola F, *The Emotional Brain and the Guilty Mind: Novel Paradigms of Culpability and Punishment* (Hart Publishing: Oxford, 2021).
Haney C, *Criminality in Context: The Psychological Foundations of Criminal Justice Reform* (American Psychological Association: Washington DC, 2020).
Hart HLA, *Punishment and Responsibility: Essays in the Philosophy of Law* (Oxford University Press: Oxford, 1968).
Kaye A, "The Secret Politics of Compatibilist Criminal Law", *Kansas Law Review*, vol. 55 (2007), pp.365–427.

Lacey N, "Socializing the Subject of Criminal Law? Criminal Responsibility and the Purposes of Criminalization", *Marquette Law Review*, vol. 99, no. 3 (2016), pp.541–557.

Norrie A, "Practical Reasoning and Criminal Responsibility: A Jurisprudential Approach", in Cornish D & Clarke R (eds), *The Reasoning Criminal: Rational Choice Perspectives on Offending* (Transaction Publishers: New Brunswick NJ, 2014).

Tonry M, "Can Desert be Just in an Unjust World?", in Simester AP, du Bois-Pedain A & Neumann U (eds), *Liberal Criminal Theory: Essays for Andreas von Hirsch* (Hart Publishing: Portland, 2014).

Journal articles

Bowlby J, Figlio K, & Young R, "An Interview with John Bowlby on the Origins and Reception of His Work", *Free Associations*, vol. 6 (1986), pp.36–64.

Bremmer JC, "Traumatic Stress: Effects on the Brain", *Dialogues in Clinical Neuroscience*, vol. 8, no. 4 (2006), pp.445–461.

Coppola F, "Bringing Social (In)Justice to the Fore of Substantive Criminal Law: A Proposal for a *Situational* Partial Excuse ('SPE')", *unpublished* (on file with author).

Duff A, "Blame, Moral Standing, and the Legitimacy of Criminal Trial", *Ratio*, vol. 23, no. 2 (2010), pp.123–140.

Evans G, Brooks-Gunn J, & Klebanov PK, "Stressing Out the Poor: Chronic Physiological Stress and the Income Achievement Gap", *Pathways, Winter* (2011), pp.16–21.

Fondacaro M, "Toward an Ecological Jurisprudence Rooted in Concepts of Justice and Empirical Research", *UMCK Law Review*, vol. 69, no. 1 (2000–2001), pp.179–196.

Gomez DV, "Duress and the Antcolony's Ethic: Reflections on the Foundations of the Defense and Its Limits", *New Criminal Law Review*, vol. 11, no. 4 (2008), pp.615–644.

Haney C, Banks C, & Zimbardo P, "Interpersonal Dynamics in A Simulated Prison", *Journal of Criminology and Penology*, vol. 1, no. 1 (1973) pp.69–97.

Lippke R, "Social Deprivation as Tempting Fate", *Criminal Law & Philosophy*, vol. 5 (2011), pp.277–291.

Manikis M, "Recognising State Blame in Sentencing: A Communicative and Relational Framework", *Cambridge Law Journal*, vol. 81, no. 2 (2022), pp.294–322.

Morse SJ, "Determinism and the Death of Folk Psychology: Two Challenges to Responsibility from Neuroscience", *Minnesota Journal of Law Science & Technology*, vol. 9, no. 1 (2008), pp.1–36.

Mousourakis G, "Character, Choice, and Criminal Responsibility", *Le Cahiers Du Droit*, vol. 39, no. 1 (1998), pp.51–73.

Norrie A, "The Limits of Justice: Finding Fault in the Criminal Law", *The Modern Law Review*, vol. 59, no. 4 (1996), pp.540–556.

Rebbe R, Sattler K & Mienko J, "The Association of Race, Ethnicity, and Poverty with Child Maltreatment Reporting", *Pediatrics*, vol. 150, no. 2 (2022), e2021053346.

Ristroph A, "How (Not) To Think like a Punisher", *Florida Law Review*, vol. 61, no. 4 (2009), pp.727–750.

Reports and websites

Lacey N, "Criminal Justice and Social Injustice", *LSE Working Paper*, No 84 (2022), available at: https://eprints.lse.ac.uk/116949/1/Lacey_criminal_justice.pdf.

3
THE RECIPROCITY OF CRIMINAL RESPONSIBILITY

Antony Duff

Accountability, answerability, and liability

This chapter is concerned with responsibility understood as "accountability".[1] To be responsible, in this sense, is to be open to being called to account for an alleged failure to act as I should. In the criminal law, I am accountable for committing a criminal offence: a criminal trial calls the defendant, *D*, to account for committing the crime specified in the indictment.

However, we must distinguish two dimensions of accountability: answerability and liability. If you accuse me of committing a wrong, for instance of breaking into a house, I can respond in one of three ways. First, I can deny the accusation altogether: I did not break into the house, and am therefore not answerable for doing so. Second, I can admit that I broke in, but offer a justification or excuse for doing so: I broke in because this was the only way to save a sick person trapped inside, or because I was plausibly threatened with serious injury if I refused to break in. In this case, I admit responsibility for breaking in – I admit that I must answer for doing so; but I offer an exculpatory answer, which (if accepted) saves me from liability to being blamed for doing so. Third, I can admit that I broke in, and admit that I had neither justification nor excuse for doing so – and that I can therefore properly be censured for it. I now admit both answerability and liability: I admit that I must answer for breaking in, and my answer is that I have no defence for doing so. (I might also respond by denying that I need answer to your accusation at all, by arguing that you have no standing thus to call me to account. This will be important later, as a way of denying responsibility without denying commission of the wrong.)

My focus is on answerability (in criminal law, in particular), rather than on liability – what it is to hold a person answerable, and the conditions under which such holdings are (il) legitimate. While theorists often use "responsibility" to encompass both answerability and liability, the distinction between them is important, and in what follows I will talk only about responsibility as answerability.[2]

We find a similar structure of accusation and response in a criminal trial. The defendant, *D*, is accused of committing a criminal offence, for instance of breaking and entering. He can respond in three ways: first, by denying the offence altogether; second, by admitting that he committed the offence, but offering a justification or an excuse for doing so – which is to admit criminal responsibility for the offence as something for which he must answer in court, but to deny criminal liability to conviction and punishment; or third, by admitting that he

DOI: 10.4324/9781003297260-5

committed the offence without justification or excuse – which is to admit both responsibility and liability. (Or he might deny that he should have to answer this charge in this court, by claiming that the court lacks jurisdiction or standing to try him: this would be to deny criminal responsibility, and thus also criminal liability, without denying the offence.)

I am responsible for an action if I can properly be called to answer for it; I am liable, to blame or condemnation, if I can properly be condemned for it. Liability to condemnation or conviction presupposes answerability: we can hold D liable for Φ only if we can claim that he is answerable for Φ. But answerability does not entail liability, although (at least in criminal law) it might create a presumption of liability. If I admit or it is proved that I committed the offence charged, i.e. that I am answerable for it, the court is entitled to presume that I am guilty, and to convict me, *unless* I offer a successful defence. However, I can admit that I am answerable, and offer a defence – an exculpatory answer that will, if accepted, block the transition from answerability to liability.[3]

Responsibility as thus understood is relational, as I will explain in part 2. It is also reciprocal, and this will be the topic of part 3. These features of responsibility will illuminate some important issues about our practices of criminal responsibility. Discussions of responsibility, within and outside criminal law, often focus on the person who is held responsible: what capacities she must have if she is to be a responsible agent – one who can be held answerable for her conduct; what her relationship to the conduct in question must be if she is to be (held) responsible for it – what she must have known or intended, whether or in what sense she must have had the capacity and opportunity to act otherwise, and so on. I will focus, however, on those who seek to hold a person responsible: what conditions must I satisfy if I am to justifiably hold another person responsible (what conditions must a court satisfy if it is to claim the authority to try this defendant), or what must be true of my relationship to her and to the conduct for which I seek to hold her responsible?

Responsibility as relational

Responsibility, understood as answerability, is doubly relational. It is relational, first, in that it is always responsibility *for* something: I must answer, and am held accountable, for some alleged wrong or failure. In criminal law, I am answerable for an alleged offence, which typically consists in some act or omission that the law defines as criminal. But, second, responsibility is always *to* someone: I am responsible for Φ to some person or body who has the right, or the standing, to call me to answer for Φ. Whenever it is claimed that A is responsible for Φ, it is always proper to ask: "to whom is A responsible for Φ?". If I seek to hold someone responsible for some alleged misdeed, I must be prepared to show not just that she is responsible for it, but that she is responsible to me.

This point is clearest in cases of role-responsibility. As a member of a football team, I am responsible to my fellow players for my conduct on the field, for turning up to matches in which I am to play, perhaps for keeping myself fit and for training: they can call me to account, and I must answer to them, for my failure or misconduct in these matters. But, first, I am not responsible for such things to a passing stranger who happens to notice my misconduct. If she seeks to call me to account for my sloppy play or for my failure to keep fit, I can properly respond not by defending myself, or by admitting my failures, but by telling her that it is not her business; I do not answer to her for these things. Second, I am not responsible to my fellow footballers for matters that fall outside the scope of our shared activity: I might have failed to submit an article on time to the journal that commissioned it, and for that I must answer to the journal's editors; but if a team-mate seeks to hold me accountable for it, I can refuse to answer (to admit, explain, justify or excuse my failure) to him for it, since it is not his business.[4] The same is true, for instance, in matters of prudence, such as one's physical or financial health: I am answerable in such matters to those who depend on me, and perhaps to my doctor for my failure to follow her advice in relation to my physical health, but I am not answerable to passing strangers who may notice my imprudent conduct and seek to call me to account for it (for eating unhealthy food, for gambling my money away) – I can tell them that it is not their business. Some would deny that this is true of moral matters, since they believe that moral wrongdoing is the business of all moral agents:[5] anyone has, in principle, the standing to call me to account for any moral wrong that I commit. Whilst this may be true of the more egregious kinds of moral wrong, I doubt that it is true of minor wrongs that we commit in our personal relationships: if I fail to do my share of domestic duties, I am answerable to my family, but not to my work colleagues, let alone to passing strangers – it is not their business.

This second kind of relationality is also evident in criminal law. If I am summoned to trial on a criminal charge, I might refuse to answer, for example refusing to enter a plea of "guilty" or "not guilty", on the grounds that the court lacks the standing to try me. The simplest basis for such a refusal is that the court lacks jurisdiction over me or over my alleged crime. If, for instance, I commit a theft whilst on holiday in Germany, I can be tried by a German court, but not by a Scottish court when I return home (though a Scottish court could extradite me to Germany for trial in a German court); for a theft committed in Germany is not a crime under Scots law and therefore falls outside the ambit of Scots criminal law, and outside the jurisdiction of Scottish criminal courts.

This raises an important question: to whom am I called to answer in a criminal court? In the extra-legal contexts of our professional or personal lives, the answer to the "to whom?" question is usually clear enough: I must answer to my fellow players for my performance in and for my (lack of) preparation for our football games; to my students, my colleagues and my employer for my discharge of (or my failure to discharge) my responsibilities as a professor; and so on. But to whom do I answer in a criminal trial? Not simply to the court, though it is the court that calls me to answer and holds me to account, but to whoever or whatever it is in whose name the court acts. In monarchies, it might look as if I am called to answer to the monarch: in England cases are listed as "*Rex v D*", as if *D* is to answer to the king. But that is hardly appropriate for polities that claim to be democracies. There, surely, I answer to the whole polity – to my fellow citizens, whose law the law is supposed to be; hence the appropriateness of American case listings as "*People v D*".

A court that summons me to trial on a criminal charge must therefore claim to be calling me to answer formally to my fellow citizens for my alleged violation of the shared values that the criminal law claims to express. "We", the citizens, collectively condemn theft as a wrong that is "public" in the sense that it concerns us all as a violation of the values that structure our shared civic life: we therefore define it through our legislature as a crime, and authorise our courts to call those who commit this wrong to public account through a criminal trial. The thief is therefore responsible for his theft to his fellow citizens collectively. But a thief might deny that he is thus responsible to the polity. As we have seen, one basis for such denial would be the claim that his alleged theft does not fall within the ambit of the polity's criminal law, and that he therefore does not fall under the jurisdiction of its courts. However, what is of more interest here is a different basis – one that is political rather than formally legal – for denying that I am responsible in this court or to this polity. The basis is that, even if my alleged crime falls within the ambit of this polity's criminal law, and within the jurisdiction of its courts, the authority to hold me to account has been undermined, and the court's standing to try me has been lost, by wrongs that I have suffered at the hands of the polity – the polity in whose name and by whose authority the court that seeks to call me to account must claim to act.

This is one way in which we can understand the problem of doing criminal justice in an unjust society. Imagine a society – perhaps one not unlike our own – in which some of those who appear in its criminal courts have suffered serious, systemic kinds of social injustice: they belong to racial, religious, or social groups whose members have been consistently excluded (whether formally or informally) from many of the rights and benefits that others enjoy in virtue of their membership of the polity, including educational or vocational opportunities, welfare provisions, political participation, and so on. Intuitively, there is something troubling about their conviction and punishment: we should feel uneasy about a criminal process that proceeds without attending to the injustices that they have suffered, and continue to suffer. The problem is to explain the grounds for such unease. Sometimes of course, the unjust conditions from which a crime flowed might ground a justification or excuse: *D*'s crime was a reasonable, justifiable response to her situation; or the pressures she faced were such that a reasonable person might well have acted as she did (either account might be offered of why the criminal law should not convict an impoverished person deprived of welfare support who steals food for her family). But it seems unlikely that such a story can be plausibly told for all the kinds of crimes committed by people who have suffered such injustices – yet we still rightly see their conviction and punishment as morally problematic. This leads some theorists to suggest that what undermines the legitimacy of their conviction is, rather, the way in which those injustices undermine the court's standing to call them to account. We could put this suggestion by saying that to explain the problem in terms of justification or excuse is to accept that such defendants are responsible to the polity for their crimes, but to block the move from responsibility to liability by positing a defence, whereas to say that the court lacks standing to try them is to suggest that they are not responsible – not responsible, that is, for these alleged crimes to these courts or to the polity in whose name the courts act. This is not to suggest, insultingly, that they are not responsible agents, or that they are not responsible for their criminal conduct; nor is it to deny that there is anyone to whom they are responsible for those crimes. It is to deny that they are answerable to the polity which has subjected them, and still subjects them, to such injustice.

But why should the injustice that I have suffered at another's hands undermine their standing to call me to account for wrongs that I commit? Something analogous does seem plausible in our informal moral interactions. Consider a relatively trivial example. You and I often arrange to meet to discuss mutual business matters. I regularly arrive late, or not at all, without apology or explanation; but you continue to make the arrangements, and to turn up yourself, because you see the meetings as valuable, despite my conduct. One day you are very late for the meeting, without warning me, and I call you vigorously to account for this: I complain about the inconvenience you have caused me, and demand an explanation and apology. You might quite reasonably reply that I am ill placed to call you to account in this way, given my own prior conduct. You might have a justification or excuse for your lateness (one that does not portray your lateness as being rendered permissible, or excusable, by my behaviour) – perhaps you were detained by an emergency and had no chance to contact me. But you might think that you need not answer to me by seeking in this way to justify or excuse your conduct, because my own misconduct has undermined my standing to call you to account in this way.

There are different accounts of just why and how my standing is thus undermined, different questions about whether it is indeed undermined, and further questions about what kinds of wrong on my part can undermine my standing – for example, must the wrongs that I have committed against you be of the same kind as, or of similar seriousness to, that for which I now seek to call you to account?. I cannot pursue these possibilities and questions in detail here,[6] but will suggest that we can usefully understand the matter in terms of reciprocity – the reciprocity not just of actions (the lack of any reciprocity in punctuality), but of responsibility. Such an explanation will help us understand why systemic social injustice can undermine the polity's standing to call to account offenders who have suffered it. It will also enable us to meet an obvious objection to such "lack of standing" arguments – that they threaten to undermine the law and the conditions necessary for any progress towards justice, and fail to do justice to the victims of these crimes. For if we simply say that the polity's standing (its courts' standing) to call such offenders to account is undermined, so that they cannot justly be tried, we then face an apparently irresoluble dilemma. If they are exempt from trial, from criminal responsibility for their crimes, the victims of those crimes (who will often themselves be victims of the same kinds of social injustice) will be left without any kind of vindication, and will thus be subjected to a further kind of victimisation. The law's crime-preventive efficacy, such as it is, will be undermined, thus creating a danger of serious social disorder and disruption. But if we therefore insist that these offenders must be prosecuted and punished, it seems that we subject them to further serious injustice. We can, I will argue, avoid the dilemma by looking more carefully at the ways in which responsibility is or should be reciprocal.

Responsibility as reciprocal

To say that responsibility is reciprocal is to say that it involves a two-way rather than just a one-way relationship: if we call someone to account, to answer, we demand something from them, an answer or an account, but we also owe something to them, something that they can properly demand of us. We can initially identify two dimensions to this reciprocity in our moral interactions.

First, if I am to call you to answer, I must be sure that you are able to answer. I must, that is, be sure (or be able to presume) that you have the rational capacities necessary to understand and to respond appropriately to the call; I must address you in terms that you can be expected to understand; I must explain what I am calling you to answer for, and why. If these conditions are not satisfied, I fail to hold you to account; if I know that they are not satisfied, I can only pretend to be calling you to account. We might add that I must be sure that it is reasonable, or fair, to expect you to answer: if, for instance, I seek to call you to account for some relatively minor wrong when I know that you have just suffered a grievous bereavement, I do successfully call you to account, but should not do so; it is unreasonable, cruel, to expect you to attend to this minor wrong when you have just suffered this loss.

Second, I must attend to your answer – to your denial that you committed the wrong, to your explanation (whether justificatory, excusatory, or confessional) of why you acted as you did; but to attend is to be ready to be persuaded – that, for instance, I should not blame you. Furthermore, I must be ready to justify my reception of your answer: I cannot just dismiss it, or close my ears to it; I must be ready to accept it, or to give reasons for rejecting it. To call you to answer, but then to fail to attend to your answer or to fail to take it seriously, is an obvious kind of injustice.

Reciprocity of this kind is an essential feature of treating others as responsible agents – that is, as people who operate within the realm of practical reason; as people who can, and who should be allowed and enabled to, answer for themselves and for their actions.[7] That is why ascriptions of responsibility, holdings to account, can be portrayed as conversations:[8] conversation is a two-way enterprise, which requires the conversers to explain themselves to each other and to attend to each other seriously. Already, then, we can see how if I am to call you to answer to me (or to an "us" in whose name I call you), I must myself be ready to answer to you: I must explain my calling, and be ready to respond to your challenge to it or to your answer to it. This might include being ready to explain by what right I call you to account, since you might challenge either the grounds on which I call you (why should I believe that you committed this wrong?) or my standing thus to call you (what makes this my business?).

We can see these same features in the structure of a criminal trial. *D*, the defendant, is called to answer a charge of criminal wrongdoing: to answer to the charge, initially by pleading "guilty" or "not guilty", then to answer for the crime if it is proved or he admits that he committed it. Proof or an admission that he committed the crime is proof or admission of criminal responsibility: he must answer for the crime. But it is not yet conclusive proof of guilt, of criminal liability to conviction and punishment: he can block the transition from responsibility to liability by offering a defence. However, if the trial is to be legitimate, as a process of calling to account, it must respect the demands of reciprocity. The court must be sure, or be able safely to presume, that *D* is competent to be tried – that he has the capacities necessary to understand and respond to the charges he faces.[9] It must ensure that he has a fair opportunity, and the necessary resources, to respond: that he knows what charge he faces, that he has access to relevant evidence, and to the assistance of counsel; that he has a fair chance to put his case to the court.[10] It must attend to any answer he gives – to any defence that he offers; it must also attend and respond to any challenge to its jurisdiction, by showing that it does have the standing to call *D* to account for this alleged crime. (This is why it can be said that both the defendant and the prosecution are called to account in a criminal trial: the prosecution must be ready to justify the charge, and to justify its bringing of the charge.)

(There might seem to be at least one significant disanalogy between criminal trials and callings to account in extra-legal moral contexts. If I call you to answer for, for instance, preventing me from getting to a meeting by blocking the road, you might respond with a would-be justification – that you were engaged in a justified protest for an important political cause. I might not accept that justification, but I must listen to it, and be ready to give reasons for rejecting it. If I am on trial for a criminal offence, by contrast, there are legal limits to the kind of defence that I will be allowed to put to the court: I will not, as it is sometimes put, "be heard" to offer a moral or political defence that is not recognised by the law. This is to say not that I will necessarily be prevented from putting the defence: but the court – even if it can't help but hear what I say – will not listen to it, will not recognise it as a relevant contribution to the trial.[11] It might be tempting to say that there is no real disanalogy here: that in moral contexts I need only attend to morally relevant answers from a person I seek to call to account, and in a criminal trial the court need only attend to answers that the law recognises as legally relevant. That would be too quick, since we still need to ask why the law should not recognise as relevant any answer that bears on the ultimate (moral) justifiability of *D*'s conduct or on its blameworthiness; but we cannot pursue this issue here.)

We can now turn back to the issue of undermined standing raised at the end of part 2: how does my or our prior misconduct towards *D*, the wrongs that I or we committed against him, undermine my or our standing now to call him to account for a wrong he has committed? Let us suppose that we do in principle have, or had, standing to call him to account: namely that, in a moral context, the wrong is our business, or that, in the criminal context, the alleged crime falls within the ambit of the polity's criminal law, and *D* falls under the legally defined jurisdiction of the court. How can that standing be undermined by my or our previous misconduct towards *D*?

The answer flows from a third dimension of reciprocity. If responsibility is reciprocal, as I have argued it is, then if I am to call *D* to answer to me, I must be ready to answer to him; if a polity is to call *D* to answer to a criminal charge, it must be ready to answer to him. We have seen already that I or we must be ready to answer *D*'s challenges to our accusations, or to our standing: but we must also be ready to answer to him for our own conduct towards him, and our standing to call him to answer is undermined insofar as we fail or refuse to do so. Thus when I seek to call you to account for your failure to turn up for our meeting, having regularly failed to turn up to previous meetings myself, what undermines my standing thus to call you is not the mere fact of my past offences of this kind: if, for instance, I had apologised for those previous failures, sought to explain them, and made a commitment to do better in future, my standing to call you to account now is not undermined. What does undermine it is my past failure to answer for (to explain, to apologise for) those past wrongs, and my refusal now to do so. Thus, when I challenge you about your failure to turn up, you might naturally respond by saying: "but look at all the times you failed to turn up". This might be not an attempt to justify or excuse your failure now, but a challenge to my standing: "how can you now claim the right to call me to account, given your past conduct?". That challenge can be met, and defused, if I can point out that I did explain and apologise for my past failures – that I answered to you for them, and can therefore properly call you to answer to me now. Further, and crucially, even if I did in the past fail to answer for my conduct, so that my standing is now undermined, I can regain it by being willing now to answer for my past wrongs: our conversation can now become a genuinely reciprocal enterprise in which we answer to each other, and I can say that, since I am now answering to you, you must be ready to answer to me.

There is of course very much more to be said about this kind of case, and in particular about what kinds of unanswered-for past wrong can undermine present standing, but it cannot be said here; we must instead see how we can understand (part of) the problem of doing penal justice in a context of serious social injustice, and see a way of resolving it, in analogous terms.

The issue of lost standing in contexts of interpersonal morality was illustrated above by cases in which my standing to call you to account for a particular present wrong is undermined by one or more past wrongs that I committed against you, and for which I have failed to apologise or answer. It could also be illustrated, in a way that brings us closer to the problem for criminal law, by more collective, patterned examples. Suppose, for instance, that I share a flat with others who have consistently treated me in oppressive, demeaning, exclusionary ways: they insult me, they do not involve me in their communal activities, they make my life in various ways difficult – yet they never apologise for this behaviour, or recognise it as something for which they should answer. I do not fight back or leave (perhaps I would find it too hard to move house), and continue to carry out my parts of the agreement that governs our flat sharing. However, one day I slip up, and forget to perform a task that is my responsibility, and my flatmates then seek to call me to vigorously censorial account for this failure. I might with justice reply, not that my failure was justified or excused by their past treatment of me (I might not believe that it is; or, more significantly for present purposes, I might believe that I anyway should not have to engage in the exercise of explaining, justifying, excusing, or answering for, my conduct to them), but that they have lost their standing to call me to account in this way, given their treatment of me. Analogously, if I belong to a group whose members have suffered persistent, systemic kinds of political, social and economic injustice; if, although formally a citizen, I have thus been excluded (partially or wholly) from many of the rights and benefits of citizenship, but such exclusion has not been recognised or remedied: I might claim that my fellow citizens, and thus the criminal courts that claim to speak in their name, have lost their standing to call me to account for a crime that I am accused of committing. I need not claim that those injustices justify or excuse my crime: rather, my claim is that they have no right to call on me to explain, justify or excuse my crime. We could put the point thus: they have hitherto failed to treat me as a fellow citizen, with the equal concern and respect that the polity owes its citizens and that they owe each other; but to call me now to answer a criminal charge in this way is to (claim to) treat me as a citizen, and to demand that I fulfil my civic obligation to answer to my fellows for my crime. So having failed to treat me as a citizen hitherto, they now seek to treat me as one in this particular matter – but they have lost the right to do so.

This is a powerful argument that victims of such systemic injustice can offer to show, not why they should be acquitted (an acquittal implies that the defendant has offered an exculpatory answer to the charge), but why they cannot legitimately be tried at all – why they cannot be expected to answer this charge in this forum. However, we can also now see how such an argument could in principle be met, and the polity's and the court's standing be regained: what is required is that the polity now be ready, and display such readiness in action, to answer to the defendant, and to the disadvantaged group to which he belongs, for the wrongs they have suffered – and thus to show that they will now treat him fully, not selectively or partially, as a citizen. I can regain my standing to call you to account for the wrong you committed against me by being ready to answer to you for the wrongs I committed against you – and by putting that readiness into action. Analogously, the polity can regain its standing to call the defendant to account by manifesting its active readiness to answer to him for the wrongs he suffered at its hands.

That might sound like fine rhetoric: but how could it be given practicable concrete form? How can a polity answer to defendants or groups who have suffered such injustice? One question here is whether this is something that could be done, at least in part, in the criminal court to which the defendant has been summoned: can we so reform the trial process that there is room for defendants to be heard to offer this kind of objection to their trial. If so, what kind of response to the objection could be given, by whom, that would allow the trial to proceed; and if the trial does proceed, should those past injustices be recognised partly in sentencing? Or should we rather look for a different forum in which this kind of challenge could be addressed, so that the court can honestly tell the protesting defendant that he must pursue this objection elsewhere, and that his trial can proceed so long as such an alternative forum is genuinely available to him? What must be clear, however, is that what is needed is not just a forum (within or outside the trial) in which such objections can be heard and addressed, but also some way in which a genuine commitment on the polity's part to address the injustices can be displayed. Only then, only by respecting the reciprocal character of responsibility as answerability, can the standing to call to account be regained.

Notes

1. G Watson, "Two Faces of Responsibility", in G Watson (ed), *Agency and Answerability: Selected Essays* (Oxford University Press: Oxford, 2004), pp. 273–55.
2. I will also be talking only about retrospective responsibility: responsibility for some past (alleged) wrong or error. I will not discuss prospective responsibility: responsibility to take care of certain matters (though retrospective responsibility usually depends on prospective responsibility, since I am held retrospectively responsible for the way in which I discharged or failed to discharge my prospective responsibilities). Nor will I discuss what it is to be a responsible, or a non-responsible or irresponsible, agent.
3. See further RA Duff, *Answering for Crime* (Hart Publishing: Oxford, 2007), ch 1.
4. More precisely, I can refuse to answer to him qua fellow member of the team: if he is also an editor of the journal, or my co-author, that makes it his business. But the central point holds good: that if he is to claim the right to call me to account for my failure, he must show that it is his business, in virtue of his relationship to me and to the matter in question.
5. E.g. TM Scanlon, *Moral Dimensions: Permissibility, Meaning, Blame* (Harvard University Press: Cambridge, 2008), pp. 139–40.
6. See B Ewing, "Do Unjust States Have the Standing to Blame? Three Reservations About Scepticism", *Oxford Journal of Legal Studies*, vol. 43, no. 2 (2022), pp. 249–72; JW Howard & A Pasternak, "Criminal Wrongdoing, Restorative Justice, and the Moral Standing of Unjust States", *Journal of Political Philosophy*, vol. 31 (2023), pp. 42–59.
7. See J Gardner, "The Mark of Responsibility", in J Gardner (ed), *Offences and Defences* (Oxford University Press: Oxford, 2007), pp. 177–200.
8. See M McKenna, *Conversation and Responsibility* (Oxford University Press: Oxford, 2012).
9. Hence the legal bar on trying someone who is not "fit to plead": see J Sprack & M Engelhardt-Sprack, *A Practical Approach to Criminal Procedure* (Oxford University Press: Oxford, 16th edn, 2019), ch 17.36.
10. Compare the "minimum rights" declared in Article 6(3) of the European Convention on Human Rights as being essential to a fair trial.
11. And I might indeed be punished for trying to put a defence that the court has ruled out: see the cases reported in S Laville, "Insulate Britain activists found guilty over London roadblock", *The Guardian*, 13 February 2023, available at: www.theguardian.com/environment/2023/feb/13/insulate-britain-activists-found-guilty-blockade.

References

Duff RA, *Answering for Crime* (Hart Publishing: Oxford, 2007).
Ewing B, "Do Unjust States Have the Standing to Blame? Three Reservations About Scepticism", *Oxford Journal of Legal Studies*, vol. 43, no. 2 (2022), pp. 249–272.
Gardner J, "The Mark of Responsibility", in Gardner J (ed), *Offences and Defences: Selected Essays in the Philosophy of Criminal Law* (Oxford University Press: Oxford, 2007).
Howard JW & Pasternak A, "Criminal Wrongdoing, Restorative Justice, and the Moral Standing of Unjust States", *Journal of Political Philosophy*, vol. 31, no. 1 (2023), pp. 42–59.
Laville S, "Insulate Britain Activists Found Guilty over London roadblock", *The Guardian* (13 February 2023).
McKenna M, *Conversation and Responsibility* (Oxford University Press: Oxford, 2012).

Scanlon TM, *Moral Dimensions: Permissibility, Meaning, Blame* (Harvard University Press: Cambridge MA, 2008).
Sprack J & Engelhardt-Sprack M, *A Practical Approach to Criminal Procedure* (Oxford University Press: Oxford, 16th edn, 2019).
Watson G, "Two Faces of Responsibility", in Watson G (ed), *Agency and Answerability: Selected Essays* (Oxford University Press: Oxford, 2004).

4

CRIMINAL RESPONSIBILITY, CIVILISATION, AND EMPIRE

Catherine L Evans

Introduction

This chapter offers a historical account of nineteenth-century debates over the limits and definition of criminal responsibility in the British Empire. It argues that Victorian understandings of "civilisation" inflected medical and legal controversies over the nature of the mind and legal responses to violence in Britain and the wider British world. By knitting together the legal histories of pluralism and insanity, the chapter draws out the political stakes of criminal responsibility during a period of imperial legal consolidation and Anglicisation. Broadly, it suggests that criminal responsibility was more than just a legal or even a medical quandary – it was also a site for the elaboration of what we might call "psychological subjecthood".

A disturbing case

When police caught William Bigg, the boy confessed to sneaking into his neighbours' farmyards to mutilate horses. After a year in jail in rural Ontario, Bigg, who was then 13 years old, returned to his family. It was not a happy reunion. Police soon caught him with money stolen from his father's desk, and Bigg was sentenced to seven years in the local penitentiary.[1] One night, after his discharge, Bigg saw his father cut himself with a paring knife. According to doctors who would later record his medical history, Bigg "was observed to become restless, nervous, pale, and to have undergone a peculiar change of demeanour".[2] He slipped next door and cut a horse's throat. He then fled to the woods, where he raped a girl who stumbled upon his hiding place. He was arrested, tried, and sentenced to death for the assault, but after ten years was pardoned and released. On his way home from prison, Bigg attacked yet another horse, cutting off parts of its tongue and slashing its belly and neck. He was arrested and transferred to Rockwood Asylum in Kingston, Ontario, in late September 1879.[3]

In 1884, Dr. Daniel Hack Tuke, a well-known English physician and expert in mental science, visited the asylum. When he returned to Britain, he brought Bigg's story with him. Tuke told it at the 1885 annual meeting of the Medico-Psychological Association, the premier professional organisation for British physicians with expertise in the diagnosis and treatment of insanity. Even for men accustomed to working with the criminally insane, Bigg's behaviour was shocking. Tuke hoped that Bigg's combination of perversion and superficial rationality would convince the assembled of the existence of a disturbing mental illness: moral insanity.[4]

DOI: 10.4324/9781003297260-6

The 1843 English *M'Naghten* case had established the legal definition of insanity that dominated Victorian criminal justice both in Britain and in its colonies.[5] This definition famously required that the accused prove that he or she was unable, due to a disease of the mind, to understand either the nature of a criminal act or that it was wrong. This standard was controversial from its inception, drawing fire from physicians who argued that it was excessively narrow and would result in the unjust punishment of mentally ill accused. But even *M'Naghten*'s many critics tended to approach moral insanity with great caution. More than any other nineteenth-century diagnosis, moral insanity forced lawyers and doctors to consider what they knew, and could ever know, about human nature. For nineteenth-century physicians, the mind's "moral" facets could include every quality and function that was not purely cognitive.[6] The ambiguity and capaciousness of moral insanity made it controversial. Could the will and desires of a person be diseased while his or her cognition remained unscathed? Moral insanity challenged traditional, legal understandings of criminal responsibility. It seemed to erase any distinction between criminality and insanity, suggesting in essence that those who were the most depraved were the least responsible for their actions. Indeed, most types of insanity raised significant questions about where to draw the line between criminality and mental illness, responsibility and irresponsibility.

Many scholars have described the late-nineteenth-century contests between physicians and lawyers over the existence of moral insanity and the proper parameters of legal responsibility.[7] Recent studies have emphasized the political valence of these debates, connecting medico-legal controversies to broader questions about mental capacity and political belonging, expressed, for instance, through concerns about the fitness of individuals and groups to vote and participate in the economy.[8] Although liability to criminal punishment could mean imprisonment or death for the convicted, a finding that a person was criminally responsible also declared their status as a rational agent capable of participating in at least some aspects of public life.[9] Criminal responsibility thus engaged what we might call "psychological subjecthood": for a person to face the full brunt of the law's judgment, he or she had to be capable of meaningful participation in civil society. Or rather, to put it in Victorian terms, *civilised society*. Late-Victorian debates about criminal responsibility, especially moral insanity, took place in the context of a broader interrogation of the fitness of racialised colonial subjects for governance through British law. The psychological consequences of civilisation, or its absence, shaped imperial understandings of responsible subjecthood in Britain and its colonies.

Civilisation and madness

The second half of the nineteenth century was a time of dizzying optimism for many Britons. Railways, steamships, and telegraph lines brought the distant corners of the empire into intimate contact, facilitating the rapid circulation of goods and people around the globe. Technological and scientific discoveries seemed to promise that this new world could be known, and through that knowledge, mastered. Among the most exciting fields of inquiry was humanity itself, made legible and, Victorian Britons hoped, changeable through the judicious application of medical, anthropological, and penological expertise. While some revelled in the thought that they were on the precipice of a bold new age, however, others were less sanguine. By the 1880s, the excitement of mid-century had begun to cool. Asylums and penitentiaries around the British Empire were crowded with incurables and recividists.

Railways jangled delicate nerves, and the hustle and bustle of city life seemed to test the limits of the refined psyche. Urban slums and rural poverty remained, apparently immune to the dazzling wealth of the Empire – these blights perhaps even spurred by the Empire's success, which attracted chancers and petty criminals to large, anonymous cities where many succumbed to vice and viciousness.

Authorities, whether in London, Melbourne, or Madras, turned to the criminal law to impose order. "The British people", one Australian journalist commented in the early twentieth century,

> have an instinctive love of 'law and order.' Where seventy or eighty persons are settled in a British community, the policeman is sure to appear, and there will never be difficulty in obtaining the services of a local tradesman or local orator as a justice of the peace.[10]

But here, a problem emerged. Were those who committed acts of violence evil, or were they ill? This had long been a core concern of common law jurisprudence, dating back to the medieval origins of the concept of felony.[11] Throughout the nineteenth century, the highest courts in England, especially the House of Lords, had considered cases in which the accused was alleged to have committed crimes while insane. In homicide, the mandatory punishment for a guilty offender was death, although this could be commuted by executive authorities. A person found not guilty by reason of insanity, in contrast, would be sent to a secure hospital to be detained "at Her Majesty's pleasure" – an indefinite term that could stretch from several months to many decades.

The putatively medical diagnosis of moral insanity drew on the Victorian concepts of racial, cultural, and religious difference encapsulated in the idea of "civilization". While there was no consensus as to the causes of moral insanity, most prominent physicians reached for an evolutionary explanation. They suggested that moral insanity was an expression of atavism – the regression of the sufferer to an earlier stage in human evolutionary development. If the civilized layers of the brain were peeled back, the primitive core was exposed. Some physicians believed that reversions of this sort were rare: spectacular mutations that could be diagnosed, and sufferers confined to asylums or otherwise controlled. Others, who were likelier to subscribe to the theories of "degeneration" that swept Western Europe in the second half of the nineteenth century, worried that entire populations were rapidly losing their grip on civilisation in response to the pressures of modern life.[12] Urbanisation, industrialisation, globalisation, and technological advances, to say nothing of the promise and peril of imperial expansion, had pushed human bodies and minds too far, too fast. Drinking, poverty, illegitimacy, feeblemindedness, and criminality of all sorts were, to these pessimistic thinkers, evidence that civilisation itself was failing. As "degenerates" proliferated, they threatened the achievements of supposedly civilised polities and undermined the civilising mission that animated Victorian imperialism.

Controversies over insanity and responsibility were not only about the fate of individual people but also about the competence of groups, often delineated by imagined racial characteristics. Charles Darwin's 1859 *Origin of Species* was quickly taken up by natural and social scientists, some of whom saw Darwinian evolutionary theory as scaffolding for older ideas about, as Nancy Stepan writes, the "fixity, antiquity, and hierarchy of human races".[13] By the end of the century, ethnologists and criminal anthropologists had proposed theories that explicitly linked criminal propensities to race, and race to heredity. For them, allusions to "savagery" or "primitivism" were not metaphors but references to real evolutionary processes. While Victorian commentators applied civilisational modifiers freely to the non-white peoples of the Empire, they also used them to describe Europeans, especially members of the poor and the working classes and those accused of terrible or motiveless violence, like William Bigg.[14] When white Britons committed "savage" crimes, they were not acting *like* savages but revealing a genuinely savage nature that evolution had not yet stamped out.

Mental science was not immune to evolutionary models in which mental and moral acuity were functions of race. Prominent English alienist Henry Maudsley, a staunch believer in degeneration, argued that moral insanity and primitivism were sides of the same coin. Maudsley saw compulsive violence as a sign of sickness among Europeans. Non-European peoples, whom he and many of his contemporaries arranged on a scale from debasement to near-civilisation, were believed to be less susceptible to moral insanity because they had a shorter evolutionary distance to fall. In one of his later works, *The Pathology of Mind* (1895), Maudsley illustrated his theory of the relationship between race and moral insanity. "The Australian savage", he wrote, ". . . clearly cannot go mad because of a breach of the moral law, nor ever present an example of true moral insanity; before he can undergo moral degeneration he must first be humanized and then civilized".[15]

Daniel Hack Tuke, who described William Bigg's case to the Medico-Psychological Association in 1885, also posited a relationship between insanity and primitivism. He echoed Maudsley's view that moral insanity, and violence generally, were the result of degeneration. The morally insane sufferer became, because of his disease, like the primitive peoples of the far reaches of the empire. "Such a man as this", wrote Tuke,

> is a reversion to an old savage type, and is born by accident in the wrong century. He would have ... been in harmony with his environment, in a barbaric age, or at the present day in certain parts of Africa, but he cannot be tolerated now as a member of civilized society. But what is to be done with the man who, from no fault of his own, is born in the nineteenth instead of a long-past century? Are we to punish him for his involuntary anachronism?[16]

As both Maudsley's and Tuke's accounts of moral insanity suggest, Victorian physicians often analogised mentally ill white Europeans and sane members of racialised groups. As Megan Vaughan argues in her work on colonial Nyasaland (Malawi), colonial psychiatrists routinely described mental pathology – or at least mental weakness, emotional volatility, and impulsivity – as the normal state of Indigenous people.[17] What could be explained as disease in Europeans could be described as intrinsic to the non-European condition. This difference had important legal consequences, not least of which was that *M'Naghten* required that a "disease of the mind" be identified as the cause of the cognitive errors that could lead to an acquittal on the ground of insanity. The question of how British law should respond to "savage" minds remained. Moral insanity cases involving white defendants like Bigg dovetailed with questions about the culpability of Indigenous subjects of the British Empire. If a white, British morally insane defendant were to be found criminally irresponsible on the ground that he or she had a "primitive" mind, what were the implications for the allegedly "uncivilised" peoples of the Empire?

Psychological subjecthood

This raises the problem of subjecthood and Empire. As Hannah Weiss Muller argues, political subjecthood and the relationship between subject and sovereign acquired new importance in the last decades of the eighteenth century, knitting an expanded and increasingly diverse empire together after the upheavals of the Seven Years' War.[18] A century later, subjecthood remained central to imperial governance, but its focus had shifted decisively inward. As Britain's colonial strategy turned away from military conquest and indirect rule toward settlement and governance through anglicised legal institutions, administrators were more confident in asserting British jurisdiction over colonial populations. As the administration of law in the Empire became more standardised, professional, bureaucratic, and ostentatiously "English", however, officials faced new challenges. If defendants were to be judged according to English legal principles, they had to be cognitively and morally capable of responsible action. Otherwise, English law would be unmasked as hypocritical, even cruel. It was relatively simple for British officials to claim sovereignty over foreign lands and peoples. Delivering British justice was another matter.

Legal, medical, and political officials struggled to distinguish between the mental and moral symptoms of brain disease and the alleged constitutional weaknesses of the Empire's "primitive" peoples. The bare assertion that a person was a British subject could not answer the question of his or her competence. Determining whom officials could govern through law required an intimate, psychological inquiry, often bolstered by expert medical and ethnological testimony. Mapping territory was not enough; the problem of responsibility focused the resources of the imperial state on the plotting of subjects' inner lives. The mind emerged as what I have described elsewhere as the Victorian Empire's "vast internal frontier".[19]

Mental science, theories of degeneration and emerging understandings of race and heredity were refashioning how Victorians saw human nature. This shifting intellectual landscape inflected how individuals and groups fared under British law at home and abroad. Institutions, too, underwent civilisational analysis. How should Britons govern an Empire of uncivilised, incompletely civilised, or tenuously civilised subjects? Competing visions of civilised British governance emerged. One faction saw most deviance as the result of disease or biological destiny, which called for medical treatment or cultural, religious, and economic uplift, not punishment. An opposing faction saw the presumption that most people were sane and responsible as a requirement of just governance, and judgment under criminal law as an affirmation of the accused's status as an autonomous subject.

James Fitzjames Stephen, the famous lawyer and legal thinker, fell into the latter camp. He saw no reason to doubt the clinical experience of Maudsley or others who argued for the existence of moral insanity. The problem, for Stephen, arose when medical men tried to argue that the law should take these differences in moral sensibility into account when it determined responsibility. "The moral sense of an English gentleman, the moral sense of an Irish peasant, the moral sense of a Hindoo, the moral sense of any two individual men, differ profoundly", he wrote. "The criminal law ... says to all alike, 'Think and feel as you please about morals, but if you do certain things you shall be hanged' ".[20] Stephen, who had made his name as the architect of the Indian Evidence Act and as a supporter of codification in England, India, Canada, and other colonies, embraced a degree of legal authoritarianism that made some of his colleagues uncomfortable. Many British jurists and physicians did not share Stephen's blithe pragmatism.[21] They asked themselves: Should British civilisation be humane, or should it be just? Could it be either without being both?

Scholars have argued that culture – what Victorians would likely have described as "civilisation" – has long been used as the basis of criminal defences in common law courtrooms. There is no formal "cultural defence" in Anglo-American jurisdictions, although many contend that such a defence exists in practice.[22] Historians, for their part, have tended to see situations in which colonial officials treated Indigenous subjects differently on cultural or racial grounds as concessions to legal pluralism, even in cases where there was no official recognition of Indigenous legal tradition.[23] Apparent deviations from British law in such cases also reflect the struggle to define responsible subjecthood, and to reckon with the implications of civilisation – or its absence – in legal assessments of a defendant's mental capacity. Viewed through this lens, the mind becomes the touchstone for jurisdictional decision making, both in the colonies and in metropolitan courts, in moral insanity and culture-based cases alike.

Australia and the "cultural defence"

An example of how nineteenth-century colonial administrators in the Australian colonies discussed cultural and civilisational difference helps to illustrate the link between psychological subjecthood and jurisdiction. Historian Lisa Ford argues that from the 1830s white settlers in the colonies grew increasingly intolerant of Indigenous exemptions from common-law authority.[24] Sir George Grey, who served terms as governor of South Australia, New Zealand, and the Cape Colony, believed that Indigenous people should be fully subject to British law, regardless of their state of civilisation. He thought that uncivilised *laws*, not biological destiny, limited the development of Indigenous societies. Aboriginal Australians were, he wrote, "as apt and intelligent as any other race of men", but their laws were so debased that "it would appear ... impossible that any nation subject to them could ever emerge from a savage state".[25] But not all colonial authorities shared Grey's vision.

Although efforts to use British law to govern Aboriginal Australians increased in the mid-nineteenth century, officials still made many formal and informal exceptions to common-law jurisdiction. Australian legal historians have noted that settler authorities were reluctant to prosecute Aboriginal people for crimes committed *inter se* even into the twentieth century.[26] Partly, this reluctance stemmed from logistical difficulties. Few white Australians spoke Indigenous languages, and racist tropes about the untrustworthiness of Aboriginal witnesses further discouraged officials from spending time and money gathering what they assumed would be faulty evidence.[27] Cases in which colonial authorities hesitated to investigate, prosecute, or punish Aboriginal Australians should not, however, be seen only as artefacts of official neglect or resource scarcity. Officials' apparent derogations from criminal-justice policies can also reveal uncertainty about the applicability of common-law standards to Aboriginal people, including thresholds of criminal responsibility. This uncertainty persisted into the late nineteenth century, decades after colonial authorities in Australia and other settler colonies proclaimed the exclusive jurisdiction of British law, and British courts, in criminal matters. This shows the potency of late-Victorian medico-legal concerns about the mental and moral effects of civilisation, whether expressed through the language of mental disease or through invocations of colonial difference.

In a case tried in the Northern Territory in 1900, Charles Dashwood, a white judge, argued that three Aboriginal men should be discouraged from pleading guilty to killing a pig with intent to steal it because he "did not favor natives being allowed to plead guilty unless it was clearly shown that they understood the nature of the charge". In the same court, on the same day, an Aboriginal man known as Long Peter was tried for the murder of another Aboriginal man, identified in colonial records as Jimmy. Jimmy died during a settling of scores between two Aboriginal communities following the accidental killing of an old woman, Long Peter's sister. Although the judge instructed the jurors that, technically, "no cognizance could be taken of individual or tribal customs as serving to excuse offenses against British law", he encouraged them to consider "the general facts as to the habits or customs prevailing among the natives". Ultimately, the jury convicted Long Peter of manslaughter and strongly recommended his pardon on the ground that his "act was the outcome of tribal custom".[28] He was released after three months. Dashwood was no warrior for Aboriginal rights, or for the respect of Aboriginal law. In 1893, he had famously sentenced ten Aboriginal defendants to death within his first three days on the Northern Territory bench.[29] Still, the widespread colonial belief that Indigenous people could not conform to foreign, "civilised" law could lead to less punitive outcomes for Indigenous defendants in some cases.

A person's alleged primitivism was certainly not universally protective in British criminal courts. Indigenous people regularly suffered imprisonment and death at the hands of colonial authorities, and accusations of primitivism and savagery could be used to justify harsh, even exemplary, punishment. The same was true of defendants whose advocates claimed they were morally insane: for some, this species of insanity seemed to demand lenience; for others, a defendant's moral insanity made them more dangerous, and justified more brutal treatment. Both kinds of cases asked government authorities, jurors, and members of the public to weigh their fidelity to a legal order that claimed to punish only those whose criminal behaviour was knowingly chosen against their growing suspicion that many who committed criminal acts in Britain and its Empire did so with impaired understanding and little choice.

Criminal responsibility was a matter internal to criminal-law jurisprudence, applicable only to defendants who had already been declared subject to British jurisdiction. Even after British courts declared their supremacy, however, debates about who was a full subject of British law continued. When accused criminals raised insanity in their defence, for instance, they asked decision-makers to determine whether courts should cede their authority to hospitals and medical personnel. In cultural-defence or legal pluralism cases, questions of political jurisdiction shaded into jurisprudential, even moral, ones, as officials contemplated the legal implications of the Empire's insistence on colonial difference. Political subjecthood brought the Empire's denizens into British courts, but determinations of psychological subjecthood – often conceived in terms of mental capacity – dictated what happened there.

To most late-Victorian Britons, the inferiority of colonised people was an axiom of imperial government. Although white, specifically white-British, supremacy was a useful justification for colonial rule, it made questions of criminal responsibility more complex. Despite its apparent contradictions, the notorious "rule of colonial difference" facilitated Britain's nineteenth-century liberal imperialism.[30] Still, though greed and violence often dispelled their scruples, the lieutenants of the Empire remained sensitive to fault lines in the ideology of British rule. In the opinion of some white Victorians, Indigenous people who committed crimes were victims of a biological legacy that they could not deny and a colonial legal order that they could not follow. Maudsley put it vividly: "A low savage in a civilized society", he wrote, "must needs fare almost as badly as a carnivorous animal would fare in a land of herbivorous animals which it was forbidden to eat".[31] Sometimes, then, British officials questioned the justice of expecting colonised people to think and act like Britons while simultaneously declaring that it was impossible for them to do so.[32]

To reiterate, there was no official "cultural defence" under British criminal law, just as moral insanity could not satisfy the *M'Naghten* conditions for legal insanity, at least not without torturing its terms. And yet, defendants did at times succeed in reducing their punishments or avoiding liability altogether by pleading civilisational incapacity: ignorance, impulsivity, emotional volatility, superstition, or moral insensibility. Arguments against defendants' responsibility advanced in British and British colonial courts might take the form of insanity pleas but could also be expressed through less formal appeals to emotion, liberal humanitarianism, or the need for legal pluralism in colonial contexts. These late-Victorian debates over the limits of legal insanity and legal pluralism or cultural accommodation were both, fundamentally, about the consequences of civilisational deficit for responsible, psychological subjecthood, and the fate of supposedly civilised law in an uncivilised world.

Conclusion

Tuke, who had hoped that Bigg's disturbing tale would at last settle the question of the existence of moral insanity, would be disappointed. Fellow physicians agreed that Bigg was ill, but continued to resist the diagnosis that purported to explain his condition. In an 1886 article, one of Bigg's Canadian physicians, Charles Kirk Clarke, argued that his patient was a "moral imbecile". Clarke claimed that this condition was not identical to moral insanity, which he dismissed as "hazy".[33] Imbecility, in the nineteenth century, implied a profound, hereditary disability manifested in systemic weakness. Perhaps Clarke hoped to distinguish Bigg, who was obviously and theatrically disturbed, from the more liminal cases in which moral insanity was often alleged, where the patient appeared sane but for their otherwise inexplicable violence.

Some physicians rejected this kind of diagnostic casuistry. Dr. David Nicolson, then superintendent of Broadmoor, Britain's premier asylum for the criminally insane, took a more pragmatic approach. Nicolson urged his colleagues to remain agnostic on the subject of moral disorders, at least in public. While he did not deny that patients might suffer from non-delusional insanity, when they committed acts of violence he preferred to leave their fates to the lawyers.

> If we were to allow the term [moral insanity] to be too influential in our minds, we would be thwarting justice, and cutting our own throats as men who were endeavouring to carry out scientific ideas: so that instead of carrying weight in the courts of law we would be laughed at.[34]

Nicolson's priority was to protect physicians' credibility, even if that required throwing some patients to the legal wolves. The morally insane were a small minority of those who committed crimes under the sway of mental disease. If physicians squandered their political capital in such cases, all mentally ill accused would pay the price.

Bigg struck no one who met him as normal. The reason he was so appealing to Tuke as a sort of test case for moral insanity – the extreme nature of his mental disorder – seems to have allowed observers to discount his case as *sui generis*: an unhelpful guide for physicians in the course of their ordinary medico-legal work. More mundane moral insanity cases, insofar as they existed, continued to vex physicians, lawyers, and administrators alike, who could not ignore the troubling consonances between the imagined psychology of the morally insane defendant and the "uncivilised" one. British lawyer Robert Lowe, in his 1844 defence of killer John Knatchbull in New South Wales on the ground of moral insanity, described his client as "one of those persons for whom laws had not been made". Such people should, he argued, "be placed under the most severe restraint" in the interest of public safety but ought not to be held legally responsible.[35] In the nineteenth-century British Empire, the possibility that law, at least as Britons knew it, had not been made for many subjects of the Crown remained a distressing possibility. Bigg was an oddity whose story, strange and terrible as it was, could be committed to the pages of medical journals and then, like Bigg himself, forgotten. Moral insanity and civilisational deficit, and the implicit threat to the integrity of criminal law in the Empire these concepts represented, could not be so easily contained.

Notes

1 CK Clarke, "The Case of William B. - Moral Imbecility", *The American Journal of Insanity* vol. 43, no. 1 (1886), p.86.
2 D Hack Tuke, *Prichard and Symonds in Especial Relation to Mental Science: With Chapters on Moral Insanity* (London, 1891), pp.103–4.
3 John Creighton to W.G. Metcalf, 23 October 1884, RG 10-291, B280641, Archives of Ontario (AO).
4 For another account of Bigg's case, see: N Rafter, "The Unrepentant Horse-Slasher: Moral Insanity and the Origins of Criminological Thought", *Criminology*, vol. 42, no. 4 (2004), p.979.
5 *M'Naghten's case* [1843] UKHL J16 (19 June 1843).
6 H Sass & S Herpertz, "Personality Disorders: Clinical Section", in GE Berrios & R Porter (eds), *A History of Clinical Psychology: The Origin and History of Psychiatric Disorders* (Athlone Press: London, 1995), p.635.
7 See, for example: CE. Rosenberg, *The Trial of the Assassin Guiteau: Psychiatry and the Law in the Gilded Age* (University of Chicago Press: Chicago, 1968); R Smith, *Trial by Medicine: Insanity and Responsibility in Victorian Trials* (Edinburgh University Press: Edinburgh, 1981); JP Eigen, *Mad-Doctors in the Dock: Defending the Diagnosis, 1760–1913* (John Hopkins University Press: Baltimore, 2016).
8 See, for example: SL Blumenthal, *Law and the Modern Mind: Consciousness and Responsibility in American Legal Culture* (Harvard University Press: Cambridge MA, 2016); R Belt, "Ballots for Bullets?: Disabled Veterans and the Right to Vote", *Stanford Law Review*, vol. 69, no. 2 (2017), p.435; R Harris, *Murders and Madness: Medicine, Law, and Society in the Fin de Siècle* (Clarendon Press: Oxford, 1989).
9 MD Dubber, "The Right to be Punished: Autonomy and Its Demise in Modern Penal Thought", *Law and History Review*, vol. 16, no.1 (1998), p.113.
10 JL Forde, *The Story of the Bar of Victoria* (Whitcombe & Tombs Ltd: Melbourne, 1913), p.10.
11 EP Kamali, *Felony and the Guilty Mind in Medieval England* (Cambridge University Press: Cambridge, 2019).
12 D Pick, *Faces of Degeneration: A European Disorder, C.1848-1918* (Cambridge University Press: Cambridge, 1993).
13 N Stepan, *The Idea of Race in Science: Great Britain, 1800-1960* (Archon Books: Hamden CT, 1982), p.49.
14 GW Stocking, *Victorian Anthropology* (Free Press: New York, 1987), p.229.

15 H Maudsley, *The Pathology of Mind: A Study of Its Distempers, Deformities, and Disorders* (Macmillan and Co: London, 1895), p.29.
16 Tuke, *Prichard and Symonds*, p.110.
17 M Vaughan, *Curing Their Ills: Colonial Power and African Illness* (Stanford University Press: Stanford CA, 1991).
18 HW Muller, *Subjects and Sovereign: Bonds of Belonging in the Eighteenth-Century British Empire* (Oxford University Press: Oxford, 2017), pp.14–15.
19 CL Evans, *Unsound Empire: Civilization and Madness in Late-Victorian Law* (Yale University Press: New Haven CT, 2021), p.3.
20 JF Stephen, *A History of the Criminal Law of England* (Macmillan and Co: London, 1883), vol I, pp.184–185.
21 KJM Smith, *James Fitzjames Stephen: Portrait of a Victorian Rationalist* (Cambridge University Press: Cambridge, 1988).
22 See, for example: D Woo, "Cultural 'Anomalies' and Cultural Defenses: Towards an Integrated Theory of Homicide and Suicide", *International Journal of the Sociology of Law*, vol. 32 (2004), p.279; A Dundes Renteln, *The Cultural Defense* (Oxford University Press: New York, 2004); W Kymlicka, C Lernestedt, & M Matravers, (eds), *Criminal Law and Cultural Diversity* (Oxford University Press: Oxford, 2014).
23 See, for example: CL Evans, "Heart of Ice: Indigenous Defendants and Colonial Law in the Canadian North-West", *Law and History Review*, vol. 36, no. 2 (2018), p.199; T Loo, "Savage Mercy: Native Culture and the Modification of Capital Punishment in Nineteenth-Century British Columbia", in C Strange (ed), *Qualities of Mercy: Justice, Punishment, and Discretion* (UBC Press: Vancouver, 1996), p.104.
24 L Ford, *Settler Sovereignty: Jurisdiction and Indigenous People in America and Australia, 1788-1836* (Harvard University Press: Cambridge MA, 2010), p.3.
25 G Grey, "A Report upon the Best Means of Promoting the Civilization of the Aboriginal Inhabitants of Australia", in The Aborigines' Committee of the Meeting for Sufferings, *Further Information Respecting the Aborigines* (London, 1842), p.25.
26 M Finnane, "'Payback', Customary Law and Criminal Law in Colonised Australia", *International Journal of the Sociology of Law*, vol. 29, no.4 (2001), p.303.
27 Finnane, "'Payback'", p.304.
28 "Circuit Court, Monday, September 24, 1900", *Northern Territory and Gazette* [Darwin], 18 September 1900, p.3.
29 T Anthony, *Indigenous People, Crime and Punishment* (Routledge: New York, 2013), p.40.
30 P Chatterjee, *The Nation and Its Fragments: Colonial and Postcolonial Histories* (Princeton University Press: Princeton, 1993).
31 Maudsley, *Pathology of Mind*, p.29.
32 HK Bhabha, *The Location of Culture* (Routledge: New York, 2012), pp.123–124.
33 Clarke, "The Case of William B. - Moral Imbecility", p.102.
34 Tuke, *Prichard and Symonds*, p.58.
35 "Supreme Court – Criminal Side", *Sydney Morning Herald* (25 January 1844), p.2.

References

Books and book chapters

Anthony T, *Indigenous People, Crime and Punishment* (Routledge: New York, 2013).
Bhabha HK, *The Location of Culture* (Routledge: New York, 2012).
Blumenthal SL, *Law and the Modern Mind: Consciousness and Responsibility in American Legal Culture* (Harvard University Press: Cambridge MA, 2016).
Chatterjee P, *The Nation and Its Fragments: Colonial and Postcolonial Histories* (Princeton University Press: Princeton NJ, 1993).
Eigen JP, *Mad-Doctors in the Dock: Defending the Diagnosis, 1760–1913* (Johns Hopkins University Press: Baltimore MD, 2016).

Evans CL, *Unsound Empire: Civilization and Madness in Late-Victorian Law* (Yale University Press: New Haven CT, 2021).
Ford L, *Settler Sovereignty: Jurisdiction and Indigenous People in America and Australia, 1788–1836* (Harvard University Press: Cambridge MA, 2010).
Forde JL, *The Story of the Bar of Victoria* (Whitcombe & Tombs Ltd: Melbourne, 1913).
Harris R, *Murders and Madness: Medicine, Law, and Society in the Fin de Siècle* (Clarendon Press: Oxford, 1989).
Kamali EP, *Felony and the Guilty Mind in Medieval England* (Cambridge University Press: Cambridge, 2019).
Kymlicka W, Lernestedt C, & Matravers M (eds), *Criminal Law and Cultural Diversity* (Oxford University Press: Oxford, 2014).
Loo T, "Savage Mercy: Native Culture and the Modification of Capital Punishment in Nineteenth-Century British Columbia", in Strange C (ed), *Qualities of Mercy: Justice, Punishment, and Discretion* (UBC Press: Vancouver, 1996).
Maudsley H, *The Pathology of Mind: A Study of Its Distempers, Deformities, and Disorders* (Macmillan and Co.: London, 1895).
Muller HW, *Subjects and Sovereign: Bonds of Belonging in the Eighteenth-Century British Empire* (Oxford University Press: Oxford, 2017).
Pick D, *Faces of Degeneration: A European Disorder, C.1848–1918* (Cambridge University Press: Cambridge, 1993).
Renteln AD, *The Cultural Defense* (Oxford University Press: New York, 2004).
Rosenberg CE, *The Trial of the Assassin Guiteau: Psychiatry and the Law in the Gilded Age* (University of Chicago Press: Chicago, 1968).
Sass H & Herpertz S, "Personality Disorders: Clinical Section", in Berrios GE & Porter R (ed), *A History of Clinical Psychology: The Origin and History of Psychiatric Disorders* (Athlone Press: London, 1995).
Smith KJM, *James Fitzjames Stephen: Portrait of a Victorian Rationalist* (Cambridge University Press: Cambridge, 1988).
Smith R, *Trial by Medicine: Insanity and Responsibility in Victorian Trials* (Edinburgh University Press: Edinburgh, 1981).
Stepan N, *The Idea of Race in Science: Great Britain, 1800–1960* (Archon Books: Hamden CT, 1982).
Stephen JF, *A History of the Criminal Law of England* (Macmillan and Co: London, 1883), vols I–III.
Stocking GW, *Victorian Anthropology* (Free Press: New York, 1987).
Tuke DH, *Prichard and Symonds in Especial Relation to Mental Science: With Chapters on Moral Insanity* (London & Churchill: London, 1891).
Vaughan M, *Curing Their Ills: Colonial Power and African Illness* (Stanford University Press: Stanford CA, 1991).

Journal articles

Belt R, "Ballots for Bullets?: Disabled Veterans and the Right to Vote", *Stanford Law Review*, vol. 69, no. 2 (2017), pp.435–90.
Clarke CK, "The Case of William B. – Moral Imbecility", *The American Journal of Insanity*, vol. 43, no. 1 (1886), pp.83–103.
Dubber MD, "The Right to Be Punished: Autonomy and Its Demise in Modern Penal Thought", *Law and History Review*, vol. 16, no. 1 (1998), pp.113–46.
Evans CL, "Heart of Ice: Indigenous Defendants and Colonial Law in the Canadian North-West", *Law and History Review*, vol. 36, no. 2 (2018), pp.199–234.
Finnane M, "'Payback', Customary Law and Criminal Law in Colonised Australia", *International Journal of the Sociology of Law*, vol. 29, no. 4 (2001), pp.293–310.
Rafter N, "The Unrepentant Horse-Slasher: Moral Insanity and the Origins of Criminological Thought", *Criminology*, vol. 42, no. 4 (2004), pp.979–1008.

Woo D, "Cultural 'Anomalies' and Cultural Defenses: Towards an Integrated Theory of Homicide and Suicide", *International Journal of the Sociology of Law*, vol. 32, no. 4 (2004), pp.279–302.

Archival material

Archives of Ontario (AO)

"Circuit Court, Monday, September 24, 1900", *Northern Territory and Gazette* [Darwin], 18 September 1900, 3.

"Supreme Court – Criminal Side", *Sydney Morning Herald*, 25 January 1844, 2.

Grey G, "A Report upon the Best Means of Promoting the Civilization of the Aboriginal Inhabitants of Australia", in The Aborigines' Committee of the Meeting for Sufferings, *Further Information Respecting the Aborigines* (London, 1842).

5
CRIMINAL RESPONSIBILITY ATTRIBUTION AS A STEP ON THE ROAD TO DESISTANCE?

Exploring Theoretical Intersections

Louise Kennefick

Critical scholars continue to decry the construct of the responsible subject of the criminal law as abstract and separate, yet little progress is made by way of doctrinal reform. This chapter argues that change is hampered by a sense of doctrinal remoteness that separates guilt-finding from the wider aims of the criminal justice system, and insulates it from progressive, evidence-based justice discourses. The study of desistance from crime has emerged as one of the most influential of such discourses, and its core premise of social contextuality speaks to the quest for a relational view of the person in critical legal scholarship. It is important to acknowledge from the outset that desistance studies do not represent a single theory, rather, the term represents a multifaceted and diverse conceptual and empirical landscape. Though a thorough review of the field is not feasible here, it is argued that engaging more closely with desistance theories has the potential to invigorate criminal law theory discourses that seek to reshape the responsible subject. Conversely, for desistance scholars aiming to expand the reach of this framework, guilt-finding is a significant and untapped area that entrenches a narrow view of the person that such frames seek to dismantle. This chapter speculates about how ideas may be exchanged across these seemingly distinct fields through the cultivation of a shared conceptual terrain with the ultimate objective of advancing social cohesion.[1]

The chapter begins with a brief tour of key arguments calling for context in doctrine as a matter of justice with a view to highlighting the juxtaposition of the force of the literature and its limited impact on doctrine itself. Reflecting on how to address this lag, the second part steps back to consider functions of criminal responsibility, forefronting the instrumental function of blame as a fundamental feature of the civil order project. The next part deploys the concept of punitiveness to highlight how the rational agency paradigm on which doctrine rests has the effect of undermining, rather than bolstering, the civil order project of our present time. Foregrounding wider criminal justice concerns, the fourth part draws on desistance studies to consider their potential to support the quest for social cohesion in

DOI: 10.4324/9781003297260-7

criminal law scholarship. Finally, brief consideration is given to the transposition of desistance theory to doctrine through the example of excuse.

The mounting case against doctrinal remoteness

It is difficult to take an interest in the future of an abstract construct in the same way that you might a flesh and bones person. Indeed, many of the complaints against the rational agency paradigm (just some of which are touched on in what follows) may be read as sharing an underlying sense that responsibility attribution based thereon simply misses the mark and, in so doing, causes unjustifiable hardship to persons and undermines communities. Literature responds with calls for a contextual understanding of personhood grounded in variable and multifaceted critiques.[2] Notwithstanding the force of such arguments, however, they appear to have little impact on doctrinal reform. My suspicion is that lack of progress has more to do with the enduring conceptual remoteness of responsibility doctrine than with the authority of the arguments themselves.

A core issue brought to light by the literature relates to the fact that the law's person does not accurately depict contemporary understandings of the human psyche, bringing into question the retributive ideal of fairness through blaming according to proportionate desert.[3] This standpoint is particularly evident in the context of defences. For example, according to Stephen Morse, the full range of capacities encompassing the human psyche sit in opposition to the narrow scope of excuse doctrine.[4] And scholarship concerning the role of emotions highlights how cognition alone, as the basis of exculpation, does not account for the complex process underpinning human decision-making.[5] In this vein, emotion theory has been drawn on to test the reasonableness component of defences like duress,[6] in addition to informing novel theories of existing defences,[7] and justifying arguments for the introduction of new categories of excuse and partial excuse, as well as greater more expansive reforms.[8] Other convincing lines draw on social psychology to question more broadly the construct of agency underpinning the law from a situationist perspective. Jon Hanson and others challenge the dominance of the "norm of reasoning" in legal discourses charging it with the mantle of "dubious ideological framework" and problematising it in a social psychological context as a "dispositionist person schema".[9]

As well as drawing on psychology, more diverse and sweeping accounts of the criminal law rely on philosophy, sociology, and critical historical perspectives to challenge the abstracted and isolated depiction of personhood therein.[10] It is impossible to do justice to such accounts here, but to note that they have been the springboard for an ever expanding and deepening critique of criminal responsibility that recognises demands for an alternative account of the person.[11] Recently, for example, Craig Reeves calls for a heteronomous (as distinct from autonomous) understanding of personhood in terms of agency, belying a greater challenge to criminal law theory:

> The task for the philosophy of criminal law is to engage in concrete utopian reflections on the possibility of a different responsibility practice in a changed form of ethical life that would be more adequate to the real psychology of persons.[12]

These lines run adjacent to a significant body of work on the law's gendered subject, which is nearing consensus on the relational nature of human personhood, in contrast to the orthodox subject of the law, though means of expression differ.[13] In a criminal law context, Ngaire Naffine deploys a critical feminist approach to interrogate and undermine conceptual orthodoxies in criminal law,[14] and Arlie Loughnan brings this particular frame to criminal responsibility, arguing that it functions to organise "key sets of relations – between self, others and the state – as relations of responsibility".[15] The relational trend is further echoed in ethics of care scholarship, which underscore close personal relationships and related responsibility over those of the individual liberal agent conception of the law.[16] Recently, for example, Jonathan Herring has argued that the law's objective ought to focus on enhancing caring relationships over individual rights, atop of an understanding of the self as relational, drawing on feminist psychology, philosophy, and sociology understandings.[17]

With the continued advancement of these relational scholarships, our understanding of the disconnect between the abstract agent and the real human person is maturing, and is made stronger by a renewed appreciation of the cultural significance of condemnation, and what it means for the real human person of the criminal law.[18] In response, some scholars have put forward novel theories that seek to take the sting out of the rational agency paradigm and to emphasise, to differing degrees, the significance of forward-looking ends.[19] Notably, Nicola Lacey and Hanna Pickard question the apparent sense of entitlement to hostile reactions against those who offend and highlight the harmful impact of this reaction.[20] The authors envisage an alternative, clinical approach to accountability whereby responsibility ascription is divested of aversive features, and punishment is deployed with a therapeutic emphasis in order to integrate justice and rehabilitative models. It is noteworthy, however, that their approach is directed less at doctrine itself and more at sentencing and its aftermath. Erin Kelly takes a step further from the justice model, arguing that public blaming is not legitimate given the gap between legal guilt and moral blameworthiness, and should be dispensed with.[21] Rather, her "harm reduction" account entails "a rights-protecting, public-safety rationale that permits us to shift burdens of rights-protection onto people who criminally threaten or violate other people's rights".[22] For Kelly, punishment without blame is justifiable in order to meet the demands of a "just social order", which involves: "fundamentally, acknowledging and addressing the basic needs and potentialities of all members of society, including those who break the law".[23] Most recently, Amanda Wilson's work on developing an ethical foundation for restorative justice draws on metapsychology to forefront the significance of guilt and shame in undermining some current practices and thinking in the field.[24] Her project is indicative of the challenge posed by alternative and emerging justice mechanisms and how they might bear on more conventional ways of understanding responsibility.

Taken together, such developments threaten the reification of guilt-finding, and its remoteness from wider criminal justice discourses. Concurrently, the argument that to undermine the hegemony of the rational agency paradigm is, in some way, to disrespect personhood is losing traction. This argument can be countered persuasively by drawing on wider justice and critical political philosophical arguments that posit respect for agency as beyond rational abstraction. Rather, such respect manifests in public institutions by supporting agency through investing in the social conditions that hone the capacity to choose, rather than requiring investment in condemnation. As Vincent Chiao notes, in "taking responsibility seriously", "acknowledging that people can render themselves liable to defensive harm through their wrongful acts does not entail discounting the rights and interests of the guilty relative to those of the innocent".[25]

Notwithstanding the force and maturity of this scholarship, doctrinal reform lags owing to the perpetuation of morality of form over morality of substance, which might be explained by a sort of *status quo* stalemate.[26] This torpor suggests that more is needed to bring doctrine within wider criminal justice discourses in order to recognise more overtly its instrumentalist duty to fulfil the criminal law's core objective to preserve civil order. Giving a more prominent position to the effective function of state blame is supported by general sentiment underpinning literature that emphasises the public duty of the law to its citizens,[27] linking it to wider justice discourses around the cultivation of social cohesion and reintegration within the penal context. To this end, the next section explores the functions of blaming, with a view to recalibrating the roles of backward- and forward-looking accounts underpinning responsibility doctrine.

Functions of criminal responsibility attribution

The criminal law seeks to preserve civil order in two ways. First, it defines our understanding of civility by marking out what is deemed uncivil or criminal (criminalisation) and, second, it reinforces the distinction by condemning (blaming and punishing) those who transgress its codes.[28] Criminal responsibility attribution feeds into the greater project at the condemnation stage, where questions of liability and culpability are measured and decided upon in order to identify the blameworthy, as a prerequisite to punishment. The conditions of responsibility are embedded in doctrine and its underlying ideas and so the latter become significant conceptual tools in coordinating social conduct.[29]

Doctrines of responsibility (*mens rea* and excuse, in particular)[30] centre around the mental state of the individual, with a view to evaluating their culpability for the harm caused.[31] Notwithstanding the prevalence of consequentialist accounts more broadly,[32] this calculation is informed by a deontological understanding of responsibility as retrospective because it revolves around the notion of desert as a means of justifying blame. One explanation for the perpetuation of the deontological account is in the way the stages of justice are categorised. The process is presented so as to insulate culpability evaluation from consequentialist considerations, because such concerns are dealt with at other stages, for instance, at the front-end in questions around prosecution, and at the back-end in sentencing considerations and related sanctions and measures. Crudely put, then, culpability evaluation appears to be concerned chiefly with sorting the guilty from the not guilty, based on an evaluation of past actions alone. This understanding monopolises perceptions of guilt-finding in wider justice discourses.

The dominance of this view tends to overshadow the fact that blaming has another important function that serves the greater civil order project, a didactic function.[33] Attributing blame also works towards securing order through seeking to influence the future behaviour of the person towards ceasing offending, and to encourage compliance in the wider community. In blaming someone, we find fault with the wrongdoer and confront them accordingly in order to elicit remorse with a view to advancing greater moral alignment.[34] We want the person who has wronged us to appreciate the moral significance of what they have done. In so doing, the hope is that their newfound understanding of their actions will produce better behaviour in the future. Drawing on moral psychology, we can see how blaming has a greater role to play in terms of effecting attitudinal and behavioural change as a method of control then is perhaps currently appreciated.[35] For instance, for George Tsai, blaming is a key mode of regulation which constructs and maintains collective reasons, motivations, and expectations that underpin our shared ethical life. That life, or "*lived experience of ethical norms* and *concrete ethical practice*" (emphasis in original)[36] is made up in part of members that have "internalized reciprocal attitudes with ethical content".[37]

Transposing Tsai's observations about blame to the attribution of criminal responsibility helps explain how ideas underpinning doctrine can inform the substantive content that shapes the attitude of the moral community in a more meaningful way. That content is unpicked in the next section, but for now it is enough to emphasise that, punishment aside, in holding someone to account for their past transgression, culpability evaluation is also transmitting an expectation to that person that they will not behave in this way again because it is blameworthy, and communicating the norms around more complex situations (e.g. where someone has a mental disorder) that it is difficult to escape liability owing to, for one reason, the fact that excuse options are restrictive in doctrine, and narrowly applied in practice. Of course, moral alignment is not always possible in reality, but we can still appreciate the point of blaming as aiming towards moral recalibration as between the person who has offended and the (so-called) law abiding majority.[38] Thinking about blaming in this way accords more readily with wider global movements in justice discourses seeking to normalise social rehabilitation and reintegration as a central aim of penality.[39] This account brings greater meaning to the notion of civil order, one more fitting for our time and place.

The next section argues that the didactic function is failing in its task to ensure order through moral alignment because the substantive content of doctrine, as based on the rational agency paradigm, incites social discord through a form of conceptual punitiveness.

The punitive credentials of rational agency

Far from a neutral phenomenon, the rational agency paradigm undermines social cohesion by making a distinct contribution to a greater punitive climate. Connecting rational agency to the concept of punitiveness at the guilt-finding phase sheds light on the nature of that contribution, and provides a shared vernacular for doctrine to take a more central role in discourses around wider criminal justice aims.

Punitiveness has become something of a prosaicism with different meanings and uses afforded it depending on what purpose it serves. For instance, it is commonly employed to encapsulate public attitudes in the context of penal populism discourses,[40] in addition to explaining complex phenomena such as methods of state control.[41] Notwithstanding its preponderance, it remains difficult to measure, and arguably under-theorised,[42] though recent scholarship has gone some way towards addressing these concerns.[43] For present purposes, I am interested in exploring punitiveness as a concept that may be understood in the context of principles of responsibility, and in the sense of capturing the underlying sentiment of the state towards those who offend.

In this regard, Stanley Cohen's definition of the term is one of the more helpful attempts at interpreting punitiveness,[44] which he characterises by the presence of "coercion, formalism, moralism and the infliction of pain on individual legal subjects by a third party".[45] More recently, Henrique Carvalho *et al*'s theorisation of punitiveness as a "phenomenological complex" has further deepened and expanded understandings of the notion by framing it as "a central feature of a range of intersecting experiences and practices, operating at a personal, symbolic, political and structural level".[46] In so doing, the authors reveal how punitiveness acts both universally and particularly; "constructing and espousing authoritarian and hostile worldviews that generate from and perpetuate a sense of insecurity on a variety of issues".[47] In particular, though Carvalho *et al* deploy their complex to capture the punitiveness beyond criminal justice, their framework can assist in articulating how doctrine plays a role in propagating wider punitive logics. They argue that punitiveness can be identified in "social attitudes, arrangements and conditions" to the degree that they encourage punitive subjectivity, support symbolic scapegoating through isolation techniques, institutionalise and strategically deploy hostile practices, and reproduce and reinforce oppressive mechanisms and structures.[48] In turn, the potency of these effects distracts from the greater societal harm that punitiveness does in terms of precipitating inequality, undermining welfare efforts, and making a key contribution to social discord through civil disengagement.[49]

Drawing on these definitions, I argue that doctrine, as the institutional language of responsibility, reinforces punitive logics through a conceptual triad of individualism, moralism, and formalism inherent in the rational agency construct. For, the agent of the criminal law is isolated (individualism) and judged (formalism) in a way that presents them as inherently corrupt and unworthy of membership of the moral community (moralism), thereby undermining social cohesion.

Individualism

Criminal responsibility has taken a decidedly individualistic turn over time, reflecting broader cultural depictions and expectations of the individual as self-constituted, self-governing, and detached from interests that relate to broader social forces and structures.[50] Criticism of individualism in criminal legal scholarship is extensive, and the core debates in the context of criminal responsibility are touched on above. For present purposes, however, I wish to emphasise how individualism, as a psychological mechanism, reveals a conceptual strategy to isolate the person, bringing divisive consequences for wider justice aims.

It is now well established in the social psychological literature that an individualistic frame represents an intrinsic human tendency to "overstate the role of individual disposition and under-appreciate the role of situation in accounting for human behaviour".[51] This tendency is innate in that it is borne from a sense of fear in the face of wrongdoing to others, and a need to understand and control the source of the fear by containing it within the subject. The rational agency paradigm reflects this tendency at a doctrinal level, and may be framed as an institutional strategy to accentuate the role of the individual and dampen the relevance of wider contexts relating to criminal behaviour. In so doing, the paradigm channels our collective and generalised anxieties around disorder and injustice, containing them within the person as the responsible source.[52] In turn, responsibilisation literature helps us to understand how dispositional bias is operationalised on a grander scale as a modus of both neoliberalism and advanced liberalism that enables a transfer of responsibility from state to person.[53]

With the problem of crime projected onto the person, the criminal justice system can contain and control the individual as a rational, blameworthy agent. Guilt-finding plays its part by cultivating a moral discourse that dichotomises people into offender (which can slip into "vile individuals" or the "anti-social or disrespectful 'other'") and non-offender (or "law abiding majority").[54] Creating opposing categories of people generates a reductivist account of the lived reality of those who come before the criminal justice system (and, indeed, the so-called "law abiding majority").[55] This state of affairs is unhelpful because it makes moral rule difficult to apply as there is no space for different interpretations of a given situation.[56] Moreover, though a sense of cohesion might emerge from identifying and isolating the criminal person, it is an insecure cohesion, and destructive, because isolation continues to feed the conditions that contribute to crime,[57] ultimately undermining social solidarity.

Moralism and formalism

Moralism tends to cultivate punitivism where there is a strong association between the wrong done to the victim and what the person who committed the wrong deserves as a result.[58] And the more morally wrongful people perceive an action to be, the more they presume intention in the perpetrator.[59] The punitive response is further reinforced by criminological findings which suggest that those who believe that criminal behaviour is the consequence of the free choice of the individual (which is a strong bias as discussed above), the more likely they are to hold punitive attitudes than those who believe that crime is a consequence of external factors.[60] As such, foregrounding rational agency as the basis of responsibility in legal doctrine feeds into punitive logics whereby the wrongfulness of the act itself is equated with the moral worth of the person.[61] The limited range of excuses available at the exculpatory stage of criminal responsibility ascription is one example where doctrine serves to reinforce this obtuse moralistic standpoint whereby the person who has transgressed is reduced to their offence as it stood at that point in time, with very limited recourse to relevant external moral concerns. The portrayal of the person as inherently morally corrupt marks the conceptual contribution of doctrine to the scapegoating of the individual in order to support a maladapted version of solidarity based on fear of crime, insecurity, and aggression.[62]

The displacement of situational, particular, and consequential moral concerns (beyond the agency paradigm) at guilt-finding to the punishment stage is often justified by a claim to formalism.[63] As an expression of formalism, the "legal guilt" construct relies on its own internal logic in order to provide a coherent account of who may be deemed blameworthy.[64] Though formalism lends an internal coherence to law, critical legal scholarship has called out its superficiality.[65] In particular, Alan Norrie's work on responsibility and punishment exposes the fact that formalism in itself is inherently moralistic.[66] He describes a "morality of form" whereby doctrine acts to superimpose legal definitions, or forms, upon considerations of wrongdoing and culpability with a view to imbedding individual freedom, but in a way that evades a substantive reckoning with the greater moral nature of the acts themselves.[67]

Moreover, the formalist account is problematic as it masks the inherent moral essence of the law's approach to decision-making through responsibility doctrine. The nature of the moral judgement at play is evident when we look at the dominant approach to understanding the concept of culpability, the "reason-responsiveness" account. Reason-responsiveness is an enduring theory,[68] whereby an agent is deemed responsible on the basis that they demonstrate the capacity to respond to their moral reasons for acting in a certain way, but they respond wrongly. The reasons, in particular, are significant here because they reveal an individual's core motivation for action which is the key to the moral assessment. As Gregory Antill puts it:

> "These reasons are important for subjective culpability because it is the agent's reasons for acting that reveal (or constitute) their "quality of will." It is the agent's will, rather

than their actions, which, according to the reasons-responsiveness theory, is the ultimate object of assessment, or grounds for our blame or resentment, of the culpable agent".[69]

The question, therefore, that the law asks in this context, is to what extent the individual's actions revealed a moral deficit in terms of appreciating the reasons why the act itself was wrongful.[70] Douglas Husak characterises this moral deficit as a faulty reasoning process and shows it breaches the gossamer of formalism to reveal a distinct version of moralism at play in assessing blameworthiness. Husak states that the agent's "deliberation is deficient in the way that supports blameworthiness most clearly when agents respond incorrectly to the balance of moral reasons *according to their own lights*."[71] It is in this sense that agents ought to have "known better" than to act as they have done, and so they "merit blame" (as the most appropriate response) as a result of their poor choice.[72] As such, it is a small step from a theory based on flawed practical reasoning, to the attribution of responsibility on the basis of a morally corrupt will. As Husak puts it: "an individual is morally responsible when her action expresses negative attitudes that reveal *something bad about her as a person*".[73] (emphasis added). And so, we can see that rather than neutralising the causticity of more obvious forms of moralism, formalism simply masks a more clandestine brand.

Casting someone as morally corrupt at the point of blame reinforces punitive logic by formalising and lending legitimacy to the categorisation (and consequent segregation) of people who offend. As a result, the person who offends is more likely to be perceived as irredeemable.[74] Desistance theory challenges this approach by showing how compliance is borne from an individual's sense that they have a way back to being accepted by the moral community, further prompting the call for a fundamental change in how the state ascribes blame.

Lessons in promoting social cohesion from desistance theory

Having demonstrated the punitive logic inherent in the rational agency paradigm, the chapter now turns to the potential role that desistance theories can play in supporting an alternative conceptual architecture for responsibility attribution, one that better aligns with the wealth of scholarship calling for change. Desistance theories have the added legitimacy of already being (at least discursively) embedded in criminal justice policy and practice, and the indicators are that they are likely to continue to inform policy formation owing to a strong evidence base and alignment with international ideals and objectives that support liberal democracy.[75]

The rise of desistance

Together with restorative justice,[76] desistance studies have made a significant cultural and practical mark in recent decades, in response to (or in the face of) more traditional criminal justice policies and practices.[77] Indeed, the prevalence of desistance theory frameworks has grown to such an extent that some would argue criminal justice is undergoing a paradigm shift.[78] Notwithstanding the complexity and challenges defining, applying, and measuring desistance,[79] it has become an accepted evidence base used to support strategies that span key stages of the criminal justice system, across a growing number of jurisdictions.[80] While questions around the extent to which practice meets policy remain pertinent,[81] a core focus has become how best to apply it in operations, and institutional strategy and practices,[82] rather than whether or not it should be applied.

The objective of desistance theory

The study of desistance emerged from life-course and developmental criminology research,[83] and is concerned with understanding the process of transitioning from offending behaviour through to reducing it either in seriousness or quantity, and to eventually ceasing it.[84] There is an acceptance that the process of changing behaviour is lengthy, complex, and contingent, and that it can be marked by distinct aspects (primary, secondary, and tertiary desistance),[85] or spheres (act, identity, and relational desistance).[86] Primary and secondary desistance relate to a reduction in offending and the assumption of a new identity as someone who does not offend, respectively, though the two are not mutually exclusive. Tertiary desistance describes the sense of belonging that emerges when the desister feels recognised by and part of the moral community.[87] Secondary and tertiary desistance, too, have been described as interrelated, as Thomas Ugelvik remarks, these two phases: "more likely develop at the same time, mutually fortifying each other in complex feedback processes that are difficult, if not impossible, to untangle empirically".[88]

The nuance around the boundaries of desistance is emblematic of the greater uncertainty around how desistance ought to be conceptualised, measured, and applied, which arguably has much to do with the fact that it is imbedded in the particular. Desistance theories are non-ideal in that they stand as an acknowledgment that everyone has a different experience of the change process, that not everyone desists, and that many (or most) desist without (or in spite of) criminal justice intervention. The approach to change is clear, in that desistance studies want to understand this process so that people can be supported in achieving and maintaining law-abiding lives. However, unlike the rational agency paradigm, such studies tend to start from a ground-up understanding of the person as embedded in the moral community, notwithstanding their transgressions. This frame has emerged from an evidence-base demonstrating that those who offend share moral values with those who do not,[89] with the implication that the former are both capable of change and deserving of supports that facilitate conditions that better empower them to exercise their values in a law-abiding way.[90] As a result, it is the barriers to living a law-abiding life that are the target of desistance theory,[91] rather than placing the responsibility for crime solely at the feet of the individual when seeking to advance social cohesion.

I have outlined above how individualism, moralism, and formalism combine to imbed a form of conceptual punitiveness in doctrinal evaluations of criminal responsibility by reinforcing an idea of the person as an "other" with a fixed character that is inherently immoral. Key findings from desistance studies may go some way towards undermining this approach by framing conceptual punitiveness as a barrier to change, thereby bolstering a new avenue for critical criminal law theory and reform pathways.

The significance of desistance theory to criminal responsibility attribution

Individualism is conceptually punitive because it separates the person from their wider moral and social context, imposing a top-down ideal of personhood as rational agency in order to evaluate culpability. Desistance theories, on the other hand, begin with seeking to understand how people change in the real world. They tend towards a "social normative" model that is founded on "values of social cooperation and harmony",[92] and recognising that change does not happen in a vacuum. Rather, because people are relational, conditions beyond the individual are connected to social-psychological processes that impact behaviour.[93] Though some desistance theories have been charged with having an individualism problem due to their focus on transformation of an individual's psyche, the structure and agency question has been well debated in the literature, and most acknowledge that there is a complex interaction happening between the two.[94] For instance, Beth Weaver describes desistance as being "inescapably relational" and conceptualised as "a process involving an interplay between 'objective', or external factors, and 'subjective', or internal factors, with different theoretical and empirical accounts of desistance prioritizing either the role of social contexts or agency in the process".[95] Recent literature describes the desistance process as a "two-way" street between individuals and the community in terms of achieving reintegration.[96]

Thinking about the relational nature of the person in the desistance process has prompted recognition of the role of justice agencies and institutions in bridging the gap between agency/individual and structure/community. A recent development in the literature adopts the concept of "recovery capital" to explain the "personal, social and community resources an individual can draw upon to support their recovery…"[97] and to turn away from offending behaviour. A key finding from this work is to highlight the significance of formal relationships, (together with resources, processes, and systems) in supporting change. Justice capital, in turn, refers to resources available to individuals from institutions. For instance, David Best *et al* introduce the notion of "institutional justice capital" which describes "the capital that institutions provide (including institutional actors) which either builds on or undermines the personal justice capital of justice-involved people".[98] In light of this research, much of the work within the criminal justice arena relates to how agencies can respond to individuals who offend in a way that supports desistance.[99] They argue that institutional justice capital is sustained by norms, just as much as rules and practices within institutions, as a means of generating "the conditions and context for growth and for building personal and social capital".[100] For the authors, institutional justice capital may be designated as positive or negative, depending on how its features "promote or diminish wellbeing and the capacity for personal growth and fulfilment".[101]

Criminal responsibility doctrine plays a significant role in sustaining the normative message of the criminal law, as a key justice institution. However, it is arguable that its role is a negative one in terms of diminishing an individual's self-efficacy through the promulgation of conceptual punitiveness. As discussed above, individualism, moralism, and formalism tend to work in tandem to craft an image of the person who offends as a fixed, and inherently bad, character, undermining social (re)integration efforts in real life through the reinforcement of hostile responses that inhibit change. For desistance theorists, people who struggle most to change behaviour are those who have bought into their identification as inherently bad or being "doomed or fated in their situation", which ultimately amounts to a feeling of lack of agency/self-efficacy.[102]

Theories of desistance, on the other hand, are bound by a more dynamic view of personhood underpinned by the idea that "people can change".[103] Moreover, key findings from secondary/identity theories of desistance demonstrate that desistance is supported where individuals are able to make their past offending behaviour part of their story towards a non-offending future.[104] They need to imagine and play out a flexible narrative that allows their understanding of themselves to change.[105] As Farrall *et al* put it: "the past cannot change but its meaning can and … frequently does. In short then, the meaning placed upon the past is a function of who one is, which in turn, is informed by who one can be."[106] This view of personhood supports change at the secondary desistance level by allowing to open the possibility of growth and redeemability, over condemnation and moral judgement all the way down.[107] Desistance-based criminal justice responses seek to embody respect for the individual and foster agency.[108] Literature suggests that though a desistance-based approach is no panacea, it offers an evidence-based framework for supporting change through the promulgation of key principles that instil hope in the individual, that acknowledge agency and reflexivity, that develop strengths, and that value and protect relationships.[109]

So, how might the site of culpability evaluation respond doctrinally to the lessons from desistance, in order to combat conceptual punitiveness?

Transplanting desistance into doctrine – [re]making excuses?

This section highlights excuse as a potential target for doctrinal reform through a desistance lens because excuse doctrine is one of the few places where circumstances beyond the person are entertained in responsibility ascription. As Lacey puts it, "excuses... mark out situations in which the internal or external conditions under which a defendant acts are such as to displace – partly or completely – the attribution of responsibility for an admittedly wrongful act."[110] As such, excuse doctrine represents one point of particularisation in the attributional process where there is a potential opening for dialogue about the nature and breadth of responsibility. Space limitations constrain a comprehensive consideration of a desistance framework in the context of individual excuses, and so this section engages in a more general, exploratory discussion as a preliminary step towards considering how criminal responsibility ascription (through excuse doctrine) may be recast to conceptually support, rather than undermine, the desistance process. In other words, how can we use findings from desistance studies to inform substantive doctrinal content so that it can fulfil its blaming function in a way that advances social cohesion rather than reinforcing punitive attitudes which undermine it? The remainder of this section considers potential advantages from two perspectives: offender-oriented benefits and community-oriented benefits.

Offender-oriented benefits

Thinking about what excuses do through a desistance lens might take us further along in the quest for a greater acknowledgement for context in questions of culpability. According to Snyder and Higgins, excuse-making, as an internal process, involves framing causal attributions for behaviour as "less central" to a person's self-image.[111] As such, explanations for wrongful action that are based on external, uncontrollable, or unintentional behaviour helps to better separate the person's sense of self from their offending.[112] Viewed this way, the literature suggests that certain forms of excuse-making can support the desistance process by allowing the person who offends to take active responsibility through a process of "neutralisation". Neutralisation was originally used as a means of explaining causes of crime,[113] however, Shadd Maruna and Ruth Mann's study highlights how it has become acknowledged as a form of normal behaviour, and one that has the potential to encourage meaningful accountability, reduce stigma, and support the development of pro-social identities.[114] Excuse-making and neutralisation suggest that coming to terms with their behaviour allows a person to build a narrative where they can make sense of what they did but leave a space for themselves to still exist as a person with worth, which then gives them a constructive way to engage their rational capacity in order to build a non-offending identity.[115] Viewing excuses in criminal law through this lens may provide a basis to tackle the problems of moralism and formalism in the law, which tend to collapse the distinction between the offence and the person, making it harder for them to self-identify, and be seen, as a person worthy of membership of the moral community.

Community-oriented benefits

From the perspective of the community, there is empirical support for the claim that the more empathetic someone feels, the less likely they are to support harsh forms of punishment. Rather, they are more likely to hold a positive attitude towards rehabilitation and reintegration of those who offend.[116] Desistance literature supports the contention that people are more likely to believe that someone can change if they have more information about the circumstances of their offending behaviour. Knowledge of context then, can support the cultivation of compassionate responses which "de-other" the person who offends.

Within excuse scholarship, much has been written about the categorisation of excuses, and what might amount to the basis of an excuse, with considerably less focus afforded to the instrumentalist function of excuses in the criminal law context, beyond the negation of culpability.[117] To imbue culpability evaluation with desistance principles would require rethinking excuse doctrine in a way that acknowledges the relational nature of personhood, and the fact that individual behaviours and decision-making is heavily influenced by psycho-social processes both acting within and beyond the person. All this is not to reject rational agency outright. For, agency itself is not at odds with desistance because desistance studies show that taking responsibility for past actions is an integral part of the change process. Rather, a desistance lens on excuse requires supplementing rational agency with reintegrative considerations. This might mean that the proportionality principle remains, but that the basis of the just deserts calculation is expanded to enhance the excusing function. The significance of excuse-making as a step towards maintaining or building a pro-social identity and igniting compassionate (over aversive) responses would also need to be considered more seriously. This perspective would forefront the functional nature of blame in terms of supporting social cohesion, and has the potential to open new directions for scholarship for instance, in the context of underpinning arguments that call for the expansion of excuse (and partial excuse) offerings on the basis of factors such as developmental immaturity, past trauma, and social deprivation.[118]

Conclusion

This chapter has stressed how calls for recognition of context as a means of redressing punitiveness are becoming more numerous and more persuasive in critical criminal law scholarship, but with little imprint on doctrinal development. To further the effort, the chapter foregrounds the greater, instrumentalist function of responsibility attribution, emphasising its significance as a fundamental feature of the civil order project. This step is significant because there is a growing awareness that the concept of rational agency, untempered, reinforces a punitive logic at the heart of criminal responsibility attribution. Punitivism undermines social cohesion, which counters the wider objective of the criminal justice system in maintaining civil order. For the law (at its guilt-finding phase) to take seriously its role in this overarching endeavour, it must do more to unearth, acknowledge, and strive to ameliorate, the harm done by conceptual punitiveness to those subject to state blame. Accordingly, viewing guilt-finding through an instrumentalist lens provides greater access for responsibility doctrine to wider criminal justice concerns and developments, but more work is needed to showcase the harm caused by conceptual punitiveness, and to present feasible avenues to support a reform agenda.

To this end, the chapter identifies desistance studies as one field that has the potential to support the quest for context and cohesion in criminal responsibility ascription. It explores the notion that desistance studies can provide guilt-finding with a more pointed objective (achieving social cohesion in a way that supports cessation of offending), and an established evidence-base to support doctrinal reform relying on concepts that promote reintegration, rather than disintegration. Excuse was identified as one potential area where desistance studies might have an impact. Further work is needed in order to consider the cogency of its application here, as well as the potential of desistance and related pro-social fields of study to apply to other doctrines of responsibility.[119]

Acknowledgements

With sincere thanks to Prof Lindsay Farmer and Prof Fergus McNeill for their valuable feedback on an earlier draft.

Notes

1 For example, Fox describes desistance studies as a "cluster of theories" or "empirical observations"; KJ Fox, "Desistance frameworks", *Aggression and Violent Behavior*, vol 63 (2022), p.1. See further, B Weaver, "Understanding desistance: a critical review of theories of desistance", *Psychology, Crime & Law*, vol. 25, no. 6 (2019), p.641.
2 For overview, see: N Lacey, *In Search of Criminal Responsibility: Ideas, Interests, and Institutions* (Oxford University Press: Oxford, 2016), pp.1–13.
3 DO Brink, "Partial Responsibility and Excuse" in HM Hurd (ed) *Puzzles in Criminal Law in Moral Puzzles and Legal Perplexities: Essays on the Influence of Larry Alexander* (Cambridge University Press: Cambridge, 2019); *Fair Opportunity and Responsibility* (Oxford University Press: Oxford, 2021); see also, F Coppola, "Context Matters: An Argument for a Socio-Contextual Model of Criminal Responsibility", in this edition.
4 SJ Morse, "Diminished Rationality, Diminished Responsibility", *Ohio State Journal of Criminal Law*, vol. 1, no. 1 (2003), p.289.
5 E.g. see F Coppola, "We are More Than our Executive Functions: on the Emotional and Situational Aspects of Criminal Responsibility and Punishment", *Criminal Law and Philosophy*, vol. 16 (2022), p.253.
6 E Spain, *The Role of Emotions in Criminal Law Defences: Duress, Necessity and Lesser Evils* (Cambridge University Press: Cambridge, 2011), ch.5.
7 G Barclay, "Law, Emotions and 'Reactive Defences'" in this edition.
8 F Coppola, *The Emotional Brain and the Guilty Mind* (Hart Publishing: Oxford, 2022).
9 J Hanson & J Jost (eds) *Ideology, Psychology, and Law* (Oxford University Press: Oxford, 2012), ch.1. See also, A Benforado & J Hanson, "The great attributional divide: How divergent views of human behavior are shaping legal policy", *Emory Law Journal*, vol. 57 (2008), p.311.
10 L Farmer, *Making the Modern Criminal Law: Criminalization and Civil Order* (Oxford University Press: Oxford, 2016); N Lacey, "In Search of the Responsible Subject: History, Philosophy and Social Sciences in Criminal Law Theory", *Modern Law Review*, vol. 64, no. 3 (2001), p.350; A Norrie, *Punishment, Responsibility, and Justice: A Relational Critique* (Oxford University Press: Oxford, 2000).

11 For overview, see A Loughnan, "The Meta-significance of Criminal Responsibility", *Critical Analysis of Law*, vol. 4, no. 1 (2017), p.31.
12 C Reeves, "Responsibility Beyond Blame: Unfree Agency and the Moral Psychology of Criminal Law's Persons" in C Lernestedt and M Matravers (eds), *Criminal Law's Person* (Hart Publishing: Oxford, 2022), p.158.
13 E.g. C Gilligan, *In a Different Voice: Psychological Theory and Women's Development* (Harvard University Press: Cambridge MA, 1982); D Meyers (ed) *Feminists Rethink the Self* (Westview Press: Boulder CO, 1997).
14 N Naffine, "Who are Law's Persons? From Cheshire Cats to Responsible Subjects", *Modern Law Review*, vol. 66, no. 3 (2003), p.346; "The Liberal Legal Individual Accused: The Relational Case", *Canadian Journal of Law and Society*, vol. 29 (2014), p.123; *Criminal Law and the Man Problem* (Hart Publishing: Oxford, 2019).
15 A Loughnan, *Self, Others and the State: Relations of Criminal Responsibility* (Cambridge University Press: Cambridge, 2019), p.265.
16 V Held, *The Ethics of Care: Personal, Political, Global* (Oxford University Press: Oxford, 2006).
17 J Herring, *Law and the Relational Self* (Cambridge University Press: Cambridge, 2019).
18 This is bolstered by a more general 'emotive turn' in criminal justice studies more broadly. E.g. C Knight, J Phillips, & T Chapman, "Bringing the feelings back: returning emotions to criminal justice practice", *British Journal of Community Justice*, vol. 14, no. 1 (2016), p.45.
19 For an overview of recent literature concerned with civilising blame, see C Mackenzie, "Culpability, blame, and the moral dynamics of social power", *Proceedings of the Aristotelean Society Supplementary Volume*, vol. 95, no.1 (2021), p.163.
20 N Lacey & H Pickard, "From the Consulting Room to the Court Room? Taking the Clinical Model of Responsibility without blame into the legal realm", *Oxford Journal of Legal Studies*, vol. 33, no. 1 (2013), p.1.
21 EI Kelly, *The Limits of Blame: Rethinking Punishment and Responsibility* (Harvard University Press: Cambridge MA, 2018).
22 EI Kelly, "Is blame warranted in applying justice?", *Critical Review of International Social and Political Philosophy*, vol. 26, no. 1 (2023), p.71 at p.77.
23 Kelly, "Is blame warranted", p.80.
24 E.g. A Wilson, "What a shame! Restorative justice's guilty secret", *The Howard Journal of Crime and Justice*, vol. 61, no.1 (2022), p.39. See also, A Norrie & A Wilson, "On Dispositional-relational Responsibility: From Punishment to Reconciliation", in this edition.
25 V Chiao, *Criminal Law in the Age of the Administrative State* (Oxford University Press: Oxford, 2018), p.252.
26 AE Taslitz, "Trying not to be like Sisyphus: Can defense counsel overcome pervasive status quo bias in the criminal justice system?", *Texas Tech Law Review*, vol. 45 (2012), p.315.
27 RA Duff, *Answering for Crime* (Hart Publishing: Oxford, 2009); Chiao, *Criminal Law*; M Thorburn, "Criminal Law as Public Law" in RA Duff & S Green (eds) *Philosophical Foundations of Criminal Law* (Oxford University Press: Oxford, 2011).
28 HM Hart Jr, "The Aims of the Criminal Law", *Law and Contemporary Problems*, vol. 23, no. 3 (1958), p.401. For an analysis of the relationship between the three stages of condemnation, punishment, and criminalisation, see A Cornford, "Rethinking the Wrongness Constraint on Criminalisation", *Law and Philosophy*, vol. 36 (2017), p.615 at pp.618–621.
29 Lacey, *In Search of Criminal Responsibility*, p.2.
30 HLA Hart explains how the two interact, framing excuse as the negative form of the mental condition requirement. HLA Hart, "Legal Responsibility and Excuses", in S Hook (ed) *Determinism and Freedom in the Age of Modern Science* (Collier Books: New York, 2nd edn, 1965), p.81.
31 Other prominent concerns of responsibility theorists centre around the questions of proximate cause and justifications, which are less relevant to the present discussion.
32 E.g. PF Strawson, "Freedom and Resentment", *Proceedings of the British Academy*, vol. XLVIII (1962), p.1. More recent developments include V McGeer, "Civilizing Blame" in JD Coates & NA Tognazzini (eds), *Blame: Its Nature and Norms* (Oxford University Press: New York, 2013), p.162. For critique see M Vargas, "Instrumentalist Theories of Moral Responsibility" in D Nelkin & D

Pereboom (eds), *The Oxford Handbook on Moral Responsibility* (Oxford University Press: Oxford, 2022); Kelly, *The Limits of Blame*.

33 E.g. RA Duff, *Punishment, Communication, and Community* (Oxford University Press: Oxford, 2001); V Tadros, *Criminal Responsibility* (Oxford University Press: Oxford, 2005), ch.3.
34 M Fricker, "What's the Point of Blame? A Paradigm Based Explanation", *Noûs*, vol. 50, no. 1 (2016), p.165.
35 In this vein, see G Tsai, "Respect and the Efficacy of Blame" in D Shoemaker (ed), *Oxford Studies in Agency and Responsibility* (Oxford University Press: Oxford, 2017), vol IV, p.248; V McGeer, "Civilizing Blame"; Fricker, "What's the Point".
36 Tsai, "Respect and the Efficacy", p.250.
37 Tsai, "Respect and the Efficacy", p.250, drawing on B Williams, *Shame and Necessity*, (University of California Press: Berkeley and Los Angeles CA, 1993).
38 Fricker, "What's the Point", p.173.
39 E.g. This sentiment is captured by the UN Research Institute for Social Development: "Designing and implementing comprehensive policies based on internationally agreed norms and standards is essential in today's era of sustainable development that pledges to leave no one behind—offering a chance for inmates and the released to be full members of society.", C Gisler, I Pruin, & U Hostettlerat, "Experiences with Welfare, Rehabilitation and Reintegration of Prisoners Lessons Learned?" *UNRISC Working Paper 2018-5*, p.3.
40 S Maruna & A King, "Once a Criminal, Always a Criminal?: 'Redeemability' and the Psychology of Punitive Public Attitudes", *European Journal on Criminal Policy and Research*, vol. 15, no. 1 (2009), p.7.
41 S Cohen, "Social Control and the Politics of Reconstruction", in D Nelken (ed) *The Futures of Criminology* (Sage Publications: London, 1994), pp.67–8.
42 For overview of various approaches, see C Hamilton, "Reconceptualising penalty: Towards a Multidimensional Measure of Punitiveness", *The British Journal of Criminology*, vol. 54, no. 2 (2014), p.321 at pp.322–323; for conceptual analysis, see R Matthews, "The Myth of Punitiveness", *Theoretical Criminology*, vol. 9, no. 2 (2005), p.175.
43 E.g. EG Pfeffer, "Conceptualizing and measuring 'punitiveness' in contemporary advanced democracies" *Regulation & Governance* (2023), early online access, available at: https://doi.org/10.1111/rego.12533.
44 Cohen, "Social Control", pp.63–88.
45 Cohen, "Social Control, pp.63–88, as summarised in Matthews, "The Myth of Punitiveness", p.178.
46 H Carvalho, A Chamberlen, & R Lewis, "Punitiveness beyond Criminal Justice: Punishable and Punitive Subjects in an Era of Prevention, Anti-Migration and Austerity", *The British Journal of Criminology*, vol. 60, no. 2 (2020), p.265 at pp.265–266.
47 Carvalho et al, "Punitiveness beyond", p.266.
48 Carvalho et al, "Punitiveness beyond".
49 E.g. D Downes & K Hansen, "Welfare and punishment in comparative perspective", in S Armstrong & L McAra (eds), *Perspectives on Punishment: The Contours of Control* (Oxford University Press: Oxford, 2006).
50 Farmer, *Making the Modern Criminal Law*, p.188. Farmer notes the recent phenomenon of the move from social responsibility to the law being involved with "identifying the conditions of individual punishability".
51 J Hanson & D Yosifon, "The situational character: A critical realist perspective on the human animal", *Georgetown Law Journal*, vol. 93, no. 1 (2004), p.6. See also "The Situation: An Introduction to the Situational Character, Critical Realism, Power Economics, and Deep Capture", *University of Pennsylvania Law Review*, vol.152 (2003), p.129.
52 JD Hanson & K Hanson, "The Blame Frame: Justifying (Racial) Injustice in America", *Harvard Civil Rights-Civil Liberties Law Review*, vol. 41 (2006), p.413.
53 See further, P Miller & N Rose, *Governing the Present: Administering Economic, Social and Personal Life* (Polity Press: Cambridge, 2008); K Juhila, S Raitakari, & C Hall (eds) *Responsibilisation at the Margins of Welfare Services* (Routledge: London, 2017).
54 A Millie, *Securing Respect: Behavioural Expectations and Anti-social Behaviour in the UK* (Bristol University Press: Bristol, 2009), p.10.

55 See generally, E Goffman, *Behaviour in Public Places; Notes on the Social Organisation of Gatherings* (The Free Press: New York, 1963).
56 Goffman, *Behaviour*, p.241.
57 E.g. G Feldman, "Neoliberalism and poverty: an unbreakable relationship" in B Greve (ed) *Routledge International Handbook of Poverty* (Routledge: London, 2019).
58 Akin to Robinson's notion of "vengeful desert" whereby the latter focuses on "the offense harm and victim suffering and sets the deserved punishment to match that of victim's harm and suffering". PH Robinson, *Distributive Principles of Criminal Law: Who Should be Punished and How Much* (Oxford University Press: Oxford, 2008), p.153.
59 D Pettit & J Knobe, "The Pervasive Impact of Moral Judgment", *Mind & Language*, vol. 24, no. 5 (2009), p.546.
60 S Maruna, "Once a Criminal, Always a Criminal?: 'Redeemability' and the Psychology of Punitive Public Attitudes", *European Journal on Criminal Policy and Research*, vol. 15 (2009), p.7.
61 We can see this sometimes in judicial statements at sentencing in the face of serious crime. For example, in a recent Northern Irish case of uxoricide, handing down a murder sentence with 18 years' imprisonment, Mr Justice O'Hara stated: "This is a significant prison sentence for a man of 62 but given the horror of what he did to his wife it is the least he deserves." A Morris, "Man who murdered wife in case fire horror jailed for at least 18 years" *The Irish Independent* (5 July 2023), available at: www.independent.ie/irish-news/man-who-murdered-wife-in-car-fire-horror-jailed-for-at-least-18-years/a836504661.html.
62 See H Carvalho & A Chamberlen on Mead, "Why punishment pleases: punitive feelings in a world of hostile solidarity", *Punishment and Society*, vol. 20, no. 2 (2017), p.217; GH Mead, "The psychology of punitive justice", *American Journal of Sociology*, vol. 23, no. 5 (1918), p.577.
63 H Stewart, "Contingency and Coherence: The Interdependence of Realism and Formalism in Legal Theory", *Valparaiso University Law Review*, vol. 30 (1995), p.3.
64 For a defence of formalism see EJ Weinrib, "Legal Formalism: On the Immanent Rationality of Law", *The Yale Law Journal*, vol. 97, no. 6 (1988), p.949.
65 E.g. R Posner, *Economic Analysis of Law* (Little, Brown, and Co: Boston MA, 4th edn, 1992); "Utilitarianism, Economics, and Social Theory", in *The Economics of Justice* (Harvard University Press: Cambridge MA and London, 1981), pp.48–75.
66 E.g. A Norrie, *Justice and the Slaughter Bench: Essay's on Law's Broken Dialectic* (Routledge: Abingdon, 2017); "Critical realism and the metaphysics of justice", *Journal of Critical Realism*, vol. 15, no. 4 (2016), p.391; *Punishment*.
67 Norrie, *Justice and the Slaughter Bench*.
68 In this vein, JM Fischer & M Ravizza, *Responsibility and Control* (Cambridge University Press: Cambridge, 1998).
69 G Antill, "Fitting the Model Penal Code into a Reason-Responsiveness Picture of Culpability", *Yale Law Journal*, vol. 131 (2022), p.1346 at p.1353.
70 Antill, "Fitting the Model", p.1355.
71 D Husak, "Retributivism and Over-Punishment", *Law and Philosophy*, vol. 41 (2022), p.169 at p.183, drawing on G Rosen: "Culpability and Moral Ignorance", *Proceedings of the Aristotelian Society*, vol. 103, no.1 (2002), p.61; and M Zimmerman, *Living with Uncertainty: The Moral Significance of Ignorance* (Cambridge University Press: Cambridge, 2008).
72 Husak, "Retributivism", p.183.
73 Husak, "Retributivism", p.183.
74 Maruna & King's findings that the public's belief in redeemability curbed their level of punitiveness was affirmed in 2020 by a more widespread study: Buron et al, "Belief in Redeemability and Punitive Public Opinion: 'Once a Criminal, Always a Criminal' Revisited" *Criminal Justice and Behavior*, vol. 47, no. 6 (2020), p.712.
75 E.g. United Nations Standard Minimum Rules for Non-custodial Measures (The Tokyo Rules) Adopted by General Assembly resolution 45/110 of 14 December 1990.
76 I am focusing on desistance studies as there is potentially more conceptual bandwidth with which to apply it to criminal responsibility doctrine. That said, the same exercise could be explored in the context of restorative justice, as the two movements are not mutually exclusive, e.g. see M Suzuki & T Jenkins, "The role of (self-)forgiveness in restorative justice: Linking restorative justice to

desistance", *European Journal of Criminology*, vol. 19, no. 2 (2022), p.202. See also, A Wilson, "What a shame!".

77 Maruna has described them as: "the fastest growing, most influential developments in academic criminology and applied criminal justice practice over the past three decades". S Maruna, "Desistance and restorative justice: it's now or never", *Restorative Justice*, vol. 4, no. 3 (2016), p.289.

78 Maruna, "Desistance"; BE Bersani & E Eggleston Doherty, "Desistance from Offending in the Twenty-First Century", *Annual Review of Criminology*, vol. 1 (2018), p.311.

79 Fox, "Desistance frameworks".

80 E.g. L Kennefick & E Guilfoyle, "An Evidence Review of Community Service Policy, Practice and Structure" (Irish Probation Service, 2022), available at: < www.probation.ie/EN/PB/0/B28C5 7C6B765BFF98025891000379F2E/$File/FOR%20PRINT%20CS%20Review_FINAL_271 022.docx.pdf; Northern Ireland Department of Justice, "Supporting Change: A Strategic Approach to Desistance" *Policy Statement*, available at: https://niopa.qub.ac.uk/bitstream/NIOPA/767/ 1/supporting-change-a-strategic-approach-to-desistance.pdf.

81 E.g. in a youth justice context, Hampson notes that though policy makers have adopted the rhetoric of desistance, more risk-based frameworks endure, see: KS Hampson, "Desistance approaches in youth justice – the next passing fad or a sea-change for the positive?", *Youth Justice*, vol. 18, no. 1 (2017), p.18.

82 E.g. J Dominey, "Probation supervision as a network of relationships: aiming to be thick, not thin", *Probation Journal*, vol. 66, no. 3 (2019), p.283.

83 RJ Sampson & JH Laub, "A life-course view of the development of crime", *The Annals of the American Academy of Political and Social Science*, vol. 602, no. 1 (2005), p.12.

84 S Farrall et al, *Criminal careers in transition* (Oxford University Press: Oxford, 2014); F McNeill et al, "How and why people stop offending: discovering desistance", *Institute for Research and Innovation in Social Services* (2012).

85 S Maruna & S Farrall, "Desistance from crime: A theoretical reformulation", *Kolner Zeitschrift fur Soziologie und Sozialpsychologie*, vol. 43 (2004), p.171; F McNeill, "Desistance and Criminal Justice in Scotland", in H Croall, G Mooney, & M Munro (eds), *Crime, Justice and Society in Scotland* (Routledge: London, 2015).

86 B Nugent & M Schinkel, "The Pains of Desistance", *Criminology and Criminal Justice*, vol. 16, no. 5 (2016), p.568; F McNeill & M Schinkel, "Tertiary or relational desistance: Contested belonging" *International Journal of Criminal Justice* (forthcoming).

87 McNeill, "Desistance and Criminal Justice in Scotland".

88 T Ugelvik, "The Transformative Power of Trust: Exploring Tertiary Desistance in Reinventive Prisons", *The British Journal of Criminology*, vol. 62, no. 3 (2022), p.623.

89 J Shapland & A Bottoms, "Reflections on social values, offending and desistance among young adult recidivists", *Punishment & Society*, vol. 13, no. 3 (2011), p.256.

90 E.g C Chouhy, FT Cullen, & HA Lee, "Social support theory of desistance", *Journal of Developmental and Life Course Criminology*, vol. 6 (2020), p.204.

91 In this vein, see Fox, "Desistance Frameworks", p.3.

92 T Ward, KJ Fox, & M Garber, "Restorative justice, offender rehabilitation and desistance", *Restorative Justice*, vol. 2, no. 1 (2014), p.24, at p.40.

93 Fox, "Desistance Frameworks".

94 E.g. S Farrall & A Calverley, *Understanding Desistance from Crime* (McGraw-Hill Education: New York, 2005). Note that some desistance theories are much more structural than others (cf. Sampson and Laub, "A life-course view of the development of crime" and S Maruna, *Making Good how ex-convicts reform and rebuild their lives* (American Psychological Association Books: Washington DC, 2001)).

95 B Weaver, "The relational context of desistance: some implications and opportunities for social policy", *Social Policy & Administration*, vol. 46, no. 4 (2012), p.395.

96 E.g. Weaver, "The relational context", p.395. More recently, McNeill uses the idea of "generative justice" to capture "… social processes and community practices involving justice-affected people that are somehow generative of relationships characterised by solidarity."; F McNeill, *Imagining Generative Justice*, Keynote address at the conference of the Howard League for Penal Reform in England and Wales, Keble College, Oxford, 13–14 September 2022.

97 D Best et al, "Justice Capital: A model for reconciling structural and agentic determinants of desistance", *Probation Journal*, vol. 68, no. 2 (2021), p.206.
98 D Best et al, "Justice Capital", p.206.
99 D Best & C Colman, "Promoting relational and strengths-based approaches to illustrating pathways to desistance and recovery", in D Best & C Coleman (eds) *Strengths-based Approaches to Crime and Substance use: From Drugs and Crime to Desistance and Recovery* (Routledge: London, 2020), p.279.
100 D Best et al, "Justice Capital".
101 D Best et al, "Justice Capital".
102 S Maruna, *Making Good: how ex-convicts reform and rebuild their lives*, p.11.
103 S Maruna, "Desistance as a Social Movement", *Irish Probation Journal*, vol. 14 (2017), p.5 at p.6.
104 R Paternoster & S Bushway, "Desistance and the Feared Self: Toward an Identity Theory of Criminal Desistance", *Journal of Criminal Law and Criminology*, vol. 99, no. 4 (2009), p.1103.
105 In this vein, see S Maruna, *Making Good*; B Hunter & S Farrall, "Emotions, Future Selves and the Process of Desistance", *British Journal of Criminology*, vol. 58, no. 2 (2018), p.291.
106 Farrall et al, *Criminal Careers in Transition*, pp.52–53.
107 S Maruna, "Desistance and Restorative Justice: it's now or never", *Restorative Justice*, vol. 4, no. 3 (2016), p.289.
108 McNeill et al, "How and Why".
109 McNeill et al, "How and Why".
110 N Lacey, "Partial Defences to Homicide: Questions of Power and Principle in Imperfect and Less Imperfect Worlds" in A Ashworth & B Mitchell (eds), *Rethinking English Homicide Law* (Oxford University Press: Oxford, 2000), p.114.
111 CR Snyder & RL Higgins, "Excuses: Their effective role in the negotiation of reality", *Psychological Bulletin*, vol. 104, no. 1 (1988), p.23.
112 S Maruna & RE Mann, "A fundamental attribution error? Rethinking cognitive distortions", *Legal and Criminological Psychology*, vol. 11, no. 2 (2006), p.155 at p.156.
113 GM Sykes & D Matza, "Techniques of neutralization: A theory of delinquency", *American Sociological Review*, vol. 22, no. 6 (1957), p.664.
114 E.g. JL Hulley, "'While this does not in any way excuse my conduct …': The role of treatment and neutralizations in desistance from sexual offending", *International Journal of Offender Therapy and Comparative Criminology*, vol. 60, no. 15 (2016), p.1711; I Masson & N Booth, "Using techniques of neutralisation to maintain contact: The experiences of loved ones supporting remand prisoners", *The Howard Journal of Crime and Justice*, vol. 61, no. 4 (2022), p.463.
115 E.g. A Ievins, *Stains of Imprisonment: Moral Communication and Men Convicted of Sex Offenses* (University of California Press: California, 2023).
116 JD Unnever & FT Cullen, "Public opinion and the death penalty" in ME Oswald, S Bieneck, & J Hupfeld-Heinemann (eds), *Social Psychology of Punishment of Crime* (John Wiley & Sons Ltd: Hoboken NJ, 2009); DA Mackey, KE Courtright, & SH Packard, "Testing the rehabilitative ideal among college students", *Criminal Justice Studies*, vol. 19, no. 2 (2006), p.153.
117 E.g. V Tadros, "The Structure of Defences in Scots Criminal Law", *Edinburgh Law Review*, vol. 7, no. 1 (2003), p.60.
118 E.g. ME Gilman, "The Poverty Defense", *University of Richmond Law Review*, vol. 47 (2013), p.495.
119 To this end, I develop the idea of recognitive justice as legitimation for a universal partial defence in a forthcoming monograph; L Kennefick, *The Boundaries of Blame: Towards a Universal Partial Defence for the Criminal Law* (Cambridge University Press, forthcoming).

References

Books and book chapters

Best D & Colman C, "Promoting Relational and Strengths-Based Approaches to Illustrating Pathways to Desistance and Recovery", in Best D & Coleman C (eds), *Strengths-Based Approaches to Crime and Substance Use: From Drugs and Crime to Desistance and Recovery* (Routledge: London, 2020).

Brink DO, "Partial Responsibility and Excuse", in Hurd HM (ed), *Puzzles in Criminal Law in Moral Puzzles and Legal Perplexities: Essays on the Influence of Larry Alexander* (Cambridge University Press: Cambridge, 2019).

Brink DO, *Fair Opportunity and Responsibility* (Oxford University Press: Oxford, 2021).

Chiao V, *Criminal Law in the Age of the Administrative State* (Oxford University Press: Oxford, 2018).

Cohen S, "Social Control and the Politics of Reconstruction", in Nelken D (ed), *The Futures of Criminology* (Sage Publications: London, 1994).

Coppola F, *The Emotional Brain and the Guilty Mind* (Hart Publishing: Oxford, 2022).

Downes D & Hansen K, "Welfare and Punishment in Comparative Perspective", in Armstrong S & McAra L (eds), *Perspectives on Punishment: The Contours of Control* (Oxford University Press: Oxford, 2006).

Duff RA, *Answering for Crime* (Hart Publishing: Oxford, 2009).

Duff RA, *Punishment, Communication, and Community* (Oxford University Press: Oxford, 2001).

Farmer L, *Making the Modern Criminal Law: Criminalization and Civil Order* (Oxford University Press: Oxford, 2016).

Farrall S & Calverley A, *Understanding Desistance from Crime* (McGraw-Hill Education: New York, 2005).

Farrall S, Hunter V, Sharpe G, & Calverley A, *Criminal Careers in Transition* (Oxford University Press: Oxford, 2014).

Feldman G, "Neoliberalism and Poverty: An Unbreakable Relationship", in Greve B (ed), *Routledge International Handbook of Poverty* (Routledge: London, 2019).

Fischer JM & Ravizza M, *Responsibility and Control* (Cambridge University Press: Cambridge, 1998).

Gilligan C, *In a Different Voice: Psychological Theory and Women's Development* (Harvard University Press: Cambridge MA, 1982).

Goffman E, *Behaviour in Public Places; Notes on the Social Organisation of Gatherings* (The Free Press: New York, 1963).

Hanson J & Jost J (eds), *Ideology, Psychology, and Law* (Oxford University Press: Oxford, 2012).

Hart HLA, "Legal Responsibility and Excuses", in Hook S (ed), *Determinism and Freedom in the Age of Modern Science* (Collier Books: New York, 2nd edn, 1965).

Held V, *The Ethics of Care: Personal, Political, Global*, (Oxford University Press: Oxford, 2006).

Herring J, *Law and the Relational Self* (Cambridge University Press: Cambridge, 2019).

Ievins A, *Stains of Imprisonment: Moral Communication and Men Convicted of Sex Offenses* (University of California Press: California, 2023).

Juhila K, Raitakari S, & Hall C (eds) *Responsibilisation at the Margins of Welfare Services* (Routledge: London, 2017).

Kelly EI, *The Limits of Blame: Rethinking Punishment and Responsibility* (Harvard University Press: Cambridge MA, 2018).

Lacey N, "Partial Defences to Homicide: Questions of Power and Principle in Imperfect and Less Imperfect Worlds", in Ashworth A & Mitchell B (eds), *Rethinking English Homicide Law* (Oxford University Press: Oxford, 2000).

Lacey N, *In Search of Criminal Responsibility: Ideas, Interests, and Institutions* (Oxford University Press: Oxford, 2016).

Loughnan A, *Self, Others and the State: Relations of Criminal Responsibility* (Cambridge University Press: Cambridge, 2019).

Maruna S, *Making Good: How Ex-Convicts Reform and Rebuild Their Lives* (American Psychological Association Books: Washington DC, 2001).

McGeer V, "Civilizing Blame", in Coates JD & Tognazzini NA (eds), *Blame: Its Nature and Norms* (Oxford University Press: New York, 2013).

McNeill F, "Desistance and Criminal Justice in Scotland", in Croall H, Mooney G, & Munro M (eds), *Crime, Justice and Society in Scotland* (Routledge: London, 2015).

Meyers D (ed), *Feminists Rethink the Self* (Westview Press: Boulder CO, 1997).

Miller P & Rose N, *Governing the Present: Administering Economic, Social and Personal Life* (Polity Press: Cambridge, 2008).

Millie A, *Securing Respect: Behavioural Expectations and Anti-Social Behaviour in the UK* (Bristol University Press: Bristol, 2009).

Naffine N, *Criminal Law and the Man Problem* (Hart Publishing: Oxford, 2019).

Norrie A, *Justice and the Slaughter Bench: Essay's on Law's Broken Dialectic* (Routledge: Abingdon, 2017).

Norrie A, *Punishment, Responsibility, and Justice: A Relational Critique* (Oxford University Press: Oxford, 2000).
Posner R, in *The Economics of Justice* (Harvard University Press: Cambridge MA and London, 1981).
Posner R, *Economic Analysis of Law* (Little, Brown, and Co: Boston MA, 4th edn, 1992).
Reeves C, "Responsibility Beyond Blame: Unfree Agency and the Moral Psychology of Criminal Law's Persons", in Lernestedt C & Matravers M (eds), *Criminal Law's Person* (Hart Publishing: Oxford, 2022).
Robinson PH, *Distributive Principles of Criminal Law: Who Should be Punished and How Much* (Oxford University Press: Oxford, 2008).
Spain E, *The Role of Emotions in Criminal Law Defences: Duress, Necessity and Lesser Evils* (Cambridge University Press: Cambridge, 2011).
Tadros V, *Criminal Responsibility* (Oxford University Press: Oxford, 2005).
Thorburn M, "Criminal Law as Public Law", in Duff RA & Green S (eds), *Philosophical Foundations of Criminal Law* (Oxford University Press: Oxford, 2011).
Tsai G, "Respect and the Efficacy of Blame", in Shoemaker D (ed), *Oxford Studies in Agency and Responsibility* (Oxford University Press: Oxford, 2017), vol IV.
Unnever JD & Cullen FT, "Public Opinion and the Death Penalty", in Oswald ME, Bieneck S, & Hupfeld-Heinemann J (eds), *Social Psychology of Punishment of Crime* (John Wiley & Sons Ltd: Hoboken NJ, 2009).
Vargas M, "Instrumentalist Theories of Moral Responsibility", in Nelkin D & Pereboom D (eds), *The Oxford Handbook on Moral Responsibility* (Oxford University Press: Oxford, 2022).
Williams B, *Shame and Necessity* (University of California Press: Berkeley and Los Angeles, 1993).
Zimmerman M, *Living With Uncertainty: The Moral Significance of Ignorance* (Cambridge University Press: Cambridge, 2008).

Journal articles

Antill G, "Fitting the Model Penal Code into a Reason-Responsiveness Picture of Culpability", *Yale Law Journal*, vol. 131 (2022), pp.1346–1384.
Benforado A & Hanson J, "The Great Attributional Divide: How Divergent Views of Human Behavior are Shaping Legal Policy", *Emory Law Journal*, vol. 57 (2008), pp.311–408.
Bersani BE & Eggleston Doherty E, "Desistance from Offending in the Twenty-First Century", *Annual Review of Criminology*, vol. 1 (2018), pp.311–334.
Best D, Hamilton S, Hall L, & Bartels L, "Justice Capital: A Model for Reconciling Structural and Agentic Determinants of Desistance", *Probation Journal*, vol. 68, no. 2 (2021), pp.206–223.
Buron AL, Cullen FT, Burton Jr. VS, Graham A, Butler LC, & Thielo AJ, "Belief in Redeemability and Punitive Public Opinion: 'Once a Criminal, Always a Criminal' Revisited", *Criminal Justice and Behavior*, vol. 47, no. 6 (2020), pp.712–732.
Carvalho H & Chamberlen A, "Why Punishment Pleases: Punitive Feelings in a World of Hostile Solidarity", *Punishment and Society*, vol. 20, no. 2 (2017), pp.217–234.
Carvalho H, Chamberlen A, & Lewis R, "Punitiveness beyond Criminal Justice: Punishable and Punitive Subjects in an Era of Prevention, Anti-Migration and Austerity", *The British Journal of Criminology*, vol. 60, no. 2 (2020), pp.265–284.
Chouhy C, Cullen FT, & Lee HA, "Social Support Theory of Desistance", *Journal of Developmental and Life Course Criminology*, vol. 6 (2020), pp.204–223.
Coppola F, "We are More Than our Executive Functions: On the Emotional and Situational Aspects of Criminal Responsibility and Punishment", *Criminal Law and Philosophy*, vol. 16 (2022), pp.253–266.
Cornford A, "Rethinking the Wrongness Constraint on Criminalisation", *Law and Philosophy*, vol. 36 (2017), pp.615–649.
Dominey J, "Probation Supervision as a Network of Relationships: Aiming to be Thick, Not Thin", *Probation Journal*, vol. 66, no. 3 (2019), pp.283–302.
Fox KJ, "Desistance Frameworks", *Aggression and Violent Behavior*, vol. 63 (2022), p. 101684.
Fricker M, "What's the Point of Blame? A Paradigm Based Explanation", *Noûs*, vol. 50, no. 1 (2016), pp.165–183.

Gilman ME, "The Poverty Defense", *University of Richmond Law Review*, vol. 47 (2013), pp.495–553.

Hamilton C, "Reconceptualising Penalty: Towards a Multidimensional Measure of Punitiveness", *The British Journal of Criminology*, vol. 54, no. 2 (2014), pp.321–343.

Hampson KS, "Desistance Approaches in Youth Justice – The Next Passing Fad or a Sea-Change for the Positive?", *Youth Justice*, vol. 18, no. 1 (2017), pp.18–33.

Hanson J & Yosifon D, "The Situation: An Introduction to the Situational Character, Critical Realism, Power Economics, and Deep Capture", *University of Pennsylvania Law Review*, vol. 152 (2003), pp.129–346.

Hanson J & Yosifon D, "The Situational Character: A Critical Realist Perspective on the Human Animal", *Georgetown Law Journal*, vol. 93, no. 1 (2004), pp.6–179.

Hanson JD & Hanson K, "The Blame Frame: Justifying (Racial) Injustice in America", *Harvard Civil Rights-Civil Liberties Law Review*, vol. 41 (2006), pp.413–480.

Hart Jr HM, "The Aims of the Criminal Law", *Law and Contemporary Problems*, vol. 23, no. 3 (1958), pp.401–441.

Hulley JL, "'While This Does Not in Any Way Excuse My Conduct …': The Role of Treatment and Neutralizations in Desistance from Sexual Offending", *International Journal of Offender Therapy and Comparative Criminology*, vol. 60, no. 15 (2016), pp.1776–1790.

Hunter B & Farrall S, "Emotions, Future Selves and the Process of Desistance", *British Journal of Criminology*, vol. 58, no. 2 (2018), pp.291–308.

Husak D, "Retributivism and Over-Punishment", *Law and Philosophy*, vol. 41 (2022), pp.169–191.

Kelly EI, "Is Blame Warranted in Applying Justice?", *Critical Review of International Social and Political Philosophy*, vol. 26, no. 1 (2023), pp.71–87.

Knight C, Phillips J, & Chapman T, "Bringing the Feelings Back: Returning Emotions to Criminal Justice Practice", *British Journal of Community Justice*, vol. 14, no. 1 (2016), pp.45–58.

Lacey N & Pickard H, "From the Consulting Room to the Court Room? Taking the Clinical Model of Responsibility without blame into the legal realm", *Oxford Journal of Legal Studies*, vol. 33, no. 1 (2013), p.1–29.

Lacey N, "In Search of the Responsible Subject: History, Philosophy and Social Sciences in Criminal Law Theory", *Modern Law Review*, vol. 64, no. 3 (2001), pp.350–371.

Loughnan A, "The Meta-Significance of Criminal Responsibility", *Critical Analysis of Law*, vol. 4, no. 1 (2017), pp.31–41.

Mackenzie C, "Culpability, Blame, and the Moral Dynamics of Social Power", *Proceedings of the Aristotelean Society Supplementary Volume*, vol. 95, no.1 (2021), pp.163–182.

Mackey DA, Courtright KE, & Packard SH, "Testing the Rehabilitative Ideal Among College Students", *Criminal Justice Studies*, vol. 19, no. 2 (2006), pp.153–170.

Maruna S & Farrall S, "Desistance from Crime: A Theoretical Reformulation", *Kolner Zeitschrift fur Soziologie und Sozialpsychologie*, vol. 43 (2004), pp.171–194.

Maruna S & King A, "Once a Criminal, Always a Criminal?: 'Redeemability' and the Psychology of Punitive Public Attitudes", *European Journal on Criminal Policy and Research*, vol. 15, no. 1 (2009), pp.7–24.

Maruna S & Mann RE, "A Fundamental Attribution Error? Rethinking Cognitive Distortions", *Legal and Criminological Psychology*, vol. 11, no. 2 (2006), pp.155–177.

Maruna S, "Desistance and Restorative Justice: It's Now or Never", *Restorative Justice*, vol. 4, no. 3 (2016), pp.289–301.

Maruna S, "Desistance as a Social Movement", *Irish Probation Journal*, vol. 14 (2017), pp.5–20.

Maruna S, "Once a Criminal, Always a Criminal?: 'Redeemability' and the Psychology of Punitive Public Attitudes", *European Journal on Criminal Policy and Research*, vol. 15 (2009), pp.7–24.

Masson I & Booth N, "Using Techniques of Neutralisation to Maintain Contact: The Experiences of Loved Ones Supporting Remand Prisoners", *The Howard Journal of Crime and Justice*, vol. 61, no. 4 (2022), pp.463–483.

Matthews R, "The Myth of Punitiveness", *Theoretical Criminology*, vol. 9, no. 2 (2005), pp.175–201.

McNeill F and Schinkel M, "Tertiary or Relational Desistance: Contested Belonging", *International Journal of Criminal*, vol. 6, no. 1 (2024), pp.47–74.

Mead GH, "The Psychology of Punitive Justice", *American Journal of Sociology*, vol. 23, no. 5 (1918), pp.577–602.

Morse SJ, "Diminished Rationality, Diminished Responsibility", *Ohio State Journal of Criminal Law*, vol. 1, no. 1 (2003), pp.289–308.

Naffine N, "The Liberal Legal Individual Accused: The Relational Case", *Canadian Journal of Law and Society*, vol. 29 (2014), pp.123–132.

Naffine N, "Who are Law's Persons? From Cheshire Cats to Responsible Subjects", *Modern Law Review*, vol. 66, no. 3 (2003), pp.346–367.

Norrie A, "Critical Realism and the Metaphysics of Justice", *Journal of Critical Realism*, vol. 15, no. 4 (2016), p.391.

Nugent B & Schinkel M, "The Pains of Desistance", *Criminology and Criminal Justice*, vol. 16, no. 5 (2016), pp.568–584.

Paternoster R & Bushway S, "Desistance and the Feared Self: Toward an Identity Theory of Criminal Desistance", *Journal of Criminal Law and Criminology*, vol. 99, no. 4 (2009), pp.1103–1156.

Pettit D & Knobe J, "The Pervasive Impact of Moral Judgment", *Mind & Language*, vol. 24, no. 5 (2009), pp.586–604.

Pfeffer EG, "Conceptualizing and Measuring 'Punitiveness' in Contemporary Advanced Democracies", *Regulation & Governance* (2023), early online access, https://doi.org/10.1111/rego.12533.

Rosen G, "Culpability and Moral Ignorance", *Proceedings of the Aristotelian Society*, vol. 103, no.1 (2002), pp. 61–84.

Sampson RJ & Laub JH, "A Life-Course View of the Development of Crime", *The Annals of the American Academy of Political and Social Science*, vol. 602, no. 1 (2005), pp.12–45.

Shapland J & Bottoms A, "Reflections on Social Values, Offending and Desistance Among Young Adult Recidivists", *Punishment & Society*, vol. 13, no. 3 (2011), pp.256–282.

Snyder CR & Higgins RL, "Excuses: Their Effective Role in the Negotiation of Reality", *Psychological Bulletin*, vol. 104, no. 1 (1988), pp.23–35.

Stewart H, "Contingency and Coherence: The Interdependence of Realism and Formalism in Legal Theory", *Valparaiso University Law Review*, vol. 30 (1995), pp.1–50.

Strawson PF, "Freedom and Resentment", *Proceedings of the British Academy*, vol. XLVIII (1962), pp.187–211.

Suzuki M & Jenkins T, "The Role of (Self-)Forgiveness in Restorative Justice: Linking Restorative Justice to Desistance", *European Journal of Criminology*, vol. 19, no. 2 (2022), pp.202–219.

Sykes GM & Matza D, "Techniques of Neutralization: A Theory of Delinquency", *American Sociological Review*, vol. 22, no. 6 (1957), pp.664–670.

Tadros V, "The Structure of Defences in Scots Criminal Law", *Edinburgh Law Review*, vol. 7, no. 1 (2003), pp.60–79.

Taslitz AE, "Trying Not to Be Like Sisyphus: Can Defense Counsel Overcome Pervasive Status Quo Bias in the Criminal Justice System?", *Texas Tech Law Review*, vol. 45 (2012), pp.315–387.

Ugelvik T, "The Transformative Power of Trust: Exploring Tertiary Desistance in Reinventive Prisons", *The British Journal of Criminology*, vol. 62, no. 3 (2022), pp.623–638.

Ward T, Fox KJ, & Garber M, "Restorative Justice, Offender Rehabilitation and Desistance", *Restorative Justice*, vol. 2, no. 1 (2014), pp.24–42.

Weaver B, "The Relational Context of Desistance: Some Implications and Opportunities for Social Policy", *Social Policy & Administration*, vol. 46, no. 4 (2012), pp.395–412.

Weaver B, "Understanding Desistance: A Critical Review of Theories of Desistance", *Psychology, Crime & Law*, vol. 25, no. 6 (2019), pp.641–658.

Weinrib EJ, "Legal Formalism: On the Immanent Rationality of Law", *The Yale Law Journal*, vol. 97, no. 6 (1988), pp.949–1016.

Wilson A, "What a Shame! Restorative Justice's Guilty Secret", *The Howard Journal of Crime and Justice*, vol. 61, no.1 (2022), pp.39–52.

Reports and websites

Gisler C, Pruin I, & Hostettlerat U, "Experiences with Welfare, Rehabilitation and Reintegration of Prisoners Lessons Learned?", *UNRISC Working Paper 2018*, no. 5.

Kennefick L & Guilfoyle E, "An Evidence Review of Community Service Policy, Practice and Structure", (Irish Probation Service, 2022), available at: www.probation.ie/EN/PB/0/B28C57C6B765BFF98025891000379F2E/$File/FOR%20PRINT%20CS%20Review_FINAL_271022.docx.pdf

McNeill F, Farrall S, Lightowler C, & Maruna S, "How and Why People Stop Offending: Discovering Desistance", *Institute for Research and Innovation in Social Services* (2012).

Northern Ireland Department of Justice, "Supporting Change: A Strategic Approach to Desistance", *Policy Statement*, available at: www.niopa.qub.ac.uk/bitstream/NIOPA/767/1/supporting-change-a-strategic-approach-to-desistance.pdf

6
RESPONSIBILITY AND "BLAMEWORTHINESS" IN CRIMINAL LAW

Claes Lernestedt & Matt Matravers

Introduction

"In the beginning there was blame. Adam blamed Eve, Eve blamed the serpent, and we've been hard at it ever since".[1]

In discussions concerning responsibility in criminal law, the language of blame, blaming, blameworthy, and blameworthiness seems to be ubiquitous. Moreover, that language appears at all stages of criminal law theorising: with respect to conduct in debates over criminalisation; in demarcating excuses and justifications; in sentencing theory; as well as in discussions of the justification of punishment overall. The terms are often used quite differently by different theorists. In sum, for all that the language is pervasive, and the concept(s) seemingly central, blameworthiness and its cognates seem to have little agreed meaning, or an agreed place, in criminal law theorising.

In part, this mirrors ways in which the term "responsibility" is deployed in criminal law theorising, not least in the way that in both cases – "responsibility" and "blameworthiness" – the prefix "moral" is common, but what it adds is contested. That said, one interesting difference in the ways in which the two concepts are treated in criminal law theory is that discussions of responsibility draw heavily on the responsibility literature in moral philosophy. That is not the case when it comes to blameworthiness. Although there is a significant philosophical literature that emphasises the contested nature of blame as "an extraordinarily rich topic",[2] this is barely acknowledged in criminal law theory.[3]

The invoking of the language of blameworthiness invites a number of questions not only as to *definition* but also as to its *function(s)*, for example:

- What kinds of entities are properly the subjects of our enquiries?
- Within the realm of apt entities, is what is to be assessed the entity itself, the entity's conduct, or some combination of both?
- Are the standards invoked against which the subject is to be assessed objective or subjective and agent-sensitive?

In short, to invoke the language of blame(worthiness) is not to appeal to concepts with agreed meanings, but to indicate a place where an argument is needed. There seems to be agreement, somehow, that a demand for something called "blameworthiness" is fundamental to respect, but there is disagreement regarding its meaning as well as its proper function. For example, consider the following famous, and seemingly clear, statement from Oliver Wendell Holmes Jr with respect to the crucial, perhaps necessary, condition for society to hold someone criminally responsible for what he or she did (and caused, etc.). In his lecture on "The Criminal Law" he famously declared,

> "It is not intended to deny that criminal liability, as well as civil, is founded on blameworthiness. Such a denial would shock the moral sense of any civilized community; or, to put it another way, a law which punished conduct which would not be blameworthy in the average member of the community would be too severe for that community to bear".[4]

Now, clearly this statement should not be interpreted as insisting that criminal liability is founded on *legal* blameworthiness, as that would amount to little more than the maxim "no crime/punishment without law" (*nullum crimen nulla poena sine lege*). This is about something else. Perhaps most importantly, someone who did not know Holmes's work might assume that whatever the remaining perplexities of his position, his declaration is important because it establishes that the yardsticks used to determine criminal liability should be *backward-looking* in the sense of looking at what has already occurred to see whether a person was worthy of – deserved – punishment or not (and if so, how much). Holmes, though, does not seem to think (only) in such a backward-looking way. He continues the passage quoted above as follows,

> "It is only intended to point out that, when we are dealing with that part of the law which aims more directly than any other at establishing standards of conduct, we should expect there more than elsewhere to find that the tests of liability are external, and independent of the degree of evil in the particular person's motives or intentions. The conclusion follows directly from the nature of the standards to which conformity is required. These are not only external, as was shown above, but they are of general application. They do not merely require that every man should get as near as he can to the best conduct possible for him. They require him at his own peril to come up to a certain height".[5]

In other words, his idea of "blameworthy" conduct here is better captured by the idea of "worth blaming", and what determines what is worth blaming are *forward-looking* considerations of what Holmes called "public policy", primarily the policy of inducing "external conformity to the law".[6] Thus, despite the apparent clarion call of the first part of the quotation, Holmes is intellectually honest enough to note two pages later that what is needed is a "reconciliation of the doctrine that liability is founded on blameworthiness with the existence of liability where the party is not to blame".[7]

What, then, is going on? Later in the chapter, we will suggest that what is going on is a form of signalling. Invoking the language of blameworthiness and its cognates is meant to signal allegiance to a compatibilist conception of responsibility and to a degree of non-consequentialism (or at least to the constraining of consequentialism). It is to indicate that the approach is not like, for example, that of JJC Smart for whom ascriptions of responsibility, as expressed in praising and blaming, are merely mechanisms by which we try to alter the future for the better.[8]

However, to get there we need several intervening steps. In the section *"Blameworthiness", and its Cognates, and Agency* we further discuss possible meanings, contents and functions of "blameworthiness" and its cognates (including the distinction between "blameworthy" and "worth blaming" mentioned above). We also start relating this vocabulary to a few possible types of agents. In the section *"Sifting" human beings*, we relate blameworthiness and responsibility by looking at three approaches to criminal blame. Finally, the last section concludes.

"Blameworthiness", and its Cognates, and Agency

"As it turns out, a significant part of achieving justice involves finding someone or something to blame for the wrongs we endure. How successful the law is in ascertaining perpetrators and doling out just desserts [sic] is a complicated question. But on March 27, 1535, one such jury in Nottinghamshire, England was able to meet that extraordinary burden by carefully identifying the particular hay in a haystack that shifted and crushed Anthony Wylde. The offending hay, having killed the deceased, was appraised, and its value was forfeited to the state to be used for charitable purposes. It was, after all, a deodand".[9]

In this section, we attempt to get a grip on the concept of "blameworthiness", by discussing some related concepts ("blaming" and "blameworthy"), and by relating them to types of potential agents: inanimate objects, plants, and non-human animals. From the perspective of today, these types of potential agents seem inapt for the language of "blameworthiness". Yet, at various times, none of these groups of potential agents was, *qua* group, excluded from responsibility and the language of blame. In the muddy complexities of these earlier times, we might find possible explanations for some of our present uses – at least for some of the ambiguities – of "blame"-related concepts.

Why do we need to think in terms of groups of agents? This is because "blameworthiness" is a *relational* concept; it comes to life only in relation to something or someone. Moreover, there is also a third element: blameworthiness only comes to life *for* something. It must stand in a relation to something, a state of affairs, that the agent could be said to have (in a relevant way) brought about.[10]

This might contribute to the original idea of *the scapegoat* being difficult to grasp for today's readers. A scapegoat was symbolically given, had bestowed upon it, all the sins and impurities of a community's individuals. The goat was then driven out into the desert, carrying these with it, and in this way, it removed these sins from the community:

"Then Aaron shall lay both his hands on the head of the live goat, and confess over it all the iniquities of the people of Israel, and all their transgressions, all their sins, putting them on the head of the goat, and sending it away into the wilderness by means of someone designated for the task. The goat shall bear on itself all their iniquities to a barren region; and the goat shall be set free in the wilderness".[11]

The scapegoat suggests that "blameworthiness" *could* be an object with some kind of inherent identity, which furthermore could be traded between individuals (perhaps in a way which a financial debt could be). However, that this is not the way blameworthiness is looked upon today is clear from how the term "scapegoat" is now used in ordinary speech: the "scapegoat" is pro definition exactly a person (or some other agent) who gets the blame for something for which he/she/it *should not be blamed*. One may take over another's debt, but one cannot take over another's blameworthiness in the same manner: it cannot, generally, be bought and sold.[12]

The words: "blaming", "blameworthy", and "blameworthiness"

To grasp the concept of "blameworthiness" and its relation to responsibility, it is worth touching upon "blaming" and "blameworthy". "Blaming" is a verb; it is an *activity*. As with consent, for example, this activity can be both inward and outward. I can blame you in my thoughts without ever letting you (or anyone else) know. I can also do and say things signalling that I am doing what we call blaming you. These things that I can do and say, while not necessary for blaming, might be thought of as a "soundtrack" of blame (characterised by harsh treatment, harsh and loud words, etc.).

What is contested, at least in current debates, is whether "blaming" *must* be in response to something that you have done (or not done) or, perhaps, something that you plainly *are* as revealed in what you have done (or not done). Similarly, it is contested whether my use of the verb "blaming" presupposes that I also, in some morally relevant way, hold you morally responsible for whatever it was that you did or failed to do.

It might seem odd to say that this is contested. After all, what is so alien in the original scapegoat is, at least in part, that the goat carries "blame" but has not done anything (to be blameworthy). Yet, as we saw in the *Introduction*, we might "blame" for forward-looking reasons, where we deem that there is "conduct worth blaming". To be effective, this must be accompanied by the soundtrack of blame – after all, it would be impossible to alter the future for the better by blaming only within one's head – but it is perhaps not blame in a profound sense, but rather a simulation of blame. In the penultimate section, on "sifting", we will return to this in relation to Strawson's influential work on responsibility and the reactive attitudes.

Turning to "blameworthy"; it is an adjective, *prima facie* closely tied to "blameworthiness". "Blameworthiness" requires that someone or something has been deemed "blameworthy" for having done something (as was noted above, there is no such thing as free-floating "blameworthiness"). And, it seems, it gets used in both backward- and forward-looking enterprises.

The former is what one might call the "traditional" interpretation; when we wish to find out (or, more adequately, to decide upon) the blameworthiness of a defendant in a criminal trial, we do this (or are at least supposed to do this) by looking *backwards*. Being "worthy of" blame here is close to *being deserving*. The latter is like the simulation of blame. Here, "blameworthy" does not mean "worthy of blame" but instead "worth blaming". It is a *forward-looking*, utilitarian construction the justification of which (if it is justified) lies in the possibility of altering the future for the better.

Blame and non-human "agents"

In this sub-section, we consider "blame-related" words in their encounters with potential agents grouped as follows: inanimate objects, plants and other living objects, and non-human animals. When we refer to them as potential agents, we need to consider them not only in their potential role as (blameworthy) aggressors, but also as victims with standing. It is worth noting that the scope of our discussion does not include the use of the language of blame to signal nothing other than (morally irrelevant) causation, as in, "the heavy snowfall was to blame for the accident, not Ulrika's driving".

Today, inanimate objects are deemed to lack what is needed for *both* backward-looking and forward-looking purposes. A chair, a haystack, or the wind in the trees, are considered neither "worthy of blame" nor "worth blaming". Historically – as with all the groups considered here – things were, at least potentially, completely different. As a brief example, consider the *deodand*, a long-lived common law figure with contested rationales. If an object, or an animal, was instrumental in the killing of a person – an ox that gored a man, a heavy object that fell, or a knife that was used to stab someone to death – it would be treated as a deodand. With variations depending on what kind of "agent" it was, the item or its monetary value was turned over to the King. There was probably more than one reason for these rules: one could imagine a mosaic of the crown's need for money, ideas related to compensation, and (mostly misplaced) ambitions in terms of objects being "blameworthy" as well as "worth blaming".[13]

When we turn to the group including living objects but not animals, things become more complicated in that an asymmetry with respect to agency starts to emerge. No one would claim that there is agency in the sense that would underpin a judgement of "worthy of blame", but there might be agency in the sense of the capacity to be a victim, and today objects such as rivers and trees have been deemed to be the carriers of rights in this sense, and thus to have the capacity required for "legal standing".[14]

Although we would not think of these kinds of living objects as "worthy of blame", the idea that some sub-set of them might be "worth blaming" is more controversial. On the face of it, it seems implausible that conveying blame on such entities would have any positive effects on anyone's (or anything's) future behaviour. Yet, recent scientific developments suggest that, for example, we might expect at least to have some small fragments of success when it comes to hard treatment in modifying the behaviour of certain kinds of fungi. That, of course, helps put pressure on argumentation that forward-looking "worth blaming" is a genuine form of "blaming".

With respect to non-human animals, it is worth pausing to consider, even if only briefly, the considerable history of such trials.[15] These present a challenge in understanding quite what was being assumed of the animal in terms of agency. When a town put up signs to tell the rats that they were expected to attend their trial, did anyone really believe that the rats could read such an invitation? Yet, some non-human animals clearly were considered "blameworthy", either as agents themselves or as carriers of malevolent agents. Thus, one explanation of animals having more skills than they should was that they had been taken over by the devil, a demon, or something similar (something which would then also serve as an explanation for the animal's behaviour).

A French case of a rooster accused of having laid eggs is interesting in this respect. The defence attorney (yes, there was one) argued *not* that the rooster *qua* rooster could not properly be a defendant, but instead that the rooster had a defence in that the rooster's laying of the eggs was *an involuntary act*. As one account puts it,

"The prosecution alleged that Satan employed witches and demons to hatch these eggs and that the creatures that emerged, usually basilisks, would torment the human race (a cock's egg was supposed to have great magical properties; a witch would favour it over even the philosopher's stone). The defense counsel did not try to deny the fact of the egg-laying. Instead, he pleaded that no evil deed had been intended. The laying of an egg was an involuntary act and, as such, not punishable by law … The cock was found guilty and sentenced to death as a sorcerer who'd assumed the shape of a bird. He and the egg were burned together at the stake".[16]

If little else of the rooster story has passed the test of time it is worth noting that the idea of involuntary acts lives on today in the criminal law, characterised as things that happen to the agent's body, not as acts originating from the agent. It is an open question whether a defence attorney today, if defending a human defendant accused of having laid eggs, would invoke the same defence.

The point is to emphasise that our current attitudes to non-human animals are different. Here the distinction between forward- and backward-looking blame again matters, and the asymmetry with respect to agency becomes more acute. Today, only a few people would talk about animals possessing the capacities necessary to be able to be held responsible – blameworthy – for something that has happened. Yet, no-one would deny that many, but not all, non-human animals can be conditioned for the future, trained by blaming (and praising) responses, and in this sense are "worth blaming" (and, indeed, "worth praising").

"Sifting" human beings

The previous section offered a whirlwind tour of some of the ways in which both backward- and forward-looking practices were directed at entities beyond human beings. This section deals with human beings. One might think that it is easier to handle. However, the group is not homogenous when it comes to ideas of (possible) agency. Two sub-groups are typically excluded from the area of eligible agents: both the *young* enough and the *mad* enough are deemed to lack something (or at least potentially lack something), and this (potential) deficit makes it troublesome to treat them as (full) agents. The two sub-groups will be returned to, not generally but by way of example, later below.

In this section, we bring together some of the ways in which the language of blame and blameworthiness intersect with the language of responsibility with respect to both meaning and function in the criminal law (and in criminal justice more widely understood). We do this, in part, by looking at the different ways in which different theorists deploy these languages.

One of the difficulties in pinning down the relationship between blameworthiness and responsibility stems from the multifarious and often vague nature of both terms. One might wonder whether blameworthiness requires responsibility, or responsibility of the particular kind found in criminal law requires blameworthiness, or whether the relationship is more distant, or even so close as to render the terms equivalent.[17]

This matters because the language of blame and blameworthiness has a role in *legitimising* criminal law and punishment. This is clear from the Holmes quote with which we began. That is, Holmes's claim that he does not intend to deny that criminal liability is founded on blameworthiness is meant to reassure and legitimise. It places the argument within "the moral sense of [a] civilized community" by denying that criminal liability falls on the blameless, although as we have seen, it is Holmes's position that it can sometimes properly do so.

How the language of blameworthiness legitimises is related to what we will call "sifting". Holmes's reader is meant to be reassured that his account will lead to the numerous persons and acts in the community being appropriately sifted, so that punishment will fall on those who are blameworthy. Yet, all the interesting and important arguments lie in how and why people and acts are sifted in one way rather than another. To say or imply that "sifting has occurred" should not in itself reassure or be taken to legitimate. Rather, it should invite further questions as to where the argument is to be found.

Although, as we noted at the start of the chapter, blameworthiness and its cognates "sift" (and ostensibly legitimate) at every stage of criminal justice – from criminalisation, through enforcement, justifications and excuses, to sentencing – our main focus here is on its role in fixing the range of people to whom criminal liability may apply. This is in part because of constraints of space, and in part because it is here that issues of blame and of responsibility overlap most extensively. To organise the discussion, we look at three "models": one consequentialist; one capacity based; and one based on practices of blaming/holding responsible.

Recall, for example, Smart's account of praise, blame, and responsibility briefly mentioned in the *Introduction*. Smart's article is also an instance of "sifting". Only, in Smart's case, the filters through which persons must pass are designed to identify those for whom it is true that being the object of praise or blame would produce good consequences. In this sense, punishment falls on those who are "worth blaming".

Such an idea is not entirely alien to contemporary liberal ears. As we saw in the section *"Blameworthiness", and its Cognates, and Agency*, it is common in training non-human animals, and even in the case of children. As one of us has put it, "I praise my 3-year-old daughter when she does the right thing, not because I believe she is a morally responsible agent who deserves to be praised, but because I want to encourage her to do the right thing again." However, extending such an approach to (genuine) blame and associating responsibility with malleability is more controversial. To continue the quote, "I do not blame her when she behaves badly – she is, after all, only 3 – but I nevertheless express what seems like blame... in order to discourage her from acting in a similar way in the future".[18]

Nicola Lacey and Hanna Pickard offer a less radical, but still revisionist, proposal that tries to secure responsibility, but detach it from "affective blame".[19] For Lacey and Pickard, responsibility is a matter of agency. Sifting picks out those entities – in their case, human beings with certain "cognitive and volitional capacities" – that are eligible for attributions of criminal culpability. However, *how* we respond to criminal acts – the soundtrack of blame – is open, and we can do so by blaming – with "hostile, negative reactive attitudes" ("affective blame") – or with "an attitude of concern, respect and compassion" ("detached blame").[20]

Lacey's and Pickard's argument for importing a clinical model of detached blame into criminal justice is revisionist, but their account of responsibility is quite traditional in the sense identified at the end of the section *The words: "blaming", "blameworthy", and "blameworthiness"*. To be responsible, and thus potentially criminally liable and blame*worthy* (even in their revised sense of blame), is to have passed some kind of capacity test with respect to one's actions.[21] Blameworthiness, then, is backward-looking since it is an evaluation of a person's capacities and actions at the time. What is distinctive about their position is that how we blame can be shaped by forward-looking considerations.

That said, and as Lacey and Pickard recognise, the seemingly straightforward claim that (appropriate) sifting has taken place by virtue of passing or failing a cognitive and volitional capacity test conceals a multitude of controversial issues as to both the nature of the capacities involved and the threshold for passing or failing. Debates over the insanity test and the correct age of criminal responsibility instantiate the difficulties of, rather than are resolved by, reference to capacity thresholds.

Although traditional and used in a widespread way in both criminal and mental health law, a capacity understanding of responsibility is not standard in moral philosophy or criminal law theory. The capacity view holds that responsibility is a property of persons. By contrast, the dominant view, largely as a result of Peter Strawson's influential paper "Freedom and Resentment", is that responsibility is to be found in our practices of holding responsible. That is, for Strawson and his followers, our lives as social animals are characterised by different responses to, for example, people and rocks. So, on the one hand, if a person deliberately stamps on my toe, my response is one of indignation and blame. If, on the other, I stub my toe on a rock I had not noticed, I can be angry, but it makes no (reflective) sense to feel indignation or to blame the rock for its having hurt me.[22]

Of course, the Strawson and capacity accounts are related in that it is in virtue of persons having (or, more precisely, being deemed to have) certain capacities that we think of them in one way and think of rocks in another, but the accounts differ in the status they give to these capacities. For capacity accounts, there is a correct, pre-legal, understanding of what it is for a person to be responsible. For Strawson, and Strawson-inspired accounts, the relevant capacities and thresholds are given by the social practices of holding responsible.

In one sense, the strength of Strawsonian accounts lies precisely in this practice-based approach to responsibility that avoids the tricky metaphysics of the free will/determinism debates. However, it leaves (at least) three worries in its wake: first, it rests on an assertion that our practices of responsibility are part of the only recognisable and stable way human beings can live together. Thus, in response to responsibility (and desert) sceptics who argue that, for example, the truth of the causal thesis shows that no-one is properly responsible for anything,[23] Strawsonians can claim that such evidence is irrelevant given the "folk psychology" on which our criminal justice practices rest, and *must* rest given the way human beings are, or powers only an "external critique" which would upend morality more generally.[24] In this sense, second, it is deaf to arguments – for example, from behavioural sciences – that purport to show that aspects of our behaviour are caused, *and* that this is relevant to attributions of responsibility. Third, although Strawson himself is careful to tie his analysis to an account of the form of life possible for human beings, his analysis has lent itself to more conventionalist understandings in which responsibility is located in "local" and familiar practices, whatever those might be. In particular, since in criminal law we clearly do have practices of holding responsible and blaming those who are "worth blaming", in addition to those who are blameworthy, it is tempting to wrap those into a (misread) Strawsonian account in which responsibility and blameworthiness are just what we say they are.

Conclusion

We began the chapter by noting that criminal law theorists often use the language of blame and blameworthiness together with the language of responsibility. In the case of the latter, they are often conscious of the associated moral and metaphysical debates and are careful to define the term as they are using it. The same is not true of the former, which is generally used much more freely as if its meaning were clear and unambiguous. We hope to have shown that this is just not the case. Moreover, we have argued that this matters because the language around blame and blameworthiness plays a *legitimising role* in, or at least lends a legitimising air to, the arguments. What follows from this is a number of recommendations; one formal and others material.

The *formal* one is boring but important (not least because of the legitimising role). The language of blame should be treated with as much care, precision, and transparency as the language of responsibility. Both require their users to define their terms in a careful way and to work within the constraints of those definitions.

The *material* requirements grow out of the last condition of the formal one. The elements of a theory that purports to justify the state establishing rules that threaten, and impose, harsh sanctions on those who contravene them, must be consistent *or* their pluralistic nature must be explained and justified. In the end, we need an account that explains why the punishment of a certain individual is legitimate.

Materially, we would suggest, that *if* and *to the extent* that ascription of responsibility is seen as a retributive venture, *then* it has to be retributive all the way down.[25] This means that one cannot allow for anything else than backward-looking considerations in the area, and there should be no place for (forward-looking) "worth blaming" as a form of "blame worthy". Furthermore, the rules for the ascription of responsibility must be *person*-sensitive as well as *science*-sensitive. That is, if and to the extent that personal blameworthiness *is* what is decisive, then the rules need to get reasonably close to the specific, unique person of flesh and blood who is to be punished. Similarly, both our conception of the person, and of the form of life appropriate for persons, need to be open to changes and not insulated from the findings of, for example, behavioural sciences.

Finally, and to return to the theme of backward- and forward-looking accounts of responsibility and blame, it is worth noting two things about the relationship of these arguments to the legitimation argument. First, criminal law theories (and, indeed, moral philosophers) are more comfortable with backward-looking, non-consequentialist, accounts. Yet, as Holmes and every plausible account of the criminal law recognises, criminal law is part of public policy and as such is forward-looking. In every jurisdiction – some much more than others – the criminal law includes, for example, offences of strict liability, so these must either be explained away as in some way anomalous or included in a more nuanced account of criminal law.

Yet, even within such an account, we must also strive to be as *correct* as possible, in a (very difficult) sense which protects against the kind of Humpty-Dumptean, relativistic free-for-all interpretations of "blameworthy" as defined by our practices of blaming. Facts do matter. This is why it is not only inefficient, but wrong, to fire several meteorologists in response to bad weather (as seems to have happened some years ago in a country not so far from where one of us is based) whatever the norms at the time. The challenge, then, is to craft an account of blameworthiness that is fact-sensitive, practical, and precise. That is not a challenge taken up in this chapter which has, rather, focused in the main on how not to do it and on what we can, and should, learn from that.

Acknowledgments

We are grateful to Derek Matravers for comments. MM is grateful to the Leverhulme Trust for a Major Research Grant – MRF-2020-090: Criminalisation and Punishment: Philosophical Theory and Practical Reality – that provided much needed time to work on this chapter. CL is equally grateful to Torsten Söderbergs stiftelse for research funding that made writing this possible.

Notes

1. C Campbell, *Scapegoat: A history of blaming other people* (Overlook Press: New York, 2012), p.15.
2. DJ Coates & NA Tognazzini, "The Contours of Blame", in DJ Coates & NA Tognazzini (eds), *Blame: Its Nature and Norms* (Oxford University Press: New York, 2012), p.26.
3. As is pointed out by David Shoemaker in the collection cited above (p.100n), Michael Moore's *Placing Blame: A General Theory of the Criminal Law* (Oxford University Press: Oxford, 1997) is one of the leading works in recent criminal law theory that, despite the title, contains no discussion of, or even an index entry for, "blame".
4. OW Holmes Jr, *The Common Law* (The Belknap Press of Harvard University Press: Cambridge MA, 2009 [1881]) p.47.
5. Holmes Jr, *The Common Law*, p.47.
6. Holmes Jr, *The Common Law*, p.46.
7. Holmes Jr, *The Common Law*, p.48.
8. JJC Smart, "Freewill, Praise, and Blame", *Mind*, vol. 70, no. 279 (1961), p.291. On Smart's approach, see RJ Arneson, "The Smart Theory of Moral Responsibility and Desert", in S Olsaretti (ed), *Desert and Justice* (Clarendon Press: Oxford, 2003).
9. T Hockstad, "The Wrong, the Wronged, and the Wrongfully Dead: Deodand law as practice of absolution", *Nebraska Law Review*, vol. 101, no. 3 (2023), p.731 at p.732.
10. In this sense, blame is analogous to responsibility. As Antony Duff puts it, "The relational conception of responsibility… [is] triadic: I am responsible *for X, to S*—to a person or body who has the standing to call me to answer for X. I am also responsible for X to S *as* Φ—in virtue of satisfying some normatively laden description that makes me responsible (prospectively and retrospectively) for X to S". RA Duff, *Answering for Crime: Responsibility and Liability in the Criminal Law* (Hart Publishing: Oxford, 2007), p.23.
11. Leviticus, 16:21–22. Definition of a scapegoat from Funk & Wagnall's Standard Dictionary of Folklore, Mythology and Legend, as quoted in Campbell, *Scapegoat*, p.37: "Any material object, animal, bird or person on whom the bad luck, diseases, misfortunes and sins of an individual or group are symbolically placed, and which is then turned loose, driven off with stones, cast into a river or the sea, etc, in the belief that it takes away with it all the evils placed upon it."
12. Cf. the figure of *the whipping boy*. The whipping boy suffered the physical punishment that should have landed on the prince. The idea was that the prince, on whom it was forbidden to lay hands in such a way, would see his friend suffering and thus realise his wrong and its consequences. In this situation, we might reasonably say that the blameworthiness was still to be found in the prince, although the punishment (and thus the outer expression of blaming) was directed at the whipping boy. Regarding the figure of the whipping boy, see e.g. Campbell, *Scapegoat*, ch.3.
13. Regarding Deodand law, see e.g. Hockstad, "The Wrong, the Wronged, and the Wrongfully Dead".
14. See e.g. M Tanasescu, "When a River is a Person: From Ecuador to New Zealand, nature gets its day in court", *Open Rivers: Rethinking Water, Place & Community*, no. 8 (2017), p.127.
15. One standard reference here is EP Evans, *The Criminal Prosecution and Capital Punishment of Animals* (Heinemann: London, 1906).
16. Campbell, *Scapegoat*, p.125f.
17. One theorist who insists on distinguishing the terms is Mitchell Berman. See, e.g. "Blameworthiness, desert, and luck", *Noûs*, vol. 57, no. 2 (2023), p.370.
18. M Matravers, *Responsibility and Justice* (Polity Press: Cambridge, 2007), p.18.
19. N Lacey & H Pickard, "From the Consulting Room to the Court Room? Taking the Clinical Model of Responsibility Without Blame into the Legal Realm", *Oxford Journal of Legal Studies*, vol. 33, no. 1 (2013), p.1.
20. Lacey & Pickard, "From the Consulting Room to the Court Room?", p.2.
21. "Potentially", because to be liable to criminal blame, one needs not only to be the kind of being eligible for blame, but also to have done something: a criminal act usually with an associated mental state such as an intention, and so on.
22. P Strawson, "Freedom and Resentment", *Proceedings of the British Academy*, vol. 48 (1962), p.1. Of course, one can momentarily feel indignant and blame the rock, but that feeling should not survive reflection.

23 For responsibility scepticism, see GD Caruso, *Rejecting Retributivism: Free Will, Punishment, and Criminal Justice* (Cambridge University Press: Cambridge, 2021); D Pereboom, "Free Will Skepticism and Criminal Punishment", in T Nadelhoffer (ed), *The Future of Punishment* (Oxford: Oxford University Press, 2013).
24 For both those responses, see SJ Morse, "Compatibilist Criminal Law", in T Nadelhoffer (ed), *The Future of Punishment*, p.107.
25 See, C Lernestedt, "Standard-Setting versus Tracking 'Profound' Blameworthinhess: What should be the Role of the Rules for Ascription of Responsibility?", in C Lernestedt & M Matravers (eds), *The Criminal Law's Person*, (Hart/Bloomsbury: Oxford, 2022).

References
Books and book chapters

Arneson RJ, "The Smart Theory of Moral Responsibility and Desert", in Olsaretti S (ed), *Desert and Justice* (Clarendon Press: Oxford, 2003).
Campbell C, *Scapegoat: A History of Blaming Other People* (Overlook Press: New York, 2012).
Caruso GD, *Rejecting Retributivism: Free Will, Punishment, and Criminal Justice* (Cambridge University Press: Cambridge, 2021).
Coates DJ & Tognazzini NA, "The Contours of Blame", in Coates DJ & Tognazzini NA (eds), *Blame: Its Nature and Norms* (Oxford University Press: New York, 2012).
Duff RA, *Answering for Crime: Responsibility and Liability in the Criminal Law* (Hart Publishing: Oxford, 2007).
Evans EP, *The Criminal Prosecution and Capital Punishment of Animals* (Heinemann: London, 1906).
Holmes Jr. OW, *The Common Law* (The Belknap Press of Harvard University Press: Cambridge MA, 2009 [1881]).
Lernestedt C, "Standard-Setting versus Tracking 'Profound' Blameworthinhess: What should be the Role of the Rules for Ascription of Responsibility?", in Lernestedt C & Matravers M (eds), *The Criminal Law's Person* (Hart/Bloomsbury Publishing: Oxford, 2022).
Matravers M, *Responsibility and Justice* (Polity Press: Cambridge, 2007).
Moore MS, *Placing Blame: A General Theory of the Criminal Law* (Oxford University Press: Oxford, 1997).
Morse SJ, "Compatibilist Criminal Law", in Nadelhoffer T (ed), *The Future of Punishment* (Oxford University Press: Oxford, 2013).
Pereboom D, "Free Will Skepticism and Criminal Punishment", in Nadelhoffer T (ed), *The Future of Punishment* (Oxford University Press: Oxford, 2013).

Journal articles

Berman MN, "Blameworthiness, Desert, and Luck", *Noûs*, vol. 57, no. 2 (2023), pp.370–390.
Hockstad T, "The Wrong, the Wronged, and the Wrongfully Dead: Deodand Law as Practice of Absolution", *Nebraska Law Review*, vol. 101, no.3 (2022), pp.731–772.
Lacey N & Pickard H, "From the Consulting Room to the Court Room? Taking the Clinical Model of Responsibility Without Blame into the Legal Realm", *Oxford Journal of Legal Studies*, vol. 33, no. 1 (2013), pp.1–29.
Smart JJC, "Freewill, Praise, and Blame", *Mind*, vol. 70, no. 279 (1961), pp.291–306.
Strawson P, "Freedom and Resentment", *Proceedings of the British Academy*, vol. 48 (1962), pp.1–25.
Tanasescu M, "When a River is a Person: From Ecuador to New Zealand, Nature Gets Its Day in Court", *Open Rivers: Rethinking Water, Place & Community*, vol. 8 (2017), pp.127–132.

7
CRIMINAL RESPONSIBILITY, MENTAL DISORDER, AND BEHAVIOURAL NEUROSCIENCE

Stephen J Morse

Introduction

Mental disorder, especially severe mental disorder, intellectual disability, and the new behavioural neuroscience are all thought to present a challenge to conventional accounts of criminal responsibility.[1] The central thesis of this chapter is that mental disorders do in some cases undermine an agent's responsibility for criminal actions, but they pose no general threat to criminal responsibility. In contrast, many people think that the new behavioural neuroscience, fuelled by neuroimaging studies, will substantially alter our concept of criminal responsibility, and may more radically eliminate it. The former problem is more familiar and reduces to the continuously contested questions of what types of mental disorder and what types of resulting functional impairments should diminish or excuse the agent's responsibility. There is little dispute, however, about the underlying premise that some mentally disordered people with such impairments should be excused. In contrast, the claims based on the new neuroscience, especially the more radical claims, are highly controversial for both conceptual and empirical reasons.

This chapter begins with a brief account of the concept of criminal responsibility, before addressing the role mental disorder plays in assessing individual cases of criminal responsibility. The bulk of the chapter addresses the challenges from neuroscience. First it discusses the scientific status of behavioural neuroscience. Then it considers two radical challenges to current conceptions of criminal responsibility that neuroscience allegedly poses: determinism and the death of agency. The question of the specific relevance of neuroscience to criminal law doctrine, practice and institutions is considered next. The penultimate section points to some areas warranting modest optimism. A brief conclusion follows.

The meaning of criminal responsibility

This chapter employs an expansive definition of criminal responsibility. Although the discussion will focus on United States law, its doctrines are similar to continental criminal law codes, albeit different structures and terminology are used.

Crimes are defined by their criteria, what lawyers term the "elements" of the offense. For our purposes, the most important are the act requirement (often misleadingly terms the "voluntary act") and a culpable mental state, the *mens rea*. The most basic definition of an act is an intentional bodily movement or omission performed in a reasonably integrated state of consciousness. For example, a reflex movement or movements performed in a state of divided or partial consciousness, such as sleepwalking, would not qualify as acts for criminal law purposes, even if they resulted in harm to another.

Mens rea is not required constitutionally for less serious, regulatory crimes, but it is almost certainly required for serious crimes involving moral turpitude.[2] *Mens rea* elements, such as purpose, intent, knowledge, conscious awareness of a substantial risk of harm (recklessness) and unreasonable *un*awareness of a substantial risk of harm (negligence) are crucial because they indicate the agent's moral indifference to the rights and interests of others. Harming another "on purpose" is almost always more morally blameworthy than harms caused carelessly.

Together, these elements are known as the *prima facie* case and must be proven beyond a reasonable doubt by the prosecution. If they are so proven, the defendant is *prima facie* criminally liable. The defendant nevertheless can avoid liability by establishing an "affirmative defence" of justification or excuse, which are also defined by their elements.

In cases of justification, otherwise prohibited conduct is considered right or at least permissible in the specific circumstances of the case. Self-defence is a classic example because the innocent victim of wrongful aggression is justified in intentionally using proportionate force to defend against the wrongful aggression. Excuses obtain if the agent is *prima facie* liable because he has done something wrong but is not responsible for that wrong. The primary generic excusing condition is lack of the capacity for rationality in the context. A classic example is legal insanity. The agent was irrational at the time of the crime because, for example, he did not know right from wrong as a result of severe mental disorder. Lack of control capacity is another, although it is conceptually and empirically more controversial than lack of capacity for rationality. The control prong of some insanity defence tests is the best example. If the agent is in touch with reality and knows right from wrong but cannot control himself as a result of severe mental disorder, he may be excused. Finally, external coercion is an excusing condition. The defence of duress is the best example. The agent is compelled by being placed in a do-it-or-else situation through no fault of his own and a person of reasonable firmness would have yielded to that threat.

In sum, criminal responsibility in this chapter means that the *prima facie* case has been proven and no affirmative defence has been established. The primary criteria are behavioural—acts and mental states. Indeed, criminal responsibility is a thoroughly folk psychological concept, one that primarily explains behaviour by mental states causing action.[3] Free will as philosophers understand the term is not a criterion for criminal responsibility in any sense.[4]

Mental disorder

In many civil and criminal legal contexts, there are special rules to respond to subjects with mental disorder, especially severe mental disorder. The usual effect of these rules is to limit the autonomy and responsibility of the person with disorder. In the criminal law, for example, an agent who is incompetent to stand trial or to plead guilty as a result of mental disorder cannot be tried or enter a plea. The most familiar criminal responsibility example is, of course, the affirmative defence of legal insanity.

Although all mental health laws have a medical condition, mental disorder, as a necessary criterion, it is never sufficient. All also include legally relevant behaviours, such as dangerousness or the inability to know right from wrong, that are the crucial reason for special legal treatment. Mental disorder alone, even if it is severe, does not justify legal intervention. As the Supreme Court has consistently re-iterated with only one exception,[5] what is meant by a mental disorder in a legal statute, is itself a legal, and not a medical, question.[6] Moreover, the legally relevant criteria are also not medical, but are normative behavioural criteria. For example, what the legally relevant criteria for legal insanity should be is clearly a matter of normative, social, and ultimately legal debate.

Recall that the two generic excusing conditions are lack of rational capacity and lack of self-regulation (or self-control) capacity. Both are legal and normative, and the latter is independent of a rationality defect. Depending on the individual jurisdiction's doctrinal approach, all make a rationality defect a criterion for the excuse of legal insanity, and a minority also include a self-regulation (control) criterion. Although this chapter is about theory rather than doctrine, a few doctrinal examples will help. The dominant rationality (cognitive) test is some form of the famous *M'Naghten* rule that asks whether as a result of mental disorder the defendant lacked the ability to know right from wrong.[7] The dominant self-regulation test is the American Law Institute's Model Penal Code formulation that grants an excuse if as a result of mental disorder a defendant lacked substantial capacity to conform his conduct to the requirements of law.[8] Self-regulation tests are less favoured because they are both difficult to conceptualise in folk psychological terms and difficult to operationalise.

As noted, there is normative controversy about every aspect of these tests. For example, what should count as a mental disorder is contested and many jurisdictions exclude recognised mental disorders such as substance-related disorder (roughly, addiction), paraphilias (sexual disorders), and psychopathy within the definition. In the right/wrong criterion, whether the wrong should be moral or legal wrong has caused countless rivers of ink to be spilled and pixels illuminated. Nevertheless, some form of the test is considered necessary in all but four U.S. states and is ubiquitous in common law and civil law jurisdictions. It is almost uniformly recognised that some people with severe mental disorders have such substantial cognitive or control defects that they are not morally and legally responsible agents if those defects play a role in the agent's practical reasoning that produces criminal conduct. The U.S. Supreme Court *has* upheld the constitutionality of a state abolishing an affirmative defence of legal insanity,[9] but with respect, the majority's reasoning is defective, and betokens a lack of understanding of how mental disorder affects behaviour. Explaining this conclusion would take us too far afield, but many have made this argument in detail.[10] Even in those few jurisdictions that have abolished the insanity defence, the law permits a defendant to use evidence of mental disorder to negate the *mens rea* required by the definition of the crime charged. But mental disorder rarely negates *mens rea*; more commonly it explains why the defendant formed it.

The factual, functional capacities for rationality and self-regulation are continuum capacities. And if they are the foundations for criminal responsibility or its lack, then criminal responsibility should also be arrayed on a continuum. But the insanity defence is binary: the defendant was or was not criminally insane at the time of the crime. This seems unfair to many because defendants not disordered enough to justify a full excuse may nonetheless seem to have been substantially behaviourally compromised at the time of the crime. This possibility may be considered at sentencing, but there it will be discretionary and may create disparate sentences in similar cases. Unfortunately, there is no generic mitigating condition of "partial responsibility" that can be considered at trial, although many have claimed that justice demands its creation.[11] At most, many jurisdictions permit evidence of mental disorder to be introduced to negate *mens rea*, albeit with restrictions, and there are a few forms of partial responsibility that apply within the law of homicide that reduce a conviction from murder to manslaughter (e.g. the doctrine of provocation/passion). In this author's view, the need for a generic partial responsibility doctrine applicable at trial is urgently needed, but there is no indication that such a reform is forthcoming.

Almost no one thinks all offenders are mentally disordered, no less severely mentally disordered, and therefore should be excused. Mental disorder can therefore negate criminal responsibility in some cases, but it poses no challenge generally to traditional conceptions of criminal responsibility that are satisfied by most offenders. This is in stark contrast to the new neuroscience, that many think will justify major changes to conceptions of criminal responsibility and will perhaps justify abolishing it altogether.

Neuroscience

A decade ago, I published a state-of-the-art review of the existing neurolaw literature.[12] The primary claim was that the major problem confronting the emerging field was the question of legal relevance. Could the translation problem be solved; could the gap be closed between the purely mechanistic discourse of neuroscience and the thoroughly folk psychological concepts of the law? This chapter will address the same issue of the potential contributions of neuroscience to law, with special emphasis on criminal justice and responsibility because these are the areas that have received the lion's share of neurolaw attention. This discussion will generalise to other applications, however. The conclusion remains the same as 10 years ago. At present, virtually no neuroscience addresses legal questions directly and little of pure neuroscience is even indirectly legally relevant. One hopes that future advances will increase the legal usefulness of neuroscience, but the notion that neuroscience will radically change the law by replacing its concepts and procedures is a chimera. At most, one can hope for incremental reforms.

The law's criteria for responsibility and competence are virtually all behavioural—acts and mental states. The most relevant neurosciences are therefore the behavioural neurosciences, such as cognitive, affective, and social neuroscience. There have been major advances in these fields since the beginning of the century when non-invasive functional magnetic resonance imaging (fMRI) to investigate brain function became widely available for non-clinical research. But again, these advances have scarcely improved the legal relevance of neuroscience.

The limits of behavioural neuroscience

Most generally, the relation of brain, mind, and action is one of the hardest problems in all science. We have no idea how the brain enables the mind, how consciousness is produced, and how action is possible.[13] The brain–mind–action relation is not a mystery because it is inherently unamenable to scientific explanation, but because the problem is so difficult. For example, we would like to know the difference between a neuromuscular spasm and intentionally moving one's arm in exactly the same way. The former is a purely mechanical motion, whereas the latter is an action, but we cannot explain the difference between the two. We know that a functioning brain is a necessary condition for having mental states and for acting. After all, if your brain is dead, you have no mental states and are not acting. Still, we do not know how mental states and action are caused.

Despite the astonishing advances in neuroimaging and other neuroscientific methods—especially in understanding sensory systems and memory—we do not have sophisticated causal knowledge of how the brain works generally. The scientific problems are fearsomely difficult. Only in the present century have researchers begun to accumulate much data from fMRI imaging. New methodological problems are constantly being discovered.[14] This is not surprising given how new the science is and how difficult these problems are. Moreover, virtually no studies have been performed to address specifically normative legal questions. There are many studies of the neural correlates of legal decision-making, but they have no normative relevance. Law should not expect too much of a young science that uses new technologies to investigate some of science's most intrinsically difficult problems and that does not directly address normative questions. Caution is warranted, although many would think the argument of this chapter is too cautious.

Neuroscience is insufficiently developed to detect specific, legally relevant, mental content. For example, it does not provide a sufficiently accurate diagnostic marker for even a severe mental disorder that might be relevant to many legal doctrines.[15] Many studies do find differences between patients with mental disorders and controls, but the differences are too small to be used diagnostically, and publication bias may have inflated the number of such positive studies.[16] There are limited exceptions for some genetic disorders that are diagnosed using genomic information or some well-characterised neurological disorders, such as epilepsy, that are definitively diagnosed using electroencephalography (EEG), but these are not the types of techniques that are central to the new neuroscience based primarily on imaging.

Let us consider the specific grounds for modesty about the achievements of behavioural neuroscience. fMRI is still a rather blunt instrument to measure brain functioning. It measures the amount of oxygenated blood that is flowing to a specific region of the brain (the blood oxygen dependent level [BOLD] signal), which is a proxy for the amount of neural activation that is occurring in that region above or below baseline activation (the brain is always and everywhere physiologically active). There is good reason to believe that the BOLD signal is a good proxy, but it is only a proxy. There is a sub-optimal time lag between when actual activation occurs and when fMRI measures it, and pinpointing the exact region where activation occurred is also far from perfect.[17] The spatial resolution problem can lead to substantial numbers of false-positive findings. These and similar technical difficulties will surely be ameliorated by technological advances, but to date, such limitations exist.[18]

There are research design difficulties. It is difficult to control for all conceivable artifacts; that is, other variables that may also produce a similar result. Consequently, there are often problems of over-inference and of invalid reverse inferences.[19] The same region of interest (ROI) may be associated with opposite behaviours, which also confounds inferences.

At present, most neuroscience studies on human beings involve small numbers of subjects, which makes it difficult to achieve statistically significant results and which undermines the validity of significant findings.[20] This problem is termed "low power". This is especially important as research increasingly uses machine learning techniques. To ensure that the algorithms derived from a subject sample are generalisable, they must be cross-validated on different populations. If sample sizes are small, the risk of error is magnified.[21] The problem of small samples will improve as the cost of scanning decreases and future studies will have more statistical power.

The types of subjects used also present a problem. Most behavioural neuroscience studies are done on college and university students, who are hardly a random sample of the population generally. Many studies use non-human animals, such a rats or primates, as subjects. Although the complexity and operation of the neural structure and function of such animals may be on a continuum with those of human beings, there is reason to question the applicability of the neuroscience of the behaviour of non-human animals to humans. The human brain is capable of language and rationality, which marks an immense difference between humans and other animals. We should be cautious about extrapolating to humans from neuroscience studies of other animals.

Most studies average the neurodata, and the average finding may not accurately describe the brain structure or function of any individual subject in the study. This leads to a more general problem about the applicability of scientific findings from group data to an individual subject, a problem called *G2i* for "group to individual".[22] Scientists are interested in how the world works generally, but law is often concerned with individual cases, and it is difficult to know how properly to apply relevant group data. If such group data are permitted, as they now are for functions such as predictions, the question is how to use probabilistic data to answer what is often a binary question, such as whether to parole a prisoner because he is deemed no longer a danger to society.

A serious question is whether findings based on subjects' behaviour and brain activity in a scanner apply to real-world situations. This is known as the problem of "ecological validity". Does a subject's performance in a laboratory while being scanned on an executive function task that allegedly measures the ability to control impulses really predict that person's ability to resist criminal offending, for example?

Behavioural neuroscientists have great flexibility in data collection, analysis, and reporting—a phenomenon termed "researcher degrees of freedom".[23] When this is coupled with low power and the multidimensionality of fMRI data, the probability of false-positive results is increased markedly.[24]

Replications are few, which is especially important for any discipline, such as law, that has public policy implications.[25] Policy and adjudication should not be influenced by findings that are insufficiently established, and replications are crucial to our confidence in a result, especially given the problem of publication bias[26] and reproducibility scepticism.[27] Indeed, replications are so few in this young science and the power of too many studies is so low that one should be wary of the ultimate validity of many results. A recent analysis suggests that more than 50 percent of cognitive neuroscience studies may be invalid and not reproducible.[28]

Drawing extended inferences from findings is especially unwarranted at present. If there are numerous studies of various types that seem valid, all converge on a similar finding, and there is theoretical reason to believe they should be consistent, then lack of replication of any one of them may not present such a large problem. For example, there are relatively few neuroscientific studies of adolescent behaviour (although it is one of the areas well-studied), but they tend to be consistent with both the developmental psychology of adolescence and the neuroanatomical evidence indicating average differences between adult and adolescent brains.[29] Such examples are now few, especially in legally and morally relevant neuroscience.

What is known about behavioural neuroscience is coarse-grained and correlational rather than fine-grained and causal.[30] Studies that show an association between a task or condition and brain structure or function do not demonstrate that the brain ROI or activity is a sensitive diagnostic marker for the condition or either a necessary, sufficient, or predisposing causal condition for the behavioural task. Any language that suggests otherwise—such as claiming that some brain region is the "neural substrate" for the behaviour—is not justifiable based on the methodology of most studies. Such inferences are only justified if everything else in the brain remained constant, which is seldom the case.[31]

What is the relevance of neuroscientific evidence to the acts and mental states that concern criminal law? If the behavioural data are not clear, then the potential contribution of neuroscience is large. Unfortunately, it is in just such cases that neuroscience at present is not likely to be of help. I term the reason for this the "clear-cut" problem.[32] Virtually all neuroscience studies of potential interest to the law involve some behaviour that has already been identified as of interest, such as addiction, and the point of the study is to identify that behaviour's neural correlates to deepen our understanding. Neuroscientists do not go on general "fishing" expeditions.[33] Such investigations presuppose that the researchers have already well-characterised and validated the behaviour under neuroscientific investigation. Cognitive, social, and affective neuroscience is thus inevitably embedded in a matrix involving allied sciences such as cognitive science and psychology. Behavioural science is virtually always the predicate for good behavioural neuroscience.[34] Consequently, neurodata can seldom be more valid than the behaviour with which it is correlated. In such cases, the neural markers might be sensitive to the already clearly identified behaviours precisely because the behaviour is so clear. Less clear behaviour is simply not studied, or the overlap in data about less clear behaviour is greater between the subjects of interest and comparison subjects. Consequently, the neural markers of clear cases will provide little guidance to resolve behaviourally ambiguous cases of relevant behaviour, and they are unnecessary if the behaviour is sufficiently clear.

In general, however, the existence of relevant behaviour will already be apparent before the neuroscientific investigation is begun. For example, some people are grossly out of touch with reality. If, as a result, they do not understand right from wrong, we excuse them because they lack such knowledge. We might learn a great deal about the neural correlates of such psychological abnormalities. But we already knew without neuroscientific data that these abnormalities existed, and we had a firm view of their normative significance.

My best hope for the future is that neuroscience and ethics and law will each richly inform the other and perhaps help reach what I term a conceptual–empirical equilibrium. I suspect that we are unlikely to make substantial progress with neural assessment of mental content, but we are likely to learn more about capacities that will bear on excuse or mitigation.

The radical challenges of neuroscience to law

Neuroscience allegedly poses two radical challenges to current law: determinism and epiphenomenalism about the mind, the no agency thesis. These are purely hypothetical, theoretical challenges at present and have virtually no practical purchase, so this chapter will deal with them briefly.

The challenge from determinism is the familiar claim that if determinism or something like it is true (e.g. physicalism plus causal closure), then no one can be responsible, a position termed "hard incompatibilism".[35] Even if our mental states play a causal role in explaining behaviour, what mental states we have and what they cause is not up to us. It is a form of ersatz agency in which no one can be responsible for anything. Many incorrectly believe that neuroscience will prove that determinism is true, but no science can do this. It is a metaphysical hypothesis about the ontology of the known universe and, roughly, a working background hypothesis for many practicing scientists. Moreover, there is a competing position within the philosophy of responsibility, "compatibilism", which holds that we have enough freedom to ground robust responsibility even if determinism is true. This is currently the dominant position among philosophers and there is no possible resolution of this metaphysical dispute. Both camps can recognise that humans are agents who act for causal reasons, but they disagree about whether action is sufficiently free to warrant ascriptions of responsibility.

Compatibilism is the theory most consistent with the approach of the ordinary person and the law to agency and responsibility and with a scientific worldview.[36] It is entirely consistent with the moral distinctions the law makes. For example, even if determinism or something quite like it is true, some bodily movements are actions and others are not. Some defendants are deluded, and most are not. These are simply undeniable facts about human behaviour that make a moral difference on deontological and consequentialist grounds.

There is simply no compelling reason to upend centuries of legal doctrine, theory, and institutions based on an armchair metaphysical theory, hard incompatibilism, that is not itself demonstrably true and whose implications are unclear. Given the history of the law, the burden of persuasion should rest with the radical critics of current doctrines, practices, and institutions. Critics of responsibility have a duty to provide the practical implications of their philosophical position, especially if they hope to institute radical change. They have an obligation to propose the details of psychology, politics, and law that would follow. Most have not done so in any real detail. Pereboom and Caruso have admirably tried, but the "medical model" they propose, which would abandon all notions of desert, including deserved punishment, in favour of a "quarantine" model of social control,[37] does not depend on the new neuroscience and has been intensely criticised.[38]

The epiphenomenal challenge is more radical. It claims that we are just a pack of neurons or victims of neuronal circumstances and that our mental states have no causal power whatsoever. On this view, minds are just the epiphenomenal foam on the neural wave. The existence of agency is thus denied, but agency is foundational for law and legal institutions. If the epiphenomenal claim is true, law and legal institutions rest on an illusion that is itself doing no work because illusory beliefs are mental states. Compatibilism cannot deflect this challenge because it begs the question against epiphenomenalism by assuming that we are agents, which is precisely what the radical challenge denies.

The question is whether mental epiphenomenalism is justified conceptually and empirically. Space precludes me from providing the full argument,[39] but the present conclusion, and probably the conclusion forever, is that we have no good conceptual or empirical grounds for thinking the epiphenomenal challenge is correct.

A final objection to the radical challenge is the unjustifiable normative implications that allegedly follow. The most common is the claim, discussed previously, that the truth of the challenge implies consequentialism, a set of ethical theories that considers the right action, which maximises good consequences. This position rejects deontology, a set of ethical theories that claims that some actions are right in themselves without regard to consequences. But if our mental states, including our reasons, are epiphenomenal and doing no work, then reasons do not have force and no normative implications follow at all. Would anyone want to live in a world without normativity (albeit the question itself makes no sense if the radical challenge is true because desires have no motivating effect but are just epiphenomena themselves)?

Agency is secure, at least for now. Neuroscience will not radically transform the law's view of the person, legal doctrine, and legal institutions for the foreseeable future and probably never.

Legal relevance

This section will assume that the scientific data being adduced to guide the law are valid. For example, it will assume that imaging data were properly acquired and interpreted. In that case, the issue will be whether the science is genuinely legally relevant. If it is not, it can be misleading and will be used primarily rhetorically.

Those who wish to understand the relevance of behavioural neuroscience to law must first understand that law is a thoroughly folk psychological institution. The primary goal of law (and morality) is to guide behaviour by giving people reasons to behave one way or another.[40] Law is thus like other forms of social interaction and control, such as ethics, etiquette, and social norms. It is addressed to creatures, us, who can understand and be guided by reasons, creatures for whom mental states in part explain their behaviour.

The criminal law is folk psychological because the primary criteria for culpability, responsibility, and competence are acts and mental states.[41] The crucial question for law and neuroscience is whether neuroscientific data are relevant to and thus help answer a legal question involving acts and mental states.

I term this the problem of "translation".[42] Neuroscience is a purely mechanistic science. Neuroscience eschews folk-psychological concepts and discourse (although neuroscientific articles are rife with dualistic discourse that suggests that regions of the brain are little homunculi that do things and that there seems to be a struggle between the self and the brain as an independent agent).[43] Neurons, neural networks, and the connectome do not have reasons. They have no aspirations, no sense of past, present, and future. They do not "do" things to each other. These are all properties of persons as agents. Legal rules are addressed to agents. Is the apparent chasm between those two types of discourse bridgeable? There will always be a problem of translation between the pure mechanisms of neuroscience and the folk psychology of law. It is the task of those doing normative neurolaw always to explain precisely how neuroscientific findings are relevant to a legal issue. No hand waving is allowed.

The brain does enable the mind and action (even if we do not know how this occurs). Facts we learn about brains in general or about a specific brain could in principle provide useful information about mental states and about human capacities in general and specific cases. Some believe that this conclusion is a category error because it fallaciously attributes to a part of the person (e.g. the brain) attributes such as rationality that are logically properties of whole persons.[44] If this view is correct, then the whole subject of neurolaw is empty. Let us therefore bracket this pessimistic view and determine what follows from the more optimistic position that what we learn about the brain and nervous system can be potentially helpful in resolving questions of criminal responsibility if the findings are properly translated.

Biological variables, including abnormal biological variables, do not per se answer any legal question because the law's criteria are not biological. Any legal criterion must be established independently, and biological evidence must be translated into the criminal law's folk-psychological criteria. That is, the advocate for using the data must be able to explain precisely how the neurodata bore on the agent's action, formed the required *mens rea*, or met the criteria for an excusing or mitigating condition. In the context of competence evaluations, the advocate must explain precisely how the neuroevidence bears on whether the subject was capable of meeting the law's functional criteria. If the evidence is not directly relevant, the advocate should be able to explain the chain of inference from the indirect evidence to the law's criteria. At present, few such data exist that could be the basis of such an inferential chain of reasoning.[45]

Even if neuroscience does seem relevant to a legal issue, the concerns with prejudice, cumulation (additional evidence that adds nothing new to evidence already adduced), and other worries about the potentially negative impact of concededly relevant evidence must be considered. Good studies have disclosed that this worry appears unjustified. With limited exceptions, decision-makers do not give undue weight to imaging data.[46] The issue is not yet resolved empirically, but the present default should be that the evidence is not prejudicial.

A pressing concern is the value added by imaging. A scan is relatively expensive and time consuming. It thus has the potential for waste and delay. Legally relevant neuroimages must be based on valid, prior behavioural science that identifies clearly the behaviour to which the brain structure or function will be correlated. This raises the problem of cumulation. For example, the law has treated adolescents differently from adults for centuries based on undoubted average behavioural differences between adolescents and adults. Now, we know from brain imaging data that adolescent and young adult brains are on average less anatomically mature than adult brains. What does this anatomical information add to what we already knew beyond some potentially causal information? It is unsurprising in light of the behavioural differences that there are brain differences, but would we believe adolescents are *not* behaviourally different if the current brain imaging data did not show a difference? Instead, we would justifiably believe that the neuroscience was not yet sophisticated enough to detect the undoubted brain differences.

Might not neuroscience be especially helpful in cases in which the behavioural evidence is unclear? The answer in principle is that of course it would be helpful, but as a practical matter it will not be because the neurodata is based on correlations with clear behavioural data, a problem I described earlier as the "clear cut" issue.[47] Where the behaviour is unclear, the neurodata will not be sufficiently sensitive to help resolve the behavioural issue even if the neurodata can distinguish the already behaviourally clear cases.

Here is an example of the current limitations of neuroscience for normative conclusions. A neuroscientist and I reviewed all the behavioural neuroscience that might possibly be relevant to criminal law adjudication and policy. With the exception of a few already well-characterised medical conditions that did not employ the new neuroscience, such as epilepsy, our review found virtually no solid neuroscience findings that were yet relevant.[48] Similar conclusions were reached after reviews of "brain reading" studies (e.g. "neural lie detection")[49] and addictions.[50]

At this point, there has been a torrential stream of articles making inflated claims for the relevance and usefulness of neuroscience to law. I have termed this phenomenon "neurohype". Professor Francis Shen terms it, "lobbyist neuroscience", in which advocates use neuroscience more aggressively and categorically for their purposes than the evidence warrants.[51] Like Professor Shen, I believe that many of the claims for the relevance of neuroscience are best characterised as more "rhetorically relevant" than genuinely relevant. For example, defence advocates in capital punishment proceedings, in which the threshold for admissibility of mitigating evidence is considerably lower than at trial, hope that the fetching images produced by "real" neuroscience will be more persuasive to decision-makers than evidence provided by apparently more suspect social and behavioural science, even if the advocate cannot say precisely how the neuroscience bears on a genuinely mitigating condition. Having a brain lesion or injury is not a mitigating condition per se. The actual relevance of such brain abnormality evidence therefore requires an account of why the brain evidence makes it more likely than not that a genuine mitigating condition, such as lack of rational capacity, obtains.

Let us conclude this section with an observation that will always be germane even if neuroscience makes huge leaps forward. For the law, actions speak louder than images with very few exceptions. The law's criteria are behavioural—actions and mental states. If the finding of any test or measurement of behaviour is contradicted by actual behavioural evidence, then we must believe the behavioural evidence because it is more direct and probative of the law's behavioural criteria except perhaps in cases of malingering (although neuroscience cannot at present reliably and validly identify malingerers).

For example, if an agent behaves rationally in a wide variety of circumstances, the agent is rational even if his or her brain appears structurally or functionally abnormal. We confidently knew that some people were behaviourally abnormal—such as being psychotic—long before there were any psychological or neurological tests for such abnormalities. In contrast, if the agent is clearly psychotic, then a potentially legally-relevant rationality problem exists even if the agent's brain looks entirely normal.

Conclusion

At present, mental disorder, especially severe disorder, plays an important role in criminal responsibility decisions in individual cases, but it presents no general challenge to traditional concepts of criminal responsibility. Neuroscience is thought to present such a challenge, but has little to contribute to more just and accurate criminal law decision-making concerning policy, doctrine, and individual case adjudication. This was the conclusion reached when I tentatively identified "Brain Overclaim Syndrome" in "Lost in Translation" well over a decade ago, and it remains true today. Despite having claimed that we should be exceptionally cautious about the current contributions that neuroscience can make to criminal law policy, doctrine, and adjudication, I am modestly optimistic about the near- and intermediate-term contributions neuroscience can potentially make to our ordinary, traditional, folk-psychological legal system. In other words, neuroscience may make a positive contribution even though there has been no paradigm shift in thinking about the nature of the person and the criteria for criminal responsibility. The legal regime to which neuroscience will contribute will continue to take people seriously as people—as autonomous agents who may fairly be blamed and punished based on their mental states and actions.

Acknowledgements

Part IV of this chapter is reprinted in revised form with the permission of the publisher, Elsevier, from, SJ Morse, "Neurolaw: Challenges and Limits", in G Meynen & H Swab (eds), *Brain and Crime, Handbook of Clinical Neurology*, Vol. 197 (Elsevier Publishers: Amsterdam, 3rd series, 2023). The author is grateful to Elsevier.

Notes

1. In the rest of this chapter, it should be understood that the term, "mental disorder", includes intellectual disability.
2. *Morisette v. United States* (1952) 342 US 246.
3. K Sifferd, "In Defense of the Use of Commonsense Psychology in the Criminal Law", *Law and Philosophy*, vol. 25, no. 6 (2006), p.571.
4. SJ Morse, "The (Non)Problem of Free Will in Forensic Psychiatry and Psychology", *Behavioral Sciences and the Law*, vol. 25 (2007), p.203.
5. *Moore v. Texas* (2017) 137 S. Ct. 1039.
6. *Kansas v. Hendricks* (1997) 521 US 346.
7. *M'Naghten's Case* (1843) 8 ER 718.
8. American Law Institute, 1985, §4.01(1).
9. *Kahler v. Kansas* (2020) 140 S. Ct. 1021.
10. E.g. SJ Morse, "Before and After Hinckley: Legal Insanity in United States", in R Mackay & W Brookbanks (eds), *Legal Insanity: International and Comparative Perspectives* (Oxford University Press: Oxford, 2023).
11. E.g. EL Johnston & V Leahey, "Psychosis, Heat of Passion, and Diminished Responsibility", *Boston College Law Review*, vol. 63 (2022), p.1227; L Kennefick, "Beyond homicide? The Feasibility of Extending the Doctrine of Partial Excuse Across All Offence Categories", *Criminal Law Forum*, vol. 33, no. 4 (2022), p.323; SJ Morse, "Diminished Rationality, Diminished Responsibility", *Ohio State Journal of Criminal Law*, vol. 1 (2003), p.289.
12. SJ Morse, "Lost in Translation? An Essay on Law and Neuroscience", in M Freeman (ed), *Law and Neuroscience* (Oxford University Press: Oxford, 2011).
13. R Adolphs, "The Unsolved Problems of Neuroscience", *Trends in Cognitive Sciences*, vol. 19, no. 4 (2015), p.173 at p.175; M Cobb, *The Idea of the Brain: The Past and Future of Neuroscience* (Basic Books: New York, 2020); PR McHugh & P Slavney, *The Perspectives of Psychiatry* (Johns Hopkins University Press: Baltimore, 2nd edn, 1998), pp.11-12.
14. CM Bennett, GL Wolford, & MB Miller, "The Principled Control of False Positives in Neuroimaging", *Social Cognitive and Affective Neuroscience*, vol. 4, no. 4 (2009), p.417; KS Button et al, "Power Failure: Why Small Sample Size Undermines the Reliability of Neuroscience", *Nature Reviews Neuroscience*, vol. 14, no. 5 (2013), p.365; A Eklund, TE Nichols, & H Knutson, "Cluster Failure: Why fMRI Inferences for Spatial Extent Have Inflated False-Positive Rates", *Proceedings of the National Academy of Sciences*, vol. 113, no. 28 (2016), p.7900; E Vul et al, "Puzzlingly High Correlations in fMRI Studies of Emotion, Personality, and Social Cognition", *Perspectives on Psychological Science*, vol. 4, no. 3 (2009), p.274. But see MD Lieberman, ET Berkman, & TD Wager, "Correlations in Social Neuroscience Aren't Voodoo: A Commentary on Vul et al.", *Perspectives on Psychological Science*, vol. 4 (2009), p.299.
15. A Francis, "Whither DSM-V?", *British Journal of Psychiatry*, vol. 195, no. 5 (2009), p.391; SJ Morse & WT Newsome, "Criminal Responsibility, Criminal Competence, and Prediction of Criminal Behavior", in SJ Morse & AL Roskies (eds), *A Primer on Criminal Law and Neuroscience* (Oxford University Press: New York, 2013); MD Rego, "Counterpoint: Clinical Neuroscience is Not Ready for Clinical Use", *British Journal of Psychiatry*, vol. 208, no. 4 (2016), p.312.
16. JP Ioannides, "Excess Significance Bias in the Literature on Brain Volume Abnormalities", *Archives of General Psychiatry*, vol. 68, no. 8 (2011), p.773.
17. AL Roskies, "Brain Imaging Techniques", in SJ Morse & AL Roskies (eds), *A Primer on Criminal Law and Neuroscience* (Oxford University Press: New York, 2013), p.37; YW Hong et al, "False-Positive Neuroimaging: Undisclosed Flexibility in Testing Spatial Hypotheses Allows Presenting Anything as a Replicated Finding", *NeuroImage*, vol. 195 (2019), p.384.
18. For sophisticated, systematic, and comprehensive reviews of the proper uses and limitations of fMRI, see NK Logothetis, "What We Can and Cannot Do with fMRI", *Nature*, vol. 453 (2008), p.869 and RA Poldrack, *The New Mind Readers: What Neuroimaging Can and Cannot Reveal About Our Thoughts* (Princeton University Press: Princeton NJ, 2018).
19. RA Poldrack, "Can Cognitive Processes be Inferred from Neuroimaging Data?", *Trends in Cognitive Sciences*, vol. 10, no. 2 (2006), p.59.

20 Button et al, "Power Failure"; D Szucs & J Ioannidis, "Empirical Assessment of Published Effect Sizes and Power in the Recent Cognitive Neuroscience and Psychology Literature", *PLOS: Biology*, vol. 15 (2017), e2000797.
21 G Varoquaux, "Cross-Validation Failure: Small Sample Sizes Lead to Large Error Bars", *NeuroImage*, vol. 180 pt A (2017), p.68.
22 DL Faigman, J Monahan, & C Slobogin, "Group to Individual (G2i) Inference in Scientific Expert Testimony", *University of Chicago Law Review*, vol. 81, no. 2 (2014), p.417.
23 JP Simmons, LD Nelson, & U Simonsohn, "False-Positive Psychology: Undisclosed Flexibility in Data Collection and Analysis Allows Presenting Anything as Significant", *Psychological Science*, vol. 22, no. 11 (2011), p.1359.
24 RA Poldrack et al, "Scanning the Horizon: Towards Transparent and Reproducible Neuroimaging Research", *Nature Reviews: Neuroscience*, vol. 18 (2017), p.115.
25 JM Chin, "Psychological Science's Replicability Crisis and What It Means for Science in the Courtroom", *Journal of Psychology, Public Policy, and Law*, vol. 20, no. 3 (2014), p.225.
26 Ioannides, "Excess Significance Bias".
27 Chin, "Psychological Science's Replicability Crisis and What It Means for Science in the Courtroom"; Open Science Collaboration, "Psychology: Estimating the Reproducibility of Psychological Science", *Science*, vol. 349, no. 6251 (2015), aac4716-1.
28 Szucs & Ioannidis, "Empirical Assessment".
29 A Galvan, *The Neuroscience of Addiction* (Cambridge University Press: Cambridge, 2017).
30 GA Miller, "Mistreating Psychology in the Decades of the Brain", *Perspectives on Psychological Science*, vol. 5, no. 6 (2010), p.716.
31 Adolphs, "The Unsolved Problems of Neuroscience".
32 Morse, "Lost in Translation?".
33 For an amusing exception, see CM Bennett et al, "Neural Correlates of Interspecies Perspective Taking in the Post-Mortem Atlantic Salmon: An Argument for Proper Multiple Comparisons Correction", *Journal of Serendipitous and Unexpected Results*, vol. 1, no. 1 (2009), p.1.
34 Y Niv, "The Primacy of Behavioral Research for Understanding the Brain", *Behavioral Neuroscience*, vol. 135, no. 5 (2021), p.601.
35 E.g. D Pereboom & GD Caruso, "Hard-Incompatibilist Existentialism: Neuroscience, Punishment, and Meaning in Life", in GD Caruso & O Flanagan (eds), *Neuroexistentialism: Meaning, Morals, and Purpose in the Age of Neuroscience* (Oxford University Press: Oxford, 2018).
36 SJ Morse, "The Neuroscientific Non-Challenge to Meaning Morals and Purpose", in GD Caruso & F Flanagan (eds), *Neuroexistentialism: Meaning, Morals, and Purpose in the Age of Neuroscience* (Oxford University Press: Oxford, 2018); SJ Morse, "Neuroscience and Criminal Law: Perils and Promises", in L Alexander & K Ferzan (eds), *The Palgrave Handbook of Applied Ethics and the Criminal Law* (Palgrave Macmillan: Cham, Switzerland, 2019).
37 Pereboom & Caruso, "Hard-Incompatibilist Existentialism".
38 SJ Morse, "Mental Disorder and Criminal Justice", in E Luna (ed), *Reforming Criminal Justice: A Report of The Academy for Justice Bridging the Gap Between Scholarship and Reform* (Academy for Justice: Phoenix AZ, 2018); SR Sehon, *Free Will and Action Explanation: A Non-Causal, Compatibilist Account* (Oxford University Press: Oxford, 2016).
39 Which can be found in other work: AR Mele, *Effective Intentions: The Power of Conscious Will* (Oxford University Press: New York, 2009); AR Mele, *Free: Why Science Hasn't Disproved Free Will* (Oxford University Press: New York, 2014); MS Moore, "Responsible Choices, Desert-Based Legal Institutions, and the Challenges of Contemporary Neuroscience", *Social Philosophy and Policy*, vol. 29, no. 1 (2012), p.233; SJ Morse, "Neuroprediction: New Technology, Old Problems", *Bioethica Forum*, vol. 8 (2015), p.128; P Nachev & P Hacker, "The Neural Antecedents to Voluntary Action: Response to Commentaries", *Cognitive Neuroscience*, vol. 6, no. 4 (2015), p.180; A Schurger, JD Sitt, & S Dehaene, "An Accumulator Model for Spontaneous Neural Activity Prior to Self-Initiated Movement", *Proceedings of the National Academy of Sciences of the U.S.A.*, vol. 109 (2012), E2904–E2913; A Schurger & S Uithol, "Nowhere and Everywhere: The Causal Origin of Voluntary Action", *Review of Philosophy and Psychology*, vol. 6 (2015), p.761.
40 S Shapiro, "Law, Morality, and the Guidance of Conduct", *Legal Theory*, vol. 6, no. 2 (2000), p.127; G Sher, *In Praise of Blame* (Oxford University Press: Oxford, 2006).

41 K Sifferd, "In Defense of the Use of Commonsense Psychology in the Criminal Law", *Law and Philosophy*, vol. 25, no. 6 (2006), p.571.
42 Morse, "Lost in Translation?".
43 L Mudrik & U Maoz, "'Me & My Brain': Exposing Neuroscience's Closet Dualism", *Journal of Cognitive Neuroscience*, vol. 27, no. 2 (2014), p.211.
44 MR Bennett & PMS Hacker, *Philosophical Foundations of Neuroscience* (Wiley-Blackwell: Hoboken NJ, 2003).
45 Morse & Newsome, "Criminal Responsibility", p.150.
46 AL Roskies, NJ Schweitzer, & MJ Saks, "Neuroimages in Court: Less Biasing than Feared", *Trends in Cognitive Sciences*, vol. 17, no. 3 (2013), p.99; NJ Schweitzer, MJ Saks, ER Murphy et al, "Neuroimages as Evidence in a Mens Rea Defense: No Impact", *Psychology, Public Policy, and Law*, vol. 17, no. 3 (2011), p.357.
47 Morse, "Lost in Translation?"
48 Morse & Newsome, "Criminal Responsibility".
49 HT Greely, "Mind Reading, Neuroscience, and the Law", in SJ Morse & AL Roskies (eds), *A Primer on Criminal Law and Neuroscience* (Oxford University Press: New York, 2013).
50 D Husak & E Murphy, "The Relevance of the Neuroscience of Addiction to the Criminal Law", in SJ Morse & AL Roskies (eds), *A Primer on Criminal Law and Neuroscience*, (Oxford University Press: New York, 2013).
51 F Shen, "Legislating Neuroscience: The Case of Juvenile Justice", *Loyola Law Review*, vol. 46 (2013), p.985. There are of course many examples of exemplary caution (e.g. AL Wax, "The Poverty of the Neuroscience of Poverty: Policy Payoff or False Promise", *Jurimetrics*, vol. 57, no. 2 (2016-2017), p.239), but these are less frequent especially in politically fraught legal contexts.

References

Cases

Kahler v. Kansas (2020) 140 S. Ct. 1021.
Kansas v. Hendricks (1997) 521 U.S. 346.
M'Naghten's Case (1843) 8 ER 718.
Miller v. Alabama, 132 S.Ct. 2455 (2012).
Moore v. Texas (2017) 137 S. Ct. 1039.
Morisette v. United States (1952) 342 US 246.
People v. Weinstein (1992) 591 N.Y.S.2d 715.
United States v Hinckley (DDC 1981) 525 F. Supp. 1342.

Books and book chapters

Bennett MR & Hacker PMS, *Philosophical Foundations of Neuroscience* (Wiley-Blackwell: Hoboken NJ, 2003).
Caruso GD, *Rejecting Retributivism: Free Will, Punishment, and Criminal Justice* (Cambridge University Press: Cambridge, 2021).
Cobb M, *The Idea of the Brain: The Past and Future of Neuroscience* (Basic Books: New York, 2020).
Davis K, *The Brain Defense: Murder in Manhattan and the Dawn of Neuroscience in America's Courtrooms* (Penguin: New York, 2017).
Feldman R, *The Role of Science in Law* (Oxford University Press: New York, 2009).
Gabriel M, *I Am Not a Brain: Philosophy of Mind for the 21st Century* (Wiley: Hoboken NJ, 2017).
Galvan A, *The Neuroscience of Addiction* (Cambridge University Press: Cambridge UK, 2017).
Greely HT, "Mind Reading, Neuroscience, and the Law", in Morse SJ & Roskies AL (eds), *A Primer on Criminal Law and Neuroscience* (Oxford University Press: New York, 2013).
Hunter JD & Nedelsky P, *Science and the Good: The Tragic Quest for the Foundations of Morality* (Yale University Press: New Haven CT and London, 2018).

Husak D & Murphy E, "The Relevance of the Neuroscience of Addiction to the Criminal Law", in Morse SJ & Roskies AL (eds), *A Primer on Criminal Law and Neuroscience* (Oxford University Press: New York, 2013).

Jones OD, "Seven Ways Neuroscience Aids Law", in Battro A, Dehaene S, & Singer W (eds), *Neurosciences and the Human Person: New Perspectives on Human Activities* (Pontifical Academy of Sciences: Vatican City, 2013).

Macmillan M, *An Odd Kind of Fame: Stories of Phineas Gage* (MIT Press: Cambridge MA, 2000).

McHugh PR & Slavney P, *The Perspectives of Psychiatry* (Johns Hopkins University Press: Baltimore, 2nd edn, 1998).

Mele AR, *Effective Intentions: The Power of Conscious Will* (Oxford University Press: New York, 2009).

Mele AR, *Free: Why Science Hasn't Disproved Free Will* (Oxford University Press: New York, 2014).

Menninger K, *The Crime of Punishment* (Viking Press: New York, 1968).

Moore MS, *Mechanical Choices: The Responsibility of the Human Machine* (Oxford University Press: New York, 2020).

Morse SJ, "New Neuroscience, Old Problems", in Garland B (ed), *Neuroscience and the Law: Brain, Mind and the Scales of Justice* (Dana Press: New York, 2004).

Morse SJ, "Lost in Translation? An Essay on Law and Neuroscience", in Freeman M (ed), *Law and Neuroscience* (Oxford University Press: Oxford, UK, 2011).

Morse SJ, "The Neuroscientific Non-Challenge to Meaning Morals and Purpose", in Caruso GD & Flanagan F (eds), *Neuroexistentialism: Meaning, Morals, and Purpose in the Age of Neuroscience* (Oxford University Press: Oxford, 2018).

Morse SJ, "Mental Disorder and Criminal Justice", in Luna E (ed), *Reforming Criminal Justice: A Report of The Academy for Justice Bridging the Gap Between Scholarship and Reform* (Academy for Justice: Phoenix AZ, 2018).

Morse SJ "Neuroscience and Criminal Law: Perils and Promises", in Alexander L & Ferzan K (eds), *The Palgrave Handbook of Applied Ethics and the Criminal Law* (Palgrave Macmillan: Cham, Switzerland, 2019).

Morse SJ, "Before and After Hinckley: Legal Insanity in United States", in Mackay R & Brookbanks W (ed), *Legal Insanity: International and Comparative Perspectives* (Oxford University Press: Oxford, 2023).

Morse SJ & Newsome WT, "Criminal Responsibility, Criminal Competence, and Prediction of Criminal Behavior", in Morse SJ & Roskies AL (eds), *A Primer on Criminal Law and Neuroscience* (Oxford University Press: New York, 2013).

Pardo M & Patterson D, *Minds, Brains, and Law: The Conceptual Foundations of Law and Neuroscience* (Oxford University Press: New York, 2013).

Pereboom D & Caruso GD, "Hard-Incompatibilist Existentialism: Neuroscience, Punishment, and Meaning in Life", in Caruso GD & Flanagan O (eds), *Neuroexistentialism: Meaning, Morals, and Purpose in the Age of Neuroscience* (Oxford University Press: New York, 2017).

Poldrack RA, *The New Mind Readers: What Neuroimaging Can and Cannot Reveal About Our Thoughts* (Princeton University Press: Princeton NJ, 2018).

Sehon SR, *Free Will and Action Explanation: A Non-Causal, Compatibilist Account* (Oxford University Press: Oxford, 2016).

Sher G, *In Praise of Blame* (Oxford University Press: Oxford, 2006).

Stone A, *Law, Psychiatry, and Morality* (American Psychological Association: Washington DC, 1984).

Wittgenstein L, *Philosophical Investigations* (Macmillan Company: New York, 1953).

Journal articles

Adolphs R, "The Unsolved Problems of Neuroscience", *Trends in Cognitive Sciences*, vol. 19, no. 4 (2015), pp.173–175.

Aharoni E, Vincent GM, Harenski CL, Calhoun VD, Sinnott-Armstrong W, Gazzaniga MS, & Kiehl KA, "Neuroprediction of Future Arrest", *Proceedings of the National Academy of Sciences of the United States of America*, vol. 110, no. 15 (2013), pp. 6223–6228.

Alimardani A & Chin JM, "Neurolaw in Australia: The Use of Neuroscience in Australian Criminal Proceedings", *Neuroethics*, vol. 12 (2019), pp.255–270

American Psychiatric Association, "American Psychiatric Association Statement on the Insanity Defense", *American Journal of Psychiatry*, vol. 140, no. 6 (1983), pp.681–688.

Bennett CM, Baird AA, Miller MB, & Wolford GL, "Neural Correlates of Interspecies Perspective Taking in the Post-Mortem Atlantic Salmon: An Argument for Proper Multiple Comparisons Correction", *Journal of Serendipitous and Unexpected Results*, vol. 1 (2009), pp. 1–5.

Bennett CM, Wolford GL, & Miller MB, "The Principled Control of False Positives in Neuroimaging", *Social Cognitive and Affective Neuroscience*, vol. 4, no. 4 (2009), pp.417–422.

Button KS, Ioannidis JPA, Mokrysz, Nosek BA, Flint J, Robinson ESJ, & Munafò MR, "Power Failure: Why Small Sample Size Undermines the Reliability of Neuroscience", *Nature Reviews Neuroscience*, vol. 14, no. 5 (2013), pp.365–376.

Catley P & Claydon L, "The Use of Neuroscientific Evidence in the Courtroom by Those Accused of Criminal Offenses in England and Wales", *Journal of Law and Biosciences*, vol. 2, no. 3 (2015), pp.510–549.

Chandler J, "The Use of Neuroscientific Evidence in Canadian Criminal Proceedings", *Journal of Law and Biosciences*, vol. 2, no. 3 (2015), pp.550–579.

Chin JM, "Psychological Science's Replicability Crisis and What It Means for Science in the Courtroom", *Psychology, Public Policy, and Law*, vol. 20, no. 3 (2014), pp. 225–238.

De Kogel CH & Westgeest EJMC, "Neuroscientific and Behavioral Genetic Information in Criminal Cases in the Netherlands", *Journal of Law and Biosciences*, vol. 2, no. 3 (2015), pp.580–605.

Delfin C, Krona H, Andiné P, Ryding E, Wallinus M, & Hofvander B, "Prediction of Recidivism in a Long-Term Follow-Up of Forensic Psychiatric Patients: Incremental Effects of Neuroimaging Data", *PLoS ONE*, vol. 14, no. 5 (2019), e0217127.

Eklund A, Nichols TE, & Knutson H, "Cluster Failure: Why fMRI Inferences for Spatial Extent Have Inflated False-Positive Rates", *Proceedings of the National Academy of Sciences*, vol. 113, no. 28 (2016), pp.7900–7905.

Faigman DL, Monahan J, & Slobogin C, "Group to Individual (G2i) Inference in Scientific Expert Testimony", *University of Chicago Law Review*, vol. 81, no. 2 (2014), pp.417–480.

Farahany NA, "Neuroscience and Behavioral Genetics in US Criminal Law: An Empirical Analysis", *Journal of Law and Biosciences*, vol. 2, no. 3 (2015), pp.485–509.

Francis A, "Whither DSM-V?", *British Journal of Psychiatry*, vol. 195, no. 5 (2009), pp.391–392.

Gaudet LM & Marchant GE, "Under the Radar: Neuroimaging Evidence in the Criminal Courtroom", *Drake Law Review*, vol. 64, no. 3 (2016), pp.577–661.

Gilbert DT, King G, Pettigrew S, & Wilson TD, "Comment on 'Estimating the Reproducibility of Psychological Science'", *Science*, vol. 351, no. 6277 (2016), p.1037-a.

Gillebaart, M, "The Operational Definition of Self-Control", *Frontiers in Psychology*, vol. 9 (2018), p.1231.

Hong YW, Yoo Y, Han J, Wager TD, & Woo CW, "False-Positive Neuroimaging: Undisclosed Flexibility in Testing Spatial Hypotheses Allows Presenting Anything as a Replicated Finding", *NeuroImage*, vol. 195 (2019), pp.384–395.

Ioannides JP, "Excess Significance Bias in the Literature on Brain Volume Abnormalities", *Archives of General Psychiatry*, vol. 68, no. 8 (2011), pp.773–780.

Johnston EL & Leahey V, "Psychosis, Heat of Passion, and Diminished Responsibility", *Boston College Law Review*, vol. 63, no. 4 (2022), pp.1227–1294.

Kennefick L, "Beyond Homicide? The Feasibility of Extending the Doctrine of Partial Excuse Across All Offence Categories", *Criminal Law Forum*, vol. 33, no. 4 (2022), pp.323–357.

Lieberman MD, Berkman ET, & Wager TD, "Correlations in Social Neuroscience Aren't Voodoo: A Commentary on Vul et al.", *Perspectives on Psychological Science*, vol. 4, no. 4 (2009), pp.299–307.

Logothetis NK, "What We Can and Cannot Do with fMRI", *Nature*, vol. 453 (2008), pp. 869–878.

Miller GA, "Mistreating Psychology in the Decades of the Brain", *Perspectives on Psychological Science*, vol. 5, no. 6 (2010), pp.716–743.

Moore MS, "Responsible Choices, Desert-Based Legal Institutions, and the Challenges of Contemporary Neuroscience", *Social Philosophy and Policy*, vol. 29, no. 1 (2012), pp.233–279.

Morse SJ, "Brain and Blame", *Georgetown Law Journal*, vol. 84 (1995), pp.527–549.

Morse SJ, "Diminished Rationality, Diminished Responsibility", *Ohio State Journal of Criminal Law*, vol. 1 (2003), pp.289–308.

Morse SJ, "The (Non)Problem of Free Will in Forensic Psychiatry and Psychology", *Behavioral Sciences and the Law*, vol. 25 (2007), pp.203–220.

Morse SJ, "Brain Overclaim Redux", *Law and Inequality*, vol. 31, no. 2 (2013), pp.509–534.

Morse SJ, "Neuroprediction: New Technology, Old Problems", *Bioethica Forum*, vol. 8 (2015), pp. 128–129.

Mudrik L & Maoz U, "Me & My Brain': Exposing Neuroscience's Closet Dualism", *Journal of Cognitive Neuroscience*, vol. 27, no. 2 (2014), pp.211–221.

Nachev P & Hacker P, "The Neural Antecedents to Voluntary Action: Response to Commentaries", *Cognitive Neuroscience*, vol. 6, no. 4 (2015), pp.180–186.

Niv Y, "The Primacy of Behavioral Research for Understanding the Brain", *Behavioral Neuroscience*, vol. 135, no. 5 (2021), pp.601–609.

Open Science Collaboration, "Psychology: Estimating the Reproducibility of Psychological Science", *Science*, vol. 349 (2015), pp.aac4716–aac4721.

Pardini DA, Raine A, Erickson K, & Loeber R, "Lower Amygdala Volume in Men is Associated with Childhood Aggression, Early Psychopathic Traits, and Future Violence", *Biological Psychiatry*, vol. 75, no. 1 (2014), pp.73–80.

Poldrack RA, "Can Cognitive Processes be Inferred from Neuroimaging Data?", *Trends in Cognitive Sciences*, vol. 10, no. 2 (2006), pp.59–63.

Poldrack RA, Monahan J, Imrey P, Reyna V, Raichle ME, Faigman D, & Buckholtz JW, "Predicting Violent Behavior; What Can Neuroscience Add?", *Trends in Cognitive Sciences*, vol. 22, no. 2 (2018), pp.111–123.

Poldrack RA, Baker CI, Durnez J, Gorgolewski KJ, Matthews PM, Munafò MR, Nichols TE, Poline JB, Vul E, & Yarkoni T, "Scanning the Horizon: Towards Transparent and Reproducible Neuroimaging Research", *Nature Reviews: Neuroscience*, vol. 18, no. 2 (2017), pp.115–126.

Rakoff JS, "Neuroscience and the Law: Don't Rush In", *New York Review of Books*, vol. LXIII (2016), pp.30–35.

Rego MD, "Counterpoint: Clinical Neuroscience is Not Ready for Clinical Use", *British Journal of Psychiatry*, vol. 208, no. 8 (2016), pp.312–313.

Rissman J, Chow TE, Reggente N, & Wagner AD, "Decoding fMRI Signatures of Real-World Autobiographical Memory Retrieval", *Journal of Cognitive Neuroscience*, vol. 28, no. 4 (2016), pp. 604–620.

Rissman J, Greely HT, & Wagner AD, "Detecting Individual Memories through the Neural Decoding of Memory States and Past Experience", *Proceedings of the National Academy of Sciences of the United States of America*, vol. 107, no. 21 (2010), pp.9849–9854.

Schurger A, Sitt JD, & Dehaene S, "An Accumulator Model for Spontaneous Neural Activity Prior to Self-Initiated Movement", *Proceedings of the National Academy of Sciences of the U.S.A.*, vol. 109 (2012), pp.E2904–E2913.

Schurger A, & Uithol S, "Nowhere and Everywhere: The Causal Origin of Voluntary Action", *Review of Philosophy and Psychology*, vol. 6 (2015), pp.761–778.

Schweitzer NJ, Saks MJ, Murphy ER, Roskies AL, Sinnott-Armstrong W, & Gaudet LM, "Neuroimages as Evidence in a Mens Rea Defense: No Impact", *Psychology, Public Policy, and Law*, vol. 17, no. 3 (2011), pp.357–393.

Shapiro S, "Law, Morality, and the Guidance of Conduct", *Legal Theory*, vol. 6, no. 2 (2000), pp.127–170.

Shen F, "Legislating Neuroscience: The Case of Juvenile Justice", *Loyola Law Review*, vol. 46 (2013), pp. 985–1018.

Sifferd K, "In Defense of the Use of Commonsense Psychology in the Criminal Law", *Law and Philosophy*, vol. 25 (2006), pp.571–612.

Simmons JP, Nelson LD, & Simonsohn U, "False-Positive Psychology: Undisclosed Flexibility in Data Collection and Analysis Allows Presenting Anything as Significant", *Psychological Science*, vol. 22, no. 11 (2011), pp.1359–1366.

Szucs D & Ioannidis J, "Empirical Assessment of Published Effect Sizes and Power in the Recent Cognitive Neuroscience and Psychology Literature", *PLOS: Biology*, vol. 15 (2017), p.e2000797.

Varoquaux G, "Cross-Validation Failure: Small Sample Sizes Lead to Large Error Bars", *NeuroImage*, vol. 180(Pt A) (2017), pp.68–77.

Vilares I, Wesley MJ, Ahn WY, Bonnie RJ, Hoffman M, Jones OD, Morse SJ, Yaffe G, Lohrenz, & Montague PR, "Predicting the Knowledge–Recklessness Distinction in the Human Brain", *Proceedings of the National Academy of Sciences of the United States of America*, vol. 114, no. 12 (2017), pp.3222–3227.
Vul E, Harris C, Winkielman P, & Pashler H, "Puzzlingly High Correlations in fMRI Studies of Emotion, Personality, and Social Cognition", *Perspectives on Psychological Science*, vol. 4, no. 3 (2009), pp.274–290.
Wax AL, "The Poverty of the Neuroscience of Poverty: Policy Payoff or False Promise", *Jurimetrics*, vol. 57 (2016–2017), pp. 239–287.
Zijlmans J, Marhe R, Bevaart F, Van Duin L, Luijks MJA, Franken I, Tiemeier H, & Popma A, "The Predictive Value of Neurobiological Measures for Recidivism in Delinquent Male Young Adults", *Journal of Psychiatry and Neuroscience*, vol. 46, no. 2 (2021), E271–E280.

Reports and websites

Presidential Commission for the Study of Bioethical Issues, *Gray Matters: Topics at the Intersection of Neuroscience, Ethics, and Society, Volume 2* (Presidential Commission for the Study of Bioethical Issues: Washington DC, 2015).
The Economist, "Open Your Mind" (25 May, 2002), p.93.
U.S. National Institutes of Health, "Funding Opportunity Announcement (FOA): Basic Research on Self-Regulation", available at: www.grants.nih.gov/grants/guide/rfa-files/rfa-ag-11-010.html

8
CRIMINAL RESPONSIBILITY IN THE ITALIAN COLONIES
The Eritrean Case (Nineteenth–Twentieth Centuries)

Emilia Musumeci

Introduction

This chapter investigates the influence of the Positivist School of Criminal Law in the evaluation of mental capacity in the Italian colonies, with a specific focus on Eritrea, the first experience of the Kingdom of Italy with African Colonialism. This area, as well as in general the colonial situation,[1] was indeed a privileged ground for developing new models of punishment between the nineteenth and twentieth centuries. Even though it is overly simplistic to see the authoritarian traces of criminal justice in Eritrea merely as a distortion of the positivist thesis, acknowledging that Italian Colonialism itself is a complex and multi-faceted phenomenon, it is nevertheless true that many fundamental principles of the Positivist School (such as that of social defence) were adopted and used by colonialists for their own ends. In addition to the adoption of methods of the ancient regime (capital punishment and corporal punishment, enormous discretion of the judge and so on), criminal justice was administered in violation of all the cardinal principles of the tradition of the penal Enlightenment: from the principle of legality to the prohibition of non-retroactivity and analogy, as well as the principle of equality before criminal law. Not by chance, the typical approach that overseas magistrates had towards the deviance of the natives in the early twentieth century and the consequent model of criminal justice to be adopted could be summarised recalling this opinion: "They have […] a deficient mind that puts them in a condition to act by instinct and tradition without reasoning."[2] With these words, Adelgiso Ravizza, in 1933 when he had become Judge of the Court of Cassation, recalled the years in which he had been a colonial magistrate,[3] describing the psychological diversity of the "truly barbaric and savage populations",[4] or rather, the tribes in Eritrea. The firm belief that the colonies in Italian Africa were populated by savages to be dominated obviously underlies the original idea of the superiority of the white race over the black race and had a decisive impact on colonial criminal law, conceived as a sort of law of a *permanent exception*.[5]

Meanwhile, the possibility of a new kind of criminal law, completely different from that in force in Italy, had been stated by some Italian legal scholars like Ugo Conti. The latter, pupil of Luigi Lucchini, following an eclectic approach,[6] declared that the indigenous people were a subject of study for a legal science separated from the others and defined as "colonial penal law". This was an integrated and interdisciplinary criminal law or "an independent, comprehensive, particularly strong legal science with biological and sociological traits: the criminal legal science" in which were intertwined "anthropology, psychology and social psychology, ethnography in relation to law and its history, the science of religions, the science of customs, social morality, etc".[7]

These approaches were particularly evident in Eritrea, in a historical phase that for Italian legal science was characterised by great changes.[8] In particular, the Zanardelli Code approved in 1889 had resulted in the adoption of a liberal code in Italy, with a significant reduction in the number of crimes and the abolition of the death penalty. Consequently, the Italian penal law was immediately perceived not suitable for Eritrean people, not only due to the obstacle to imposing written codes instead of the indigenous customary law. Moreover, there was underlined the supposed impossibility to use legal concepts and abstract categories, imagined for a *superior* society, also for colonised people, frequently represented as belonging to *inferior* races with savage and immoral customs.

Cesare Lombroso's proposal and the Italian criminal law debate

The debate on criminal responsibility in the colonies occurred at a crucial stage for Italian legal science. The birth of the Positivist School took place from the second half of the nineteenth century, putting in crisis what seemed, from Beccaria onwards, to be unshakable certainties in the criminal legal field, starting from a system built on the concept of free will and a conception of mental insanity based on it. In other words, the problem was: why should we punish those who have not consciously and really chosen to commit a crime?

More specifically, Lombroso came to deny the existence of free will because he was so strongly influenced by scientific positivism: believing in a "religion of the facts", he attempted to certify scientific differences not only between criminals and "normal" people,[9] but also between different types of criminals.[10]

The most emblematic example of this belief is provided by the famous "discovery"[11] attributed to Lombroso of the "median occipital fossa" in the skull of Giuseppe Villella, a 70-year-old brigand from Calabria under suspicion of robbery, who died in prison. In 1872, during a "cold grey November morning" (as his daughter, Gina Lombroso, remembered it),[12] while he was examining the skull, Lombroso found a strange anomaly: on the occipital part, where the spine would normally be found on a human skull, there was instead a distinct depression that he called the median occipital fossa.[13] This anomaly, which Lombroso described as the "birth certificate"[14] of criminal anthropology, explained the existence of crime through atavism,[15] (from Latin *atavus*, or ancestor), coinciding with the return to an ancestral and lower stage of evolution, and becoming the emblem of a new legislative framework designed to frame a real science of the abnormal. After that, Lombroso theorised the inborn physical and psychological characteristics of criminals, asserting that a criminal was, since birth, "a miserable variety of man ... more pathological than the insane".[16] In sum, this was the premise of his theory of the born criminal.

Obviously, Lombroso's thesis had an impact on the legal science of his time; with the principal purpose of making criminal law a real social science, disengaging from the "a priori legal syllogistic system",[17] the Positivist School was developed in Italy in the nineteenth century against the Enlightenment rationalism of criminal law, represented by the various doctrinal currents generically called the Classical School. This School considered crime to be a mere consequence of the breach of a legal rule, and as an event arising from the free and voluntary human being's choice. The Positivist School was strenuously opposed to this abstract and unhistorical rationalism, which led to an "immutable" law separated from context, the Positivists' primary intention being not only to deny scientifically the existence of free will, but also to expunge any metaphysical element from the criminal justice system, thereby delivering "law in real life".[18]

The main impact of the Positivist School was on the questions relating to the philosophical foundations of criminal responsibility, and the relationship between crime and punishment. It is informative to consider the ensuing intense debate over free will,[19] which involved the Classical School of Francesco Carrara, who firmly proclaimed the existence of human freedom, as opposed to the Positivist School of Cesare Lombroso, who denied it.

Since the existence of free will was denied, the criminal act was consequently, in the eyes of Lombroso, "an unfortunate natural production, a form of disease",[20] which as such deserved *care and segregation*, rather than *punishment and revenge*. An improvement in the criminal justice system and in the fight against crime in the community (that had become an illusory game in which criminality was becoming ever stronger) could therefore be achieved, according to Lombroso, only if morality were thrown down from "the frail altar of free will, to which it was elevated by metaphysicians".[21] In particular, according to the most eminent pupil of Lombroso, Enrico Ferri, criminal law would have to be reformed on the basis of the following guidelines: (a) replacing individual liability (*imputabilità*) with a form of "social responsibility" (released from the concept of free will); (b) redefining the purpose of punishment, not as compensation but as a special preventive measure in defence of society; (c) individualising punishment and eliminating the maximum sentence prescribed by law; (d) recognising the importance of the criminal, instead of the abstract crime.

In Eritrea: a two-speed criminal law?

The "colonial situation" became, especially for the followers of the Positivist School, a real laboratory in which to experiment solutions for subjugating defenceless populations that would otherwise have been unacceptable in the homeland context.

The Italian colonial experience in the Horn of Africa officially began in 1882, when there was established the transfer to the Italian State of "private property" of all the territories of the Bay of Assab, which Giuseppe Sapeto had purchased in 1869 by some local bosses, on behalf of the shipowner Raffaele Rubattino of the Colonial Company.[22] This is the first territorial area of the Eritrean colony, which was established in 1890.[23]

After the *civilising mission*[24] that had often concealed imperialistic and exploitative policies of the first colonial period of the sixteenth and seventeenth centuries, this second expansionist phase (eighteenth–nineteenth centuries), which also involved Italy, included the export not only of religious beliefs, but also cultural. But this project also hid the view that colonised peoples were not *subjects* but *objects* of the law applied to them.[25] We can therefore ask ourselves what kind of criminal law to apply and, above all, how to assess the criminal responsibility of these peoples and how to punish their crimes. If the Zanardelli Code had been issued "too early"[26] to adopt the new theories of the Positivist School, as Lombroso complained, the Ferri Project inevitably arrived too late. In other words, after the resounding defeat of the Positivist School in the 1889 Zanardelli Code, which was clearly liberal and more responsive to theories supported by the Classical School, the Colonial Penal legislation seemed the first real opportunity to see Lombroso's theories applied to a criminal law in force.

Regardless the "philanthropic ideals"[27] on colonialism in Eritrea manifested by some intellectuals and politicians in Italy, we must not forget that behind the paternalistic spirit of the Western countries, there was, indeed, a strong feeling of cultural and racial superiority, which qualified Eritreans not only inferior but also "not-adults" and, as such, to be subdued. However, the need to develop a different law suitable for the "savage" populations of Eritrea seems to clash with the liberal and Enlightenment values of the legal system adopted in Italy.

The Italian's laws were not applied in Eritrea for several reasons: first, it was considered too advanced with respect to the barbaric conditions of the indigenous populations, and too ineffective and moderate with respect to the deviance of these territories. Therefore, the first Eritrean penal code, although formally approved in 1908, never entered into force as it was not translated into Arabic or Amharic. Furthermore, the penal code clashed with a reality of customary law present in African territories.

In the absence of a written and universally accepted law, Italy carried out a type of criminal justice entirely different from that practiced in the motherland. Under the sign of emergency, all the victories of liberal criminal law were forgotten in favour of a penal policy for natives that disrupted the system of penalties and the concept of mental insanity. More specifically, there were compressed judicial guarantees and the legal principles adopted in the Italian penal code (i.e. certainty, and proportionality of punishment). The result was a real *two-speed criminal law* applied by the "brave colonial magistrates":[28] guaranteeing and liberal penal justice for compatriots and highly repressive penal law and strict penalties for the natives.

This authoritarian trait was particularly significant in relation to the evaluation of the criminal responsibility of *savage people*[29] firmly convinced not only that their psychic condition was different from that of civilised peoples but also that "in black Africa, the punishment sanctioned for the various crimes committed by the natives, had to take into account a particular objective situation that affected their *imputability*".[30]

From responsibility to the *infantilisation* of indigenous people

Faced with the crime of the "savage", therefore, the Italian colonial magistrates adopted three different possible solutions to decide on criminal responsibility. First, the Eritrean judges avoided resorting to psychiatric categories, choosing to force, from a technical–legal point of view, the concept of wilful misconduct or malicious intent (*dolo*) and its possible lack, as provided for by article 45 of the Zanardelli Penal Code. Keeping in mind the notion of *mens rea*, it is believed that the indigenous people were not responsible for the crimes committed because, beyond the voluntary nature of their commission, "the crimes of savages [should] be considered more antisocial and therefore to be subjected to a special preventive treatment, which is anti-juridical, as they lack the essential extreme of intentionality".[31]

In other words, the perceived backwardness of the subjects would have affected the wilful element that guided the action as in the decision assessed by the Asmara Court of Assizes, *Gabrù v. Macrù* (President and compiler D'Amelio) of 4 December 1905, where it is observed that sometimes "the malicious intention exists, but it is darkened, abnormal, or bound by a morbid or irresistible impulse" and, at other times "it is completely lacking".[32] However, this was not a determined approach, since the magistrates were not able to deny, at least technically, that the wilfulness or the specific malicious intent in murder (*animus necandi*) still existed even when the hand of the murderer was guided by *savage* reasons falling "into the orbit of inherited beliefs, fanaticisms and prejudices".[33] In other words, according to the judges, these kinds of homicides, even originated by superstitions or prejudices, were nevertheless committed with malice.

Noting the inadequacy of the thesis of the lack of malicious intent or conscious intentionality, the judges in Eritrea chose the path of emphasising total or partial mental insanity. Some decisions established that in cases of "crimes perpetrated by savages for savage ethnic stimuli, the intelligence is wholly or partly deficient; the brain is darkened by old prejudices [...] and lacking in moral ideas".[34]

Thus, for instance, partial mental insanity has been used by various decisions, including the judgment of 21 August 1906, *Alfai v. Sottu*, to overcome an important problem: applying "the most advanced code in the world to completely savage people".[35] However, with the ruling of 28 October 1902 (*Ismail Abubaker and others*), there was stated the impossibility to confuse the incivility of an entire people with the partial mental insanity, which must refer to an individual pathological condition. In this case, however, it was decided that the accused was anyway not responsible since "the state of slavery in which he lived from birth [...] and of having had no other will than that of the master" had caused "an arrest of his psychic development" making him "irresponsible, according to art. 45 cod. pen., of criminal acts committed in obedience to an order from the master, against which he did not know how to rebel".[36]

Therefore, the judges in Eritrea attempted to solve the problem of criminal responsibility from another point of view: where it was not possible to invoke the total or partial mental insanity, the judges relied on the non-conformity of the crime of the savages. This was especially applied in certain tribes (i.e. Cunama) with a supposed different conception of the crime and the punishment due to the intrinsic "moral and social conditions" of the natives as well as their "ethnic characteristics". In other words, where a pathological condition could not be glimpsed, there was a reference to the "lack of discernment", the ability, even in a physiological condition, "to distinguish good from evil".[37] Specifically, it was found that the social status of the Baza tribe, as well as in all the "primitive people",[38] entailed the recognition in them of "a very limited discernment like that of children".[39]

In this regard, for their crimes, the "savages" have been considered eternal children and equated, for the purposes of responsibility, with minors under the age of 14 who can act with or without *discernment*.[40] For the psychiatry of the time, this was a *physiological* and *not a pathological* condition relating to the rational faculties in which intelligence, free will, and feeling must be included.

This approach, also shared by Judge Mariano d'Amelio, was strongly affected by the dictates of the Positivist School and the idea of a substantial coincidence between born criminal and savage, whose mental capacity could even be compared to that of a child. The administration of justice in Eritrea, more than adopting theses of colonial psychiatry (think of what were considered typical indigenous diseases such as cases of "religious paranoia", "hysteria or self-suggestion for possession", or "nervous contagion"), chose to expand the areas of physiological mental incapacity to bring the condition of the savage back to that of the minor.

There was a real *infantilisation* of the indigenous people. However, the paternalistic perfective adopted in Eritrea did not lead towards a model of mild criminal justice. In other words, comparing an indigenous person to a minor should have involved a model of justice inspired by principles of re-education of the convict. Traditionally, in fact, juvenile criminal justice provides for lighter sentences than those provided for adults. In the Eritrean justice system, paradoxically, an opposite result was reached.

What kind of punishment for "irresponsible people"?

Despite the *infantilisation* process, criminal justice was administered in the Italian overseas in an extremely repressive way. For example, the death penalty was retained for the purpose of general intimidation. The motivation was again linked to concepts of racial superiority/inferiority in the belief that these populations considered savage and primitive, with their limited cognitive abilities, could understand only force and violence. For the same reason, corporal punishments were maintained in the Eritrean colony,[41] by then abandoned in the motherland. For example, the maintenance of corporal punishments in the form of *curbasciate* (flogging) was justified by the judge of the Court of Appeal of Asmara, Ranieri Falcone, based on an alleged "less painful sensitivity of the natives",[42] as well as a greater repressive efficacy.

To this was added the possibility of applying the *indeterminate sentence* along the lines of the traditional indigenous penalty called *taazir*[43] and a model of punishment based on *dangerousness* rather than *imputability*.

The *indeterminate sentence*,[44] in fact, was a type of penalty with non-predefined outlines for which the judge had to evaluate the guilt of the accused, remaining entrusted with the task of specifying its duration[45] to the institution of execution of the sentence.[46] This approach had already introduced by the well-known German psychiatrist Emil Kräpelin in his provocative writings entitled *The Abolition of the Measure of Punishment*, according to which "the science of crime" and consequently also criminal justice, should "focus less on the crime and more on the criminal man".[47] According to another approach, the idea of indeterminacy of the sentence entailed greater discretion for the judge who could even choose, as Mariano D'Amelio underlined, "among the penalties of arrest, fine and flogging, the one that he considered most suited to personal conditions of the accused".[48]

In both approaches to the *indeterminate sentence*, there was however an evident reference to what was theorised by the Positivist School of criminal law.[49] It is no coincidence that the new Eritrean criminal law code in 1908, which never came into force, was presented in parliament by one of the followers of this school, Raffaele Garofalo. The latter, on that occasion, reiterating the need for a criminal law based on "unequal treatment"[50] between Italians and indigenous people, supported the introduction of the obligation, in the new code, to "be locked up in a criminal asylum or in another institution" in case of recognised irresponsibility due to mental insanity, with the consequent impossibility of "being definitively released only when judged *harmless*".[51]

This obligation, in the eyes of Garofalo, was required due a specific reason:

> in a simpler population than ours, and in which there is no idea of the extent that psychiatry has given to the concept of madness, it would make a very strange impression, and it would seem an inexplicable thing, the liberation of a criminal from any bond. Common sense, which is not lacking in African people, although less civilized than

ours, suggests that if there is an irresponsible due insanity defence, if not punished, he must at least be restrained.[52]

Conclusion

In conclusion, we must ask ourselves whether what happens in the Italian colonies can be considered a posthumous victory of Lombroso and his school which, failing to break through its theses in liberal Italy, can finally find a sequel here. Beyond Garofalo's approach, who has always been attested to reactionary and authoritarian positions, to the point of being considered the most conservative wing of the Positivist School, overseas magistrates had been more Lombrosian than Lombroso himself.

It is a simplistic reading of Lombroso's theories to reduce his work excessively and solely to the attempt to identify criminals through their external aspects or atavism. The "criminal man" imagined by Lombroso was more complex and multi-faceted than a "primitive man", or a sort of walking museum piece. Indeed, considering Lombroso's work on the whole, we see that atavism constituted a milestone in his research, but it was not the ultimate solution to the ambitious question about the origins of crime. By analysing the structure of *Criminal Man*, several theories on the explanation of crime have been gradually refined, according to clinical case studies that range from the initial thesis of the born criminal as a savage, to the theory of the political criminal and *mattoid* (an ambivalent kind of deviance between genius and insanity), and "occasional criminals", defined *criminaloids*. In addition, Lombrosian research focused not only on criminal faces or their cranial shapes, as is usually thought, but also on all physical and psychological characteristics, eventually including their language, both verbal (slang) and body (tattoos), and even on their artefacts. He even analysed several biographies of great writers, artists, politicians, and poets, with the aim of understanding the "secret of deviance", or rather, why some people emerged from the quiet pathways of so-called "normality", for either negative (criminal) or positive (men of genius) reasons.

The explanation of crime proposed by Lombroso was not in fact crystallised in a theory but was constituted instead by a composite picture in which the causes of criminal agency, while often having a biological substrate, overlapped, and intersected each other: to atavism was added moral insanity and epilepsy, giving rise to a multi-faceted explanation of crime.[53]

Furthermore, despite the explanation for biological crime in which even the ethnic-racial factor could play a role, the latter was not prominent in the reflection of Lombroso who, like other scientists of the time, automatically assumed the existence of "white and coloured" races without embracing the scientific racism prone to the *hygiene of the races* like Gobineau and Chamberlain, considered by the followers of the Positivist School as a "fanatic"[54] attitude. At the same time, as has been observed, "Lombroso did not legitimize the racist uses of his theories, to which, on the contrary, he constantly accompanied reform proposals in the economic and social field, however often vague, unrealistic or even misleading".[55]

As evidence of this, we add the anti-colonial character of Lombroso who on several occasions was critical of the violent colonial policy of the Kingdom of Italy. Lombroso's words in this regard are significant, where he defined "absolutely barbaric"[56] colonial politics and the attempt to subjugate entire peoples through bloody wars.[57] This could be said to be one of the many contradictions that crossed the thought and work of Lombroso, an atheist and Jewish socialist in favour of capital punishment, theoretician of the inferiority of women and a convinced supporter of the intellectual work of his daughters, and so on.

In particular, the colonial judges took from the Positivist tradition only what they needed, eliminating all progressive and secularised instances and emphasising concepts and theories in an exclusively repressive way, to create with every available means a new kind of criminal justice suited to the Italian colonialism marked by the model of the *enemy criminal law*.

Specifically, the choices made in the Italian colonies were certainly the fertile ground for experimenting with a repressive and authoritarian right or a sort of "try-out" of what would later emerge in Italy with the advent of the fascist regime. It is no coincidence that Mariano d'Amelio, the undisputed protagonist of colonial criminal justice, became one of the most influential judges under the Fascist regime.[58] Shortly thereafter, with the advent of the fascist regime,[59] true or presumed mental diseases (from *political mania* to paranoia passing through hysteria) were used to intern in asylums many political opponents of the regime. In a similar vein, a racist and colonialist ideology created the conditions for the adoption a real "racial law".[60]

Notes

1 On this topic, for a comparative approach, see recently, the special issue on S Falconieri (ed), "Droit et Folie en Situation Colonial: Perspectives Impériales Comparées (xixe-xxe siècle)", *Clio@Themis*, vol. 23 (2022), available online: https://journals.openedition.org/cliothemis/2555.
2 A Ravizza, *Cenni di Giurisprudenza Penale Eritrea*, in *Studi in Onore di Mariano d'Amelio* (Foro Italiano: Rome, 3rd edn, 1933), p.202.
3 Cf. C Giorgi, "Magistrati d'Oltremare", *Studi Storici*, vol. 51, no. 4 (2010), p.856.
4 Ravizza, *Cenni di Giurisprudenza Penale Eritrea*, p.202.
5 L Martone, *Diritto d'Oltremare: Legge e Ordine per le Colonie del Regno d'Italia* (Giuffrè: Milano, 2008), p.3.
6 Cf. A Mazzacane, "Conti Sinibaldi, Ugo" (entry), in *Dizionario Biografico degli Italiani*, 1983, 28, available online: www.treccani.it/enciclopedia/ugo-conti-sinibaldi_%28Dizionario-Biografico%29/.
7 U Conti, *Diritto Penale Coloniale: Linee Generali*, extract from the journal '*Rivista Penale*', 1910, LXXII, IV. (Utet: Turin, 1910), p.5.
8 Obviously, in this epoch the problem of penal reform was dealt not only by Italy but also by the most important Western countries. On this topic see M Pifferi, *Reinventing Punishment: A Comparative History of Criminology and Penology in the Nineteenth and Twentieth Centuries* (Oxford University Press: Oxford, 2016).
9 C Lombroso, *L'uomo Delinquente in Rapporto All'antropologia, Giurisprudenza e alle Discipline Carcerarie: Aggiuntavi la Teoria della Tutela Penale del Prof. Avv. F. Poletti* (Bocca: Turin, 2nd edn, 1878), p.50.
10 C Lombroso, *L'Uomo Delinquente in Rapporto All'antropologia, alla Giurisprudenza ed alle Discipline Carcerarie* (Bocca: Turin, 5th edn, 1896), vol I, pp.274–278.
11 "This was not merely an idea, but a revelation": C Lombroso, "Introduction", in G Lombroso Ferrero (ed), *Criminal Man, according to the Classification of Cesare Lombroso* (GP Putnam's Sons: New York, 1911), p.xiv.
12 G Lombroso Ferrero, *Criminal Man According to the Classification of Cesare Lombroso* (GP Putnam's Sons: New York, 1911), p.15.
13 On the discovery of Villella's fossa, see especially M Renneville, "Un Cranio che fa Luce? Il Racconto della Scoperta dell'Atavismo Criminale", in S Montaldo & P Tappero (eds), *Il Museo di Antropologia Criminale Cesare Lombroso* (Utet: Turin, 2009), pp.107–112.
14 C Lombroso, "Discours d'Ouverture au VI Congrés d'Anthropologie Criminelle", in *Comptes-rendus du VI Congrès International d'Anthropologie Criminelle: Turin, 28 avril-3 mai 1906* (Bocca: Turin, 1908), p.6.
15 See R Villa, *Il Deviante e i suoi Segni: Lombroso e la Nascita dell'Antropologia Criminale* (FrancoAngeli: Milan, 1985), pp.144–149.

16 C Lombroso, "Esistenza di una Fossa Occipitale Mediana nel Cranio di un Delinquente", (1871) 1 *Rendiconti del Reale Istituto Lombardo di Scienze e Lettere* 41.
17 C Lombroso, E Ferri, R Garofalo, & G Fioretti, *Polemica in Difesa Della Scuola Criminale Positiva* (Zanichelli: Bologna, 1886), p.I.
18 U Spirito, *Storia del Diritto Penale Italiano da Cesare Beccaria ai Giorni Nostri* (Sansoni: Florence, 3rd edn 1974), p.25.
19 See especially E Musumeci, *Cesare Lombroso e le Neuroscienze: un Parricidio Mancato: Devianza, Libero Arbitrio, Imputabilità tra Antiche Chimere ed Inediti Scenari* (FrancoAngeli: Milan, 2012), pp.151–173.
20 C Lombroso, "Prefazione del Traduttore", in J Moleschott (ed), *La Circolazione della Vita. Lettere Fisiologiche di Jac: Moleschott in Risposta alle Lettere Chimiche di Liebig, traduzione sulla quarta edizione tedesca pubblicata con consenso dell'autore dal Prof. Cesare Lombroso* (Brigola: Milan, 1869), p.ix.
21 Lombroso, "Prefazione del traduttore", p.ix.
22 Cf. N Labanca, *Oltremare: Storia dell'Espansione Coloniale Italiana* (Il Mulino: Bologna, 2002).
23 The colonisation of Eritrea took place over the course of about sixty years and ended in 1941 with the passage of the territories under Italian dominion under the control of the military administration (British Military Administration of Eritrea) after the African defeats of Italy during the Second World War.
24 See I Rosoni, *La Colonia Eritrea: La Prima Amministrazione Coloniale Italiana (1880-1912)* (Eum: Macerata, 2006), pp.27–28.
25 In particular, "in the colonial context, the term *subjects* had a meaning of removal of the political subjectivity of the colonized, who were 'subjects' in the exclusively negative sense of the term, i.e. only as *subjected*": L Martone, "Il Diritto Coloniale" (entry), in *Enciclopedia Treccani: Il Contributo Italiano alla Storia del Pensiero: Diritto* (Istituto dell'Enciclopedia Treccani: Rome, 2012) available online: www.treccani.it/enciclopedia/il-diritto-coloniale_%28Il-Contributo-italiano-alla-storia-del-Pensiero:-Diritto%29/.
26 C Lombroso, "Troppo presto", in C Lombroso, A Berenini, & V Rossi (eds), *Appunti al Nuovo Codice Penale* (Bocca: Torino, 2nd edn, 1889).
27 Cf. O De Napoli, "Colonialism through penal deportation in the Italian political and legal debate: from the Unification to the beginning of the colonial enterprise", *Quaderni Fiorentini per la Storia del Pensiero Giuridico Moderno*, vol. 49, no. 1 (2020), p.209.
28 Cf. L Martone, *Giustizia coloniale: Modelli e Prassi Penale per i Sudditi d'Africa dall'Età Giolittiana al Fascismo* (Jovene: Naples, 2002), p.22.
29 Martone, *Diritto d'Oltremare*, p.58.
30 Martone, *Diritto d'Oltremare*, p.58.
31 Ravizza, *Cenni di Giurisprudenza Penale Eritrea*, p.204.
32 Ravizza, *Cenni di Giurisprudenza Penale Eritrea*, p.204.
33 Ravizza, *Cenni di Giurisprudenza Penale Eritrea*, p.204.
34 Ravizza, *Cenni di Giurisprudenza Penale Eritrea*, p.205.
35 Ravizza, *Cenni di Giurisprudenza Penale Eritrea*, p.205.
36 A Ravizza, "L'Ordinamento Legislativo della Colonia Eritrea", *Rivista Penale*, vol. LXXX, (1914), pp.5–53.
37 Ravizza, *Cenni di Giurisprudenza Penale Eritrea*, p.206.
38 Ravizza, *Cenni di Giurisprudenza Penale Eritrea*, p.206.
39 *Gaia v. Issa*, Asmara Court of Assizes, 20 May 1905.
40 On this category see G Pace Gravina, *Il Discernimento dei Fanciulli: Ricerche sulla Imputabilità dei Minori nella Cultura Giuridica Moderna* (Giappichelli: Turin, 2000), and more recently, G Pace Gravina, "'A-t-on, dans un âge si tendre, une volonté certaine?': "dubbi" e "certezze" sull'imputabilità minorile tra Otto e Novecento", *Quaderno di Storia del Penale e della Giustizia*, no. 2 (2020), pp.167–176.
41 F Martini, *Allegati alla Relazione sulla Colonia Eritrea* (Tip. Camera dei Deputati: Rome, 1913), vol II, p.215.
42 R Falcone, *Disegno di Codice Penale da Pubblicarsi nella Colonia Eritrea, con le Modificazioni Disposte dall'Articolo 2 della legge 24 Maggio 1903: Relazione sul Libro Primo*, in *Relazione sulla Colonia Eritrea di Ferdinando Martini*, Allegato 29 (Tip. Camera dei Deputati: Rome, 1913), p.613.

43 Cf. A Ravizza, "Pena Indeterminata ed Individualizzazione di Pena nel Diritto Indigeno Eritreo", *La Scuola Positiva*, vol. V, no. 4 (1914), p.295.
44 On the dilemmas of the *indeterminate sentence*, see especially M Pifferi, *L'Individualizzazione della Pena: Difesa Sociale e Crisi della Legalità Penale tra Otto e Novecento* (Giuffré: Milan, 2013), pp.30–33.
45 Cf. A Mazzacane, *Oltremare: Diritto e Istituzione dal Colonialismo all'Età Postcoloniale* (Cuen: Naples, 2006), p.264.
46 Ravizza, "Pena indeterminata", p.294.
47 Ravizza, "Pena indeterminata", p.293.
48 M D'Amelio, "Di Alcuni Caratteri della Legislazione in Libia", *La Scuola Positiva*, vol. V (1914), pp. 9–10.
49 For a comparative approach on this issue, see recently M Pifferi (ed), *The Limits of Criminological Positivism: The Movement for Criminal Law Reform in the West, 1870-1940*, (Routledge: Abingdon-New York, 2022).
50 R Garofalo, "Il Codice Penale della Colonia Eritrea", *Rivista Coloniale*, vol. VI (1909), p.139.
51 Garofalo, "Il Codice Penale della Colonia Eritrea", p.138.
52 Garofalo, "Il Codice Penale della Colonia Eritrea", p.138.
53 See also M Gibson, *Born to Crime. Cesare Lombroso and the Origins of Biological Criminology* (Praeger: Westport CT, 2002), p.ix.
54 H Kurella, "L'Importanza dell'Opera di Cesare Lombroso nella Sociologia", in *L'Opera di Cesare Lombroso nella Scienza e nelle sue Applicazioni* (Bocca: Turin, 1908), p.318.
55 M Nani, "Lombroso e le Razze", in S Montaldo & P Tappero (eds), *Cesare Lombroso Cento Anni Dopo* (Utet: Turin, 2009), p.174.
56 C Lombroso, *Il Momento Attuale* (Casa Editrice Moderna: Milan, 1903), p.28.
57 Cf. L Sansone, *La Galassia Lombroso* (Laterza: Rome-Bari, 2022), pp.63–64.
58 On the nature of the fascist criminal justice, see S Skinner (ed), *Fascism and Criminal Law: History, Theory, Continuity* (Hart: Oxford-Portland, 2015), and L Lacchè (ed), *Il Diritto del Duce: Giustizia e Repressione nell'Italia Fascista* (Donzelli: Rome, 2015).
59 See M Petracci, *I Matti del Duce: Manicomi e Repressione Politica nell'Italia Fascista* (Donzelli: Rome, 2014).
60 See S Falconieri, *La legge della Razza: Strategie e Luoghi del Discorso Giuridico Fascista* (Il Mulino: Bologna, 2012).

References

Books and book chapters

Conti U, *Diritto Penale Coloniale: Linee Generali*, extract from the journal 'Rivista Penale', 1910, LXXII, IV. (Utet: Turin,1910).
Falconieri S, *La Legge della Razza: Strategie e Luoghi del Discorso Giuridico Fascista* (Il Mulino: Bologna, 2012).
Gibson M, *Born to Crime. Cesare Lombroso and the Origins of Biological Criminology* (Praeger: Westport CT, 2002).
Kurella H, *L'importanza dell'Opera di Cesare Lombroso nella Sociologia*, in Amadei G. et al. (ed), *L'Opera di Cesare Lombroso nella Scienza e nelle sue Applicazioni* (Bocca: Turin, 1908).
Labanca N, *Oltremare:Storia dell'Espansione Coloniale Italiana* (Il Mulino: Bologna, 2002).
Lacchè L (ed), *Il Diritto del Duce: Giustizia e Repressione nell'Italia Fascista* (Donzelli: Rome, 2015).
Lombroso C, "Introduction", in Lombroso Ferrero G (ed), *Criminal Man, According to the Classification of Cesare Lombroso* (GP Putnam's Sons: New York, 1911).
Lombroso C, "Prefazione del traduttore", in Moleschott J (ed), *La circolazione della vita. Lettere fisiologiche di Jac: Moleschott in risposta alle lettere chimiche di Liebig, traduzione sulla quarta edizione tedesca pubblicata con consenso dell'autore dal Prof. Cesare Lombroso* (Brigola: Milan, 1869).
Lombroso C, "Troppo Presto", in Lombroso C, Berenini A, & Rossi V (eds), *Appunti al Nuovo Codice Penale* (Bocca: Torino, 2nd edn,1889).
Lombroso C, *L'Uomo Delinquente in Rapporto all'Antropologia, alla Giurisprudenza ed alle Discipline Carcerarie* (Bocca: Turin, 5th edn, 1896).

Lombroso C, *L'Uomo Delinquente in Rapporto all'Antropologia, Giurisprudenza e alle Discipline Carcerarie: Aggiuntavi la Teoria della Tutela Penale del Prof. Avv. F. Poletti* (Bocca: Turin, 2nd edn, 1878).
Lombroso C, Ferri E, Garofalo R, & Fioretti G, *Polemica in Difesa della Scuola Criminale Positiva* (Zanichelli: Bologna, 1886).
Lombroso Ferrero G, *Criminal Man According to the Classification of Cesare Lombroso* (The Knickerbocker Press: New York, 1911).
Martini F, *Allegati alla Relazione sulla Colonia Eritrea* (Tip. Camera dei Deputati: Rome, 1913).
Martone L, *Diritto d'Oltremare: Legge e Ordine per le Colonie del Regno d'Italia* (Giuffrè: Milano, 2008).
Martone L, *Giustizia Coloniale: Modelli e Prassi Penale per i Sudditi d'Africa dall'Età Giolittiana al Fascismo* (Jovene: Naples, 2002).
Mazzacane A, *Oltremare: Diritto e Istituzione dal Colonialismo all'Età Postcoloniale*, (Cuen: Naples, 2006).
Musumeci E, *Cesare Lombroso e le neuroscienze: un parricidio mancato. Devianza, libero arbitrio, imputabilità tra antiche chimere ed inediti scenari* (FrancoAngeli: Milan, 2012).
Nani M, "Lombroso e le razze", in Montaldo S & Tappero P (eds), *Cesare Lombroso cento anni dopo* (Utet: Turin, 2009).
Pace Gravina G, *Il Discernimento dei Fanciulli: Ricerche sulla Imputabilità dei Minori nella Cultura Giuridica Moderna* (Giappichelli: Turin, 2000).
Petracci M, *I Matti del Duce: Manicomi e Repressione Politica nell'Italia Fascista* (Donzelli: Rome, 2014).
Pifferi M (ed), *The Limits of Criminological Positivism: The Movement for Criminal Law Reform in the West, 1870–1940* (Routledge: Abingdon & New York, 2022).
Pifferi M, *L'Individualizzazione della Pena: Difesa Sociale e Crisi della Legalità Penale tra Otto e Novecento* (Giuffré: Milan, 2013).
Pifferi M, *Reinventing Punishment: A Comparative History of Criminology and Penology in the Nineteenth and Twentieth Centuries* (Oxford University Press: Oxford, 2016).
Ravizza A, *Cenni di Giurisprudenza Penale Eritrea*, in *Studi in onore di Mariano d'Amelio* (Foro Italiano: Rome, 1933), vol. III.
Renneville M, 'Un Cranio che fa Luce? Il Racconto della Scoperta dell'Atavismo Criminale', in Montaldo S & Tappero P (eds), *Il Museo di Antropologia criminale Cesare Lombroso* (Utet: Turin, 2009).
Rosoni I, *La Colonia Eritrea. La Prima Amministrazione Coloniale Italiana (1880–1912)* (Eum: Macerata, 2006).
Sansone L, *La Galassia Lombroso* (Laterza: Rome-Bari, 2022).
Skinner S (ed), *Fascism and Criminal Law: History, Theory, Continuity* (Hart: Oxford-Portland, 2015).
Spirito U, *Storia del Diritto Penale Italiano da Cesare Beccaria ai Giorni Nostri* (Sansoni: Florence, 3rd edn, 1974).
Villa R, *Il Deviante e i suoi Segni: Lombroso e la Nascita dell'Antropologia Criminale* (FrancoAngeli: Milan, 1985).

Journal articles

D'Amelio M, "Di Alcuni Caratteri della Legislazione in Libia", *La Scuola Positiva*, vol. V (1914), pp.9–22.
De Napoli O, "Colonialism through Penal Deportation in the Italian Political and Legal Debate: from the Unification to the Beginning of the Colonial Enterprise", *Quaderni Fiorentini per la Storia del Pensiero Giuridico Moderno*, vol. 49 (2020), pp.185–220.
Falconieri S (ed), "Droit et Folie en Situation Colonial: Perspectives Impériales Comparées (xixe-xxe siècle)", *Clio@Themis*, vol. 23 (2022), available at: www.journals.openedition.org/cliothemis/2555
Garofalo R, "Il Codice Penale della Colonia Eritrea", *Rivista Coloniale*, vol. VI (1909), p.139.
Giorgi C, "Magistrati d'Oltremare", *Studi Storici*, vol. 51, no. 4 (2010), pp.855–879.
Lombroso C, "Discours d'Ouverture au VI Congrés d'Anthropologie Criminelle", in Bureau du Secrétariat - Institut de Médecine Legal Turin, Comptes-rendus du VI Congrès International d'Anthropologie Criminelle : Turin, 28 avril-3 mai 1906 (Bocca : Turin, 1908), pp.XXXI-XXXVI.

Lombroso C, "Esistenza di una Fossa Occipitale Mediana nel Cranio di un Delinquente", *Rendiconti del Reale Istituto Lombardo di Scienze e Lettere*, vol. IV, no. II, part. I, (1371), pp.37–41.

Pace Gravina G, "'A-t-on, dans un âge si tendre, une volonté certaine?': "dubbi" e "certezze" sull'imputabilità minorile tra Otto e Novecento", *Quaderno di Storia del Penale e della Giustizia*, vol. 2 (2020), pp.167–176.

Ravizza A, "L'ordinamento legislativo della colonia eritrea", *Rivista Penale*, vol. LXXX, (1914), pp.5–53.

Ravizza A, "Pena indeterminata ed individualizzazione di pena nel diritto indigeno eritreo", *La Scuola Positiva*, vol. V, no. 4 (1914), pp.293–302.

Encyclopaedia entries

Martone L, "Il Diritto Coloniale" (entry), in *Enciclopedia Treccani. Il Contributo Italiano alla Storia del Pensiero: Diritto* (Istituto dell'Enciclopedia Treccani: Rome, 2012), available at: www.treccani.it/enciclopedia/il-diritto-coloniale_%28Il-Contributo-italiano-alla-storia-del-Pensiero:-Diritto%29/

Mazzacane A, "Conti Sinibaldi, Ugo" (entry), in *Dizionario Biografico degli Italiani*, 1983, 28, available at: www.treccani.it/enciclopedia/ugo-conti-sinibaldi_%28Dizionario-Biografico%29/

9

ON DISPOSITIONAL–RELATIONAL RESPONSIBILITY

From Punishment to Reconciliation

Alan Norrie and Amanda Wilson

For a critical account of criminal responsibility

We wish to challenge the orthodox account of criminal responsibility and, through its immanent critique, to offer a theoretical and practical alternative. Models of responsibility give form to the overall aims and practices of the criminal justice system and different models reflect these differently. The dominant model of crime, blame, and punishment entails a view of the responsible individual organised around a person's choice, capacity, or character. The resulting "penal equation" (crime plus responsibility equals punishment) involves a weak, attributional responsibility concept that is at odds with the dispositional–relational model we propose. In holding a person responsible, and subject to blame and punishment, orthodox criminal responsibility produces a "punctualist" or "actualist" (a momentary) account of the act and actor that short-circuits the human capacity for transformative change at the interconnected levels of the individual and the social. Dispositional–relational responsibility, by contrast, nurtures both by showing the psychological depth, social relationality, and possibilities for change that accompany a person taking responsibility for past actions.

We do not argue for such a model as a better way of rationalising existing punishment practices but rather as a reason to move away from these as the dominant form of criminal justice. Processes involving restoration and reconciliation suggest other ways of addressing violation that lead to real personal responsibility for acts and to constructive change in the social world. The two are fundamentally interconnected and not reducible to one or the other. We see responsibility complexly as both dispositional and relational and as pressing for different legal responses than those connected with justifying punishment. A dispositional–relational model of responsibility takes us away from standard legal devices involving individual culpability, blame, and holding a person responsible.

We start with how the philosophical question of responsibility is dealt with generally in the legal field. An individual's choice, character, or capacity constitutes variously the personal quality that inheres in that individual and licenses blame and punishment. We find none of these models for attributing responsibility convincing because they are all based on attributing blame to an individual for an act done. As between them, we think however that the character conception is more persuasive, albeit in orthodox legal theory's typically narrow terms. This is because it relates the question of responsibility to a more general understanding of the actor and what informed her act. Choice and capacity approaches may also have their place, but by themselves are not able to secure a sufficient link between a culpable actor and an act. Yet, when we probe the theory which leads to a character approach, we find that it too is fundamentally lacking.[1] We show this in the next section where we analyse the philosophical issues underlying the justification of criminal responsibility. This brings out weaknesses in the orthodox approach by means of an immanent critique which we use in the third section to launch our own substantive, dispositional–relational, approach to responsibility.

Engaging the hierarchical account of responsibility

Underlying how questions of criminal responsibility are shaped is a deep philosophical literature that cannot be avoided, that helps to understand what is wrong with extant doctrines and suggests why a dispositional–relational approach is important. In modern times, that literature is shaped by how we understand human freedom in a determined universe. A central response that is particularly relevant to criminal responsibility involves arguing for ways in which the one is compatible with the other. Positions focus on how characteristic features of human moral psychology combine to produce an entity that possesses sufficient freedom to be responsible for its acts. Among these are a number of what has been called "mesh theories",[2] where contributions by Harry Frankfurt[3] and Gary Watson[4] lie at the core of the debate.[5] The former writes of a hierarchy of first- and second-order desires in which higher-level desires can be identified with who a person is and therefore why she is responsible for what she does. The latter takes issue with the former's focus on a hierarchy of desires, arguing that the human "mesh" is one in which desires interact with a valuational system reflecting what the individual sees as valuable, good, or desirable.[6]

These are important arguments for law because they underpin a sophisticated understanding of criminal responsibility, as we see in Victor Tadros's[7] work. We begin by considering his account of hierarchical responsibility and then his Watson-based development of a valuational account. We argue in this section however, that this account reveals immanent problems for attributing criminal responsibility as a matter of individual blameworthiness. Second, we show in the following section how a critique of the character account leads us beyond it to a substantively different account of responsibility, which we describe as dispositional–relational. We indicate briefly in a final section how such a model takes us away from blameworthiness and towards restorative and reconciliative approaches.

Linking action to a person

Criminal law holds an agent responsible for her actions, but only, Tadros argues, if they are reflective of her as an agent. Action by choice does not provide sufficient moral information by which to judge responsibility. For this reason, agency must be related to character. While the latter is not the immediate focus of responsibility attribution, it is an associated requirement for judging action.[8] Linking action and character is the range of mental phenomena which make the former possible and the latter relevant. The starting point is intention in relation to action, which concretises beliefs and desires together with the motivating reasons which underpin them. These are all relevant to thinking about responsibility, but the need for motivating reasons raises a question. Can such reasons be connected to the person if the desire that motivates the reason is not "properly reflective of the agent *qua* agent"?[9] Tadros gives the simple example of an action that is the result of a person having her drink spiked, but this is just one illustration of a general problem, that a person may not be identified with her actions and their motivating reasons. Tadros describes this as a problem of "alienation", and he probes it initially in terms of Frankfurt's hierarchical account of responsibility.[10]

The basic argument is that we need to know not only if a person acted from a motivating reason, but also that such a reason can be connected to the agent more deeply. Frankfurt's way to deal with this is to consider those higher-order volitions or desires of an agent which organise lower-level action-oriented reasons or desires for action, that is, a hierarchy of reasons. This however leads to a problem of a regress in which we might question why the higher-level decisions are themselves intrinsically connected to the agent, or if they do not need a further and higher level to finally make the link. The way out of this provided by Watson is to argue that what we should look for at a higher level consists not of further reasons or desires but of values, and their relationship to reasons. The existence of values addresses the problem of regress because "the scheme of values of the agent is so closely interwoven into the nature of the agent *qua* agent that there is no further possible account of agency that could be used to undermine responsibility".[11] The realm of values is something that agents cannot escape, and there is nothing beyond it at a higher level to which one could refer. One "can give up a set of values only in the light of some other set of values that one does accept".[12] Values, in this view, ground motivating reasons in line with who an agent is. This perhaps solves the problem of the regress of reasons or desires, but does a reliance on underlying values not cause its own problems? Can it resolve the problem of alienation, that is, now, that one could be as alienated from one's values as one is from one's motivating reasons?

The problem of value alienation

What would it mean to say that one was alienated from a particular value? Consider the example of a person revolted by his materialistic values and approach to life. Such a person, says Tadros, "may recoil from his materialism" but, still living with it, be said to accept it. His values would, in such a situation, be flexible so that he is not genuinely alienated from his actions, though he claims he is. It would only be "if he attempts to become less materialistic and reasonably fails that we can truly say ... that [he] is alienated from his materialism".[13] But is this true? Might the recoil from materialism that ultimately goes unaddressed not *also* be a sign of (a deeper) alienation from values?

This issue is brought out if we consider how a person's values develop over time.[14] At T1, *A* happily pursues materialistic goals without a thought for the outcome in terms of planetary well-being or lack of resources for others. Later at T2, *A* realises his materialism leads to planetary or social degradation and seeks to change his life. He finds, however, that despite his best efforts he is trapped by his social milieu. Alternatively, let us say that his understanding of how he should live does lead to consistent and far-reaching changes in his life. In these situations, at what point is *A* alienated from his values? The initial response might be to say that he is only alienated from his values at T2, when he realises that his materialism is unsustainable, and either fails or succeeds to change. Might we also say, however, that he was already alienated from them at T1, but just did not know it at that time? The interesting point is to think about how this might look to *A* himself. Questioned at T1 about whether he is alienated from his values, he might well look blankly at the questioner. Questioned at T2, however, with the dawning realisation of what he knows now, he might say that he is alienated now, at the point of change, but he also now realises that he was alienated at T1, though he did not then know it.

The problem is that values sit complexly within human agents taken at one point in time, but especially over time. Post hoc realisation is always possible, both for itself and as the sign that values may be held provisionally or subject to revision in the present. Linking this to responsibility for one's value-based actions, Tadros notes that "the value to which the desire is connected must not be alienated from the general system of values that the agent adopts",[15] but he sets this against the qualification that values need not be consistently held. Values may generally operate "in a consistent set", yet from such a set, "one value may be alienated".[16] Moral agents are, perhaps, not just as consistent as they ought to be, and backsliding is an evident possibility. But if one value can be alienated, what about two or more? And further, what about situations where people live with deeply contradictory alternative values? For example, they might genuinely value non-materialism but cannot resist "consumer therapy".

Such situations point to the possibility of deep-seated splits between what we value, think, and do, coexisting within us. This is what underlies the example of alienated materialism: that someone might only realise later (at T2) that the acts, reasons, and values on which he acted previously (at T1) were fundamentally wrong. Only at the later time does he appreciate, perhaps with bitter regret, the alienation from underlying values which he now realises (with hindsight at T2) that he lived with. Looking back, he realises that, say, social, cultural, and ideological forces led him to be materialistic, and *it was these that were responsible for him acting as he did*. The values, in other words, that are present and realised at T2 may be present but unactualised at T1, yet latent or immanent in the person at the earlier point. Alienation from such values was present at both T1 and T2, but only realised to be such at the later time. Note how the issue raises a question about responsibility in the italicised phrase above. Could it be that the recognition of subsisting value conflict and change might significantly undermine the idea of individual responsibility? We return to this question below.

The problem of unconscious motivation

Before doing so, however, we should like to address a linked issue. A second problem about how people hold values arises in relation to the question of what we *consciously* know. With our alienated materialist, we are concerned with a person whose values at T1 are latent and immanent rather than realised and actual. Such latent values appear as a simple present absence at T1, but as an absent presence at that time with the hindsight afforded at T2. *A* only becomes conscious of them at the later point. Talk of knowledge that exists as immanent and latent yet unconscious at T1, but capable of being realised and conscious at a later point reveals similarities to how the relationship between the conscious and unconscious is understood in psychoanalytical theory.

Such theory also raises questions for the account of how desires and values mesh together, and therefore of responsibility. If we are going to talk of the values that structure our motivations and beliefs, what are we to make of a realm of unconscious psychological life that the person can at best only know imperfectly, with values sedimented in the psyche yet hard to bring into consciousness? Do we need to know what such values are and how they relate to a person's expressed values in order to identify her responsibility for an act? If we do, what does it say about a person's responsibility at T1 if she acted from motives unconscious at that time, though brought into consciousness at T2?

We think that questions of identity, values, and responsibility ought to take the relationship between the conscious and the unconscious into account, in ways we will draw out below. Staying with Tadros, however, we note that he rejects this. He is interested in a person's psychology, and he wishes to recognise the role of time and change in affecting a person's mind, but he steers clear of "any deep level and hidden desires" in favour of what he calls "attributes of the mind of the agent".[17] For psychoanalytic thought, this is a distinction without a difference, since the attributes of the agent's mind contain both conscious and unconscious elements. For Tadros, per contra, "the relevant kind of explanation is precisely to be distinguished from explanation in terms of the agent's 'unconscious self', if indeed there is such a thing".[18] If there is no such thing, then of course there is no problem, but the experience that many people have of discovering deep-seated motivations which relate to present conduct, or simply of dramatic dreams which deserve interpretation suggests otherwise.

Psychoanalytical explanations for Tadros "are to be distinguished from the kind of explanation that refers to the reasons that D recognised at the time of action";[19] but if reasons can be acted on that are unrecognised by the agent at the time of action, does that make them any the less reasons (in line with values, etc.)? He similarly suggests that talk of responsibility involves looking at "*rational* explanation as distinct from scientific or deep psychological explanation", appealing to "the agent's ability to evaluate his action".[20] But psychoanalysis is also in favour of rational explanation and the need to evaluate one's actions.[21] The concept of the unconscious is in line with this but extends "the range and application of the concepts of belief and desire"[22] and, we might add, values. It just sees the human mind as more complex and less transparent, as involving different modes of reflection,[23] and, we will argue in the next section, this leads to a different account of responsibility.

In any case, the ruling out of unconscious reasons *ab initio* provides further fuel to our main point, that legal conceptions of responsibility may be troubled by questions of value, value alienation, and identity across time. Psychoanalytic accounts represent just one kind of ethical case where people may re-evaluate (i.e. differently value) their past acts in terms of what they know now. We will argue that such different cases of value alienation and unconscious motivation require a more complex account of responsibility that takes law in a different direction to the standard one of the criminal courts.

Responsibility in light of the above

So far, we have spoken about how values may change historically but not yet fully about the impact of such change on responsibility. Let us return to the question of the person who changes his values, sees his past values negatively, and as alienated in light of his present ones. To be responsible for an action, it must, per Tadros, reflect "on the agent *qua* agent" and the reason behind the action must be motivated by a desire that is appropriately connected to the agent's value system. It is however recognised that an agent may not hold consistently or coherently to values in their value system. There are two main demands in this theory. The first is that the agent's actions "cannot be alienated from" his value system.[24] The second, in line with our discussion above, is that one cannot know about an agent's responsibility except by looking at his identity over time, for whether:

"a particular feature of the agent's psychology truly reflects his agency ... depends upon the history of the agent. A consequence of this is that whether a desire is reflective of agency cannot be understood simply by investigating the psychology of the agent at the time at which the action was performed. How the agent came to have that psychology will also be important in establishing responsibility".[25]

We can initially see this argument as leading to a problematic and a non-problematic responsibility scenario. The non-problematic scenario is where a person identifies with a particular set of values but inconsistently so. She knows she ought to do *x* according to her values but due to weakness of will she does *y*. Reflecting on this value conflict, she comes to accept that she is complacent about her values and choices. Though she holds still to value *x*, she recognises that doing *y*, inconsistent with *x*, is part of her value system. For example, *B* is a professed vegetarian but cannot resist the odd bacon sandwich: she values animal life highly, in principle, but prone to backsliding and is inconsistent in applying her values in practice. She must accept she is still, non-ideally, a meat-eater, and therefore complicit in the killing of animals. She may also have to accept she is somewhat hypocritical and accept judgment as such, but in all this, there is no problem in thinking through the question of her responsibility for what she values, thinks, feels, and does.

This non-problematic scenario may however be taking things superficially. Introducing the time factor, a more problematic responsibility case is one in which *B* ate meat at T1 and then became a convinced vegetarian at T2. Considering previous discussion is she *responsible* for meat-eating at T1? The quick answer may seem to be that she is but consider the following. With benefit of the moral hindsight afforded by a change of values at T2, *B* now rejects meat-eating not only at T2 but also, looking back, at T1 and regards her actions at that time as the result of a profound but latent alienation in her values. On our argument about time and changed values above, this alienation suggests that she is responsible for her (vegetarian) food choices at T2 but not responsible for her (carnivorous) choices at T1. She now sees her eating choices at T1 as the mark of a deep alienation in her value system at the earlier time. The alienation is backdated to T1 in line with the need to look at the person's value system as a whole and over time. It is fundamental to view any value system in such a way, so it seems to follow that *B* is not responsible for her food choices at T1, at least if we pursue the logic of the Frankfurt–Watson account of responsibility.

Dispositional–relational responsibility

Could it really be the case that a person's value conversion at T2 could undermine responsibility for wrongful action at T1? Could a present moral change undermine a past wrongdoing in this way? We think that the argument for hierarchical and value responsibility is important in understanding how legal responsibility works, but when pushed, we think it leads to the conclusion we have outlined. We think its immanent logic undermines rather than supports an argument in favour of criminal responsibility as this is normally cast. Its account of individual responsibility does not ultimately work. We will argue, in light of this, that a different account of responsibility is necessary and possible and that this would suggest a different perspective on how legal process should operate. In this section we explain why we argue for a dispositional–relational approach by considering how it relates first to personal identity and then to individual responsibility. We end the section by considering a possible objection.

Dispositional–relational identity

Our starting point is located in an understanding of human identity as individual, social, and relational. As a general observation about human being, we would say that it develops through something like four different kinds of relations: (1) relations to nature; (2) the social and institutional relations which constitute us, and which our agency in turn constitutes; (3) our interpersonal relations with family, friends etc; and (4) the intra-psychic structures of our minds, our internal mentalities. These four sets of relations (or "planes" as Bhaskar has it[26]) are interrelated and also combine with other aspects such as our genetic make-up to produce our unique individual identity. Yet this complex synchronic picture of who we are still misses the crucial diachronic element that we exist in time and place. We become who we are through the human life cycle (the "seven ages") and in historical time and geographical space. Because our being develops inside different relations and geo-temporally, our experience of being can be one of significant change over the course of a life. We are born into the world in one time and place and die in another having been subjected to internal changes through the human life cycle and the impact of external changes as the external world evolves. Over the course of a life, change is both endogenous (the growth, maturing, and decline of an ageing person) and exogenous (the influence of changing social and geo-historical settings), and these changes are always interrelated to produce our concrete individuality.

This means that our identity as evolving and complex beings may involve complex changes in our character, dispositions, and values over time. It is inevitably the case that we will be unaware of some things influencing us, not understand or anticipate the impact of these on us or hold unconsciously to understandings which shape our action. In all such cases, we will not recognise, understand, or master factors creating our identity including our values, or we may only do so with hindsight. Because identity is relational it is importantly changeable, but not simplistically pluralistic. Every individual has both internal developmental capacities and a relationship to what lies "outside" us. The model of dispositional–relational identity indicates the importance of change in response to an environment, the sense of the irreducible individuality of each human being, and the possibility, but not the certainty, of understanding a life's development, usually only in retrospect. Identity, and therefore character, involves both the process of developing dispositions and values and of reflecting on how these develop. From that conception of an evolving "meta-reflexive"[27] identity involving both change and making sense of it, human beings may change from T1 to T2 and a person's essential responsibility involves making sense of change at the different times. To be dispositionally responsible is therefore to be able to reflect on one's changing relational identity, values, and actions and to take responsibility for them. For that reason, we call identity and the ensuing sense of responsibility both dispositional and relational.

Dispositional–relational responsibility

With this approach, how responsibility is understood changes. We can see this if we compare our position to the conventional character approach, where dispositions are settled expressions of character which can make a person worthy of censure. In that model, they are the basis for holding someone to account through punishment (the choice and capacity models having been shown to be inadequate). This approach is insufficient to reflect the sense of an individual's real responsibility to understand her evolving or changing dispositions, which requires a focus on how a person comes to be who she is, and can be, rather than qualifying her for punishment for a one-off act. Since no one chooses their character, it is a criticism of the existing character/disposition model that how a person is responsible for their character remains unclear. Our account fills that gap by seeing dispositions as changing over time so that responsibility is less about paying a price for what one did and more about reflecting on how one came to do it. This kind of responsibility is one in which one takes responsibility for understanding and, if need be, changing one's character rather than being held responsible and censured for it as the "responsibility proxy" for one's acts.

Here is how we think responsibility should be reconfigured, taking our previous example of the vegetarian *B*. *B* looks back on her past settled disposition to eat meat and finds herself deeply alienated from it. This places her not so much in a position of denying responsibility for her past as one of ambivalence and conflict about it. On the one hand, *B* thinks her past meat-eating was not really "hers". It clashes with values she now takes to have been immanent within her even if she did not previously recognise them. She was brought up, say, in a family and a culture which took meat-eating for granted. Values around animal killing and eating handed down to her later seem abhorrent and alien. Since meat-eating was done by someone with very different values to those *B* holds now; since she condemns her previous values; and since they were culturally or ideologically acquired rather than personally adopted, she does not hold herself responsible for them. That is one side of the story.

On the other hand, *B* must acknowledge that while she was brought up in a culture that normalised animal killing and eating, for many years she went along with it. The person that she is now, in very important ways, is the same person who ate meat in the past. Though *B* finds her past actions abhorrent and cannot endorse them (then or now), they were a significant part of her past agential being – and they remain a part of who she is now as a person with a past, as well as a present and future. Her past victims, the sentient animals whose lives were taken that she might eat, remain her victims, albeit they became such without moral reflection on her part. There was, she now sees, moral damage in her past, and might say she was herself damaged, but she was also a participant in the damage taking place. On this view, *B* should regret her past, and in regretting it, take responsibility for it in appropriate ways. These might involve both critically evaluating her past, engaging appropriately with family members who encouraged it, and finding ways to be respectful and challenging of animal suffering in the present. The upshot is an ambivalence around responsibility, where *B* thinks that in one way she was not responsible for her past acts – others in her family, the culture, etc., were; but in another way, it leaves her to regret what she did, to understand how she came to be that person, and what she now should do about it.[28] Acting on her regret is a form of taking responsibility in its own right. *B* owes it to herself as a person with values, to herself as a person over time, to those in her family and social group, and to the animals themselves to address her past in the present and with an eye on the future.

The result of this exploration of responsibility for alienated (and it could also be unconscious) past deeds is twofold. The first is analytical. Responsibility cannot be "punctualist" or "actualist", that is a matter of directly linking specific action with an individual mind, its reasons and values, without thinking about time and the possibility of previously unrealised, alienated values. Against an "actualist" approach to the phenomena of values and agency, we need a "depth realist" approach which can ground present actions and values in their emergence in a structured past.[29] Reasons and values placed under question by alienation over time provide an ambivalent basis for responsibility ("yes, I did it"/ "no, cultural conditions made me do it"), and this needs to be faced in thinking through how we deal with the issue.

The second is more processual and practical in light of the first. The upshot of a finding of responsibility in these situations involves a different kind of reaction or judgment. It is not one of straightforward censure at one point in time, but of relating a person's past, present, and future to their actions. In this form, responsibility for violative acts becomes a questioning and regretful commitment to investigate what I did in the light of who I was and now am. Outcomes concern not punishment as sanction for a past act but the reflective making of amends (insofar as one can) for past wrongdoing. In that sense, we would say that responsibility should start from an individual's subjective understanding and commitment to setting things to right rather than a community's objective belief in censure focused on punishment. Responsibility does not take the attributional and retributional form of being "held responsible" for a past act but the reflective subjective form of "taking responsibility" for it. It ceases in criminal justice terms to be punitive and becomes restorative or reconciliative.

An objection considered

Dispositional–relational identity generates a model of responsibility adequate to a situation where humans have to understand and negotiate their past and present morally and emotionally, and with an eye to the future. It challenges our existing practices around censure and punishment in terms of responsibility for an act and mental state at a particular point in time, thinking about the historical depth of a person entailed by a dispositional–relational model. Is such a model possible? Earlier, we noted that the kind of past–present–future model of responsibility we sought brought into play the relevance of psychoanalytical explanation. Surely, it will be said, if we take up an account of responsibility which can extend to the unknown or the unconscious, we are doomed to achieve *no* account of *any* individual's responsibility for her acts here and now. We have sailed too close, perhaps, to the kind of therapeutic or behaviouristic model of human behaviour which denies responsibility.

We think not, and we would invoke Freud's own account of responsibility to show our general direction of travel. Of the need to take responsibility for one's dreams, he wrote:

> "What else is one to do with them? Unless the content of the dream (rightly understood) is inspired by alien spirits, it is part of my own being. If I seek to classify the impulses that are present in me according to social standards into good and bad, I must assume responsibility for both sorts..."[30]

How can one be responsible for the unconscious psychological process that occurs in dreams, which are surely a sign of deep dispositions over which one has no control? For Freud, one is *not* responsible for one's dreams in that one should blame oneself for having a bad dream or congratulate oneself for a good one. The dream nonetheless shows something about what the dreamer thinks unconsciously about her conscious life. Taking responsibility for one's dreams is not being "held responsible" for them but learning and changing by taking them seriously. The dream is a conduit to a better understanding of one's dispositional and relational identity and responsibility resides in working through what it tells us so that we may move forward, from one time to another, in our lives. Transferring the argument from dream to act, let us say a bad, violative one, dispositional–relational responsibility is not about blame and punishment (being "held responsible") but about linking the act to who I am, why it was wrong, what its effects were, how I could have done it, what I would need to change to not repeat it, changing the environment which made it possible, and what I would need to do now to repair it.[31] Dispositional–relational responsibility is thus linked to restorative and reconciliative trends in criminal justice, though we believe these need to be theoretically developed.[32]

Dispositional–relational responsibility: two implications

In this section, we make two points about dispositional–relational responsibility, one concerning its psychological foundations, the other concerning its social significance.

Psychological foundations

Though not in such terms, a seminal psychological example of dispositional–relational responsibility for wrongdoing is found in Hans Loewald's account of superego formation and its relation to guilt.[33] In simplified terms, superego formation represents for him a core moment in the development of personal identity when a person starts to be able to organise herself and her different dispositions in a more or less coherent way. It involves capacity for more complex levels of psychical organisation of one's past, present, and future. Psychological maturity in its turn involves taking responsibility for oneself through "appropriating or owning up to one's needs and impulses as [one's] own…being responsive…facing and bearing the guilt for [acts]…and being again at one"[34] with oneself and one's world. It thus provides the basis for dispositional–relational responsibility since it makes it possible for a person to understand, organise, and re-align (take responsibility for) her dispositions in a social setting.

This is a process that emphasises the search for wholeness and continuity in a changing world. Loewald speaks of why we would feel bad for violating another and how we should deal with the aftermath. He speaks as we have just seen of "bearing guilt" (feeling bad) but also of "being again at one" (seeking to come to terms with what we have done). He calls the superego, which is the attempt to develop a single identity from a variety of competing claims, and which he believed to be a supreme human achievement, an "atonement structure". But note what he meant by this: "atonement" is the sense of reconciling oneself, of being "at one", with what one has done ("at-one-ment"). This links his metapsychology with the most thoughtful of punishment theorists, Herbert Morris, who has written of taking responsibility for wrong done as a "need to make amends, to mend what has been damaged, and to be at one again with others".[35] If successful, this "is atonement, *being at one with*"[36] oneself and others. These psychological ideas underlie and affirm the concept of dispositional–relational responsibility, and, as with Morris, they indicate a critique of orthodox ideas of blame and punishment.[37] They also point us importantly to the relationship of reconciliation between individual and social change, as below.

Sociological implications

The second point to make, briefly, is that dispositional–relational responsibility is always also about social or "contextual" responsibility, because our dispositions are related to who we are in particular social settings, in the several planes of our social, relational, and interpersonal being. Dispositional–relational responsibility both affirms individual responsibility and sets it in a complex space between the individual and the social. We are historical and relational beings constituted by the social world which we in turn constitute. A commitment to changing oneself is therefore already ex hypothesi *both* a commitment to redressing harms one may have done and to change the social setting that enabled, conditioned, or caused them. In this way, individual dispositional–relational responsibility has as its interconnected counterpart the need for a sense of social responsibility to intervene in ways that improve social settings through effective means of intervention.

The following all too common example demonstrates why. A man violates his female partner at T1. She reports it to the police. He is arrested and charged with domestic assault. At T2 he is held to account by the criminal law for the domestic abuse at T1; he is deemed responsible for it and following the finding of guilt, in an extreme case, is incarcerated. After serving his sentence he marries again but six months later starts violating his second wife at T3. This sadly familiar[38] scenario illustrates precisely what dispositional–relational responsibility offers over and against a "punctualist" or "actualist" criminal responsibility holding the perpetrator responsible and punishing him for his violence. The latter does not consider the temporal relation between past (T1), present (T2), and future (T3). The repetition of violence indicates how dispositions may be sedimented in character, and that such sedimentation requires addressing. We say it *can be addressed*, but only as a kind of dispositional–relational responsibility, a sort of "quantum guilt"[39] rather than just a repeat offending. In failing to consider this problem of repetition, i.e. other than as an occasion for increased punishment, orthodox accounts of criminal responsibility obscure the nature of such sedimented dispositions, the context for their existence, and how they might be addressed. How is it that the man is able to violate his partner? What is it about the social world and its gender relations that enables this to happen quite systematically? And what is it about both the social world and the individual's psyche that means that holding him to account and imposing punishment does not stop the violation from repeating? These questions take us through and beyond criminal law's limited and limiting penal equation (crime plus responsibility equals punishment[40]) and invite us to consider a different approach that would see human violation as the need for a person to address their dispositions, values, and actions and ultimately take responsibility for them.

What is at stake here are questions of restoration and reconciliation – how it is that we reconcile violation at the individual (intra-psychic, interpersonal) *and* social (contextual) level thereby achieving restorative and reconciliative at-one-ment.[41] Violative relationships need to be worked through between perpetrator and victim, perpetrator and social context, and the victim with the social too. Social as well as individual assumptions about the permissibility of attitudes linked to violation are all part of why people act. This requires that a response to violation must be responsive to the moral psychology of whole, flawed, persons in their relational context – their past, present, and future dispositions, their capacity for growth and change, their agency in relation to the social world that both constitutes who they are and which they, in turn, constitute. Dispositional–relational responsibility lies at the heart of such reconciliation. It recognises that dispositions are both practiced and organised by individuals and that societies encourage or enable them. It represents the coming together of powers and capacities for transformative change both within individuals and beyond in the broader social world. It invokes a sense of responsibility that is active and constructive rather than punitive and repetitive of the past.

Conclusion

We started this chapter with an immanent critique of criminal responsibility as its practice is most powerfully (we think) understood in legal theory in the Frankfurt, Watson, and Tadros view. Out of this, we proposed and developed an account of dispositional–relational responsibility as a response to the failures of a narrow "punctualist" or "actualist" understanding. These contrasting models have different theoretical and practical implications. We then identified two key, interrelated implications of dispositional–relational responsibility. First is the interconnection of dispositional–relational and contextual (social) responsibility. Second is the relationship between such responsibility and the idea of atonement (in the sense of "at-one-ment") and the connection then to restoration and reconciliation as both individual and social. The contours of a reconciliative approach require further refinement than space provides here,[42] but our aim has been to show that dispositional–relational responsibility demands an approach that is attentive to both the individual *and* the social context and indicates a different way of addressing wrongdoing than censure and punishment. We also think it important that the argument emerges immanently from critique of the existing best theoretical model we could find.

The penal equation that characterises criminal law's approach to violation relies on a weak, attributional responsibility concept that is at odds with our dispositional–relational identity as human beings. In *holding* a person responsible, criminal responsibility short-circuits our capacity for transformative change at the individual and social level. Dispositional–relational *taking* responsibility, by contrast, nurtures both. If we are convinced by such a model, then its depth and potential at both the individual and the social levels demand that we take restoration and reconciliation seriously. It would not be enough, for example, to cast restorative process in an institutionally friendly manner, law's adjunct or junior partner. The move from punishment to restoration and reconciliation via dispositional–relational responsibility has important implications for a system based on crime and punishment. It asks us all to imagine other possibilities that lead to real personal responsibility for one's acts *and* constructive change in the world rather than processes based on punishment leading only to the repetition of past behaviours. The whole point of our dispositional–relational approach is that these two elements, the individual and the social, come as a pair.

Acknowledgements

A first version of this chapter was presented at the Max Planck Institute for the Study of Crime, Security and Law in Freiburg in September 2022 as part of a workshop on "Rethinking the Social Environment in Criminal Law Theory and Doctrine".

Notes

1. The character approach is attractive as a means of broadening our understanding of why a person might act, and in that regard the dispositional–relational approach takes off from and presses beyond it. Its own limit in terms of continued individualisation of responsibility around a person's character or settled dispositions is brought home in a savage way in Texas death penalty cases where it is used to justify execution over imprisonment. The perpetrator is argued to have an irredeemably bad character (see C Deambrogio, *Judging Insanity, Punishing Difference: A History of Mental Illness in the Criminal Court* (Stanford University Press: Stanford, 2024)).
2. The main essays in the postwar debate are collected in G Watson (ed), *Free Will* (Oxford University Press: Oxford, 2nd edn, 2003) and a more recent set is in R Kane (ed), *The Oxford Handbook of Free*

Will (Oxford University Press: Oxford, 2nd edn, 2011). The idea of "mesh" theories, meaning a theory which synthesises psychological processes to produce the possibility of sophisticated human agency, is developed in M McKenna, "Contemporary Compatibilism: Mesh Theories and Reasons-Responsive Theories", in Kane (ed), *Oxford Handbook of Free Will* and M McKenna and J Coates, "Compatibilism" and "Compatibilism: State of the Art", *Stanford Encyclopedia of Philosophy* (2019), available at: https://plato.stanford.edu/entries/compatibilism/. The latter contains a helpful supplement of "state-of-the-art" discussions on compatibilism. We find the idea of mesh theories interesting because one of us has written, in the line of dialectical theory, of human life as caught up in a "material meshwork of being", that is being "existentially involved in processes of change and becoming" (see A Norrie, *Dialectic Difference: Dialectical Critical Realism and the Grounds of Justice* (Routledge: Abingdon, 2010), p.30). This relational approach to the meshing of social, historical, and individual agency takes us well beyond the focus of compatibilist free will theory but the different focus on what the human mesh is helps draw out the different starting points. Ours is reflected in the dispositional–relational approach to responsibility developed below.
3   H Frankfurt, "Freedom of the Will and the Concept of the Person" in G Watson (ed), *Free Will*.
4   G Watson, "Free Agency" in G Watson (ed), *Free Will*.
5   A sharp alternative within this debate is to argue from "free will scepticism", i.e. that there is no free will so that retribution in the form of backwards looking "basic desert" is unjustified (D Pereboom, *Wrongdoing and the Moral Emotions*, (Oxford University Press: Oxford, 2021). If the aim is then "to secure forward-looking goals such as the moral reform of the wrongdoer" (Pereboom, *Wrongdoing*, p.26), we agree. We think the dispositional–relational approach to responsibility is best suited to achieve this – by relating past violation to present day self-critical reflection and the eventual possibility of atonement ("at-one-ment") as described below. Pereboom links basic desert to anger, which we see as a primitive and punitive emotion licensing retributive thinking, but we think a very different "mature" retributivism not involving censure and punishment is possible, based on love, restoration, and reconciliation (see A Norrie, "Taking Guilt Seriously" in I Solanke (ed), *On Crime, Society and Responsibility: The Work of Nicola Lacey* (Oxford University Press: Oxford, 2021)).
6   Watson, "Free Agency".
7   V Tadros, *Criminal Responsibility* (Oxford University Press: Oxford, 2005).
8   Tadros, *Criminal Responsibility*, p.9.
9   Tadros, *Criminal Responsibility*, p.32.
10 Tadros, *Criminal Responsibility*, p.31–42.
11 Tadros, *Criminal Responsibility*, p.39.
12 Tadros, *Criminal Responsibility*, p.39.
13 Tadros, *Criminal Responsibility*, p.38.
14 Tadros, *Criminal Responsibility*, p.41.
15 Tadros, *Criminal Responsibility*, p.39.
16 Tadros, *Criminal Responsibility*, p.40.
17 Tadros, *Criminal Responsibility*, p.28.
18 Tadros, *Criminal Responsibility*, p.28.
19 Tadros, *Criminal Responsibility*, p.28.
20 Tadros, *Criminal Responsibility*, p.28.
21 J Lear, *Open Minded: Working Out the Logic of the Soul* (Harvard University Press: Cambridge, 1998); J Lear, *Freud* (Routledge: London, 2nd edn, 2015).
22 R Bhaskar, *The Possibility of Naturalism: A Philosophical Critique of the Contemporary Human Sciences* (Harvester: Brighton, 1979), p.123.
23 Lear, *Freud*, ch.1.
24 Tadros, *Criminal Responsibility*, p.41.
25 Tadros, *Criminal Responsibility*, p.41.
26 R Bhaskar, *Dialectic: The Pulse of Freedom* (Verso: London, 1993).
27 Bhaskar, *Dialectic*.
28 This is a more complex form of regret than that canvassed by Bernard Williams (see B Williams, *Moral Luck* (Cambridge University Press: Cambridge, 1981), though we might think that underlying his account there is a conception of what we would call here "metaphysical regret".

29 Bhaskar, *Possibility of Naturalism*.
30 S Freud, "Some Additional Notes on Dream Interpretation as a Whole" in *The Standard Edition of the Complete Psychological Works of Sigmund Freud* (1925), vol XIX, pp.127–38 at p.133.
31 C Reeves, "What Punishment Expresses", *Social and Legal Studies*, vol. 28, no. 1 (2019), p.31; C Reeves, A Norrie & H Carvalho, "Between Persecution and Reconciliation: Criminal Justice, Legal Form and Human Emancipation" in E Christodoulidis, R Dukes, & M Goldoni (eds), *Handbook on Critical Legal Theory* (Edward Elgar: Cheltenham, 2019).
32 A Wilson, "General Terms of Comparison: Two Cores of the Restorative Justice Apple", in T. Gavrielides (ed) *Comparative Restorative Justice* (Springer: New York, 2021); A Wilson, "What a Shame! Restorative Justice's Guilty Secret", *Howard Journal of Crime and Justice*, vol. 61, no. 1 (2022), p.39.
33 A Norrie, "Animals Who Think and Love: Law, Identification and the Moral Psychology of Guilt" *Criminal Law and Philosophy*, vol. 13 (2019), p.515; Norrie, 'Taking Guilt'; Wilson, 'What a Shame'.
34 HW Loewald, *Papers on Psychoanalysis* (Yale University Press: New Haven, 1980), pp.392–393.
35 H Morris, *On Guilt and Innocence: Essays in Legal Philosophy and Moral Psychology* (University of California Press: Berkeley, 1976), p.100.
36 Morris, *On Guilt*, p.100, emphasis added.
37 A Wilson, "Guilt Beyond Guilt: From Political Theory to Metaphysics with Herbert Morris" *Modern Law Review*, vol. 84, no. 1 (2021), p.89.
38 Notwithstanding the reality that many domestic violations never get reported in the first place, and those that do are rarely prosecuted, let alone lead to convictions.
39 Wilson, "Guilt Beyond".
40 A Norrie, "The Limits of Justice: Finding Fault in the Criminal Law", *Modern Law Review*, vol. 59, no. 4 (1996), p.540; A Norrie, *Law and The Beautiful Soul* (Routledge: Abingdon, 2005), ch.5.
41 Space prohibits further development of this point but in short order, we are interested in the relationship between the restorative and the reconciliatory in a way that gives restorative justice a fully reconciliatory dimension and (thus) does not tailor restorative responses to institutional settings often given their overall shape by criminal punishment either in theory or in practice. For more, see Wilson, "General Terms"; Wilson, "Guilt Beyond"; Wilson, "What a Shame"; A Wilson, *Restoring Restorative Justice* (Oxford University Press: Oxford, *forthcoming*).
42 For instance, a developed conception of community would be essential. For an ethically real account of reconciliation as it pertains to restorative justice, see Wilson, *Restoring Restorative*.

References

Books and book chapters

Bhaskar R, *The Possibility of Naturalism: A Philosophical Critique of the Contemporary Human Sciences* (Harvester: Brighton, 1979).
Bhaskar R, *Dialectic: The Pulse of Freedom* (Verso: London, 1993).
Deambrogio C, *Judging Insanity, Punishing Difference: A History of Mental Illness in the Criminal Court* (Stanford University Press: Stanford, 2024).
Frankfurt H, "Freedom of the Will and the Concept of the Person", in Watson G (ed), *Free Will* (Oxford University Press: Oxford, 2nd edn, 2003).
Freud S, "Some Additional Notes on Dream Interpretation as a Whole", in *The Standard Edition of the Complete Psychological Works of Sigmund Freud XIX* (1925).
Kane R (ed), *The Oxford Handbook of Free Will* (Oxford University Press: Oxford, 2nd edn, 2011).
Lacey N, *State Punishment: Political Principles and Community Values* (Routledge: London, 1988).
Lacey N, *In Search of Criminal Responsibility: Ideas, interests, and institutions* (Oxford University Press: Oxford, 2016).
Lear J, *Open Minded: Working Out the Logic of the Soul* (Harvard University Press: Cambridge MA, 1998).
Lear J, *Freud* (Routledge: London, 2015).
Loewald HW, *Papers on Psychoanalysis* (Yale University Press: New Haven CT, 1980).

McKenna M, "Contemporary Compatibilism: Mesh Theories and Reasons-Responsive Theories", in Kane R (ed), *The Oxford Handbook of Free Will* (Oxford University Press: Oxford, 2nd edn, 2011).

Morris H, *On Guilt and Innocence: Essays in Legal Philosophy and Moral Psychology* (University of California Press: Berkeley CA, 1976).

Norrie A, *Law and The Beautiful Soul* (Routledge: Abingdon, 2005).

Norrie A, *Dialectical Critical Realism and the Grounds of Justice* (Routledge: Abingdon, 2010).

Norrie A, "Taking Guilt Seriously", in Solanke I (ed), *On Crime, Society and Responsibility: The Work of Nicola Lacey* (Oxford University Press: Oxford, 2021).

Pereboom D, *Wrongdoing and the Moral Emotions*, (Oxford University Press: Oxford, 2021).

Reeves C, Norrie A, & Carvalho H, "Between Persecution and Reconciliation: Criminal Justice, Legal Form and Human Emancipation", in Christodoulidis E, Dukes R, & Goldoni M (eds), *Handbook on Critical Legal Theory* (Edward Elgar: Cheltenham, 2019).

Tadros V, *Criminal Responsibility* (Oxford University Press: Oxford, 2005).

Watson G (ed), *Free Will* (Oxford University Press: Oxford, 2nd edn, 2003).

Williams B, *Moral Luck* (Cambridge University Press: Cambridge, 1981).

Wilson A, "General Terms of Comparison: Two Cores of the Restorative Justice Apple", in Gavrielides T (ed), *Comparative Restorative Justice* (Springer: New York, 2021).

Wilson A, *Restoring Restorative Justice* (Oxford University Press: Oxford, forthcoming).

Journal articles

Norrie A, "The Limits of Justice: Finding Fault in the Criminal Law", *Modern Law Review*, vol. 59, no. 4 (1996), pp.540–556.

Norrie A, "Animals Who Think and Love: Law, Identification and the Moral Psychology of Guilt", *Criminal Law and Philosophy*, vol. 13 (2019), pp.515–544.

Reeves C, "What Punishment Expresses", *Social and Legal Studies*, vol. 28, no. 1 (2019), pp.31–57.

Wilson A, "Guilt Beyond Guilt: From Political Theory to Metaphysics with Herbert Morris", *Modern Law Review*, vol. 84, no. 1 (2021), pp.89–117.

Wilson A, "What a Shame! Restorative Justice's Guilty Secret", *Howard Journal of Crime and Justice*, vol. 61, no. 1 (2022), pp.39–52.

Encyclopaedia entries

McKenna M & Coates J, "Compatibilism" and "Compatibilism: State of the Art" *Stanford Encyclopedia of Philosophy* (2019), available at: www.plato.stanford.edu/entries/compatibilism/

10
FROM CASUISTRY TO THE GENERAL PART

The Conception of Criminal Responsibility from the *ius commune* to the Penal Codes (Twelfth–Nineteenth Centuries)

Michele Pifferi

Introduction

A renewed interest in casuistic reasoning is sparked by both historians and criminal law scholars. The former have highlighted its significance and intertwined development in medieval theology and law and the expediency of resorting to the rule/exception paradigm to legitimate Machiavellian political ideas.[1] The latter have argued the potential of casuistry for judicial decision-making in national and international criminal law.[2] The relationship between casuistic reasoning and criminal law is not new. Legal historians have long regarded medieval criminal law in continental Europe as casuistic – a definition vastly used yet rarely explained – and are used to juxtaposing its characteristics to a more systematic and principled modern criminal law typically embedded in penal codes.[3]

This chapter will investigate the origins and development of the notion of criminal responsibility in late medieval legal sources and its modern shift from a casuistic to a principled conception, linked to the formation and institutionalisation of the modern state since the XVI century. The chapter will be divided into three main parts: the first will be focused on the *ius commune* doctrine (XII to XVI centuries) and the gradual elaboration of the theory that penally indictable conducts imply either malice (*dolus*) or negligence (*culpa*) and should not refer to purely objective causal inferences.[4] This notion meant the rejection of the early medieval idea of strict responsibility, the reinterpretation of Roman law texts, the recognition of responsibility theories formulated by canon lawyers, and the definition of specific criminal law notions of responsibility as distinguished from the private law ones used by Roman law. The method usually employed by legal scholars and judges was a casuistic approach whereby different and variable circumstances of cases and persons involved were carefully considered to balance the claim of the public powers not to leave any offences unpunished and the more rational idea that only volitional conduct should be criminalised. The second part of the chapter will concern the systematisation of the rules of criminal responsibility within a theoretical framework that is no longer reliant or dependent on cases but driven by principles and rules. This new methodological and theoretical approach was associated with the consolidation of state sovereignty, which, in the field of criminal justice, took the form of more extended and hierarchically prevailing penal legislation enacted by European rulers between the XVI and the late XVIII centuries (e.g. the *Constitutio Criminalis Carolina* of 1532; the *Constitutio Criminalis Theresiana* of 1768). The third part of the chapter will refer to the central role played by the notion of criminal liability based on free will in the general part of the penal codes enacted in the late XVIII and XIX centuries. Before the rise of criminological positivism challenged the moral notion of responsibility and free will, penal liberalism had elaborated an idea of liability perfectly consistent with the values and visions of individual autonomy upon which the functioning of society rested. This model could no longer be case-oriented but necessitated a normative and general definition of criminal responsibility.

The medieval casuistic description of criminal responsibility

The turn of the XI and XII centuries represented a watershed in European legal history characterised by the central role of legal scholarship, the gradual rediscovery of Roman law as an authoritative basis of legal reasoning, the foundation of universities, the coexistence of the universalistic *ius commune* with particularistic sources, and the creation of classical canon law.[5] Late medieval jurists were confronted with three main positions regarding criminal responsibility. First, Roman law had elaborated neither a general notion of criminal intent nor a theory of culpability. The *Corpus Iuris Civilis* provided some norms and rules referring to volition and wilfulness (*voluntas* and *animus*) as essentials of certain offenses, although variously and inconsistently.[6] Second, the legacy of Germanic law and early medieval law (V to XI centuries) was mainly dominated by the idea of strict responsibility and by purely objective criteria of accountability.[7] Third, the statutes of medieval cities, especially regarding homicide or other serious crimes, largely provided for (capital) punishment as a consequence of the material causation of the fact, regardless of any consideration of *mens rea*.[8]

Through their steady and sophisticated interpretive work on different sources, late medieval jurists contributed to distinguishing voluntary from involuntary crimes, identifying different degrees of volition (malice aforethought; malice; more and less serious levels of negligence), and turning judicial discretion to more moderate and fair decisions based on the intensity of the offender's intention. This theoretical process was greatly influenced by canon lawyers, whose key role in shaping the modern notion of responsibility has long been thoroughly recognised by legal historians.[9] For this chapter, it should be emphasised that the canon law doctrine enhanced the subjective element of any unlawful conduct through casuistic reasoning. The origins of such stress on volition rather than on material fact should be traced back to the penitential books written since the end of the XI century when the sacramental character of penance was clearly established and the Fourth Lateran Council of 1215 prescribed the obligation of yearly confession. The *Summae confessorum*, far from being a predetermined catalogue of punishments to be applied to sinners, was a combination of theology and canon law, of moral and legal discourses based on the idea that the wide discretion in imposing penances given to confessors was a necessary means to flexibly adjust penalties to the individuals' peculiarities and the circumstances of each situation to help sinners' salvation.[10] The casuistic method was crucial to these texts as, by case-driven reasoning, abstract definitions and strict top-down impositions were avoided, and, on the contrary, rules' application was relativised, adapted to variable cases, and individualised.[11] Penitential books employed casuistry to distinguish voluntary from involuntary crimes and to differently graduate the sanction according to the degree of volition's intensity, especially regarding homicide.[12] Raymond of Peñafort, in his *Summa de casibus poenitentiae* written in 1216,[13] after defining homicide as a man's killing by a man, distinguishes spiritual homicide, in which someone is spiritually and in a fictitious way killed such as by hating, bad counselling, or denigrating, from corporal homicide. Corporal homicide can be perpetrated by words or by facts and can be committed in four ways (justice, necessity, case, and volition). Accidental or unintentional homicide can be differentiated by whether the doer was engaging in unlawful conduct (*dabat operam illicitae rei*) and should therefore be responsible for the unintended consequences of his or her act or whether he or she was engaging in lawful conduct. In this second case, whether due diligence was observed should be further considered because, if it was not, the perpetrator should be held responsible for the event. Raymond then discusses further cases and examples to clarify whether the canon law penalty of irregularity should be applied.[14] This casuistry, rather than establishing binding precedents and rules for the confessors, served the purpose of accurately examining each sin, deeply understanding the inner attitude of doers and judging accordingly.

This same casuistic reasoning was then applied to the study of offences and punishments by jurists who, by interpreting the Roman and the canon law sources as well as the city statutes, laid the foundations for the development of public criminal justice in the medieval communes of the late Middle Ages.[15] Since the XII century, the rules of the increasingly inquisitorial criminal procedure were shaped by legal doctrine to define the judges' remit and the purpose of their discretionary power, the hierarchical value of evidence, and the different punishments to be applied.[16] Substantial criminal law – and guilt definition and attribution as an essential part thereof – was neither elaborated as an autonomous subject matter nor investigated through insightful conceptualisation. In the *tractatus de maleficiis* (such as those of Alberto da Gandino or Angelo Gambiglioni) and in the many *practicae criminales*, procedural matters and problems took centre stage. Rather than providing abstract definitions of malice or negligence, legal scholars were interested in clarifying what form or intensity of guilty mind was relevant in specific cases; or, in the many forms in which an offence could be realised, how the subjective element should be proved or why it should imply a more severe or lenient sentence. A case-based approach was followed, whose main purpose was to make the judges aware of the need to consider singularities not contemplated by abstract norms reasonably.[17] By providing examples and suggesting solutions for future cases, penal casuistry rested on distinctions, exceptions, and limitations of laws belonging to a pluralistic legal system within which every judicial decision, due to the lack of definite general principles of responsibility, should always resort to equity, namely, to a fair assessment of the cases' circumstances.[18] Gambiglioni, for instance, distinguishes four types of arson according to the different intensity of volition (committed with malice; gross, slight, or very slight negligence), which were in turn differentiated and punished depending on the place of the crime (*locus commissi delicti*, such as within or outside the city-wall; in a private or public place) and the victim's social status.[19]

Singularities notwithstanding, casuistic reasoning allowed jurists to emphasise the fundamental role of intention as a condition of punishability, the possibility of distinguishing malice from negligence and of graduating their intensity, and the impact of such differences regarding proportionality of punishment.[20] Giulio Claro, for instance, writing his criminal law treatise in the mid-XVI century when these ideas had become consolidated, distinguished between simple homicide (*simplex homicidium*), committed without the quality of deliberate intention (*sine qualitate animi deliberati*), and homicide deliberately committed (*deliberatum*). Simple homicide can be committed in four ways (necessity, case, negligence, or malice). Claro points out that it is a common opinion among jurists and has also become a prevailing case-law rule that a homicide committed without malice should be punished more mildly than one maliciously perpetrated. Deliberate homicide is committed not with a simple intention (which can be triggered by an outburst of anger or by a brawl) but with more meditated malice (by aforethought malice, by deceit, by treachery, and by contract killing) and is, therefore, more regrettable.[21] In the pluralistic medieval legal order, different sources such as Roman law, Canon law, feudal law, merchants' law, city-states' law, and customary law were in force at the same time without any hierarchical criterium and there was no monopolistic state-like political power able to impose legal certainty by means of laws binding all of the different courts. By contrast, different courts were operating on the same territory with different and usually not overlapping jurisdictions. In such a system characterised by simultaneous and multiple layers of normativity, resorting to casuistry and scrutiny of intentionality centred on the peculiarities of facts represented the method to inductively bring out some rules. There was no general theory of criminal responsibility that should be rigidly followed, such as a scheme within which peculiarities of behaviours and facts should be forced or normalised. It was not a matter of abstract legal principles to which the variety of life had to (fictitiously) be made to match. In contrast, casuistry permitted flexible assessment of the quality and quantity of guiltiness in each situation.[22] Theoretical subtleties on the many different shapes that guilt could take in distinct cases and on how they should be proven and punished were the method followed to infer, from the multifaceted reality, rules based on the pivotal dimension of *mens rea*. Moreover, the attention to the peculiarity of the case, allowed to gradually shift from an objective theory of conduct-outcome causality to an insightful analysis of volition and foreseeability.[23] The binding force of such rules rested on the reliability and soundness of legal casuistic reasoning rather than on the authority and coerciveness of the laws, and their credibility and likelihood of being applied by judges depended on the persuasiveness and logical rigour of casuistic distinctions. The philosophical and cultural rationale of such a casuistic construction of volition-based criminal responsibility lies in (and corresponds to) the growing concern for individual conscience and free will shared by both theologians and jurists (above all by canonists) since the XII century.[24] The vision of human agency based on moral freedom and rational choices brought about by the "papal revolution", with its theological and legal underpinnings,[25] also affected the secular sphere of criminal responsibility by inextricably linking the degree of guilt and punishment to intention.[26] For all the different underlying justifications displayed by jurists of the *ius commune* to hold offenders accountable – be it retribution, deterrence, or correction – both the nature and intensity of criminal intent had to be carefully appraised.[27]

The theorisation of criminal responsibility in the XVI century

A shift from a case-based approach to a more systematic one occurred in criminal law in the XVI century. Four main reasons can be argued for such methodological change. First, criminal law started being taught as an autonomous discipline in many European universities.[28] This resulted from the scientific maturity reached by criminal law, considered sufficiently developed and based on its own rules and concepts. However, the subject had to be theoretically elaborated, rationally analysed, and systematically reorganised to be better taught and studied. Given the penetrating control over universities exercised by public authorities in the Middle Ages, recognising an academic space for criminal law was also functional in allowing trained jurists to be employed in the state criminal justice apparatus.[29] Second, the new methodological approach of legal humanism clamoured for the reshaping of all legal disciplines systematically and rationally, starting with general principles from which solutions for specific cases could be deductively determined. Such a rationalisation claim affected both the teaching method and the way legal books were written,[30] including – as we shall see – some criminal law treatises. Third, the XVI century was characterised by the issuing of criminal laws (e.g. the *Carolina* of 1532 in the Holy Roman Empire; the *Ordonnance sur le fait de la Justice of Villers-Côtterêts* of 1539 in France; the criminal laws enacted by Philippe II in the Netherlands in 1570[31]) that made the sovereigns' purpose of hegemonic control over the administration of criminal justice more explicit and penetrating, even though their efforts to exclude the validity of other concurring norms were not completely successful.[32] Finally, by deeply investigating the relationship between sin and crime, punishment and penance, Spanish Second Scholasticism significantly contributed to emphasising guiltiness and criminal law getting rid of any residual idea of strict liability disconnected from moral agency.[33] Moreover, jurists and theologians of the School of Salamanca highlighted the moral implications of any laws,[34] penal ones included. Their insistence on the moral duty to comply with penal laws enacted by rulers[35] strengthened the link between the authoritative power of the sovereign and the subjective element of guilt. For the thinkers of the Second Scholasticism, who embraced the idea of imputation as the moral evaluation of an action prohibited by a rule, responsibility was the consequence of the binding force of the law.[36] The notion of culpability (both in internal and external forums) and the authoritativeness of penal laws mutually reinforced each other. Even though their reasoning was still casuistic, sometimes they also resorted to synthetic considerations, such as when Antonio Gomez identified the three constituents of any crime in intentionality, the materiality of the fact, and legal provision inflicting a punishment.[37]

The interplay of these factors can be seen in Tiberio Deciani's *Tractatus criminalis*, which has long been considered the first formulation of the general part of criminal law.[38] In the introductory chapters, Deciani (1509–1582), who had been a criminal law professor at the University of Padua and served the interests of the Republic of Venice as a diplomat and jurist, clearly points out that for a better understanding of the subject, abstract reasoning rather than casuistic reasoning had to be followed, starting with the analysis of the general elements common to all the different crimes. By drawing upon Aristotelian logic and applying to the concept of crime the same methodological approach that other jurists were experimenting with in the concepts of contract and property,[39] Deciani provides an abstract theory of crime comprising (1) the analysis of its material, efficient, formal, and final causes; (2) its definition; and (3) the study of its substantial, natural, and accidental elements.[40] Within this framework, criminal responsibility plays a key role: volition (*voluntas*) is, together with human facts, the material cause of a crime; guilty mind (either malice or negligence) is one of the constituent elements of a crime's definition; volition and intention to commit a crime (*animus delinquendi*) are substantial elements of any crime along with the positive law prohibiting a conduct, the material fact, and the unlawfulness of the fact. Moreover, in the first book focused on the explanation of some terms, Deciani had already defined and clarified the proper meaning of both malice and negligence. In particular, the specific meaning of criminal intent (*dolus in criminalibus*) and its difference from contract fraud – two concepts rather confused in Roman sources – are elucidated: *mens rea* is a quality that, when absent, either there is no punishable offence (as in the case of fortuitous events) or the offence should be punished more mildly (as when committed on an impulse).[41] The concept of *dolus* entails the idea of purpose and is a vice of volition, while *culpa* (negligence) is a vice of intellect and memory lacking a previous harmful intention (*nulla praecedente nocendi intentione*).[42] Deciani further discusses theoretical and theological fine distinctions between volition, intention, and purpose in a chapter focused on homicide with considerations that can be applied to all offences.[43] The originality of Deciani's general part and its emphasis on the guilty mind lie more in the order of the discourse than in its contents. The systematic approach, abstract reasoning, condensation of scattered opinions and rules into a logical deductive sequence, and first (defective as it may appear) attempt to shift from casuistry to rules are the very reasons for the importance of the *Tractatus* for the development of modern criminal law. Regarding criminal responsibility, the acquisition of Deciani's methodological turn can be summarised in two main points. First, no crime is conceivable without a guilty mind. Second, malice and negligence have specific meanings in criminal law, connoting different levels of responsibility, which entail corresponding and proportionate penalties.[44] Such rules, as a consequence, should guide both the judges, who can no longer adhere to the idea of strict liability or avoid a deep and equitable investigation of the subjective element of the offence, and the lawmakers, whose criminalisation choices should not eschew the condition of *mens rea*.

The criminal law doctrine of the late *ius commune* has elaborated a theory of responsibility that, as flexible and adjustable to cases' circumstances as it may be, nevertheless considers individual volition a constitutive element of every crime. The methodological turn towards a general theory of crime, however rudimentary it may be in the XVI century, delineates a discursive space within which the essence of crime is conceived and defined as an act inherently intentional.

The principle of culpability and the codification process

It took time for this systematic approach to become established and for jurists to develop an elaborated theory of culpability as one of the essential subjects of the general part of criminal law. In the European legal tradition, there was a doctrinal and philosophical phase of formation of the general part that preceded the late-eighteenth to early-nineteenth century normativisation of its materials into the formal shape of penal codes.[45] In such a theoretical framework, the criteria for being held criminally responsible were thoroughly elaborated by a legal science whose method was at odds with casuistry and oriented, by contrast, to build deductive conceptual pyramids moving from general and abstract principles to their embodiment in specific cases.[46] The transition from the old regime to modern society, summarised by Maine's move from status to contract and described by Weber in terms of historical legal development from casuistry to systematisation,[47] brought about what Lacey defined as capacity responsibility.[48] The impact of liberalism and individualism on late-eighteenth and nineteenth century criminal law triggered a detailed examination of the forms of criminal intent as manifestations of the deliberate choice to violate the laws. In a sociopolitical and economic framework centred around free will and rational decisions of equal individuals, self-determination became pivotal: while in contract law autonomy was positively assumed as the driver of the free market, in criminal law the notion of criminal responsibility embodied the opposite meaning of a deviant volition worth being punished.[49]

Unsurprisingly, criminal law scholars focused on theories of culpability and legality as general premises of any penal system: principles of imputability had to be framed as normative provisions so that the whole structure of the penal code coherently reflected the *mens rea* as a necessary (and ordinary) condition of any penal intervention. The free will of equal and rational individuals whose contractual choices and property rights' enjoyment were granted by the civil code was also the key element of the penal code whose justification rested on the assumption of individual moral agency. Since the penal Enlightenment, the finely elaborated theory of the guilty mind, grounded on philosophical and metaphysical principles, has been closely related to the claim of the principle of legality paving the way to the incorporation (and graduation) of criminal intent in the general part of penal codification. In so doing, reformers were pursuing multiple goals. By overcoming penal casuistry, they were shaping a philosophical and metaphysical theory of culpability that corresponded to the pivotal importance of individual volition and rationality as functioning conditions of the legal order. Moreover, an abstract, general definition of the guilty mind implied a graduation of blameworthiness (from malice aforethought to slight negligence) that should be reflected in proportionate punishments. Finally, by fostering the normativisation of these categories of responsibility into penal codes' general part, reformers emphasised their importance in terms of individual guarantees: judges could no longer disregard the rules of culpability defined by the articles of the penal code, nor could they inflict disproportionate and arbitrary punishments inconsistent with the culpability rules. The connection between a theoretical system of penal law based on the clarification of the different degrees of criminal intent and the issuing of a penal code is openly explained by Gaetano Filangieri, one of the most important enlightened Italian reformers. In the third book of his *The Science of Legislation*, published in 1783, Filangieri describes the "rule" according to which the legislator should state the lowest, medium, and maximum degrees of malice and negligence. He then argues that judges should be bound to inflict the kind of punishment proportioned to such a scale of responsibility as defined by the law. It is exactly such "metaphysical science" that "makes easy what will always seem impossible to the casuist, who does not have the eye to discover those first links from which the huge and complicated chain proceeds". The path towards a perfect penal system cannot but lead to the final enactment of a penal code in which arbitrary punishments will be banished, and the law will never permit the judges to act as if they were legislators. General principles enshrined in a penal code fulfil the aim that in the old feudal regime seemed politically impossible: an equal and just proportion between crimes and punishments.[50]

Conclusion

The shift from a casuistic to a principled notion of criminal responsibility inaugurated by late-eighteenth century reformers contributed to informing the penal rules of the European *Rechtsstaat* and the English rule of law of the XIX century. The image of an autonomous individual as the master of his rational choices and therefore held accountable for her or his crimes and the abstract categorisation of forms of criminal responsibility characterised the development of continental and codified criminal law until the end of the century. This harmonious combination of theories and laws, such a simplified narrative of the guilty mind and its proportionate punishment, was questioned by the discovery of the criminal man in the

1870s.[51] Only when criminal anthropology and criminological positivism criticised abstract theories of imputability completely disconnected from the peculiarities of the individual delinquent and openly negated the existence of free will was the very idea of criminal responsibility undermined. By embracing determinism, criminologists tried to replace responsibility with dangerousness as the rationale for the imposition of punishment: they did not succeed, but contributed to reshaping the liberal notion of criminal intent.[52]

Funding

This contribution is part of the italian MUR Research Project PRIN2022 "Casiustry" and rule-based approach in criminal law. Historical perspectives, current devlopments (2022PLENEZ), Funded by European Union NextGenerationEU.

Notes

1 See, e.g. C Ginzburg, "Ein Plädoyer für den Kasus", in J Süßmann, S Scholz, G Engel (eds), *Fallstudien: Theorie – Geschichte – Methode* (Trafo: Berlin, 2007), pp.29–48; C Ginzburg & L Biasiori (eds), *A Historical Approach to Casuistry. Norms and Exceptions in a Comparative Perspective* (Bloomsbury: London, 2019); S Tutino, *Uncertainty in Post-Reformation Catholicism: A History of Probabilism* (Oxford University Press: Oxford, 2017); S Di Giulio & A Frigo (eds), *Kasuistik und Theorie des Gewissens. Von Pascal bis Kant* (De Gruyter: Berlin/Boston, 2020); E Corran, *Lying and Perjury in Medieval Practical Thought: A Study in the History of Casuistry* (Oxford University Press: Oxford, 2018); JC Passeron & J Revel (eds), *Penser par cas* (Éditions de l'École des hautes études en sciences sociales: Paris, 2020).

2 See, e.g. M Cupido, "The Casuistry of International Criminal Law: Exploring A New Field of Research", *Netherlands Journal of Legal Philosophy*, vol. 44, no. 2 (2015), p.116; M Cupido, "Facing Facts in International Criminal Law. A Casuistic Model of Judicial Reasoning", *Journal of International Criminal Justice*, vol. 14, no. 1 (2016), p.1; A Di Martino, "The importance of being a case. Collapsing of the law upon the case in interlegal situations", *The Italian Law Journal*, vol. 7, no. 2 (2021), p.961.

3 See, e.g. JM Carbasse, *Introduction historique au droit pénal* (Presses Universitaires de France: Paris, 1990), pp.185–186; F Tomas y Valiente, *El derecho penal de la Monarquía absoluta (siglos XVI-XVII-XVIII)* (Tecnos: Madrid, 1969), p.89; E Schmidt, *Einführung in die Geschichte der deutschen Strafrechtspflege* (Vandenhoeck & Ruprecht: Gottingen, 4th edn, 1995), p.148; M Sbriccoli, "Giustizia criminale", in *Storia del diritto penale e della giustizia. Scritti editi e inediti (1972-2007)* (Giuffrè: Milano, 2009), p.13.

4 The chapter is focused on the history of the European continental legal system; the importance of *mens rea* in English medieval criminal law has been thoroughly investigated by EP Kamali, *Felony and the Guilty Mind in Medieval England* (Cambridge University Press: Cambridge, 2019).

5 See P Grossi, *A History of European Law* (Wiley Blackwell: Chichester, 2010), pp.19–38.

6 See C Gioffredi, *I principi del diritto penale romano* (Giappichelli: Torino, 1970); GP Demuro, *Il dolo: Svolgimento storico del concetto* (Giuffrè: Milan, 2007), vol I, pp.23–78.

7 See R Sorice, "La dialettica tra volontario e involontario nella dimensione penale pregregoriana: l'omicidio *sponte commissum* nei Penitenziali e nei *Capitularia* carolingi", *Rivista Internazionale di Diritto Comune*, vol. 29 (2018), p.45.

8 See, e.g. M Lucchesi, *Si quis occidit occidetur. L'omicidio doloso nelle fonti consiliari (secoli XIV-XVI)* (Cedam: Padova, 1999).

9 See, e.g. S Kuttner, *Kanonistische Schuldlehre von Gratian bis auf die Dekretalen Gregors IX. Sistematisch auf Grund der handschriftlichen Quellen dargestellt* (Biblioteca Apostolica Vaticana: Città del Vaticano, 1935); L Kéry, *Gottesfurcht und irdische Strafe. Der Beitrag des mittelalterlichen Kirchenrechts zur Entstehung des öffentlichen Strafrechts* (Bohlau: Köln, 2006); O Descamps, "Quelques remarques sur la distinction entre homicide volontaire et homicide involontaire en droit canonique médiéval", in O Condorelli, F Roumy, & M Schmoeckel (eds), *Der Einfluß des*

Kanonistik auf die europäische Rechtskultur. Straf– und Strafprozessrecht (Bohlau: Köln, 2012), vol III, pp.108–134; H Pihlajamäki & M Korpiola, "Medieval Canon Law: The Origins of Modern Criminal Law", in M Dubber (ed), *The Oxford Handbook of Criminal Law* (Oxford University Press: Oxford, 2014), pp.201–224.

10 See, e.g. TN Tentler, "The Summa for confessors as an instrument of social control", in C Trinkaus, HA Oberman (eds), *The Pursuit of Holiness in Late Medieval and Renaissance Religion* (Brill: Leiden, 1974), pp.103–126.

11 See P Grossi, "Somme penitenziali, diritto canonico, diritto comune", *Annali della Facoltà giuridica di Macerata*, vol. 1 (1966), p.95.

12 J Guyader, "Aux origines canoniques de la responsabilité pénale: volonté coupable et pénitence dans les crimes contre les personnes d'après Burchard de Worms", in J-L Thireau (ed), *Le droit entre laïcisation et neo-sacralisation* (PUF: Paris, 1997), pp.87–107; S Menzinger, *Finzioni del diritto medievale* (Quodlibet: Macerata, 2023) pp.27–61.

13 See S Kuttner, "Zur Entstehungsgeschichte des Summa de casibus poenitentiae des hl. Raymund von Penyafort", *Zeitschrift der Savigny-Stiftung für Rechtsgeschichte. Kanonistische Abteilung*, vol. 39 (1953), p.419.

14 R of Peñafort, *Summa de casibus poenitentiae* (Cambridge, Corpus Christi College, MS 247), f.133. [ca 1200–1299]

15 See M Sbriccoli, "Legislation, Justice and Political Power in Italian Cities, 1200-1400", in, *Storia del diritto penale*, pp.47–72; R Fraher, "The theoretical justification for the new criminal law of the high Middle Ages: «Rei publicae interest, ne crimina remaneant impunita»", *University of Illinois Law Review*, vol. 1984, no.3 (1984), p.577; M Vallerani, *Medieval Public Justice* (Catholic University of America Press: Washington DC, 2012).

16 See M Meccarelli, "Criminal law: Before a state monopoly", in H Pihlajamäki, MD Dubber, M Godfrey (eds), *The Oxford Handbook of European Legal History* (Oxford University Press: Oxford, 2018), pp.632–655.

17 See, e.g. A Tiraqueau, *De poenis Legum ac Consuetudinum Statutorumque temperandis, aut etiam remittendis, et id quibus, quotque ex causis*, in, *Tractatus varii* (G Rovillum: Lugduni, 1587), p.256 § 23; P di Castro, *In Primam Codicis partem Commentaria* (apud Lucam Antonium Iuntam: Venetiis 1582), p.137 § 3; A Tartagni, *Consiliorum liber secundus* (Ex officina Damiani Zenarii: Venetiis, 1578), Cons CXL, p.116 § 4.

18 See, e.g. A Laingui, *La responsabilité pénale dans l'ancien droit (XVIe-XVIIIe siècle)* (Librairie générale de droit et de jurisprudence: Paris, 1970), pp.19–20.

19 A Gambiglioni, *Tractatus de maleficiis, cum additionibus Augustini Bonfrancisci Ariminensis* (Flackenburg: Coloniae, 1599) § *Incendiario*, p.324.

20 See, e.g. the classical studies of W Engelmann, *Die Schuldlehre der Postglossatoren und Ihre Fortentwicklung. Eine historisch-dogmatische Darstellung der kriminellen Schuldlehre der italienischen Juristen des Mittelalters seit Accursius* (Duncker & Humblot: Leipzig, 1895), and A Löffler, *Die Schuldformen des Strafrechts in vergleichend-historischer und dogmatischer Darstellung* (CL Hirschfeld: Leipzig, 1895), pp.136–181; more recently, see R Sorice, *Vittime colpevoli e colpevoli innocenti. Ricerche sulle responsabilità penali nell'età del diritto comune* (Bologna University Press: Bologna, 2018).

21 G Claro, *Volumen, alias Liber Quintus* (IA de Antoniis Librarii: Venetiis, 1570), p.22.

22 See, R Volante, "Argomentazione senza principi nel diritto comune", in C Latini (ed), *Argomentazione e lessico nella tradizione giuridica* (Giappichelli: Torino, 2022), pp.37–58; D De Concilio, "Soggettività e qualificazione del fatto. L'indagine del *factum intrinsecum* tra diritto e teologia nel XII secolo: due casi di studio e spunti per una ricerca", *Historia & Ius*, vol. 22, paper 9 (2022), p.1; R Sorice, "La teoria del *versari in re illicita* nel pensiero di Giovanni d'Andrea: *dolus generalis?*", *Zeitschrift der Savigny-Stiftung für Rechtsgeschichte: Kanonistische Abteilung*, vol. 105, no. 1 (2019), p.99.

23 See G Rossi, *Ordinatio ad casum: Legal Causation in Italy (14th – 17th centuries)* (Vittorio Klostermann: Frankfurt am Main, 2023), p.219.

24 See L Siedentop, *Inventing the Individual: The Origins of Western Liberalism* (Harvard University Press: Cambridge MA, 2014).

25 See HJ Berman, *Law and Revolution: The Formation of the Western Legal Tradition* (Harvard University Press: Cambridge MA, 1983).

26 B Tierney, *The Idea of Natural Rights: Studies on Natural Rights, Natural Law, and Church Law, 1150-1625* (Scholars Press: Atlanta, 1997), p.56.

27 See, e.g. F Grunert, "'Punienda ergo sunt maleficia.' Zur Kompetenz des öffentlichen Strafens in der Spanischen Spätscholastik", in F Grunert, K Seelmann (eds), *Die Ordnung der Praxis. Neue Studien zur Spanischen Spätscholastik* (Max Niemeyer Verlag: Tübingen, 2001), pp.313–332; M Pifferi, "Per giustizia e per salvezza. Qualche riflessione sulla polifunzionalità della pena tra medioevo ed età moderna", *Quaderni di diritto e politica ecclesiastica*, vol. 22 (2019), p.3.

28 The first criminal law course (*lectura criminalium*) was delivered in 1509 at the University of Bologna by Ippolito Marsigli. On the importance of such criminal law courses see, e.g. H Coing, "L'insegnamento del diritto nell'Europa dell'Ancient Regime", *Studi Senesi*, vol. 82 (1970), p.186; M Pifferi, *Generalia delictorum: Il Tractatus criminalis di Tiberio Deciani e la "parte generale" di diritto penale* (Giuffrè: Milan, 2006), pp.65–90.

29 See P Nardi, "Relations with Authority", in H De Ridder-Symoens (ed), *A History of the University in Europe* (Cambridge University Press: Cambridge, 1992), vol I, pp.77–107; H Coing, "Die juristische Fakultät und ihr Lehrprogramm", in H Coing (ed), *Handbuch der Quellen und Literatur der neueren europäischen Privatrechtsgeschichte* (CH Beck'sche: Munich, 1973), vol I, pp.85–90.

30 See, e.g. V Piano Mortari, *Diritto logica metodo nel secolo XVI* (Jovene: Napoli, 1976); PJ du Plessis & JW Cairns (eds), *Reassessing Legal Humanism and its Claims: Petere Fontes?* (Edinburgh University Press: Edinburgh, 2016).

31 See LT Maes, "Die drei grossen europäischen Strafgesetzbücher des 16. Jahrhunderts. Eine vergleichende Studie", *Zeitschrift der Savigny-Stiftung für Rechtsgeschichte: Germanistische Abteilung*, vol. 94 (1977), p.207.

32 See R Martinage, *Histoire du droit pénal en Europe* (PUF: Paris, 1998), pp.21–26; W Reinhard, *Geschichte der Staatsgewalt: Eine vergleichende Verfassungsgeschichte Europas von den Anfängen bis zur Gegenwart* (CH Beck: Munich, 2nd edn, 2000), pp.291–305.

33 See H Maihold, *Strafe für fremde Schuld? Die Systematisierung des Strafbegriffs in der Spanischen Spätscholastik und Naturrechtslehre* (Böhlau: Köln, 2005); H von Weber, "Zur Entwicklung des gemeinen deutschen Strafrechts unter besonderer Berücksichtigung spanischer Einflüsse", in *L'Europa e il diritto romano: Studi in memoria di Paolo Koschaker* (Giuffrè: Milan, 1954), vol I, pp.337–355; Pifferi, *Generalia delictorum*, pp.308–322.

34 See, e.g. M Villey, "La promotion de la loi et du droit subjectif dans la Seconde Scolastique", in P Grossi (ed), *La Seconda Scolastica nella formazione del diritto privato moderno* (Giuffrè: Milan, 1973), pp.53–71.

35 See A De Castro, *De potestate legis poenalis. Libri duo* (In aedibus Viduae et Haeredum Ioannis Stelsii: Antuerpiae, 1568).

36 See A Giuliani, "Imputation et justification", *Archives de philosophie du droit*, vol. 22 (1977), p.85.

37 A Gomez, *Variarum Resolutionum Iuris Civilis, Communis et Regii Commentaria*, t III, *de Delictis* (Ex typographia Felicis Mosca: Neapoli, 1718), c 3 *De Homicidio*, § 30, 81.

38 See, e.g. F Schaffstein, "Tiberius Decianus und seine Bedeutung für die Entstehung des Allgemeinen Teils im Gemeinen deutschen Strafrecht", in *Abhandlungen zur Strafrechtsgeschichte und zur Wissenschaftsgeschichte* (Scientia Verlag: Aalen, 1986), pp.199–226; Pifferi, *Generalia delictorum*. The *Tractatus*, made of nine books, was first published posthumously by his son in 1590 and presumably written in 1572; its so called "general part" refers to the first five chapters of the second book.

39 See, e.g. F Mantica, *Vaticanae lucubrationes de tacitis et ambiguis conuentionibus* (Ex typographia Vaticana: Romae, 1609), esp. p.5 and pp.26–35 for the substantial, natural and accidental elements of any contract. On the elaboration of a general theory of contract, see P Cappellini, "Sulla formazione del moderno concetto di 'dottrina generale del diritto'", *Quaderni fiorentini per la storia del pensiero giuridico moderno*, vol. 10 (1981), pp.323–354; P Grossi, "Sulla 'natura' del contratto (qualche nota sul 'mestiere' di storico del diritto, a proposito di un recente 'corso' di lezioni)", *Quaderni fiorentini per la storia del pensiero giuridico moderno*, vol. 15 (1986), p.593; M Lipp, *Die Bedeutung des Naturrechts für die Ausbildung der Allgemeinen Lehren des deutschen Privatrechts* (Duncker & Humblot: Berlin 1980), esp. pp.91–104.

40 See T Deciani, *Tractatus criminalis* (Apud Franciscus de Franciscis Senensem: Venetiis, 1590), vol I, 18r–20r.

41 Deciani, *Tractatus*, I, ch 4 § 9, 6.

42 Deciani, *Tractatus*, I, ch 6 § 5, 11 and § 16, 12.
43 Deciani, *Tractatus*, IX, ch. 27, 410–411.
44 See X Rousseaux, "From Case to Crime. Homicide Regulation in Medieval and Modern Europe", in H Schlosser & D Willoweit (eds), *Neue Wege strafrechtsgeschichtlicher Forschung* (Böhlau: Köln, 1999), pp.143–166.
45 See, e.g. K Tiedemann, "Zum Verhältnis von allgemeinem und besonderem Teil des Strafrechts", in G Arzt, G Fezer, U Weber, E Schlüchter, D Rössner (eds), *Festschrift für Jürgen Baumann zum 70. Geburtstag 22. Juni 1992* (Gieseking: Bielefeld, 1992), pp.7–20; M Schmoeckel, "Der Allgemeine Teil in der Ordnung des BGB", in M Schmoeckel, J Rückert, R Zimmermann (eds), *Historisch-kritischer Kommentar zum BGB, I, Allgemeiner Teil, §§ 1–240* (Mohr Siebeck: Tübingen, 2003), pp.123–165; on the connection between rationalisation and systematisation of European legal systems in Weber's conception of historical legal development, see TE Huff, "Max Weber's comparative and historical sociology of law. The Developmental Conditions of Law", in A Sica (ed), *The Routledge International Handbook on Max Weber* (Routledge: London & New York, 2023), pp.339–352.
46 See, e.g. JSF Böhmer, *Elementa iurisprudentiae criminalis. Editio tertia* (Ex officina Fritschiana: Halae at Bernburgi, 1743), ch II *De natura et indole delictorum*, p.17; GJF Meister, *Principia iuris criminalis Germaniae communis* (IC Dieterich: Gottingae, 1798), pp.19–22; CR Köstlin, *System des deutschen Strafrechts: Allgemeiner Teil* (Laupp: Tübingen, 1855); FM Renazzi, *Elementa iuris criminalis. Liber I. De delictis generatim* (Joannes Generosus Salomoni: Romae, 1774) chs V–VIII, p.74; on Renazzi's theory of culpability see M Cavina, "Il dolo latente nell'animo. Filippo Maria Renazzi nel dibattito giuridico intorno alla graduazione del dolo fra XVIII e XIX secolo", in MR Di Simone, C Frova, & P Alvazzi del Frate (eds), *Filippo Maria Renazzi: Università e cultura a Roma tra Settecento e Ottocento* (il Mulino: Bologna, 2019), pp.227–239.
47 H Maine *Ancient Law* (Cambridge University Press: Cambridge, 2013 [1861]); M Weber, *Economy and Society. An Outline of Interpretive Sociology*, edited and translated by G Roth & C Wittich (University of California Press: Berkley CA, 1978), pp.655–657.
48 N Lacey, *In Search of Criminal Responsibility: Ideas, Interests, and Institutions* (Oxford University Press: Oxford, 2016).
49 See L Farmer, *Making the Modern Criminal Law: Criminalization and Civil Order* (Oxford University Press: Oxford, 2016), pp.163–203; P Costa, *Il progetto giuridico: Ricerche sulla giurisprudenza del liberalismo classico* (Giuffrè: Milan 1974), vol I, esp pp.357.
50 G Filangieri, *La scienza della legislazione* (C Derriey: Parigi, 1853), pp.224–225.
51 See, e.g. D Garland, *Punishment and Welfare. A History of Penal Strategies* (Ashgate: Aldershot, 1985); RF Wetzell, *Inventing the Criminal: A History of German Criminology, 1880–1945* (University of North Carolina Press: Chapel Hill, 2000); M Gibson, *Born to Crime: Cesare Lombroso and the Origins of Biological Criminology* (Praeger: Westport, 2002); M Pifferi, *Reinventing Punishment: A Comparative History of Criminology and Penology in the Nineteenth and Twentieth Centuries* (Oxford University Press: Oxford, 2016).
52 See M Pifferi, "From responsibility to dangerousness? The failed promise of penal positivism", in M Pifferi (ed), *The Limits of Criminological Positivism: The Movement for Criminal Law Reform in the West, 1870-1940* (Routledge: London, 2022), pp.255–279.

References

Books and book chapters

Berman HJ, *Law and Revolution: The Formation of the Western Legal Tradition* (Harvard University Press: Cambridge MA, 1983).
Böhmer JSF, *Elementa iurisprudentiae criminalis. Editio tertia* (Ex officina Fritschiana: Halae at Bernburgi, 1743).
Carbasse JM, *Introduction historique au droit pénal* (Presses Universitaires de France: Paris, 1990).
Cavina M, "Il dolo latente nell'animo. Filippo Maria Renazzi nel dibattito giuridico intorno alla graduazione del dolo fra XVIII e XIX secolo", in Di Simone MR, Frova C, & Alvazzi del Frate P (eds), *Filippo Maria Renazzi: Università e cultura a Roma tra Settecento e Ottocento* (il Mulino: Bologna, 2019).

Claro G, *Volumen, alias Liber Quintus* (IA de Antoniis Librarii: Venetiis, 1570).
Coing H, "Die juristische Fakultät und ihr Lehrprogramm", in H Coing (ed), *Handbuch der Quellen und Literatur der neueren europäischen Privatrechtsgeschichte* (CH Beck'sche: Munich, 1973), vol I.
Corran E, *Lying and Perjury in Medieval Practical Thought: A Study in the History of Casuistry* (Oxford University Press: Oxford, 2018).
Costa P, *Il progetto giuridico: Ricerche sulla giurisprudenza del liberalismo classico* (Giuffrè: Milan 1974), vol I.
De Castro A, *De potestate legis poenalis. Libri duo* (In aedibus Viduae et Haeredum Ioannis Stelsii: Antuerpiae, 1568).
Deciani T, *Tractatus criminalis* (Apud Franciscus de Franciscis Senensem: Venetiis, 1590), vol I.
Demuro GP, *Il dolo: Svolgimento storico del concetto* (Giuffrè: Milan, 2007), vol I.
Descamps O, "Quelques remarques sur la distinction entre homicide volontaire et homicide involontaire en droit canonique médiéval", in Condorelli O, Roumy F, & Schmoeckel M (eds), *Der Einfluß des Kanonistik auf die europäische Rechtskultur. Straf- und Strafprozessrecht* (Bohlau: Köln, 2012), vol III.
di Castro P, *In Primam Codicis partem Commentaria* (apud Lucam Antonium Iuntam: Venetiis 1582).
Di Giulio S & Frigo A (eds), *Kasuistik und Theorie des Gewissens. Von Pascal bis Kant* (De Gruyter: Berlin/Boston, 2020).
du Plessis PJ & Cairns JW (eds), *Reassessing Legal Humanism and its Claims: Petere Fontes?* (Edinburgh University Press: Edinburgh, 2016).
Engelmann W, *Die Schuldlehre der Postglossatoren und Ihre Fortentwicklung. Eine historisch-dogmatische Darstellung der kriminellen Schuldlehre der italienischen Juristen des Mittelalters seit Accursius* (Duncker & Humblot: Leipzig, 1895).
Farmer L, *Making the Modern Criminal Law: Criminalization and Civil Order* (Oxford University Press: Oxford, 2016).
Filangieri G, *La scienza della legislazione* (C Derriey: Parigi, 1853).
Gambiglioni A, *Tractatus de maleficiis, cum additionibus Augustini Bonfrancisci Ariminensis* (Flackenburg: Coloniae, 1599).
Garland D, *Punishment and Welfare. A History of Penal Strategies* (Ashgate: Aldershot, 1985).
Gibson M, *Born to Crime: Cesare Lombroso and the Origins of Biological Criminology* (Praeger: Westport, 2002).
Ginzburg C & Biasiori L (eds), *A Historical Approach to Casuistry: Norms and Exceptions in Comparative Perspective* (Bloomsbury: London, 2019).
Ginzburg C, "Ein Plädoyer für den Kasus", in Süßmann J, Scholz S, & Engel G (eds), *Fallstudien: Theorie – Geschichte – Methode* (Trafo: Berlin, 2007).
Gioffredi C, *I principi del diritto penale romano* (Giappichelli: Torino, 1970).
Gomez A, *Variarum Resolutionum Iuris Civilis, Communis et Regii Commentaria*, t III, *de Delictis* (Ex typographia Felicis Mosca: Neapoli, 1718), c 3 *De Homicidio*, § 30.
Grossi P, *A History of European Law* (Wiley Blackwell: Chichester, 2010).
Grunert F, "'Punienda ergo sunt maleficia.' Zur Kompetenz des öffentlichen Strafens in der Spanischen Spätscholastik", in Grunert F & Seelmann K (eds), *Die Ordnung der Praxis. Neue Studien zur Spanischen Spätscholastik* (Max Niemeyer Verlag: Tübingen, 2001).
Guyader J, "Aux origines canoniques de la responsabilité pénale: volonté coupable et pénitence dans les crimes contre les personnes d'après Burchard de Worms", in Thireau J-L (ed), *Le droit entre laïcisation et neo-sacralisation* (PUF: Paris, 1997).
Huff TE, "Max Weber's Comparative and Historical Sociology of Law. The Developmental Conditions of Law", in Sica A (ed), *The Routledge International Handbook on Max Weber* (Routledge: London & New York, 2023).
Kamali EP, *Felony and the Guilty Mind in Medieval England* (Cambridge University Press: Cambridge, 2019).
Kéry L, *Gottesfurcht und irdische Strafe. Der Beitrag des mittelalterlichen Kirchenrechts zur Entstehung des öffentlichen Strafrechts* (Bohlau: Köln, 2006).
Köstlin CR, *System des deutschen Strafrechts: Allgemeiner Teil* (Laupp: Tübingen, 1855).
Kuttner S, *Kanonistische Schuldlehre von Gratian bis auf die Dekretalen Gregors IX. Sistematisch auf Grund der handschriftlichen Quellen dargestellt* (Biblioteca Apostolica Vaticana: Città del Vaticano, 1935).

Lacey N, *In Search of Criminal Responsibility: Ideas, Interests, and Institutions* (Oxford University Press: Oxford, 2016).
Laingui A, *La responsabilité pénale dans l'ancien droit (XVIe-XVIIIe siècle)* (Librairie générale de droit et de jurisprudence: Paris, 1970).
Lipp M, *Die Bedeutung des Naturrechts für die Ausbildung der Allgemeinen Lehren des deutschen Privatrechts* (Duncker & Humblot: Berlin 1980).
Löffler A, *Die Schuldformen des Strafrechts in vergleichend-historischer und dogmatischer Darstellung* (CL Hirschfeld: Leipzig, 1895).
Lucchesi M, *Si quis occidit occidetur. L'omicidio doloso nelle fonti consiliari (secoli XIV-XVI)* (Cedam: Padova, 1999).
Maihold H, *Strafe für fremde Schuld? Die Systematisierung des Strafbegriffs in der Spanischen Spätscholastik und Naturrechtslehre* (Böhlau: Köln, 2005).
Maine H, *Ancient Law* (1861) (Cambridge University Press: Cambridge, 2013).
Mantica F, *Vaticanae lucubrationes de tacitis et ambiguis conuentionibus* (Ex typographia Vaticana: Romae, 1609).
Martinage R, *Histoire du droit pénal en Europe* (PUF: Paris, 1998).
Meccarelli M, "Criminal Law: Before a State Monopoly", in Pihlajamäki H, Dubber MD, Godfrey M (eds), *The Oxford Handbook of European Legal History* (Oxford University Press: Oxford, 2018).
Meister GJF, *Principia iuris criminalis Germaniae communis* (IC Dieterich: Gottingae, 1798).
Menzinger S, *Finzioni del diritto medievale* (Quodlibet: Macerata, 2023).
Nardi P, "Relations with Authority", in H De Ridder-Symoens (ed), *A History of the University in Europe* (Cambridge University Press: Cambridge, 1992), vol I.
Passeron JC & Revel J (eds), *Penser par cas* (Éditions de l'École des hautes études en sciences sociales: Paris, 2020).
Piano Mortari V, *Diritto logica metodo nel secolo XVI* (Jovene: Napoli, 1976).
Pifferi M, "From Responsibility to Dangerousness? The Failed Promise of Penal Positivism", in Pifferi M (ed), *The Limits of Criminological Positivism: The Movement for Criminal Law Reform in the West, 1870–1940* (Routledge: London, 2022).
Pifferi M, *Generalia delictorum: Il Tractatus criminalis di Tiberio Deciani e la "parte generale" di diritto penale* (Giuffrè: Milan, 2006).
Pifferi M, *Reinventing Punishment: A Comparative History of Criminology and Penology in the Nineteenth and Twentieth Centuries* (Oxford University Press: Oxford, 2016).
Pihlajamäki H & Korpiola M, "Medieval Canon Law: The Origins of Modern Criminal Law", in Dubber M (ed), *The Oxford Handbook of Criminal Law* (Oxford University Press: Oxford, 2014).
Reinhard W, *Geschichte der Staatsgewalt: Eine vergleichende Verfassungsgeschichte Europas von den Anfängen bis zur Gegenwart* (CH Beck: Munich, 2nd edn, 2000).
Renazzi FM, *Elementa iuris criminalis. Liber I. De delictis generatim* (Joannes Generosus Salomoni: Romae, 1774).
Rossi G, *Ordinatio ad casum: Legal Causation in Italy (14th – 17th centuries)* (Vittorio Klostermann: Frankfurt am Main, 2023).
Rousseaux X, "From Case to Crime. Homicide Regulation in Medieval and Modern Europe", in Schlosser H & Willoweit D (eds), *Neue Wege strafrechtsgeschichtlicher Forschung* (Böhlau: Köln, 1999).
Sbriccoli M, "Giustizia criminale", in *Storia del diritto penale e della giustizia. Scritti editi e inediti (1972–2007)* (Giuffrè: Milano, 2009).
Sbriccoli M, "Legislation, Justice and Political Power in Italian Cities, 1200–1400", in *Storia del diritto penale e della giustizia. Scritti editi e inediti (1972–2007)* (Giuffrè: Milano, 2009).
Schaffstein F, "Tiberius Decianus und seine Bedeutung für die Entstehung des Allgemeinen Teils im Gemeinen deutschen Strafrecht", in *Abhandlungen zur Strafrechtsgeschichte und zur Wissenschaftsgeschichte* (Scientia Verlag: Aalen, 1986).
Schmidt E, *Einführung in die Geschichte der deutschen Strafrechtspflege* (Vandenhoeck & Ruprecht: Gottingen, 4th edn, 1995).
Schmoeckel M, "Der Allgemeine Teil in der Ordnung des BGB", in Schmoeckel M, Rückert J, & Zimmermann R (eds), *Historisch-kritischer Kommentar zum BGB, I, Allgemeiner Teil, §§ 1-240* (Mohr Siebeck: Tübingen, 2003).
Siedentop L, *Inventing the Individual: The Origins of Western Liberalism* (Harvard University Press: Cambridge MA, 2014).

Sorice R, *Vittime colpevoli e colpevoli innocenti. Ricerche sulle responsabilità penali nell'età del diritto comune* (Bologna University Press: Bologna, 2018).

Tartagni A, *Consiliorum liber secundus* (Ex officina Damiani Zenarii: Venetiis, 1578), Cons CXL.

Tentler TN, "The Summa for Confessors as an Instrument of Social Control", in Trinkaus C & Oberman HA (eds), *The Pursuit of Holiness in Late Medieval and Renaissance Religion* (Brill: Leiden, 1974).

Tiedemann K, "Zum Verhältnis von allgemeinem und besonderem Teil des Strafrechts", in Arzt G, Fezer G, Weber U, Schlüchter E, & Rössner D (eds), *Festschrift für Jürgen Baumann zum 70. Geburtstag 22. Juni 1992* (Gieseking: Bielefeld, 1992).

Tierney B, *The Idea of Natural Rights: Studies on Natural Rights, Natural Law, and Church Law, 1150–1625* (Scholars Press: Atlanta, 1997).

Tiraqueau A, *De poenis Legum ac Consuetudinum Statutorumque temperandis, aut etiam remittendis, et id quibus, quotque ex causis*, in *Tractatus varii* (G Rovillum: Lugduni, 1587).

Tomas y Valiente F, *El derecho penal de la Monarquía absoluta (siglos XVI-XVII-XVIII)* (Tecnos: Madrid, 1969).

Tutino S, *Uncertainty in Post-Reformation Catholicism: A History of Probabilism* (Oxford University Press: Oxford, 2017).

Vallerani M, *Medieval Public Justice* (Catholic University of America Press: Washington DC, 2012).

Villey M, "La promotion de la loi et du droit subjectif dans la Seconde Scolastique", in Grossi P (ed), *La Seconda Scolastica nella formazione del diritto privato moderno* (Giuffrè: Milan, 1973).

Volante R, "Argomentazione senza principi nel diritto comune", in Latini C (ed), *Argomentazione e lessico nella tradizione giuridica* (Giappichelli: Torino, 2022).

von Weber H, "Zur Entwicklung des gemeinen deutschen Strafrechts unter besonderer Berücksichtigung spanischer Einflüsse", in *L'Europa e il diritto romano: Studi in memoria di Paolo Koschaker* (Giuffrè: Milan, 1954), vol I.

Weber M, *Economy and Society. An Outline of Interpretive Sociology*, edited and translated by Roth G & Wittich C (University of California Press: Berkley CA, 1978).

Wetzell RF, *Inventing the Criminal: A History of German Criminology, 1880–1945* (University of North Carolina Press: Chapel Hill, 2000).

Journal articles

Cappellini P, "Sulla formazione del moderno concetto di 'dottrina generale del diritto'", *Quaderni fiorentini per la storia del pensiero giuridico moderno*, vol. 10 (1981), pp.323–354.

Coing H, "L'insegnamento del diritto nell'Europa dell'Ancient Regime", *Studi Senesi*, vol. 82 (1970), pp.179–193.

Cupido M, "Facing Facts in International Criminal Law. A Casuistic Model of Judicial Reasoning", *Journal of International Criminal Justice*, vol. 14, no. 1 (2016), pp.1–20.

Cupido M, "The Casuistry of International Criminal Law: Exploring A New Field of Research", *Netherlands Journal of Legal Philosophy*, vol. 44, no. 2 (2015), pp.116–132.

De Concilio D, "Soggettività e qualificazione del fatto. L'indagine del *factum intrinsecum* tra diritto e teologia nel XII secolo: due casi di studio e spunti per una ricerca", *Historia & Ius*, vol. 22, no. paper 9 (2022), pp.1–42.

Di Martino A, "The Importance of Being a Case. Collapsing of the Law Upon the Case in Interlegal Situations", *The Italian Law Journal*, vol. 7, no. 2 (2021), pp.961–984.

Fraher R, "The theoretical Justification for the New Criminal Law of the High Middle Ages: 'Rei publicae interest, ne crimina remaneant impunita'", *University of Illinois Law Review*, vol. 1984, no. 3 (1984), pp.577–595.

Giuliani A, "Imputation et justification", *Archives de philosophie du droit*, vol. 22 (1977), pp.85–96.

Grossi P, "Somme penitenziali, diritto canonico, diritto comune", *Annali della Facoltà giuridica di Macerata*, vol. 1 (1966), pp.95–134.

Grossi P, "Sulla 'natura' del contratto (qualche nota sul 'mestiere' di storico del diritto, a proposito di un recente 'corso' di lezioni)", *Quaderni fiorentini per la storia del pensiero giuridico moderno*, vol. 15 (1986), pp.593–619.

Kuttner S, "Zur Entstehungsgeschichte des Summa de casibus poenitentiae des hl. Raymund von Penyafort", *Zeitschrift der Savigny-Stiftung für Rechtsgeschichte. Kanonistische Abteilung*, vol. 39 (1953), pp.419–434.

Maes LT, "Die drei grossen europäischen Strafgesetzbücher des 16. Jahrhunderts. Eine vergleichende Studie", *Zeitschrift der Savigny-Stiftung für Rechtsgeschichte: Germanistische Abteilung*, vol. 94 (1977), pp.207–217.

Pifferi M, "Per giustizia e per salvezza. Qualche riflessione sulla polifunzionalità della pena tra medioevo ed età moderna", *Quaderni di diritto e politica ecclesiastica*, vol. 22 (2019), pp.3–19.

Sorice R, "La dialettica tra volontario e involontario nella dimensione penale pre-gregoriana: l'omicidio *sponte commissum* nei Penitenziali e nei *Capitularia* carolingi", *Rivista Internazionale di Diritto Comune*, vol. 29 (2018), pp.45–64.

Sorice R, "La teoria del *versari in re illicita* nel pensiero di Giovanni d'Andrea: *dolus generalis?*", *Zeitschrift der Savigny-Stiftung für Rechtsgeschichte: Kanonistische Abteilung*, vol. 105, no. 1 (2019), pp.99–152.

Archival materials

of Peñafort R, *Summa de casibus poenitentiae* (Corpus Christi College, MS: Cambridge 247) [ca 1200-1299].

PART II

Doctrines and Principles of Criminal Responsibility

11
LAW, EMOTIONS, AND "REACTIVE DEFENCES"

Grant Barclay

Introduction

"They had been brought up in a tradition that told them in one way or another that the life of the mind and the life of the senses were separate and, indeed, inimical; they had believed, without ever having really thought about it, that one had to be chosen at some expense of the other. That the one could intensify the other had never occurred to them".[1]

Over the last few decades, there has been an increasing interest in discussing the role that emotions can be said to play in the various parts of the criminal justice system in legal scholarship.[2] Indeed, it is probably fair to say that, insofar as there is a relationship between law and society, there is necessarily also a relationship between law and humanity, and thus between law and emotions. Emotions are, after all, an essential part of the human condition.[3] Some scholarship has focused on humanising the criminal justice process itself, arguing for a justice policy which is emotionally literate and recognises the importance of participation in the process for both victims and offenders alike.[4] Other work has focused on the ability of emotions in judicial decision-making to "fix" and "sustain" judicial attention upon the impact of laws to the rights of an affected individual or group.[5] Such work highlights that emotions can be utilised by judges as a useful tool for critical engagement when considering potential rights violations, usually in the context of determining human dignity.[6] Other work still has examined the use of narrative and emotion in legal processes more generally, focusing on the admissibility of victim impact statements as testimony to provide/improve context.[7]

These works necessarily have as their focus the ways in which we might incorporate emotions into the criminal justice process, as humans interacting within that institutional space. My own interest in emotions focuses on their value to substantive criminal law theory, and how our understanding of emotions might shape notions of culpability and hence legal doctrine. I have focused my research on what I call "reactive defences"[8] in Scotland, which encompasses the defences of duress,[9] necessity, and self-defence. In particular, I have found myself considering the question: to what extent can and should emotions play a role in characterising and hence formulating substantive criminal law defences like necessity, duress, and self-defence? In other words, what role do emotions play in determining criminal responsibility in the context of defences?

Questions like these form part of a growing scholarship examining the role of emotions in various facets of criminal law doctrine.[10] Classic, voluntarist accounts of culpability tend to focus on the concept of choice as being paramount to the kind of rational agency for which application of the criminal law should be focused, but exclude consideration of the factors that might bear on the authenticity of that choice.[11] Theories of culpability which account for emotions are therefore necessarily wider in scope, aiming to encompass those factors which might be seen as choice-limiting, with some even including socio-environmental factors as part of this assessment.[12] Taking such a normative account as a starting point, scholarship which aims to utilise emotions theory in doctrinal analysis is therefore focused on identifying which current criminal law doctrines are doing a poor job at conveying the authentic human experience. The topic of criminal law defences is an area ripe for such analysis because the very notion of the availability of a defence to criminal conduct engenders the intersection of multiple, often incongruent and competing, aims of criminal justice, some of which compel the law towards a more inauthentic outlook on human behaviour.

My aim in this chapter is to contribute to this scholarship by introducing another research question: insofar as self-defence is comparable to other defences with an emotional component – such as necessity and duress – to what extent does self-defence have an emotional component, and to what extent should this inform our understanding of these other defences in any potential future reforms? This question is of particular significance as the vocabulary found in discussions of duress and necessity is often very different to that found in discussions of self-defence.

Space precludes a full analysis of this and related questions in this chapter; instead, I have two more modest goals. The first is to establish the existence of a normative category of defences which is responsive to emotions, known as reactive defences, to which duress, necessity and self-defence all belong. The second goal is to suggest that this normative categorisation might be utilised in conjunction with novel paradigms of culpability, particularly those that feature emotions as a constituent part, to make broader claims about other, related criminal law doctrines. Specifically, I suggest that a focus on the emotional component of self-defence may allow us to rethink the exclusion of duress and necessity defences from charges of murder. With this contribution, I hope to further scholarship which promotes an understanding of emotions in defences which is attentive to the feelings[13] experienced by the actor and yet sensitive to the positive declarations of responsibility being made when a person acts in situations of extreme pressure.

Paradigms of culpability

In her seminal work on the topic, Coppola explains that classic accounts of criminal responsibility adopt a compatibilist perspective of personhood in evaluating culpability, which is to say that free will is not a prerequisite for culpability.[14] On this view, persons are culpable for the actions they cause, even if external factors have contributed to the production of such actions, because all humans still possess a margin of freedom which allows them to act in a non-compelled way. This freedom, from which culpability attributions derive, is understood through two essential aspects of personhood: individual autonomy and rationality. Hart provides a classic example of this voluntarist theory with the statement that persons should have the capacity and fair opportunity to conform their actions to the law.[15]

Coppola locates the origin of this dominant paradigm of culpability in the growing adherence to individualism as an ideology.[16] Indeed, the concepts of individualism and voluntarism are mutually affirming in that it is to the individual alone that voluntarist theories state we should look to determine culpability, by examining their rational choice unaffected by broader notions of culture or society.[17] On this account, it is easy to see why capacity assumed the vaulted (and solitary) position in culpability assessments that it has. The doctrinal implications for this theory are clear: factors like emotions are relevant only insofar as they can be said to remove cognition, for if cognition remains, culpability can (and should) be ascribed. We can see this play out in various jurisdictions' homicide laws, where some form of provocation/loss of control and diminished capacity style defences operate to mitigate the culpability of persons who would otherwise be guilty of murder.[18]

The problem with the voluntarist theory is that it is rationalist to a fault – it assumes that persons who possess sound mental capacity are able to act freely upon their choices and are given a fair opportunity to avoid wrongdoing. Cognition in the context of personhood under voluntarism is thus reduced to rationality and individual autonomy.[19] As Coppola puts it: "Culpability ascriptions are fundamentally based on the assumption that cognitive powers of reason and control allow people to grasp the guiding force of legal norms and conform their behaviour to them."[20] This is a problem because while legal doctrines shaped by voluntarism have proliferated across jurisdictions, an ever-increasing amount of research has established that various sociological and neuroscientific factors do in fact operate to encumber decision-making in a meaningful way.[21] One particular strand of this research concerns explaining how emotions can be said to affect decision-making, with the modern consensus being that emotions are cognitive in nature and thus responsive to reason.[22] This research therefore suggests that greater attention should be paid to these additional factors which form part of our reasoning processes in culpability attribution assessments. Scholars such as Gardner have since written about the rationality of emotions as a useful guide to assessing responsibility in the context of excusing offenders who act "in the thrall of" an emotion.[23] Emotions, he argues, are rational in nature and responsive to reason. We are compelled to act precisely because the action corresponds to an underlying belief set that we, as rational choosing agents, align with. Emotions are thus suitable bases for normative and hence legal blame and ought to be considered in relation to responsibility assessments that test the reasonableness of our reactions to stressful stimuli.

In addition to theoretical work, the cognitive theory of emotions[24] has also encouraged doctrinal work examining specific areas of the law and how they might be reformed to take into consideration this modern understanding of emotions and their influence on culpability. In relation to defences specifically, previous work has looked at reforming duress to be more in line with cognitive theories of emotion,[25] and the creation of new (partial) defences which aim at the law recognising a broader spectrum of emotional reactions as reasons for criminal action.[26] One area of the law of defences which seems to have evaded such analysis is the law of self-defence, presumably owing to the defence's typical characterisation as a justification. Indeed, as Duff notes in his discussion of emotions in defences, if the reason for exculpation is that the action is justified or permissible,[27] the agent's motivations become irrelevant as what matters for justification is the presence of pre-defined external circumstances.[28] However, it seems that there are good reasons why a closer inspection of self-defence under emotions theories would be a fruitful endeavour. Specifically, not all examples of self-defence are rightly to be understood as justified.[29] This suggests that in at least some cases of self-defence the emotional component *is* important. In any case, it seems undeniable that self-defence as a normative concept has an emotional component in all cases, irrespective of whether the legal assessment is to be focused on the agent or the circumstances. Thus, an analysis of self-defence might provide value to doctrinal analyses of other, similar defences, like duress and necessity. The next section will demonstrate in what ways these defences are similar, and why all three might be thought of as forming a category known as "reactive defences".

Reactive defences

Here, I provide a brief sketch of the legal landscape covering "reactive defences" so called, with a view to establishing a close factual nexus between self-defence, necessity, and duress. Establishing this nexus will help to explain why rationalisations based on emotions are interlinked between the defences, thereby enabling further comparisons on this basis.

Of the numerous substantive criminal law defences, only a few can be characterised by the presence of some external, stressful stimuli which operates to produce a reaction within the agent, thereby motivating them to commit an offence. It is this reaction to external factors which provides the agent's immediate reasons for acting, and hence the rationale for exculpation. Important for present purposes is the fact that not just any reaction will suffice. The law tends to reserve exculpation for reactions based on fear, whereas actions based on other emotions such as anger do not qualify for the same exculpatory treatment.[30] Determining the precise contours of these reactions is therefore of importance. What kinds of reactions can generate condonation from the legal system to instances of law breaking which even include, in the case of self-defence, homicide? What kinds of rights and/or values must be at stake before the law will excuse or permit intentional criminal acts? These are important questions to consider, and necessarily raise further questions about the relationship between such defences.

I refer to this small subset of defences as "reactive defences".[31] Their limited number is perhaps explained by the fact that modern substantive criminal law is usually unconcerned with the agent's motives, with such considerations typically being considered in later stages of the trial.[32] Indeed, reactive defences appear to occupy an interesting space in the criminal justice process as a whole, insofar as their underlying rationale is one which has typically been reserved for consideration as part of the sentencing process as pleas in mitigation, after the substantive criminal law portion of the trial has ended. To that end, the concept of provocation appears to best correspond to this division of criminal procedure, finding a niche application as a partial defence in UK jurisdictions to charges of murder,[33] as well as applying generally as a plea in mitigation to other offences.

Duress, necessity, and self-defence as conventionally understood all involve the kind of motivational claim outlined above, but unlike provocation they result in complete exculpation through an acquittal. Beyond this initial commonality, it is not always clear what the precise basis for distinguishing these defences is. Traditional understandings of duress and necessity locate their distinction in whether the stressful stimulus, that is to say the threat, originates from a human or natural origin,[34] but this does not correspond to how the defences have been utilised by courts where human threats can ground cases of necessity.[35] A more accurate distinction might be found in whether the agent retains some level of choice over their ultimate criminal conduct, as is the case in necessity, or whether they instead relinquish all control by obeying the commands of another (duress).[36] While a distinction based on the presence of a choice in the criminal conduct undertaken is certainly far more defensible than one based on the origin of the threat, it seems somewhat disingenuous to suggest that the criminal path is unclear in most necessity type cases such that they will typically offer more than one (criminal) choice: in reality the criminal choice is usually singular and obvious. These conceptual difficulties have led Spain to argue that a singular, reformulated defence of duress should cover those situations where threats impel fear, and that fear constitutes a reasonable emotional reaction to the circumstances.[37] In contrast, necessity would operate in a residual, justificatory capacity as a utilitarian-styled lesser evils defence, where the accused acts to minimise harm irrespective of their emotional state.[38]

Self-defence appears to differ from both duress and necessity on the basis that it involves an initial aggressor who, by their attack on the agent, creates an entitlement for the agent to respond with defensive force against that aggressor to ward off the attack. Nevertheless, this theoretical division is not always so neat: if what matters is that a person has a duty to defend themselves from potentially lethal violence,[39] the circumstances under which such a duty arises are surely irrelevant and thus such a duty should hypothetically also arise in circumstances of duress and necessity.[40] Indeed, the strict requirement of these defences that the threat avoided was one of death or serious injury would point towards this conclusion. If, conversely, what matters in creating that duty or entitlement to defend in self-defence cases is the conduct of the initial aggressor, then what really seems to be at play is a retributivist understanding of self-defensive conduct, classically understood as the "forfeiture theory", whereby the deceased can be said to have forfeited their right to life by disregarding the agent's own right to life through their initial attack.[41] Of course, this logic enters an inescapable quagmire in trying to explain how self-defensive action is allowed against innocent aggressors, such as children or those with mental disorders.[42] This conceptual incoherence might be seen to indirectly bolster claims for other reactive defences to operate against charges of murder, although there has never been much of a judicial appetite for this extension in the UK.[43] Nevertheless, at a practical level the requirement that the self-defender respond with force against the aggressor appears to have been abandoned in some jurisdictions, with the defence being made available to those who "commit an offence" to avoid an attack.[44]

The precise lines to be drawn between each defence is therefore a site of much debate. In the context of emotions theory, what seems to emerge from a survey of these defences at a doctrinal level is a difference predicated on perspective. In self-defence cases, we are concerned with the reasonableness of a person's self-defensive action in relation to the actions of another; in duress and necessity cases by contrast, the language suggests we should be concerned with the reasonableness of a person's *reaction* to stressful circumstances.[45]

Despite linguistic differences, however, in normative terms the defences seem very similar. Duff speaks of duress having a strong justificatory dimension, because the actor's emotional motivation, reasons for acting, and weighing of the reasons for and against so acting must all be justified, even if it is ultimately impermissible to commit the offence.[46] However, this normative dimension appears to be at odds with practical reality. Indeed, Duff's example to explain this point is analogous to *R v Hudson & Taylor*,[47] a position which was definitively overruled in *R v Hasan*.[48] Interestingly though, the above description seems apt to also describe excusatory self-defence: if the circumstances are not as the agent believed, we might say that a defence of self-defence can only be available where the actor's emotional motivation, reasons for acting, and weighing of the reasons for and against so acting must all be justified, even if ultimately the agent's actions are to be deemed impermissible (but nevertheless excusable). Dissatisfaction with the normative (and practical) boundaries between these defences has also encouraged previous attempts to amalgamate them all into one, singular defence,[49] but such proposals have not picked up any momentum.

Far more might be said about the normative divisions between the recognised reactive defences, but for the purposes of this chapter it suffices to demonstrate that there is a factual nexus which supports a normative connection between each reactive defence; one based on the presence of a reaction to external circumstances which the law recognises as a suitable ground for eliminating an agent's criminal responsibility. The main point of distinction between reactive defences on this basis in practice is the extent to which the external circumstances are dispositive of the matter, in relation to the emotions experienced. This particular axis therefore suggests that an understanding of reactions and emotions in self-defence is of importance to broader analyses of culpability in reactive defences generally, and thus worthy of further consideration.

The emotional self-defender

In this last section I aim to briefly examine self-defence through a doctrinal lens to establish an emotional foundation for its legal doctrine. Space precludes a full examination (indeed the primary purpose of this chapter is to argue that such further work is a worthy endeavour), and so Scotland is provided as a focal point; partly as a legal system with which the writer is familiar, but also one which features a rich common law tradition.[50] Indeed, the reactive defences in Scots law are all found in the common law, based on judicial precedent and the writings of key legal figures throughout Scottish legal history, known as institutional writers.[51] The prominence of these writings is, at least in part, due to a lack of reported decisions during this time, with many of the institutional writers being practising lawyers/judges who would record the decisions of cases of which they were a part in their writing.[52] I see this peculiar tradition within the common law as offering a unique perspective for contextual analysis of legal doctrine: the commentaries of judges and institutional writers are invariably far richer in vocabulary, and perhaps more varied in the sources that may be drawn upon in any given case,[53] than their statutory counterparts.

The limitations of this analysis must be acknowledged, lest this chapter be taken to otherwise suggest that self-defence is primarily a defence of emotion, and that doctrinal sources refer to it as such. Rather, the focus of this exercise is to explore which principles might be transferable to other reactive defences, despite a tendency to *downplay* emotional characteristics in legal doctrine. Indeed, generally the emotional aspect of self-defence has been overlooked in Scottish legal doctrine. The historical sources, while occasionally referencing feelings of apprehension or fear in treatments of self-defence, focus on the accused having a duty[54] or entitlement[55] to resist. However, even the early historical sources refer to the emotional content of self-defence in a way which can be seen to influence the doctrine being expounded. Writing in the seventeenth century, Mackenzie describes threats of death being sufficient to ground self-defence on the basis that "there is a greater fear from some threats than from wounds, and therefore, seeing it is lawful to kill those who assault us with wounding, why not and {also} him who threatens?"[56] One century later, Hume tells us that it would be unreasonable to expect due temperance and moderation from a person who was attacked on the public highway, such that they could not be expected to adhere to any kind of proportionality when retaliating.[57] Of particular importance, Hume states that if the highway rogue were to demand their property, they might still have a defence since one would have reason "to dread all sorts of violence on refusal, or even delay to comply".[58] Nevertheless, Hume tells us that self-defence is committed from necessity to save one's life, and cannot be relied upon where a person kills to avoid "some great indignity".[59] In these cases, the accused "must answer for this vice of temper" and rely on a less favourable plea.[60]

There is thus a sense from Hume's treatment that fear might exculpate fully in self-defence, but that anger and its related motivations could not. Mackenzie's account appears to align with this view, and later treatments also speak of the reasonableness of one's "alarm" as being dispositive of the plea.[61] Modern caselaw also refers to fear or apprehension as being a consideration when determining the validity of an accused's self-defence plea.[62] As with the normative foundation of reactive defences then, what seems to connect reactive defences in terms of emotional content is the presence of fear. These legal sources, interpreted through a broader theory of culpability, may therefore introduce a different dimension for examining the validity of emotional responses in other reactive defences. Most prominently, the Scottish self-defence doctrine understood through a broader understanding of culpability, and as part of a broader category of reactive defences, may suggest that the exclusion of duress and necessity pleas from charges of murder can no longer be sustained on public policy grounds alone.

The public policy argument is often produced as a trump card in response to normative theories of the relationship between reactive defences which demonstrate that favouring self-defence over the others for such charges is unprincipled. The idea is that, while the law accepts that citizens will sometimes find themselves in intolerable circumstances, it nevertheless cannot tolerate exculpating the taking of life. Theoretically, we might explain such an argument as being that under no circumstances can killing under duress or necessity be considered a rationally attractive option: it is simply not an option we can consider in our reasons for acting.[63] If, however, we understand culpability as involving a broader idea of personhood – one which includes the emotional lives of still rational agents – and if further we accept that fear provides an explanatory component for the rational attractiveness of killing in at least some circumstances, we may have to finally accept, *simpliciter*, the proposition that a reasonable fear of death can exculpate the taking of life to avoid it. Whether this entails allowing duress and necessity as defences to charges of murder or amplifies those calls for a generic partial defence[64] (of which self-defence may have to form a part) is another matter entirely.

Conclusion

Contemporary scholarship has identified an important role for emotions in criminal culpability, one that challenges the traditional voluntarist understanding and perhaps compatibilism more generally. This challenge invites us to engage in broader discussions about how concepts such as choice and will interact and influence culpability assessments. Such a paradigm shift also requires us to reconsider various aspects of criminal law doctrine. Of particular significance are those defences involving the blameworthiness of persons who commit offences in the kinds of extraordinary circumstances which engender strong emotional responses and can thus be regarded as reactive defences. This chapter has argued that an analysis of the emotional relationship between reactive defences is not only viable, but indeed necessary for understanding the normative concerns that such defences embody. One avenue for further exploration, introduced here, is how a broader understanding of the emotional content of self-defence, previously under-scrutinised, might be employed to help answer difficult policy-related questions in relation to reactive defences more generally.

Acknowledgements

My thanks to Chloë Kennedy and Dalia Malek for their helpful feedback on earlier drafts of this chapter.

Notes

1 J Williams, *Stoner* (Vintage Books: London, 2003), p.205.
2 Although the roots of this scholarship are far richer: see Aristotle, *The Nicomachean Ethics*, translation by D Ross (Oxford University Press: Oxford, 2009), 1105b, pp.29–30, discussing the nature of emotions in the voluntariness of action.
3 The essentiality of emotions is relatively uncontroversial, but the precise nature and scope of emotions is part of a larger, more rigorous debate concerning the history of emotions. One of the key research questions in this field of literature is to what extent emotions are socially constructed, versus evolutionary and hence universal. For a general introduction and overview, see J Plamper, *The History of Emotions: An Introduction* (Oxford University Press: Oxford, 2015). For general introductions from proponents of culturalism in understanding emotions, see K Barclay, "State of the Field: The History of Emotions", *The Journal of the Historical Association*, vol. 106, (2021), p.456; BH Rosenwein, "Emotions: Some Historical Observations", *History of Psychology*, vol. 24, no. 2 (2021), p.107.
4 C Tata & F Jamieson, "Just Emotions? The Need for Emotionally-Intelligent Justice Policy", *Scottish Justice Matters*, vol. 5, no. 1 (2017), p.32; C Tata, "Humanising Punishment? Mitigation and 'Case-cleansing' Prior to Sentencing", *Oñati Socio-Legal Series*, vol. 9, no. 5 (2019), p.659. Cf. J Gormley & C Tata, "Remorse and Sentencing in a World of Plea Bargaining" in S Tudor et al (eds), *Remorse and Criminal Justice: Multi-Disciplinary Perspectives* (Routledge: London & New York, 2022), pp.40–66, considering the value of the absence or presence of remorse on sentencing decisions.
5 E Kidd White, "On Emotions and the Politics of Attention in Judicial Reasoning" in A Amaya & M Del Mar (eds), *Virtue, Emotion and Imagination in Law and Legal Reasoning* (Hart Publishing: Oxford, 2020), pp.101–120.
6 Although care must be taken to avoid focusing on the wrong aspects, or from the wrong perspectives, as wholesale prescriptions of emotions to the judicial role pay insufficient attention to the normative situation of the law: Kidd White, "On Emotions and the Politics of Attention", pp.103-104.
7 SA Bandes, "Empathy, Narrative, and Victim Impact Statements" *The University of Chicago Law Review*, vol. 63, no. 2 (1996), p.361.
8 A term inspired by the late Professor Gerry Maher, then Commissioner at the Scottish Law Commission, to describe necessity, coercion (Scottish terminology for duress), self-defence and provocation in the Commission's Seventh Programme of Law Reform (Scot Law Com No 198 (2005)), at para 2.47.
9 Known as coercion in Scotland.
10 Notable works include S Pillsbury, *Judging Evil: Rethinking the Law of Murder and Manslaughter* (NYU Press: New York, 1998); B Berger, "Emotions and the Veil of Voluntarism: The Loss of Judgment in Canadian Criminal Defences", *McGill Law Journal*, vol. 51 (2006), p.99; E Spain, *The Role of Emotions in Criminal Defences: Necessity and Duress* (Cambridge University Press: Cambridge, 2011); RA Duff, "Criminal Responsibility and the Emotions: If Anger and Fear Can Exculpate, Why Not Compassion?", *Inquiry: An Interdisciplinary Journal of Law and Philosophy*, vol. 58, No. 2 (2015), p.189.
11 For classic examples, see JL Austin, "A Plea for Excuses: The Presidential Address", *Proceedings of the Aristotelian Society*, vol. 57, no. 1 (1957), p.1; and HLA Hart, "Legal Responsibility and Excuses" in *Punishment and Responsibility: Essays in the Philosophy of Law* (Clarendon Press: Oxford, 1968), pp.28–53. More recent (yet still classic) examples include CO Finkelstein, "Duress: A Philosophical Account of the Defense in Law", *Arizona Law Review*, vol. 37 (1995), p.251 and PH Robinson, "Criminal Law Defenses: A Systematic Analysis", *Columbia Law Review*, vol. 82, no. 2 (1982), p.199 at pp.225–226. This position is discussed in more detail below.

12 For a classic example, see R Delgado, "'Rotten Social Background': Should the Criminal Law Recognize a Defense of Severe Environmental Deprivation?", *Law & Enquiry*, vol. 3, no. 1 (1985), p.9.
13 "Feelings" here is understood as a cognitive awareness and appraisal of an emotional response. Anything less would appear to lack the sort of capacity that even traditional voluntarist accounts require for culpability. For a terminological overview of "feeling" in relation to "emotion", see F Coppola, *The Emotional Brain and the Guilty Mind: Novel Paradigms of Culpability and Punishment* (Hart Publishing: Oxford, 2021), p.93.
14 Coppola, *The Emotional Brain*, p.13.
15 Hart, *Punishment and Responsibility*, pp.28–53, particularly at p.44 (the law is a "choosing system").
16 Hart, *Punishment and Responsibility,* see chapter 2 generally, but particularly pp.48–60.
17 Cf. Meyers, arguing that autonomous selves are relational selves who learn to be so through interactions with others, highlighting that we are constituted within historical and social frameworks: D Meyers, *Self, Society, and Personal Choice* (Columbia University Press: New York, 1989), pp.189–202.
18 Scotland still utilises the common law provocation defence originally found in JHA Macdonald ("Being agitated and excited, and alarmed by violence, I lost control over myself, and took life, when my presence of mind had left me, and without thought of what I was doing": in J Walker & DJ Stevenson (eds), *A Practical Treatise on the Criminal Law of Scotland*, (W Green: Edinburgh, 5th edn, 1948), p.94) whereas England & Wales have replaced provocation with a statutory loss of control defence (ss 54–56 Coroners and Justice Act 2009). The Model Penal Code recommends a defence of "extreme mental or emotional disturbance": §210.3(1)(b).
19 Diana Meyers has provided a feminist critique of the traditional understanding of autonomy which views the idea as a continuum rather than as binary: "Personal Autonomy and the Paradox of Feminine Socialization", *Journal of Philosophy*, vol. 84, no. 11 (1987), p.619 at p.624. See also SJ Brison, *Aftermath* (Princeton University Press: New Jersey, 2022), pp. 59-64 on the necessity of retraining one's responses after trauma to recover diminished or lost autonomy.
20 Coppola, *The Emotional Brain*, p.42.
21 W Hirstein et al, *Responsible Brains: Neuroscience, Law, and Human Culpability* (MIT Press: Michigan, 2018), p.69, note that a "responsible act" requires the mind to be free of both internal and external pressures not initiated by the agent.
22 This literature begins with S Schachter & JE Singer, "Cognitive, Social and Physiological Determinants of Emotional States", *Psychological Review*, vol. 69, no. 5 (1962), p.379. For a fuller overview of the competing understandings of emotions, see DM Kahan & MC Nussbaum, "Two Conceptions of Emotion in Criminal Law", *Columbia Law Review*, vol. 96, no. 2 (1996), p.269.
23 J Gardner, "The Logic of Excuses and the Rationality of Emotions", Journal *of Value Inquiry*, vol. 43 (2009), p.315.
24 Used here as a generic term to cover all those theories of emotion based in cognition, rather than any specific one.
25 Spain, *The Role of Emotion in Criminal Law Defences.*
26 Duff, "Criminal Responsibility and the Emotions", (arguing for an compassion based excuse defence for those who assist their loved ones to commit suicide); SJ Morse, "Excusing and New Excuse Defenses: A Legal and Conceptual Review", *Crime and Justice*, vol. 23 (1998), p.323 and SJ Morse, "Diminished Rationality, Diminished Responsibility", *Ohio State Journal of Criminal Law*, vol. 1, no.1 (2002), p.289 (arguing for a "generic doctrine of partial excuse" defence which would respond to our increased understanding of human behaviour); P Catley, "The Need For a Partial Defence of Diminished Capacity and the Potential Role of the Cognitive Sciences in Helping Frame That Defence", in S Ligthart et al (eds), *Neurolaw: Advances in Neuroscience, Justice & Security* (Palgrave Macmillan: Switzerland, 2021) (arguing for a generic partial defence which rejects the traditionally understood binary of capacity).
27 On permissibility, see RA Duff, *Answering for Crime* (Hart Publishing: Oxford, 2009), p.266; S Uniacke, *Permissible Killing* (Cambridge University Press: Cambridge, 1994), p.14.
28 Duff, *Answering for Crime*, p.215. This argument builds on an understanding of the justification/ excuse distinction which is based on the "acoustic separation" of rules for courts and rules for

citizens: M Dan-Cohen, "Decision Rules and Conduct Rules: On Acoustic Separation in Criminal Law", *Harvard Law Review*, vol. 97, no. 3 (1984), p.625; P Alldridge, "Rules for Courts and Rules for Citizens", *Oxford Journal of Legal Studies*, vol. 10, no. 4 (1990), p.487.

29 For arguments on self-defence understood as an excuse, see: CO Finkelstein, "Self-Defense as a Rational Excuse", *University of Pittsburgh Law Review*, vol. 57 (1996), p.621; GP Fletcher, "Domination in the Theory of Justification and Excuse", *University of Pittsburgh Law Review*, vol. 57 (1996), p.553; CJ Rosen, "The Excuse of Self-Defense: Correcting A Historical Accident on Behalf of Battered Women Who Kill", *American University Law Review*, vol. 36, no.1 (1986), p.11.

30 Angry reactions tend to offer only partial exculpation or mitigation.

31 An alternative term is "rationale-based defences": M Dsouza, *Rationale-Based Defences in Criminal Law* (Hart Publishing: Oxford, 2017).

32 Motives and general character do, however, appear to have played a much larger role in the trial process historically. For an example, Elizabeth Papp Kamali has undertaken an extensive review of the concept of "felony" in Medieval England which demonstrates that early juries would consider the particular circumstances of a case (as well as the general character of the offender) when determining whether the accused had the necessary "felonious" state of mind for guilt: *Felony and the Guilty Mind in Medieval England* (Cambridge University Press: Cambridge, 2019).

33 The existence of a mandatory life sentence for charges of murder in both Scotland and England and Wales has precipitated the need for such partial defences which operate to "reduce" murder charges to charges of culpable homicide and manslaughter, respectively, thereby granting the judge sentencing discretion in those cases deemed to warrant it.

34 *Moss v Howdle* 1997 JC 123 at p.127 per Lord Justice-General Rodger, affirming the judgment of Lord Hailsham LC in the English case of *R v Howe* [1987] AC 417 at p.429. From secondary literature see, for example: MD Bayles, "Reconceptualising Necessity and Duress", *Wayne Law Review*, vol. 33 (1987), p.1191; J Dressler, "Exegesis of the law of Duress: Justifying the Excuse and Searching for its Proper Limits", *Southern California Law Review*, vol. 62, no. 5 (1989), p.1331 at p.1348; A Wertheimer, *Coercion* (Princeton University Press: New Jersey, 1987), p.146; G Williams, *Criminal Law: The General Part* (Stevens & Sons Ltd: London, 2nd edn, 1961), p.757; Law Reform Commission of Ireland, Consultation Paper: "Duress and Necessity" (Ireland: LRC CP 39, 2006), para 1.01, available at: www.lawreform.ie/_fileupload/consultation%20papers/Duress%20and%20Necessity%20CP.pdf.

35 See e.g. *Tudhope v Grubb* 1983 SCCR 350 (Scotland); *R v Willer* (1986) 83 Cr App R 225 (England & Wales).

36 J Chalmers & F Leverick, *Criminal Law Defences and Pleas in Bar of Trial* (W Green/Scottish Universities Law Institute: Edinburgh, 2006), para 5.02.

37 Spain, *The Role of Emotion in Criminal Law Defences*, p.263.

38 Spain, *The Role of Emotion in Criminal Law Defences*, p.283.

39 The language of "duty" is particularly prominent in historical Scottish texts. See, e.g. Sir George Mackenzie, OF Robinson (ed), *The Laws and Customs of Scotland in Matters Criminal* (1678) (The Stair Society: Edinburgh, 2012) vol. 59, Title XI, p.2; W Forbes, *The Institutes of the Law of Scotland* (1722 and 1730) (Edinburgh Legal Education Trust: Edinburgh, 2012), p.630; D Hume, *Commentaries on the Law of Scotland* (1800) (Law Society of Scotland: Edinburgh, 1986) vol I, p.217 (discussed below).

40 For necessity, see the infamous English maritime cannibalism case *R v Dudley and Stephens* (1884) 14 QBD 273 where necessity was rejected as a defence to murder.

41 For a more detailed analysis, see F Leverick, *Killing in Self-Defence* (Oxford University Press: Oxford, 2006), p.44.

42 Leverick, *Killing in Self- Defence*.

43 *R v Dudley and Stephens* (1884) 14 QBD 273; *R v Howe* [1987] AC 417; *Collins v HM Advocate* 1991 JC 204; *R v Abdul-Hussain* [1999] Crim LR 570; Cf. *Re A (Children)* [2001] Fam 147; *HM Advocate v Anderson* (Unreported, 2006).

44 Canadian Criminal Code, §34(1). The provision itself is silent, while the brief description, explanation, and commentary of the provision all refer to an individual's use of force. However, this term is never explicated, and indeed there is no suggestion that this force must be directed at the initial aggressor – only that it is utilised for the purpose of defending or protecting oneself or another

from use or threat of force, and that the force used is reasonable in the circumstances. There is therefore seemingly nothing preventing this provision applying when a person uses force on another, or indeed commits another crime to escape an attack.

45 Language in these cases focuses on an "overborne will" and "concessions to human frailty": See, e.g., *Thomson v HMA* 1983 JC 69 at 77; *Moss v Howdle* 1997 JC 123 at 129; *Lord Advocate's Reference (No 1 of 2000)* 2001 JC 143 at paras [38] and [42]. Indeed, this is a phenomenon not localised to Scotland, but apparent in many common law jurisdictions, such as England & Wales (e.g. *R v Hudson & Taylor* [1971] 2 QB 202 at 206) and Canada (e.g. *R v Perka* [1984] 2 SCR 232 at 249).
46 Duff, "Criminal Responsibility and the Emotions", p.198.
47 [1971] 2 QB 202.
48 [2005] 2 AC 467. Lord Bingham there agreed with Glanville Williams' view that the decision in *Hudson* was "indulgent": at 494, citing G Williams, *Textbook of Criminal Law* (Stevens & Sons: London, 2nd edn, 1983), p.636.
49 CMV Clarkson, "Necessary Action: A New Defence" [2004] Crim LR 81.
50 For an excellent overview of the nature and origins of this tradition, see L Farmer, *Criminal Law, Tradition and Legal Order: Crime and the Genius of Scots Law, 1747 to the Present* (Cambridge University Press: Cambridge, 1997), pp. 21–56; C Kennedy, "Declaring Crimes", *Oxford Journal of Legal Studies*, vol. 37, no. 4 (2017), p.741.
51 For an extensive (and critical) overview, see JW Cairns, "Institutional Writings in Scotland Reconsidered", in AKR Kiralfy & HL MacQueen (eds), *New Perspectives in Scottish Legal History* (Frank Cass & Co: London, 1984), pp.76–117, particularly at p.88 and p.98; and more recently JW Cairns, "The Moveable Text of Mackenzie: Bibliographical Problems for the Scottish Concept of Institutional Writing" in JW Cairns & OF Robinson (eds), *Ancient Law, Comparative Law and Legal History: Studies in Honour of Alan Watson* (Hart Publishing: Oxford and Portland, Oregon, 2001), pp.235–248. John Blackie has also provided an accessible overview, albeit focused on the particular writings of Stair, a private lawyer: JWG Blackie, "Stair's Later Reputation as a Jurist", in DM Walker (ed), *Stair Tercentenary Studies*, (The Stair Society: Edinburgh, 1981), vol. 33, pp.207–227.
52 Blackie, "Stair's Later Reputation as a Jurist", at p.213.
53 Or at least more transparent.
54 Mackenzie, *MC*, Title XI, 2; Forbes, *Institutes*, p.630; Hume, I, p.217–18.
55 A Alison, *Principles of the Criminal Law of Scotland* (Blackwood: Edinburgh, 1832), p.133; AM Anderson, *The Criminal Law of Scotland* (Bell and Bradfute: Edinburgh, 2nd edn, 1904), p.17.
56 Mackenzie, *MC*, Title XI, p.3.
57 Hume, I, p.218.
58 Hume, I, p.220.
59 Hume, I, p.223.
60 Hume, I, p.226.
61 Macdonald, *A Practical Treatise*, p.106.
62 *HMA v Doherty* 1954 JC 1; *Elliott v HMA* 1987 JC 47; *Jones v HMA* 1990 JC 160; *Pollock v HMA* 1998 SLT 880.
63 Duff, "Criminal Responsibility and the Emotions", p.201.
64 See note 26 above.

References

Cases

Collins v HM Advocate 1991 JC 204.
Elliott v HMA 1987 JC 47.
HM Advocate v Anderson (Unreported, 2006).
HMA v Doherty 1954 JC 1.
Jones v HMA 1990 JC 160.
Lord Advocate's Reference (No 1 of 2000) 2001 JC 143.

Moss v Howdle 1997 JC 123.
Pollock v HMA 1998 SLT 880.
R v Abdul-Hussain [1999] Crim LR 570.
R v Dudley and Stephens (1884) 14 QBD 273.
R v Hasan [2005] 2 AC 467.
R v Howe [1987] AC 417.
R v Hudson & Taylor [1971] 2 QB 202.
R v Perka [1984] 2 SCR 232.
R v Willer (1986) 83 Cr App R 225.
Re A (Children) [2001] Fam 147.
Thomson v HMA 1983 JC 69.
Tudhope v Grubb 1983 SCCR 350.

Books and book chapters

Allison A, *Principles of the Criminal Law of Scotland* (William Blackwood: Edinburgh, 1832).
Anderson AM, *The Criminal Law of Scotland* (Bell and Bradfute: Edinburgh, 2nd edn, 1904).
Aristotle, *The Nicomachean Ethics*, translation by D Ross (Oxford University Press: Oxford, 2009).
Blackie JWG, "Stair's Later Reputation as a Jurist", in Walker DM (ed), *Stair Tercentenary Studies* (The Stair Society: Edinburgh, 1981), vol. 33.
Brison SJ, *Aftermath: Violence and the Remaking of a Self* (Princeton University Press: Princeton NJ, 2022).
Cairns JW, "Institutional Writings in Scotland Reconsidered", in Kiralfy AKR & MacQueen HL (eds), *New Perspectives in Scottish Legal History* (Frank Cass & Co: London, 1984).
Cairns JW, "The Moveable Text of Mackenzie: Bibliographical Problems for the Scottish Concept of Institutional Writing", in Cairns JW & Robinson OF (eds), *Ancient Law, Comparative Law and Legal History: Studies in Honour of Alan Watson* (Hart Publishing: Oxford and Portland OR, 2001).
Catley P, "The Need For a Partial Defence of Diminished Capacity and the Potential Role of the Cognitive Sciences in Helping Frame That Defence", in Ligthart S, van Toor D, Kooijmans T, Douglas T & Meynen G (eds), *Neurolaw: Advances in Neuroscience, Justice & Security* (Palgrave Macmillan: Switzerland, 2021).
Chalmers J & Leverick F, *Criminal Law Defences and Pleas in Bar of Trial* (W Green: Edinburgh, 2006).
Coppola F, *The Emotional Brain and the Guilty Mind: Novel Paradigms of Culpability and Punishment* (Hart Publishing: Oxford and New York, 2021).
Dsouza M, *Rationale-Based Defences in Criminal Law* (Hart Publishing: Oxford, 2017).
Duff RA, *Answering for Crime* (Hart Publishing: Oxford, 2009).
Farmer L, *Criminal Law, Tradition and Legal Order: Crime and the Genius of Scots Law, 1747 to the Present* (Cambridge University Press: Cambridge, 1997).
Forbes W, *The Institutes of the Law of Scotland* (1722 and 1730) (Edinburgh Legal Education Trust: Edinburgh, 2012).
Gormley J & Tata C, "Remorse and Sentencing in a World of Plea Bargaining", in Tudor S, Weisman R, Proeve M, & Rossmanith K (eds), *Remorse and Criminal Justice: Multi-Disciplinary Perspectives* (Routledge: London & New York, 2022).
Hart HLA, "Legal Responsibility and Excuses", in *Punishment and Responsibility: Essays in the Philosophy of Law* (Clarendon Press: Oxford, 1968).
Hirstein W, Sifferd KL, & Fagan TK, *Responsible Brains: Neuroscience, Law, and Human Culpability* (MIT Press: Michigan, 2018).
Kidd White E, "On Emotions and the Politics of Attention in Judicial Reasoning", in Amaya A & Del Mar M (eds), *Virtue, Emotion and Imagination in Law and Legal Reasoning* (Hart Publishing: Oxford, 2020).
Leverick F, *Killing in Self-Defence* (Oxford University Press: Oxford, 2006).
Papp Kamali E, *Felony and the Guilty Mind in Medieval England* (Cambridge University Press: Cambridge, 2019).

Plamper J, *The History of Emotions: An Introduction* (Oxford University Press: Oxford, 2015).
Macdonald JHA with Walker J & Stevenson DJ (eds), *A Practical Treatise on the Criminal Law of Scotland* (W Green: Edinburgh, 5th edn, 1948).
Mackenzie G with Robinson OF (ed), *The Laws and Customs of Scotland in Matters Criminal* (1678) (The Stair Society: Edinburgh, 2012), vol. 59.
Meyers D, *Self, Society, and Personal Choice* (Columbia University Press: New York, 1989).
Pillsbury S, *Judging Evil: Rethinking the Law of Murder and Manslaughter* (NYU Press: New York, 1998).
Spain E, *The Role of Emotions in Criminal Defences: Necessity and Duress* (Cambridge University Press: Cambridge, 2011).
Uniacke S, *Permissible Killing* (Cambridge University Press: Cambridge, 1994).
Wertheimer A, *Coercion* (Princeton University Press: Princeton NJ, 1987).
Williams G, *Criminal Law: The General Part* (Steven & Sons Ltd: London, 2nd edn, 1961).
Williams G, *Textbook of Criminal Law* (Stevens & Sons Ltd: London, 2nd edn,1983).
Williams J, *Stoner* (Vintage Book: London, 2003).

Journal articles

Alldridge P, "Rules for Courts and Rules for Citizens", *Oxford Journal of Legal Studies*, vol. 10, no. 4 (1990), pp.487–504.
Austin JL, "A Plea for Excuses: The Presidential Address", *Proceedings of the Aristotelian Society*, vol. 57, no. 1 (1957), pp.1–30.
Bandes SA, "Empathy, Narrative, and Victim Impact Statements", *The University of Chicago Law Review*, vol. 63, no. 2 (1996), pp.361–412.
Barclay K, "State of the Field: The History of Emotions", *The Journal of the Historical Association*, vol. 106, no. 371 (2021), p.456–466.
Bayles MD, "Reconceptualising Necessity and Duress", *Wayne Law Review*, vol. 33, no. 4 (1987), pp.1191–1220.
Berger B, "Emotions and the Veil of Voluntarism: The Loss of Judgment in Canadian Criminal Defences", *McGill Law Journal*, vol. 51 (2006), pp.99–126.
Clarkson CMV, "Necessary Action: A New Defence", (2004) Crim LR 81.
Dan-Cohen M, "Decision Rules and Conduct Rules: On Acoustic Separation in Criminal Law", *Harvard Law Review*, vol. 97, no. 3 (1984), pp.625–637.
Delgado R, "'Rotten Social Background': Should the Criminal Law Recognize a Defense of Severe Environmental Deprivation?", *Law & Enquiry*, vol. 3, no. 1 (1985), pp.9–90.
Dressler J, "Exegesis of the Law of Duress: Justifying the Excuse and Searching for its Proper Limits", *Southern California Law Review*, vol. 62, no. 5 (1989), pp.1331–1386.
Duff RA, "Criminal Responsibility and the Emotions: If Anger and Fear Can Exculpate, Why Not Compassion?", *Inquiry: An Interdisciplinary Journal of Law and Philosophy*, vol. 58, no. 2 (2015), pp.189–220.
Finkelstein CO, "Duress: A Philosophical Account of the Defense in Law", *Arizona Law Review*, vol. 37 (1995), pp.251–285.
Finkelstein CO, "Self-Defense as a Rational Excuse", *University of Pittsburgh Law Review*, vol. 57 (1996), pp.621–649.
Fletcher GP, "Domination in the Theory of Justification and Excuse", *University of Pittsburgh Law Review*, vol. 57 (1996), pp.553–578.
Gardner J, "The Logic of Excuses and the Rationality of Emotions", *Journal of Value Inquiry*, vol. 43 (2009), pp.315–338.
Kahan DM & Nussbaum MC, "Two Conceptions of Emotion in Criminal Law", *Columbia Law Review*, vol. 96, no. 2, pp.269–374.
Kennedy C, "Declaring Crimes", *Oxford Journal of Legal Studies*, vol. 37, no. 4 (2017), pp.741–769.
Meyers D, "Personal Autonomy and the Paradox of Feminine Socialization", *Journal of Philosophy*, vol. 84, no. 11 (1987), pp.619–628.
Morse SJ, "Excusing and New Excuse Defenses: A Legal and Conceptual Review", *Crime and Justice*, vol. 23 (1998), pp.323–406.

Morse SJ, "Diminished Rationality, Diminished Responsibility", *Ohio State Journal of Criminal Law*, vol. 1, no. 1 (2002), pp.289–308.

Robinson PH, "Criminal Law Defenses: A Systematic Analysis", *Columbia Law Review*, vol. 82, no. 2 (2005), p.199.

Rosen CJ, "The Excuse of Self-Defense: Correcting A Historical Accident on Behalf of Battered Women Who Kill", *American University Law Review*, vol. 36, no. 1 (1986), pp.11–56.

Rosenwein BH, "Emotions: Some Historical Observations", *History of Psychology*, vol. 24, no. 2 (2021), pp.107–111.

Schachter S & Singer JE, "Cognitive, Social and Physiological Determinants of Emotional States", *Psychological Review*, vol. 69 (1962), pp.379–399.

Tata C, "Humanising Punishment? Mitigation and 'Case-cleansing' Prior to Sentencing", *Oñati Socio-Legal Series*, vol. 9, no. 5 (2019), pp.659–683.

Tata C & Jamieson F, "Just Emotions? The Need for Emotionally-Intelligent Justice Policy", *Scottish Justice Matters*, vol. 5, no. 1 (2017), pp.32–33.

Reports

Law Reform Commission of Ireland, *Consultation Paper: "Duress and Necessity"* (Ireland: LRC CP 39, 2006).

Scottish Law Commission, Seventh Programme of Law Reform (Scot Law Com No 198 (2005)).

12
RECKLESSNESS AND NEGLIGENCE IN THE CRIMINAL LAW

Marcia Baron

Introduction

Disagreements abound over whether negligence should suffice for criminal liability. Parties to the dispute all agree that recklessness should suffice, but they differ on whether negligence ever should. The debate is encumbered by tacit disagreement about just how recklessness and negligence differ, disagreement that is rarely noted except insofar as someone says with respect to a putative example of negligence, "But that isn't negligence. That is recklessness!" This encumbrance is surprising because, particularly in the US, where the debate is a lively one, the parties to the dispute anchor their discussion in the Model Penal Code (MPC) definitions.[1] Given this point of agreement, and given how influential the MPC discussion of culpability levels has been, perhaps we can advance the debate of whether negligence should suffice for criminal liability by taking a close look at the MPC definitions of negligence and recklessness, with an eye to saying, "if you are working with these definitions, at least this much is clear: ...", and thus reduce disagreement about how recklessness and negligence differ.

The discussion may have other benefits as well: readers who do not see the MPC definitions as providing a useful anchor may find that my discussion helps them pinpoint why they think the definitions are not apt. And for those unfamiliar with the debate and a little shaky on the concept of *mens rea*, I provide a brief overview of that concept and of the *mens rea* requirement. In short, my chapter should be helpful in three ways (beyond offering that brief overview): first, it sheds light on how, on the MPC definitions, negligence and recklessness differ; second, it addresses some objections to allowing negligence to suffice for criminal liability; third, it may lead those who find the definitions and perhaps the distinction itself not particularly helpful to respond by articulating what they find misguided about them.

In this chapter, I take a close look at the definitions, so as to gain clarity on what, according to the MPC, the difference between acting recklessly and acting negligently is. There are unclarities in the definitions, and we need to figure out how these should be resolved. My aim in this chapter is thus to probe the MPC definitions, note and try to resolve the unclarities, and then bring out some of the implications of these clarifications for the debate over whether negligence suffices for criminal liability.

Before doing so, some background is needed. In the next section, I explain the backdrop for the distinction in the MPC between acting recklessly and acting negligently. Doing so calls for explaining the idea of *mens rea*, and the *mens rea* requirement.

The *mens rea* requirement[2]

It is a basic tenet of criminal law that, with the exception of strict liability crimes, a conviction requires not only proof that the defendant committed an act[3] prohibited by law, but also proof of this other thing, the *mens rea*. The Latin translates to "guilty mind". The idea is that the mere doing of the action does not make the person culpable.[4] After all, it might have been an accident. So, the *mens rea* requirement says that to be convicted of a crime, it is not enough that one committed the prohibited action; one must also have (or more precisely, have had at the time one acted) a guilty mind.[5]

To better understand the *mens rea* requirement, it helps to contrast the modern conception of *mens rea* to an earlier conception.[6] In earlier eras, culpability in Anglo-American law was linked to having a "wicked mind," and the term "*mens rea*" captured that notion. The modern conception, by contrast, does not predicate culpability on a wicked mind (or anything else that smacks of an overall character assessment) but instead on some "mental element" (that then has to be specified) that shows the person to be at fault for the action.[7] Moreover, it is part of the modern conception of *mens rea* that it attaches to the crime with which one has been charged (more precisely, to the elements of the crime).

The modern notion thus pegs culpability strictly to the crime with which the person is charged.[8] If one sets out to steal something and in the course of so doing, inadvertently causes a fire,[9] one may be guilty of theft but not arson. Doing *A* on purpose and in the course of doing *A*, causing *B*, does not entail that one did *B* on purpose.

Implicit in what I have said so far in this section is something that I should make explicit, namely, different crimes call for different culpability (or *mens rea*) specifications. The *mens rea* requirement for reckless homicide should be (and normally is) that the defendant acted recklessly; but for murder, more has to be required by way of *mens rea* than just *recklessly* causing a death. The Model Penal Code provides four options: purposely, knowingly, recklessly, and negligently. The idea of these four options is that legislators can specify which of the four is required for the particular offence (with the option of requiring a different *mens rea* for one element of an offence than for another element of the same offence). The default is recklessness: if no *mens rea* is indicated, the requirement is satisfied by showing that the defendant acted recklessly. These *mens rea* standards also form a hierarchy. The *mens rea* requirement for a particular offence is satisfied by a higher *mens rea*, but not by a lower one. Thus, if the *mens rea* required is negligence, a defendant who acted recklessly would satisfy the requirement. But if the *mens rea* is recklessness, negligence would not suffice to establish that the *mens rea* requirement has been met.

The point of the Model Penal Code list and, more fundamentally, the significance of the *mens rea* requirement, becomes more vivid if we consider *Regina v Cunningham*, an English case from the 1950s.[10] Mr. Cunningham was short on cash, and decided to steal the coins from a gas meter in the cellar of the house where he was due to live shortly. The house had originally been a single unit but was now divided, with a porous ("honeycomb") wall in the cellar separating the two sides of the house. Cunningham wrenched the meter from the wall, took the coins, and although there was a stop tap within a couple of feet of the meter, he did not turn it to stop the gas from flowing. Enough gas escaped through the wall that someone asleep in the other side of the house, Sarah Wade, was partially asphyxiated. Cunningham was charged with a property crime—two counts of larceny of a gas meter and its contents—to which he pled guilty. But he was also charged with another crime. The charge was that he "unlawfully and maliciously caused to be taken by Sarah Wade a certain noxious thing, namely coal gas, so as thereby to endanger her life". He pled not guilty to that charge and when he was convicted, appealed it on the ground that the instruction to the jury was incorrect. The issue was the term "maliciously". The judge told the jury that in the statute under which Cunningham was charged, "maliciously" meant "wickedly doing something which he has no business to do and perfectly well knows it."[11]

Cunningham's appeal succeeded. Cunningham had the *mens rea* for the crimes of ripping the gas meter from the wall and stealing the coins, but that does not show that he had the *mens rea* for the other crime. That he intentionally ripped the meter from the wall to steal the coins—that he had a "guilty mind" with respect to the property damage and the theft—does not show that he had a guilty mind with respect to causing Sarah Wade to be partially asphyxiated. The issue of whether he caused this injury maliciously is not settled by pointing to the fact that he wickedly did something that he had no business doing and knew he had no business doing.

We can see that the trial judge got it wrong. But what should the jury direction have been? If before they can convict Cunningham of the crime, they need to find that he maliciously caused Sarah Wade to be partially asphyxiated, the jurors need guidance on how "maliciously" is to be understood.

The Court of Appeal held that the jury should have been instructed that for Cunningham to be guilty of the crime, either he has to have intended to poison his neighbour, or he has to have foreseen that the removal of the gas meter might cause injury to someone, but then gone ahead and removed it anyway. The latter, known in British criminal law theory as "Cunningham recklessness", is the reigning view of recklessness for purposes of criminal law.[12] Recklessness, thus understood, requires "foresight" or awareness of risk.[13] So, according to the Court, Cunningham had to have either intended to cause her harm or have recklessly caused it—specifically, have foreseen that his action might injure someone but then gone ahead despite that.

This is much better than the trial judge's direction to the jury. But one might find it troubling if a conviction for any crime, other than minor property crimes, is ruled out unless it can be shown that the defendant foresaw that what he was doing might cause someone serious harm. Cunningham caused the partial asphyxiation of Sarah Wade. But a conviction was ruled out if it simply did not occur to him that this might happen. Do we really want to say, one might ask, that one cannot be guilty of such a crime, where one caused considerable harm, and where the risk should have been obvious, just because one did not foresee the harm? In some cases that will be fine; the defendant didn't foresee it because it was very hard to foresee. Or, they didn't foresee it because of some handicap that made it very hard for them to foresee it. But what if they didn't foresee it because they were just totally unconcerned—they were, as we might say in ordinary parlance, reckless?

This is a concern many have had. Surely, it is claimed, the mere fact that the person did not foresee the risk is not enough to preclude culpability.[14] Some have argued that recklessness should not be understood as requiring awareness of the risk.[15] There has been a voluminous debate on this in the United Kingdom.[16] In the US, too, this was an issue, especially prior to the Model Penal Code.

The Model Penal Code handles the problem by defining recklessness so as to require awareness of risk, but then offering a separate culpability level of negligence that does not require it. The MPC approach deftly clears up a question that dogged many courts, while at the same time allowing for criminal liability for negligence. Some would take issue with the MPC approach, however, because they think the possibility of criminal liability for negligence should be foreclosed.[17] This will be discussed further in Section 4.

What is the difference between acting recklessly and acting negligently?

According to the Model Penal Code,

> "A person acts recklessly with respect to a material element of an offense when he consciously disregards a substantial and unjustifiable risk that the material element exists or will result from his conduct. The risk must be of such a nature and degree that, considering the nature and purpose of the actor's conduct and the circumstances known to him, its disregard involves a gross deviation from the standard of conduct that a law-abiding person would observe in the actor's situation".[18]

> "A person acts negligently with respect to a material element of an offense when he should be aware of a substantial and unjustifiable risk that the material element exists or will result from his conduct. The risk must be of such a nature and degree that the actor's failure to perceive it, considering the nature and purpose of his conduct and the circumstances known to him, involves a gross deviation from the standard of care that a reasonable person would observe in the actor's situation".[19]

The main difference between acting recklessly and acting negligently, on these definitions, is that the person who acts recklessly consciously disregards a substantial and unjustifiable risk, whereas the person who acts negligently is not aware of the risk (to put it a bit too simply) but should be aware of it. (Too simply, because there is unclarity as to what exactly it is that the person who acts negligently isn't aware of. I'll speak to that shortly.) The meaning of "should be aware" is elaborated in the next sentence of the definition of negligence, which also serves to explain what counts as a substantial and unjustifiable risk: "the risk must be of such a nature and degree that the actor's failure to perceive it...involves a gross deviation from the standard of care that a reasonable person would observe in the actor's situation". So, for the failure to perceive the risk to meet the requirement for negligence, it has to involve a gross deviation from the standard of care that a reasonable person would observe in the actor's situation.

The second sentence in the definition of *recklessness* says something similar, but not identical, about the risk: "the risk must be of such a nature and degree that...its disregard involves a gross deviation from the standard of conduct that a law-abiding person would observe in the actor's situation".

For both recklessness and negligence, a gross deviation from the relevant standard is required (*nota bene*: too often it is ignored).[20] But the relevant standards are not identical. For recklessness, it is the standard of conduct that a law-abiding person would observe in the actor's situation; for negligence, it is the standard of care that a reasonable person would observe in the actor's situation. There are two differences: standard of conduct vs. standard of care, and law-abiding person vs. reasonable person. The first difference makes some sense: the term "conduct" does have a clearer application when someone consciously disregards a risk than when someone fails to perceive (or notice) a risk. By contrast, the second difference between the two parallel sentences is puzzling. Why "law-abiding" in the case of recklessness, and "reasonable" in the case of negligence? I wish I knew. Nothing in the Comments provided by the framers suggests a reason for this disparity. Almost all scholarly opinions I have read or heard are that the disparity, unlikely though this seems, is a fluke.[21] I will so regard it and treat "reasonable person" as the appropriate term for each.

Let's sum up where we are at this point on what negligence and recklessness are and how they differ. The key difference is that the reckless actor[22] consciously disregards a substantial and unjustifiable risk, whereas the negligent actor is not aware of the risk, and should be aware of it ("should be" in the sense that a reasonable person would be aware of it). It is important not to forget that one does not count as negligent simply by virtue of not being aware of what a reasonable person would be aware of. It takes more than that. The risk must be such that "the actor's failure to perceive it...involves a *gross deviation* [my emphasis] from the standard of care that a reasonable person would observe in the actor's situation". Otherwise, the conduct does not count as negligent (nor, of course, as reckless).

There is something else to note: the risk must be such that "the actor's failure to perceive it, *considering the nature and purpose of his conduct and the circumstances known to him* [my emphasis], involves a gross deviation from the standard of care that a reasonable person would observe in the actor's situation". Thus, we are to take into account the nature and purpose of the actor's conduct in assessing whether the failure to perceive the risk involves this gross deviation, and we are also to factor in the circumstances known to the actor. The same qualification is included in the definition of recklessness.

There is an ambiguity in what I pinpointed as the "key difference" between negligence and recklessness two paragraphs back. I'll focus on it as an unclarity in the MPC definition of recklessness. I'll first present it as Douglas Husak has,[23] but then will reframe it in the way I think it needs to be framed, given the MPC definition of recklessness.

Exactly what, Husak asks, must the reckless defendant believe concerning the risk? We know he has to be aware of a substantial and unjustifiable risk. But is it that he has to be aware of a risk that, in fact, is substantial and unjustifiable? Or does he have to be aware that it is substantial and unjustifiable? Husak's reply is as follows: while "no clear answer emerges from positive law", it is plausible to suppose that the defendant "must be aware of a risk, aware that it is substantial, and also aware of the facts that make it unjustifiable" yet may reach "a different normative conclusion about its justifiability".[24] Thus, for a person to count, on the MPC definition, as acting recklessly, it has to be the case that he or she is aware of the risk, aware that it is substantial, and aware of the facts that make it unjustifiable, but it is compatible with acting recklessly, Husak thinks (again, on the MPC definition), that the actor believes that it is justifiable.[25]

I disagree, but it is easy to view it as Husak does if we frame the issue as he did and ask: what must the reckless person believe? Or, of what exactly must the reckless person be aware? Suppose, however, that we frame it in terms not of awareness or belief, but conscious disregard.[26] The question then is as follows: what is it that one (consciously) disregards when one acts recklessly?

It makes a difference. When we take seriously "consciously disregards" in the MPC definition of recklessness, it becomes clear that one cannot count as acting recklessly if one was aware of the risk and the features that render it unjustified, thought about the risk, and reached the normative conclusion that the risk was justified. *There has to be something* that the reckless person consciously disregards. But what could it be, if one arrived at that normative conclusion? Someone who is aware of the risk and that it is substantial,[27] and is aware of the facts that make it unjustifiable, but reaches the conclusion that taking the risk is justified, does not disregard anything. He has thought about the matter and determined that the risk is justified. Thus, according to the MPC, he cannot count as acting recklessly.

A possible wrinkle: what if he came to the conclusion that the risk is justified, but came to it by dishonest means, i.e. by talking himself into believing it is justified, reasoning in roughly the manner of W.K. Clifford's shipowner?[28] Arguably this should suffice for recklessness, rather as wilful ignorance is allowed to suffice for knowledge. If he in effect realised it was an unjustifiable risk but talked himself into believing it wasn't—pushed himself to focus on this feature of the situation, and not that one—it is plausible to count this as recklessness. But that is the only circumstance, as I see it, where someone could qualify as acting recklessly while believing that the risk he is taking is justified.

In disagreeing with Husak on this, I am not taking the position that the reckless person has to reach the conclusion, "what I'm doing is unjustifiable, but I'll do it anyway". She might do so, but that is not essential for the conduct to count as reckless. The following, I take it, would also count as acting recklessly: the person sees there to be a substantial risk and consciously disregards it, neither judging: "it is justifiable to go ahead", nor "it is not justifiable to go ahead". In such a scenario, she would be aware that the risk might not be justifiable. Why do I say this? Because it is *part of what it is for something to be a substantial risk* that if one does not judge it to be justifiable, yet attends to it enough that one counts as consciously disregarding it, one *has to be aware that it may not be justifiable*. Thus, although recklessness does not require that one saw the risk to be unjustifiable, it does involve some sense that it is not, or may not be, justifiable.

In sum, one counts as having acted recklessly only if one consciously disregarded a substantial and unjustifiable risk, where that means that one disregarded something that one (a) saw to be a risk and (b) did not see to be justified. One sees the risk, does not see it to be justified (or sees it to be justified only because one has talked oneself into believing it is), and goes ahead anyway.

With that clarified, let's consider the implications for negligence. Presumably, alongside cases where one is not aware of the risk and should have been (where "should have" is understood as explained above), the following would count as acting negligently: one is aware of the risk but not aware of its seriousness, yet should have been. (It is because of this that I noted earlier that it is a bit of an oversimplification to say that when one acts negligently, one is not aware of the risk. The negligent actor might be aware of the risk, just not aware of its seriousness). Within this type we have two subtypes:[29] those where one is aware of the factors that render it unjustifiable but draws the wrong normative conclusion, and those where one is not aware of (some of) those factors. In each case, for this to count as negligence, it has to be the case that one should have been aware, where "should have" has the meaning explained above: in not being aware, one deviates from the standard of care that a reasonable person in the actor's situation would have observed—and the deviation has to be gross.

There is a further question about recklessness that needs to be addressed. What is the time frame for this conscious disregard of the risk? A related question concerns negligence: what is the time frame for failing to be aware of the risk? Concerning recklessness, I take it that the relevant time frame is from when I first thought of so acting, up to and including when I did so act. If I consciously disregarded the risk at any point in that time, and did not revisit the matter and reach the conclusion that the risk is justified, then if the other conditions are met for recklessness, I count as having acted recklessly.[30]

Likewise with negligence: if I act negligently, the time when I am not aware of the risk but should have been, is when I am thinking of so acting, when I so act, and the time in between. If I was aware of the risk long before I thought about taking this action, my awareness back then does not suffice to meet the requirement for recklessness that one have consciously disregarded the risk (though it might provide some evidence that in fact I was aware of it when I was considering whether to so act).

Some implications for the current debate on negligence

Larry Alexander and Kimberly Ferzan, proponents of the view that negligence should never suffice for criminal liability,[31] write the following in a response to discussions of their lead article, "Against Negligence Liability": "We claim that criminal law cannot blame and punish for misperception or misestimation".[32] The claim misleads in two ways. The first is that the criminal law does not punish for the *mens rea* alone, so of course it cannot punish for misperception or misestimation. Punishing for misperception or misestimation is not up for consideration at all. Conviction and thus punishment require the commission of a prohibited act, or the omission of a required act. The criminal law punishes for *that*, done with this *mens rea* (whatever *mens rea* is required for this type of offence).[33]

The second problem, and the one I want to focus on, is this: to say that someone acts negligently is to say much more than that the person misperceived or misestimated something. This is true if we rely on the Model Penal Code definition; it is true in ordinary discourse, as well. It is so obvious that it should not need to be mentioned. But it does need to be reiterated because of claims such as Alexander and Ferzan's. What I quoted from them is their reply to the discussions of their lead essay, in which they wrote the following:

> "What presumably makes the negligent actor culpable is that he underestimates the risk his act creates; whereas, a 'reasonable'—that is nonculpable—person would not have underestimated the risk and, as a consequence, would not have acted as did the negligent actor".[34]

The book from which their essay is drawn quotes the Model Penal Code definition of negligence as representative of the view of negligence they are explaining.[35]

What close attention to the MPC definition of negligence discloses, however, is that negligence, as there defined, *is no mere misperception or misestimation*. And what makes the actor culpable is not simply that the person underestimates the risk. Negligence as articulated by Ferzan and Alexander is not negligence as defined by the MPC. Nor is it a notion of negligence that anyone seriously considering the position that negligence sometimes should be the required *mens rea* would do well to utilise. It is well suited for anyone who has already made up their mind that negligence should not suffice for criminal liability and wants to lead others to think likewise. But it is not well suited for serious discussion of the question of whether negligence should so suffice.

Negligence, as defined by the MPC, is not a matter of carefully calculating a risk but alas getting it wrong. Crucially, it involves a deviation from a standard of care: one is not taking the care, the precautions, that one should take. And it is more than that: it involves a *gross* deviation from the standard of care of a reasonable person. Alexander and Ferzan treat negligence as if it were just a matter of making a mistake or being stupid. No wonder they believe that negligence should never suffice for criminal liability.

Conclusion

In this chapter, I have sought to shed light on what recklessness and negligence are, according to the Model Penal Code. I rely on the MPC definitions because in the debate about whether negligence should suffice for criminal liability, they are the definitions that are relied on. Not everyone who relies on them fully endorses them, certainly, but they provide the anchor, the lingua franca. It is convenient that they are, in that minimal sense, agreed on; and yet, as I have tried to bring out, some components of the definition are too often ignored or given short shrift. In particular, that recklessness requires a conscious disregard of the risk is often ignored. This has implications for just what acting recklessly is, on the MPC definition, how it differs from acting negligently, and how various cases are to be categorised—as acting recklessly, or acting negligently (or neither). In addition, while it is true that negligence involves not being aware of something one should be aware of, the force of the "should" is often missed, and treated by some opponents of negligence liability as if the implicit norm were merely epistemic. On the MPC definition, it is not merely that. The failure will indeed be in part a failure to notice, or a failure to remember, or a failure to put two and two together and see the danger in what one is about to do, but in each case, these do not constitute negligence unless they involve a gross deviation from a standard of care that a reasonable person would observe. In each case, the problem is more fundamentally a failure to take care to avoid harm to others.

Acknowledgements

An earlier version of this chapter was presented to the Purdue University Philosophy Department (in October 2022); a yet earlier version was presented as a keynote at the 15th International Conference on Deontic Logic and Normative Systems in July 2021. I am grateful to discussants at both events for their helpful comments and to the organisers for inviting me. I am grateful as well to Alexander Greenberg for his astute written comments. I only wish that I had the time and the space to adequately address all the comments. Thanks too to Kyle Stroh for editorial assistance, to Louise Kennefick for helpful suggestions on the semi-final version, and to David Prendergast for catching an embarrassing typo just in time before the paper went to press.

Notes

1 American Law Institute, *Model Penal Code and Commentaries*, 2.02 (2). For an explanation of the Model Penal Code, see PH Robinson & MD Dubber, "The American Model Penal Code: A Brief Overview", *New Criminal Law Review*, no. 10 (2007), p.319.

2. The first three paragraphs of Section 2 overlap somewhat with my "Negligence and the *Mens Rea* Requirement," *Jahrbuch für Recht und Ethik/Annual Review of Law and Ethics*, Themenschwerpunkt: Strafrecht und Rechtsphilosophie, Gedächtnisschrift für Joachim Hruschka, vol. 27 (2019), p.325.

3. Two clarifications: first, the requirement is that there be a voluntary act (an action done under duress counts; an action done under hypnosis does not). Second, "committed an act" is understood to include omissions.

4. A quick clarification, lest I mislead: *mens rea* is necessary but not sufficient for culpability. Imagine that the prosecution has shown that the defendant committed the prohibited action and had the required *mens rea*. The defendant might nonetheless have an affirmative defence, for example, that she acted under duress. For ease of expression, in this paper I'll be using "culpable" as shorthand for "culpable barring an affirmative defence".

5. The famous Latin phrase is *actus non facit reum nisi mens sit rea*, i.e. "an act does not make [a person] guilty, unless the mind be guilty." J Dressler, *Understanding Criminal Law* (Lexis-Nexis: New Providence NJ, 7th edn, 2015), p.117.

6. For more (much more) on the history, see PH Robinson, "A Brief History of Culpability Distinctions in Criminal Law", *Hastings Law Journal*, no. 31 (1979-80), p.815.

7. Some would say "mental state" instead of "mental element". For my reasons for not so framing it, see my "Negligence, *Mens Rea*, and What We Want the Element of *Mens Rea* to Provide", *Criminal Law and Philosophy*, vol. 14, no. 1 (2020), p.69.

8. Felony murder, still on the books in the US and often utilised by prosecutors, is best seen as at odds with what I am calling the "modern" notion. One can be convicted of felony murder if one accidentally causes a death in the course of committing a different felony, e.g. robbery. It is as if the *mens rea* for robbery transferred over to the act of causing another's death.

9. See *Regina v. Faulkner* (1877) 13 Cox CC 550.

10. *Regina v. Cunningham* (1957) 2 Q.B. 396.

11. *Cunningham*, p.400.

12. It is of course subject to interpretation in subsequent case law. For a pertinent case, see *R v G & another* [2003] UKHL 50.

13. For a time, "Caldwell recklessness", which did not require awareness of risk, replaced "Cunningham recklessness". See, *inter alia*, AP Simester & WJ Brookbanks, *Principles of Criminal Law* (Thomson Reuters: Wellington, 5th edn, 2019), Ch 4; RA Duff, "*Caldwell* and *Lawrence*: The Retreat from Subjectivism", *Oxford Journal of Legal Studies*, vol. 3, no. 1 (1983), p.77; F Stark, *Culpable Carelessness* (Cambridge University Press: Cambridge, 2016); K Amirthalingam, "Caldwell Recklessness is Dead; Long Live Mens Rea's Fecklessness", *The Modern Law Review*, vol. 67, no. 3 (2004), pp.491, and G Williams, "Recklessness Redefined", *Cambridge Law Journal*, vol. 40, no. 2 (1981), p.252.

14. See RA Duff, "Recklessness and Rape," *The Liverpool Law Review*, vol. 3, no. 2 (1981), p.49; M Baron, "I Thought She Consented", *Philosophical Issues*, vol. 11, no. 1 (2001), p.1.

15. See Duff, "Recklessness and Rape".

16. See the articles by Duff, Amirthalingam, and Williams cited in notes 13 and 14.

17. Some might take issue with it on other grounds. Drawing on some of Antony Duff's work, one might question whether awareness of risk has the significance that is accorded it by treating negligence as involving less culpability than recklessness. See, in addition to "*Caldwell* and *Lawrence*," his "Two Models of Criminal Fault," *Criminal Law and Philosophy*, vol. 13 (2019), p.643. For discussion of Duff's view in "Two Models," see A Greenberg, "Awareness and the Recklessness/Negligence Distinction", forthcoming in *Criminal Law and Philosophy*.

18. American Law Institute, *Model Penal Code and Commentaries*, 2.02 (2) (c).

19. ALI, *MPC and Commentaries*, 2.02 (2) (d).

20. E.g. "as the Model Penal Code puts it, negligence is the imposition of a 'substantial and unjustifiable risk,' the latter being defined as a risk the taking of which would violate the 'standard of care that a reasonable person would observe in the actor's situation'". MS Moore & HM Hurd, "Punishing the Awkward, the Stupid, the Weak, and the Selfish: The Culpability of Negligence", *Criminal Law and Philosophy*, vol. 5, no. 2 (2011), p.147. Moore and Hurd are by no means unusual in ignoring the fact that a gross deviation from the standard is required for negligence.

21 See for example KW Simons, "Should the Model Penal Code's *Mens Rea* Provisions Be Amended?" *Ohio State Journal of Criminal Law*, vol. 1 (2003), p.179, esp. note 24, and the *MPC and Commentaries*, 2.02, p.242, note 27, indicating that the standard of recklessness "requires the same discriminations demanded by the standard of negligence".

22 "Reckless actor" (and "reckless person") should be understood as shorthand for "the person who has acted recklessly". I do not mean to attribute a character trait of recklessness to the person. One can, after all, act recklessly yet out of character. One need not be reckless to (occasionally) act recklessly. Ditto for "negligent actor".

23 In D Husak, "Negligence, Belief, Blame and Criminal Liability: The Special Case of Forgetting", *Criminal Law and Philosophy*, vol. 5, no. 2 (2011), p.199.

24 Husak, "Negligence, Belief, Blame", p.208.

25 He illustrates: "Thus a defendant who realizes a hurricane is approaching and has been strongly advised to evacuate his family is not reckless if he believes, however foolishly, that the storm poses only a minor risk. But a defendant who believes that his own selfish pursuits justify imposing huge risks on his family may still be reckless" (Husak, "Negligence, Belief, Blame", p.208). I take it that this would be the case even if it were not his own selfish pursuits; it could be pursuits on behalf of another person.

26 That Husak is following the MPC definition of recklessness is evident on p.200, where he appends a footnote citing the MPC, Sections 2.02(2)(c) and (d) to his explanation of the difference between recklessness and negligence. I should note that he does introduce the paragraph with "superficially, the contested issue is easily described"; but he doesn't ever retract the claim that the difference between recklessness and negligence is "the presence or absence of consciousness or awareness" (p.200). His point, rather, in saying "superficially" seems to be that the difference is a lot less clear than it initially looks. I agree with Husak that it needs clarification but think that the problem is more easily addressed once we focus on "consciously disregards".

27 In *Crime and Culpability: A Theory of Criminal Law* (Cambridge University Press: Cambridge, 2009), Larry Alexander and Kimberly Kessler Ferzan (with Stephen Morse) claim that "substantial" is superfluous: all that matters is that it is unjustifiable (pp.25–27). When I last wrote on this topic (in my "Negligence, *Mens Rea*, and What We Want the Element of *Mens Rea* to Provide"), I was on board. If it is unjustifiable, wouldn't that settle it? Why would it need also to be substantial? I now think, however, that "substantial" may not be superfluous. Consider cases where both of the following obtain: the probability of X is low, and if X did happen, it would not be catastrophic, or even very serious. The risk is thus not substantial. And yet given the nature of the activity, the risk may be unjustifiable. On the MPC definition, these would be unjustified insubstantial risks, and would, unlike unjustified substantial risks, not suffice for recklessness. Thus, it looks like the MPC framers knew what they were doing when they wrote "substantial and unjustifiable": "substantial" is not superfluous. The actor would not have the required *mens rea* if the risk they took was, although not justified, insubstantial.

28 WK Clifford, "The Ethics of Belief," in *The Ethics of Belief and Other Essays* (Prometheus Books: Amherst NY, 1999). The shipowner was troubled by doubts about whether his ship was safe for its voyage across the Atlantic without first undergoing an expensive overhaul, and actively sought to dissuade himself from his inconvenient worries. At the time that the ship set sail he believed that it was seaworthy, but he believed this only because he had succeeded in silencing his doubts, having told himself that "Providence ... could hardly fail to protect all these unhappy families that were leaving their fatherland to seek better times elsewhere" (Clifford, *The Ethics of Belief*, p.70). I discuss the shipowner example in my "Justification, Excuse, and the Exculpatory Power of Ignorance", in R Peels (ed), *Perspectives on Ignorance from Moral and Social Philosophy* (Routledge: New York, 2017), pp.53–76.

29 And perhaps more, since the risk has to be both substantial and unjustifiable, on the MPC definition. See note 27, above.

30 As noted above, if I did revisit the matter and came to the conclusion that the risk is justified, but, like Clifford's shipowner, arrived at the conclusion by dishonest means, this too could count as acting recklessly. It is not entailed by the MPC definition of recklessness, but I believe it is compatible with it.

31 As explained above, this way of putting it is a bit misleading, because satisfying the *mens rea* requirement does not by itself suffice for criminal liability; one might act (e.g.) recklessly but have a defence

(such as involuntary intoxication). I word it this way because it is customary, but more accurate than "suffice for criminal liability" would be "satisfy the *mens rea* requirement" for that crime.

32 L Alexander & KK Ferzan, "Reply", in PH Robinson et al, *Criminal Law Conversations* (Oxford University Press: Oxford, 2009), p.291.

33 Alexander and Ferzan are not the only scholars to speak in a way that suggests that when we ask whether X should suffice for criminal liability, we are asking whether the criminal law can punish for X. I draw attention to the way their claim misleads not to single them out but because I think such framing may slightly throw us off in our discussion of whether negligence should ever suffice for criminal liability.

34 L Alexander & KK Ferzan, "Against Negligence Liability," in *Criminal Law Conversations*, p.273.

35 Alexander & Ferzan, *Crime and Culpability*, pp.69–70.

References

Cases

Regina v Cunningham (1877)13 Cox CC 550.
Regina v. Faulkner (1877)13 Cox CC 550
R v G & another (2003) UKHL 50.

Books and book chapters

Alexander L & Ferzan KK, "Against Negligence Liability", in Robinson PH, Garvey S, & Ferzan KK (eds), *Criminal Law Conversations* (Oxford University Press: Oxford, 2009).

Alexander L & Ferzan KK, "Reply", in Robinson PH, Garvey S, & Ferzan KK (eds), *Criminal Law Conversations* (Oxford University Press: Oxford, 2009).

Alexander L & Ferzan KK (with Morse S), *Crime and Culpability: A Theory of Criminal Law* (Cambridge University Press: Cambridge, 2009).

American Law Institute, *Model Penal Code and Commentaries: (Official Draft and Revised Comments)* (ALI: Philadelphia PA, 1962).

Baron M, "Justification, Excuse, and the Exculpatory Power of Ignorance", in Peels R (ed), *Perspectives on Ignorance from Moral and Social Philosophy* (Routledge: New York, 2017).

Clifford WK, "The Ethics of Belief", in Clifford WK (ed), *The Ethics of Belief and Other Essays* (Prometheus Books: Amherst NY, 1999).

Dressler J, *Understanding Criminal Law* (Lexis-Nexis, 7th edn, 2015).

Simester AP & Brookbanks WJ, *Principles of Criminal Law* (Thomson Reuters: Wellington, New Zealand, 5th edn, 2019).

Stark F, *Culpable Carelessness: Recklessness and Negligence in the Criminal Law* (Cambridge University Press: Cambridge, 2016).

Journal articles

Amirthalingam K, "Caldwell Recklessness is Dead; Long Live Mens Rea's Fecklessness", *The Modern Law Review*, vol. 67, no. 3 (2004), pp.491–500.

Baron M, "'I Thought She Consented'", *Philosophical Issues*, vol. 11, no. 1 (2001), pp.1–32.

Baron M, "Negligence and the *Mens Rea* Requirement", *Jahrbuch für Recht und Ethik /Annual Review of Law and Ethics*, Themenschwerpunkt: Strafrecht und Rechtsphilosophie, Gedächtnisschrift für Joachim Hruschka, vol. 27 (2019), pp.325–344.

Baron M, "Negligence, *Mens Rea*, and What We Want the Element of *Mens Rea* to Provide", *Criminal Law and Philosophy*, vol. 14, no. 1 (April 2020), pp.69–89.

Duff RA "Two Models of Criminal Fault", *Criminal Law and Philosophy*, vol. 13 (2019), pp.643–665.

Duff RA, "*Caldwell* and *Lawrence*: The Retreat from Subjectivism", *Oxford Journal of Legal Studies*, vol. 3, no. 1 (Spring, 1983), pp.77–98.

Duff RA, "Recklessness and Rape", *The Liverpool Law Review*, vol. 3, no. 2 (1981), pp.49–64.

Greenberg A, "Awareness and the Recklessness/Negligence Distinction", Criminal Law and Philosophy, vol. 18 (2024), pp.351–367.
Husak D, "Negligence, Belief, Blame and Criminal Liability: The Special Case of Forgetting", *Criminal Law and Philosophy,* vol. 5, no. 2 (2011), pp.199–218.
Moore MS & Hurd HM, "Punishing the Awkward, the Stupid, the Weak, and the Selfish: The Culpability of Negligence", *Criminal Law and Philosophy,* vol. 5, no. 2 (2011), pp.147–198.
Robinson PH & Dubber MD, "The American Model Penal Code: A Brief Overview", *New Criminal Law Review*, vol. 10, no. 3 (2007), pp.319–341.
Robinson PH, "A Brief History of Culpability Distinctions in Criminal Law", *Hastings Law Journal*, vol. 31, no. 4 (1979–80), pp.815–853.
Simons KW, "Should the Model Penal Code's *Mens Rea* Provisions Be Amended?", *Ohio State Journal of Criminal Law,* vol. 1 (2003), pp.179–205.
Williams G, "Recklessness Redefined", *Cambridge Law Journal*, vol. 40, no. 2 (1981), pp.252–283.

13
THE DENIAL/DEFENCE AND OFFENCE/DEFENCE DISTINCTION

Rehabilitating Gardner to Answer the Incorporationist Challenge

David Campbell

Introduction

Is there any substantive difference between denials and defences? Incorporationism is sceptical about such claims. After all, denials and defences both go to the merits of the case and if successful, operate to deny the claimant or prosecutor a verdict in their favour.[1] There is no formal, logical, or structural difference between denials and defences, incorporationists say. This presents an excellent challenge to those who would maintain there is a denial/defence distinction or an offence/defence distinction.

The burden assigned by incorporationists, to those who seek to challenge them – as will be explained shortly – is to produce a theory of defences which adequately explains the precise difference between a denial and a defence. Now, a fully developed theory of defences cannot be articulated in the space of one short chapter, but this chapter will posit the kernel of a novel(ish) theory of defences with a particular focus on justifications. This will provide sufficient fodder to enliven a challenge to the incorporationist position.

The theory of defences advanced here is described as novel(ish). This is because rather than reinventing the wheel, it advances from the work of John Gardner. Gardner drew upon Joseph Raz's work on practical reasoning to develop a sophisticated theory of justifications. This chapter also turns to Raz as the starting point for the development of the novel(ish) theory of defences. It then proceeds to consider Gardner's model and identifies some "wrinkles" therein. The chapter offers a rehabilitation of Gardner's model which irons out those wrinkles. It does so by building upon an underdeveloped distinction noted by Raz in *Practical Reason and Norms* between well-groundedness and reasonableness.[2] The theory advanced here can thereby be described as Gardnerian, albeit not Gardner's own theory.

The novel(ish) theory advanced provides an answer to the question incorporationists pose by identifying a difference of kind between denials and defences. In this way, the supposed implications of the incorporationist position are debunked. As will become apparent however, the central logical claim of incorporationism withstands this debunking. The supposed implications of the incorporationist position are merely shorn from the logical claim. This has the effect of denuding the incorporationist challenge of its bite. What remains is a logical truth, but a trivial one.

Preliminaries

This chapter offers a positive contribution in its proposal of a novel(ish) theory of defences which provides the basis for recognising the substantive distinctions at play between denials/defences and offences/defences.[3] It does so through the vehicle of a rehabilitated Gardnerian view used to counter the incorporationist challenge. The most elegant expression of incorporationism is provided by Luís Duarte d'Almeida. It is useful therefore for the chapter to adopt this strongest expression as the foil against which to prosecute the arguments here.

It is important that when the terms "defence" and "denial" are used, they have the same meaning incorporationists ascribe to them.[4] The topic of defences – be they tortious or criminal – is fraught with ambiguity and polysemic usages. It is vital therefore that extra care is taken to ensure that both sides of the debate speak to the same issues and concepts.

Therefore, every effort will be made to ensure the incorporationist definitions will be faithfully relied upon. Denials and defences are considered to have at least one commonality, namely: "both kinds, if successful, will prevent the claimant or prosecutor from succeeding *on the merits*"[5] (i.e. not merely on a procedural basis). This then provides us with a fairly robust working definition of defences as those circumstances which go to the merits of the case and are not reducible to denials.[6]

As will be seen in the next section, the incorporationist challenge sets its opponents the task of developing a theory of defences; in other words, a theory which demonstrates a substantive distinction between denials and those "merits-relative liability-defeating considerations that are not 'denials' ".[7] While a full-bodied theory of defences is beyond the space available here, the chapter develops a theory of the central case of defences – justifications.

The incorporationist challenge is levelled at both crime and tort because both are thought to deal in denials and defences. Therefore, throughout the chapter, reference will be made sometimes to crime, sometimes to tort, and sometimes to both. Nothing of substance is intended by the choice of one or the other where it arises.

To begin the substantive work of the chapter, let us briefly outline the challenge and consider the implications and burdens that flow from it.

The challenge, its implications, and burdens

The essence of the challenge is drawn for us in the following passage, which warrants quoting here *in extenso*:

> "Consider the tort of battery…[where *a*, *b*, *c* are elements of the tort]… . If we use '*x*', '*y*' and '*z*' to stand for the admissible defences, we can articulate the following representation of the conditions on which a verdict for the claimant ('*VC*') depends:
>
> **If *a* and *b* and *c* and *not x* and *not y* and *not z*, then** *VC*
>
> … . Under this model, however, the absence or negation of each admissible defence—'*not x*', '*not y*', '*not z*'—is shown to play *precisely* the same role as the presence or

assertion of each element—'*a*', '*b*', '*c*'—of the tort. There is no difference in function between the two subsets of relevant circumstances. The members of the subset {*not x, not y, not z*} are—just like the members of the subset {*a, b, c*}—'elements' proper *of the condition* of VC".[8]

The primary implication of incorporationism, of course, is that there is no substantive distinction between denials and defences. Therefore, if this chapter is to challenge this view, then a theory of defences which demonstrates that distinction will be needed. Incorporationists propose that if incorporationism is true, then it will prove to be the case that "there is no relevant line to draw between 'denials' and 'defences'".[9] They claim that the incorporationist position demonstrates "that the two labels fail to track any deeper distinction of kinds of circumstances",[10] and that it will be evident that there is no "fundamental" or "basic" distinction at play. This must be so per incorporationism because "a defendant who denies an element of the tort in which the claimant sues—arguing, for example, that element *a* is *not the case*—seems to be doing exactly the same as a defendant who invokes a defence",[11] and thereby it becomes apparent "that there is ultimately no deeper difference between those two subsets of relevant circumstances".[12]

The chapter will now proceed to offer a theory of defences which identifies a substantive distinction between denials and defences. The foundation of this theory is to be found in the work of Joseph Raz and a conundrum he identified in our assessments of practical reasoning. The chapter will therefore begin with a brief exposition of Razian theory and draw out an overlooked aspect therein: the distinction between being well grounded in reason and being reasonable. This distinction will be built upon to distinguish denials from defences, with direct application to distinguishing offences from defences.

A theory of defences

Razian theory

Joseph Raz has provided us with tools to assess the practical reasoning of an agent. He does so by way of determining whether an agent acted for an undefeated or for a defeated reason. The question of whether or not a reason is defeated is one which concerns the outcome of any conflict of reasons. Standardly, the solution to such conflicts is provided by a consideration of the "strength" of the reasons, where the stronger reason outweighs the weaker and so stands to be considered as undefeated.

Perhaps the most significant contribution Raz has made to our understanding of reasons is to identify a distinction between first-order reasons and second-order reasons.[13] First-order reasons are quite simply reasons to φ or not to φ. Second-order reasons are different. They are reasons to act or refrain from acting on reasons.

As noted, when reasons conflict, the solution to such conflict is usually found through recourse to the strength of such reasons, such that the stronger reason prevails and may be considered an undefeated reason. This appears to satisfactorily explain how to assess the conflict of first-order reasons with other first-order reasons, or second-order reasons with other second-order reasons. However, when first-order reasons conflict with second-order reasons, a different "calculus" applies. The solution, Raz tells us, is that the conflict is no longer resolved by recourse to the internal strength of the reasons, but rather by virtue of the positional power of the second-order reasons.

This "calculus" provides us with a neat and clear-cut tool for assessing an agent's conduct, particularly as such assessments relate to law, as legal obligations are an archetypal form of second-order exclusionary reasons. While neat and clear-cut, this calculus isn't entirely satisfactory. Raz recognises this difficulty:

> "When the application of an exclusionary reason leads to the result that one should not act on the balance of reasons, that one should act for the weaker rather than the stronger reason which is excluded, we are faced with two incompatible assessments of what ought to be done. This leads normally to a peculiar feeling of unease, which will show itself when we wish to censure a person who acted on the balance of reasons for disregarding the exclusionary reason and when we have to justify someone's acting on an exclusionary reason against claims that the person concerned should have acted on the balance of reasons".[14]

So, some determinations under the calculus are clear-cut, while others are much trickier and we are left with "unease", as Raz puts it, when the first-order internal strength analysis and the second-order positional calculus generate conflicting results, the one to φ and the other not to φ. Should the agent comply with the weightier first-order reason or the unexcluded weaker reason which survived the exclusionary effect of the second-order calculus?

We are left then with a puzzle of how to make full-bodied assessments regarding the praise or censure of an agent. In an important paragraph Raz considers:

> "A person's action can be judged as being *well grounded in reason* or not according to whether there actually are reasons for performing the action. It can also be assessed as *reasonable* or rational according to whether the person had reasons to believe that there were reasons for his action. It is the world which guides our action, but since it inevitably does so through our awareness of it, our beliefs are important for the explanation and assessment of our behaviour".[15] [emphasis added]

This is an important acknowledgement of the central place awareness holds in evaluating an agent's conduct, where we can judge said conduct to be: (1) actually well-grounded in reason; and (2) rational or reasonable. These are dissociable assessments, recognition of which – it is proposed – solves Raz's conundrum.

On the one hand, we have a well-grounded in reason assessment which considers – via the Razian second order calculus – which undefeated reasons apply and whether or not the agent conformed to those reasons. This, without more, informs us as to the well-groundedness or otherwise of the agent. This is a purely objective assessment.

On the other hand, we must adopt a subjective epistemic ambit when assessing whether or not one acted reasonably and consider the facts and evidence *available* to the agent, not just the facts or reasons that actually applied. To do this, we must work within the epistemic world of the agent and operate solely on the basis of what evidence was available to them, not what was objectively known or knowable.

These two assessment types are dissociable. For any one action we can assess both the well-groundedness and the reasonableness of the agent. They may concur in that the determination may be that the agent acted reasonably and was well-grounded in reason. Likewise, they may diverge.

For our present purposes, let us focus on the scenario of an agent who is not well-grounded in reason but has acted reasonably. If the agent within their epistemic bounds discerns and acts for a reason that any of us (so bounded) would also discern as undefeated, then we can only assess them as having acted in as rational and reasonable a manner as possible. It is not open to us to assess them as rationally poor even though they may not be well-grounded in reason.

From this exposition and analysis of Razian theory, we can discern two kinds of assessments of the practical reasoning of an agent. One is an objective assessment of an agent's conformance with the dictates of reason, as determined through the operation of the second-order reasons' calculus. The other is an assessment conducted within the subjective epistemic ambit of the agent addressing itself to the compliance or otherwise to the subjectively discerned weightier reason.

To develop this division into a theory of defences which meets the incorporationist challenge and explains a substantive distinction between denials and defences, we will make use of John Gardner's groundbreaking and field-setting work on justifications.

Gardnerian justifications

As will become apparent, a number of wrinkles arise in Gardner's theory which this chapter will seek to iron out. These wrinkles, however, don't undermine the extraordinary advancement he has made to our understanding of the nature of justifications, as the core features of his theory are excellent and adopted. Instead, the rehabilitation work offered here is conceived of as advancing his theory rather than replacing it. Let us begin by briefly outlining that theory.

Building upon a Razian conception of reasons, Gardner proposes justification to be built upon guiding and explanatory reasons.[16] Guiding reasons are essentially what one ought to do, and explanatory reasons are offered as an account of why one acted in a particular way. On this view, justification (a combination of what one did and why one did it) resides in the coherence of guiding and explanatory reasons, while dissonance between these two reasons gives rise to unjustified action.

For Gardner then, justification is something of a combined objective/subjective assessment where

> no action or belief is justified unless it is true *both* that there was an applicable (guiding) reason for so acting or so believing *and* that this corresponded with the (explanatory) reason why the action was performed or the belief held.[17]

The nature of a justification then is: (1) that there was an applicable guiding reason; and (2) this corresponded with the explanatory reason.[18]

Giving concrete form to this theory through use of an example may be helpful here. To begin with a trivial scenario, Gardner reuses Raz's example of an agent choosing to leave their umbrella at home even though it will rain as a scenario of unjustified action.[19] This is because there was a guiding reason to bring one's umbrella (which we can assume stands undefeated) and yet when asked to explain their actions, their explanatory reason will have been that they acted for a defeated reason. In this way, there is a dissonance between the guiding and explanatory reasons. Therefore, the agent was unjustified to do as they did, albeit trivially so.

Consider now a more serious example of a meretricious self-defence.[20] Agent (A) sees their nemesis (N) attacking a victim (V). A guiding reason is therefore provided by the weighty reason that attends defending others from attack. Now, in this scenario A does act and does stop the attack on V but he does so to exact revenge on N. Therefore, his explanatory reason does not cohere with the guiding reason and he thereby also acted in an unjustified manner.

While this is indeed a sophisticated model, there are however a number of wrinkles arising. Let us now move to consider them, each in turn.

Wrinkles in Gardner's theory

There are three aspects of Gardner's theory that will be critiqued in this section, namely:

(1) The objective discernment of guiding reasons;
(2) The position justifications hold in the hierarchy of rationality; and
(3) The view that justifications offer permissions to violate legal norms.

Firstly, it will be argued that the commitment to the objective discernment of guiding reasons is ill-fitting with the model of assessing both what an agent did and *why* they did it. Flowing from this, the position afforded justifications in Gardner's hierarchy of defences will be demonstrated as insecure. Finally, the view that justifications offer permissions will be interrogated and found wanting.

However, all is not lost: the dissociable Razian assessments of well-groundedness and reasonableness will be proposed as a route to ironing out those wrinkles and rehabilitating Gardnerian justifications. This will reveal a novel(ish) theory of defences which addresses the implications of the incorporationist challenge by demonstrating differences of kind between denials and defences.

Objective guiding reasons?

To recapitulate, in order to be justified, there must be a guiding reason (i.e. an undefeated reason) and the agent must have acted for that guiding reason. For Gardner, determination of which reasons are guiding is done from an entirely objective epistemic position. This has some unfortunate permutations.

Consider the following trolley problem; a trolley hurtling down the track and the track diverges with five people stuck on one spur but nobody on the other. Our agent has the means to divert the trolley through use of the lever. Above the lever reads a sign:

> If you pull the lever the train will be diverted to the empty spur

Now let us assume this instruction is a lie, and in fact the opposite is true. For Gardner, the agent who came upon the scene, read the sign, and responded to it by pulling the lever will have been unjustified in doing so. This is because although the agent responded to all the evidence available to them in as rational a manner as possible, they did not act for the objectively discernible guiding reason. This is a disquieting result *per se* but more troubling still, is how this stands in tension with a central objective of Gardner's enterprise, namely challenging the act/actor distinction.

In drawing out the fact that justifications entail a consideration of both what an agent did and why they did it, Gardner is countering some widely held views that justificatory defences relate to acts, while excusatory defences relate to actors. One of his aims then is to eschew such views. Now, it is reasonable that the trolley scenario may fail a pure act assessment or a "what one did" analysis, but once we consider why an agent acted, we are addressing ourselves to how an agent reasons, which can only sensibly be done on the basis of the evidence available to them.

Having made clear that being justified is not just a matter of what one did but also why they did it, it is unfortunate Gardner didn't give this realisation the full import it deserves, namely: it is an assessment of an agent's action upon their reasoning, rather than simply an assessment of reasons and one's conformity thereto. To equate one with the other is problematic. Because it is an assessment of reasoning, it is sensibly bounded by the subjective epistemic ambit.

Consider our vengeful putative defender (A) earlier. He has brought about a beneficial result for the victim (V). However, he acted in pursuit of his vengeful desires, not in pursuit of the applicable guiding reason. In assessing the agent then, it was determined that there is a dissonance between the guiding and explanatory reasons, with such dissonance constituting unjustifiedness. So, it is not enough to just happen to be in conformity with applicable guiding reasons in order to be right, nor does it negate the agent's unjustifiedness. Gardner is incorrect not to recognise the converse also holds, namely where one happens to be in nonconformity but their actions were entirely justified. In other words, where the agent came to as rational a conclusion as possible but were mistaken by virtue of some unknowable facts, such as in the Trolley problem, they cannot be thought less of.

The conformity assessment of the Razian well-groundedness calculus (detailed earlier) is "objective" and has no necessary reference to what was subjectively known or knowable to the defendant. However, assessments of reasoning are necessarily bounded by the subjective epistemic world, albeit assessed against the standard created by the community viewpoint. I suggest then that Gardner is wrong to consider that an agent who comes to as rationally sound a conclusion as possible should be thought of as being unjustified because of some fact unavailable to them (or perhaps anyone in the same situation) at the time. This is to confuse non-conformity with unjustifiedness. The former is a matter of well-groundedness or otherwise, and thereby perfectly acceptable as an objective assessment, and the latter is not so, because it is an assessment of reasoning, not reasons.

Hierarchy of rationality

In Gardner's work on defences, he draws for us a hierarchy. For Gardner, what he describes as the phenomenal self will prudently seek to escape the negative consequences of wrongdoing and therefore be quite content to rely on any liability-blocking claim that will do the job. However, the basic responsibility of the noumenal self will draw a hierarchy which *ceteris paribus* a rational agent will seek to abide by: firstly, the rational agent will attempt to justify any wrongdoing; secondly, failing justification, they will seek to excuse the wrongdoing; and thirdly, at the nadir or base of the hierarchy of priority, the rational agent will cast doubt on their own basic responsibility.[21]

Returning again to the trolley problem, it is troubling that the agent who pulls the lever ought to be assessed as rationally inferior and merely entitled to a second-tier defence of an excuse as opposed to a justification. If the hierarchy is one of rationality, the fact that one who has been as rationally perfect as anybody would have been, in the same circumstances, is not at the zenith therefore casts doubt on the security of justification as occupying the apex position of the hierarchy.

It is true that the agent is not in conformance with the objective dictates of reason and may be in breach of the relevant norm(s), but that is well accounted for by a determination of one having engaged in the "wrongdoing" which they are seeking to justify. For that objective non-conformance to go to justification as well would be to engage in double counting. To see how this is so, consider the agent in the trolley problem, *supra*. They objectively did the wrong thing in pulling the lever. We can apply the Razian calculus and determine them to be in non-conformance with what reason demands. We can thus assess them as having done wrong or engaged in "wrongdoing". If we are to consider their objective non-conformance a second time in assessing whether or not the agent was justified in their wrongdoing, then this would be to count the objective non-conformance twice. What motivates us in seeking a justification is to assess the reasoning which led the agent into such non-conformance.

Permission view

Gardner proposes a justificatory defence entails a permission to breach a legal duty such that:

> "By default, in the eyes of the law, a criminal prohibition excludes from consideration all competing reasons. It constitutes an absolute duty. The provision by the law of a justificatory defence unexcludes a certain reason or a certain range of reasons in favour of the prohibited action and returns the reason or reasons so unexcluded to the pool of reasons that engage in a simple conflict of weight with the duty, and are capable of either outweighing or being outweighed by it. In my fancy lingo, justificatory defences in law are cancelling permissions".[22]

This formulation sees defences as occupying a permissive scope hewn from the otherwise mandatory legal norm. The reasons then in favour (or against) the relevant action, such as say, use of force in self-defence, are weighed on a purely first-order basis because the cancelling permission returns the reasons from the protected realm of the second-order plane to the first-order balance.

Permissions certainly do exist, but they cannot sensibly be said to be defences. Permissions go to the question of whether or not one was in conformance with the requirements of the legal norm. To rely on a permission is to say one was allowed to do as they did and therefore, they did no wrong. This must be the case because if one is under a legal prohibition, we may describe this as "D must not X". If one has a permission to act, this is described as "D may X". Now, it is a matter of plain logic that if D may X, it cannot be the case that D must not X. Such permissions, it is accepted, do exist, but they must be denials.

Now, it may be countered that Gardner isn't quite going so far as to say D may act on the reason in favour of the relevant action, rather he is just saying that the reasons in favour are unexcluded and returned to the balance. The reasons for or against so acting remain to be weighed. They are simply stripped of the "positional strength" of second-order reasons. If denials are claims of having acted in conformance with a legal norm, but justifications cancel only the obligatoriness of the legal norm (as this counter might suggest), then we have advanced no further. An obligation stripped of its obligatoriness is no longer an obligation, and cannot be breached. If no obligation can be breached, a claim of a cancelling permission – even under these lights – can only amount to a denial and not a defence.

This highlights a problem of internal coherence for Gardner in that he wishes to defend the offence/defence or denial/defence distinction, and yet simultaneously claim justifications to be permissions. To adhere to both of these propositions is not coherently available to him.

Rehabilitation

All of the above "wrinkles" in Gardner's theory can be ironed out by recognising and building upon the distinction between being well-grounded in reason and being reasonable. These are the two principal assessments of agency discerned from Razian theory, namely determinations of well-groundedness and reasonableness. Because applicable guiding reasons are not subjectively created and exist objectively outside of whether or not a given agent recognises such reasons (i.e. they are facts), conformity or otherwise with said reasons (well-groundedness) is a matter susceptible to purely objective assessments. In contrast to this, reasonableness entails an assessment of the reasoning of the agent, which is necessarily informed by what reasons the agent was aware of.

This is why we may say assessments of reasonableness are subjectively bounded albeit they are not wholly subjectively determined. We don't take the subject's reasoning as good or right simply because they thought they had reason to do as they did or simply because they failed to grasp the full import of the subjectively discernible guiding reason, as that would be to put the cart before the horse. Rather, it is an assessment *of* the agent's practical rationality precisely because it does not adopt the agent's valuing of reasons on its face. In conducting such assessment, we do not take on the agent's world view or ideological perspective, we simply work within the agent's epistemic world, including the evidence that was available to her at the time she exercised the agency which is being assessed. The limitation of scope applied is epistemic rather than perspectival.

The core of Gardner's theory of justification is sound. To be justified is indeed to act *for* an undefeated reason. The suggestion for rehabilitation offered here lies in recognising that this is a reasonableness rather than a well-groundedness assessment, and therefore that this is an assessment conducted within the epistemic world of the agent. This is not some sort of lesser or modified version of the second-order well-groundedness calculus. It is a dissociable assessment kind.

Once this tweak is made, it helps to iron out the wrinkles identified. Limiting our assessment to the epistemic world of the defendant is more fitting for evaluations of the reasoning of agents. It better secures the position of justification in a hierarchy of rationality whilst simultaneously avoiding the pitfall of double counting any non-conformance. Finally, and perhaps most usefully for the enterprise of this chapter, it avoids the notion of justifications as permissions, and the incompatibility that arises therefrom with the proposal of a denial/defence or an offence/defence distinction. More succinctly, it identifies justifications as species of reasonableness assessments while offences (and denials) are recognised as species of well-groundedness assessments.

To sum up, the kernel of a novel-ish theory of defences offered here identifies a substantive difference between denials and defences. Denial assessments operate within an objective epistemic ambit and they address themselves to the question of conformance thereto. These are assessments of well-groundedness. Defence assessments operate within a subjective epistemic ambit and they address themselves to the question of compliance thereto. These are assessments of reasonableness.

This model answers the incorporationist challenge in that it demonstrates a "deeper difference" between denials and defences, than "mere… convenient labelling". And it also explains "what, precisely the difference between 'denials' and 'defences' is". This demonstration of differences of kind is not however fatal to the incorporationist challenge. While this theory of defences addresses the proposed implications of the incorporationist challenge, it is not clear how this detracts in even the slightest degree from the logical truth of the "simple descriptive model" quoted *in extenso* earlier in the chapter. It seems eminently clear that although there may be differences of kind between denials and defences, an absence of a defence is still required for a verdict in favour of the claimant or prosecutor.

A route to understanding this may be available to us by calling upon a skill newly developed across the western world during the pandemic: baking! (And in particular the baking of banana bread.) Consider the recipe:

Ingredients

285g/10oz plain flour
1 tsp bicarbonate of soda
½ tsp salt
110g/4oz butter, plus extra for greasing
225g/8oz caster sugar
2 free-range eggs
4 ripe bananas, mashed
85ml/3fl oz buttermilk (or normal milk mixed with 1½ tsp lemon juice or vinegar)

1 tsp vanilla extract

Method

1. Preheat the oven to 180C/350F/Gas 4.
2. Sift the flour, bicarbonate of soda and salt into a large mixing bowl.
3. In a separate bowl, cream the butter and sugar together until light and fluffy.
4. Add the eggs, mashed bananas, buttermilk and vanilla extract to the butter and sugar mixture and mix well. Fold in the flour mixture.
5. Grease a 20cm x 12.5cm/8in x 5in loaf tin (2lb) and pour the banana bread mixture into the tin.
6. Transfer to the oven and bake for about an hour, or until well-risen and golden-brown.
7. Remove from the oven and cool in the tin for a few minutes, then turn out onto a wire rack to cool completely before serving.[23]

It is true that the ingredients of flour, eggs, butter, etc., are necessary elements of the recipe. Likewise, it is true that in order to be successful and the cake to bake, the presence of heat from the oven is also a necessary element. However, it doesn't follow that there aren't "fundamental" and "basic" distinctions between the ingredients of the cake and the heat from the oven. There are relevant lines to be drawn and deep distinctions at play that are not mere matters of "convenient labelling".[24] Conversely, these deep distinctions leave the truth of the categorisation of both heat and flour as necessary elements of the recipe untouched.

Such is also the case of the truth of incorporationism and the truth of there being fundamental and deep distinctions at play between denials and defences. We can disassociate the two, and so, if the supposed implications don't follow – as this chapter argues – we are left with a sound, erudite, unimpeachable, logical truth but it is one denuded of import or substance. It is true, but trivially so.

Notes

1. Non-merits-relative bases would include procedural blocks such as double jeopardy.
2. J Raz, *Practical Reason and Norms* (Oxford University Press: Oxford, 2nd edn, 1999).
3. Duarte d'Almeida notes this as "long recognised as a central issue in the philosophy of criminal law, the distinction between offences and defences has yet to be satisfactorily explained." In L Duarte d'Almeida, "'O Call Me Not to Justify the Wrong': Criminal Answerability and the Offence/Defence Distinction", *Criminal Law and Philosophy*, vol. 6, no. 2 (2012), p.227.
4. Indeed, this is noted by L Duarte d'Almeida, "Defining Defences", in A Dyson, J Goudkamp & F Wilmot-Smith (eds), *Defences in Tort* (Hart Publishing: Oxford, 2015), p.37 where he opines "whoever wishes to take issue with the incorporationist view must use the relevant terms in the same sense".
5. Duarte d'Almeida, "Defining", p.48.
6. Duarte d'Almeida, "Defining", p.49.
7. Duarte d'Almeida, "Defining", p. 50.
8. Duarte d'Almeida, "Defining", p.39.
9. Duarte d'Almeida, "Defining", p.36.
10. Duarte d'Almeida, "Defining", p.37.
11. Duarte d'Almeida, "Defining", p.40.
12. Duarte d'Almeida, "Defining", p.44.
13. This is recognized as "one of Raz's most important philosophical insights" and "the foundation upon which much of his work in legal and political as well as in practical philosophy is built". Cf. SR Perry, "Second-Order Reasons, Uncertainty and Legal Theory", *Southern Californian Law Review*, vol. 62 (1989), p.913 and has been described as "perhaps the most significant work in jurisprudence since H.L.A. Hart's *The Concept of Law*." Cf. W Edmundson, "Book Review", *Law and Philosophy*, vol. 12, no. 3 (1993), p.329.
14. Raz, *PRN*, p.41.
15. Raz, *PRN*, p.22.
16. J Gardner, "Justifications and Reasons", in *Offences and Defences* (Oxford University Press: Oxford, 2007).
17. Gardner, *Offences and Defences*, p.94.
18. Gardner, *Offences and Defences*, Ch 5.
19. J Gardner, "Wrongs and Faults", *The Review of Metaphysics*, vol. 59, no. 1 (2005), p.95.
20. Defence of others is standardly understood to be part of this defence.
21. Gardner, *Offences and Defences*, Ch 4.
22. J Gardner, "Justification Under Authority", *Canadian Journal of Law and Jurisprudence*, vol. 23, no.1 (2010), p.71 at p.80.
23. BBC Good Food, "Easy Banana Bread", available at: www.bbc.co.uk/food/recipes/bananabread_85720.
24. Duarte d'Almeida, "Defining", p.44.

References

Duarte d'Almeida L, "'O Call Me Not to Justify the Wrong': Criminal Answerability and the Offence/Defence Distinction", *Criminal Law and Philosophy*, vol. 6 (2012), pp.227–245.

Duarte d'Almeida L, "Defining Defences", in Dyson A, Goudkamp J, & Wilmot-Smith F (eds), *Defences in Tort*, (Hart Publishing: Oxford, 2015).

Edmundson W, "Rethinking Exclusionary Reasons: A Second Edition of Joseph Raz's [Book Review]", *Law and Philosophy*, vol. 12, no. 3 (1993), pp.329–343.
Gardner J, "Justification Under Authority", *Canadian Journal of Law and Jurisprudence*, vol. 23, no. 1 (2010), pp.71–98.
Gardner J, "Justifications and Reasons" in *Offences and Defences: Selected Essays in the Philosophy of Criminal Law* (Oxford University Press: Oxford, 2007).
Gardner J, "Wrongs and Faults", *The Review of Metaphysics*, vol. 59, no. 1 (2005), pp.95–132.
Perry SR, "Second-Order Reasons, Uncertainty and Legal Theory", *Southern California Law Review*, vol. 62 (1989), pp.913–994.
Raz J, *Practical Reason and Norms* (Oxford University Press: Oxford, 2nd edn, 1999).

14

THE CRIMINAL LAW OF TRIAGE

A Rights-Based Approach to Justificatory Defences

Ivó Coca-Vila

Introduction

The COVID-19 global pandemic has triggered a deep discussion about the legal consequences of distributing scarce medical resources in dilemmatic situations. While the question of the criminal liability of public officials in charge of managing health budgets has been given short shrift,[1] the question of how doctors should make life and death decisions in situations of shortage (triage) has become the focus of several criminal law scholars.[2] The contemporary triage debate involves the following three dilemma scenarios:

(1) Triage *ex ante*: Two people, (A) and (B), arrive at the intensive care unit (ICU) at the same time. There is only one available ventilator, so the doctor should either withhold the ventilator from (A) to give it to (B) or withhold the ventilator from (B) to give it to (A). Both patients have the capacity to benefit from it and both will die if not treated immediately.
(2) Triage *ex post*: (A) arrives at the ICU and is immediately placed on the last available ventilator. Although their recovery prospect is low, treatment is medically indicated, and they would have the chance to benefit from it. Then (B) arrives, who also needs to be placed on a ventilator. (B)'s prospect for recovery is higher than (A)'s, but the only way for the doctor to treat (B) is to withdraw the ventilator from (A), which means condemning them to death. If (B) is not treated, they will also die.
(3) Triage *ex ante* pre-emptive: (A) arrives at the ICU and there is only one available ventilator. (A) could benefit from treatment, but their prospect of recovery is low. To avoid using the ventilator and having to triage, the doctor withholds treatment from (A) to allow a future patient with a better prospect of recovery to be treated.

It is widely accepted within the framework of continental criminal law systems that doctors hold a guarantor position with regard to their patients, which means that their omissions leading to death are considered to be equivalent to active causation of the result (commission by omission).[3] In other words, doctors who (knowingly) withhold medical treatment are criminally liable for those deaths. The same conclusion applies to triage *ex post*. The doctor who withdraws the ventilator to save the newly arrived patient with a better prospect of recovery would be liable for the death of the first patient. And the same applies to the triage *ex ante* pre-emptive scenario: the doctor who does not attend the only patient present is killing them (commission by omission).

However, these conclusions are of a purely *prima facie* nature. They are reached without considering the conflict situation in which doctors act. The *all-things-considered* judgement as to whether these doctors are, in fact, committing legal wrongs must be made considering the competing interests or rights of all patients involved in the triage scenario. In other words, deciding whether doctors are criminally liable ultimately depends on whether their actions can be covered by a justificatory defence, in particular, by the so-called *collision of duties defence* and the *necessity defence*.

The overall aim of this chapter is to provide an overview of the recent discussion among continental criminal law scholars about triage and, in particular, to offer a critique of the most recent approaches that propose a maximising-utilitarianism reading of the justificatory defences.[4] Contra those who argue that both the triage *ex post* and the triage *ex ante* pre-emptive scenarios are justified, and that the doctor in the triage *ex ante* scenario should treat the person with the best recovery prospect or the best life expectancy, I will argue that the system of justificatory defences and, in general, the conduct rules in criminal law, are not tailored to the maximisation of any (medical) resource. In other words, whether an action is criminally liable is not determined by whether a medical resource has been maximised from a collective perspective. In particular, I will argue that in the triage *ex ante* scenario, the doctor acts in accordance with the (criminal) law by saving either one of the patients involved, and that both triage *ex post* and triage *ex ante* pre-emptive constitute criminally liable behaviour and should be punished accordingly.

Justifying utility-maximising killing

In recent years, many authors have proposed a utility-maximising reading of criminal justificatory defences in triage situations. So, where resources are scarce and doctors must allocate them, the assessment of their decisions should be based on the principle of maximisation. In other words, the justification of doctors' action via the necessity or collision of duties defences would depend on whether doctors adopted decisions that optimised outcomes in terms of lives saved or the number of years of life saved. According to this view, criminal law should not deviate from the (profoundly utilitarian) logic that inspires medical triage guidelines, at least, not in extraordinary situations such as a pandemic. In such exceptional situations, the (criminal) law should be subordinated to public health considerations.[5] While some authors allude to a classically utilitarian reasoning,[6] others try to found the maximising reading of the justificatory defences on a Rawlsian conceptualist reasoning: doctors should adopt utility-maximising allocation because this is the solution that citizens would rationally adopt behind a hypothetical "veil of ignorance" that prevents them from knowing which position they will take in the dilemma.[7] Let's see what these authors propose in the three scenarios described above.

Triage ex ante

In the triage *ex ante* scenario, the doctor must decide to whom to allocate the last ventilator between two patients that need it immediately (same urgency). The doctor is a special guarantor with respect to each patient. Both patients want to be treated and the untreated one will die immediately. This sort of dilemma has been traditionally conceptualised by continental criminal law scholars as a "collision of duties":[8] the guarantor is bound by two (criminal law) duties to act, however, those duties cannot be fulfilled cumulatively, but only alternatively. The doctor can save either (*A*) or (*B*), but not both. Whatever they do, at the very least, will be in breach of a duty to act.

The collision of duties defence is generally considered to be a justificatory defence that releases a person from criminal liability for a crime of omission. Since the law cannot require the impossible ("ought implies can"), guarantors do not commit any legal wrong if they fulfil the higher-ranking duty. The ranking must be decided by a comparative judgement of legal interests underlying both conflicting duties. When this balance of interests results in a technical tie, i.e. both duties are considered to be of equal-rank, guarantors act in accordance with the law by fulfilling either one of them (disjunctive or alternative duty). Although some authors aim to condition guarantors' decisions procedurally, for example, by obliging them to flip a coin, there is a broad consensus among criminal law scholars that if the duties at stake are of equal-rank and the guarantor fulfils one of them, the omission is justified regardless of the reason or motive behind the choice. Thus, no one commits homicide just because they have chosen whom they save based on a deplorable motive.[9]

Thus, the key question in triage *ex ante* scenarios is whether it is possible to establish a ranking of duties, so that doctors are compelled to treat a specific patient, or whether, as has traditionally been held, when human lives in immediate risk are at stake, doctors are free to decide who to treat, since it is a conflict between equal-rank duties. As mentioned, in the wake of the COVID-19 crisis, many criminal law scholars have argued that conflicting duties in triage *ex ante* scenarios must be ranked, as this would be essential to achieving the most efficient allocation of scarce medical resources. In particular, three factors have been proposed as a way of reaching such a ranking. First, some authors want to rank the duties according to the recovery prospect of each patient, understood as the likelihood of overcoming the specific disease that justifies treatment with the ventilator.[10] That is, assuming that both patients have a sufficiently high recovery prospect for ventilator treatment to be indicated (non-futile treatment), doctors must save those patients with the better recovery prospects. In favour of taking into account this factor, a classical prioritisation factor in almost all (legally non-binding) clinical triage guidelines, it is argued that only by taking prospect for recovery into consideration can an efficient use of lifesaving medical resources be ensured. Second, some authors, such as Elisa Hoven, suggest that the patient's life expectancy should also be considered when ranking duties.[11] Based on the notion of "fair innings", famously introduced into the public health discussion by John Harris in his seminal *The Value of Life*,[12] Hoven states that when recovery prospects are similar, life expectancy should be the key criterion for deciding which duty doctors must fulfil. Doctors must treat the patient who has not already reached the years of life that are considered reasonable to live. Third, Tatjana Hörnle proposes using vaccination status as a decision criterion where patients' recovery prospects are identical.[13] She appeals to a fairness argument:

those who in the past have attached more importance to avoiding the risks of vaccination or other inconveniences than to the prospect of reducing the likelihood of a potentially fatal disease through vaccination must in return accept that their own decisions become a prioritisation criterion in the absence of better alternatives.[14]

Although requiring patients to take responsibility for their own healthcare decisions does not obey a utilitarian logic, it does also imply breaking the equality of duties in cases of *ex ante* triage.

What are the legal consequences of taking these three factors into consideration in the case of *ex ante* triage? It means that, contrary to what has been classically defended by criminal law scholars, doctors would not have the freedom to choose between two equal-rank duties. They would be obliged to fulfil the higher-ranking duty—that is, they must save the patient with the best recovery prospect or, in the case of equivalence, the patient with the best life expectancy, or the vaccinated patient. Although it is not always stated clearly enough, prioritising duties implies that doctors performing lower-ranking duties would not be justified in failing to treat the legal-preferred patient (killing by omission). Thus, the doctor who saves the patient with the lower recovery prospect would be criminally liable for killing a patient in a non-justified way and should be punished accordingly. The same applies to the doctor who saves the patient who has already exhausted his fair innings, or the doctor who treats the unvaccinated patient to the detriment of the one who is vaccinated.

Triage ex post

In the triage *ex post* scenario, the doctor considers discontinuing a treatment already started with a ventilator in order to reallocate that ventilator to a patient who has just arrived with a (much) better recovery prospect. Criminal law scholars, at least in the continental debates, have traditionally held that withdrawing treatment in such circumstances is tantamount to killing the first patient, and that this cannot be justified on the basis of any justificatory defence.[15]

This conclusion is based on the following three premises. First, it is assumed that discontinuing treatment that has already begun involves the violation of a right of the treated person, different, therefore, to the (mere) expectation of recovery, which the patient who has not yet been treated may have. Withholding and withdrawing treatment are not equivalent, at least not from a criminal law point of view. Second, withdrawing treatment can only be justified by appealing to the necessity defence. This means that such an active interference on a legal sphere (withdrawing treatment) can only be justified when doctors safeguard interests that substantially outweigh the ones they harm. Third, given that human lives are always of equal worth, the difference in the recovery prospect between the intubated patient and the one who has just arrived does not establish a relevant difference. Most continental criminal law scholars, in addition to denying the justification, are unwilling to accept an exculpation of the doctor who performs *ex post* triage.[16] Their actions, in short, should be punished.

The prohibition on *ex post* triage is considered by a growing number of scholars to be deeply contrary to the maximising-utilitarian logic that should govern the allocation of medical resources in cases of extreme scarcity.[17] For this reason, they propose a new reading of the dilemma that would make it possible to consider withdrawing treatment to be justified in order to save patients with better recovery prospects. The basic premises are as follows: first, for criminal law, there should be no distinction between acting and omitting, since certain omissions are punished in the same way as actions. Second, the fact that the first patient is already connected to the ventilator does not give them any better right to treatment than any other citizen may have.[18] Three arguments are advanced in favour of this second premise. First, the right to be ventilated is a purely positive right (to participate in a fair distribution of a scarce resource); it is not a negative right (to life). Second, the ventilator is a public resource that requires constant monitoring by a medical team for its operation, so it is never integrated into the patient's legal sphere as a bodily right. Therefore, the medical team would always retain the power to redistribute it. And third, forbidding *ex post* triage may also result in unnecessary *ex ante* pre-emptive triage.

What are the consequences of accepting the above two premises? If we look at it in detail, it implies that the situation of *ex post* triage would not differ in any way from that of *ex ante* triage. Regardless, doctors must still choose between two duties, and by fulfilling either of them would act in a justified manner.[19] For some authors, there would even be a duty to perform *ex post* triage: if the recovery prospect of the treated patient is much worse than that of the new one, the doctor would be required to perform the higher-rank duty and, therefore, to disconnect the first patient.[20] Their killing would be justified by appealing to the collision of duties defence.

Triage ex ante pre-emptive

In the triage *ex ante* pre-emptive scenario, the doctor decides not to perform their duty to attend to a current patient, so that the ventilator the patient with a better recovery prospect would use is kept free. In short, it is a matter of withholding treatment to avoid having to perform *ex post* triage at a later date.

Structurally, we are faced here with a conflict between a duty to treat the patient and a "prospective duty"[21] to be able to care for a future non-identified patient. Given that the only duty whose infringement generates criminal liability is the former, it has traditionally been stated that here the guarantor must fulfil the actual (not the hypothetical) duty. Their future omission would not be criminally liable, due to lack of capacity to act ("ought implies can"). However, this solution also makes the supporters of maximising-utilitarian solutions uncomfortable. In their opinion, we would be faced here with a conflict to be resolved by comparing the various interests at stake:[22] if the probability of a new patient arriving with a much better recovery prospect is high, and the current patient has a poorer prospect or is of advanced age, the doctor could justifiably (invoking the necessity defence) infringe their duty and deny treatment. Postponing ventilator allocation is then the solution that maximises its use.

A rights-centred system of justificatory defences

The readings of the justificatory defences underlying the conclusions presented in the preceding section have the charm of simplicity: they seek to ensure an allocation of medical resources under the rule of maximisation. Surely, this is also the logic that inspires most (non-binding) medical guidelines on triage. However, as I have argued elsewhere in detail,[23] conceiving of justificatory defences as tools in the service of the maximisation of a certain value—e.g. the number of survivors, life years, quality-adjusted life years ("QALYs"), whereby that value is aggregated beyond the borders of people—is unconvincing. The challenge for the liberal justificatory defences system is far more complex than maximising the safeguarding of interests in aggregated terms: it is to find solutions to conflicts that respect all of the individuals involved, as *rights holders*.[24] In short, a legitimate solution to a conflict cannot be an alleged maximising interest of a holistic entity; instead, each of the individuals involved and, in particular, the one who will ultimately bear the cost of the conflict, must be respected as autonomous rights holders.[25]

Note that the classical objections to the utilitarian reading cannot be circumvented by appealing to the Rawlsian veil of ignorance or to an *ex ante* consent that leads to maximising solutions. A justificatory defences system must be able to explain to the specific individual in the specific conflict why their claim or right should yield to that of their fellow. To argue that behind a veil of ignorance all citizens would have agreed to the maximising solution ("utilitarianism from behind the veil of ignorance") is, again, not to take the rights of the individual concerned seriously.[26] The right to life of the person suffering from a congenital chronic lung disease does not lose one iota of normative status by the fact that the rival patient has a better recovery prospect. And this, contrary to the exceptionalism approach, is still true in times of pandemic.[27] As Weyma Lübbe has convincingly shown,[28] explaining to the first patient that, behind a veil of ignorance, they would have consented to the maximising allocation is only slightly less unsatisfactory than relying on the alleged maximising interest of a collective in the classical utilitarian sense.

The imponderability of human life

A fundamental principle in the rights-based understanding of the justificatory defences for which I am arguing is the imponderability of human life.[29] Two sub-principles are derived from this principle: first, the quantitative accumulation of lives does not alter the comparative value of any one of them (prohibition of addition). This is convincingly shown in the political philosophy of John Taurek, which is widely accepted on this point among continental criminal law scholars.[30] Second, there is no difference in worth between two human lives (prohibition of grading or ranking). All lives, in short, have the same (imponderable) value.

The principle of the qualitative imponderability of human lives has been accepted by continental scholars when applying both the necessity and the collision of duties' defence. The idea is as follows: when two human lives are at stake in a conflict situation, the urgency in both cases being similar, the conflicting interests are equivalent. Any qualitative difference among human lives (social utility, age, prospect of recovery, nationality, etc.) does not, under any circumstances, allow for a ranked difference between interests to justify the sacrifice of one of the parties. The right to life of either of the parties involved cannot yield simply because the other life at stake is considered more valuable in the eyes of a holistic entity. Let us see what the consequences are of taking seriously the principle of the imponderability of human life in the three triage scenarios presented above.

In the triage *ex ante* scenario, taking the (qualitative) imponderability of human life seriously implies that—assuming both patients wish to be treated and both have similar urgency—the doctor is faced with two equal-rank duties. This means, then, that neither the different prospects of recovery nor different life expectancies are relevant factors in the ranking of duties. From a criminal law perspective, the doctor in the triage *ex ante* scenario will always have the power to choose which duty they fulfil (disjunctive or alternative duty). If they save one of the patients, even if they treat the oldest patient or the one with the lower recovery prospect, they will be acting justifiably and will not be (all things considered) criminally liable.[31]

That the doctor saves one of the two patients is the only interest shared by both patients in the conflict situation and thus the only reason that the untreated patient must accept their death if they are not treated. It is the price they must pay in the specific case in order not to lose their option for treatment from the outset.[32] However, what if the doctor decides based on an immoral, e.g. racist, motive? I would argue that—for the purposes of justifying the killing by omission—that fact is irrelevant. Faced with two equal-rank duties, the doctor acts justifiably by attending to one of the patients, their motive being completely irrelevant from a criminal liability perspective. It is a different matter whether, as some authors have proposed,[33] it makes sense to criminalise decision-making based on unacceptable motives, e.g. discrimination based on disability or ethnicity. The wrong committed by the doctor would, then, not be a killing, but a legal wrong against the fairness of the decision-making procedure.

Is a ranking of duties based on vaccination status compatible with a rights-based understanding of the collision of duties defence? Yes, but there is a strong (practical) reason not to take this factor into consideration. As citizens freely decide not to be vaccinated and thus contribute to the conflict, it seems fair that they should bear the primary cost of the conflict. In fact, this same logic underlies self-defence. However, if we take into account patients' vaccination status, we should also take into account any other autonomous decisions by patients that have contributed to their current health status (drugs, tobacco, etc.). In addition, we would have to assess how autonomous the endangerment was (which is particularly complex when it comes to the use of addictive substances) and how much it affects the current state of health (causality). This is, in practical terms, almost impossible.[34] Therefore, the doctor in the triage *ex ante* scenario who chooses to save the unvaccinated patient is also acting in accordance with the (criminal) law. Their omission is justified by the collision of duties' defence.

Taking the principle of the imponderability of human life seriously also means denying the possibility of justifying the practice of *ex ante* pre-emptive triage. *Ex ante* pre-emptive triage can only be justified where the doctor's current infringement of a duty of care allows a substantially outweighing interest to be safeguarded, i.e. in accordance with the parameters of the necessity defence. Since neither the prospect for recovery nor a patient's life expectancy are allowable criteria for distinguishing between lives, relying on those factors in the case we are concerned with here—triage *ex ante* pre-emptive—is criminally forbidden.[35] In short, the doctor (guarantor) who does not attend to the elderly patient is criminally liable for killing that patient (by omission), and must be punished accordingly. For the same reason, the practice of *ex post* triage cannot be justified using the necessity defence.[36] The interests of the two patients are equivalent, so the only (theoretical) way to justify withdrawing treatment would be to appeal to the collision of duties' defence. However, as I will show below, this is also unconvincing.

The consolidation of survival expectations

Those who defend the justification of *ex post* triage rely on two arguments. First, they argue that acting and omitting are equivalent under the criminal law, since there are omissions that are punished as actions. Second, they argue that the patient who is already being treated with the ventilator has no better right to the resource than any other citizen. I will argue that the first argument is right, but the second is wrong, which means that *ex post* triage cannot be justified under any circumstances. In what follows, I will try to show why.

As I have argued in more detail elsewhere,[37] a regulatory system has a reasonable interest in reducing situations of uncertainty regarding the rights (and their strength) of the people involved. This is especially true in life and death situations. From the very moment a shipwrecked person reaches the float that has just been thrown to them and is going to prevent them from drowning, they consolidate their expectation of survival in the form of a right to the float. Thus, to take the life preserver away once they already have it—regardless of whether that is read as an action, an omission, or an intermediate form[38]—not only means letting them die, but it means killing them. This is widely recognised by continental criminal law scholars.[39] This also explains why the patient who is already being treated has a stronger claim to the ventilator than a patient waiting to be treated. Although the exact moment at which the patient consolidates their expectation of survival is highly controversial,[40] it is plausible to assert that from the very moment the doctor assigns a particular ventilator to a particular patient, that patient consolidates their claim to treatment in the form of a right to life.[41] This clearly applies to cases of allocation of personal ventilators, which are used at home and understood as bodily parts,[42] but it also applies to cases of ventilators used in ICUs. And this is likely to be the case even if the initial allocation of the ventilator was unfair.[43] Discontinuing treatment, then, does not merely mean not saving the patient, but killing them. The equivalence thesis between withholding and withdrawing in the criminal law debate ignores the normative meaning of assigning a resource: it turns a mere expectation of survival into an authentic right to be saved.

Contrary to the thesis defended here, others argue that the expectation of survival is based on a mere positive right to participate in an equitable distribution of a scarce resource (for example, a ventilator).[44] In short, there is no general right to healthcare in classical negative terms. This is true, although an expectation based on a mere positive right can be consolidated into a right to life in the strong sense. This is evident when it comes to the implantation of a human organ. Although the patient initially only has a right to participate in a fair sharing of organs, once implanted, they consolidate their right. And the same applies to other medical treatments. Would anyone deny that deactivating an already implanted pacemaker is a form of killing if it leads to the non-consented death of the patient?[45] While the right to a pacemaker is originally a mere positive right, once implanted, its interruption constitutes a form of killing. The ventilator, unlike the life preserver in the example above, requires frequent supervision by a medical team (monitoring and maintenance). This, however, is not a decisive argument against what is argued here. Once the patient is connected to the ventilator, they consolidate the expectation of life-saving treatment in the form of a right, not only over the ventilator, but also over all of the services provided by the medical team. That the right has been consolidated is clear if we consider a patient who is not provided with mandatory follow-up care: the nurse who does not change the ventilator's oxygen cylinder is not *failing to save* the patient, but is instead *killing* them, in the same way that they would be killed if someone turns the ventilator off. The intubated patient has, from a criminal law perspective, a right to the medical services necessary to keep the ventilator working.

Thus, I am arguing that there is a crucial normative difference between *ex ante* triage and *ex post* triage situations. In the former, there are several patients with a normatively identical expectation of treatment. In the latter, the patient who is already treated has a right to the ventilator that the newly arrived patient lacks. From a normative point of view, the first patient is no longer in need, while the second patient is still in a situation of need.[46] This being the case, depriving the first patient of the ventilator means shifting to them a misfortune that currently affects only the newly arrived patient. Should we take a kidney from a healthy person walking down the street to provide to a patient who urgently needs one? Such an act could only be theoretically justified under the strict logic of the necessity defence, that is, when the damage to the healthy person's interest would be compensated by safeguarding an essentially outweighing interest. As I have argued above, since neither the prospect for recovery nor a patient's life expectancy are allowable criteria in assessing the value of a human life, *ex post* triage cannot be justified—not even in a pandemic situation—from the perspective of the criminal law. The doctor who discontinues treatment commits homicide, which, as a rule, must be punished.

Conclusion

The system of justificatory defences should not aim to maximise scarce medical resources, but to allocate them in the best fair way, taking into account all subjects involved on an equal footing as rights holders. This means that in the *ex ante* triage scenario, where the doctor has to allocate the last ventilator to one of two patients in equally urgent situations, the doctor can choose which patient to treat. Killing (by omission) the untreated patient is justified. Neither the patient's recovery prospect nor life expectancy are relevant factors in the context of a rights-based reading of the conflict of duties as a justificatory defence. Although responsibility for vaccination status could be taken into account in determining the value differences between interests, there are practical reasons against ranking duties on this basis. *Ex ante* pre-emptive triage, i.e. not treating a patient in order to save a scarce resource for a future patient with a better prognosis, cannot be justified. It is a form of killing that deserves punishment. The same applies to *ex post* triage. This cannot be justified under any circumstances. The patient who has already been treated has consolidated their right (e.g. to a ventilator) and to interrupt this treatment is an unjustified form of killing.

Acknowledgements

I am grateful to Ángela Buquet Cebada for helpful suggestions and excellent research assistance.

Notes

1 While it is clear that the doctor who must choose between which two patients to save is, at least *prima facie*, killing the untreated patient, criminal law scholars usually deny that public officials who decide, for example, how many ventilators to buy, are criminally liable for deaths in triage cases. On the obstacles to moving up in the hierarchical healthcare structure and attributing death results by macro-triage, see e.g. S Schürch, *Rationierung in der Medizin als Straftat* (Helbing und Lichtenhahn: Basel, 2000), pp.204–211.
2 E Hilgendorf, E Hoven, & F Rostalski, *Triage in der (Strafrechts-) Wissenschaft* (Nomos: Baden-Baden, 2021); T Hörnle, S Huster, & R Poscher, *Triage in der Pandemie* (Mohr Siebeck: Tübingen, 2021); I Coca-Vila, "Triaje y colisión de deberes jurídico-penal. Una crítica al giro utilitarista", *InDret*, no. 1 (2021), p.166; I Coca-Vila,"Strafrechtliche Pflichtenkollision als Institut der Maximierung der Zahl der Überlebenden?", *Goltdammer's Archiv für Strafrecht*, vol. 168, no. 8 (2021), p.446.
3 Continental criminal law doctrine usually distinguishes between two kinds of duties to act: the *duty of guarantee*, based on a special relationship between actor and victim (voluntary undertaking, parental/family, creation of the victim's peril, etc.), and the general *duty of solidarity*. For more on

this, see JM Silva Sánchez, "Criminal Omissions: Some Relevant Distinctions", *New Criminal Law Review*, vol. 11, no. 3 (2008), p.452; K Ambos, "Omissions", in K Ambos, J Roberts, T Weigend, & A Heinze (eds), *Core Concepts in Criminal Law and Criminal Justice* (Oxford University Press: Oxford, 2019), p.20.

4 Maximizing-utilitarianism prescribes that in every situation an agent should act to produce a feasible outcome that maximizes the overall utility of the situation. In the context of this contribution, this means that a doctor should allocate resources to save the greatest number of human lives or the greatest number of years of human life in the aggregate.

5 I de Miguel Beriain, *The Ethical, Legal and Social Issues of Pandemics: An Analysis from the EU Perspective* (Springer: Cham, 2022), Ch. 5.

6 K Gaede, M Kubiciel, F Saliger & M Tsambikaki, "Rechtmäßiges Handeln in der dilemmatischen Triage Entscheidungssituation", *Medstra*, no. 3 (2020), p.129.

7 E Hoven, "Berücksichtigung von Lebensalter und Lebenserwartung – ein Nachtrag", in E Hilgendorf, E Hoven, & F Rostalski (eds), *Triage in der (Strafrechts-) Wissenschaft* (Nomos: Baden-Baden, 2021), p.185; E Hoven, "Die »Triage«-Situation als Herausforderung für die Strafrechtswissenschaft", *Juristen Zeitung*, vol. 75, no. 9 (2020), p.449.

8 I Coca-Vila, "Self-Driving Cars in Dilemmatic Situations: An Approach Based on the Theory of Justification in Criminal Law", *Criminal Law and Philosophy*, vol. 12, no. 1 (2018), p.59.

9 For discussion on that, see I Coca-Vila, "Self-Driving Cars", p.63. For a different point of view in the philosophical literature, see R Dworkin, *Justice for Hedgehogs* (Harvard University Press: Cambridge, MA, 2011), pp.281–284: there are limits when making decisions, since there are certain grounds of preference that respect for humanity rules out.

10 See e.g. M Pantaleón Díaz, "Justificación penal, sacrificio y unas abejas", *ADPCP LXXV* (2022), p. 589; H Frister, *Strafrecht. Allgemeiner Teil*, 10ª ed. (2023), p.327.

11 Hoven, "Berücksichtigung von Lebensalter und Lebenserwartung – ein Nachtrag"; Hoven, "Die »Triage«-Situation als Herausforderung für die Strafrechtswissenschaft".

12 See J Harris, *The Value of Life: An Introduction to Medical Ethics* (Routledge: London and New York, 1985), p.91: "the fair innings argument requires that everyone be given an equal chance to have a fair innings, to reach the appropriate threshold but, having reached it, they have received their entitlement. The rest of their life is the sort of bonus which may be cancelled when this is necessary to help others reach the threshold". For saving younger lives, see also P Singer & L Winkett, "In a Pandemic, Should We Save Younger Lives?", in U Schüklenk & P Singer (eds), *Bioethics: An Anthology* (Wiley: Hoboken, 4th edn, 2021), pp.399–402.

13 T Hörnle, "Priorisierung von Geimpften?", *Ethik in der Medizin*, vol. 34 (2022), p.481.

14 Hörnle, "Priorisierung von Geimpften?", p.492.

15 I Coca-Vila, "La justificación penal de la desconexión letal de aparatos médicos. A propósito de la reasignación de respiradores en contextos dilemáticos (triaje ex post)," *Revista Penal*, no. 49 (2022), p.7.

16 See e.g. FP Schuster, "Coping with Moral Dilemmas in German Criminal Law Theory and Justice: Classical Cases and Modern Variants", *Criminal Law Forum*, vol. 34 (2023), p.237. It would not be possible to excuse the doctor by appealing to an excusing necessity (duress) defence, since they neither save a person closely related to them (family member), nor save a greater number of lives than the one they condemn to death.

17 See e.g. T. Horter, "Überlegungen zum Verhältnis der Kriterien „Dringlichkeit" und „Erfolgsaussicht" im Rahmen der Entscheidung über die Verteilung lebenserhaltender Ressourcen", *Medstra*, no. 1 (2023), p.10.

18 T Hörnle, "Ex-post-Triage: Strafbar als Tötungsdelikt?", in T Hörnle, S Huster & R Poscher (eds), *Triage in der Pandemie* (Mohr Siebeck: Tübingen, 2021).

19 F Rostalski, "(Straf-)Rechtliche Verantwortlichkeit in Fällen der Triage. Zugleich eine funktional-rechtsvergleichende Betrachtung", in E Hilgendorf, E Hoven, & F Rostalski (eds), *Triage in der (Strafrechts-) Wissenschaft* (Nomos: Baden-Baden, 2021), p.265.

20 In this vein, see e.g. E Hoven, "Die »Triage«-Situation als Herausforderung für die Strafrechtswissenschaft", *Juristen Zeitung*, vol. 75, no. 9 (2020), p.454, fn.55.

21 C Cordelli, "Prospective Duties and the Demands of Beneficence", *Ethics*, vol. 128, no. 2 (2018), p.272.

22 Pantaleón Díaz, "Justificación penal, sacrificio y unas abejas".

23 Coca-Vila, "Self-Driving Cars".
24 For a communitarian (relational) approach to triage, see J Herring, "The Ethical Conflicts of the COVID Pandemic in Criminal and Medical Law", *Anatomia Do Crime*, vol. 12 (2021), p.29.
25 G Duttge,"Update im Medizinstrafrecht – Entscheidungen und Tendenzen-?", in Institut für Rechtsfragen der Medizin (ed), *Aktuelle Entwicklungen im Medizinstrafrecht* (Nomos: Baden-Baden, 2021), p.13; D von der Pfordten, "Five Elements of Normative Ethics – A General Theory of Normative Individualism", *Ethic Theory and Moral Practice*, vol. 15, no. 4 (2012), p.449.
26 Coca-Vila,"Strafrechtliche Pflichtenkollision als Institut der Maximierung der Zahl der Überlebenden?".
27 Even in exceptional times, such as a pandemic, the state is bound to safeguard the foundations of the legal system. It is not possible to admit exceptions without changing the rule. For discussion, see Coca-Vila "Triaje y colisión de deberes jurídico-penal", pp.192–195. For another view, see de Miguel Beriain, *The Ethical, Legal and Social Issues of Pandemics*, p.131: "in the midst of a pandemic that has killed thousands of people, it is reasonable to abstract from the usual conceptual framework that we use to configure the state of necessity".
28 W Lübbe, "Where Should Rationing Go? Philosophical Aspects", in F Breyer, H Kliemt, & F Thiele (eds), *Rationing in Medicine: Ethical, Legal and Practical Aspects* (Springer: Berlin/Heidelberg/New York, 2002), p.105.
29 For discussion, see Coca-Vila, "Self-Driving Cars", p.70. For a different point of view in the philosophical literature, see J Glover, *Causing Death and Saving lives* (Penguin: London, 2001), pp.104–107.
30 JM Taurek, "Should the Numbers Count?", *Philosophy & Public Affairs*, vol. 6, no. 4 (1977), p.293.
31 FP Schuster, "Coping with Moral Dilemmas".
32 Further, see Coca-Vila, "Conflicting Duties in Criminal Law", *New Criminal Law Review*, vol. 22, no. 1 (2019), p.34 at pp.63–64.
33 R Merkel and S Augsberg, "Die Tragik der Triage – straf- und verfassungsrechtliche Grundlagen und Grenzen", *Juristen Zeitung*, vol. 75, no. 14 (2020), p.704.
34 J Herring, *Medical Law and Ethics* (Oxford University Press: Oxford, 2022); A Engländer, "Impfverzicht als Abwägungsfaktor bei der Triage?", in J Bülte et al. (eds), *Festschrift für Gerhard Dannecker zum 70. Geburtstag* (Beck: München, 2023), p.603.
35 In a similar vein, see de Miguel Beriain, *The Ethical*, pp.127–128; and Liddell et al, "Who gets the ventilator? Important legal rights in a pandemic", *Journal of Medical Ethics*, no. 46 (2020), p.421 at pp.423–424.
36 U Neumann, "Necessity/Duress", in MD Dubber & T Hörnle (eds), *The Oxford Handbook of Criminal Law* (Oxford University Press: Oxford, 2014), p.583.
37 Coca-Vila, "La justificación penal de la desconexión letal de aparatos médicos. A propósito de la reasignación de respiradores en contextos dilemáticos (triaje ex post)".
38 What is relevant is not the phenomenological nature of human behaviour, nor whether the double-prevention should be read as an action, as omission, or as a *tertium genus*. What is decisive is whether the subject is interfering in the legal sphere of others by violating a right (to life) or whether they are only infringing a duty of solidarity by not helping those in need. In detail, see Coca-Vila, "Self-Driving Cars", pp.74–77. For the philosophical discussion, see in this vein, HM Malm, "Killing, Letting Die, and Simple Conflicts", *Philosophy & Public Affairs*, vol. 18, no. 3 (1989), p.238.
39 JM Silva Sánchez, "Interrupción de cursos salvadores ajenos dentro de la propia esfera de organización: un problema de justificación", in M da Costa Andrade, M João Antunes & S Aires de Sousa (eds), *Estudos em homenagem ao Prof. Doutor Jorge de Figueiredo Dias* (Universidade de Coimbra: Coimbra, 2011), vol II, p.979.
40 A McGee & D Carter, "The Equivalence Thesis and the Last Ventilator", *Journal of Applied Philosophy*, vol. 39, no. 2 (2022), p.297.
41 Schuster "Coping with Moral Dilemmas".
42 JM Reynolds, L Guidry-Grimes & K Savin, "Against Personal Ventilator Reallocation", *Cambridge Quarterly of Healthcare Ethics*, vol. 30, no. 2 (2021), p.272; S Aas & D Wasserman, "Bodily Rights in Personal Ventilators?", *Journal of Applied Philosophy*, vol. 39, no. 1 (2022), p.73.
43 In this vein, see DP Sulmasy & J Sugarman, "Are Withholding and Withdrawing Therapy Always Morally Equivalent?", *Journal of Medical Ethics*, vol. 20, no. 4 (1984), p.220. The question of

whether the patient who obtains through illicit means to be treated also deserves to be protected against withdrawal of ventilation is more complex. To the extent that their treatment may be seen as an unjust threat on another patient, withdrawal of treatment in self-defence may be justified.
44 Hörnle, "Ex-post-Triage: Strafbar als Tötungsdelikt?".
45 For discussion, see T Huddle & FA Bailey, "Pacemaker Deactivation: Withdrawal of Support or Active Ending of Life?", *Theoretical Medicine and Bioethics*, vol. 33, no. 6 (2012), p.421.
46 In the case presented by McGee & Carter, "The Equivalence Thesis and the Last Ventilator", p.7, in which a doctor must choose which patient to disconnect so that both patients do not die in the case of a sudden reduction of oxygen supply to the hospital, both patients are (again) in a situation of need. This is an *ex ante* triage scenario and the doctor can withdraw either patient to save the other.

References

Books and book chapters

Ambos K, "Omissions", in Ambos K, Roberts J, Weigend T, & Heinze A (eds), *Core Concepts in Criminal Law and Criminal Justice* (Oxford University Press: Oxford, 2019), pp.17–53.

de Miguel Beriain I, *The Ethical, Legal and Social Issues of Pandemics: An Analysis from the EU Perspective* (Springer: Cham, 2022).

Duttge G, "Update im Medizinstrafrecht – Entscheidungen und Tendenzen–?", in Institut für Rechtsfragen der Medizin (ed), *Aktuelle Entwicklungen im Medizinstrafrecht* (Nomos: Baden-Baden, 2021).

Dworkin R, *Justice for Hedgehogs* (Harvard University Press: Cambridge MA, 2011).

Engländer A, "Impfverzicht als Abwägungsfaktor bei der Triage?", in Bülte J, Dölling D, Haas V, & Schuhr J (eds), *Festschrift für Gerhard Dannecker zum 70. Geburtstag* (Beck: München, 2023).

Frister H, *Strafrecht. Allgemeiner Teil* (Beck: München, 10th edn, 2023).

Glover J, *Causing Death and Saving Lives* (Penguin: London, 2001).

Harris J, *The Value of Life: An Introduction to Medical Ethics* (Routledge: London and New York, 1985).

Herring J, *Medical Law and Ethics* (Oxford University Press: Oxford, 2022).

Hilgendorf E, Hoven E, & Rostalski F (eds), *Triage in der (Strafrechts-) Wissenschaft* (Nomos: Baden-Baden, 2021).

Hoven E, "Berücksichtigung von Lebensalter und Lebenserwartung – ein Nachtrag", in Hilgendorf E, Hoven E, & Rostalski F (eds), *Triage in der (Strafrechts-) Wissenschaft* (Nomos: Baden-Baden, 2021).

Hörnle T, "Ex-post-Triage: Strafbar als Tötungsdelikt?", in Hörnle T, Huster S, & Poscher R (eds), *Triage in der Pandemie* (Mohr Siebeck: Tübingen, 2021).

Hörnle T, Huster S, & Poscher R (eds), *Triage in der Pandemie* (Mohr Siebeck: Tübingen, 2021).

Lübbe W, "Where Should Rationing Go? Philosophical Aspects", in Breyer F, Kliemt H, & Thiele F (eds), *Rationing in Medicine: Ethical, Legal and Practical Aspects* (Springer: Berlin/Heidelberg/New York, 2002), pp.105–117.

Neumann U, "Necessity/Duress", in Dubber MD & Hörnle T (eds), *The Oxford Handbook of Criminal Law* (Oxford University Press: Oxford, 2014), pp.583–606.

Rostalski F, "(Straf-)Rechtliche Verantwortlichkeit in Fällen der Triage. Zugleich eine funktional-rechtsvergleichende Betrachtung", in Hilgendorf E, Hoven E, & Rostalski F (eds), *Triage in der (Strafrechts-) Wissenschaft* (Nomos: Baden-Baden, 2021).

Schürch S, *Rationierung in der Medizin als Straftat* (Helbing und Lichtenhahn: Basel, 2000).

Silva Sánchez JM, "Interrupción de cursos salvadores ajenos dentro de la propia esfera de organización: un problema de justificación", in da Costa Andrade M, João Antunes M, & Aires de Sousa M (eds), *Estudos em homenagem ao Prof. Doutor Jorge de Figueiredo Dias* (Universidade de Coimbra: Coimbra, 2011), vol II.

Singer P & Winkett L, "In a Pandemic, Should We Save Younger Lives?", in Schüklenk U & Singer P (eds), *Bioethics: An Anthology* (Wiley: Hoboken NJ, 4th edn, 2022), pp.399–402.

Journal articles

Aas S & Wasserman D, "Bodily Rights in Personal Ventilators?", *Journal of Applied Philosophy*, vol. 39, no. 1 (2022), pp.73–86.

Coca-Vila I, "La justificación penal de la desconexión letal de aparatos médicos. A propósito de la reasignación de respiradores en contextos dilemáticos (triaje ex post)", *Revista Penal*, vol. 49 (2022), pp.7–25.

Coca-Vila I, "Triaje y colisión de deberes jurídico-penal. Una crítica al giro utilitarista", *InDret*, vol. 1 (2021), pp.166–202.

Coca-Vila I, "Strafrechtliche Pflichtenkollision als Institut der Maximierung der Zahl der Überlebenden?", *Goltdammer's Archiv für Strafrecht*, vol. 168, no. 8 (2021), pp.446–461.

Coca-Vila I, "Conflicting Duties in Criminal Law", *New Criminal Law Review*, vol. 22, no. 1 (2019), pp.34–72.

Coca-Vila I, "Self-Driving Cars in Dilemmatic Situations: An Approach Based on the Theory of Justification in Criminal Law", *Criminal Law and Philosophy*, vol. 12, no. 1 (2018), pp.59–82.

Cordelli C, "Prospective Duties and the Demands of Beneficence", *Ethics*, vol. 128, no. 2 (2018), pp.272–401.

Gaede K, Kubiciel M, Saliger F, & Tsambikaki M, "Rechtmäßiges Handeln in der dilemmatischen Triage Entscheidungssituation", *Medstra*, vol. 3 (2020), pp.129–137.

Herring J, "The Ethical Conflicts of the COVID Pandemic in Criminal and Medical Law", *Anatomia Do Crime*, vol. 12 (2021), pp.13–33.

Hörnle T, "Priorisierung von Geimpften?", *Ethik in der Medizin*, vol. 34 (2022), pp.481–495.

Horter T, "Überlegungen zum Verhältnis der Kriterien „Dringlichkeit" und „Erfolgsaussicht" im Rahmen der Entscheidung über die Verteilung lebenserhaltender Ressourcen", *Medstra*, vol. 3 (2023), pp.10–18.

Hoven E, "Die »Triage«-Situation als Herausforderung für die Strafrechtswissenschaft", *Juristen Zeitung*, vol. 75, no. 9 (2020), pp.449–454.

Huddle T & Bailey FA, "Pacemaker Deactivation: Withdrawal of Support or Active Ending of Life?", *Theoretical Medicine and Bioethics*, vol. 33, no. 6 (2012), pp.421–433.

Liddell K, Skopek JM, Palmer S, Martin S, Anderson J, Sagar A, "Who Gets the Ventilator? Important Legal Rights in a Pandemic", *Journal of Medical Ethics*, vol. 46 (2020), pp.421–426.

Lorenz H & Turhan E, "The Pandemic and Criminal Law – A Look at Theory and Practice in Germany", *Bialystok Legal Studies*, vol. 26, no. 6 (2021), pp.9–14.

Malm HM, "Killing, Letting Die, and Simple Conflicts", *Philosophy & Public Affairs*, vol. 18, no. 3 (1989), pp.238–258.

Mcgee A & Carter D, "The Equivalence Thesis and the Last Ventilator", *Journal of Applied Philosophy*, vol. 39, no. 2 (2022), pp.297–312.

Merkel R & Augsberg S, "Die Tragik der Triage – straf- und verfassungsrechtliche Grundlagen und Grenzen", *Juristen Zeitung*, vol. 75, no. 14 (2020), pp.704–714.

Pantaleón Díaz M, "Justificación penal, sacrificio y unas abejas", *ADPCP*, vol. LXXV (2022), pp.589–683.

Reynolds JM, Guidry-Grimes L, & Savin K, "Against Personal Ventilator Reallocation", *Cambridge Quarterly of Healthcare Ethics*, vol. 30, no. 2 (2021), pp.272–284.

Schuster FP, "Coping with Moral Dilemmas in German Criminal Law Theory and Justice: Classical Cases and Modern Variants", *Criminal Law Forum*, Early Online Access, vol. 34, (2023), pp.1–34.

Silva Sánchez JM, "Criminal Omissions: Some Relevant Distinctions", *New Criminal Law Review*, vol. 11, no. 3 (2008), pp.452–469.

Sulmasy DP & Sugarman J, "Are Withholding and Withdrawing Therapy Always Morally Equivalent?", *Journal of Medical Ethics*, vol. 20, no. 4 (1994), pp.218–222.

Taurek JM, "Should the Numbers Count?", *Philosophy & Public Affairs*, vol. 6, no. 4 (1977), pp.293–316.

von der Pfordten D, "Five Elements of Normative Ethics – A General Theory of Normative Individualism", *Ethic Theory and Moral Practice*, vol. 15, no. 4 (2012), pp.449–471.

15
RESPONSIBILITY OVER CRIME AND TORT

Matthew Dyson

The line between tort and crime

Origins

The present divides between tort and crime is a relatively modern invention and was created in different legal systems by different means. A single coherent concept of responsibility is not necessarily obvious across those systems. For example, it is not clear that ancient lawyers thought about what would become criminal law in anything like the same way lawyers do now;[1] the same is true about whatever "responsibility" might mean over time. For instance, many "penal" elements existing inside the Roman law of delict, such as multiple of the loss being awarded for theft, and noxal surrender of slaves and sons in power. In the early common law, "crime" and "tort", as we call them now, were equally valid ways for a victim to pursue justice for a wrongful act.[2] The choice, made by the victim, seems to have been between *compensation* and *vengeance*.[3] Similarly, French law seems to have made a formal distinction between civil and criminal from the approach to codification at the end of the eighteenth century.[4] *Responsabilité*, a modern word closest to "responsibility", was not then known. Even today, French does not have a technical word like "liability", and in the earlier period one might realistically speak of *repression pénale* and *réparation civile*; that is, either process or outcome, rather than doctrinal arrangement.[5] To some in Germany, the distinction between private law and criminal law is actually one of the great achievements of the nineteenth century.[6] The distinction is complex, but turns particularly on the personal guilt that criminal law requires but civil law does not. Two smaller European legal systems recognised this distinction also quite late. Medieval Swedish law did not distinguish between tort and crime per se, but between wrongs to individuals and wrongs to society.[7] Wrongs to individuals were often remedied by the *bot*, a tariff system of compensation to the victim, but which also went in equal measure to the King and the county. This system remained in the landmark Law Code of 1734, though academic work began to refer separately to civil and criminal law and procedure. Reform ultimately led to the practical coupling of tort and crime, in that the rules on compensating for damage caused by criminal acts were put in the criminal code since no civil code yet existed.[8] That arrangement, theoretically distinguishing between tort and crime but practically merging them continued until 1972 when a civil liability statute was at last passed. It might also be that smaller legal systems have had less need to distinguish: it is only in the last hundred years or so that Scotland has developed separate jurisdictions, procedures and penalties for tort and crime, which in turn has led to some differences of substantive legal rules.[9]

In fact, procedural interactions have been a reason for, and expression of, the relationship between tort and crime. Which court could try disputes, and hear appeals; what remedies were available; what rules of evidence and procedure applied; and how concurrent, or consecutive forms of litigation on the same facts might be resolved, were quintessentially procedural questions. More than substantive questions, such as the content of the prohibitions against theft or the requirement to compensate the victim, these procedural questions needed clear and technical answers. Substantive questions might be ignored or given temporary or vague answers, but procedural ones required a response to allow the litigation to proceed. They might also be areas where instrumental arguments work more easily. For example, on the one hand, requiring a criminal court to proceed before a civil claim in a civil court, and on the other hand, giving that criminal court the power to handle that civil claim is an efficient solution.

By the nineteenth century, most Western legal systems had begun to divide between crime and tort. Some grand claims have been made, such as in England when Lord Mansfield said: "there is no distinction better known, than the distinction between civil and criminal law".[10] Those grand claims are not always very illuminating, especially when, as in that case, they are made in the context of a highly disputed application of the rule. Indeed, even if a distinction is known, as Jeremy Bentham noted, its precise contours might not be clear at all.[11]

Definitions

In the context of tort and crime, in some legal systems the term "responsibility" has a particular meaning. *Liability* or *responsibility* as concepts in use from the 1950s at least in the common law showed a new formulation of criminal doctrine. This intellectual structure for both areas of law moved away from moralised statements of the law. HLA Hart, for instance, writing in 1967, made significant philosophical advances in this direction.[12] Hart separated out different forms of responsibility, particularly with respect to roles, causes, liability, and capacity. His work in the 1960s marked a theoretical position the doctrinal law could have aspired to follow, but it in fact moved towards focusing on a separate and less normative concept of liability. Instead, in English law, voluntariness was moved into physical components instead but crimes had multiple *mens rea* elements; more complex parts to offences, narrower and less open-textured objective tests. Criminal offences were drafted in quite specific terms, certainly more specific than the burgeoning tort of negligence. However, as applied by the courts, the role of responsibility has been much simpler.

In the common law tradition, the closest one gets to expressing any theory is that "responsibility" shows what *D* is *responsible* for as a condition of assessing what *D* is *culpable* for. Responsibility is essentially a form of attributability: that a person's voluntary act brought about a thing means that the thing can be attributed to him and he is responsible for it. It is therefore the larger part of *actus reus* in traditional terminology. By contrast, culpability demonstrates the blameworthiness of *D*'s conduct. However, that tradition is not uniform. It is also a somewhat simplistic approach and criminal theorists have taken the role of responsibility somewhat wider, in a number of different directions.

Outcomes

This different conceptual role responsibility is playing in crime and in tort still leads to the same place: liability, that is, the requirement to answer the law's demand. That said, the law might demand different things from each area of law. In the modern world, tort law has few remedies, and certainly fewer than criminal law. Historically the difference was less marked, with physical punishment being more generally restricted to criminal law, with imprisonment for debt being an exception open to the civil law in some legal systems into the nineteenth century. Being precise and universal is difficult. For example, *penalties*, meant to punish, are most strongly associated with criminal law; at the same time, outwardly similar *awards of money*, such as "damages", meant to undo loss, are more strongly associated with civil law. Injunctions are generally known within the laws of property and contract, but common law legal systems will impose them within tort law as well, to protect persons and property. Other legal systems might do so only within property law and for reasons connected to constitutional rights or human rights. One famous *non-compensatory money award* in common law systems is punitive damages (or "exemplary damages"). These are damages awarded to the claimant to punish the defendant, not to compensate for losses. They are rare and controversial in England, where they originated.[13] They are more common in most states of the USA, though still not entirely routine, and more recently have been held to be restricted by the Constitution, including a guidelines' ratio of 4:1 compared to compensatory damages being a sign of the award violating due process.[14] Claims for "pure distress" or "moral harm" can do similar work, if normally for smaller sums, and some civilian legal systems debate what should be done.[15] By contrast, many legal systems will reduce, forego, or change the form of punishment where compensation has taken place.[16]

Substantive comparison of responsibility

Vehicles for responsibility

The same events might give rise to one, or both, of criminal and civil liability. There is no clear position across legal systems, but the assumption seems to be that one might separately talk of a responsibility under or enforced by criminal law, and a different responsibility under civil law. Torts and criminal offences share some common structural elements. Both typically ask some questions about capacity, attribution to the defendant, unlawfulness or wrongfulness, fault, causation and outcomes (depending on the crime), and defences. Each element might have different content, or significance.[17]

On some rare occasions, the same root prohibition might lead to both forms of responsibility. That might be the case where one form of action was later copied in another area of law, such as the tort of trespass to the person budding into a crime of battery centuries ago. But a more modern example might be where a statute creates a prohibition which is then enforced by more than one area of law. The Protection from Harassment Act 1997 in England and Wales is an example of that: a duty not to harass others (s. 1), enforced by a criminal offence for breaching that duty (s. 2), and by civil liability for any losses caused by the breach (s. 3).

Outside those rare examples, formal unity of the names and structures of civil wrongs and criminal offences is not common. Civilian legal systems normally have specific named crimes with specific conditions, but often general clauses for tort liability; common law systems tend to be narrower on both sides, having named torts as well as named crimes. The reason seems to be partly historical, grounded in legal theory and practice from the seventeenth century on, and solidified in codification: it might reflect a lesser role specificity plays in communicating a civil wrong, compared to criminal offences.

Principles

There are many principles at play in each of tort and crime, but three examples are particularly important in understanding the border between the two.

First, some legal systems have principles reflecting the priority of an area of law. Some expressly, or impliedly, put criminal law above civil law, for instance, though that might mean many different things in practice. Relatedly, criminal responsibility is often characterised as the tool of last resort, the *ultima ratio*, so criminalisation should only happen when other modes of law are insufficient to protect the relevant interests.[18] This is also sometimes linked to a principle of "subsidiarity", that the criminal law is there to provide support to existing interests within civil law: it is unclear whether subsidiarity is part of, derived from, or just closely related to *ultima ratio*.[19]

Second, a principle of unity of the legal system holds that the contents of the system should be coherent, though this does not necessarily in fact require that all objects have the same meaning in all areas of law.[20] What it does seem to mean, at a minimum, is that the criminal law should not prohibit what private law requires. On some occasions, it does appear that the criminal law might prohibit what private law would otherwise permit.

Third, in some legal systems, only constitutionally accepted purposes of the criminal law can justify criminalisation. What is now regarded as the classic formulation of this comes from German law: that criminal laws protect "legally protected goods" (*Rechtsgüter*).[21] Theories of limits on criminalisation based on harm[22] do some of the same work in common law legal systems, along with other constraints. By contrast, there is often not a clear relationship between the theories in criminal law and in tort law.[23] Indeed, there seems to be a lot greater variation, and uncertainty, in what justifies and explains tort law, than what does so for criminal law. Further examples of normative questions include the role of tort and crime in "deterring wrongdoing or harm" (criminal law phrasing) or "incentivising avoiding harm" (typically a tort law phrasing), and how that kind of policy-based reasoning appears in liability.

Civil law is often framed in terms of being unlawful, or wrongful.[24] "Wrongful" suggests an interference with another's right, but there are then many embedded questions about rights, interests, and interferences that require unpacking. Little detailed work has been done on comparing unlawfulness across tort and crime. There are many crimes which also give rise to tort liability, and vice versa; there are also many opposite cases. Focusing only on tort as a loss allocation system would highlight its inefficiency, and beg questions on why some conduct and not others is tortious, if both lead to loss.

While a particular criminal wrong might mirror a civil wrong (whether in the form of a general clause, or a nominate tort such as in the common law), that alone tells us very little. Mirroring does not reflect much about responsibility. However, legal systems all go further in integrating the fact patterns. Some common law systems would say breaching a statute was per se evidence of negligence, or would use the tort of breach of statutory duty to decide if a statute which does not on its face impose civil liability should nonetheless do so. In Sweden, there appears to be no integrating provision, creating civil liability where there is a crime, but as a matter of fact many criminal offences will mirror civil liability.[25] In France, deeper integration occurs through the unity of criminal and civil fault, a judicial doctrine tweaked by legislation in 2000 (discussed below). German law has §823(2) BGB (*Bürgerliches Gesetzbuch*, or German Civil Code) which replicates the general provision (§823(1)) for anyone who commits a breach of a statute that is intended to protect another person. The difficulty then is to determine which statutes are intended to protect another, but that list will certainly include some criminal statutes. The Dutch and Spanish rules are the most integrative. Dutch law's key definition of an unlawful act is as, amongst other things, "an act or omission in violation of a duty imposed by written law" and all criminal laws must be in written form (in addition, breaching social standards of due care also generates liability).[26] Spain makes its integration even more obvious: article 109(1) of the Spanish Criminal Code provides that:

"The carrying out of an act prescribed by the law as *delito* or *falta* obliges reparation, according to law, for the damage and losses caused by it".[27]

That is, the law turns on damage being caused and the facts also happen to be a criminal offence. This is quite a remarkable link between tort and crime, and in part, was what was thought to justify the placing of civil law norms in the criminal code in 1848, a situation that was originally intended to be temporary, until a Spanish civil code could be passed.[28]

Damage and fault

Lawyers in civilian systems often begin from the starting point that whereas tort law's substantive components focus more upon damage, criminal law focuses more on culpability for wrongful conduct. This is why, for instance, crimes exist which prohibit conduct which does not lead to harm, but tort law generally does not.[29] Examples within criminal law include liability for attempts, conspiracy, and encouraging others to commit crime. Some legal systems have even created offences of endangerment, of risking harm to another even without it materialising. These are well known in driving offences, which might or might not be criminal, but in some jurisdictions they go further. Examples include Spain and Germany, where offences of endangerment have been created in addition to their well-known home in road traffic, covering, for instance, environmental offences and offences against the public health. Risk-taking or risk-imposition might also impose strict liability in tort for things like dangerous products (in many countries), hazardous activities (in many civil law jurisdictions, and some of the USA), and even commercial services (in Brazil).[30] In those situations, however, loss must result in order for a defendant to be liable.

A further significant difference is the possibility of liability without personal fault. Strict liability criminal offences are generally rejected in civilian jurisdictions, personal guilt or culpability being required. Many common law legal systems permit "strict liability" if the legislature uses clear words to impose it. However, they also use "strict liability" in a much wider sense. It is not liability *regardless of fault*, as it is in private law, rather it means there is at least one physical element in the offence without a corresponding fault element. That an offence requires little to no fault is common for public welfare offences, such as food safety; for example, a defendant might not need to know of the unsafeness of the food, only to intentionally sell it. In addition, even some serious offences, like murder, might not require fault about death, but be "constructed" on intending serious harm. In general, in common-law systems that permit strict liability, it is rare for sentences of imprisonment to be imposed without having established *mens rea*. Conversely, almost every tort-law system recognises instances of strict liability; liability for defective products[31] and for road traffic accidents resulting in personal injuries[32] being perhaps the most conspicuous examples.

One of the simplest justifications for punishment is that the conduct was blameworthy. Civilian legal systems add another component, and some common law theorists seek the same, that one should not be punished beyond one's culpability (that is, for conduct she could not avoid). This plays out in many ways across the law, but one example is capacity. Generally, criminal law imposes standards on the mental capacity of a defendant which are mostly or completely absent from tort law. Criminal law normally has a set age below which children either cannot be liable, or cannot be punished, while tort law tends to have no age limit, or a flexible one.[33] According to one instrumental view, this is due to the logic of tort law being different to that of criminal law, namely that it is about allocating the cost of accidents. By contrast, decisions about punishment do not entail a choice between two individuals with respect to a finite resource like money: either the wrongdoer gets punished, or she does not, but neither of these alternatives makes the victim better or worse off financially. On the contrary, tort law is a "zero-sum game": the claimant loses what is awarded to the defendant, and vice versa. Being restrictive in the imposition of punishment (requiring culpability, avoiding disproportionate penalties, etc.) is less problematic than denying compensation on the same grounds and this is, in turn, why strict liability requires other forms of justification than simple culpability about that element of the offence. And a common law system might accept strict liability about some elements of the crime, requiring fault for other elements, instead of accepting negligence or a reverse standard of proof.

Causation

There have also been some interesting overlaps in the law of causation, a classic place to consider responsibility. Wherever the law seeks to respond to harm, it will have to establish that a particular person(s) caused the harm specified, but only in some systems do tort and crime use the same test. Most legal systems start out with requiring "but for" causation: without that event, the prohibited outcome would not have happened. This is potentially under-inclusive, so some systems accept causation even without it, particularly where proof is practically very difficult. It is also likely to be over-inclusive, suggesting a further stage is necessary to truncate liability. It is at this further stage that significant divergence occurs. In the common law, there is a second stage which might conveniently, though not completely accurately, be called "legal causation": tort law tends to focus on foreseeability and intervening acts, while criminal law talks of a substantial and operating cause. The tests appear somewhat similar, though the use of different language appears to be deliberate. In fact, the criminal law test calls on "common sense" and physical descriptions of events more, perhaps to aid jury decisions. French law is quite distinctive, using a somewhat flexible concept of "directness" as well as a number of presumptions about causation in both tort and crime. German law is particularly intricate. Criminal law requires objective attribution, including objective unforeseeability, objective unavoidability and harm not being covered by the protective ratio of the infringed norm. Civil law under §823(1) BGB divides causation into the causing of injury to the absolute right (*haftungsbegründende Kausalität*), and that that injury to the right caused harm (*haftungsausfüllende Kausalität*); such a division is not necessary where the provision of the BGB does not protect such rights, as is the case in §826. However, the civil methods to then restrict "but for" causation (in Germany and other Continental European systems, the *Äquivalenztheorie*) are less extensive than in criminal law. In particular, it appears that the civil law rarely uses one of that approach's ostensibly key elements, the *Adäquanztheorie* theory, to disprove causation: according to this theory damage which is highly unusual and which could not have been foreseen by an ideal observer will not be sufficient. Some legal systems have formally connected causation across both areas. In 1970, the Dutch *Hoge Raad* adopted the limiting condition of "reasonable imputation" of the outcome to the event; in 1978, it said criminal law should use the same standard. In Spain, the adoption of a single limiting theory on causation happened the other way around: criminal law scholarship and jurisprudence adopted the "objective imputation" theory first, followed some time later by the Civil Chamber of the *Tribunal Supremo*. This theory is technically a normative assessment of facts and their attribution to an individual, which works as a functional equivalent to "legal causation" in common-law jurisdiction.

Defences

Another classic instance of the substantive overlap of tort and crime is in defences. For instance, while tort and crime typically both accept that there are justifications, it is not clear that every system's tort law accepts excuses while crime typically does. There are three approaches to the comparison of defences.

First, a system may have no sustained attempt to compare or link tortious and criminal law defences, as in England, Scotland and Australia. This leaves some defences applying in crime, but apparently not in tort, like duress. Some use the same term but have different meanings. In England, the House of Lords decided that self-defence had a different test in tort than in crime.[34]

Second, systems may have links which are variable or uncertain. The French and Swedish positions are quite nuanced, but it appears that while the same defences are recognised in tort and crime, there is no need to apply them in the same way in both areas.[35]

Third, a legal system may create some unity of defences across both tort and crime. This is the approach in German law, where criminal law uses defences from BGB and tort law uses defences from the *StGB* (*Strafgesetzbuch*, the Criminal Code), apparently in an example of a "hard" use of the unity of the legal system.

Procedural expressions of responsibility

The reluctance to use state power to punish without sufficient grounds covers the higher substantive components of criminal liability, and the greater procedural protections for the defendant in criminal trials. Typically, the defendant has protections against self-incrimination, double-jeopardy, and weaker forms of evidence like hearsay or illegally obtained evidence. Legal systems tend to state that the defendant is innocent unless found otherwise. In the common law, this means the prosecutor, normally a state actor or delegate, has the burden of proof of liability. In many civilian systems, it is not necessarily correct to say the state must prove liability, but it is clear that the defendant does not normally need to disprove it. Instead, the judge must be "certain" of that liability, and the office of the investigating judge is a significant feature of some civilian legal systems. For some, especially common law legal systems, there is a difference in the standard of proof: civil claims must be proven on the balance of probabilities, so 51% or more likely; while criminal prosecutions must be proven "beyond reasonable doubt", a much higher standard, though without a specific figure of probability. Unlike reluctance to use state power in criminal law, in tort, erroneously upholding a claim is as onerous for the defendant as erroneously dismissing it is for the claimant, so the standard of proof treats both errors as equally undesirable.[36]

In the modern state, criminal investigation, prosecution and punishment is normally handled by the state. Some legal systems, both civilian and common law, permit private parties to prosecute, or force the state to prosecute, though there are typically protections against. In tort, private parties (potentially including the state in its private capacity) decide whether to litigate and can waive liability, while most legal systems do not give a victim the right to waive prosecution for most crimes.

There may also be structural differences, such as criminal law being more likely to feature lay decision-makers or fact-finders, at least in the common law, such as juries or lay magistrates. The state might also be involved in different degrees of ensuring the legal system is accessible to all, by paying for advocates or similar.

Civil liability and criminal procedures

The right of the victim to constitute herself as a *penal* prosecuting party is most often, though not necessarily, associated with the possibility existing in most systems to *accumulate* to the criminal proceedings the victim's *civil* claim for compensation, so that she becomes a "*partie civile*" in the criminal trial. This method has been stated to exist in all Germanic, Romanistic and Nordic jurisdictions,[37] but not in the common law. While this is true in a general sense, there are very important differences in the way the system actually functions in each of the jurisdictions that recognise it.

Hence, for instance, in countries like Spain, most compensation claims by victims of crime will usually be dealt with within the criminal proceedings, following special rules located in the Spanish Criminal Code, not the Civil Code,[38] and will even be handled by the public prosecutor, unless the victim renounces or reserves her claim.[39] The situation in France does not have the same default stage but is otherwise similar. Conversely, in Germany, a very similar system known as the *Adhäsionsverfahren* or "adhesion procedure"[40] appears to be very rarely used in practice.

The possibility to join a civil claim inside criminal proceedings is not normally used in common law systems. Instead, the criminal courts issue their own criminal form of compensation, at least for simple cases, and following the broad thrust of tort law but without having to follow the detailed tort rules. For example, while individual powers to award compensation go back centuries in England, the first *general* power of English criminal courts to award compensation was created in 1972, and now exists under the Sentencing Code 2020. These powers are not the same as tort compensation, for example they are limited by the defendant's means and can exist even when civil liability does not for the same facts.

Prescription

Another aspect of responsibility, on the border of substance and procedure, that might be illuminating, concerns prescription and limitation periods. Some common law legal systems do not have prescription or limitation periods for criminal law at all, outside minor offences (as in England). There the responsibility of the criminal law for serious offences is not ended by time. By contrast, most legal systems do have prescription periods for criminal law. Do legal systems change the civil prescription or limitation period where the conduct is both a tort and a crime? France, the Netherlands and Germany do not.[41] On the other hand, there are countries where the criminal element behind the harm significantly affects the length of time within which a civil claim can be brought. Such an effect is well known in Scandinavia, Greece and Italy, for instance[42], which is also the case in Portugal.[43] The Spanish system is particularly extreme, with prescription periods varying from one year for "pure" civil liability to five years (fifteen until 2015) for "*ex delicto*" liability. Formally in England the criminal character of offences can be relevant to applying the discretion to extend civil limitation but in practice rarely is.[44]

Timing rules and binding rules

A final point to be examined in this section relates to the extent to which tort and criminal proceedings on the same facts are *coordinated* in order to avoid contradictory outcomes.[45]

The French system provides perhaps the best example of procedural coordination, where a clear hierarchy of criminal over civil proceedings is recognised. Firstly, no claim on facts which suggest a criminal offence may have been committed are generally allowed to proceed: *le criminel tient le civil en l'état*, the criminal procedure holds the civil matter in place.[46] The foundations of this principle are uncertain, but it seems most likely to be based on a desire to avoid contradictory outcomes, linked to the procedural fact that civil claims are channelled first into criminal procedures.

Secondly, a criminal court decision creates a *res judicata* over later litigation on the same matter.[47] This means that, within limits, once a criminal court has determined a fact (occasionally even a legal issue) within criminal law a later civil court is bound by it. More recently, an exception was created for certain types of negligence within criminal law: from 2000 a new art. 4-1 of the *Code de procédure pénale* was inserted stating that a criminal court declaring the absence of non-intentional fault under article 121-3 of the Criminal Code does not prevent a later civil claim. But it is important to understand that this is an exception, for non-intentional wrongs, which officially created, for the first time in a century, two levels of *chose jugée* (otherwise known as res judicata) in France.

English law provides a useful counterpoint, as there is no automatic suspension nor binding impact of the criminal conviction. On timing, the court will instead weigh the seriousness and relevance of the offence against the merits of proceeding normally with the civil claim.[48] On binding effect, English law has only allowed convictions to be *admissible*, let alone determinative, since 1968. The Civil Evidence Act 1968 made convictions admissible in respect of the facts upon which they must have been founded, and made them binding in defamation claims.

Conclusion

Responsibility as a summary term for the generation of liability has fascinating overlaps and separations across criminal law and tort law. The conditions of liability and the principles behind them are often separated but lead to the same form, liability. There seems to be little clear pattern to the connections and separations between them across legal systems, though more local structures are more easily identified. Significantly more work needs to be done to explore and catalogue all these instances. That will also require inter-category work from a range of scholars. At present, conflict and ignorance often prevail in the relationship of tort to crime, particularly in a legal world whose actors increasingly specialise. For instance, it has been said by Lasser[49] to be:

> "...almost unthinkable for a French academic who specializes in administrative law to study —never mind say anything about— the private law (civil) courts. This is the very meaning and purpose of the rigid French distinction between the 'pénalistes' and the 'civilistes'..."

Acknowledgements

With thanks in particular to Marta Pantaleón Díaz and the Kathrin Nickel.

Notes

1. See J Lindgren, "Why the Ancients May Not Have Needed a System of Criminal Law", *Boston University Law Review*, vol. 76 (1996), p.29.
2. See generally DJ Seipp, "The Distinction between Crime and Tort in the Early Common Law", *Boston University Law Review*, vol. 76 (1996), p.59; JB Ames, *Lectures on Legal History and Miscellaneous Legal Essays* (Harvard University Press: Cambridge, MA, 1913), ch II, III, and IV.
3. On Spain, see M Roig Torres, *La reparación del daño causado por el delito (aspectos civiles y penales)* (Tirant lo Blanch: Valencia, 2000), pp.32–38.
4. O Descamps, *Les origines de la responsabilité pour faute personnelle dans le Code civil de 1804* (LGDJ: Paris, 2005), pp.204–213; J Bell & D Ibbetson, *European Legal Development: The Case of Tort* (Cambridge University Press: Cambridge, 2012), pp.72–73.
5. See, e.g. G Viney, *Introduction à la responsabilité* (LGDJ: Paris, 4th edn, 2019), pp.181–184.
6. P Hellwege & P Wittig, "Delictual and Criminal Liability in Germany", in M Dyson (ed), *Comparing Tort and Crime* (Cambridge University Press: Cambridge, 2015), p.124.
7. S Friberg & M Sunnqvist, "Crime and Tort in Sweden", in Dyson, *Comparing Tort and Crime*, pp.174–183.
8. Friberg & Sunnqvist, "Crime and Tort", p.180.
9. J Blackie & J Chalmers, "Mixing and matching in Scottish Delict and Crime", in Dyson, *Comparing Tort and Crime*, pp.286–313.
10. *Atcheson v. Everitt* (1775) I Cowp. 382, 391; 98 ER 1142, 1147, per Lord Mansfield, in respect of oaths.
11. "[N]o settled line can be drawn between the civil branch and the penal", in J Bentham, *Limits of Jurisprudence Defined* (Columbia University Press: New York, CW Everett edn, 1945), p.298.
12. HLA Hart, *Punishment and Responsibility: Essays in the Philosophy of Law* (Oxford University Press: Oxford, second impression, 2008), passim, and see, e.g. ch 5, 8, Postscript.
13. *Rookes v Barnard* [1964] AC 1129, 1225-27. See further J Goudkamp & D Nolan (eds), *Winfield and Jolowicz on Tort* (Sweet & Maxwell: London, 20th edn, 2020), paras. 23-012 to 23-024.
14. *BMW of North America, Inc. v Gore* 517 U.S. 559 (1996).
15. See, e.g. H Koziol & V Wilcox (eds), *Punitive Damages: Common Law and Civil Law Perspectives* (Springer: Vienna, 2009); N Rosenvald, *As funções da responsabilidade civil: a reparação e a pena civil,* (Saraiva: São Paulo, 3rd edn, 2017).
16. E.g. 167 of the Austrian Penal Code.
17. E.g. M Pantaleón Díaz, "Imputación objetiva e imprudencia en el Derecho anglosajón", in F Pérez Álvarez (ed), *Propuestas penales: nuevos retos y modernas tecnologías* (Universidad de Salamanca: Salamanca, 2016), pp.147–62.
18. See, e.g. N Jareborg, "Criminalization as Last Resort (Ultima Ratio)", *Ohio State Journal of Criminal Law*, vol. 2 (2005), p.521; D Husak, "Applying Ultima Ratio: A Skeptical Assessment", *Ohio State Journal of Criminal Law*, vol. 2 (2005), p.535.

19 Cf. M Dubber, "Theories of Crime and Punishment in German Criminal Law", *American Journal of Comparative Law*, vol. 53, no. 3 (2005), p.692; C Roxin, *Strafrecht: Allgemeiner Teil. Grundlagen, Der Aufbau der Verbrechenslehre* (Beck'sche Vertragsbuchhandlung: Munich, 3rd edn, 1997), vol. I, pp.26–27; T Vormbaum, "Fragmentarisches Strafrecht in Geschichte und Dogmatik", *Zeitschrift für die gesamte Strafrechtswissenschaft* 123 Heft 4 (2011), pp.667–669.
20 M Kloepfer, *Verfassungsrecht: Grundlagen Staatsorganisationsrecht, Bezüge zum Völker- und Europarecht* (Beck: Munich, 2011), vol. I, para. 10.141; E Deutsch, *Haftungsrecht* (Heymanns: Cologne, 1976), vol. 1, pp.89–97.
21 Cf. BVerfGE, arts. 92, 1, 13; BVerfGE, arts. 126, 170, 197.
22 E.g. JS Mill, *On Liberty* (1859).
23 See, e.g., the discussion in P Hellwege & P Wittig, "Delictual liability and criminal accountability in German law", in Dyson, *Comparing Tort and Crime*, pp.128–132.
24 Or if not framed in those terms, is understood to represent something to be corrected.
25 See generally S Friberg & M Sunnqvist, "Crime and Tort in Sweden", in Dyson, *Comparing Tort and Crime*, pp.173–222.
26 I Giesen, F Kristen, & R Kool, "The Dutch crush on compensating crime victims", in Dyson, *Comparing Tort and Crime*, pp. 320–328.
27 *Delito* marks out the more serious crimes, *falta* the less serious ones. See also LECrim, art. 100.
28 JF Pacheco, *El Código Penal* (Edisofer: Madrid, 2000 [1867]), p.279.
29 G Viney, *Introduction à la responsabilité* (LGDJ: Paris, 4th edn, 2019), pp.183–185.
30 See generally, M Dyson (ed), *Regulating Risk through Private Law* (Intersentia: Cambridge, 2018).
31 See Council Directive 85/374/EEC on the approximation of the laws, regulations and administrative provisions of the Member States concerning liability for defective products, [1985] OJ L210.
32 See, e.g. the French *Loi n° 85-677 du 5 juillet 1985*, or the Spanish *Real Decreto Legislativo 8/2004, de 29 de octubre*.
33 See M Pantaleón Díaz, "Children's Liability in Negligence", *Journal of European Tort Law*, vol. 9, no. 1 (2018), pp.29–39.
34 In *Ashley v Chief Constable of Sussex Police* [2008] UKHL 25; [2008] 1 AC 962 (HL), [17]-[18] cf. [76]. see generally on defences, Dyson, Comparing Tort and Crime.
35 See, e.g. JM Busto Lago, *La antijuridicidad del daño resarcible en la responsabilidad civil extracontractual* (Tecnos: Madrid, 1998), pp.246–414.
36 JC Bayón Mohíno, "Epistemología, moral y prueba de los hechos: hacia un enfoque no benthamiano", *Revista Jurídica Mario Alario D'Filippo* vol. 2, no. 4 (2010), pp.12–17.
37 E Hoegen & M Brienen, *Victims of Crime in 22 European Criminal Justice Systems: The Implementation of Recommendation (85) 11 of the Council of Europe on the Position of the Victim in the Framework of Criminal Law and Procedure* (Wolf Legal Productions: Nijmegen, the Netherlands, 2000), p.27.
38 Dyson, *Explaining Tort and Crime*, ch. 6.
39 *Ley de Enjuiciamiento Criminal*, art. 108.
40 *Strafprozessordnung*, paras. 403–406c.
41 C von Bar, *The Common European Law of Torts* (Oxford University Press: Oxford, 2000), vol. I, para. 618.
42 von Bar, *The Common European Law of Torts*, paras. 619–620.
43 Civil Code, art. 498(3).
44 See *A v Hoare* [2008] UKHL 6 (HL); Limitation Act 1980, ss. 2, 11 and 33.
45 See generally Dyson, *Explaining Tort and Crime*, ch. 6–8.
46 Viney, *Introduction à la responsabilité*, pp.298–305.
47 Viney, *Introduction à la responsabilité*, pp.305–371.
48 CPR, 23 PD, paras. 11A1—11A.4.
49 M De S.-O.-L'E Lasser, *Judicial Deliberations: A Comparative Analysis of Judicial Transparency and Legitimacy* (Oxford University Press: Oxford, 2004), p.6.

References

Cases

A v Hoare [2008] UKHL 6 (HL).
Ashley v Chief Constable of Sussex Police [2008] UKHL 25; [2008] 1 AC 962 (HL).
Atcheson v Everitt (1775) I Cowp. 382; 98 ER 1142.
BMW of North America, Inc. v Gore 517 U.S. 559 (1996).
Rookes v Barnard [1964] AC 1129.

Legislation

BVerfGE, arts.92, 1, 13 (Germany).
BVerfGE, arts.126, 170, 197 (Germany).
Civil Code, art.498(3) (Portugal).
Civil Evidence Act 1968 (England and Wales).
Council Directive 85/374/EEC (EU).
CPR, 23 PD, paras.11A1—11A.4 (England and Wales).
LECrim, art.100 (Spain).
Ley de Enjuiciamiento Criminal, art.108 (Spain).
Limitation Act 1980, ss.2, 11, and 33 (England and Wales).
loi n° 85–677 du 5 juillet 1985 (France).
Real Decreto Legislativo 8/2004, de 29 de octubre (Spain).
Strafprozessordnung, paras.403–406c (Germany).

Books and book chapters

Ames JB, *Lectures on Legal History and Miscellaneous Legal Essays* (Harvard University Press: Cambridge MA, 1913).
Bell J & Ibbetson D, *European Legal Development: The Case of Tort* (Cambridge University Press: Cambridge, 2012).
Bentham J, *Limits of Jurisprudence Defined* (Columbia University Press: New York, CW, Everett edn, 1945).
Binding K, *Die Normen und ihre Übertretung Eine Untersuchung über die rechtmässige Handlung und die Arten des Delikts. Band 1: Normen und Strafgesetze* (Felix Meiner: Hamburg, 4th edn, 1922).
Blackie J & Chalmers J, "Mixing and Matching in Scottish Delict and Crime", in Dyson M (ed), *Comparing Tort and Crime* (Cambridge University Press: Cambridge, 2015).
Bonfils P, *L'action civile. Essai sur la nature juridique d'une institution* (Presses Universitaires d'Aix-Marseille: Marseille, 2000).
Busto Lago JM, *La antijuridicidad del daño resarcible en la responsabilidad civil extracontractual* (Tecnos: Madrid, 1998).
De S.-O.-l'E Lasser M, *Judicial Deliberations: A Comparative Analysis of Judicial Transparency and Legitimacy* (Oxford University Press: Oxford, 2004).
Descamps O, *Les origines de la responsabilité pour faute personnelle dans le Code civil de 1804* (LGDJ: Paris, 2005).
Deutsch E, *Haftungsrecht* (Heymanns: Cologne, 1976), vol. I.
Dyson M (ed), *Comparing Tort and Crime* (Cambridge University Press: Cambridge, 2015).
Dyson M (ed), *Regulating Risk through Private Law* (Intersentia: Cambridge, 2018).
Dyson M (ed), *Unravelling Tort and Crime* (Cambridge University Press: Cambridge, 2014).
Dyson M, *Explaining Tort and Crime* (Cambridge University Press: Cambridge, 2022).
Feinberg J, *The Moral Limits of Criminal Law: Harm to Others* (Oxford University Press: New York, 1984), vol. I.
Francisco Pacheco JF, *El Código Penal* (Edisofer: Madrid, 1867 reprint,, 2000).
Friberg S & Sunnqvist M, "Crime and Tort in Sweden", in Dyson M (ed), *Comparing Tort and Crime* (Cambridge University Press: Cambridge, 2015).

Giesen I, Kristen F, & Kool R, "The Dutch Crush on Compensating Crime Victims", in Dyson M (ed), *Comparing Tort and Crime* (Cambridge University Press: Cambridge, 2015).
Goudkamp J & Nolan D (eds), *Winfield and Jolowicz on Tort* (Sweet & Maxwell: London, 20th edn, 2020).
Goudkamp J, *Tort Law Defences* (Hart Publishing: Oxford, 2013).
Hart HLA, *Punishment and Responsibility: Essays in the Philosophy of Law* (Oxford University Press: Oxford, 2nd Impression, 2008).
Hellwege P & Wittig P, "Delictual and Criminal Liability in Germany", in Dyson M (ed), *Comparing Tort and Crime* (Cambridge University Press: Cambridge, 2015).
Kloepfer M, *Verfassungsrecht: Grundlagen Staatsorganisationsrecht, Bezüge zum Völker- und Europarecht* (Beck: Munich, 2011), vol. I.
Koziol H & Wilcox V (eds), *Punitive Damages: Common Law and Civil Law Perspectives* (Springer: Vienna, 2009).
Mill JS, *On Liberty* (Cambridge University Press: Cambridge, 2012 [1859]).
Pantaleón Díaz M, "Imputación objetiva e imprudencia en el Derecho anglosajón", in Pérez Álvarez F (ed), *Propuestas penales: nuevos retos y modernas tecnologías* (Universidad de Salamanca: Salamanca, 2016).
Roig Torres M, *La reparación del daño causado por el delito (aspectos civiles y penales)* (Tirant lo Blanch: Valencia, 2000).
Rosenvald N, *As funções da responsabilidade civil: a reparação e a pena civil* (Saraiva: São Paulo, 3rd edn, 2017).
Roth H, "'§140' and '§149'", in Friedrich Stein F & Jonas M (eds), *Kommentar zur Zivilprozessordnung* (Mohr Siebeck: Tübingen, 2006).
Roxin C, *Strafrecht: Allgemeiner Teil. Grundlagen, Der Aufbau der Verbrechenslehre* (Beck'sche Vertragsbuchhandlung: Munich, 3rd edn, 1997), vol. I.
Tolsada Y, *Aspectos civiles del nuevo Código Penal* (Dykinson: Madrid, 1996).
Viney G, *Introduction à la responsabilité* (LGDJ: Paris, 4th edn, 2019).
von Bar C, *The Common European Law of Torts* (Oxford University Press: Oxford, 2000), vol. I.

Journal articles

Bayón Mohíno JC, "Epistemología, moral y prueba de los hechos: hacia un enfoque no benthamiano", *Revista Jurídica Mario Alario D'Filippo*, vol. 2, no. 4 (2010), pp.15–34.
Boston University Law Review, vol. 76 (1996), Symposium Vols. 1 & 2.
Cane P, "The General/Special Distinction in Criminal Law, Tort Law and Legal Theory", *Law and Philosophy*, vol. 26, no. 5 (2007), pp.465–500.
Dubber M, "Theories of Crime and Punishment in German Criminal Law", *American Journal of Comparative Law*, vol. 53, no. 3 (2005), pp.679–707.
Dyson M, "Connecting Tort and Crime: Comparative Legal History in England and Spain since 1850", *Cambridge Yearbook of European Legal Studies*, vol. 11 (2009), pp.247–288.
Husak D, "Applying Ultima Ratio: A Skeptical Assessment", *Ohio State Journal of Criminal Law*, vol. 2, no. 2 (2005), pp.535–545.
Jareborg N, "Criminalization as Last Resort (Ultima Ratio)", *Ohio State Journal of Criminal Law*, vol. 2, no. 2 (2005), pp.521–534.
Lindgren J, "Why the Ancients May Not Have Needed a System of Criminal Law", *Boston University Law Review*, vol. 76, nos. 1–2 (1996), pp.29–56.
Pérez Álvarez F, "Children's Liability in Negligence", *Journal of European Tort Law*, vol. 9, no. 1 (2018), pp.25–33.
Seipp DJ, "The Distinction between Crime and Tort in the Early Common Law", *Boston University Law Review*, vol. 76, nos. 1–2 (1996), pp.59–88.
Vormbaum T, "Fragmentarisches Strafrecht in Geschichte und Dogmatik", *Zeitschrift für die gesamte Strafrechtswissenschaft*, vol. 123, no. 4 (2011), pp.660–690.
Widener Law Journal, vol. 17, No. 3 (2008) Symposium on Crimtorts.

16
CRIMINAL RESPONSIBILITY FOR MARKET MISCONDUCT

Lindsay Farmer

Introduction

Markets are usually seen as sites of responsibility. Individuals make deals based on their own judgments of value – their self-interest – and it is in this collective pursuit of individual self-interest that the social value of the market is seen to lie.[1] While the focus of discussions of the market is usually on either the goods that the market is presumed to deliver, or on the means by which it does so (how the rational, self-interested individual makes choices), it is important to note that this is also about responsibility. The individual is presumed to be responsible for their own decisions – good or bad – and they are responsible because they are presumed to be acting in a rational and calculated way. It is even argued by some that the market makes people responsible, imposing a kind of "market discipline" to root out bad or untrustworthy individuals. To be sure, the law steps in to protect certain classes of persons (or to regulate certain types of contracts) – consumers, employees and so on – but this is seen as an exception to the general rule of individual responsibility. This is especially so in financial markets where judgments of value are based purely on profit and calculation. We are encouraged to invest in stocks and shares, to "play" the market, but at the same time reminded that it is not a game and that we do so at our own risk: the value of investments, we are constantly reminded, can go down, as well as up. You are responsible for your losses as well as your potential gains, and if you cannot bear that risk, you should not get involved.

At the same time, markets are unpredictable. They operate in unexpected ways and are full of mechanisms that diffuse or reduce responsibility. On the one hand, there are so-called bubbles and crashes. These are moments when prices become hugely inflated and investors rush to buy, even when the prospect of profit is unlikely at best – perhaps leading to the inevitable crash.[2] While these are seen as exceptional occurrences, they happen with sufficient regularity to require explanation by economists, who then do so in terms of "animal spirits" or "irrational exuberance" – precisely the kind of emotions that are supposed to be absent from normal market transactions.[3] These are moments when rationality is displaced and so cannot be explained within the normal terminology of the discipline. Even in normal times, though, the market is spoken about as if it operates autonomously, independent of the wishes or expectations of participants.[4] The market is an actor – it moves or reacts or speaks in ways which take the focus away from individual action and fault and which escape the control of (or is incapable of being influenced by) any one individual. The market in this sense is neither responsible nor irresponsible – merely a device that processes information from thousands of individual transactions – and yet the responsibilities of the individuals who conduct these transactions, some more powerful than others, are somehow displaced.[5] The market is thus also increasingly seen as a place of irresponsibility, creating the conditions for fraudulent or criminal conduct as competitive markets incentivise bad behaviour and provide opportunities to exploit others.[6]

Under these conditions, some of the normal assumptions about responsibility are displaced. If the successful trader is lionised for their individual genius in identifying and exploiting opportunities, the person who loses money is often seen as the victim of the caprices of an unpredictable market.[7] In the cases of crashes and bubbles, the event itself is seen as too large to be the responsibility of any single person. It is a market event, but the market cannot be responsible – in the sense of being accountable – as "market discipline" breaks down and the result is impunity.[8] The market, in an important sense, increasingly becomes a mechanism of irresponsibility, where the relationship between individual actions and outcomes becomes increasingly hard to pin down.[9]

This raises a particular set of questions when it comes to imposing criminal responsibility for market misconduct – that is to say conduct which breaches rules of criminal law regulating forms of market activity. Why is it that the model of rational agency which is taken to be characteristic of market agency, and which seems to have much in common with models of rational agency in the criminal law, does not lead to more prosecutions (or more successful prosecutions) where the misconduct of individuals has caused harm? How can we hold individuals criminally responsible for market misconduct when markets seem to diffuse that responsibility? These questions have had a particular salience in recent years when the increased formal criminalisation of market misconduct (especially, but not exclusively, in financial markets) has not been accompanied by a corresponding increase in numbers of individuals actually being held criminally responsible for their conduct. More specifically, there are two kinds of problems.[10] First, there is a difficulty with applying a "criminal law" model of fault based on knowledge or foresight of particular (harmful) outcomes. Are market outcomes foreseeable – or what does foreseeability even mean in the context of markets? What kind of knowledge, in other words, should give rise to culpability? There are difficulties around proving recklessness in a market context, when speculative conduct is, by its nature, a matter of risk-taking. What is excessive risk-taking in this context? If this is judged only by market norms, then criminal law will simply collapse into economics, but there seem to be no other ways of judging this. Second, there are questions about the presence or absence of moral fault. Is it fair to criminalise those who were only acting in a way the market expected them to act? Is there sufficient moral fault in forms of market misconduct? If it is sometimes suggested that this is a matter of the "moral ambiguity" of market misconduct, it is not disputed that this is offered as an explanation for the failure to pursue more criminal prosecutions.[11] Neither of these "responsibility problems" are unique to market misconduct but, as I shall attempt to show, there are institutional features of markets which give rise to particular difficulties in relation to these questions.

The aim of this chapter, then, is to explore the relationship between models of agency in criminal law and in economic theory – between *homo juridicus* and *homo economicus* – with a view to exploring theoretical issues around criminal responsibility for market misconduct. There are two main sections. In the first section, I look critically at the models of agency to explore their similarities and differences. In the next section, I then look more closely at institutional features of markets to examine agency in markets more specifically and the features of markets that hinder the attribution of liability. The paper then concludes by setting out some more general considerations that might guide further research in this area.[12]

Homo economicus/homo juridicus

It has been suggested that there is an affinity between the economic subject (*homo economicus*) and the responsible subject of criminal law (*homo juridicus*), as both rely on a model of the rational, egoistic, individual as the irreducible basis for social action.[13] In both cases, the fundamental model of agency is the individual who chooses on the basis of interests which only they are presumed to know (or be capable of knowing). In the market, this leads to profit or loss; in criminal law, the choice to break the law (to pursue illegitimate interests or legitimate interests by illegitimate means) leads to justified punishment. This might lead us to expect that the "responsibility problems" identified above might be illusory. On the one hand, if market conduct is rational, in the sense that individuals weigh all possible future outcomes before deciding to break the law (in the expectation of greater profit), then we might expect that (other things being equal) models of criminal liability would work in relation to market misconduct. Alternatively, law and economics would argue that market misconduct might be subject to "market discipline" – in effect "priced out" of properly functioning markets – and thus that there would be no need for criminal law. However, as we noted above, this does not seem to be the case, and so it necessary to reflect further on *homo economicus* and *homo juridicus* and the relation between them.

Homo economicus

There is some debate about the origins of the term *homo economicus*.[14] The idea of economic man can arguably be traced back to the work of Adam Smith and his famous claim that:

> "It is not from the benevolence of the butcher, the brewer, or the baker, that we expect our dinner, but from their regard to their own interest. We address ourselves, not to their humanity but to their self-love, and never talk to them of our own necessities but of their advantages".[15]

This has shaped the modern understanding of markets as institutions which co-ordinate the actions of rational, self-interested, individuals: while a collective good might emerge from market exchanges, social relationships within markets are more narrowly conceived in instrumental terms, as individuals pursue personal profit. The idea of there being a specific kind of economic rationality, however, is more usually attributed to John Stuart Mill. In an essay published in 1836, he described the subject of the science of political economy:

> "It does not treat of the whole of man's nature as modified by the social state, nor of the whole conduct of man in society. It is concerned with him solely as a being who

desires to possess wealth, and who is capable of judging of the comparative efficacy of means for obtaining that end".[16]

The aim of this, he was clear, was not to identify some fundamental quality of human nature, but to produce a model of economic action – as consumption and exchange – by stripping out other kinds of motivations or desires. This was necessary not because "any political economist was ever so absurd as to suppose that mankind really are (sic) thus constituted, but because this is the mode in which science must necessarily proceed".[17] By identifying this specific form of rationality, it would be possible then to explore the influence of institutions on economic behaviour. This project was consistent with the project of political economy as a science for the exploration of the impact of particular laws or institutions on the production of wealth.[18] In this sense, the calculating economic individual defined the limits of government, whose role was that of creating the conditions in which the production of wealth (the market) might flourish. Thus, while Mill generally favoured *laissez-faire* (or non-intervention in markets), he also maintained both that certain kinds of government intervention were essential, and that such a system could only work if individuals had developed practical experience and judgment (character) so as to be capable of pursuing their own interests. Economic man, in other words, was not born, but was constructed through careful government intervention informed by the science of political economy.

The understanding of the term *homo economicus* – and the ends which this concept served – changed significantly over the course of the twentieth century as the discipline of economics (as distinct from political economy) developed.[19] Contemporary *homo economicus* is seen as a hypothetical agent who possesses "perfect rationality": complete information about available options, perfect foresight of possible consequences, and the capacity to identify the option which maximises their personal utility. While the agent is still an abstraction, it is clear that they are conceived of in terms of quite specific attributes reflecting the assumptions which shape much contemporary economic theory. This can be illustrated by considering the work of Gary Becker, the Chicago School economist, who is often seen as giving one of the clearest articulations of a contemporary understanding of *homo economicus* – developing this account specifically in relation to the criminal law.[20] Becker argued that "a person commits an offense if the expected utility to him exceeds the utility he could get by using his time and other resources at other activities."[21] From the point of view of the actor, the decision whether or not to perform an action was a straightforward calculation of costs and benefits based on the information available to that actor at that point in time, and the ends that they wanted to pursue. The decision to commit a "crime" was thus framed in economic terms as a question of whether the individual might expect to maximise any "profit" from their decision – with any potential penalty simply being seen as part of the calculation. Punishment, or the likelihood of punishment, was thus a "price" that might be factored in – and so from the point of view of the state the penalty should be adjusted to the level at which it is marginally more "costly" than any expected benefit from criminal activity – thus deterring the calculating individual from committing the crime.

This economic theory of deterrence continues to be influential, particularly as a model in theories of market regulation and the use of administrative sanctions, as well as in criminological theories such as situational crime prevention.[22] Consistently with Becker's account, deterrence is conceived of as having two dimensions. On the one hand, there are sanctions, which should be more costly than any expected profit from the conduct. On the other, the aim is to design the market environment in such a way as to create incentives for good behaviour. It is worth noting that Becker drew connections between his model of deterrence and the work of penal theorists such as Bentham and Beccaria who, he argued, had applied a similar sort of "economic" rationality when they argued that punishment should be set at a level which might deter a criminal, but no higher.[23] However, these superficial similarities should not blind us to some important ways in which Becker's conception reflects a different understanding of the relationship between law and the market.

One key difference is that while Bentham and Beccaria appealed to a naturalistic psychology of the individual as a utility maximiser (that is to say, maximising pleasure and minimising pain), for Becker *homo economicus* is not a description of a psychological state of mind but of a model of market (or economic) rationality.[24] Becker effectively argues that all "rational" conduct can be understood as economic conduct – and thus that it can be understood by means of economic analysis.[25] The focus is not individual psychology but how the logic of the market (supply and demand) might be applied to other areas of social life. Thus, if Bentham and Beccaria understood society as being composed of morally responsible (pleasure-seeking) individuals who pursued their interests within a framework provided by the law, Becker effectively reverses this such that legal rationality can only be conceived of as operating in economic terms – and any calculation is thus "economic". His is also a neoliberal project of marketisation, as the costs and benefits of any putatively rational social practice, from crime and punishment to love and marriage, can be tested in terms of this economic model – and the market model extended into these areas of social life. While Becker's approach might then appear to have more in common with Mill's concept of economic man, there is another important difference. For Mill, as we have seen, the purpose of abstraction was as a means of testing the effectiveness of certain laws or governmental measures on the growth of wealth, and it was assumed that the sphere of the market was separate from that of government (or politics), and assumed the sovereignty of the political over the economic.[26] For Becker, by contrast, the effectiveness of the market is axiomatic, and his aim is that of subjecting non-economic behaviour to an economic rationality (making other areas of social life economically intelligible). The function of *homo economicus* on this model is not that it can act as a limit to governmental action, but that by demonstrating how economic rationality is a model for understanding social life more generally it can show how areas of social life can be governed by demonstrating what kind of incentive/stimulus might work best. Far from treating the individual as the irreducible foundation of social action, the individual subject is conceived as "circulating or fungible human capital instrumentalised by itself, society, economy and the state".[27] *Homo economicus* thus only has an affinity with the individual of law to the extent that law itself can be reduced to a form of economic rationality. It is thus now necessary to consider this in relation to *homo juridicus*.

Homo juridicus

My starting point here is that criminal responsibility should be understood as a legal institution – that is to say as a way of designating subjects to whom criminal liability can be attributed.[28] The model of the legal person (*homo juridicus*) thus implies a certain kind of anthropology: that "persons are capable of being guided by norms and may accordingly be answerable for their conduct when they breach those norms".[29] Legal responsibility in general is thus organised around the idea that legal subjects are autonomous and capable of regulating their own conduct in relation to others and capable of responding to general norms. This is a model of responsible agency which is an abstraction, identifying certain natural or institutional features that are treated as legally relevant.[30] Thus, this model of responsibility may be based either on a naturalistic psychology (that this reflects how individuals in fact think and act) or may be based on normative claims (it is how individuals ought to act), or even some combination of both.[31] Criminal responsibility may track accounts of moral responsibility, but these are not foundational – in the sense that we should not start by asserting (as many criminal law theorists do) a "pre-legal" account of moral responsibility and seeking to understand the criminal law in these terms. By contrast, I would argue that we should understand the responsibility practices of the criminal law and look at how these appeal to understandings of moral responsibility to organise the discipline of criminal law and establish its moral and political legitimacy.[32]

The function of criminal responsibility is thus to define the scope of responsibilities and to identify persons capable of being held to account in law. This has two dimensions. On the one hand, this requires the specification of *responsibilities* (norms/standards of conduct) which are defined with respect to an understanding of a person capable of adapting their conduct to norms and planning their conduct over time. In the modern law, these take the form of general rules which specify prohibited conduct (your responsibilities to others; the responsibilities attaching to certain roles or activities), and also certain mental states (what the responsible person should know or foresee). On the other hand, the forms of *responsibility* reflect institutional structures (what can be proved and how) as well as ideas about the individual – and political choices about the distribution of responsibility (or interests).[33] In modern criminal law, these are organised around conceptions of character, capacity, outcome, and risk. Criminal responsibility is thus an institutional understanding of the capacities and expectations of legal persons and what they can be held responsible for in law.

Even from this brief summary we can see that there are important differences between *homo economicus* and *homo juridicus*, particularly in the neoliberal version developed by Becker. In spite of superficial similarities around the idea of the rational, calculating individual, they are developed for different ends. The idea of *homo economicus* is not, in the end, an account of the subject of the market, but is an attempt to isolate individual decisions, and possible outcomes of those decisions, as the unit of social analysis. It is not, ultimately, even a theory of the market so much as an abstract model of calculation. *Homo juridicus* is also, to be sure, an abstraction – a model of the rational individual which disregards or downplays the impact of social context or "non-rational" motives on decision-making. However, even as an abstraction, it carries within itself a certain idea of subjectivity – the autonomous self-directed subject who is governed through law (i.e. who is expected to exercise a degree of autonomy in deciding whether or not to conform with general norms). The choice, in other words, to regulate an area of social life by means of law implies the recognition of a certain kind of actor who has a freedom to choose. Of course, the individualisation of fault in criminal law can create situations in which the law might disregard social factors which contribute to certain kinds of conduct, or in which individuals are "responsibilised" for the structural problems created by capitalist economy.[34] This, however, is less a matter of affinities between the different models of rationality than a consequence of the growing "marketisation" of the social order and the increased reliance on the criminal law to deal with social inequalities. A final point that we might make here concerns the "meaning" of different actions. For Becker, from the perspective of economics, there is only conduct and stimulus – and *homo economicus* is the actor who responds to stimulus in a way which is judged to be rational from the point of view of economic theory. Yet it is clear both that actions have different social meanings – a crime, however defined, is different from an economic transaction, which is different from an act of friendship, and so on – but also that how we choose to respond to certain kinds of conduct (through criminal law, by administrative action, through pricing and so on) also carries different social meanings. The functions of criminal responsibility are broader than "pricing", and it is important to bear this in mind as we turn to look at agency in markets and how criminal responsibility might be more sensitive to this particular institutional context.

Markets and market misconduct

Often markets are understood as a kind of semi-mystical process (a natural or spontaneous order) which co-ordinates social conduct through the aggregation of individual transactions.[35] In practice, however, markets are more complex institutions for distributing social goods, allowing buyers and sellers to meet and agree conditions for the sale or exchange of those goods. Markets are more discrete and bounded institutions which are normally regulated in some way – and arguably can only function because they are embedded within these larger constraints.[36] These regulations might set conditions on what can be sold, where it can be sold, who can participate. There are then, in addition to these factors, rules preventing cheating, regulating competition, or outlawing certain kinds of exploitative bargains, and so on.[37]

These broader features of markets might have an impact on agency in different ways, and I want to focus on two of these.[38] First, market relations are always embedded in existing social relations.[39] This means that those engaging in market transactions are part of business and social networks which shape how they do business (loyalty to existing customers, trusting certain people, and so on). While this is normally pointed to as showing how markets and morals are intertwined (i.e. markets are not necessarily amoral places), it also means that these "social" factors might make the decisions of actors less "rational".[40] A person might continue to trade with someone they know to be in financial trouble out of a sense of obligation, or might accept a slightly lower offer if they know a person.[41] Equally, a person might feel pressured to act in a certain way because of the expectations of the social network or organisation that they belong to – and so do something that they know to breach the regulations of the market, or even to be illegal. Alternatively, traders may be tempted to use market mechanisms to exploit the vulnerabilities of others, conduct that might be "rational", but nonetheless in breach of laws or regulations governing markets.[42] Second, competition means that people trade under conditions of uncertainty because of the unforeseeable effects of interactions, unpredictable innovations, and the contingency of other actors' choices.[43] This is not only a matter of reasonable or calculable risk, but the genuine unknowability of outcomes even if actors are intending to maximise outcomes. One of the challenges that the recognition of uncertainty poses is understanding the importance of expectations as "creative responses to situations that are based on contingent interpretations of what the future holds" – and often, the fact that a certain outcome occurs is taken as evidence that it was foreseeable.[44] Economic models are focused on the implications of errors made in valuing certain assets, and the effect this has on competition in the market as a whole – so that individual decisions, even when manifestly wrong, are treated only as if they were rational at the time, and as information to be processed by the market as a whole. However, from the perspective of individual agency, the question is how we might judge certain "errors" to be reasonable or unreasonable – or even, in certain circumstances, culpable.

If these are already complex questions, it is arguably the case that these issues are exacerbated by certain institutional features of financial markets – which is also where many of the new criminal laws have been introduced.[45] One factor is that the products traded in financial markets have become increasingly complex. Since the deregulation of the financial industry in the 1980s, financial products have been "packaged" in increasingly complex and innovative instruments, such as derivatives, where what is sold is not a debt itself, but a contract related to the future value of an underlying product (often itself based on certain "bundles" of other financial products) which allows traders to bet on movements in prices. This introduces new factors of risk and complexity into financial markets because the complexity of the instruments can make it difficult to assess the underlying value of the asset, which in turn makes it hard to assess the actual level of risk. A second factor is the automation of trading, which is increasingly conducted online using algorithms programmed to buy and sell at high speeds. However, increasing the speed and volume of trading not only introduces new elements of risk into financial markets, but also raises questions about who is trading (and with whom), and indeed whether it is possible to focus on individual transactions.[46] Choices here are embedded in the technology, and so responsibility might have to be conceived of in different ways. A third significant (though perhaps unrelated) factor that we should note is the lack of moral hazard for many participants in financial markets. While, as I noted at the start, it is assumed that the rational economic actor is responsible because they face the risk of loss, as well as profit, in fact, for many actors in financial markets, liability may be limited. Financial institutions may have limited liability, meaning that any loss would fall on shareholders rather than the corporation itself, or those working for it; deposits in banks are insured by governments or guaranteed by central banks; and, finally, as it was famously noted during the financial crisis, some institutions were considered "too big to fail", which meant the governments stepped in to bail them out because of the wider social consequences of financial failure.[47] As a consequence, the scope of responsibility is increasingly poorly defined – and this also contributes to the sense that financial markets are privileged spaces in which actors can "pursue self-serving profit without fear of moral disgrace".[48]

These reflections on agency in markets raise questions about how we might think about criminal responsibility which, as we saw above, have been based on an account of autonomous agency which assumes that actors are capable of knowing the consequences of their actions and assessing future risks.

Conclusion

In conclusion, I want to reflect on the significance of these issues of embeddedness, uncertainty, and moral hazard, and their implications for thinking about responsible agency, for as we have seen these raise questions about the relationship between individual agency and larger market systems. This, in turn, has consequences for how we might think about criminal responsibility given the divergences between conceptions of *homo economicus* and *homo juridicus*.

The first set of considerations relate to the question of uncertainty – for example in establishing evidence of excessive recklessness in a market context. As we have seen, one of the consequences of recognising the presence of uncertainty is that it undermines claims to rational agency in markets (especially financial markets). The rightness or wrongness of a decision cannot be judged by the market under conditions of uncertainty because there are no empirical grounds for assuming that, on average, market actors are correct. From the perspective of economic theory, particularly neoliberal economic theory, there are no real grounds for distinguishing between more or less serious instances of recklessness, as both might be putatively "rational" (based on the best information available to the actor at the time of acting, in pursuit of ends deemed reasonable at the time), or alternatively embedded in norms of conduct that do not offer an independent standard of judgment (what other traders might do). Indeed, the recklessness or otherwise of particular conduct might only become clearer at a later point in time depending on how the market reacts to particular alternatives – something encouraged by regulation, which is focused on addressing undesirable outcomes, rather than undesirable conduct. In these circumstances, the grounds on which conduct might be judged criminally reckless become narrow if the law concedes the grounds of judgment to economics or norms of market conduct.[49] Rather than seeking to track economic models of agency, it is necessary to think about establishing new grounds of legal responsibility because if the criminal law seeks to apply a standard account of recklessness based on knowledge and foreseeability of outcomes, it runs into the same difficulties with uncertainty as economic theory. Here, it is perhaps important to start from the point of view of how we might "responsibilise" markets – that is, to think about "the working of those markets as *markets*" before we attempt to responsibilise individuals in those markets.[50] The key point here, as illustrated by the discussion above, is that economic theory seems to offer no perspective from which to judge the moral quality of conduct – or perhaps, going further, that the qualities of conduct (good or bad market conduct) are themselves shaped by features of the market as an institution. In these circumstances, the function of criminal law is that of enforcing the kind of "morally meaningful" standards that allow trading to take place. This claim also appeals to the older tradition of political economy discussed earlier in the chapter in which the role of law and government was not to leave the market to its own devices, but to seek impose standards and regulate in the most effective way. Criminal laws directed against market misconduct are only likely to be effective if they take seriously the task understanding modern markets.

Acknowledgements

Funding for this research was generously provided by the Leverhulme Trust (Grant No. MRF 2018-075). Earlier versions of this chapter were presented at seminars at the University of Edinburgh and the University of Helsinki. I am very grateful to all the participants in those seminars for their comments. I would especially like to thank Esko Yli-Hemminki, Heli Korkka-Knuts, and Arlie Loughnan for their comments and feedback on the paper.

Notes

1. A Smith, *The Wealth of Nations* (Penguin: Harmondsworth, 1999 [1776]).
2. H Vogel, *Financial Market Bubbles and Crashes: Features, Causes and Effects* (Palgrave Macmillan: London, 3rd edn, 2021); R Aliber & CP Kindleberger, *Manias, Panics and Crashes: A History of Financial Crises* (Palgrave Macmillan: London, 7th edn, 2015).
3. The term "animal spirits" is attributed to John Maynard Keynes; "irrational exuberance" to Robert Shiller. See G Akerlof & R Shiller, *Animal Spirits* (Princeton University Press: Princeton, NJ, 2009). The FSA (UK), for example, referred to "a self-reinforcing cycle of irrational exuberance"

in their analysis of the causes of the 2008 crash (quoted in N Ryder, *The Financial Crisis and White Collar Crime: The Perfect Storm?* (Edward Elgar: Cheltenham, 2014), p.19.
4 M Watson, *The Market* (Agenda Publishing: Newcastle, 2018).
5 F Hayek, *Law, Legislation and Liberty* (Routledge: London, 2013 [1973]), ch.10; P Mirowski & E Nik-Kah, *The Knowledge We Have Lost in Information: The History of Information in Modern Economics* (Oxford University Press: Oxford, 2016).
6 See e.g. G Akerlof & R Shiller, *Phishing for Phools: The Economics of Manipulation and Deception* (Princeton University Press: Princeton NJ, 2015).
7 See e.g. M Poovey, "Stories We Tell about Liberal Markets. The Efficient Market Hypothesis and Great-Men Narratives of Change", in S Gunn & J Vernon (eds), *The Peculiarities of Liberal Modernity in Imperial Britain* (University of California Press: Berkeley CA, 2011).
8 The US Department of Treasury referred to a "significant erosion of market discipline" in their analysis of the causes of the financial crash (quoted in Ryder, *Financial Crisis*, p.19).
9 S Veitch, *Law and Irresponsibility* (Hart Publishing: Oxford, 2007).
10 I am concerned here primarily with conceptual or definitional questions of how criminal responsibility for market misconduct might be formulated. There are, of course, further problems relating to the proof of misconduct, and whether or not there is a political desire to prosecute or punish those who are responsible. These are not the primary focus of this chapter.
11 E.g. S Shapiro, *Wayward Capitalists: Targets of the Securities and Exchange Commission* (Yale University Press: New Haven CT, 1984).
12 This chapter is part of a larger project looking at understandings of market misconduct and how we might criminalise it. Questions of substantive law and corporate liability will be looked at as part of this project.
13 This connection also seems to draw unlikely support from critical scholars such as Alan Norrie who has argued that the development of criminal responsibility is functional for modern Western capitalism as the individualisation of fault enabled governance through the criminal law. For Norrie, the connection points to the influence of the economic on legal thought and the construction of an ideology in which individuals are "responsibilised" for the structural problems created by capitalist economy: AW Norrie, *Crime, Reason and History: A Critical Introduction to Criminal Law* (Weidenfeld & Nicolson: London, 1st edn, 1993), ch. 1.
14 See J Persky, "The Ethology of *Homo Economicus*", *Journal of Economic Perspectives*, vol. 9, no. 2 (1995), p.221; M Bee and M Demarais-Tremblay, "The Birth of *Homo Oeconomicus*: The Methodological Debate on the Economic Agent from JS Mill to V Pareto", *Journal of the History of Economic Thought*, vol. 45. No. 1 (2023), p.1. The precise term is usually attributed to the Italian economist Vilfredo Pareto, *Manual of Political Economy* (Oxford University Press: Oxford, 2014 [1906]) at para 28, however see now Bee & Demarais-Tremblay (p.10) suggesting that the precise term was first used by the French economist Claude Jannet in 1878.
15 Smith, *Wealth of Nations*, Bk.I, ch. 2, p.19.
16 JS Mill, "On the Definition of Political Economy" *London and Westminster Review*, no. 1 (1836) (October), p.12.
17 Mill, "Definition", p.13.
18 Persky, "*Homo Economicus*", pp.224–226. See also L Farmer, "Responsibility, Criminalisation and Political Economy", in I Solanke, *On Crime, Society and Responsibility in the Work of Nicola Lacey* (Oxford University Press: Oxford, 2021), pp.206–209.
19 See the discussion of *homo economicus* in M Foucault, *The Birth of Biopolitics* (London: Palgrave Macmillan, 2008), Lectures 10 and 11.
20 G Becker, "Crime and Punishment: An Economic Approach", *Journal of Political Economy*, vol. 76, no. 2 (1968), p.169; *The Economic Approach to Human Behaviour* (University of Chicago Press: Chicago, 1976).
21 Becker, "Crime and Punishment", p.176.
22 A Ogus, "Regulation and its Relation with the Criminal Justice Process", in H Quirk et al (eds), *Regulation and Criminal Justice* (Cambridge University Press: Cambridge, 2010); DB Cornish and RVG Clarke, *The Reasoning Criminal. Rational Choice Perspectives on Offending* (Springer-Verlag: Berlin, 1986).
23 For discussion see B Harcourt, *The Illusion of Free Markets: Punishment and the Myth of Natural Order* (Harvard University Press: Cambridge MA, 2011), chs.1, 5 & 6.

24 It is important to note that some economic theory challenges this model, arguing that rationality is "bounded" focusing on decision-making processes rather than outcomes. See G Wheeler, "Bounded Rationality", in EN Zalta (ed.), *Stanford Encyclopedia of Philosophy* (Fall 2020 Edition), available at: https://plato.stanford.edu/archives/fall2020/entries/bounded-rationality/.
25 "Rational" can be understood broadly as "non-random" in the sense that anything non-random (even so-called irrational conduct) can be explained by an economic model.
26 W Brown, *Undoing the Demos: Neoliberalism's Stealth Revolution* (Zone Books: New York, 2015), ch.3.
27 Brown, *Undoing the Demos*, p.97. See also Mirowski & Nik-Khah, *The Knowledge We Have Lost* for an extended discussion of the movement from the rational actor to the decision, with the market conceived of as a vast information-processing machine.
28 This is a summary of the argument in L Farmer, *Making the Modern Criminal Law: Criminalisation and Civil Order* (Oxford University Press: Oxford, 2016), ch.6. See also C Thornhill, "Guilt and the Origins of Modern Law", *Economy & Society*, vol. 43, no. 1 (2014), p.103.
29 Farmer, *Making*, p.168.
30 Note that one of the criticisms of law and economics – Becker – is often that it misunderstands or misrepresents the moral nature of human conduct. My point here is not that moral conduct should be a starting point, but that if we regulate through criminal law, it is necessary to treat individuals as though they are choosing.
31 Wheeler, "Bounded Rationality" para 1.4; cf. G Fletcher, *Basic Concepts in Criminal Law* (Oxford University Press: Oxford, 1998), ch.5.
32 E.g. through the justification of punishment.
33 N Lacey, *In Search of Criminal Responsibility: Ideas, Institutions and Interests* (Oxford University Press: Oxford, 2017); A Loughnan, *Self, Others and the State* (Cambridge University Press: Cambridge, 2019).
34 Norrie, *Crime Reason and History*; Harcourt, *The Illusion of Free Markets*.
35 C Taylor, *Modern Social Imaginaries* (Duke University Press: Durham NC, 2004), ch.5; Watson, *The Market*, p.7: "The market concept thus calls to mind the image of a coordinating mechanism that can bring about overall systemic coherence without the need to plan that coordination into existence".
36 They may be centralised or decentralised (e.g. when we talk about the labour market or housing market).
37 See e.g. J Beckert, "The Social Order of Markets", *Theory & Society*, vol. 38 (2009), p.245; N Fligstein, *The Architecture of Markets* (Princeton University Press: Princeton, NJ, 2001), esp ch.2; N Fligstein & L Dauter, "The Sociology of Markets", *Annual Review of Sociology*, vol. 33 (2007), p.105; L Farmer, "Taking Market Crime Seriously", *Legal Studies*, vol. 42, no.3 (2022), p.508.
38 Note also M Callon, *The Laws of the Markets* (Blackwell: Oxford, 1998) on how agency is "framed" in markets (i.e. what can be seen or count as agency from the perspective of markets).
39 M Granovetter, "Economic Action and Social Structure: The Problem of Embeddedness", *American Journal of Sociology*, vol. 91, no. 3 (1985), p.481; J Beckert, "Trust and Markets", in R Bachmann & A Zaheer (eds) *Handbook of Trust Research* (Edward Elgar: Cheltenham, 2006). He argues that trust is constitutive of markets if standard economic assumptions about perfect information do not hold (at p.318).
40 M Fourcade & K Healy, "Moral Views of Market Society" *Annual Review Sociology*, vol. 33 (2007), p.285.
41 C Zaloom, *Out of the Pits: Traders and Technology from Chicago to London* (University of Chicago Press: Chicago, 2006).
42 Akerlof & Shiller, *Phishing for Phools*.
43 J Beckert, *Imagined Futures: Fictional Expectations and Capitalist Dynamics* (Harvard University Press: Cambridge, MA, 2016), ch.3.
44 Beckert, *Imagined Futures*, p.36.
45 See L Herzog, "Introduction", in L Herzog (ed), *Just Financial Markets? Finance in a Just Society* (Oxford University Press: Oxford, 2017), esp. at pp.13–20.
46 D Mackenzie, *Trading at the Speed of Light* (Princeton University Press: Princeton NJ, 2021); JW Williams, *Policing the Markets: Inside the Black Box of Securities Enforcement* (Routledge: London, 2012).

47 Herzog, "Introduction", p.15. See also B Garrett, *Too Big to Jail: How Prosecutors Compromise with Corporations* (Harvard University Press: Cambridge MA, 2016).
48 T Jackson, *Impunity and Capitalism: The Afterlives of European Financial Crises, 1690-1830* (Cambridge University Press: Cambridge, 2022), p.5. He goes on (pp.5–6) to argue that capitalism also "depended on the creation of privileged zones of action where certain actors could pursue dangerous and destructive economic activities without fear of legal repercussion".
49 And it has been argued that markets should be further deregulated in order to improve information flows.
50 D Campbell, "Note: What is Wrong with Insider Dealing", *Legal Studies*, vol. 16, no. 185 (1996), p.192.

References

Books and book chapters

Akerlof G & Shiller R, *Animal Spirits: How Human Psychology Drives the Economy, and Why it Matters for Global Capitalism* (Princeton University Press: Princeton NJ, 2009).
Akerlof G & Shiller R, *Phishing for Phools: The Economics of Manipulation and Deception* (Princeton University Press: Princeton NJ, 2015).
Aliber R & Kindleberger CP, *Manias, Panics and Crashes: A History of Financial Crises* (Palgrave Macmillan: London, 7th edn, 2015).
Becker G, *The Economic Approach to Human Behaviour* (University of Chicago Press: Chicago, 1976).
Beckert J, "Trust and Markets", in Bachmann R & Zaheer A (eds), *Handbook of Trust Research* (Edward Elgar: Cheltenham, 2006).
Beckert J, *Imagined Futures: Fictional Expectations and Capitalist Dynamics* (Harvard University Press: Cambridge MA, 2016).
Brown W, *Undoing the Demos: Neoliberalism's Stealth Revolution* (Zone Books: New York, 2015).
Callon M, *The Laws of the Markets* (Blackwell: Oxford, 1998).
Cornish DB & Clarke RVG, *The Reasoning Criminal. Rational Choice Perspectives on Offending* (Springer-Verlag: Berlin, 1986).
Farmer L, "Responsibility, Criminalisation and Political Economy", in Solanke I (ed), *On Crime, Society and Responsibility in the Work of Nicola Lacey* (Oxford University Press: Oxford, 2021).
Farmer L, *Making the Modern Criminal Law: Criminalisation and Civil Order* (Oxford University Press: Oxford, 2016).
Fletcher G, *Basic Concepts in Criminal Law* (Oxford University Press: Oxford, 1998).
Fligstein N, *The Architecture of Markets: An Economic Sociology of Twenty-First-Century Capitalist Societies* (Princeton University Press: Princeton NJ, 2001).
Foucault M, *The Birth of Biopolitics* (Palgrave Macmillan: London, 2008).
Garrett B, *Too Big to Jail: How Prosecutors Compromise with Corporations* (Harvard University Press: Cambridge MA, 2016).
Harcourt B, *The Illusion of Free Markets: Punishment and the Myth of Natural Order* (Harvard University Press: Cambridge MA, 2011).
Hayek F, *Law, Legislation and Liberty* (Routledge: London, 2013 [1973]).
Herzog L, "Introduction", in Herzog L (ed), *Just Financial Markets? Finance in a Just Society* (Oxford University Press: Oxford, 2017).
Jackson T, *Impunity and Capitalism: The Afterlives of European Financial Crises, 1690–1830* (Cambridge University Press: Cambridge, 2022).
Lacey N, *In Search of Criminal Responsibility: Ideas, Institutions and Interests* (Oxford University Press: Oxford, 2017).
Loughnan A, *Self, Others and the State: Relations of Criminal Responsibility* (Cambridge University Press: Cambridge, 2019).
Mackenzie D, *Trading at the Speed of Light* (Princeton University Press: Princeton NJ, 2021).
Mirowski P & Nik-Kah E, *The Knowledge We Have Lost in Information: The History of Information in Modern Economics* (Oxford University Press: Oxford, 2016).
Norrie AW, *Crime, Reason and History: A Critical Introduction to Criminal Law* (Weidenfeld & Nicolson: London, 1st edn, 1992).

Ogus A, "Regulation and its Relation with the Criminal Justice Process", in Quirk H, Seddon T, & Smith G (eds), *Regulation and Criminal Justice: Innovations in Policy and Research* (Cambridge University Press: Cambridge, 2010).

Pareto V, *Manual of Political Economy* (Oxford University Press: Oxford, 2014 [1906]).

Poovey M, "Stories We Tell about Liberal Markets. The Efficient Market Hypothesis and Great-Men Narratives of Change", in Gunn S & Vernon J (eds), *The Peculiarities of Liberal Modernity in Imperial Britain* (University of California Press: Berkeley CA, 2011).

Ryder N, *The Financial Crisis and White Collar Crime: The Perfect Storm?* (Edward Elgar: Cheltenham, 2014).

Shapiro S, *Wayward Capitalists: Targets of the Securities and Exchange Commission* (Yale University Press: New Haven CT, 1984).

Smith A, *The Wealth of Nations* (Penguin: Harmondsworth, 1999 [1776]).

Taylor C, *Modern Social Imaginaries* (Duke University Press: Durham NC, 2004).

Veitch S, *Law and Irresponsibility: On the Legitimation of Human Suffering* (Hart Publishing: Oxford, 2007).

Vogel H, *Financial Market Bubbles and Crashes: Features, Causes and Effects* (Palgrave Macmillan: London, 3rd edn, 2021).

Watson M, *The Market* (Agenda Publishing: Newcastle, 2018).

Williams JW, *Policing the Markets: Inside the Black Box of Securities Enforcement* (Routledge: London, 2012).

Zaloom C, *Out of the Pits: Traders and Technology from Chicago to London* (University of Chicago Press: Chicago, 2006).

Journal articles

Becker G, "Crime and Punishment: An Economic Approach", *Journal of Political Economy*, vol. 76, no. 2 (1968), pp.169–217.

Beckert J, "The Social Order of Markets", *Theory & Society*, vol. 38, no. 245 (2009), pp.245–269.

Bee M & Demarais-Tremblay M, "The Birth of *Homo Oeconomicus*: The Methodological Debate on the Economic Agent from JS Mill to V Pareto", *Journal of the History of Economic Thought*, vol. 45, no. 1 (2023), pp.1–26.

Campbell D, "Note: What is Wrong with Insider Dealing", *Legal Studies*, vol. 16, no. 2 (1996), pp.185–199.

Farmer L, "Taking Market Crime Seriously", *Legal Studies*, vol. 42, no. 3 (2022), pp.508–524.

Fligstein N & Dauter L, "The Sociology of Markets", *Annual Review of Sociology*, vol. 33 (2007), pp.105–128.

Fourcade M & Healy K, "Moral Views of Market Society", *Annual Review Sociology*, vol. 33 (2007), pp.285–311.

Granovetter M, "Economic Action and Social Structure: The Problem of Embeddedness", *American Journal of Sociology*, vol. 91, no. 3 (1985), pp.481–510.

Mill JS, "On the Definition of Political Economy", *London and Westminster Review*, vol. 4, no. 1 (October 1836), pp.1–29.

Persky J, "The Ethology of *Homo Economicus*", *Journal of Economic Perspectives*, vol. 9, no. 2 (1995), pp. 221–231.

Thornhill C, "Guilt and the Origins of Modern Law", *Economy & Society*, vol. 43, no. 103 (2014), pp.103–135.

Encyclopaedia entries

Wheeler G, "Bounded Rationality", in Zalta EN (ed), *Stanford Encyclopedia of Philosophy* (Fall 2020 Edition), available at: www.plato.stanford.edu/archives/fall2020/entries/bounded-rationality/.

17
ELEMENTS OF BLAMEWORTHINESS IN THE LAW OF HOMICIDE
Harmfulness, Wrongness, and Culpability

Stuart P Green

Introduction

The concept of blameworthiness plays a central role in the retributive theory of criminal law, serving both negative and positive functions.[1] It functions negatively in the sense of restraining criminalisation: unless an agent's conduct is blameworthy, it is considered unjust to impose criminal punishment. Blameworthiness also functions positively in the sense of providing a good, if not conclusive, reason *for* criminalisation. But what exactly makes conduct blameworthy? In this chapter, I seek to develop a framework for thinking systematically about that question. In particular, I identify a collection of basic "elements" to which the concept of blameworthiness can be reduced.

The three elements I shall be concerned with are *harmfulness, wrongness,* and *culpability.* All three terms appear widely in the literature of criminal law theory, as does *blameworthiness* itself, but they have often been used inconsistently and without clear definition. What one theorist calls "culpability" another calls "wrongness," and vice versa.[2] Concepts that should be understood as analytically distinct are conflated. One or more key elements are left out. The relationship among the three concepts is insufficiently explained.

Ideally, the kind of framework I wish to construct could be used to analyse the blameworthiness of criminal conduct of all types, including offences as varied as homicide, rape, theft, bribery, drink-driving, indecent exposure, and fishing without a license. But accommodating such a wide range of offences would involve a larger and more complex task than is possible within the limited space of this chapter.

Instead, I shall focus on the ways in which blameworthiness inheres in the conduct that underlies the homicide offences specifically. For three reasons, homicide seems like a good place to start. First, it has a claim to being the most serious of all crimes. Second, it is in a sense a paradigm of criminal offending generally, reflecting the irreversible, non-negotiable, and non-compensable harms and wrongs it entails.[3] Third, homicide law is exceptionally sensitive to variations in blameworthiness. The basic harm that homicide entails—namely, the death of another human being—is invariable. Yet whether and to what extent one who causes such death should be viewed as blameworthy for such conduct will reflect a wide variety of factors, involving a range of possible mental states and justifying or excusing conditions.

Basic elements of blameworthiness

This part describes the three basic moral elements that, I claim, are relevant to whether and how a given act should be deemed morally blameworthy. I make no claim, however, that any of the three elements is a necessary or sufficient condition for attributing moral blame, let alone imposing criminal liability. My goal is simply to offer an account of what these elements mean and how they relate to each other.

Some commentators have sought to describe the moral content of criminal acts with reference to only two, or even just one, of these three elements.[4] In my view, however, such "conceptual parsimony" has led to an "impoverished" discourse.[5] As the discussion below demonstrates, each of the three elements, though interrelated, has its own independent normative significance.

Harmfulness

In the context of criminal law theory, we are used to thinking of harmfulness in connection with the liberal Harm Principle, the idea that the criminal law is, in Mill's language, "rightfully exercised" only when intended to prevent harm (or possibly offence) to others (or possibly self).[6] But, in addition to playing a key role in defining the limits of state power in a liberal society, harmfulness also plays a central part in defining the blameworthiness that retributive theory demands before criminal penalties can justly be imposed.[7] More needs to be said, however, about what it means for an act to be "harmful".

Joel Feinberg, in *Harm to Others*, used the term "harm" in two distinct senses, both of which incorporated the concept of "setbacks to interests", in particular, setbacks to welfare interests (such as life, health, and property).[8] Harm in the first sense consisted of setbacks to interest *simpliciter*, without regard to whether the act that caused it was wrongful. For example, if X causes Y's death in a justified use of self-defence, he causes harms to Y in this first sense, even though his act was not wrongful. Indeed, harms in this sense need not even be caused by a human agent. Y's interests can be set back by natural, non-human causes, such as an earthquake, a hurricane, or an attack by a wild animal. In such cases, there is typically no moral agent to blame.[9]

Elsewhere in *Harm to Others*, however, Feinberg also identified a second sense of "harm".

> To say that A has harmed B in this [second] sense is to say much the same thing as that A has wronged B, or treated him unjustly. One person *wrongs* another when his indefensible (unjustifiable and inexcusable) conduct violates the other's right.[10]

Thus, if X had killed Y in the lawful exercise of his right to self-defence, X would not have harmed Y in the second sense of the term, since he would not have wronged him.

Later, in *Harmless Wrongdoing*, Feinberg revised his terminology, abandoning the idea of harming simply as wronging, and instead distinguishing between harms as setbacks-to-interest *simpliciter* (which he refers to as harms$_1$) and harms as setbacks-to-interest that are also wrongful (referred to as harms$_2$).[11] From the limited perspective of criminalisation theory, there is perhaps some reason to define harms in this compound sense.[12] But for purposes of the current project, it makes little sense to do so. After all, the whole point of my project is to reduce blameworthiness to its "basic elements" or "constitutive parts". By combining harms and wrongs into a single concept of "wrongful harms", we lose the ability to do so. In the remainder of this chapter, then, I shall use the term "harm" in the original sense of Feinberg's harm$_1$ – namely, as a setback to interests, and ask separately whether such setback was wrongful.

So, how does harm in this sense inform the concept of blameworthiness? We can say, in general, that the greater the harm caused by X's act, the greater his blameworthiness.[13] For example, all else being equal (that is, holding constant X's intention, motive, and perhaps the probability that his act will cause harm), X will typically deserve more blame for causing V's death than for stealing his bicycle, in part because the first act involves a more significant setback to V's interests than the second (it also involves a more significant wrong, as we shall see below).

There are cases, however, where it may not be so easy to say whether a setback to interest has occurred. For example, imagine that B suffers from a painful and incurable disease, and that A is her nurse. If A administers B a lethal dose of morphine, causing her death, has A caused B harm? In such a case, there might well be an argument that, given the desperate state of her health, B was in fact "better off dead", and that she therefore did not suffer any setback to interests. If so, we should conclude that B was not harmed.

Wrongness

Wrongness, as I shall use the term here, refers to the fact that a given actor's conduct: (1) infringes or violates another's moral (or legal) rights; or (2) contravenes a free-standing moral (or legal) principle. Key to understanding the concept of wrongness is a basic distinction between acts that are wrongful "*pro tanto*" and those that are wrongful "all-things-considered". To say that an act is *pro tanto* wrongful is to say that it is wrong only provisionally. Although its violation of some right or principle contributes to its wrongness, further analysis is needed to determine its overall wrongness. To say, by contrast, that an act is wrong all-things-considered is to say that it is wrong conclusively, without consideration of any further factors. In determining whether the act is wrong all-things-considered, we will have to ask if its *pro tanto* wrongness is outweighed or overridden by other factors that indicate the rightness of the act.

An analogous way to conceive of the distinction between *pro tanto* and all-things-considered wrongness is in terms of the distinction, originally made by Judith Thomson, between "infringing" a right and "violating" a right.[14] As Thomson explains, conduct that is opposed to another's right infringes it, while conduct that is also wrong violates it. Thus, imagine that A has killed B. As an initial matter, we can say that B has had his right to life *infringed*. And if we further determined that A's act was unjustified and unexcused, and that B's right to life was therefore *violated*, we should conclude that A was acting wrongly all-things-considered. But if it turns out that A was justified in killing B—say, because A was defending himself or a third party from an unprovoked attack from B—then we should conclude that B did not have his right to life violated and that A's act was not all-things-considered wrong.

In the case of justified self-defence, the distinction between *pro tanto* and all-things-considered wrongness is relatively straightforward (though determining whether the defensive act really *was* justified may not be straightforward at all). But what about cases of arguably justified killing where B was not an aggressor and A's act was not defensive? Suppose that, as in the "typical" lifeboat or trolley case, *A* causes the death of *innocent B* to save the lives of innocents *C, D,* and *E*. Here, it is obvious that *B*'s right to life has been infringed. But has it also been violated? From a deontological perspective, it is hard to see how it has not been. On the other hand, it may seem strange to say that *A*'s conduct was *wrongful*, since he did what was, from a consequentialist perspective, arguably, the "right thing". So, here is a case where we cannot say whether a given act should be viewed as all-things-considered wrongful without reference to a deeper theory of what makes acts wrongful in the first place (a task that is obviously beyond the scope of the current project).

What about where *A* has caused *B*'s death with *B*'s prescriptively valid *consent*? Here again, we can say that *A* has committed a *pro tanto* wrong and infringed *B*'s right to life. It seems doubtful, however, that *A* has *violated* *B*'s right. That is because consensual harms are normally viewed as non-wrongful, a concept that finds its most famous expression in the common law maxim of *volenti non fit injuria*.[15] Thus, where *A* has *B*'s valid consent to the infliction of some harm, I think we can ordinarily say that *A*'s act was not wrongful all-things-considered.

Difficult questions concerning wrongness also arise in the context of *duress*. Imagine, for example, that *A* killed *B* because he was threatened by *C* with death unless he did so. *A*'s act would still be wrongful *pro tanto*, but would it properly be considered wrongful all-things-considered? Would *A* have violated *B*'s rights, or would he merely have infringed them? There is a debate in the literature over how we should understand the moral status of acts committed under duress. A few commentators (a minority) maintain that such acts (including, presumably, homicide[16]) should be understood, all things considered, as justified, and therefore non-wrongful.[17] Most scholars, though, maintain that duress is merely an excuse and does not override *A*'s reasons not to act, suggesting that *A*'s act remains wrongful (though the fact that he was under duress may negate or minimise his *culpability*, as discussed below).[18]

Now imagine a case in which *A*, while driving lawfully and with all appropriate care, hits and kills a pedestrian crossing the street (we can assume that the pedestrian was also without fault; it was truly a freak accident). The pedestrian suffers harm and, I would say, his rights have not merely been infringed, but also violated. Does that mean that *A*'s act was wrongful? I believe it does. The fact that *A* was not even reckless or negligent with respect to the pedestrian does not change that (though, as we'll see below, the fact that *A* lacked *mens rea* will again negate his *culpability*).

There is, of course, a great deal more that could be said about the concept of wrongness, but space constraints allow only a few brief additional points. First, killing is obviously only one of innumerable ways in which *A* can wrong another. While it is hardly possible to identify every type of wrongness here, it is worth noting that certain kinds of wrongness are so familiar and archetypical that we have specific labels for them. For example, we can talk about *A*'s doing a wrong to *B* by lying, cheating, stealing, coercing, exploiting, breaking a promise, or being disloyal.

Second, as in the case of harms, it is possible to rank wrongs in terms of seriousness. For example, *X* will typically deserve more blame for the wrong involved in taking *V*'s (innocent) life than for the wrong involved in stealing his bicycle.

Third, though the two concepts are analytically distinct on my account, wrongness is largely derivative of harmfulness. One of the clearest ways to violate another's rights is to subject him to an unwarranted or unjust harm, such as death, injury, or loss of property.

Fourth, although much wrongful conduct is also harmful, not all is. For example, subjecting others to racial epithets or the unconsented-to sight of public sex may well cause them offense, but typically not a setback to interests, and therefore not harm.

Fifth, there are also wrongful acts that do not involve a violation of rights. Consider the act of being rude, which consists of failing to treat other people with the basic respect that they deserve. Robert Audi gives the example of a man with a heavy sweater who wrongs his friend by not lending him his coat when both are caught in a freezing hotel lobby.[19] The man seems to have acted wrongfully even though his friend did not have a "right" to the loan of the coat.

Finally, there are cases in which the wrongness of an actor's conduct derives, to some degree, from the fact that he violated a legal prohibition. This is a kind of wrongness that plays a key role in defining an important class of criminal offences loosely known as *mala prohibita*, but it is of only marginal importance in the context of homicide law.

Culpability

To say that a moral agent is *culpable*, on my account, is to say that he is properly held responsible for some morally bad act. That his *act*, in turn, is culpable means that it was performed by an agent who is properly held responsible (for its badness). The concept of culpability is thus essentially one of attribution. Culpability is central to the concept of blameworthiness because it is the part that is most directly relevant to the concepts of choice and agency.[20]

On my account, such culpability can be understood as requiring that three basic conditions be met: (1) that the act was performed with a mental element such as purpose, knowledge, recklessness, or perhaps negligence; (2) that the actor was mentally and physically competent to perform the act; and (3) that the act performed was itself bad or wrongful.[21]

Let us look first at the subjective mental element requirement. To determine if X was culpable in the case of result crimes such as homicide, we will want to ask if X intended to achieve the prohibited result, knew that it was likely to occur, was aware of the risk that it would occur, or should have been aware of such a risk. Thus, a driver who, when driving lawfully and with all appropriate care, hits and kills a pedestrian who is crossing the street has not performed a culpable act, since the act was not performed with the required mental element.

The kinds of mental elements that appear in criminal offence definitions are often arrayed along a continuum of seriousness, under which, *ceteris paribus*, intentional crimes are viewed as more serious than reckless crimes, reckless crimes as more serious than negligent crimes, and so forth.[22] This is true generally in the case of homicide. There are also offences, which we call strict liability crimes, that require no proof that they were performed with a particular mental state. As such, these offenses do not require a showing of culpability.

Some commentators have used the term "culpability" to refer exclusively to such mental elements. The Model Penal Code, for example, uses the term in its "elemental" sense to refer to purpose, knowledge, recklessness, and negligence.[23] In previous work, I also used culpability in this limited sense.[24] I now believe that culpability should be understood as a more complex concept than previously acknowledged. Beyond the mental element, it reflects at least two (and possibly three) additional factors.

The first of these factors is that X had the mental and physical capacity to act freely and responsibly. A person who is deemed to be insane, for example, is not properly considered culpable for his acts, even if such acts were intentional or knowing. The same could be said when the actor is a young child.

The second component of culpability is that the act performed by *X* be wrongful. Indeed, it is nonsensical, linguistically, to say that a person is "culpable" for performing a good or morally neutral act. Moreover, unlike intention and knowledge, the mental elements of recklessness and negligence (assuming that negligence is even properly considered a mental element[25]) have badness already "baked in".[26] There is thus a sense in which the concept of culpability is dependent on, or derivative of, the concept of wrongness, just as wrongness itself is often derivative of harmfulness.

There is also another aspect of blameworthiness that deserves mention here, though there is hardly room to discuss it in detail—and that is motive.[27] There are three contexts in which motive might play a role in defining blameworthiness, or the lack of it. One is where a person does the "right thing" but for the "wrong reason" (think of Kant's shopkeeper, who passes up the chance to shortchange a customer only because he worries it would hurt his business).[28] Although interesting from a moral perspective, it seems doubtful that this is the sort of blame that is relevant to attributions of criminal liability. A second context in which motive plays a role in defining blameworthiness (or lack thereof) is where a person does the "wrong thing" for the "right reason" (think of the person who steals bread to feed his family, or perhaps the sailor who kills one shipmate in order to save three others).[29] Here, motive plays a potentially exculpatory role, and certainly could be relevant to judgements of criminal liability. Third, are cases in which a person does the wrong thing for a *particularly bad* reason (think of the person who kills to further terroristic or racist ends).[30] Here, motive has the potential to aggravate blameworthiness.

This raises an interesting question: How exactly does motive fit into the tripartite framework I have been sketching? Are motives relevant to an act's harmfulness, to its wrongness, to its culpability, or to some combination of the three? Imagine three cases in which *A* kills *B*. In case 1, he is motivated by racism or antisemitism. In case 2, he is motivated by his benevolent desire to alleviate what he perceives, incorrectly, as *B*'s suffering. In case 3, *A* has neither a particularly bad motive nor a particularly good one. In all three cases, the harm to *B* is basically the same: *B* loses his life. The wrong to *B* is roughly the same as well: *B*'s right to life is violated. If there is a difference in blameworthiness among the three cases, it is likely in the realm of culpability. Just as it is more culpable for *A* to kill *B* intentionally than recklessly, I think we can say that it is more culpable for *A* to kill *B* with a bad motive than with a good one (whether and how the criminal law ought to take account of such distinctions, though, raise different questions).

We also need to consider the role that culpability plays in defining defences. In my discussion of wrongness above, I argued that, if *A* caused *B*'s death with *B*'s prescriptively valid consent, *A* has not violated *B*'s rights, and normally has not done an all-things-considered wrongful act. And because the act was not wrongful, it also should not be viewed as culpable, since, on my account, wrongness is an essential component of culpability.

What about cases of necessity? Imagine that *A, B, C, D,* and *E* are stranded at sea on a lifeboat that is large enough to hold only four of them, and *A* intentionally kills innocent *B* to save the others (who are also innocent).[31] As suggested above, there are debates about whether *A*'s act should be regarded as morally wrongful, reflecting deeper debates about consequentialist vs. deontological ethics. Although *B*'s rights were clearly violated, *A* might nevertheless have done the right thing in killing him. We cannot say for sure whether *A*'s act was culpable until we settle on what properly counts as wrongness.

Finally, what if *A* kills innocent *B* under threat that he himself will be killed unless he does so? As indicated above in the discussion of wrongness, I believe that *A*'s act *should* be regarded as wrongful all-things-considered. But there is an argument that *A* should nevertheless be relieved of liability. Explaining exactly why this is so, however, is a complicated matter. Perhaps the best that can be said for now is not that *A*'s act in killing *B* is not wrongful or harmful, but simply that it seems somehow too much, under the circumstances, to expect *A* to defy the threat and allow himself to be killed. Hence, the understanding that the criminal law defence of duress constitutes a "concession to human frailty".[32]

Interrelationship of harmfulness, wrongness, and culpability

Having considered the concepts of harmfulness, wrongness, and culpability in isolation, we now need to examine their interrelationship. We need to ask which of these elements can exist in the absence of the others: we need to consider if harmfulness can exist without wrongness, wrongness without harmfulness, harmfulness without culpability, culpability without harmfulness, culpability without wrongness, or wrongness without culpability.

Relation between harmfulness and wrongness

As we saw above, part of the difficulty in sorting out the relation between harmfulness and wrongness arises from ambiguities in how the terms have been used, including the dual distinctions between harms$_1$ and harms$_2$ (in Feinberg's idiom) and wrongs *pro tanto* and wrongs all-things-considered. If my attempt in the previous part to clarify these concepts was at all successful, the task here should be a bit easier.

Harmfulness without wrongness

Can an act entail harms without being wrongful? Consider, again, the case in which an aggressor is killed by a defender acting in self-defence. It seems clear that such an act does entail harm$_1$, since the aggressor's interest in life has obviously been set back. We can also say that the defender's act was wrong *pro tanto* in the sense that it infringed the aggressor's right to life. The act does not, however, count as wrongful all-things-considered, since it was not wrong conclusively: the defender had a lawful right of self-defence.

An act can also entail harms$_1$ without being even *pro tanto* wrongful. Consider a case in which *A* and *B* have competing businesses (say, they both own pizza parlours on the same block). And let us imagine that *A*'s product and service are so much better than *B*'s, his prices so much lower, and his marketing so much more effective that *B* is driven out of business. *B* has obviously been harmed: his interests have been set back, and *A* was largely the cause. But, given that *A* has used legitimate business methods to achieve his success, I think we should say that *B* has not been wronged, even in the *pro tanto* sense of the term (unless perhaps one is a Marxist and is opposed in principle to a competitive market economy). Thus, we can conclude that an act can be harmful$_1$ without being wrongful in either the *pro tanto* or all-things-considered senses of the term.

Wrongness without harmfulness

Given that an act can be harmful without being wrongful, does the converse hold true as well? Can an act be wrongful without being harmful?

The answer, I think, is yes, though such cases are not easy to find. Consider, first, a case in which *A*, without justification or excuse, lies or breaks a promise to *B*. Assume further that *B* was: unaware of the lie or broken promise; was aware of it but did not rely on it; or relied on it but in a manner that turned out, through a fluke, to be to his benefit. In such a case, we should say that there was no actual harm to *B*.

This does not count as a true case of harmless wrongdoing, however. When *A* lied or broke his promise to *B*, he presumably *intended* to cause *B* harm, and he created a *risk* that *B* would be harmed. The fact that, in the event, he did not actually do so, does not make his act harmless in the morally relevant sense we are looking for.

What we are looking for is a case in which *A* does a wrongful act while neither intending harm nor risking it. This is what happens in cases of so-called harmless trespass. If *A* goes onto *B*'s land without his permission, he has violated *B*'s right to exclusive possession and enjoyment of his land. But he has done so in a way that may neither cause, nor be intended to cause, nor even risk, a setback to *B*'s interests.

Trespass constitutes a relatively minor form of wrongdoing, however. Could an act of homicide also be harmlessly wrongful? Possibly. Consider again the case of Nurse *A*, who kills his suffering patient *B*. Imagine that *B* has made clear that, despite the pain she suffers, she wishes to go on living for as long as possible. Yet Nurse *A* believes that *B* is misguided to persist in this manner. In killing *B*, Nurse *A* has done an act that is clearly wrongful: he killed *B* without her consent and therefore violated her right to life. But there is a plausible argument that *A*'s act was neither harmful nor intended to cause harm, insofar as *B*, saved from excruciating pain, was "better off dead than alive". Given such a case, I think we can conclude that even an act of homicide can be wrongful without being harmful.[33]

Relation between harmfulness and culpability

What about the relation between harmfulness and culpability? Can an act be harmful without being culpable, or culpable without being harmful?

Harmfulness without culpability

Recall that, to be culpable, an act must satisfy at least three elements: (1) it must be performed with the mental element of purpose, knowledge, recklessness, or negligence; (2) the actor must be mentally and physically competent; and (3) the act performed must be bad or wrongful. The question now is whether an act can be harmful without satisfying one or more of these conditions.

Surely, it can. Consider, first, a variation of the case involving the actor Alec Baldwin, who in 2021 accidentally shot to death the cinematographer Halyna Hutchins on the set of a film they were making. The act obviously caused harm: Hutchins, an apparently healthy woman in the prime of her life, suffered the ultimate setback to interests. Was Baldwin's act also culpable?

In the actual case, the record is unclear.[34] For the purposes of this analysis, however, let us imagine that, before firing the gun, Baldwin had taken every appropriate caution and acted in accordance with every required safety protocol. Despite his precautions, the fatal shooting still occurred (we can imagine that the gun had been sabotaged by a malicious third party in a manner that made it virtually impossible for Baldwin to detect). In such a case, I think we should say that Baldwin's act was non-culpable insofar as the requisite mental element was absent. Similarly, if Baldwin had acted intentionally but did so while suffering from schizophrenic auditory hallucinations (say, he believed that God had told him to end Hutchins' life), then once again we should conclude that his act was not culpable, despite the fact that it was both harmful (in the sense of setting back Hutchins' interests) and wrongful (in the sense of violating her right to life).

An act can also be harmful without being culpable insofar as the act performed was not wrong or violative of any rights. Recall the case of the pizza shop proprietor *A*, who through legitimate business methods, drove his competitor *B* out of business. *A*'s act was harmful to *B*. It was also intentional and competent, but because it was not even *pro tanto* wrongful, it should not be regarded as culpable. Further, what about where *A* acts in justified self-defence, causing the death of his aggressor? Here, *A*'s act would be *pro tanto* wrongful, but such wrongness would be outweighed or overridden by other factors that indicate its rightness, or at least its non-wrongness. And, because such an act is not all-things-considered wrongful, it also should not be considered culpable.

Culpability without harmfulness

Given that acts can be harmful without being culpable, we need to ask if the converse also holds true, if an act can be culpable without being harmful. The discussion above described a case in which a nurse caused the death of a patient whose physical condition was so bad that he was deemed "better off dead". The act was performed intentionally, the nurse was competent, and the act violated the patient's rights. The nurse's act was therefore clearly culpable (and also wrongful all-things-considered). Yet, under the "better off dead" assumption, the act did not set back the patient's interests; it was therefore not harmful. We can thus conclude that, just as an act can be wrongful without being harmful, it can also be culpable without being harmful.

Relation between culpability and wrongness

In this final section, we consider whether an act can be culpable without being wrongful, or wrongful without being culpable.

Culpability without wrongness

Can an act be culpable without being wrongful? Under the account of culpability offered above, in which wrongness was identified as a component of culpability (along with the agent's competence and his *mens rea*), it would seem to follow that an act *cannot* be culpable unless wrongful. And for purposes of the criminal law, that syllogism should suffice. For example, an act done in the exercise of justified self-defence, though performed intentionally and voluntarily by a competent agent, should, in virtue of its non-wrongfulness, also be regarded as non-culpable.

But perhaps there are some kinds of non-wrongful acts that should still be regarded as culpable. Consider a person who saves another's life or performs some other beneficent act but does so for the "wrong reason" (say, he acts solely, or primarily, out of a desire for monetary reward or community adulation). I think there is a plausible argument that such a person is culpable, and deserves blame, even though his acts do not qualify as wrongful. As

I have noted, however, this sort of motive-derived culpability is not likely to be particularly relevant in the context of the criminal law.

Wrongness without culpability

Finally, we need to consider whether an act can be wrongful without being culpable. For that purpose, imagine that Y is walking innocently down the street, minding his own business, when X jumps out of the bushes and, without justification, shoots at him causing his death. Now consider three variations:

(1) When X_1 shot at Y he was suffering from schizophrenia and obeying the hallucinatory voices he heard in his head telling him that God wanted him to shoot Y.
(2) When X_2 shot at Y, he was doing so under compulsion. A third party, Z, had threatened to kill X_2 unless he killed Y.
(3) When X_3 shot at Y, he was the victim of an elaborate hoax. X_3 was an actor on a movie set. The movie's director and crew had conspired to have him serve as their innocent agent in killing their enemy, Y. X_3 had been told by the director that the next scene required him to jump out of the bushes, aim a prop gun at Y, and pull the trigger. In fact, and unbeknownst to X_3, the gun contained a live cartridge. Moreover, when X_3 shot at Y he was following all the usual safety protocols that apply on movie sets. When he pulled the trigger, he had good reason to believe that the gun was loaded with blanks, not live cartridges, and that his firing the gun would pose no threat to Y's life or body.

In case 1, X_1's mental incapacity relieves him of culpability. However, his act was still all-things-considered wrongful; Y's right to life was not merely infringed, it was also violated. In case 2, X_2 was coerced into killing Y. For the reasons explained above, he should again be relieved of culpability. His act was again wrongful, though; it still violated Y's rights. Finally, in case 3, X_3 lacked the *mens rea* necessary to be culpable; his act of killing Y was neither purposeful, knowing, reckless, nor even negligent. Was his act nevertheless wrongful? Although some commentators may disagree,[35] I think the better view is that even given his lack of *mens rea*, X_3's act remains wrongful.

Conclusion

In this chapter, I have sought to develop a conceptual framework for analysing the underlying blameworthiness of acts prohibited by the criminal law. More work obviously needs to be done to flesh out the basic elements of harmfulness, wrongness, and culpability—on their own, in relation to each other, and with respect to criminal law defences, such as consent, duress, and necessity. The framework would also need to be expanded to account for criminal offences beyond just homicide. My hope is that the foundation I have laid here proves sufficiently sound to make such additional theorising worth pursuing.

Acknowledgements

For helpful comments on an earlier draft, I am grateful to Louise Kennefick and Alex Sarch.

Notes

1. See RA Duff, "Towards a Modest Legal Moralism", *Criminal Law & Philosophy*, Vol. 8 (2014), p.217 at p.229.
2. Cf. L Alexander & KK Ferzan, *Crime and Culpability: A Theory of Criminal Law* (Cambridge University Press: Cambridge, 2009) with AP Simester, *Fundamentals of Criminal Law: Responsibility, Culpability, and Wrongdoing* (Oxford University Press: Oxford, 2021) and AP Simester & A von Hirsch, *Crimes, Harms, and Wrongs: On the Principles of Criminalisation* (Hart Publishing: Oxford, 2011). See also M Berman, "'Blameworthiness' and 'Culpability' Are Not Synonymous: A Sympathetic Amendment to Simester", forthcoming in *Criminal Law and Philosophy*.
3. On such character, see SE Marshall & RA Duff, "Criminalisation and Sharing Wrongs", *Canadian Journal of Law and Jurisprudence*, vol. 11, no. 1 (1998), p.7.
4. See note 2 above.
5. The language is borrowed from A Sarch, "Too Objective for Culpability?", *Criminal Law and Philosophy*, vol. 18, no.1 (2023), pp. 19-44. at text accompanying note 67 (objecting to practice of treating wrongness as "the only relevant normative concept in one's legal moralist view").
6. See JS Mill, *On Liberty* (Cambridge University Press: Cambridge, 2012 [1859]), p.22. See also J Feinberg, *The Moral Limits of the Criminal Law* (Oxford University Press: New York, 1984, 1988, 1989, 1990), vol. I, vol. II, vol. III, vol. IV.
7. See generally J Hampton, "How You Can Be Both a Liberal and a Retributivist", *Arizona Law Review*, vol. 37, no. 1 (1995), p.105. For an attempt to dissociate the harm principle from retributivism, see P Tomlin, "Retributivists! The Harm Principle is Not for You!", *Ethics*, vol. 124, no. 2 (2014), p.272.
8. Feinberg, vol. I, p.37.
9. I put to the side cases in which a person's harms are the result of a mix of human and non-human factors, as where a human agent was responsible for leaving open the gate to the lion's den at the zoo or for using shoddy construction materials in buildings that collapse in an earthquake.
10. Feinberg, vol. I, p.34.
11. Feinberg, vol. IV, xxvii–xxix.
12. For a discussion of such reasons, see RA Duff, "Harms and Wrongs", *Buffalo Criminal Law Review*, vol. 5, no. 1 (2001), p.13.
13. In the interest of space, the discussion here is limited to paradigm cases of homicide in which an actor's conduct causes (and not merely risks) the death of another (rather than self), a state that normally entails a serious (indeed, the ultimate) setback to a person's interests (as opposed to mere offence).
14. See JJ Thomson, "Some Ruminations on Rights", in W Parent (ed), *Rights, Restitution, and Risk* (Harvard University Press: Cambridge MA and London, 1986), at p.51. For a criticism of this approach, to which there is not space to respond here, see J Oberdiek, "Lost in moral space: On the infringing/violating distinction and its place in the theory of rights", *Law and Philosophy*, vol. 23, no. 4 (2004), p.325.
15. "To one who consents, no wrong is done." See generally MM Dempsey, "The *Volenti* Maxim" in A Müller & P Schaber (eds), *The Routledge Handbook of the Ethics of Consent* (Routledge: London, 2018), p.194.
16. The common law traditionally denied a defendant charged with murder the duress defence that was available with respect to other offences, such as theft and trespass. Though it should be noted that both the American Law Institute and the Law Commission of England and Wales have recommended that the no-duress-defence-for-homicide rule be abrogated. See *Model Penal Code* § 2.09; Law Commission for England and Wales, *Murder, Manslaughter, and Infanticide* (Law Com No 304, 2006), at p.116.
17. See, e.g. P Westen & J Magnifico, "The Criminal Defence of Duress: A Justification, Not an Excuse – And Why it Matters", *Buffalo Criminal Law Review*, vol. 6, no. 2 (2003), p.833.
18. See, e.g. K Huigens, "Duress is Not a Justification", *Ohio State Journal of Criminal Law*, vol. 2, no. 1 (2004), p.303. See also M Berman, "The Normative Function of Coercion Claims", *Legal Theory*, vol. 8, no. 1 (2002), p.45.

19. R Audi, "Wrongs within Rights", *Philosophical Issues*, vol. 15, no.1 (2005), p.121 at p.129, cited in A du Bois-Pedain, "The Wrongfulness Constraint in Criminalisation", *Criminal Law and Philosophy*, vol. 8 (2014), p.149 at p.161.
20. See F Stark, *Culpable Carelessness: Recklessness and Negligence in the Criminal Law* (Cambridge University Press: Cambridge 2016), p.142.
21. Another factor that might affect culpability, which will be considered briefly below, is motive.
22. There is a complex literature that seeks to explain the rationale for such a hierarchy. See, e.g. RA Duff, "Two Models of Criminal Fault", *Criminal Law and Philosophy*, vol. 13, no. 4 (2019), p.643.
23. *Model Penal Code* § 2.02 (General Requirements of Culpability).
24. Most recently, in SP Green, *Criminalizing Sex: A Unified Liberal Theory* (Oxford University Press: Oxford 2020), p.41.
25. Some scholars have argued that negligence should not be considered a form of culpability. See, e.g., Alexander & Ferzan, *Crime and Culpability*, pp.69–85.
26. Under the Model Penal Code, for example, both recklessness and negligence are defined in terms of consciously disregarding, or failing to be aware of, a substantial and *unjustifiable* risk, a risk that involves a "gross deviation from the standard of conduct that a law-abiding person would observe in the actor's situation." See MPC 2.02(2)(c) (emphasis added).
27. For commentary on the role, if any, that motive should play in defining crimes generally, see RA Duff, "Principle and Contradiction in the Criminal Law: Motives and Criminal Liability", in RA Duff (ed), *Philosophy and the Criminal Law: Principle and Critique* (Cambridge University Press: Cambridge, 1998), p.156; J Horder, "On the Irrelevance of Motive in Criminal Law" in J Horder (ed), *Oxford Essays in Jurisprudence – Fourth Series* (Oxford University Press: Oxford, 2000), p.173; D Husak, "Motive and Criminal Law" in D Husak, *The Philosophy of Criminal Law: Selected Essays* (Oxford University Press: Oxford, 2010), p. 53.
28. Discussed in M Sandel, *Justice: What's the Right Thing to Do?* (Farrar, Straus & Giroux: New York, 2010), p.212.
29. See M Walzer, "Political Action: The Problem of Dirty Hands", *Philosophy and Public Affairs*, vol. 2, no.2 (1973), p.160.
30. See SP Green, "Motive as an Aggravating Circumstance in the Law of Intentional Homicide", *Loyola of Los Angeles Law Review*, vol. 56, no. 1 (2023), p.173.
31. Presumably, he saves himself as well; though we can change the facts to make A more clearly altruistic; perhaps the boat will hold only *three* people, and after killing B, A then also kills himself.
32. See, e.g. *R v Howe* [1987] A.C. 417, 432 (1987) (opinion of Lord Hailsham).
33. For an analogous case of rape, see J Gardner & S Shute, "The Wrongness of Rape", originally in J Horder (ed), *Oxford Essays in Jurisprudence, 4th Series* (Oxford University Press: Oxford, 2000), p.193, reprinted in J Gardner, *Offences and Defences: Essays in the Philosophy of Criminal Law* (Oxford University Press: Oxford 2007), p.1.
34. In January 2023, Baldwin was charged by New Mexico prosecutors with involuntary manslaughter, which requires a showing of recklessness or negligence. In April 2023, the involuntary manslaughter charges were dropped. At the same time, prosecutors indicated that there could still be a decision to refile charges.
35. See, e.g. Simester, *Fundamentals of Criminal Law*, pp.54–57 (describing a class of "intention-dependent wrongs").

References

Books and book chapters

Alexander L & Ferzan KK, with Morse S, *Crime and Culpability: A Theory of Criminal Law* (Cambridge University Press: Cambridge, 2009).

Dempsey MM, "The *Volenti* Maxim", in Müller A & Schaber P (eds), *The Routledge Handbook of the Ethics of Consent* (Routledge: Abingdon, 2017).

Duff RA, "Principle and Contradiction in the Criminal Law: Motives and Criminal Liability", in Duff RA (ed), *Philosophy and the Criminal Law: Principle and Critique* (Cambridge University Press: Cambridge, 1998).

Feinberg J, *The Moral Limits of the Criminal Law: Harm to Others* (Oxford University Press: New York, 1984), vol I.

Feinberg J, *The Moral Limits of the Criminal Law: Offense to Others* (Oxford University Press: New York, 1988), vol II.

Feinberg J, *The Moral Limits of the Criminal Law: Harm to Self* (Oxford University Press: New York, 1989), vol III.

Feinberg J, *The Moral Limits of the Criminal Law: Harmless Wrongdoing* (Oxford University Press: New York, 1990), vol IV.

Gardner J & Shute S, "The Wrongness of Rape", originally in Horder J (ed), *Oxford Essays in Jurisprudence* (Oxford University Press: Oxford, 4th series, 2000), reprinted in Gardner J, *Offences and Defences: Essays in the Philosophy of Criminal Law* (Oxford University Press: Oxford, 2007).

Green SP, *Criminalizing Sex: A Unified Liberal Theory* (Oxford University Press: New York, 2020).

Horder J, *Excusing Crime* (Oxford University Press: Oxford, 2004).

Mill JS, *On Liberty* (Cambridge University Press: Cambridge, 2012 [1859]).

Sandel M, *Justice: What's the Right Thing to Do?* (Farrar, Straus & Giroux: New York, 2010).

Simester AP, *Fundamentals of Criminal Law: Responsibility, Culpability, and Wrongdoing* (Oxford University Press: Oxford, 2021).

Simester, AP & von Hirsch A, *Crimes, Harms, and Wrongs: On the Principles of Criminalisation* (Hart Publishing: Oxford, 2011).

Stark F, *Culpable Carelessness: Recklessness and Negligence in the Criminal Law* (Cambridge University Press: Cambridge, 2016).

Tadros V, *Wrongs and Crimes* (Oxford University Press: Oxford, 2016).

Thomson JJ, "Some Ruminations on Rights", in Parent W (ed), *Rights, Restitution, and Risk* (Harvard University Press: Cambridge MA and London, 1986).

Journal articles

Audi R, "Wrongs within Rights", *Philosophical Issues*, vol. 15, no. 1 (2005), pp.121–139.

Bayles M, "Character, Purpose and Criminal Responsibility", *Law and Philosophy*, vol. 1, no. 1 (1982), pp.5–20.

Berman M, "The Normative Function of Coercion Claims", *Legal Theory*, vol. 8, no. 1 (2002), pp.45–89.

Cornford A, "Rethinking the Wrongness Constraint on Criminalisation", *Law and Philosophy*, vol. 36 (2017), pp.615–649.

Du Bois-Pedain A, "The Wrongness Constraint in Criminalisation", *Criminal Law and Philosophy*, vol. 8 (2014), pp.149–169.

Duff RA, "Towards a Modest Legal Moralism", *Criminal Law and Philosophy*, vol. 8 (2014), pp.217–235.

Duff RA, "Harms and Wrongs", *Buffalo Criminal Law Review*, vol. 5, no. 1 (2001), pp.13–45.

Duff RA, "Two Models of Criminal Fault", *Criminal Law and Philosophy*, vol. 13 (2019), pp.643–665.

Green SP, "Motive as an Aggravating Circumstance in the Law of Intentional Homicide", *Loyola of Los Angeles Law Review*, vol. 56 (2023), pp.173–183.

Hampton J, "How You Can Be Both a Liberal and a Retributivist", *Arizona Law Review*, vol. 37 (1995), pp.105–116.

Horder J, "On the Irrelevance of Motive in Criminal Law", in Horder J (ed), *Oxford Essays in Jurisprudence* (Oxford University Press: Oxford, 4th Series, 2000).

Huigens K, "Duress is Not a Justification", *Ohio State Journal of Criminal Law*, vol. 2 (2004), pp.303–314.

Husak D, "Motive and Criminal Law", in Husak D (ed), *The Philosophy of Criminal Law: Selected Essays* (Oxford University Press: Oxford, 2010).

Marshall SE & Duff RA, "Criminalization and Sharing Wrongs", *Canadian Journal of Law & Jurisprudence*, vol. 11, no.1 (1998), pp.7–22.

Oberdiek J, "Lost in Moral Space: On the Infringing/Violating Distinct and its Place in the Theory of Rights", *Law and Philosophy*, vol. 23, no. 4 (2004), pp.325–346.

Sarch A, "Too Objective for Culpability?", *Criminal Law and Philosophy*, vol. 18, no.1 (2023), pp.19–44.

Tomlin P, "Retributivists! The Harm Principle is Not for You!", *Ethics*, vol. 124, no. 2 (2014), pp.272–298.

Walzer M, "Political Action: The Problem of Dirty Hands", *Philosophy and Public Affairs*, vol. 2, no. 2 (1973), pp.160–180.

Westen P & Mangiafico J, "The Criminal Defence of Duress: A Justification, Not an Excuse—And Why it Matters", *Buffalo Criminal Law Review*, vol. 6, no. 2 (2003), pp.833–950.

18
CRIMINAL INSANITY AND MENTAL DISORDER
Reconsidering the Relation

Linda Gröning

Introduction

Mental disorders[1] are relevant to legal decisions in different ways. A person's mental disorder may confer legal privileges as well as limitations in self-determination related to paternalistic interventions. In this context, the legal doctrine of criminal insanity is fundamental.[2] This doctrine concerns a defendant's lack of capacity for responsible action and is found in most legal orders.[3] It defines the justifiable use of punishment, steers decisions about compulsory treatment, and is one of the most controversial legal constructs in the legal discourse today.[4]

A key challenge concerns how the doctrine of criminal insanity within current criminal justice systems is associated with psychiatric constructs and categorisations of mental disorders. While based on normative ideas of agency and its limitations, today forensic psychiatry informs much of the doctrine's practical legal meaning. Psychiatric diagnoses and symptoms of severe mental disorders are commonly utilised by judges and jurors, as premises for judgements about who is criminally accountable and who is not. A significant number of those acquitted by reason of insanity are diagnosed with schizophrenia,[5] and psychosis symptoms such as delusions are considered legally relevant.[6] Being "psychotic" is even deemed central to a common Western idea of criminal insanity.[7] The challenge is that there is a mismatch between the law's normative starting points, and the practical legal relevance of psychiatric and diagnostic constructs. This mismatch produces confusion about the law's meaning, results in unequal legal treatment of offenders with mental disorders, and generally concerns the rights of people with mental disorders and disabilities.[8]

There are, however, different legal approaches to the relevance of mental disorders for criminal accountability. Following the Anglo-American paradigm, most countries have modelled their criminal insanity doctrines on a "mixed model". Such a model requires both a specific condition, i.e. a mental disorder, and that this disorder influenced the commission of the crime, where the latter typically involves impairments in the capacity to understand and/or to control one's actions.[9] Norwegian law provides an interesting challenge to this paradigm, as it identifies criminal insanity exclusively with a specific condition, i.e. a sufficiently serious state of mental disorder, disregarding how it influenced the crime.[10]

With Norwegian law as a backdrop, this chapter will discuss, and revisit, the current association between legal concepts of criminal insanity and psychiatric notions of mental disorders. The chapter will be structured as follows. First, some starting points about criminal insanity will be presented. Thereafter, the key characteristics of the Norwegian criminal insanity doctrine will be outlined. On this basis, the next section will seek to rationalise the "Norwegian model", i.e. to justify why an acquittal by reason of criminal insanity should not require that defendant's mental disorder influenced their commission of the crime. A key argument, however, is that legal definitions, evaluations, and judgments of criminal insanity should not be determined by psychiatric constructs. This chapter will thus further propose that we should move beyond current Norwegian law, and better concretise *legally* which functional impairments are relevant for criminal unaccountability. Finally, some brief concluding remarks are provided.

Starting points

An important starting point for further discussion is that criminal insanity is a legal doctrine that is normatively and socially constructed for certain criminal law purposes. Thus, while this doctrine today relates to discussions in several disciplines, most obviously in philosophy and mental health,[11] it has a specific legal rationale. In brief, it identifies those defendants whom it seems unfair to blame for their unlawful acts, because of their mental state at the time of the act. In this regard, all versions of the insanity doctrine reflect a fundamental principle of justice: not all offenders deserve to be blamed and punished.

The insanity doctrine is conceptually related to the basic principle of fault that "only those who could and should have acted differently should be blamed and held criminally responsible". This principle tells us that criminal law is focused on *acts* and *culpability* and finds support in the rule of law.[12] Therefore, the insanity doctrine identifies those who cannot reasonably be understood as accountable for their actions, because these actions cannot be attributed to the individual as a rational, responsible agent. It is thus primarily impairments in practical rationality that are considered relevant to criminal insanity, and specifically in capacities of recognising and responding to reasons for actions (provided by legal and moral norms).[13] If these capacities are sufficiently impaired in a defendant, it makes sense to say that "it wasn't their fault, they couldn't help it".

From such a fault-based perspective, criminal insanity is most adequately considered an *excuse* in the doctrinal structure of the criminal law. An acquittal by reason of insanity requires first that someone has committed a criminalised act, i.e. has acted in violation of the criminal law (*actus reus*) with the prescribed *mens rea*, and second that there is no justification that should make the act lawful (such as necessity). When someone is acquitted by reason of insanity, it is because they should not be blamed *even though they have committed a crime that cannot be justified*.

Through the principle of fault, criminal accountability is ultimately preconditioned in the individual's moral responsibility for their act. This moral dimension of accountability concerns the individual's ability to understand and respect the justifications and preconditions that inform the penal code, and in turn to use these insights as a guide for action. In this sense, accountability is a matter of the individual's ability to be responsible for acting in permissible ways and in accordance with the norms communicated by the penal code. Criminal law is based on the premise that legal adults possess this capacity and that they may, for this reason, be held accountable for their acts.

Criminal law's precondition of individuals as responsible agents is informed by a range of assumptions which ultimately boil down to a metaphysical rationale stating that humans have the capacity for *freedom* and *reason* in thought and action (a rationale that is clearly reflected in above-mentioned paradigmatic Anglo-American standards concerning the individual's ability to understand and control their own actions). These two preconditions of freedom and reason are closely interconnected. Accountability presupposes freedom in the fundamental sense that the individual is in control of their body and can act in accordance with their intentions. This premise is, however, not particular to the concept of accountability, but a general precondition for criminal law's conceptualisation of acts, upon which the entire theory of criminal responsibility rests. Freedom must ultimately also be considered in relation to the capacity for reason. Criminal insanity above all concerns impairments in the individual's ability to understand and assess their acts in a given situation.[14]

The law must always transform concepts into concrete and applicable rules and standards. Thus, any system's definitions of criminal insanity must rely on proxies. Young age and immaturity, severe mental disorder and disabilities and consciousness disorders are across jurisdictions considered candidates to impair these capacities, although the specific legal criteria vary. Most countries require, as explained, that the relevant impairments influenced the specific crime, while Norway suggests that such influence is not relevant.

This normative rationale of the criminal insanity doctrine finally entails that there is no evident connection between legal concepts of criminal insanity and psychiatric notions of mental disorder. The current legal paradigm also takes as a clear starting point that having a psychiatric diagnosis is not sufficient for criminal insanity, and as a matter of principle neither is it necessary. It is always the defendant's mental *state* at the time of the act that matters, and "mental disorder" is relevant only in terms of insanity-relevant functional impairments. As explained above, however, psychiatric constructs are of significant practical importance. Norwegian law is interesting here as it seemingly proposes a close connection between law and psychiatry.

The Norwegian approach to criminal insanity

Key characteristics of the model: mental disorder as a criminal insanity proxy

The Norwegian insanity doctrine differs from the insanity doctrines of most countries insofar as it does not operate with any requirement of a causal link between mental disorder and crime. To refer to Michael Moore's distinction between weak and strong relevance of mental disorder for accountability,[15] Norway applies the strong relevance position. In Norway, all that matters is that the defendant was mentally disordered with specified impairments at the time of the act. Whether and how the defendant's condition influenced the commission of the crime is not relevant in the courts' insanity assessment.[16]

The Norwegian approach came to the attention of the wider international audience through the case concerning Anders Behring Breivik, who killed 77 people in Oslo and at Utøya on 22 July 2011.[17] At that time, section 20 of the Norwegian Penal Code equated criminal insanity with being "psychotic". As such, the previous rule was often referred to as a "medical model". This rule required that the defendant while committing the crime was in a mental *state* of psychosis, characterised by severe impairments in reality understanding.

That the defendant had a psychiatric diagnosis, such as schizophrenia, was not sufficient for criminal insanity.[18]

In the aftermath of the Breivik case, a law reform process was initiated, and a new insanity rule came into force on 1 October 2020.[19] In this reform, the criterion "psychotic" was removed and replaced by criteria allowing for more judicial discretion. More specifically, the determination of criminal insanity now requires a *two-step evaluation*. First, it must be considered whether the defendant's condition fulfils one or more of the mental disorder criteria specified in the second paragraph of the rule, where the criterion "severely deviant state of mind" is especially meant to include psychotic states.[20] Second, it must be evaluated whether the defendant was "unaccountable due to" his or her condition, where emphasis shall be given to the "degree of the person's failure in appreciation of reality and functional capacity". This rule thus makes it clear that criminal insanity is not a matter of the defendant's diagnosed mental disorder as such, but of certain legally relevant functional impairments present at the time of the act. Nonetheless, there should be no consideration of how this state of mental disorder influenced the crime.[21] And as before, being psychotic is still centrally relevant for insanity.

In this sense, Norwegian law uses mental disorder as a proxy for criminal insanity, and thus demonstrates a strong association between criminal law and psychiatry. The elements that the courts should emphasise in their evaluations, the degree of failure in reality understanding and functional ability, and how these elements are explained by the legislator, also clearly reflect medical terminology. At the same time there is little *legal* clarification of these impairments, and why and how they matter to criminal unaccountability.[22] As, I will return to below, there is a need to provide precisely such a clarification.

The background and justifications for the Norwegian approach

To identify criminal insanity exclusively with some version of a state of mental disorder has a long tradition in Norwegian law. Already by 1842, the Criminal Code was to a certain extent built upon such a model, and it was fully established in 1929, when the 1902 Penal Code was revised.[23] In the 1902 Penal Code, the relevant legal criterion for criminal insanity was initially "sinnssyk", which translated precisely means "insane". The core of the criterion, however, pointed to those who would have been understood today as being (medically) psychotic.[24] This "sinnssyk" criterion was removed in an amendment in 1997, when the criterion "psychotic" was introduced. This was done to move away from antiquated and potentially stigmatising labels, as the criterion psychotic was considered to reflect adequate medical terminology.[25] This "psychotic" criterion was retained without change in the 2005 Penal Code, until the Breivik case triggered legal reform.

The establishment of the medical model in Norway was largely justified by arguments about *legal certainty* and an *adequate functional division* between the legislature, the courts and the experts.[26] The idea was that questions regarding exemption from punishment should depend as little as possible on the judges' own discretion. Therefore, conditions of criminal insanity should be described and defined by the legislator in terminology that is recognised in psychiatry.[27] In Norwegian criminal law, this focus on legal certainty and the role of the legislator has traditionally been strong.[28] It is also important to note that the Norwegian insanity doctrine – like the doctrines of most other countries – emphasises impairments in understanding and control of action as central for criminal insanity. Being psychotic has been the proxy for insanity because a psychotic person has been assumed to lack the ability of reality understanding and self-regulation needed for practical reasoning. Moreover, the general justifications for identifying criminal insanity (only) with certain serious disorders has been tied to both retributive and preventive aims of punishment. The principle of fault, as introduced above, has here been a central part of the justification for psychosis as a proxy for insanity.[29] In addition, the Norwegian insanity model has been justified by arguments of crime prevention, i.e. that there is no benefit in holding accountable those who are in a severely confused and abnormal state of mind.[30]

Most importantly, however, the establishment of the specific Norwegian model must be understood in the light of the *development of psychiatry* in Norway, and its influence on the legal understanding of insanity. The establishment and early development of the medical model in Norway was accompanied by scientific optimism, and a belief that insanity could be identified by psychiatry, through scientific methods.[31] The influence of psychiatry in law has been particularly evident since the establishment of the criterion "psychotic" that provided a certain "medicalisation" of the insanity problem. Before the law reform in 2020, judges relied, to a significant extent, on the experts. In many insanity cases regarding the criterion "psychotic", the legal verdicts have been justified through clinical and diagnostic evaluations.[32] As in many other countries, paranoid schizophrenia has in recent years been the most frequent diagnosis where experts have concluded that the defendant was psychotic and insane.[33] Although the law reform also radically changed the role of the experts, by limiting their mandate to strictly clinical evaluations, their diagnostic evaluations have continued to influence criminal insanity verdicts. Through the 2020 reform, Norwegian law has in addition opened the door to wide judicial discretion and thus moved away from its original emphasis on legal certainty.

Rationalising the "Norwegian model"

Hence, Norwegian law recognises the paradigmatic idea of practical reasoning as a prerequisite for being a responsible agent in the eyes of criminal law, but at the same time denies a causality requirement. Norwegian law thus seemingly adopts what Michael Moore has called a *status excuse*, where "madness as a status generally excuses those suffering from it for all of their actions."[34] It is true that Norwegian law adopts the strong-relevance approach to mental illness, and in this sense a status excuse. I propose, however, the Norwegian model is not adequately explained by this approach.

First, Moore's status excuse approach may give the impression that Norwegian law does not take into account that symptoms and impairments of a diagnosed mental disorder, unlike the excusing status of infancy, typically fluctuate over time so that the severity of this disorder is not static. However, Norwegian law strongly emphasizes that criminal insanity must be assessed with reference to the *severity of relevant impairments at the time of the crime*. A person with a diagnosis of psychosis disorder may thus be criminally sane at the time of the act, and therefore be punished, and then become severely psychotic in prison (but without relevance for the insanity issue). A person with a severe mental disorder is also principally acknowledged as an agent unless, at a certain time, they have insanity-relevant functional impairments that are understood to be sufficiently severe. This is somewhat different from a pure status excuse that conceptually excludes some individuals from being subject to criminal law. Norwegian law also has different statutory rules for different kinds of agency in different contexts. Thus, criminal insanity at the time of the crime does not rule out that people with severe mental disorder can, for instance, be competent to contract or to make a last testament.

I suggest that the key rationale for the specific Norwegian model lies not at the conceptual but at the practical, epistemological level. As discussed, Norwegian law "solves" the causality problem at a legislative level by assuming that sufficiently serious and legally relevant disorders, when present, *generally* impair practical reasoning. With such an assumption, it recognises that there will always be epistemic (and evidential) insecurity in determining whether and how a mental disorder influenced a crime. The premise is that it is not epistemically possible to isolate one aspect of irrationality (i.e. a particular action) from a person's general mental status (which can then be rational). Therefore, one could argue, Norwegian law does it right to free judges and experts from the very difficult task of evaluating causality, and only attributes the defendant's impaired practical reason to his or her condition *while* committing the crime.

Instead, the Norwegian model suggests that the insecurity about whether the defendant's mental disorder influenced crime should weigh "in favour of the accused". Such an approach may have some principled advantages over the paradigmatic mixed-model approach, because it may better hinder disparate legal treatment of two equally functionally impaired defendants who commit different types of crimes and have different manifestations of their symptoms. It may also be better to help courts single out those who should be considered insane. At the least, the Norwegian approach does not assume that a seriously disordered and functionally impaired individual, whose delusions somehow do not satisfy causality criteria, can commit a crime based on practical reasoning. Nor does it principally allow for an insanity verdict if a crime seemed to be a result of the disorder, where the delusions morally justified the criminal act, even if the defendant's overall functioning *at the time of the act* was good.

It is, however, difficult to assess the quality of an insanity model on a theoretical level alone. Any insanity doctrine operates within a legal system and must be considered in view of its practical implementation, involving the system's functional divisions, the agents involved, its procedural organisation and evidential doctrines. In this regard, Norway is in no way perfect in its regulation of insanity. Although I see some advantages in an insanity model that does not operate with a causal link requirement, I do not defend Norwegian law on insanity as such. On the contrary, there is a need to move beyond the current Norwegian law that, like many other countries, increasingly associates insanity in legal practice with psychiatric constructs.

Moving beyond Norwegian law

The challenging association between legal and psychiatric constructs

The Norwegian insanity doctrine emphasises, as described, an assessment of the severity of impairments in reality understanding and functional capacity at the time of the act, which seems defensible in principle. However, in legal practice these impairments are linked to psychiatric diagnoses and symptoms. Norway has, in this regard, a practice similar to most current criminal justice systems, where the experts typically utilise diagnosis manuals (including the ICD-10/11 and DSM5) as the basis for their evaluation of a defendant's mental state. In Norway, it is to date required from the standard mandate for forensic psychiatrists that they must base their evaluation on diagnosis according to ICD-10. Such a practice is as such defensible, to prevent experts from "diagnosing" someone as mentally ill to justify compulsory measures, without any "objective" basis. The European Court of Human Rights has even stated that it is a violation of human rights not to anchor in "objective medical expertise" legal decisions about preventive compulsory confinement of defendants deemed unaccountable.[35]

The problematic issue, however, is not that the experts utilise diagnostic classifications, but how *legal* judgements rely upon these. From the normative point of view, diagnostic categories are not legally relevant, and are too broad and heterogeneous to guide insanity verdicts (that is most people with schizophrenia are not criminally insane). Still, Norwegian legal practice reveals that the experts' diagnostic conclusions, especially about the presence of a psychosis disorder, are decisive for legal conclusions.[36] Some diagnoses, for example personality disorders, are also formally and explicitly excluded from the Norwegian insanity doctrine.[37]

Of even more direct practical legal relevance than diagnoses are symptoms. More concretely, positive psychosis symptoms are of key relevance in criminal proceedings, delusions in particular. The rationale is then that these symptoms are evidence of the defendant's *legally relevant* functional impairments in reality understanding and functional capacity – as proxies for criminal insanity. However, in current Norwegian law, this link between symptoms and relevant impairments is blurry. Further, symptoms are subject to great variation, and can also present in healthy individuals.[38] It is to a large degree unclear both how the relevant impairments should be defined, and how they relate to psychiatric symptoms. How should we for instance define "impaired reality understanding" in the criminal law context? Should we give it a psychiatric or a legal definition, and in either case, what should that definition be?

In Norwegian law, impaired reality understanding seems to be meant as a matter for psychiatric assessment. Here, impaired reality understanding relates to the core understanding of being psychotic, but psychosis lacks unequivocal defining criteria. The mental health discourse instead includes several different clinical and theoretical perspectives on what it means to be psychotic.[39] This may allow for great clinical discretion, and – in the absence of clear legal definitions – a problematic variation across similar individual cases. In such a situation, there may also be a risk that diagnostic and legal assessments heavily influence each other, so that the experts may reach a diagnostic conclusion of the relevant diagnosis, symptoms and impairments in those cases where they find the accused to be criminally insane. Hence, it seems that, most of all, we need *legal* clarifications to reach a satisfactory criminal insanity doctrine.

The necessity of legal clarifications

I propose that it is possible and desirable to develop a clearer legal explanation of the relevant functional impairments for the criminal insanity doctrine than what Norwegian law – or any other system – currently provides. I argue that we may then take as a point of departure the Norwegian model as an *ideal regulation model*, i.e. a model that defines insanity exclusively as a matter of certain functional impairments being present at the time of the act – but without a causality requirement. Such an ideal model does not require these criteria to be specified in "medical" terms but may utilise an "ordinary language approach". To clarify the content of such a doctrine, we are forced back to considering the relation in law between legal concepts of criminal insanity and medical notions of mental disorder. We must also consider the roles of judges (and jurors) and experts in the assessments and judgements about who is accountable and not – and on what grounds.

Ultimately, in every system, it is the court's task to decide whether accountability has been proven. The court must assess the evidence that has been presented about the perpetrator's mental condition at the time of action, and forensic experts hold a central position in most systems – disregarding the specific content of the insanity doctrine. The more medicalised the insanity doctrine is, the more weight seems to attach to the experts' statements. If, as before in Norwegian law, the criterion for insanity was to be psychotic, then if a perpetrator were to be considered psychotic according to the expert witnesses' assessment, it seems reasonable that the judge would rely in this conclusion in her verdict. However, such a solution may, as discussed, have the consequence that judges' conclusions vary with clinical diagnoses – so that there is not static legal threshold that applies equally to all.

Here a rule that does not use terminology with strict medical references but employs a more general terminology invites more independent legal assessments. This is how the Norwegian rule *is meant to function*. The idea is then that the judge must question the expert witness on their assessments of, e.g. impaired functionality, severity of symptoms, and mental disorders at the time of action, but then the judge must assess whether the perpetrator's condition is so severe as to fulfil the legal standard for unaccountability. Such a rule may thus function as a connector between diagnostic and legal assessments. However, there are, as discussed above, some translation problems with such a division of labour. In fact, these translation problems seem similar to those that could result from a mixed model approach and evaluation of the influence of a disorder on a specific crime.

If we desire a clear and foreseeable rule, it seems that we should emphasise either further medicalisation of the criminal insanity doctrine, or revitalisation of this doctrine as a matter of law. In my view, we should start to engage in legal, empirical and conceptual work to seek clarification of the legal point of view – i.e. what impairments matter to the law and why. After this legal clarification is complete, relevant legal constructs and assumptions may be informed by understandings from mental health or other research about the empirical aspects of the relevant phenomena. Here, transdiagnostic and dimensional studies of mental disorders are of particular interest. Such studies may help to enlighten the complexity of legally relevant diagnoses, symptoms, and impairments, and to evaluate the law's assumptions about mental disorders.[40] On this basis, we may also eventually seek to develop a criminal insanity doctrine that is centred on clearly defined functional impairments, explained in common language, and does not lean upon diagnostic classifications at all.

Concluding remarks

To conclude, there are different ways of implementing similar ideas about who is criminally accountable (and who is not) in legal rules, doctrines, and practices. Across different countries, however, the legal doctrine of criminal insanity has become a hybrid construct, developed in the interplay between criminal law and psychiatry. There are also common challenges concerning how law associates criminal insanity with diagnoses of mental disorders. I have discussed the possibility of developing an alternative approach to the law's association between criminal insanity and mental disorder that emphasises legal clarification of the relevant functional impairments, rather than a further medicalisation of criminal insanity.

To add a final note: such a revisiting of the key doctrine of criminal law should, in my view, also involve reconsidering the label "criminal insanity". This label is commonly utilised in Anglo-American discourse, but it does not, to my knowledge, refer to any concrete legal standard in any country working under the Anglo-American legal tradition. Further, many civil law countries, Norway included, are today utilising alternative terms in their legal standards, such as variations of criminal unaccountability. At the same time, the use of the label "criminal insanity" may further increase the problematic nature of the law's reliance upon psychiatric notions of mental disorders. I believe that legal decisions about who is and who isn't "criminally insane" will continue to lean upon psychiatric classifications for a while. Thus, we can at least attempt to leave this label behind in the international research discourse about criminal unaccountability.

Notes

1. Unless otherwise specified, "mental disorder" is used in the paper as a general label for pathologic mental phenomena at different levels of abstraction (e.g. disorders, syndromes, symptoms, and functional impairments).
2. S Yeo, "The Insanity Defense in the Criminal Laws of the Commonwealths of Nations", *Singapore Journal of Legal Studies* (2008), p.241; SJ Morse, "Legal Insanity in the Age of Neuroscience", in S Moratti & D Patterson (eds), *Legal Insanity and the Brain: Science, Law and European Courts* (Hart Publishing: Oxford, 2016), pp.239–276.
3. R Mackay & W Brookbanks (eds), *The Insanity Defense – International and Comparative Perspectives* (Oxford University Press: Oxford, 2022).
4. S Adjorlolo, HCO Chan, & M DeLisi, "Mentally disordered offenders and the law: Research update on the insanity defense, 2004-2019", *International Journal of Law and Psychiatry*, vol. 67 (2019), 101507.
5. LA Callahan et al, "The volume and characteristics of insanity defense pleas: an eight-state study", *Bulletin of American Academy of Psychiatry and Law*, vol. 19, no. 4 (1991), p.377; AG Crocker et al, "The National Trajectory Project of Individuals Found Not Criminally Responsible on Account of Mental Disorder in Canada. Part 2: The People behind the Label", *The Canadian Journal of Psychiatry*, vol. 60, no. 3 (2015), p.106; G Tsimploulis et al, "Schizophrenia and Criminal Responsibility: A Systematic Review", *The Journal of Nervous and Mental Disease*, vol. 206, no. 5 (2018), p.370.
6. CA Skeie & K Rasmussen, "Assessment of causal associations between illness and criminal acts in those who are acquitted by reason of insanity", *Tidsskrift for den Norske legeforening*, vol. 135, no. 4 (2015), p.327; KE Bloch, "Untangling Right from Wrong in Insanity Law: Of Dogs, Wolves & God", *Hastings Law Journal*, vol. 73, no. 4 (2022), p.947.
7. MS Moore, "The Quest for a Responsible Responsibility Test: Norwegian Insanity Law After Breivik", *Criminal Law, Philosophy*, vol. 9 (2015), p.645.
8. See UN Doc A/HRC/10/48; T Minkowitz, "Rethinking criminal responsibility from a critical disability perspective: The abolition of insanity/incapacity acquittals and unfitness to plead, and beyond", *Griffith Law Review*, no. 23 (2014), p.434; PM Gooding & T Bennett, "The Abolition of the Insanity Defense in Sweden and the United Nations Convention on the Rights of Persons With Disabilities: Human Rights Brinksmanship or Evidence It Won't Work?", *New Criminal Law Review*, vol. 21, no. 1 (2018), p.141.
9. Mackay & Brookbanks, *The Insanity Defense*.
10. L Gröning, "Criminal insanity in Norwegian Law", in Mackay & Brookbanks, *The Insanity Defense*, pp. 295–315.
11. L Gröning et al, "Remodelling criminal insanity: Exploring philosophical, legal, and medical premises of the medical premises of the medical model used in Norwegian law", *International Journal of Law and Psychiatry*, vol. 81 (2022), 101776.
12. See also L. Gröning, "Regulating Criminal Unaccountability - From Concepts to Defensible Legal Standards", *Bergen Journal of Criminal Law & Criminal Justice*, vol. 12, no. 1 (2015), pp. 1–31.
13. See inter alia, DO Brink, "Situationism, responsibility, and fair opportunity", *Social Philosophy and Policy*, vol. 30, no. 1-2 (2013), p.121; SJ Morse, "Rationality and responsibility", *Southern Californian Law Review*, vol. 74, no.1 (2000), p.251; Morse, *Legal insanity in the age of neuroscience*.

14 Cf. SJ Morse, "Mental Disorder and Criminal Law", *Journal of Criminal Law and Criminology*, vol. 101, no. 3 (2011), p.885.
15 Moore, "The Quest for a Responsible Responsibility Test".
16 L Gröning, "Has Norway abandoned its medical model? Thoughts about the criminal insanity law reform post 22 July", *Criminal Law Review*, no. 3 (2021), pp. 191–202; Gröning, *Criminal Insanity in Norwegian Law*.
17 The final judgment of Anders Behring Breivik in the 22 July-case: TOSLO-2011-188627-24- RG-2012-1153, available in English at: https://lovdata.no/info/information_in_english.
18 See further L Gröning, UK Haukvik, & KH Melle, "Criminal Insanity, Psychosis and Impaired Reality Testing in Norwegian Law", *Bergen Journal of Criminal Law & Criminal Justice*, vol. 7, no. 1 (2019), p.27.
19 This statutory rule follows from the penal code section 20, second and third paragraph. An English translation of the penal code is available at: https://lovdata.no.
20 The relevant criteria are listed in section 20 of the Penal Code, second paragraph: (a) a severely deviant state of mind; (b) a severe mental disability; and (c) a severely impaired consciousness. In addition to psychotic states, the criterion in letter a may also include conditions that are equally serious as psychotic states, meausured in relation to how they affect the reality understanding and cognitive functional capacities of the defendant.
21 See also Gröning, "Has Norway abandoned its medical model?", p. 200.
22 For a further discussion about this ambivalence between criminal insanity as a legal and medical construct, see Gröning, "Criminal Insanity in Norwegian Law", pp.312-315.
23 On the historical development of the medical model, see SA Skålevåg, *Utilregnelighet: En historie om rett og medisin* (Pax forlag: Oslo, 2016).
24 The criterion also included intellectual disability of high degree and serious levels of autism spectrum disorders.
25 See L Gröning, "Utilregnelighetsreglenes moderne historie", in *Rett i vest - Festskrift til 50-årsjubileet for jurist-utdanningen ved Universitetet i Bergen* (Fagbokforlaget: Bergen, 2019), p.317.
26 On this matter for a comparative perspective, see L Gröning et al, "Constructing criminal insanity: The roles of legislators, judges and experts in Norway, Sweden and the Netherlands", *New Journal of European Criminal Law*, vol. 11, no. 3 (2020), p.390.
27 See the Preparatory Work regarding the Penal code, Ot.prp. no. 87 (1993–1994), p.28. See also the official Norwegian report, Ministry of Justice and Public Security, "NOU 2014:10 Skyldevne, sakkyndighet og samfunnsvern" (2014), p.91.
28 See L Gröning, J Husabø, & J Jacobsen, *Frihet, Forbrytelse og Straff: En systematisk fremstilling av norsk strafferett* (Fagbokforlaget: Bergen, 2nd edn, 2019), pp.63–65.
29 "NOU 2014:10", p.111. See also Gröning et al., *Frihet, Forbrytelse og Straff*, pp.485–486.
30 "NOU 2014:10", pp. 85–86. See also L Gröning and GF Rieber Mohn, "NOU 2014:10 – Proposal for New Rules Regarding Criminal Insanity and Related Issues, Norway post-22 July", *Bergen Journal of Criminal Law and Criminal Justice*, vol. 3, no. 1 (2015), p.109.
31 See Skålevåg, *Utilregnelighet*, pp.128–129.
32 See further Gröning et al, "Criminal Insanity, Psychosis and Impaired Reality Testing in Norwegian Law".
33 See the annual reports from the Norwegian Board of Forensic Medicine available at: https://sivilrett.no/arsmeldinger.339263.no.html.
34 Moore, "The Quest for a Responsible Responsibility Test", p.681.
35 *Denis and Ivrine v. Belgium*, Judgment from the European Court of Human Rights 01.06.2021 (appl. no. 62819/17 and 63921/17).
36 See for an overview, Gröning et al, "Criminal Insanity, Psychosis and Impaired Reality Testing in Norwegian Law", pp.37–39.
37 The exclusion of personality disorders is explicitly stated in the preparatory work, see Prop. 154 L (2016-2017) pp. 8, 13, 67, 76. This exclusion has also been confirmed by the Supreme court, see Judgment from the Norwegian Supreme Court from 23 June 2023: HR-2023-1243-A, section 39. See also Gröning, "Criminal Insanity in Norwegian Law", pp. 308–309.
38 B Kråkvik et al, "Prevalence of auditory verbal hallucinations in a general population: A group comparison study", *Scandinavian Journal of Psychology*, vol. 56, no. 5 (2015), p.508; MMJ Linszen

et al, "Occurrence and phenomenology of hallucinations in the general population: A large online survey", *Schizophr*, vol. 8 (2022), p. 41.
39 See for a discussion about this matter, Gröning et al, "Criminal Insanity, Psychosis and Impaired Reality Testing in Norwegian Law", pp.27–59.
40 See also Gröning et al, "Remodelling criminal insanity", p.5.

References

Cases and official documents

Norwegian Board of Forensic Medicine, "Annual Reports", available at: www.sivilrett.no/arsmeldinger.339263.no.html.
Ministry of Justice and Public Security, "Prop. 154 L (2016–2017)".
Ministry of Justice and Public Security, *NOU 2014:10 Skyldevne, sakkyndighet og samfunnsvern* (2014).
UN Doc A/HRC/10/48 (UN General Assembly, 2009).
Preparatory work regarding the Penal code, Ot.prp. no. 87 (1993–1994).
Denis and Ivrine v. Belgium, 01.06.2021 (appl. no. 62819/17 and 63921/17).
Judgment of Anders Behring Breivik in the 22 July-case: TOSLO-2011-188627-24- RG-2012-1153, available at: https://lovdata.no/info/information_in_english.
Judgment from the Norwegian Supreme Court 23 June 2023: HR-2023-1243-A, avaliable at https://lovdata.no/dokument/HRSTR/avgjorelse/hr-2023-1243-a.

Books and book chapters

Gröning L, "Utilregnelighetsreglenes moderne historie", in Giertsen J, Reinsertsen Konow B-E, Husabø EJ, & Iversen ØL (eds), *Rett i vest – Festskrift til 50-årsjubileet for jurist-utdanningen ved Universitetet i Bergen* (Fagbokforlaget: Bergen, 2019).
Gröning L, "Criminal Insanity in Norwegian Law", in Mackay R & Brookbanks W (eds), *The Insanity Defense: International and Comparative Perspectives* (Oxford University Press: Oxford, 2022).
Gröning L, Husabø J, & Jacobsen J, *Frihet, Forbrytelse og Straff: En systematisk fremstilling av norsk strafferett* (Fagbokforlaget: Bergen, 2nd edn, 2019).
Mackay R & Brookbanks W (eds), *The Insanity Defense: International and Comparative Perspectives* (Oxford University Press: Oxford, 2022).
Morse SJ, "Legal Insanity in the Age of Neuroscience", in Moratti S & Patterson D (eds), *Legal Insanity and the Brain: Science, Law and European Courts* (Hart Publishing: Oxford, 2016).
Skålevåg SA, *Utilregnelighet: En historie om rett og medisin* (Pax forlag: Oslo, 2016).

Journal articles

Adjorlolo S, Chan HCO, & DeLisi M, "Mentally Disordered Offenders and the Law: Research Update on the Insanity Defense, 2004–2019", *International Journal of Law and Psychiatry*, vol. 67 (2019), 101507, pp.1–11.
Bloch KE, "Untangling Right from Wrong in Insanity Law: Of Dogs, Wolves & God", *Hastings Law Journal*, vol. 73, no. 4 (2022), pp.947–974.
Brink DO, "Situationism, Responsibility, and Fair Opportunity", *Social Philosophy and Policy*, vol. 30, nos. 1–2 (2013), pp. 121–149.
Callahan LA, Steadman HJ, McGreevy MA, & Robbins PC, "The Volume and Characteristics of Insanity Defense Pleas: An Eight-State Study", *Bulletin of American Academy of Psychiatry and Law*, vol. 19, no. 4 (1991), pp. 377–382.
Crocker AG, Nicholls TL, Seto MC, Charette Y, Côté G, & Caulet M, "The National Trajectory Project of Individuals Found Not Criminally Responsible on Account of Mental Disorder in Canada. Part 2: The People behind the Label", *The Canadian Journal of Psychiatry*, vol. 60, no. 3 (2015), pp. 106–116.

Gooding PM & Bennett T, "The Abolition of the Insanity Defense in Sweden and the United Nations Convention on the Rights of Persons With Disabilities: Human Rights Brinksmanship or Evidence It Won't Work?", *New Criminal Law Review*, vol. 21, no. 1 (2018), pp.141–169.

Gröning L, "Tilregnelighet og utilregnelighet: begreper og regler", *Nordisk Tidsskrift for Kriminalvidenskab*, vol. 102, no. 2 (2015), pp.112–148.

Gröning L, "Has Norway Abandoned Its Medical Model? Thoughts About the Criminal Insanity Law Reform Post 22 July", *Criminal Law Review*, vol. 3 (2021), pp.191–202.

Gröning L, "Regulating Criminal Unaccountability – From Concepts to Defensible Legal Standards", *Bergen Journal of Criminal Law & Criminal Justice*, vol. 12 no. 1 (2015), pp.1–31.

Gröning L, Haukvik UK, & Melle KH, "Criminal Insanity, Psychosis and Impaired Reality Testing in Norwegian Law", *Bergen Journal of Criminal Law & Criminal Justice*, vol. 7, no. 1 (2019), pp.27–59.

Gröning L, Haukvik UK, Meynen M, & Radovic S, "Constructing Criminal Insanity: The Roles of Legislators, Judges and Experts in Norway, Sweden and the Netherlands", *New Journal of European Criminal Law*, vol. 11, no. 3 (2020), pp.390–410.

Gröning L, Haukvik UK, Morse SJ, & Radovic S, "Remodelling Criminal Insanity: Exploring Philosophical, Legal, and Medical Premises of the Medical Model Used in Norwegian Law", *International Journal of Law and Psychiatry*, vol. 81 (2022), pp.101776.

Gröning L & Rieber Mohn GF, "NOU 2014:10 – Proposal for New Rules Regarding Criminal Insanity and Related Issues, Norway Post-22 July", *Bergen Journal of Criminal Law & Criminal Justice*, vol. 3, no. 1 (2015), pp. 109–131.

Kråkvik B, Larøi F, Kalhovde AM, Hugdahl K, Kompus K, Salvesen, Stiles TC, & Vedul-Kjelsås E, "Prevalence of Auditory Verbal Hallucinations in a General Population: A Group Comparison Study", *Scandinavian Journal of Psychology*, vol. 56, no. 5 (2015), pp.508–515.

Linszen MMJ, de Boer JN, Schutte MJL, Begemann MJH, de Vries J, Koops S, Blom RE, Bohlken MM, Heringa SM, Dirk Blom J, & Sommer IEC, "Occurrence and Phenomenology of Hallucinations in the General Population: A Large Online Survey", *Schizophrenia (Heidelb)*, vol. 8, no. 41 (2022), pp. 1–41.

Minkowitz T, "Rethinking Criminal Responsibility from a Critical Disability Perspective: The Abolition of Insanity/Incapacity Acquittals and Unfitness to Plead, and Beyond", *Griffith Law Review*, vol. 23 (2014), pp.434–466.

Moore MS, "The Quest for a Responsible Responsibility Test: Norwegian Insanity Law After Breivik", *Criminal Law and Philosophy*, vol. 9 (2015), pp.645–693.

Morse SJ, "Rationality and Responsibility", *Southern California Law Review*, vol. 74 (2000), pp.251–268.

Morse SJ, "Mental Disorder and Criminal Law", *Journal of Criminal Law and Criminology*, vol. 101, no. 3 (2011), pp.885–968.

Skeie CA & Rasmussen K, "Assessment of Causal Associations Between Illness and Criminal Acts in Those Who are Acquitted by Reason of Insanity", *Tidsskrift for den Norske legeforening*, vol. 135, no. 4 (2015), pp.327–330.

Tsimploulis G, Niveau G, Eytan A, Giannakopoulos P, & Sentissi O, "Schizophrenia and Criminal Responsibility: A Systematic Review", *The Journal of Nervous and Mental Disease*, vol. 206, no. 5 (2018), pp. 370–377.

Yeo S, "The Insanity Defense in the Criminal Laws of the Commonwealths of Nations", *Singapore Journal of Legal Studies* (2008), pp.241–263.

19
COMPARING CRIMINAL AND CIVIL RESPONSIBILITY
Contextualising Claims to Distinctiveness

Chloë Kennedy

Introduction

Criminal responsibility is typically thought to be distinctive in some important senses. For example, criminalisation is often described as a measure of last resort, to be used only in relation to conduct which merits punishment and whose prohibition helps further the idiosyncratic aims of criminal law. Yet, as I seek to show in this chapter, maintaining the purported distinctiveness of criminal responsibility, as compared to civil responsibility, is fraught with difficulty. More specifically, I argue that in each of the three areas I examine – the substantive basis for responsibility, the process governing the attribution of responsibility, and the aims and effects[1] of these two forms of responsibility – there is an evident tension between the desire to demarcate the boundary between civil and criminal responsibility clearly and the desire (or at least the tendency) to blur this boundary in practice.

In making this argument, I draw on my work on sexual wrongs and legal responses to them, focusing particularly on the United Kingdom, and I interpret 'responsibility' expansively to include liability to compensation.[2] In fact, I go so far as to discuss the availability of government compensation for (some) criminal injuries without trial via the Criminal Injuries Compensation Scheme (CICS). Though this form of compensation does not depend on the attribution of individual responsibility, it is a form of state responsibility that intersects with criminal and civil responsibility in important ways, so it deserves to be considered. Together, these examples provide timely illustrations of the challenges involved in establishing and maintaining distinctive but complementary spheres of criminal and civil responsibility, including how to decide when criminal and/or civil responsibility is appropriate; the difficulties involved in defining wrongs identically across spheres of responsibility; the 'justice gaps' that emerge when definitions do diverge; and, finally, the complex relationship between the aims and effects of criminal and civil responsibility, particularly in the context of sexual offences where injury, culpability, and wrongdoing are closely bound together. Taken as a whole, these examples show that comparing civil and criminal responsibility, and placing both forms of responsibility into context, provides a nuanced appreciation of the apparent distinctiveness of criminal responsibility *and* the tendency of this distinctiveness to be called into question.

Substantive basis for responsibility

Many contemporary academics and lawyers are concerned with trying to answer the questions of when and why conduct ought to be criminalised and there is now a very large body of literature on the topic. One popular view is that crimes are in some sense public wrongs and torts are in some sense private wrongs.[3] On this view, it might be said that criminal wrongs protect public or collective interests and civil wrongs protect private or individual interests. Yet in the case of interpersonal wrongs – wrongs between persons, rather than against systems, or institutions, for example – it is usually a given that there are individual interests at stake. The real challenge in determining whether criminalisation is justifiable in this context is therefore identifying what makes an interest simultaneously individual and public.

One response to this challenge is to hold that an interest which is simultaneously individual and public is one a society could not allow to be flouted without betraying the values by which it claims to define itself.[4] Assuming interests of this kind could be agreed and identified, however, it is not clear they should all be protected via criminal law, which is typically considered to have graver consequences than other forms of legal regulation. One solution is to stipulate that only sufficiently serious values should qualify,[5] which in liberal democracies would include those deemed sufficiently serious via the relevant political and institutional mechanisms. However, this solution can raise a few difficulties. The first is the phenomenon of "carceral progressivism" by which criminal law emerges as the main way of addressing social problems but, paradoxically, is also recognised to be the source of many social problems.[6] The second is the tokenistic use of criminal law to signal to a society, or some cohort within it, that its concerns are being taken seriously by its politicians. This can result in criminal laws proliferating and some offences becoming doubly criminalised (i.e. punishable by new legislation when they are already punishable by law), possibly at the expense of more meaningful action.[7]

Another response is to ensure that the interpersonal wrongs caught by the criminal law track the wrongs recognised in the civil law, with perhaps more stringent fault requirements. This, it has been argued, would maximise determinacy and ensure consistency in matters such as property ownership.[8] This approach would not necessarily address the problems outlined above, though, and would need to take account of the specific desiderata that typically attach to criminal laws, such as a high degree of prospective clarity. The need for prospective clarity might mean, for example, that it is not appropriate to define crimes with reference to the experiences of, or effects on, *particular* victims, which can be difficult to predict.[9] More generally, public laws, including criminal law, typically focus on the conduct of the defendant and, in contrast to private law, less frequently require injury or loss (even if injuries are sometimes presumed in private law, as I discuss further below).[10] Finally, policy considerations, like public health goals, occupy a different and more prominent place in criminal law, such that consent to the potentially offending conduct does not always play the same role as it does in civil law.[11] Taking account of these factors, it might be that criminal wrongs do not, and should not, address exactly the same conduct as similar civil wrongs.[12] This would not necessarily mean that criminal wrongs would be incapable of generating civil liability but, rather, that the civil law governing interpersonal wrongs might be wider in scope than the criminal.

Turning to civil and criminal wrongs that are, at least theoretically, identical in scope, discrepancies can arise due to the way these wrongs are interpreted and applied in practice. Three recent civil actions for rape in Scotland help illustrate this point. In the first action, the court held that: "whether the act [rape] was to be viewed as criminal or delictual [i.e.

tortious], no material distinction arose in respect of its constituent elements".[13] The second case confirmed this, making clear that the elements of liability should be interpreted in line with the legislation governing the modern law of sexual offences, i.e. the Sexual Offences (Scotland) Act 2009.[14] As defined by the 2009 Act, the offence of rape comprises three elements that must be proved by the prosecution: (i) the intentional or reckless penile penetration of another person's vagina, anus or mouth; (ii) lack of consent to that penetration; and (iii) a lack of reasonable belief in consent on the part of the accused.[15] Given the purported identity of the civil and criminal wrongs, it might be expected that a pursuer suing for rape would need to prove these three elements. Yet in the first of these cases, *DC v DG and DR*, the court left open the possibility that the defender might have avoided civil liability for rape if he held merely an honest belief in consent.[16] Without access to the full case papers it is not clear how or why this possibility emerged. It may simply be a consequence of the parties' pleadings[17] and the fact that there was, at the time, no modern authority concerning the issue of proof of rape in civil proceedings.[18] Certainly, in the two civil rape cases that have followed, *AR v Coxen* and *AB v Diamond*, there is no reference to an honest belief in consent in the case reports.

It is worth noting, however, that according to the most recent version of the CICS, only injuries that are caused intentionally or recklessly are compensable.[19] Depending on how 'recklessly' is interpreted,[20] this means there is potential substantive discord between the criminal wrong, which can be committed negligently, and the eligibility criteria of the CICS, as well as potential discord between the civil wrong and the crime with which it is supposed to correspond.[21] There are other differences between the scope of sexual offences and the injuries compensable under the CICS, too. For example, CICS compensation is only available for "sexual assault to which a person did not in fact consent",[22] but some kinds of sexual activity, such as sexual activity involving children, are criminal even when they are factually consensual.[23] Furthermore, it is not clear whether consent that is obtained in a criminal manner – by deception, for example – would constitute consent 'in fact' and thus be excluded by the scheme. An earlier attempt to obtain compensation for deceptive sexual conduct failed because none of the crimes potentially applicable at the time were held to be crimes of "violence", a condition of the scheme. In particular, bigamy and procuring a woman to have unlawful sexual intercourse by false pretences did not qualify even though the 'married' parties had sex and the deceived woman suffered mental injury.[24] More recently, the UK Ministry of Justice has indicated that it does not plan to expand the CICS to include crimes which cause psychological and emotional trauma but are not "violent" in nature,[25] which invites questions about both the meaning of violence and whether and why the scheme should be limited to these crimes.

As this section has shown, the question of when conduct should constitute both a criminal and civil wrong is not easily answered. Furthermore, where congruent wrongs do exist substantive correspondence is not always maintained. These discrepancies are undesirable simply on the basis that they seem arbitrary, but additional difficulties come to light when some of the other purported differences between civil and criminal responsibility are taken into account. If, as I suggest below, the aims and effects of civil and criminal responsibility are not clearly distinct, then discrepancies in the substance of civil and criminal wrongs can generate potential "justice gaps" – situations where someone wronged finds they lack any, or any appropriate, redress.[26] More specifically, if criminal injuries compensation is the only redress available from a set of functionally comparable remedies (and the fact that criminal injuries compensation is a remedy of last resort means this could be the case),[27] then it matters that the scope of injuries compensable under the scheme is narrower than the scope of criminal and civil wrongs.

Nevertheless, substantive identity between civil and criminal wrongs can cause a separate set of problems. These problems emanate from a sense that there is something undesirable or illegitimate about concurrent civil and criminal liability and with claims for compensation which precede criminal prosecution. This sense of undesirability or illegitimacy, and some counterarguments to it, are considered in the following two sections.

Process for attributing responsibility

Reflecting the sense that there is something undesirable about concurrent liability, in several jurisdictions where congruent, or broadly congruent, wrongs are subject to separate criminal and civil processes, there have been, or are, rules and practices prioritising criminal prosecution over civil suits[28] and other routes to compensation.[29]

To take the latter point first, compensation under the CICS does not depend on a conviction,[30] but failing to report the crime to the police as soon as is reasonably practicable or to co-operate as far as is reasonably practicable in bringing an assailant to justice are grounds for reducing or withholding an award.[31] These requirements, and the two-year limitation period, create particular problems in the case of sexual offences due to the fact that reporting to the police is likely to be 'delayed', and might occur after disclosure to some other party,[32] if it happens at all.[33] Again, the UK Ministry of Justice has indicated that it does not intend to dispense with or amend these criteria, explaining that the proportion of claims rejected for being out of time is small, and that a large proportion of 'late' sexual offence applications are successful (claims officers have some discretion here).[34] While these statistics may be encouraging, they do not take account of the problem of poor knowledge of the scheme[35] or, more importantly for present purposes, the tendency for victims to be advised against applying for compensation, either via civil proceedings or the CICS, for fear that this would prejudice any criminal proceedings.[36]

To be clear, there may be pragmatic reasons to delay bringing a civil or criminal injuries compensation claim until after the resolution of any criminal prosecution. For example, it might be possible to rely on a conviction in subsequent proceedings,[37] and the defendant's right to avoid self-incrimination might create evidentiary difficulties in civil actions that precede a potential criminal trial.[38] But there are downsides (to the victim) in delaying, too, including the fact that waiting for a criminal prosecution to end is not considered an "exceptional circumstance" which might allow a CICS claim beyond the two-year limitation period to proceed.[39] Though these pragmatic considerations are important, they are less significant from the point of view of this chapter than two additional reasons victims are encouraged to delay seeking compensation, which centre on the perceived illegitimacy of prior or parallel compensation claims.

First, it appears still to be the case that victims who raise a civil action or pursue a compensation claim before, or instead of, criminal prosecution are perceived as lying for financial gain. As such, there is evidence that prior or contemporaneous compensation claims are used by defence lawyers in criminal trials to try to undermine the credibility of the complainant.[40] The insinuation, or even accusation, that women are 'gold diggers' has a long history in relation to civil actions brought by women who have suffered sexual or amatory wrongs at the hands of men.[41] Despite its longevity, however, the trope is undermined by both the modest compensation available under the CICS,[42] and the difficulty of enforcing orders for civil damages.[43]

Another reason concurrent liability is seen as illegitimate is the perception that it is unfair for the accused to undergo separate criminal and civil proceedings in respect of the same conduct, particularly when they have been acquitted or a potential prosecution is not commenced or is dropped (as occurred in the Scottish civil rape cases). The arguments offered to support this view include: the accused is effectively tried for the same crime twice; when the civil case is proved this is tantamount to being found guilty via a non-criminal trial;[44] and the defender in a civil trial is not afforded the same rights they would have in criminal proceedings (and if the first two arguments hold the 'denial' of these rights is problematic).[45] In formal legal terms, these arguments may not carry much weight. Yet if, as I suggest below, criminal and civil responsibility are not always clearly differentiated in their aims and effects, then things are more complicated.

Of course, in several jurisdictions, criminal and civil proceedings involve different rules of evidence and different standards of proof, namely beyond reasonable doubt and on the balance of probabilities, respectively.[46] But it is not obvious that this distinction is up to the task of unequivocally distinguishing the two processes, especially when, as I explain below, civil suits are sometimes seen as substitutes for 'successful' criminal prosecutions. There is also evidence that the civil standard of proof is sometimes interpreted differently when the subject matter of the trial is a serious criminal wrong, such as a sexual offence. For example, it has been said, following older authority, that while the "burden [*sic*] of proof" in civil cases is the balance of probabilities, the "more serious the allegation then the greater degree of certainty which is necessary in order for the jury to be satisfied that the case is proved".[47] More recently, the court in *DC v DG and DR* stated that: "the gravity of an allegation might require proof by evidence of particular weight" and "the more grave the allegation… the greater the requirement that the evidence be cogent". In the circumstances of the case before it, the court held that: "in applying the civil standard of proof, the evidence should be carefully examined and scrutinised".[48] Similarly, a year and a half later, it was argued for the defender in *AR v Coxen* that the gravity of the allegation called for evidence of "quality and weight" and that this evidence should be "carefully examined and scrutinised". The judge agreed that the evidence should be scrutinised carefully but added that: "[f]or the avoidance of doubt…the standard of proof is not elevated by the nature of the allegation concerned".[49]

These arguments and judicial comments convey a sense that something more than regular proof on the balance of probabilities is required in civil trials for serious criminal wrongs, and leading texts on evidence law suggest the same.[50] To gain a deeper understanding of why there may be discomfort with applying the regular civil standard, we need to look at the purportedly different aims and effects of civil and criminal law.

Aims and effects of attributing responsibility

The most commonly cited distinction between criminal and civil responsibility is that the former makes the accused vulnerable to punishment whereas the latter merely exposes them to civil liability (often compensation). This difference in consequences is understood to reflect the ostensibly distinct aims of criminal and civil responsibility: while the aims of punishment are retribution, deterrence and censure, compensation aims to restore (albeit imperfectly) the person who has been wronged to their former position. Functionally, things are not so clear-cut, though. As is well-recognised, civil law can exhibit punitive characteristics and pursue 'criminal law' aims. This is most apparent in the case of punitive damages but is also evident in a wider array of civil rules and remedies,[51] which historically has included remedies that it may seem strange (to modern eyes) to describe as punitive, such as marriage.[52]

Thinking about congruent wrongs in particular, there is a sense in which both civil and criminal responsibility express and convey the same message, namely that a person is proved to have engaged in conduct that is criminal and that this merits condemnation.[53] As "Miss M", the pursuer in the case of *AR v Coxen*, put it: "[i]t has taken me five years to get justice, and for society to send Stephen Coxen a message that what he did was wrong."[54] The notion that a civil suit might constitute justice for a crime experienced coheres with research showing that criminal punishment is just one of a range of legal responses which victims consider redress.[55] The civil suit might even be considered redress for the prior failed criminal prosecution when it follows an acquittal or decision not to prosecute. For example, in the most recent Scottish civil case, the pursuer was clear that she "wanted justice and to redress what she believed was her being let down by the criminal court".[56] Even the aims and effects of the CICS overlap functionally with both civil and criminal responsibility, even though an award does not depend on a conviction and the offender does not pay the compensation. This crossover is reflected in the rationales of the scheme, which include acknowledging harm and expressing public sympathy, and the way the scheme has been characterised as contributing towards the state fulfilling its obligations to enforce the criminal law and protect individual rights.[57]

The capacity for criminal compensation to constitute an expression of sympathy is worth considering in more detail because it points to one particularly knotty feature of the compensation/punishment nexus, namely the way that damages for dignitarian or emotional harm – the kind of harms that often arise in sexual offence cases but also elsewhere – blur the line between civil and criminal responsibility in at least three ways. First, punitive damages for particularly culpable wrongdoing can also be conceptualised as compensation for the additional dignitarian or emotional harms this conduct causes.[58] Second, even when emotional or dignitarian damages are given for the underlying wrong, rather than the malice or other culpable attitude that accompanies it (assuming these can easily be separated), the award resembles criminal punishment as theorised by some authors. For example, according to Jean Hampton, punishment serves to remedy the injury to the victim's honour caused by the crime.[59] Finally, where emotional or dignitarian harm is presumed, this places the emphasis on the wrongdoer's conduct, rather than its effects on the victim, and, as noted above, this is a hallmark of criminal law.

Turning back to sexual wrongs, all these complexities can be seen in action. For example, in *BXB v Watch Tower and Bible Trace Society of Pennsylvania*, counsel for the claimant argued that aggravated damages should be awarded for "the violation and humiliation" she had suffered and the "disgraceful way" the defendant had denied the rape.[60] In the judge's view, it did not matter whether this award was characterised as aggravated damages or compensation for the degradation and humiliation suffered.[61] These comments show that aggravated damages, which have an affinity with punitive damages,[62] can be considered as potentially distinct from, but also functionally equivalent to, compensation for emotional or dignitarian harm. Furthermore, civil damages and state compensation for sexual offence victims are available for the wrong, irrespective of any separately proved psychological consequences (though additional compensation for these is available).[63] This implies either that the wrong is compensable *per se* or that the compensable harms are presumed to occur when the wrong is suffered.

I would suggest that the presence of these complexities in sexual offence cases is partly attributable to some of the peculiarities of these crimes as they are now defined and understood. As others have argued, these offences are wrongful in the (unlikely) absence of harm,[64] but dignitarian harms can reliably be predicted to occur when the wrong is experienced.[65] Furthermore, culpability and wrongdoing are not easily separable in the context of these offences. As Findlay Stark has put it, culpability does not necessarily act as a kind of "blaming glue" that binds the defendant to independently wrongful behaviour in these offences; on some views, it is part of what makes the conduct wrongful. In other words, (in)astuteness to lack of consent is not necessarily an additional 'check' on the wrongful conduct (i.e. non-consensual sexual activity) but part of what *makes* this conduct wrongful.[66]

With this in mind, it is perhaps easier to see why concurrent liability for sexual offences is not exactly like concurrent liability for other crimes. In the wake of the Scottish rape suits, one personal injury lawyer asked (rhetorically) why a civil claim for rape following an acquittal should be considered different to a civil claim for serious injury or death when the driver has been acquitted of careless or dangerous driving.[67] The answer, I think, is that injury, culpability and wrong do not come apart in the same way in the case of sexual offences as they do in the context of other crimes. To take the example of death or injury by dangerous driving, it is uncontroversial to say the relevant injury or death was sustained, even if the driver was not committing a culpable wrong when they caused it. It may be that there would be no liability for these outcomes if the driving were completely fault-free but the potential to decouple culpability and injury in this context seems significant. It is also perhaps less clear that such a driver could be said to have wronged any specific individual if they did not cause them injury or death (though they may have committed a crime by engaging in the careless conduct).[68] To my mind, these are important differences and help explain why it is less easy to sustain the purported distinctiveness of criminal responsibility vis-à-vis civil responsibility in sexual offence cases.

Concluding thoughts

In this chapter, I have aimed to offer a succinct account of what I consider to be some of the main points of contention that arise in attempting to distinguish criminal and civil responsibility, with a particular emphasis on sexual offences. The analysis also suggests that this contention, and the challenges to which it gives rise, are products of time and place insofar as ideas about what constitutes a public wrong and decisions about which conduct meets the relevant criteria are dynamic. Furthermore, changes in the expectations placed upon criminal law have ramifications for their interaction with the expectations placed on civil law and indeed other avenues for securing compensation. Attempts to downplay the significance of overlaps between civil and criminal responsibility are not always convincing and, perhaps unsurprisingly, they are especially unconvincing when they depend on the support of other imperfectly differentiated distinctions.

These other purported distinctions and the ways they are hard to sustain are similarly context specific. For example, the decision to sue someone for a sexual offence after, or instead of, their being subject to criminal prosecution must be understood in light of the various ways the criminal justice system does not serve victims of sexual assault well.[69] Likewise, the reality that criminal prosecution, conviction, and punishment remain the forms of justice most commonly desired by victims of sexual offences should be born in mind when evaluating the possibility that civil responsibility, or even a claim for compensation from the government, might be an adequate substitute for criminal responsibility.[70] Allowing civil suits to replace or take priority over criminal trials would both confirm and exacerbate the sense that the criminal justice system is not the right place to pursue these kinds of wrong.[71] It would also potentially enable wealthy offenders to avoid the more burdensome sanctions of the criminal law.[72]

Finally, and perhaps most challengingly, discussions about the relationship between criminal and civil responsibility now take place in a context of increasingly mainstream awareness of the limitations of criminal law and the damage the criminal justice system causes.[73] Perhaps reflecting the paradox of "carceral progressivism" I outlined earlier, sexual offences and the other forms of gender-based violence that have caught the attention of legislators recently have been central to this debate.[74] Though there is no space to consider these developments here, this is new and important terrain on which the purported distinctiveness of criminal responsibility is ripe for scrutiny. The challenge for those decrying the criminal justice system is to show how civil justice or any of the alternatives posited (or not yet imagined) can avoid the challenges that face any project of governance and, if so, how this can be squared with the acknowledged need for accountability.[75]

Acknowledgements

Thanks to Katie Barclay, Dan Carr, Karamvir Chadha, James Chalmers, Matt Dyson, Nikki Godden-Rasul, Arantxa Gutiérrez Raymondova, Eamon Keane, Johnnie MacLeod, and Findlay Stark for feedback on a draft of this chapter. Thanks also to the Durham Centre for Law and Philosophy for hosting a discussion of a draft of this chapter. Finally, thanks to Arlie Loughnan for valuable editorial feedback.

Notes

1. I include aims and effects because both are important to a contextualised understanding of law and how it operates in the world. For an argument against focusing on effects, see K Barker, "Punishment in Private Law – No Such Thing (Any More)", in E Bant et al (eds), *Punishment and Private Law* (Hart Publishing: Oxford and New York, 2021).
2. I have excluded some areas of law that might otherwise be relevant to the discussion, such as civil preventive orders (see, e.g., A Ashworth & L Zedner, "Preventive Orders: A Problem of Undercriminalization?", in RA Duff et al (eds), *The Boundaries of the Criminal Law* (Oxford University Press: Oxford, 2010)) and some concepts that are used in determining criminal and civil responsibility, such as causation, secondary liability, and defences (M Dyson, "Tortious Apples and Criminal Oranges", in M Dyson (ed), *Comparing Tort and Crime: Learning from Across and Within Legal Systems* (Cambridge University Press: Cambridge, 2015)).
3. Dyson, "Tortious Apples", p. 419.
4. RA Duff, "Torts, Crimes and Vindication: Whose Wrong is It?", in M Dyson (ed), *Unravelling Tort and Crime* (Cambridge University Press: Cambridge, 2014).
5. Another formulation is "first order" interests: V Chiao, "Equality, Assurance and Criminalization", *Canadian Journal of Law & Jurisprudence*, vol. 27, no. 1 (2014), p.5.

6 B Levin, "Carceral Progressivism and Animal Victims", in L Gruen & J Marceau, *Carceral Logics: Human Incarceration and Animal Confinement* (Cambridge University Press: Cambridge, 2022).
7 A Tickell, "'We feel your pain': The politics of recognition, fair labelling and the Protection of Workers (Retail and Age-restricted Goods and Services) (Scotland) Act 2021", *Judicial Review* (2022), p.115.
8 R Stevens, "Private Rights and Private Wrongs", in Dyson (ed), *Unravelling Tort and Crime*, p.123.
9 AK Eisenberg, "Criminal Infliction of Emotional Distress", *Michigan Law Review*, vol. 113, no. 5 (2015), p.607.
10 JCP Goldberg & BC Zipursky, *Recognizing Wrongs* (Belknap Press of Harvard University: Cambridge, Massachusetts, 2020), ch.6. See J Oberdiek, "The Wrong in Negligence", *Oxford Journal of Legal Studies*, vol. 41, no. 4 (2021), p.1174 for an argument that the wrong of negligence does not require injury, even if the tort does.
11 KW Simons, "Consent and the Assumption of Risk in Tort and Criminal Law", in Dyson (ed), *Unravelling Tort and Crime*.
12 For some thoughts on how these considerations bear on the criminalisation of deceptive sex, see C Kennedy, "Criminalising Deceptive Sex: Sex, Identity and Recognition", *Legal Studies*, vol. 41, no. 1 (2021), p.91.
13 *DC v DG and DR* 2018 SC 47 at para 267 (to be clear, the words in square brackets are mine).
14 *AR v Coxen* 2018 SLT (Sh Ct) 355 at para 152. Both these points were endorsed in *AB v Diamond* [2022] SC Edin 4 at para 70.
15 Sexual Offences (Scotland) Act 2009, s 1.
16 At paras 1, 271, 339, 342.
17 Despite agreeing that there was no material distinction between the civil and criminal wrongs (para 267), counsel for one of the defenders appears to have suggested that the belief could be reasonable or honest (para 271). As a matter of fact, the judge found that the defenders held neither an honest nor a reasonable belief in consent.
18 Para 268. See also J Blackie, "Interaction of Crime and Delict in Scotland", in Dyson (ed), *Unravelling Tort and Crime*, p. 370. For reflections on the position in English law, see N Godden-Rasul, "Claims in Tort for Rape: A Valuable Remedy or Damaging Strategy?", *King's Law Journal*, vol. 22, no. 2 (2011), p.157.
19 The Criminal Injuries Compensation Scheme (2012), Annex B: Crimes of Violence, para 2. The preceding (2008) scheme did not include this requirement. Both schemes are available here: www.gov.uk/government/publications/criminal-injuries-compensation-scheme-1996-2001-and-2008.
20 H Power, "Towards a Redefinition of the *Mens Rea* of Rape", *Oxford Journal of Legal Studies*, vol. 23, no. 2 (2003), p.379.
21 These are a small number of Scottish cases but the suggestion that the civil and criminal law of sexual assault could justifiably be aligned has been made elsewhere: Simons, "Consent and the Assumption of Risk".
22 CICS (2012), Annex B, para 2. The 2008 scheme also excluded victims who "consented in fact but [were] deemed in law not to have consented" (para 9).
23 Sexual Offences (Scotland) Act 2009, Part 4; Sexual Offences Act 2003, various sections. This fact has led some critics to argue for greater alignment between the criminal law and the scope of the CICS e.g. Smith et al, "The Criminal Injuries Compensation Scheme & Sexual Offences" (2019), available at: https://repository.lboro.ac.uk/articles/report/The_Criminal_Injuries_Compensation_Scheme_and_sexual_offences_Research_briefing/9768158/1/files/17499323.pdf>, pp.17–18; V Baird, "Victims Commissioner 2020/21 Annual Report" (2021), p.31, available at: https://victimscommissioner.org.uk/document/annual-report-of-the-victims-commissioner-2020-to-2021/.
24 *Gray v The Criminal Injuries Compensation Board* 1999 SC 137, appealing decisions made in 1992.
25 Ministry of Justice, "Criminal Injuries Compensation Scheme Review" (2020), paras 64–65, available at: https://consult.justice.gov.uk/digital-communications/criminal-injuries-compensation-scheme-review-2020/.
26 On justice gaps, see C McGlynn & N Westmarland, "Kaleidoscopic Justice: Sexual Violence and Victim-Survivors' Perceptions of Justice", *Social & Legal Studies*, vol. 28, no. 2 (2019), p.179.

27 Baroness Newlove, "Compensation Without Re-Traumatisation: The Victims' Commissioner's Review into Criminal Injuries Compensation" (2019), p.5, available at: https://victimscommissioner.org.uk/document/compensation-without-re-traumatisation-the-victims-commissioners-review-into-criminal-injuries-compensation/.
28 M Dyson, *Explaining Tort and Crime: Legal Development Across Laws and Legal Systems 1850-2020* (Cambridge University Press: Cambridge, 2022), ch.7.
29 I do not discuss criminal compensation orders, which sometimes accompany a conviction, because these are used sparingly and in simple cases of property or pecuniary loss: Dyson, *Explaining Tort and Crime*, pp.300–307; P Cane & J Goudkamp, *Atiyah's Accidents, Compensation and the Law* (Cambridge University Press: Cambridge, 2018), pp.286–287.
30 CICS (2012), para 9.
31 CICS (2012), paras 23, 24.
32 Smith et al, "The Criminal Injuries Compensation Scheme", p.10.
33 Cane & Goudkamp, *Atiyah's Accidents*, p.301.
34 Ministry of Justice, "Review", paras 74, 96.
35 This problem has been exacerbated by one victim successfully suing a victims' charity for failing to advise him properly about aspects of the CICS (*D v Victim Support Scotland* 2018 SLT (Sh Ct) 91). Since this ruling, Victim Support and Rape Crisis Scotland have retracted most of their advice and support relating to the scheme: Newlove, "Compensation Without Re-Traumatisation", pp.14–16; Smith et al, "The Criminal Injuries Compensation Scheme", p.19.
36 Newlove, "Compensation Without Re-Traumatisation", pp.11, 73; A Jay et al (Independent Inquiry into Child Sexual Abuse panel), "Accountability and Reparations: Investigation Report" (2019), p.26, p.70, available at: www.iicsa.org.uk/reports-recommendations/publications/investigation/accountability-reparations; T Lininger, "Is It Wrong to Sue for Rape?", *Duke Law Journal*, vol. 57, no. 6 (2008), p.1557.
37 Dyson, *Explaining Tort and Crime*, ch.8.
38 J Blackie & J Chalmers, "Mixing and Matching in Scottish Delict and Crime", in Dyson (ed) *Comparing Tort and Crime*, pp.279–8; Dyson, "Tortious Apples", p.457; Lininger, "Is it Wrong to Sue for Rape?", p.1579.
39 Ministry of Justice, "Review", para 93.
40 Lininger, "Is it Wrong to Sue for Rape?"; Newlove, "Compensation Without Re-Traumatisation", p.75.
41 See, e.g. S Robertson, "Seduction, Sexual Violence, and Marriage in New York City, 1886-1955", *Law and History Review*, vol. 24, no. 2 (2006), p.331 at p.368; J Hasday, *Intimate Lies and the Law* (Oxford University Press: Oxford, 2019), pp.104–110.
42 The tariff now used values injuries less than civil law compensation: Cane & Goudkamp, *Atiyah's Accidents*, p.297, p.303; Dyson, *Explaining Tort and Crime*, p.307.
43 Scottish Women's Rights Centre, "SWRC Inform: Civil Damages", available at: www.scottishwomensrightscentre.org.uk/resources-guides/1544374244_civil-damages-guide.pdf.
44 Versions of these arguments were made and rejected in the aftermath of two of the Scottish cases: S Waiton, "Do Civil Rape Cases Mark 'Destruction of Justice'?", *Scottish Legal News* (2018), available at: www.scottishlegal.com/articles/dr-stuart-waiton-civil-rape-cases; Scottish Women's Rights Centre and JustRight Scotland, "Civil Cases for Rape are Access to Justice, Not Destruction of Justice" (2018), available at: www.scottishwomensrightscentre.org.uk/files/swrc-and-jrs-response-to-stuart-waiton-article-1.pdf. For a longer discussion, see J Stapleton, "Civil Prosecutions – Part 1: Double Jeopardy and Abuse of Process", *Tort Law Journal*, vol. 7 (1999), p.244 and J Stapleton, "Civil Prosecutions – Part 2: Civil Claims for Killing or Rape" *Torts Law Journal*, vol. 8 (2000), p.15.
45 Cane & Goudkamp, *Atiyah's Accidents*, p.285, noting the argument.
46 This is not the case in all jurisdictions and is a relatively recent development in others. Dyson, "Tortious Apples", p.457; Blackie, "Interaction", p.378.
47 Quoting the judge at first instance but upholding these jury directions: *G v Williams* 1995 WL 1083931 at 8.
48 At paras 272–274.
49 At para 155.
50 J Chalmers et al state that: "the more serious or unusual the allegation made in civil proceedings the more cogent, clear, or careful and precise will be the evidence needed to satisfy the civil standard"

(*Walker and Walker: The Law of Evidence in Scotland* (Bloomsbury Professional: Edinburgh, 5th edn, 2020), para 4.3.1). W Courtney & J Goudkamp write that: "although the standard of proof in the civil law is always the balance of probabilities, that standard is more difficult to meet where serious wrongdoing is alleged" ("Punishment and Private Law", in Bant et al (eds), *Punishment and Private Law*, p.11). Similar comments have been made in childcare cases but the House of Lords has held that the applicable standard of proof is the "balance of probability, neither more nor less". The court acknowledged that there may be civil proceedings whose nature makes it appropriate to apply the criminal standard (so, not an intermediate or more demanding civil standard) but did not include childcare proceedings in this category because they are not intended to punish or deter: *B (Children) (Sexual Abuse: Standard of Proof), Re* [2008] UKHL 35.

51 Courtney & Goudkamp, "Punishment and Private Law"; J Goudkamp & E Katsampouka, "Punitive Damages and the Place of Punishment in Private Law", *Modern Law Review*, vol. 84, no. 6 (2021), p.1257; Goldberg & Zipursky, *Recognizing Wrongs*.
52 M Murray, "Marriage as Punishment", *Columbia Law Review*, vol. 112, no. 1 (2013), p.1.
53 F Stark, "Tort Law, Expression, and Duplicative Wrongs", in PB Miller & J Oberdiek (eds), *Civil Wrongs and Justice in Private Law* (Oxford University Press: Oxford, 2020).
54 S Carrell, "Scottish Civil Court Rules that Acquitted Man Did Rape Student", *The Guardian* (4 October 2018).
55 Jay et al, *Accountability and Reparations*; McGlynn and Westmarland, "Kaleidoscopic Justice".
56 *AB v Diamond* at paras 85–86.
57 Cane & Goudkamp, *Atiyah's Accidents*, ch.12.
58 M O DeGirolami, "Reconstructing Malice in the Law of Punitive Damages", *Journal of Tort Law*, vol. 14, no. 1 (2021), p.193.
59 M Galanter & D Luban, "Poetic Justice: Punitive Damages and Legal Pluralism", *American University Law Review*, vol. 42 (1992), p.1394 at p.1397.
60 [2020] 4 WLR 42 at para 204.
61 Chamberlain J, at para 207.
62 E Descheemaker, "Rationalising Recovery for Emotional Harm in Tort Law", *Law Quarterly Review*, vol. 134 (2018), p.602 at pp.607–608.
63 CICS (2012), Tariff of Injuries, Part B; *AB v Diamond* para 93–94.
64 J Gardner & S Shute, "The Wrongness of Rape", in J Horder (ed), *Oxford Essays in Jurisprudence: Fourth Series* (Oxford University Press: Oxford, 2000).
65 O Kamir, "A Dignitarian Feminist Jurisprudence with Applications to Rape, Sexual Harassment and Honor Codes", in R West & C Bowman, *Research Handbook on Feminist Jurisprudence* (Edward Elgar: Northampton MA, 2019).
66 Stark, "Duplicative Wrongs", p.450.
67 C Kelly, "Rape Survivor Awarded Damages by Civil Court" (2022), available at: www.thorntons-law.co.uk/knowledge/rape-survivor-awarded-damages-by-civil-court.
68 On some views, such a driver has wronged those they endangered. See Oberdiek, "The Wrong in Negligence", pp.1175–1176.
69 Baird, *2020/21 Annual Report*, pp. 12–15.
70 McGlynn & Westmarland, "Kaleidoscopic Justice"; Jay et al, "Accountability and Reparations".
71 Lininger, "Is it Wrong to Sue for Rape?". Although Lininger seems hesitant to endorse the priority of criminal proceedings, he suggests that evidence that a victim contacted a civil attorney before law enforcement and a time lapse between the offence and filing a criminal complaint should militate in favour of allowing victim impeachment (p.1630). Stapleton, "Civil Prosecutions – Part 2".
72 Galanter and Luban, "Poetic Justice", p.1426.
73 ME Kim, "Anti-Carceral Feminism: The Contradictions of Progress and the Possibilities of Counter-Hegemonic Struggle", vol. 35, no. 3 (2020), p.309; D Purnell, *Becoming Abolitionists: Police, Protests, and the Pursuit of Freedom* (Verso: London, New York, 2021).
74 C McGlynn, "Challenging Anti-Carceral Feminism: Criminalisation, Justice and Continuum Thinking", *Women's Studies International Forum*, vol. 93, no. 102614 (2022).
75 C Kennedy, "Crime, Reason and History: A Critical Introduction to Criminal Law", in C Kennedy & L Farmer (eds), *Leading Works in Criminal Law* (Routledge: Abingdon, 2023).

References

Legislation

Sexual Offences (Scotland) Act 2009
Sexual Offences Act 2003

Cases

AB v Diamond [2022] SC Edin 4
AR v Coxen 2018 SLT (Sh Ct) 355
B (Children) (Sexual Abuse: Standard of Proof), Re [2008] UKHL 35
BXB v Watch Tower and Bible Trace Society of Pennsylvania [2020] 4 WLR 42
DC v DG and DR 2018 SC 47
D v Victim Support Scotland 2018 SLT (Sh Ct) 91
Gray v The Criminal Injuries Compensation Board 1999 SC 137
G v Williams 1995 WL 1083931

Books and book chapters

Ashworth A & Zedner L, "Preventive Orders: A Problem of Undercriminalization?", in Duff RA, Farmer F, Marshall SE, Renzo M, & Tadros V (eds), *The Boundaries of the Criminal Law* (Oxford University Press: Oxford, 2010).

Barker K, "Punishment in Private Law – No Such Thing (Any More)", in Bant E, Courtney W, Goudkamp J, & Paterson JM (eds), *Punishment and Private Law* (Hart Publishing: Oxford & New York, 2021).

Blackie J & Chalmers J, "Mixing and Matching in Scottish Delict and Crime", in Dyson M (ed), *Comparing Tort and Crime* (Cambridge University Press: Cambridge, 2015).

Blackie J, "Interaction of Crime and Delict in Scotland", in Dyson M (ed), *Unravelling Tort and Crime* (Cambridge University Press: Cambridge, 2014).

Cane P & Goudkamp J, *Atiyah's Accidents, Compensation and the Law* (Cambridge University Press: Cambridge, 2018).

Chalmers J, Ross ML, & Callander I, *Walker and Walker: The Law of Evidence in Scotland* (Bloomsbury Professional: Edinburgh, 5th edn, 2020).

Courtney W & Goudkamp J, "Punishment and Private Law", in Bant E, Courtney W, Goudkamp J, & Paterson JM (eds), *Punishment and Private Law* (Hart Publishing: Oxford & New York, 2021).

Duff RA, "Torts, Crimes and Vindication: Whose Wrong is It?", in Dyson M (ed), *Unravelling Tort and Crime* (Cambridge University Press: Cambridge, 2014).

Dyson M, "Tortious Apples and Criminal Oranges", in Dyson M (ed), *Comparing Tort and Crime* (Cambridge University Press: Cambridge, 2015).

Dyson M, *Explaining Tort and Crime* (Cambridge University Press: Cambridge, 2022).

Gardner J & Shute S, "The Wrongness of Rape", in Horder J (ed), *Oxford Essays in Jurisprudence: Fourth Series* (Oxford University Press: Oxford, 2000).

Goldberg JCP & Zipursky BC, *Recognizing Wrongs* (Belknap Press of Harvard University: Cambridge, Massachusetts, 2020).

Hasday J, *Intimate Lies and the Law* (Oxford University Press: Oxford, 2019).

Kamir O, "A Dignitarian Feminist Jurisprudence with Applications to Rape, Sexual Harassment and Honor Codes", in West R & Bowman C, *Research Handbook on Feminist Jurisprudence* (Edward Elgar: Northampton MA, 2019).

Kennedy C, "Crime, Reason and History: A Critical Introduction to Criminal Law", in Kennedy C & Farmer L (eds), *Leading Works in Criminal Law* (Routledge: Abingdon, 2023).

Levin B, "Carceral Progressivism and Animal Victims", in Gruen L & Marceau J (eds), *Carceral Logics: Human Incarceration and Animal Confinement* (Cambridge University Press: Cambridge, 2022).

Purnell D, *Becoming Abolitionists: Police, Protests, and the Pursuit of Freedom* (Verso: London & New York, 2021).
Simons KW, "Consent and the Assumption of Risk in Tort and Criminal Law", in Dyson M (ed), *Unravelling Tort and Crime* (Cambridge University Press: Cambridge, 2014).
Stark F, "Tort Law, Expression, and Duplicative Wrongs", in Miller PB & Oberdiek J, *Civil Wrongs and Justice in Private Law* (Oxford University Press: Oxford, 2020).
Stevens R, "Private Rights and Private Wrongs", in Dyson M (ed), *Unravelling Tort and Crime* (Cambridge University Press: Cambridge, 2014).

Journal articles

Chiao V, "Equality, Assurance and Criminalization", *Canadian Journal of Law & Jurisprudence*, vol. 27, no. 1 (2014), pp.5–25.
DeGirolami MO, "Reconstructing Malice in the Law of Punitive Damages", *Journal of Tort Law*, vol. 14, no. 1 (2021), pp.193–240.
Descheemaker E, "Rationalising Recovery for Emotional Harm in Tort Law", *Law Quarterly Review*, vol. 134 (2018), pp.602–626.
Eisenberg AK, "Criminal Infliction of Emotional Distress", *Michigan Law Review*, vol. 113, no. 5 (2015), pp. 607–662.
Galanter M & Luban D, "Poetic Justice: Punitive Damages and Legal Pluralism", *American University Law Review*, vol. 42, no. 4 (1992), pp.1393–1463.
Godden-Rasul N, "Claims in Tort for Rape: A Valuable Remedy or Damaging Strategy?", *King's Law Journal*, vol. 22, no. 2 (2011), pp.157–182.
Goudkamp J & Katsampouka E, "Punitive Damages and the Place of Punishment in Private Law", *Modern Law Review*, vol. 84, no. 6 (2021), pp.1257–1293.
Kennedy C, "Criminalising Deceptive Sex: Sex, Identity and Recognition", *Legal Studies*, vol. 41, no. 1 (2021), pp.91–110.
Kim ME, "Anti-Carceral Feminism: The Contradictions of Progress and the Possibilities of Counter-Hegemonic Struggle", vol. 35, no. 3 (2020), pp.309–326.
Lininger T, "Is It Wrong to Sue for Rape?", *Duke Law Journal*, vol. 57, no. 6 (2008), pp.1557–1640.
McGlynn C & Westmarland N, "Kaleidoscopic Justice: Sexual Violence and Victim-Survivors' Perceptions of Justice", *Social & Legal Studies*, vol. 28, no. 2 (2019), pp.179–201.
McGlynn C, "Challenging Anti-Carceral Feminism: Criminalisation, Justice and Continuum Thinking", *Women's Studies International Forum*, vol. 93, no. 102614 (2022).
Murray M, "Marriage as Punishment", *Columbia Law Review*, vol. 112, no. 1 (2013), pp.1–65.
Oberdiek J, "The Wrong in Negligence", *Oxford Journal of Legal Studies*, vol. 41, no. 4 (2021), pp.1174–1196.
Power H, "Towards a Redefinition of the *Mens Rea* of Rape", *Oxford Journal of Legal Studies*, vol. 23, no. 2 (2003), pp.379–404.
Robertson S, "Seduction, Sexual Violence, and Marriage in New York City, 1886–1955", *Law and History Review*, vol. 24, no. 2 (2006), pp.331–373.
Stapleton J, "Civil Prosecutions – Part 1: Double Jeopardy and Abuse of Process", *Tort Law Journal*, vol. 7 (1999), pp.244–262.
Stapleton J, "Civil Prosecutions – Part 2: Civil Claims for Killing or Rape", *Torts Law Journal*, vol. 8 (2000), pp.15–40.
Tickell A, "'We Feel Your Pain': The Politics of Recognition, Fair Labelling and the Protection of Workers (Retail and Age-restricted Goods and Services) (Scotland) Act 2021", *Juridical Review* (2022), pp.115–123.

Reports and websites

Baird V, *Victims Commissioner 2020/21 Annual Report*, available at: www.victimscommissioner.org.uk/document/annual-report-of-the-victims-commissioner-2020-to-2021/.
Carrell S, "Scottish Civil Court Rules that Acquitted Man Did Rape Student", *The Guardian* (4 Oct 2018).

Jay A, Evans M, Frank I, & Sharpling D (Independent Inquiry into Child Sexual Abuse panel), *Accountability and Reparations: Investigation Report* (2019), available at: www.iicsa.org.uk/reports-recommendations/publications/investigation/accountability-reparations.

Kelly C, "Rape Survivor Awarded Damages by Civil Court", *Thorntons LLP Website* (2022), available at: www.thorntons-law.co.uk/knowledge/rape-survivor-awarded-damages-by-civil-court.

Ministry of Justice, *Criminal Injuries Compensation Scheme Review* (2020), available at: www.consult.justice.gov.uk/digital-communications/criminal-injuries-compensation-scheme-review-2020/.

Newlove, *Compensation Without Re-Traumatisation: The Victims' Commissioner's Review into Criminal Injuries Compensation* (2019), available at: www.victimscommissioner.org.uk/document/compensation-without-re-traumatisation-the-victims-commissioners-review-into-criminal-injuries-compensation/.

Scottish Women's Rights Centre and JustRight Scotland, "Civil Cases for Rape are Access to Justice, Not 'Destruction of Justice'" (2018), available at: www.scottishwomensrightscentre.org.uk/files/swrc-and-jrs-response-to-stuart-waiton-article-1.pdf.

Scottish Women's Rights Centre, *SWRC Inform: Civil Damages,* available at: www.scottishwomensrightscentre.org.uk/resources-guides/1544374244_civil-damages-guide.pdf.

Smith O, Daly E, & Herriot C, *The Criminal Injuries Compensation Scheme & Sexual Offences* (2019) available at: www.repository.lboro.ac.uk/articles/report/The_Criminal_Injuries_Compensation_Scheme_and_sexual_offences_Research_briefing/9768158/1/files/17499323.pdf.

The Criminal Injuries Compensation Scheme (2012), available at: www.gov.uk/government/publications/criminal-injuries-compensation-scheme-1996-2001-and-2008.

20
CRIMINAL RESPONSIBILITY UNDER CHANGING KNOWLEDGE CONDITIONS

Arlie Loughnan

The knowledge conditions on which the criminal law depends – broadly, its epistemic frame – are undergoing a profound change. There are four salient features of this change. First, recent decades have seen a massive increase in the quantum of knowledges that bear on, or have potential to bear on, criminal law, from the "hard" sciences like the cognitive sciences, to social scientific knowledges about the multiple effects of victimisation, exclusion, and disadvantage on individuals and communities. In addition, the rise of technical knowledges like generative artificial intelligence opens new and as yet unknown epistemic frontiers. Second, knowledges are increasing in complexity, with rapid developments and new specialisms generating novel processes of validation and impacting relations between lay and expert knowledges. Increased complexity in knowledge conditions relates not just to new findings and fields, but newly legitimated knowledges, such as the experiential knowledge of crime victims. Third, the increase in quantum and complexity of knowledge is giving rise to enhanced dynamism or even churn in knowledge which has destabilising effects. Fourth, there is reduced trust in knowledge, evidenced in amplified doubts about knowledge and knowledge-holders. Stretching across these four salient features of change is a more nebulous but equally important dynamic – perceptions about exponential change in knowledge conditions.

These four features of the changing knowledge context of the criminal law have already attracted scholarly attention. In evidence law studies, scholars have recognised the different ways practitioners and courts have responded to growth in the number of experts, greater specialisation within disciplines, increasing complexity in scientific fields, and amplified potential for criticism from either within or beyond the law.[1] Among criminal law scholars, attention has focussed on changes in scientific knowledge and its complexity, with particular emphasis on the rapidly developing fields of cognitive science. Thus, some scholars consider the compatibility of scientific insights and moral-cum-legal precepts like fault, on which responsibility ascription practices rest.[2] In relation to criminal responsibility, these discussions are oriented around the old chestnuts of free will, compatibilism, determinism, and consciousness, and tend to be philosophical in tone, mining the new developments in scientific knowledges to rehearse disagreements about action, agency, and causation. And while criminal legal engagement with the cognitive sciences goes beyond these issues, insufficient attention has been given to *other* changes in knowledge conditions, such as developments in social science knowledge and the wider impacts of the increasing complexity of knowledge.

The implications of these changing conditions go beyond, and are broader and more diffuse, than extant criminal legal scholarly engagement would suggest. Knowledge conditions form the epistemic frame of the criminal law. As Nico Stehr argues, knowledge may be understood as capacity for action, meaning that the effects of knowledge are open, dependent on particular configurations of social, economic, and intellectual structures.[3] In the context of the criminal law, it is possible to see that, beyond the particular evidentiary rules and practices that govern criminal trials, knowledge conditions constitute the "setting" or context for the criminal law and determine its conditions of possibility. For instance, knowledge conditions encompass lay knowledge (unsystematised extra-legal understandings and beliefs), such as that held by the jury, that is an integral part of criminal processes, albeit often depicted as a matter of background.[4] Knowledge conditions of the criminal law are significant because, as Nicola Lacey argues, one of the functions of criminal law practices like responsibility ascription is knowledge coordination.[5] As this indicates, knowledge conditions are properly part of the social, historical, political, and institutional context in which criminal law doctrines and practices have life, and, as such, are of interest to critical criminal law scholars such as myself.[6]

Recognising the role of responsibility for crime in coordinating knowledge, and drawing on examples relating to violence by and against women, in this chapter, I explore the significance of changing knowledge conditions for criminal responsibility. I suggest that these changing knowledge conditions pose a challenge to the structure of the responsibility inquiry, that is, the way criminal responsibility is "done". As is well-recognised, individuals (and corporations) are called to account across a structure of conduct, fault, and defences (in the common law world, *actus reus*, *mens rea*, and justifications and excuses). In Alan Norrie's words, the *mens rea/actus reus* dyad is a "prevalent and continuing way of doing criminal responsibility", with defences working to reduce or remove individual responsibility (partial responsibility or non-responsibility).[7] Changing knowledge conditions challenge (or have the potential to challenge) three key dichotomies – offence and defence, perpetrator and victim, and responsibility and non-responsibility – across which the inquiry into individual responsibility for crime is structured. These dichotomies, which are conceptual and operational, reflect the ideational (if not ideological) organisation of the criminal law around a particular idea of the legal subject and around particular liberal political precepts. The significance of changing knowledge conditions on criminal responsibility is a slice of a wider issue, in which the legitimation of criminal law practices more broadly, and the coherence and standing of the criminal law, are at stake.

Changing knowledge conditions for criminal law practices

It is increasingly apparent that the knowledge conditions in which criminal law practices are embedded are undergoing profound change. Set against a backdrop of a larger and complex epistemological space marked by multifarious and intricate developments, and as noted above, there are four salient features of these changing knowledge conditions – increased quantum, greater complexity, enhanced dynamism, and reduced trust. To this four-part frame must be added an overarching dynamic – perceptions about exponential change in knowledge conditions. These four features of the knowledge context in which criminal law practices are situated are connected to each other and to other wider epistemic dynamics. The increased quantum of knowledge – across multiple domains – is linked to changing power relations and the re-organisation of social, political, and economic systems in the contemporary context ("knowledge societies").[8] Greater complexity in knowledges is connected to changes in understandings of, and attitudes to, expertise, truth, trust in authority, the structure of disciplines (and the nature of interdisciplinarity), and professionalism. Increased quantum and greater complexity are leading to an enhanced dynamism or churn in knowledges, exposing the partiality of knowledge at any one moment in time, with a question mark looming over what is accepted wisdom today as it may be debunked tomorrow. In addition, the contemporary knowledge context is marked by reduced trust in knowledge and amplified doubts about the veracity of knowledge and the independence or objectivity of knowledge-holders.

Growth in the quantum and complexity of scientific knowledges has attracted most of the criminal legal scholarly attention given to changing knowledge conditions. To date, this attention has been largely focussed on assessing the implications of developments in rapidly developing fields of cognitive science like neuroscience for the criminal law ("neurolaw"). Broadly, the cognitive sciences seek to explain individual action through a focus on the interaction of the brain and the environment.[9] Thus, in relation to criminal responsibility, the concern is that the *actus reus/mens rea* way of "doing" criminal responsibility is grounded in tacit moral-cum-legal beliefs about human subjectivity that might be disrupted by insights from these other knowledges.[10] Arguments about the relevance of the cognitive sciences to law have weaker and stronger versions, but, in general terms, advances in these brain sciences – the so-called science of antisocial behaviour – are said to provide objective or provable bases for matters such as diminished responsibility, sentencing (mitigation and aggravation), fitness to plead, and the age of criminal responsibility.[11] As contributions to this debate indicate, neuroscience has huge and increasing potential impact on criminal law practices.[12]

Growth in the quantum of knowledge in which criminal law practices are embedded is not confined to developments in one set of scientific specialisms, however. And, even given the relevance of the cognitive sciences to criminal legal practices, there is a risk entailed in too narrow a focus on the impact of a particular type of knowledges on responsibility ascription (or in other aspects of criminal law decision-making). Beyond the cognitive sciences, other "hard" sciences bear on criminal law practices, and there have been major developments here as well. For example, developments in the field of genetics and epigenetics have also accelerated.[13] This was evident in a 2023 high-profile case of wrongful conviction in NSW, leading to the exoneration of a mother, Kathleen Folbigg, who had been convicted of the homicides of her four babies who died over a period of 10 years, and who had served 20 years in prison.[14] As Folbigg had exhausted her appeal options, her exoneration followed two special inquiries, between which research relating to a genetic variant that was found in two of the children advanced so rapidly that it came to cast reasonable doubt over the convictions merely two years after it was found not to do so.[15] While reactions to this outcome focused on the particular issue of the safety of criminal verdicts and the need for better scientific literacy on the part of criminal law, lawyers, and courts,[16] the broader issue is the impact on the legitimation of criminal law practices of enhanced dynamism or churn in knowledge conditions, as I discuss below.

Another obvious area of massive growth as well as increased complexity is the rise of digital or technological knowledges including machine learning and generative artificial intelligence (GenAI). This is a new knowledge frontier, the implications of which are continuing to unfold.[17] The criminal legal attention given to these developments has focussed on the implications for criminal justice processes, such as policing, detection, and judging as well as practices of risk assessment relevant to probation and parole.[18] But, beyond this, other issues are already emerging. In relation to criminal responsibility, these issues include whether and how AI systems or agents can be brought within the reach of the criminal law as perpetrators, and what the implications of this would be for punishment.[19] More broadly, the ramifications of the rise of technical knowledges for evaluative systems like criminal law are still largely unknown. What is evident is that technological knowledges have a radical and diffused impact on the epistemic framework of the criminal law; while these knowledges have an instrumental dimension (as they are understood as tools that perform certain tasks), they also have distinct regulative dimensions associated with specific values such as managerialism, efficiency, effectiveness, and accountability.[20] Further, the rise of technical knowledges casts other knowledge from human decision-making – in the criminal law context, by experts, juries, and judges – in new light, effectively constructing a new type of knowledge – non-AI knowledge or human-made knowledge.

Moving beyond scientific and technical knowledges, it is possible to see that growth in the quantum and complexity of social scientific knowledge is equally significant for criminal law. Recent decades have seen major developments in sociological, criminological, anthropological, and other knowledges that are informed by empirical studies into the effects of violence, victimisation, abuse, addiction, and other matters, on individuals and communities.[21] These studies span the full range of issues in contemporary criminal law and justice. Although rarely acknowledged in any aggregated way, these knowledges are having a decisive impact on legal understandings of criminal conduct, criminogenic factors, desistance, and related issues.[22] Some of these social-scientific knowledges cluster around the idea of trauma, broadly, the idea that exposure to adverse experiences, particularly early in life, has life-changing impacts, including on psychological capacities, self-awareness, decision-making, integration of the self, and physical health.[23] While the origins of trauma studies are in the field of psychiatry (and relate to clinical conditions like PTSD), the study of trauma and its effects now goes well beyond discrete diagnostic categories. Indeed, it is notable that trauma has come to have a clear interdisciplinary cast, as the significance of the relationship between the individual, community, and their environment has come into sharper focus.[24] Some of these social scientific knowledges posit a novel understanding of human subjectivity and agency, and I return to this point below.

A useful illustration of the significance for the criminal law of change in social scientific knowledge is provided by the social and legal problem of intimate partner violence (in which most but not all victim-survivors are women). Successive waves of expert knowledge, each building on each other, have radically reconstructed criminal justice understandings of and responses to sustained violence and abuse. From the development of the idea of battered women's syndrome in the 1970s, to coercive control in recent years, experts have sought to explain and account for women's responses to violence. While traditionally these experts were psychologists and psychiatrists (reinforcing the pathologisation and individualisation of women's responses to abuse), more recently, a new set of knowledges have arisen – around social framework and social entrapment, in which individual responses to violence are set in a broad social context – that involve social workers, criminologists, and others as experts.[25] This development has been based on enhanced recognition of the structural aspects of violence against women as gender violence (encompassing historical failings in police responses, for instance). This development in understandings of violence against women is marked by the increasing interdisciplinarity of the knowledges in which criminal law practices are embedded, and this hints at changing expectations about the different knowledges that might be relevant to criminal law practices like responsibility ascription, as I discuss below.

Change in the knowledge conditions in which criminal law practices are situated relates not just to new findings and fields, but to newly legitimated knowledges. This is an aspect of the complexity of the knowledge conditions in the current era. Newly legitimised knowledges include knowledges of Indigenous peoples in settler colonial contexts, for example, which may be called on criminal matters concerning Indigenous laws, kinship arrangements, punishment, land and cosmology, and other matters.[26] The rise of these knowledges is already impacting on evidence law, changing rules relating to the admission and validation of expert opinion evidence, for instance,[27] but its significance is broader. These newly legitimised knowledges are shaking up the epistemological relations between legal and extra-legal knowledges, what may be assumed and what must be proved, and by whom. As this suggests, part of the complexity in the knowledge conditions for criminal law relates to the ways in which knowledges are being reconstructed, and I pick this point up again below.

A preeminent example of newly legitimated knowledge relates to lived experience knowledge – of violence, victimisation, and the like[28] – which has become part of the process and legitimation of law reform, with law and justice reform projects now routinely including lived experience representatives.[29] Of this wider plank of knowledges, experiential knowledge of crime is perhaps the most prominent. The rise of this knowledge is connected to the development of victims' movements around the world in the period since the 1970s. Victims' movements have created new social actors – victim-survivors and their families – who are now thought to have privileged access to the "truth" about crime, and whose views are enabled through technologies like victim impact statements, as well as social and political activism. This type of knowledge has profoundly altered legal understandings of crime and impacted on the development of the criminal law, for example in relation to the creation of new offences such as image-based abuse.[30] As I argue in relation to the practice of naming laws after victims of homicide, victim-survivor knowledge holders – who can be thought of as lay-experts in criminal justice and policy – are already altering the landscape in which criminal law is discussed, developed, enacted, and reformed, receiving attention from media agencies and politicians, and being consulted in police, political, and other responses to crime.[31]

The fourth salient feature of changing knowledge conditions is perhaps the most significant: reduced trust in knowledge and knowledge-holders. Reduced trust in knowledge is part of a wider and more complex shift that has taken place over the twentieth century, as modernity has given way to late, second, or advanced modernity.[32] This is a seismic shift, through which relations between individuals and the state have been radically reconstructed, as declining faith in political institutions, and rising perceptions of insecurity, have led to a recalibration of politics and identities.[33] Scholars of late modernity have identified a foundational shift – from automatic trust in experts, to self-conscious or calculated trust[34] – as central to this change. Over this period, scientific knowledge has been subject to large-scale demystification and science studies scholars have argued that science (and technology) no longer stand far above common knowledge, a situation that has been contrasted with the high-water mark of scientific infallibility, the post-World War II era.[35] Overlaid onto the developments is the more recent advent of the spectre of post-truth, a nebulous notion that evokes an idea of crisis in shared understandings that underpin social practices including law.[36]

To this point in the discussion, I have provided an overview of the changing knowledge conditions in which criminal law practices are embedded. While within the confines of this chapter, it has only been possible to offer a sketch, I hope I have done enough to suggest the significance of these changing conditions for the criminal law. While particular insights from certain fields have received attention from some scholars, these insights have been examined in isolation, both from other knowledges and from a wider appreciation of their impact on the criminal law. By contrast with the analyses that focus on the growth in, or predicted dominance of, one new set of scientific knowledges on criminal law practices, the significance of changes in knowledge conditions arises from a *combination* of factors – the growth in quantum of knowledge, increased complexity, enhanced dynamism or churn, and reduced trust in knowledge, as well as the connected issue of perceptions about exponential change in knowledge. This means that these changes need to be assessed together – as changes in knowledge conditions *as such*. These changes pose particular challenges for criminal responsibility, and it is to this that I now turn.

Challenges for criminal responsibility

The changing knowledge conditions sketched out in the preceding section have implications for criminal responsibility. As mentioned above, the inquiry into responsibility for crime – the way criminal responsibility is "done" – takes a particular form, with individuals called to account across a structure of conduct, fault, and defences. I suggest that changing knowledge conditions challenge (or have the potential to challenge) three key dichotomies – offence and defence, perpetrator and victim, and responsibility and non-responsibility – across which the inquiry into individual responsibility for crime is organised. These dichotomies, which are ideational (if not ideological), conceptual and operational, are central to the construction of criminal responsibility in the modern criminal law. This way of structuring the criminal responsibility inquiry reflects the normative commitments of the criminal law to a particular idea of the legal subject – characterised by autonomy, rationality, and agency – and to liberal political notions of a minimalist criminal law and individual fairness in punishment.[37]

Offence and defence

The offence/defence dichotomy is cardinal to criminal responsibility. As Norrie writes, the "architectonic of offence (*mens rea* plus *actus reus*) and defence" is a way of "doing" criminal responsibility.[38] This way of "doing" criminal responsibility corresponds to a division of labour in the courtroom: broadly, resting on a presumption of responsibility, that the prosecution is required to prove the elements of the offence (conduct and fault), and defence council is required to raise defences to support a finding of non- or partial responsibility. The offence/defence dichotomy is formal – in any positive law system, the precise division between the elements of an offence and elements of defences is contingent[39] – and abstract, because any overly neat or easy division is belied by the various rules of evidence and proof that govern prosecution practices and the conduct of criminal trials, and consideration of the many different types of claims that may be thought of as "defences".[40] Nonetheless, it is possible to recognise the significance of the idea that general prohibitions or rules relating to conduct ("conduct rules") are distinct from the arguments made to defeat them in specific instances ("decision rules").[41] And this reveals that the dichotomy between offence and defence reflects a hallmark of the modern criminal law – that anyone can commit any offence – that is itself central to the coherence and rationality of the law in the current era.

In what ways might changing knowledge conditions pose a challenge to the offence/defence dichotomy? The challenge relates to the prospective inapplicability or even incoherence of the normative standards of conduct encoded in offence definitions. There seem to be at least three ways this might play out. First, developing understandings of human cognitive capacities may give rise to demands that offences be particularised in new ways that encompass exculpatory factors (an example might be something like "demented driving").[42] Second, the integration of AI and other technological knowledges may mean that what is now thought about as augmented offending demands a corresponding notion of augmented responsibility (which could be thought about as "AI-assisted responsibility").[43] Third, deepening sociological knowledge around matters such as historical disadvantage, discrimination, and trauma may put pressure on stand-alone defences, such that new hybrid offence/defences are necessary to capture greater nuance in legal appreciation of exculpatory factors (here, an example might be something like failing to prevent abuse of a child while in an abusive relationship).[44]

Models for exceptions to the general idea of a separation between offence and defence already exist in various systems of criminal law. In the common law world, examples such as infanticide, both an offence and a partial defence to a charge of murder, and voluntary manslaughter resulting from a successful defence of diminished responsibility, properly occupy a hybrid status.[45] In my own work, I have called these hybrids atypical responsibility forms, on the basis that elements such as offence and defence, conduct and fault, and justification and excuse, that are usually separate, are mixed together.[46] I have argued that these hybrids developed either primarily, or in significant ways, in relation to women's responsibility for crime, with women's violence (e.g. against children) and violence against women (e.g. intimate partner violence) prompting the creation of these hybrid forms on the face of the criminal law to accommodate the distinctiveness of women's responsibility for crime.[47] These hybrids provide an attractive solution to the "problem" of different types of responsibility, indicating that may be labelled as partial responsibility in fact represents a difference in *kind* – not merely "less than" but qualitatively different from – captured only by the interweaving of offence and defence elements.

While it may seem speculative at this moment in time, it is possible to imagine a future criminal law in which offences and defences are further integrated into each other, and responsibility is further personalised. The rapid development and use of personal data in other contexts has enhanced the way that individualised risk assessments occur in contexts like insurance.[48] It does not seem far-fetched that future developments in this space might individualise conduct like lawful driving, such that my particular capacities, my vehicle, and the particular driving conditions will together determine the boundary between non-criminal and criminal conduct. Similarly, it might be possible that knowledges about the common coincidence of a particular type of offending *and* a particular defence give rise to demands for more and more hybrids, for instance in relation to drug-related crime (in which the chemical effects of a particular drug, the individual, and the conduct are all connected). And as these hypotheticals suggest, such novel criminal legal forms transcend the dichotomy between objective and subjective fault, as well as the dichotomy between offence and defence.

Perpetrator and victim

The second dichotomy to which changing knowledge conditions pose a challenge is that between the perpetrator and victim. By this I mean that the perpetrator or defendant, who is the focus of the responsibility inquiry, is treated as not being a victim, unless and until a defence is raised that depends on victimisation – or perhaps not until arguments in mitigation at sentencing (for example the defence of diminished responsibility raised in response to a murder charge). The dichotomy between the perpetrator and victim is fundamental to the modern criminal law, reflecting the criminal legal idea of the subject – as "already responsible",[49] that is, a subject who is both assumed and required to be responsible. As I have argued elsewhere, the self of criminal responsibility is generally constructed in a "thin" way, around notions of rationality, autonomy, and agency, a construction which permits moral and legal condemnation of their conduct through the criminal law.[50] This construction of the legal subject has particular effects in criminal law. As Ngaire Naffine writes, treating individuals as rational and agentic in systems such as that of criminal law has an "ennobling" effect,[51] and the reasoning individual becomes a "powerful mechanism of ideological legitimation" for the criminal law.[52]

Changing knowledge conditions challenge this dichotomy in that the substantive content of some new knowledges undermines, or has the potential to undermine, the viability of the idea of the "already responsible" legal subject on which it rests. Put another way, the normative commitment to the rational, autonomous, and agentic legal subject may be threatened by the increasing implausibility of this idea as a matter of description. There are several ways this might occur. On the one hand, increasingly sophisticated understandings of brain development are coming to show genuine differences in individuals' capacities.[53] This means that fewer individuals will be able to be assumed to be responsible and more will need to be carved out from the reach of the criminal law (in normative terms, offered exemptions as opposed to excuses). For example, contemporary research into the multiple and pervasive effects of foetal alcohol spectrum disorder (FASD) indicates that this condition is analogous to intellectual disability,[54] meaning individuals with this condition might come to be thought of as outside the reach of the criminal law. On the other hand, the rise of knowledges such as those emerging from trauma-informed studies reveals the deep and complex enmeshment of offending *and* victimisation.[55] These studies show the ways in which trauma impacts the development of identity and capacity such that individuals are distinctive kinds of selves, created in and through trauma. And this means that in some cases an abstract idea of a perpetrator of a serious crime who is not already a victim in some as yet unspecified culpability-relevant sense becomes tenuous.

The dichotomy between perpetrator and victim has already broken down in the context of violence against and violence by women. Scholarly work and advocacy and legal practice in intimate and personal violence recognises a conceptual and practical category of "primary victims", acknowledging that women who are alleged to have committed an offence may nonetheless be primarily *victims* of crime – either because they have retaliated against their abuser (and been charged with for example assault), or because the offending is in response to victimisation (e.g. drug offences, prostitution). It is in this context that the idea of "victims who kill" has emerged in homicide law and policy. The idea of "victims who kill" is that women who are charged with killing their abusers are properly understood as victims of that abuse who have resorted to killing the abuser for failure of other options, including help from the state (in the form of police).[56] These ideas about the enmeshment of the identities of perpetrator and victim responds to a need – to have different categories in which to think and work in relation to violence against and by women. These developments provide a model for criminal responsibility, in which any abstract ideas about agency and autonomy are thoroughly contextualised in individual and social circumstances.

Responsibility and non- or partial responsibility

The dichotomy between responsibility and non- or partial responsibility is between outcomes of criminal process. While it is sometimes assumed that responsibility and non-responsibility are merely flip sides of the (moral-evaluative) inquiry into responsibility, a close assessment reveals that these criminal law spaces look different. As I have argued elsewhere, ascriptions of responsibility and non-responsibility, attendant rules of evidence and procedure, the temporal logics of responsibility and non-responsibility and what I called the effects of ascriptions of responsibility and non-responsibility, expose meaningful differences between responsibility and non-responsibility practices.[57] These differences are epistemic as well as ontological: findings of responsibility, determining that the defendant did the act with the requisite mental state (conduct and fault), are treated as generally "knowable".[58] This means that they are the subject of lay knowledge: lay people are competent to identify and evaluate responsibility, and there is no need for additional informational resources to be enlisted in the process of determining responsibility.[59] By contrast, and reflecting its nominally exceptional nature, non- and partial responsibility requires expert knowledge, which is adduced at trial in the form of expert evidence, buttressing claims to exemption sought by individuals via defences.

How might changing knowledge conditions challenge the dichotomy between responsibility and non- or partial responsibility? There seem to be at least two ways. First, the challenge arises from the ways in which the content of changing knowledges undermines fundamentally the idea of a responsible subject on which distinct forces operate to reduce or remove responsibility. This means that, rather than the conceptualise and operationalise of the responsibility inquiry across the categories of responsibility and non- and partial responsibility, a new category of individual(ised) responsibility might be needed. This category of responsibility – responsibility 2.0? – would be neither responsibility, non-responsibility nor partial responsibility. Rather it would be a new beast altogether, a hyper-personalised construct, resisting or sitting above, the dichotomies which currently organise the approach to criminal responsibility in the modern law of crime.[60]

Second, changing knowledge conditions challenge the dichotomy between responsibility and non- or partial responsibility by redrawing the boundary between expert knowledge and lay or non-expert knowledge. In broad terms, the criminal responsibility dyad corresponds to a dichotomy between a synthesised moral-cum-legal knowledge, naturalised in the criminal law doctrines and practices relating to conduct and fault, on the one hand, and a more heterogenous category of specialist knowledges – traditionally, the psy-knowledges of psychiatry and psychology, but now also the growing array of science and social science knowledges discussed in this chapter – that may be used to reduce or remove individual responsibility via defences, on the other hand.[61] The rationale for relying on expert evidence to assess non-responsibility and partial responsibility is that it addresses matters lying beyond the competence of ordinary people (in the form of the jury) to evaluate.[62] As matters of specialist or exclusive knowledge gradually come to be understood and accepted by non-experts, the boundary between expert knowledge and lay knowledge shifts. This is significant for the criminal law because it impacts what a jury – the quintessential organ of lay knowledge – can be assumed to know, on the one hand, and what may be the subject of expert evidence, on the other.

As this discussion suggests, taken together the legitimation of criminal responsibility practices. Legitimation concerns the "law's claim to correctness, force and social priority", as Scott Veitch puts it.[63] As Lacey argues, criminal responsibility serves the coordination and legitimation needs of the criminal law, meaning that it provides a symbolic resource for the criminal legal system, enabling it to be regarded as a system of justice, rather than one of sheer force.[64] In Lacey's words, "criminal responsibility … is an idea which is located within a social practice of criminalization, which itself is necessarily located within an institutional framework and structured by the imperatives of legitimation and coordination".[65] Knowledge coordination is thus core to the functions of the criminal law in the current era – and changes to knowledge conditions strike at the heart of that function. Compromised legitimacy of criminal law decision-making erodes the trust in and authority of government and impacts the social and moral standing of legal and other actors, institutions, and processes.

This chapter has argued that changing knowledge conditions pose a profound challenge for criminal responsibility. By contrast with existing scholarship assessing the implications of developments in one knowledge domain, I have focussed on the broader features of the knowledge conditions that form the setting for criminal law. I suggested that the challenges arise not from just one particular type of knowledge (archetypically, the cognitive sciences), but from the sheer mass of expert knowledges in which criminal law practices are embedded, as well as greater complexity, and enhanced dynamism or churn in the knowledge domain, and reduced trust in knowledge. I suggested that, going beyond the consideration of the implications for the moral-cum-legal precepts on criminal law depends, these changing conditions pose a challenge to the way responsibility in criminal law is structured – across offence and defence, perpetrator and victim, and responsibility and non- or partial responsibility. The changing knowledge conditions of the current era impact on the legitimacy of criminal responsibility ascription (and decision-making more broadly).

In the midst of the changes that are considered in this chapter, it becomes hard to be confident about the degree of change (how does it differ from past periods of significant change?). While knowledge is always in a state of flux, and law has never been hermetically sealed away from developments in extra-legal fields, the current moment seems to be a decisive one. At this point in time, the structure of the inquiry into criminal responsibility – made up of the dichotomies discussed in this chapter which are themselves based on normative commitments to particular ideas about legal subjectivity and certain liberal political precepts – is not just independent of insights from the cognitive sciences and interdisciplinary learnings (about complex trauma, cumulative disadvantage, brain development, colonisation, and intersectionality etc.), but up *against* these learnings.[66] The position of being up against an ever-growing body of extra-legal knowledges is adversely impacting the legitimation of criminal responsibility.

The effects of this changing knowledge context on criminal law go well beyond responsibility ascription (and indeed beyond criminal law). This changing knowledge context impacts all aspects of criminal law decision-making, broadly conceived, including law-making, policy development, adjudication, and evaluation under criminal law. This points up the complexity of the changes canvassed in this chapter. What role is left for criminal law under these changed knowledge conditions? Perhaps a much-reduced role, oriented around its symbolic or crime prevention functions? And what is left of the values of consistency and generality in the criminal law? What is clear is that a broader inquiry is needed – examining the knowledge context as such – which would bring knowledge onto the radar of critical criminal law scholars. This chapter is a contribution to that endeavour.

Acknowledgements

I would like to thank Allan McCay and Sabine Selchow for comments on an earlier version of this chapter and Grace Roodenrys for excellent research assistance.

Notes

1 See for discussion G Edmond & D Mercer "Experts and Expertise in Legal and Regulatory Settings" in D Mercer & G Edmond (eds), *Expertise in Law and Regulation* (Routledge: London, 2004), p.9. See more generally S Jasanoff, *Science at the Bar: Law, Science, and Technology in America* (Harvard University Press: Cambridge MA, 1997).
2 This is a growing field: see for example MS Moore, *Mechanical Choices: The Responsibility of the Human Machine* (Oxford University Press: Oxford, 2020) and "Relating Neuroscience to Responsibility: Comments on Hirstein, Sifferd, and Fagan's Responsible Brains", *Criminal Law and Philosophy*, vol. 16, no. 2 (2022), p.283; S Morse, "Lost in Translation?: An Essay on Law and Neuroscience", *Law and Neuroscience: Current Legal Issues*, vol. 13 (2011), p.529; NA Vincent, "On the Relevance of Neuroscience to Criminal Responsibility", *Criminal Law and Philosophy*, vol. 4, no. 1 (2010), p.77.
3 See N Stehr, *Knowledge Societies* (Sage Publications: London, 1994).
4 See A Loughnan, *Manifest Madness: Mental Incapacity in Criminal Law* (Oxford University Press: Oxford, 2012) (on lay knowledge of mental incapacity).
5 See generally N Lacey, *In Search of Criminal Responsibility: Ideas, Interests and Institutions* (Oxford University Press: Oxford, 2016). Lacey's argument is part of a sophisticated analysis of the significance of criminal responsibility as serving functions of knowledge coordination and legitimation, with criminal law understood as a regulatory system governing individual and group behaviour.
6 On critical scholarly approaches to criminal law, see Lacey, *In Search of Criminal Responsibility*, p.176; see also D Nelken, "Critical Criminal Law", *Journal of Law and Society*, vol. 14, no. 1 (1987), p.105 at pp.109–11.
7 A Norrie, "Legal Form and Moral Judgement: Euthanasia and Assisted Suicide", in RA Duff et al (eds), *The Structures of Criminal Law* (Oxford University Press: Oxford, 2011), p.139.
8 See generally P Burke, *The Social History of Knowledge Vol II: From the Encyclopedia to Wikipedia* (Polity Press: Cambridge, 2012), pp.266–275.
9 See G Meynen, "Forensic Psychiatry and Neurolaw: Description, Developments, and Debates", *International Journal of Law and Psychiatry*, vol. 65 (2019), 101345.
10 See for discussion, NA Farahany & JE Coleman Jr, 'Genetics, Neuroscience, and Criminal Responsibility', in NA Farahany (ed), *The Impact of Behavioral Sciences on Criminal Law* (Oxford University Press: Oxford, 2009), pp.183–185.
11 For an overview, see JA Chandler et al, "Neurolaw Today – A Systematic Review of the Recent Law and Neuroscience Literature", *International Journal of Law and Psychiatry*, vol. 65 (2019), 101341 at pp.1–13. Even advocates of the relevance of these knowledges for criminal law admit that the sciences are in their infancy, and, in practice, courts have shown caution in admitting evidence that seeks to undercut individual responsibility.
12 See e.g. A McCay in this collection (in relation to neurotechnology).
13 For discussion in relation to law, see LA Baker et al, "Behavioral Genetics: The Science of Antisocial Behavior", *Law & Contemporary Problems*, vol. 69, nos. 1–2 (2006), p.7; BY Cheung & SJ Heine,

"The Double-Edged Sword of Genetic Accounts of Criminality: Causal Attributions from Genetic Ascriptions Affect Legal Decision Making", *Personality and Social Psychology Bulletin*, vol. 41, no. 12 (2015), p.1723.
14 See New South Wales Department of Communities and Justice, *Report of the Inquiry into the Convictions of Kathleen Megan Folbigg* (report, 2019), available at: https://2019folbigginquiry.dcj.nsw.gov.au/documents/Report_of_the_Inquiry_into_the_convictions_of_Kathleen_Megan_Folbigg.pdf; *Folbigg v Attorney General New South Wales* (2021) 391 ALR 294.
15 See *Inquiry into the convictions of Kathleen Megan Folbigg – Final Report* [2023] (8 November 2023). Changes in the psychological reading of Folbigg's diaries from the first trial also played a part Inquiry's finding that her convictions were unsafe.
16 See for discussion, "Forensic Psychology, Law and the Folbigg case: A Conversation with Professor Gary Edmond and Dr Sharmila Betts", *University of New South Wales* (2023), available at: www.unsw.edu.au/news/2023/10/forensic-psychology--law-and-the-folbigg-case; see also A Loughnan & M O'Connor, "Monstrous Mothering: Understanding the Causes of and Responses to Infanticide", *Journal of Law and Medicine*, vol. 30, no. 1 (2023), p.48.
17 For a general discussion of some of these implications, see A Azhar, *Exponential: Order and Chaos in an Age of Accelerating Technology* (Milton Keynes: Penguin, 2021).
18 See e.g. B Custers, "AI in Criminal Law: An Overview of AI Applications in Substantive and Procedural Criminal Law" in B Custers & E Fosch-Villaronga (eds) *Law and Artificial Intelligence: Regulating AI and Applying AI in Practice* (Springer: The Hague, 2022); A Sachoulidou, "Algorithmic Criminal Justice: Is It Just a Science Fiction Plot Idea?" in A Kornilakis et al (eds), *Artificial Intelligence and Normative Challenges: International and Comparative Legal Perspectives* (Springer: Cham, 2023).
19 See F Lagioia & G Sartor, "AI Systems Under Criminal Law: A Legal Analysis and a Regulatory Perspective", *Philosophy and Technology*, vol. 33 (2020), p.433.
20 See e.g. F Contini, "From the Rule of Law to the Rule of Technology? The Institutional Implications of the Digital Transformation of Courts", in S Turenne & M Moussa (eds), *Research Handbook on Judging and the Judiciary* (Edward Elgar Publishing: Cheltenham, 2023).
21 For critical discussion, see G Edmond, "Thick Decisions: Expertise, Advocacy and Reasonableness in the Federal Court of Australia", *Oceania*, vol. 74, no. 3 (2004), p.190; R van Krieken, "Law's Autonomy in Action: Anthropology and History in Court", *Social & Legal Studies*, vol. 15, no. 4 (2006), p.574.
22 A ready if not recent example is the "broken windows" theory of policing; see JQ Wilson & GL Kelling, "Broken Windows", *The Atlantic* (March 1982), available at: www.theatlantic.com/magazine/archive/1982/03/broken-windows/304465/.
23 This is an enormous field: see e.g. D Bolton et al, "Long-Term Effects of Psychological Trauma on Psychosocial Functioning", *Journal of Child Psychology and Psychiatry*, vol. 45, no. 5 (2004), p.1007.
24 See for discussion K Menzies, "Understanding the Australian Aboriginal Experience of Collective, Historical and Intergenerational Trauma", *International Social Work*, vol. 62, no. 6 (2019), p.1522.
25 See for discussion J Tolmie et al, "Social Entrapment: A Realistic Understanding of the Criminal Offending of Primary Victims of Intimate Partner Violence", *New Zealand Law Review*, vol. 2 (2018), p.181; H Douglas et al, "Social Entrapment Evidence: Understanding Its Role in Self-Defence Cases Involving Intimate Partner Violence", *UNSW Law Journal*, vol. 44, no. 1 (2020), p.324.
26 See for discussion C Cunneen & S Rowe, "Changing Narratives: Colonised Peoples, Criminology and Social Work", *International Journal for Crime, Justice and Social Democracy*, vol. 3, no. 1 (2014), p.49.
27 In general terms, expert evidence is an exception to the prohibition on opinion evidence; in the Australian context, see Uniform Evidence Act 1995 (Cth), s 79(1). A separate section provides for specific ways of validating Indigenous expert knowledges. On expert evidence generally, see KA Martire & G Edmond "Rethinking Expert Opinion Evidence", *Melbourne University Law Review*, vol. 40, no. 3 (2017), p.967.
28 With its origins in disability advocacy ("nothing about us without us"), the lived experience movement seeks to foster individual empowerment and enhance the responsiveness of social services in social change: see B Sandhu, "The Value of Lived Experience in Social Change: The Need for Leadership and Organisational Development in the Social Sector", *The Lived Experience* (2017),

available at: https://thelivedexperience.org/wp-content/uploads/2017/07/The-Lived-Experience-Baljeet-Sandhu-VLE-full-report.pdf.
29. See e.g. the NSW Lived Experience Expert Advisory Group on Sexual Violence, formed in 2023, as part of the *National Plan to End Violence Against Women and Children 2022-2032* and the Standing Council of Attorneys-General *Work Plan to Strengthen Criminal Justice Responses to Sexual Assault 2022-27*.
30. See for discussion T Crofts, "Refining the Contours of Intimate Image Abuse Offences" in GM Caletti & K Summerer (eds), *Criminalizing Intimae Image Abuse: A Comparative Perspective* (Oxford University Press: Oxford, 2024), p.121.
31. See A Loughnan, 'Eponymous Law', Peter Brett QC Memorial Lecture, University of Melbourne 2023, available at: www.youtube.com/watch?v=0UTDN8VZz3M.
32. On modernity and late modernity (or reflexive modernity), see U Beck, *Risk Society: Towards a New Modernity* (Sage Publications: London, M Ritter trans, 1992); A Giddens, *The Consequences of Modernity* (Stanford University Press, Stanford CA, 1990) and *Modernity and Self-Identity: Self and Society in the Late Modern Age* (Stanford University Press: Stanford CA, 1991).
33. See e.g. U Beck & E Beck-Gernsheim, *Individualization Institutionalized: Individualism and Its Social and Political Consequences* (Sage Publications: London, 2002).
34. See Giddens, *Modernity and Self-Identity* and *Consequences of Modernity*.
35. See H Collins & R Evans, *Rethinking Expertise* (University of Chicago Press: Chicago IL, 2007).
36. For consideration of the implications of this for law, see L Mason, "Idealism, Empiricism, Pluralism, Law: Legal Truth After Modernity" in A Condello & T Contina (eds) *Post-Truth, Philosophy and Law* (Routledge: London, 2019), pp.93–111.
37. See further A Loughnan, *Self, Others and the State* (Cambridge University Press: Cambridge, 2019), pp.50–53; see also L Farmer, *The Making of the Modern Criminal Law: Criminalization and the Civil Order* (Oxford University Press 2016).
38. See A Norrie, *Crime, Reason and History: A Critical Introduction to Criminal Law* (Butterworths: Oxford, 2001) p.139; see also RA Duff, *Answering for Crime: Responsibility and Liability in the Criminal Law* (Hart Publishing: Oxford, 2007).
39. See G Williams, "Offences and defences", *Legal Studies*, vol. 2, no. 3 (1982), p.233.
40. See L Duarte d'Almeida, "'O Call Me Not to Justify the Wrong': Criminal Answerability and the Offence/Defence Distinction", *Criminal Law and Philosophy*, vol. 6, no. 2 (2012), p.227.
41. See M Dan-Cohen, "Decision Rules and Conduct Rules: On Acoustic Separation in Criminal Law", *Harvard Law Review*, vol. 97, no. 3 (1984), p.625.
42. Offending by individuals with dementia is also discussed in N Websdale, *Fatal Family Violence and the Dementias: Grey Mist Killings* (Routledge: London, 2024) (forthcoming).
43. For discussion of the related issue of AI legal personality, see GI Zekos, *Advanced Artificial Intelligence and Robo-Justice* (Routledge: London, 2022), pp. 222–232.
44. For discussion of the problems with prosecutions in this context, see J Tolmie et al, "Criminalising Parental Failures: Documenting Bias in the Criminal Justice System", *New Zealand Women's Law Journal*, vol. 3 (2019), p.136.
45. See A Loughnan, "The Strange Case of the Infanticide Offence/Defence", *Oxford Journal of Legal Studies*, vol. 32, no. 4 (2012), p.685 and "From Carpetbag to Crucible: Reconceptualising Diminished Responsibility Manslaughter" in B Livings et al, (eds), *Mental Condition Defences and the Criminal Justice System: Perspectives from Law and Medicine* (Cambridge Scholars Publishing: Cambridge, 2015), pp.339–64.
46. See Loughnan *Self, Others and the State*, ch.6.
47. Loughnan, *Self, Others and the State*, ch.6.
48. See e.g. Z Bednarz & K Manwaring, "Keeping the (good) faith: Implications of emerging technologies for consumer insurance contracts", *Sydney Law Review*, vol. 43, no. 4 (2021), p.455.
49. See D Rabin, *Identity, Crime, and Legal Responsibility in Eighteenth-Century England* (Palgrave MacMillan: London, 2004).
50. See further Loughnan *Self, Others and the State*, pp.63–65.
51. See N Naffine, "In Defence of the Responsible Subject", *Australian Journal of Legal Philosophy*, vol. 34 (2009), p.222 at p.227.

52 See Norrie, *Crime, Reason and History*, p.176, this is the "juridical subject", in Norrie's words: see pp.16–24; see also Farmer, *The Making of the Modern Criminal Law*, p.168 (on the juridical subject and the modern subject).
53 These developments may impact on the age of criminal responsibility: see Crofts and McDiarmid contributions to this collection.
54 On FASD, see N Brown & S Greenspan "Diminished culpability in fetal alcohol spectrum disorders (FASD)", *Behavioral Sciences & the Law*, vol. 40, no. 1 (2022), p.1.
55 This is an enormous field: see e.g. L Hiromoto, "Childhood Trauma: Basis for the Insanity Defense and Other Mitigating Theories in Light of Trauma-Linked Biocognitive Deficiencies", *University of Illinois Law Review Online* (2020), p.41; M Randall & L Haskell, "Trauma-Informed Approaches to Law: Why Restorative Justice Must Understand Trauma and Psychological Coping", *Dalhousie Law Journal*, vol. 36, no. 2 (2013), p.501.
56 See further Loughnan, *Self, Others and the State*, ch.6.
57 Loughnan, "Asking Different Responsibility Questions".
58 Loughnan, "Asking Different Responsibility Questions".
59 Loughnan, "Asking Different Responsibility Questions".
60 Under this construct, blame may be detached rather than affective: see N Lacey & H Pickard, "From the Consulting Room to the Court Room? Taking the Clinical Model of Responsibility Without Blame into the Legal Realm", *Oxford Journal of Legal Studies*, vol. 33, no. 1 (2023), p.1.
61 On the difficulty of reconciling these knowledges, see D Hodgson, "Guilty Mind or Guilty Brain? Criminal Responsibility in the Age of Neuroscience", *Australian Law Journal*, vol. 74, no. 10 (2000), p.661.
62 As Antony Duff argues as part of his broader analysis of responsibility as "answerability", denials of responsibility (or "agent exemptions") implicate someone other than the defendant: it falls to a "third party" – not the defendant him or herself – to make the case on their behalf: see Duff, *Answering for Crime*, pp.286–287.
63 See S Veitch, *Law and Irresponsibility: On the Legitimation of Human Suffering* (Routledge: London, 2007), p.97.
64 See Lacey, *In Search of Criminal Responsibility*, pp.19–20, p.137.
65 Lacey, *In Search of Criminal Responsibility*, p.190.
66 See also C Lernsedt and M Mattravers in this volume in relation to the need for "science-sensitive" blaming practices.

References

Books and book chapters

Azhar A, *Exponential: Order and Chaos in an Age of Accelerating Technology* (Penguin: Milton Keynes, 2021).

Beck U, *Risk Society: Towards a New Modernity* (Translated by Ritter M) (Sage Publications: London, 1992).

Beck U & Beck-Gernsheim E, *Individualization Institutionalized: Individualism and Its Social and Political Consequences* (Sage Publications: London, 2002).

Burke P, *The Social History of Knowledge Volume II: From the Encyclopedia to Wikipedia* (Polity Press: Cambridge, 2012).

Collins H & Evans R, *Rethinking Expertise* (University of Chicago Press: Chicago IL, 2007).

Contini F, "From the Rule of Law to the Rule of Technology? The Institutional Implications of the Digital Transformation of Courts", in Turenne S & Moussa M (eds), *Research Handbook on Judging and the Judiciary* (Edward Elgar Publishing: Cheltenham, 2023).

Crofts T, "Refining the Contours of Intimate Image Abuse Offences", in Caletti GM & Summerer K (eds), *Criminalizing Intimae Image Abuse: A Comparative Perspective* (Oxford University Press: Oxford, 2024).

Custers B, "AI in Criminal Law: An Overview of AI Applications in Substantive and Procedural Criminal Law", in Custers B & Fosch-Villaronga E (eds), *Law and Artificial Intelligence: Regulating AI and Applying AI in Practice* (Springer: The Hague, 2022).

Duff RA, *Answering for Crime: Responsibility and Liability in the Criminal Law* (Hart Publishing: Oxford, 2007).
Edmond G & Mercer D, "Experts and Expertise in Legal and Regulatory Settings" in Mercer D & Edmond G (eds), *Expertise in Law and Regulation* (Routledge: London, 2004).
Farahany NA & Coleman Jr JE, "Genetics, Neuroscience, and Criminal Responsibility", in Farahany NA (ed), *The Impact of Behavioral Sciences on Criminal Law* (Oxford University Press: Oxford, 2009).
Farmer L, *The Making of the Modern Criminal Law: Criminalization and the Civil Order* (Oxford University Press: Oxford, 2016).
Giddens A, *The Consequences of Modernity* (Stanford University Press: Stanford CA, 1990).
Giddens A, *Modernity and Self-Identity: Self and Society in the Late Modern Age* (Stanford University Press: Stanford CA, 1991).
Jasanoff S, *Science at the Bar: Law, Science, and Technology in America* (Harvard University Press: Cambridge MA, 1997).
Lacey N, *In Search of Criminal Responsibility: Ideas, Interests and Institutions* (Oxford University Press: Oxford, 2016).
Loughnan A, *Manifest Madness: Mental Incapacity in Criminal Law* (Oxford University Press: Oxford, 2012).
Loughnan A, "From Carpetbag to Crucible: Reconceptualising Diminished Responsibility Manslaughter", in Livings B, Reed A, & Wake N (eds), *Mental Condition Defences and the Criminal Justice System: Perspectives from Law and Medicine* (Cambridge Scholars Publishing: Cambridge, 2015).
Loughnan A, *Self, Others and the State* (Cambridge University Press: Cambridge, 2019).
Mason L, "Idealism, Empiricism, Pluralism, Law: Legal Truth After Modernity", in Condello A & Contina T (eds), *Post-Truth, Philosophy and Law* (Routledge: London, 2019).
Moore MS, *Mechanical Choices: The Responsibility of the Human Machine* (Oxford University Press: Oxford, 2020).
Norrie A, *Crime, Reason and History: A Critical Introduction to Criminal Law* (Butterworths: Oxford, 2001).
Norrie A, "Legal Form and Moral Judgement: Euthanasia and Assisted Suicide", in Duff RA, Farmer L, Marshall SE, Renzo M, & Tadros V (eds), *The Structures of Criminal Law* (Oxford University Press: Oxford, 2011).
Rabin D, *Identity, Crime, and Legal Responsibility in Eighteenth-Century England* (Palgrave MacMillan: London, 2004).
Sachoulidou A, "Algorithmic Criminal Justice: Is It Just a Science Fiction Plot Idea?", in Kornilakis A, Nouskalis G, Pergantis V, & Tzimas T (eds), *Artificial Intelligence and Normative Challenges: International and Comparative Legal Perspectives* (Springer: Cham, 2023).
Stehr N, *Knowledge Societies* (Sage Publications: London, 1994).
Veitch S, *Law and Irresponsibility: On the Legitimation of Human Suffering* (Routledge: London, 2007).

Journal articles

Baker LA, Bezdjian S, & Raine A, "Behavioral Genetics: The Science of Antisocial Behavior", *Law & Contemporary Problems*, vol. 69, no. 1–2 (2006), pp.7–46.
Bednarz Z & Manwaring K, "Keeping the (Good) Faith: Implications of Emerging Technologies for Consumer Insurance Contracts", *Sydney Law Review*, vol. 43, no. 4 (2021), pp.455–487.
Bolton D, Hill J, O'Ryan D, Udwin O, Boyle S, & Yule W, "Long-Term Effects of Psychological Trauma on Psychosocial Functioning", *Journal of Child Psychology and Psychiatry*, vol. 45, no. 5 (2004), pp.1007–1014.
Brown N & Greenspan S, "Diminished Culpability in Fetal Alcohol Spectrum Disorders (FASD)", *Behavioral Sciences & the Law*, vol. 40, no. 1 (2022), pp.1–13.
Chandler JA, Harell N, & Potkonjak T, "Neurolaw Today – A Systematic Review of the Recent Law and Neuroscience Literature", *International Journal of Law and Psychiatry*, vol. 65 (2019), 101341.
Cheung BY & Heine SJ, "The Double-Edged Sword of Genetic Accounts of Criminality: Causal Attributions from Genetic Ascriptions Affect Legal Decision Making", *Personality and Social Psychology Bulletin*, vol. 41, no. 12 (2015), pp.1723–1738.

Cunneen C & Rowe S, "Changing Narratives: Colonised Peoples, Criminology and Social Work", *International Journal for Crime, Justice and Social Democracy*, vol. 3, no. 1 (2014), pp.49–67.

Dan-Cohen M, "Decision Rules and Conduct Rules: On Acoustic Separation in Criminal Law", *Harvard Law Review*, vol. 97, no. 3 (1984), pp.625–677.

Douglas H, Tarrant S, & Tolmie J, "Social Entrapment Evidence: Understanding Its Role in Self-Defence Cases Involving Intimate Partner Violence", *UNSW Law Journal*, vol. 44, no. 1 (2020), pp.324–356.

Duarte d'Almeida L, "'O Call Me Not to Justify the Wrong': Criminal Answerability and the Offence/Defence Distinction", *Criminal Law and Philosophy*, vol. 6, no. 2 (2012), pp.227–245.

Edmond G, "Thick Decisions: Expertise, Advocacy and Reasonableness in the Federal Court of Australia", *Oceania*, vol. 74, no. 3 (2004), pp.190–230.

Hiromoto L, "Childhood Trauma: Basis for the Insanity Defense and Other Mitigating Theories in Light of Trauma-Linked Biocognitive Deficiencies", *University of Illinois Law Review Online* (2020), pp.41–52.

Hodgson D, "Guilty Mind or Guilty Brain? Criminal Responsibility in the Age of Neuroscience", *Australian Law Journal*, vol. 74, no. 10 (2000), pp.661–680.

Lacey N & Pickard H, "From the Consulting Room to the Court Room? Taking the Clinical Model of Responsibility Without Blame into the Legal Realm", *Oxford Journal of Legal Studies*, vol. 33, no. 1 (2023), pp.1–29.

Lagioia F & Sartor G, "AI Systems Under Criminal Law: A Legal Analysis and a Regulatory Perspective", *Philosophy and Technology*, vol. 33 (2020), pp.433–465.

Loughnan A, "The Strange Case of the Infanticide Offence/Defence", *Oxford Journal of Legal Studies*, vol. 32, no. 4 (2012), pp.685–711.

Loughnan A & O'Connor M, "Monstrous Mothering: Understanding the Causes of and Responses to Infanticide", *Journal of Law and Medicine*, vol. 30, no. 1 (2023), pp.48–57.

Martire KA & Edmond G, "Rethinking Expert Opinion Evidence", *Melbourne University Law Review*, vol. 40, no. 3 (2017), pp.967–998.

Menzies K, "Understanding the Australian Aboriginal Experience of Collective, Historical and Intergenerational Trauma", *International Social Work*, vol. 62, no. 6 (2019), pp.1522–1534.

Meynen G, "Forensic Psychiatry and Neurolaw: Description, Developments, and Debates", *International Journal of Law and Psychiatry*, vol. 65 (2019), 101345.

Moore MS, "Relating Neuroscience to Responsibility: Comments on Hirstein, Sifferd, and Fagan's Responsible Brains", *Criminal Law and Philosophy*, vol. 16, no. 2 (2022), pp.283–298.

Morse S, "Lost in Translation?: An Essay on Law and Neuroscience", *Law and Neuroscience: Current Legal Issues*, vol. 13 (2011), pp.529–562.

Naffine N, "In Defence of the Responsible Subject", *Australian Journal of Legal Philosophy*, vol. 34 (2009), pp.222–227.

Nelken D, "Critical Criminal Law", *Journal of Law and Society*, vol. 14, no. 1 (1987), pp.105–117.

Randall M & Haskell L, "Trauma-Informed Approaches to Law: Why Restorative Justice Must Understand Trauma and Psychological Coping", *Dalhousie Law Journal*, vol. 36, no. 2 (2013), pp.501–533.

Tolmie J, Smith R, Short J, Wilson D, & Sach J, "Social Entrapment: A Realistic Understanding of the Criminal Offending of Primary Victims of Intimate Partner Violence", *New Zealand Law Review*, vol. 2 (2018), pp.181–217.

Tolmie J, Te Aho F, & Doolin K, "Criminalising Parental Failures: Documenting Bias in the Criminal Justice System", *New Zealand Women's Law Journal*, vol. 3 (2019), pp.136–182.

van Krieken R, "Law's Autonomy in Action: Anthropology and History in Court", *Social & Legal Studies*, vol. 15, no. 4 (2006), pp.574–590.

Vincent NA, "On the Relevance of Neuroscience to Criminal Responsibility", *Criminal Law and Philosophy*, vol. 4, no. 1 (2010), pp.77–98.

Websdale N, *Fatal Family Violence and the Dementias: Grey Mist Killings* (Routledge: London, 2024).

Williams G, "Offences and Defences", *Legal Studies*, vol. 2, no. 3 (1982), pp.233–256.

Reports and websites

Loughnan A, "Eponymous Law", Peter Brett QC Memorial Lecture, University of Melbourne (2023), available at: www.youtube.com/watch?v=0UTDN8VZz3M

New South Wales Department of Communities and Justice, *Report of the Inquiry into the Convictions of Kathleen Megan Folbigg* (report, 2019), available at:https://2019folbigginquiry.dcj.nsw.gov.au/documents/Report_of_the_Inquiry_into_the_convictions_of_Kathleen_Megan_Folbigg.pdf

New South Wales Departmenrt of Communities and Justice, *Inquiry into the convictions of Kathleen Megan Folbigg - Final Report* [2023] (8 November 2023), available at https://2022folbigginquiry.dcj.nsw.gov.au/content/dam/dcj/2022-folbigg-inquiry/documents/Report_of_the_2022_Inquiry_into_the_convictions_of_Kathleen_Megan_Folbigg.pdf

Sandhu B, "The Value of Lived Experience in Social Change: The Need for Leadership and Organisational Development in the Social Sector", *The Lived Experience* (2017), available at: https://thelivedexperience.org/wp-content/uploads/2017/07/The-Lived-Experience-Baljeet-Sandhu-VLE-full-report.pdf

Wilson JQ & Kelling GL, "Broken Windows", *The Atlantic* (March 1982), available at: www.theatlantic.com/magazine/archive/1982/03/broken-windows/304465/

Zekos GI, *Advanced Artificial Intelligence and Robo-Justice* (Routledge: London, 2022).

21
FORMS OF DURESS AS DEFENCE AND MITIGATION

Martin Wasik

Introduction

Duress by threats and duress of circumstances are closely related defences in English law. Duress by threats is of very long standing, while duress of circumstances has been developed more recently, being a restricted form of a necessity defence.[1] In 2015, a further defence was added to the mix, but limited to defendants who have committed an offence as a consequence of their being a victim of human trafficking, modern slavery, or exploitation. All three defences are tightly circumscribed in law. This chapter considers these old and new forms of duress, both in terms of the ascription of criminal responsibility and, since such defences often fail at trial, their likely impact upon sentencing outcome.

Duress as a defence and criminal responsibility

Duress by threats arises where the defendant has committed the offence while subject to irresistible pressure, while duress of circumstances covers the situation where the defendant has committed the offence in the belief that it was necessary to avoid dire consequences (rather than by reason of a direct threat). An example of the former is the case of *Hudson and Taylor*,[2] in which two teenage girls gave evidence at a trial stating that they did not know the man charged and could not identify him as the offender. The accused was acquitted, but the young women were later charged with perjury. They admitted that they had lied in court, but said that they had been threatened with violence by various men, one of whom was in the public gallery when they gave their evidence. The Court of Appeal quashed their convictions for perjury on the basis that the judge should have left the defence of duress to the jury. An example of the latter defence, duress of circumstances, is the case of *Willer*[3] where the defendant drove his car in a dangerous manner in order to escape from a gang of between 20 and 30 youths. They surrounded the vehicle, shouting abuse and threatening to kill Willer and his passenger, and one of them entered the car and started to grapple with the passenger. The defendant drove his car on to the pavement to escape, into a shopping precinct and then to the nearest police station, where he reported what had happened. The Court of Appeal quashed the defendant's conviction, because the potential defence had wrongly been withdrawn from consideration by the jury.

These two defences are common law rather than statutory. They are tightly restricted, and are subject to limitations, applying only where:

(i) the defendant (or someone close to the defendant) has been subjected to a threat of death or grievous bodily harm;
(ii) the defendant reasonably believed that threat to be imminent;
(iii) there was no realistic opportunity for the defendant to seek help from the police;
(iv) a person of reasonable firmness in the defendant's position (but sharing relevant characteristics such as their age and gender) would have given in to the threat and acted in the same way as the defendant; and
(v) the defendant has not created the terms of his or her own defence, such as by being a member of a criminal group in circumstances where they were aware (or ought to have been) that pressure might be applied upon them to commit an offence.

A further important limitation is that neither form of the defence is available to a defendant charged with murder as a principal offender.

Although these defences are available to reflect the moral principle that duress which significantly curtails the defendant's freedom of choice can expunge personal blame and criminal responsibility, the various limitations listed above are such that, in reality, defences of duress by threats or duress of circumstances are very unlikely to succeed. Neither *Hudson and Taylor* nor *Willer* were cases where a duress defence set before the jury resulted in an acquittal. These decisions simply state that, on the facts, there was in the view of the appeal court enough evidence for the defence to have been considered. Even so, in later cases, including the leading authority of *Hasan*,[4] it has been suggested that the appeal court in *Hudson and Taylor* was too generous to the defendants, because a perceived threat to witnesses in a courtroom could not reasonably be regarded as imminent, and they could easily have sought the protection of the police.

There are strong moral arguments for permitting a defence where a defendant's will has been overborne by threats, at least in circumstances where a reasonable person in the defendant's situation would have done the same thing. But there are also strong policy arguments against that approach. It is of course likely that criminals will target individuals who are vulnerable to threats, and it is said that to acquit in such cases would simply encourage further threats to be made. The law must therefore take a deterrent approach to encourage those threatened by criminals to resist, and to take immediate steps to inform the police about the threat. It is said that to allow the defence would permit unlawful demands by criminals to prevail over the legitimate rules (threats) of the criminal law. These arguments become stronger the more serious the offence committed. A different argument against the defence is that duress is easy for a defendant to claim but can be very difficult for the prosecution to disprove beyond reasonable doubt. As the Court of Appeal expressed it in the recent case of *Johnson*[5] (where the defendant was charged with perjury and perverting the course of justice but claimed unsuccessfully at trial to have been acting under duress from her partner in the context of a coercive and controlling relationship), one danger of relaxing the strict parameters of duress is that it would create "an open-ended defence which would be difficult or impossible to disprove".[6]

Sometimes these competing concerns have led to radical suggestions for reform, such as:

(i) duress should be abolished as a defence and simply treated as a mitigating factor (and a partial defence in murder cases) in a similar manner to provocation/loss of control; or
(ii) if duress is retained as a defence, it should be for the defendant to prove on the balance of probability.[7]

There seems little prospect of these or any other radical changes being accepted in the foreseeable future, and duress (in either of its forms) is likely to continue to be a defence available more often in theory than in reality.

Duress as a sentencing consideration

Given that the substantive law on duress is well settled, in this chapter I am concerned primarily in exploring cases of "imperfect" duress, which offer no defence but may still make a difference to the sentence imposed. As Jeremy Horder has put it,[8] there are many questions of degree in duress cases (degree of threat, degree of immediacy, degree of seriousness of crime) which may make duress a more appropriate consideration for the sentencing stage than the trial. A background of threats/intimidation is a common feature of criminal cases in general and, if the defendant has been convicted of the offence charged, it may be possible to rely upon that background as a mitigating feature. In a "near-perfect" case of duress a lenient sentence would be appropriate. It is a striking fact (though rarely mentioned by commentators) that the two defendants in *Hudson and Taylor* both received conditional discharges, a remarkably lenient disposal for perjury in the face of the court. Consider again *Willer*, where the threat was severe and immediate, the defendant's response seems reasonable in the circumstances, and police assistance was sought immediately. In that case, following Willer's change of plea to guilty, the judge imposed an absolute discharge, which is the mildest penalty available to a criminal court in England.[9] In other cases, however, where the facts fall far short of a duress defence, the mitigation may make little or no difference to sentencing outcome.

There are some appellate sentencing authorities which refer to the relevance of threats/intimidation across a variety of offences, although no case deals with the issue in any detail, and the area is largely unexplored in academic writing. One example is *Taonis*,[10] where the defendant smuggled cannabis in his baggage (street value about £42,000) into the country, but only after having been beaten and tortured, and further threatened that his female partner would also be tortured. Upon arrest, he assisted the authorities in every way, and promptly pleaded guilty. He appealed against his sentence of four years imprisonment. In the Court of Appeal, it was observed that Taonis had followed his defence lawyer's "wise and correct advice" to plead guilty and to put the duress "into the scales in mitigation". Scarman LJ, having noted that the defendant did have opportunity to alert the authorities to what was going on before he imported the drugs, nonetheless found that:

"The sentence was altogether too severe. We are clear that there had to be a term of immediate imprisonment. But there were mitigating factors which would make it quite wrong to treat this appellant as a vehicle for deterring others".

The sentence was halved to two years on appeal, one of the larger reductions to be found in the reported cases. It seems from the case report that Taonis pleaded guilty on the basis of the duress, and that the factual basis was agreed by the prosecution for sentencing purposes. If the defendant's account of duress is not accepted by the prosecution, the proper course is for the judge to conduct a trial of the issue (known as a *Newton* hearing), hearing evidence from the defendant and other witnesses if required. As at a full trial the defence bears an evidential burden on the issue, but then the prosecution must disprove it beyond reasonable doubt.

It is clear that duress may be deployed at the sentencing stage even if the defence has been run unsuccessfully at trial. In *Robinson*,[11] the defendants, both young women aged 17, on return from a holiday in Jamaica, hid bags of cocaine in their luggage, but were stopped at Manchester Airport. They claimed that while in Jamaica their money was stolen, and they were approached by men who asked them to take something back with them to the UK. They were told they would be shot if they refused, and would be watched while in the airports and on the plane. Their defences of duress failed at trial. The Court of Appeal said that the legal advice they had been given to run the defence was "horribly wrong", and "a hopeless venture", presumably because in fact they had plenty of opportunity to alert the authorities. The defendants, of course, had lost the one-third discount on their sentence which would have been applied if they had admitted their guilt straight away. In light of all this (mainly the poor legal advice), the sentence was reduced from four years to three and a half years on appeal.

These cases preceded the sentencing guideline on *Drug Offences*. In the modern era, many of the Sentencing Council's offence guidelines recognise duress as potentially relevant to sentence. This may take effect in the guideline in different ways – as a listed consideration affecting the level of the defendant's culpability, or as a matter of personal mitigation, or sometimes both. The relevant guideline on *Drug Offences* (effective from April 2021 but replacing an earlier version) employs both. It says that the defendant plays a "lower role" in terms of culpability if he or she was "engaged by pressure, coercion, intimidation, grooming and/or control". The same guideline then lists among potential mitigating factors that the defendant's involvement in the offence was "due to pressure, intimidation or coercion falling short of duress", *unless* this factor has already been taken into account in determining the defendant's culpability. The issue of duress is obviously regarded as potentially important, but one which must not be double-counted in the sentencing exercise.

If, as in *Robinson*, a duress defence has failed at trial, the judge should make it clear when passing sentence whether, and if so how much, weight in mitigation is being accorded to that issue. This is apparent from *Maloney*,[12] where a 19-year-old man with a clean record was convicted of possession of cocaine with intent to supply. It was accepted that he had previously acted as an innocent courier of packages. On this occasion, he suspected that the package contained drugs, but when he asked questions, he was threatened by gang members into going ahead. The package contained cocaine with a street value of £400,000. On appeal against his sentence of ten years' imprisonment, Treacy J in the Court of Appeal said that the judge's sentencing remarks had been rather brief, and he had failed to explain whether he interpreted the jury's verdict (i) as meaning that the duress claim had been wholly false, or (ii) whether there had been significant pressure falling short of a defence, or (iii) whether the nature of the threats was accepted but the defendant's failure to alert the authorities had precluded the defence. In any event, the sentence was reduced to eight years, in part to reflect the pressure that had been applied and in part that Maloney had been a one-off courier and had provided names and other information to the police. A sentencer in this situation is entitled to rely upon the evidence heard at the trial to interpret the jury's verdict, but if there remains real uncertainty over the proper basis for sentence, the judge must adopt the version most favourable to the defence.[13] An example of a defendant contesting a charge of causing death by dangerous driving on the basis of duress of circumstances (rather than duress by threats) is *Stallard*.[14] The defence was rejected by the jury, and on appeal the Court of Appeal held that this must have been (i) on the basis that the defendant's account (that he was being chased by another vehicle) was a lie, or (ii) although true, a person of reasonable firmness would have taken other steps to avoid the situation. These cases indicate that judges, so far as they can, should explain why the defence failed, and what mitigating value, if any, remains.

Another illustrative area is the smuggling of contraband into prison. In *Batt*,[15] a 60-year-old woman was given a sentence of three years' imprisonment for taking a small quantity of heroin (4.9g) into prison for her son. She had contested the case unsuccessfully, saying that she had been threatened that her son would otherwise be attacked in prison. The Court of Appeal noted that the duress defence had failed before being raised in mitigation, but that the judge had accepted the defendant's account. Buxton LJ said that "exceptional circumstances" were required to justify the suspension of a prison sentence,[16] and a defendant being subjected to threats was "part of the general pattern of many cases of this sort". The Court was, however, more impressed with other significant mitigation (Batt was suffering from depression and was a suicide risk following family tragedies), and she had already served a year in prison before the appeal was heard. As a result of these matters taken together, the sentence was reduced to two years, and suspended. Other cases confirm that this form of drug offending is regarded as extremely serious, so that a background of threats will usually make little headway as mitigation. In *Happe*,[17] a 71-year-old woman's sentence of 30 months was upheld for taking 38g heroin and 14g of cannabis into prison to her son, a serving prisoner. The defendant had been warned anonymously over the phone that her son owed a "debt" to another prisoner, and two men came to her home and said that her son would be harmed if she did not take the package into prison. The judge conducted a *Newton* hearing as to the issue of duress, and accepted her account. There was other mitigation, including the defendant's advanced age, medical issues, clean record, and her caring responsibilities for a disabled daughter. Despite the "desperately sad" circumstances, the seriousness of the offence, including the amount of the drugs involved, meant that the sentence was correct and, without the mitigation, would have been "much longer". In *Hynes*,[18] the defendant threw a bag containing 100g of heroin and 25g of cannabis over the perimeter wall of a prison. He pleaded guilty to an attempt to supply those drugs, but on the basis that he had acted under threat from others. On the morning of the offence, he had been pulled into a car by two men and told that if he did not comply, he or his partner would be seriously injured. Hynes had good reason to believe the threats, having previously been attacked by the same people. His home had also been damaged and broken into, forcing him to move house. Those matters had been reported to the police. A sentence of five years' imprisonment was upheld by the Court of Appeal, noting that the sentencing judge had already reduced the sentence from a starting point of seven years to take account of the mitigation.

Further examples arise from minimum sentence cases. In English law, statute provides for a minimum sentence of five years for the possession of certain kinds of firearm, unless the court takes the view that there were "exceptional circumstances" relating to the offence or to the offender which justify not imposing the minimum sentence. In *Culpepper*,[19] the defendant was found in possession of a Browning self-loading pistol containing ammunition. It was accepted that he had stored the gun for a few days because he owed money to his drug supplier, who had forced him to store the gun, together with drugs, at his home. The judge found that there were "exceptional circumstances" and imposed a sentence of two years. The Court of Appeal, however, raised the sentence up to the five-year minimum, holding that being subjected to pressure of that kind was not unusual, and so fell well short of being "exceptional". This approach was approved in *Greenfield*,[20] where the Court of Appeal held that "exceptional circumstances" should only be found in rare cases, and that judges must not be swayed by sympathy for the defendant. The reasoning here is the particular need for deterrence in relation to gun crime—clearly the Parliament's intention in creating the minimum sentence. By contrast, the sentencing decision of *Ram*[21] involved house burglary, where the Court of Appeal held that a different minimum sentence provision (of three years for the third residential burglary) ought not to apply where the defendant had committed the most recent burglary in company with the very man who was putting him in fear. In contrast to some of the earlier cases, this outcome might be considered generous, given that the defendant was involved in continuing joint criminal activity and presumably had plenty of earlier opportunity to report what was going on to the police.[22]

Compulsion and modern slavery

International agreements impose an obligation on states to combat human trafficking. In particular, Article 26 of the *Council of Europe Convention on Action against Trafficking in Human Beings* requires that the UK:

> "... in accordance with the basic principles of its legal system, [ought to] provide for the possibility of not imposing penalties on victims [of trafficking] for their involvement in unlawful activities, to the extent that they have been compelled to do so".

In 2011, the European Union (of which, at that time, the UK was a Member State) adopted a directive on trafficking in human beings. Prior to the coming into force of the Modern Slavery Act 2015 (see below), in cases where there was evidence that a person was the victim of modern slavery or human trafficking, the Crown Prosecution Service might decide not to prosecute or, in the event of prosecution the defendant might try to run the defence of duress. In 2012 in *N*,[23] the Court of Appeal held that Article 26 offered no blanket immunity to victims of trafficking. Each case required the careful exercise of prosecutorial discretion. The Director of Public Prosecutions issued guidance for prosecutors for this purpose. The Court of Appeal said that if a prosecution did go ahead, it was open to the defence to make an application to stay that prosecution as a form of abuse of process. So, in practice, there were three different ways of achieving the Article 26 objective of "not imposing penalties on victims": (i) non-prosecution (ii) stay of prosecution, and (iii) defence of duress. Failing all these, as *N* also makes clear, a lesser degree of coercion can still be relevant to sentence. Although an additional potential defence has since been introduced (see below), these options all remain available.[24]

The modern slavery act defence

The Modern Slavery Act 2015, with effect from 31 July of that year, introduced by section 45 a novel statutory defence (or, rather, two distinct defences depending upon the age of the defendant) for persons who commit an offence as a consequence of their slavery or exploitation. The defence is designed to assist and protect victims, and to provide them with a mechanism whereby they can confess in safety. It applies in England and Wales but does not extend to Scotland.[25]

If the defendant is aged 18 or over the defence will succeed if:

(i) the defendant was compelled to do the act that constitutes the offence;
(ii) the compulsion is attributable to slavery or relevant exploitation; and
(iii) a reasonable person in the same situation (and with the defendant's relevant characteristics) would have no realistic alternative but to do the act in question.

If the defendant is aged under 18, the test is different, and the defence will succeed if:

(i) the defendant committed the act that constitutes the offence as a direct consequence of being, or having been, a victim of slavery or relevant exploitation; and
(ii) a reasonable person in the same situation (and with the defendant's relevant characteristics) would have no realistic alternative but to do the act in question.

The modern slavery defence is modelled on the defence of duress. As a legislative approach that was perhaps inevitable, but modern slavery is not simply duress by another name. Modern slavery can involve an almost complete extinction of the victim's autonomy and the loss of opportunity to escape from the situation of servitude that they find themselves in. It is arguable that the modern slavery defence should be seen as more akin to a loss of capacity defence. Where a victim of trafficking commits what would otherwise be regarded as a criminal offence, their entire situation of desperation is relevant to their potential liability rather than, as with duress, the issue being whether the offence was committed as a result of a specific threat which sapped the will of the defendant on that occasion, or was committed in the spur of the moment in order to escape from a specific threat. There is a resonance here with Baroness Hale's approach in *Hasan*, where she accepted the general case for strict parameters being applied to the defence of duress, but argued that different considerations ought to apply to a defendant who commits an offence when trapped within a continuing violent or abusive relationship. As Laird[26] rightly points out, requiring (adult) victims of slavery and trafficking to show the same level of fortitude as "normal people" is very problematic given the extreme nature of their circumstances. Whether a reasonable person would have thought that there was a realistic alternative to committing the offence in question seems an inappropriate question, given that the trafficked victim may be in a situation of "learned helplessness"[27] akin to the battered spouse. It is understandable that a trafficked victim may fail to take an opportunity to escape their traffickers and might well think that going to the police would lead to their own prosecution and deportation, rather than providing sanctuary.[28]

Be that as it may, we have the defence which we have. By comparison with duress, the new defence is more generous in that it does not require that the compulsion took the form of threats of death or very serious harm. However, in other respects the defences are very similar in that they both require a reasonable standard of fortitude in resisting the threats. The defendant's relevant characteristics can be taken into account, but these are limited by the statute to age, gender, and any physical or mental illness or disability. This again mirrors the approach in duress.[29] As far as causation is concerned, for adults the compulsion to commit the offence must be "attributable" to the slavery or relevant exploitation, but for those under 18 the offence must be a "direct consequence" of slavery or relevant exploitation. It is unclear whether this different wording is significant. The new defence is much narrower than duress in that it only applies to victims of slavery or relevant exploitation and, very importantly in practice, it is unavailable in relation to a wide range of offences. Over 100 offences to which the defence cannot be run are listed in schedule 4 to the Act while, as we have seen, duress is unavailable only in murder cases. In principle, then, for many trafficked victims (including child victims) the section 45 defence is simply not available, and they will have to fall back on the duress defence or hope for non-prosecution or a stay of proceedings. Further, if the relevant offence was committed before the 2015 Act came into force, the new defence is unavailable. In the case of *Joseph*,[30] the Court of Appeal rejected an argument that the requirements of the defence of duress should be relaxed in some way so as to cater for old cases where the defence in section 45 would have been applicable, but the offence occurred before the Act was in force. The Court said that the 2015 Act was not retrospective and the law of duress was well settled. Finally, as with duress, the defendant bears an evidential burden, and it is for the prosecution to disprove the section 45 defence beyond reasonable doubt.

Procedure and problems with the defence

If a person intends to rely on the section 45 defence, the proper procedure is for a "first responder" (usually the police, Border Force, a social worker or a charity such as Barnardo or the Salvation Army) to refer the case *via* the National Referral Mechanism (NRM) to a Single Competent Authority (SCA) within the Home Office to determine whether the evidence shows that the person is in fact a victim of trafficking or modern slavery. Referrals to the SCA are currently running at around 10,000 cases each year.[31] This whole process has been the subject of regular criticism by the Court of Appeal, which called the NRM a "tick-box exercise" in *Brecani*.[32] The SCA produces a "conclusive grounds" decision in due course. If there is a positive finding by the SCA, the CPS will review the case. A prosecution is then unlikely, and the defendant will thereby avoid the risk of criminal liability. The CPS is not, however, bound by the SCA assessment, and may decide to prosecute anyway, requiring the defendant to then rely upon the section 45 defence or duress if available, or to plead guilty. Prosecution may occur where the CPS believes it to be in the public interest to take the case to trial, considering matters such as (i) the seriousness of the offence, (ii) the apparent degree of coercion involved, and (iii) the degree of nexus between the trafficking and the offending. The Court of Appeal upheld the decision of the CPS to prosecute in *EK*[33] for a combination of these reasons. The Court of Appeal in *Brecani* held that a conclusive grounds' decision cannot be put before a jury at a trial, nor could an SCA caseworker give expert evidence as to their findings because caseworkers are "minor civil servants" and therefore not qualified as expert witnesses. This decision was greeted with some consternation by defence lawyers,[34] given SCA reports are regularly put before the appeal courts.

Despite its other limitations, the section 45 defence can be deployed for drugs' offences, and that is where it has been most used so far. These cases include importation and possession with intent to supply Class A drugs, matters which attract heavy sentences on conviction. The defence is also available in cases involving cultivation of cannabis. The classic example is the "gardener", discovered by the police locked inside a cannabis factory, who has been required to work unpaid to look after the plants as a means of paying off a "debt" owed to those who have exploited him or her. The section 45 defence may be of value here, since the defence of duress is confined to threats of death or serious injury and does not extend to false imprisonment.[35] The section 45 defence has also been relied upon in "county lines" drugs' cases (with variable success), in false documents' cases, and miscellaneous others.

There is a large number of appellate cases where facts indicating that the defendant was the victim of slavery or trafficking have not emerged until after the person was convicted or pleaded guilty to the offence. In these cases, the Court of Appeal has been prepared to hear fresh evidence, in the form of an SCA report, and then to decide whether the conviction must be quashed because (i) a defence under section 45 would likely have succeeded on the facts, or (ii) an application to stay the prosecution on abuse of process grounds would have succeeded. Some of these cases have been reconsidered years after the conviction took place and indeed long after the sentence has been served. One such example is *AFU*,[36] where a Vietnamese national was found tending the plants in a cannabis factory. He was prosecuted and pleaded guilty in 2016, but the Court of Appeal in 2023 quashed his conviction. The Court was very critical of the failures of the authorities to check whether the defendant was the victim of trafficking, and concluded that there had been an abuse of process since a section 45 defence would have succeeded. In *BYA*,[37] decided in 2022, the defendant had pleaded guilty to false identity document offences in 2009. Having regard to a much later SCA report, the Court of Appeal concluded that the offences had been committed when the defendant, who had been trafficked and forced to work as a prostitute for six years, was trying to flee her traffickers, and that if the CPS had known of the circumstances, it would not have prosecuted. A failure to identify people trafficking cases early enough has clearly been a problem, but it is hoped that with extensive training of practitioners and judges in these matters and the raised profile of the issue of people trafficking in the news, and, for that matter, in popular literature and television dramas,[38] such cases are much less likely now to be overlooked.

Victim trafficking as a sentencing consideration

As with the discussion on duress above, I turn now to consider "imperfect" cases, namely where the defendant has been prosecuted and a section 45 defence has not been run or has failed, or where the defence is unavailable either because the offence is excluded by the 2015 Act, or because it was committed before the Act came into force.

In the first group of cases, circumstances of exploitation affecting the defendant operated as important mitigation. In *D*,[39] the defendant admitted dealing in Class A drugs, and had a significant criminal record for dishonesty offences. His custodial sentence of two years and six months was, however, reduced to 18 months and suspended on appeal in light of a decision letter from the SCA stating that when the defendant committed the drugs' offences he had been exploited and recruited into a county lines gang by a dealer to whom he owed money. The defendant, who suffered from cerebral palsy, had been injured and threatened and forced to watch over a quantity of money and drugs. Recently, he had freed himself from the criminal connections, and had turned his life around. It is significant here that the SCA report was admissible in relation to sentence but (following *Brecani*) would not have been admissible at trial. Another example is *HF*,[40] where the defendant had also been involved in drug dealing. An SCA report found that he had been trafficked in 2019 in the sense that violent criminals had exploited him. On this occasion, it was said that the same people were still involved, but it had been accepted by the defence that a section 45 defence was unavailable because the defendant had had opportunity to seek help from the police. These issues had been canvassed at the sentencing hearing, along with the defendant's youth (he was 18 at the time of the offending) and immaturity, but the Court of Appeal reduced the final sentence from 36 months to 30 months because it felt that insufficient weight had been given to those mitigating factors.

In the next group of cases, despite there being evidence of exploitation, the appeal court found that the mitigation was limited in scope and that the sentencing court had already given appropriate effect to it. In *Miller-Cross*,[41] the defendant, aged 23 and with previous convictions, was convicted of possession of Class A drugs with intent to supply and possession of criminal property. He ran a section 45 defence at his trial and, because this case preceded the ruling in *Brecani*, the jury was told of the content of the SCA report. The report said that the defendant had been recruited against his will into a gang, and had been stabbed in the leg when he tried to break that connection. He had then been taken to a different part of the country and coerced into drug dealing. Nonetheless, the defence was rejected by the jury. The defendant received a sentence of five years and four months. The Court of Appeal confirmed that it was a matter for the sentencing judge to assess the relevance to sentence of pressure short of a defence, but that, taken on the whole, the sentence was not excessive. A slightly different case was *Ahmed*,[42] where the defendant had pleaded guilty to fraud against a background of dishonest offending. The Court of Appeal considered an SCA determination that she was the victim of trafficking by criminal associates of hers. The Court of Appeal refused leave to appeal, holding that the circumstances now advanced by the defendant could and should have been raised at her sentencing hearing. She had not been under direct threat from the other people involved. She was able to move about freely and had ample time to seek help had she wished to.

In the final group of cases the mitigation was found to be of limited value because of the lack of a clear nexus between the trafficking or exploitation (which was accepted to have occurred) and the offence. A striking case is *Spence*,[43] where the defendant was convicted of murder when aged 18, the murder taking place when he was 16 years old. He had previous convictions for drug offences. There was an SCA determination in 2022 that the defendant was a victim of modern slavery in the sense that he had been the victim of criminal exploitation. The Court of Appeal thought it remarkable that there had been no mention of these matters at the trial (which had lasted 48 days), and that even if the exploitation went to explain the defendant's involvement in drug dealing, it was irrelevant to his involvement in the murder. He was young and immature but there was nothing to suggest that he had been pressured into the killing. In *AUL*,[44] the defendant, now aged 26, was convicted of dealing in Class A drugs. It was accepted that he had been trafficked from North Africa to Spain when he was 15 years old. He then came to the UK and was settled with a supportive foster family. Aged 20, however, he left the family and began to live on the streets, used drugs, and became involved in drug dealing. There was an NRM report before the Court of Appeal with a finding that the defendant had been trafficked within the UK, but the Court was dismissive of that report, saying that it had been "uncritical" and that the defendant's account of what had happened after he left the foster home was inconsistent and unreliable. The Court found that the defendant had received money for dealing in drugs and spent his "earnings" as he wished, and so could have abandoned his criminal lifestyle had he wished to do so.

Conclusions

In an article published over 50 years ago, Peter Glazebrook pointed out that although there was (and still is) no general defence of necessity in English criminal law, there are other ways in which the law handles "the plea of necessity" when it arises.[45] A range of juristic techniques are utilised. These involve the various use of discretionary powers—to not prosecute, or to stay a prosecution which has been begun or, most importantly, devices of pardoning or exercising mercy through sentencing. The duress and modern slavery defences provide a similar and striking example of the different routes by which the criminal justice system may "provide for the possibility of not imposing penalties", to quote Article 26 of the Convention. The defendant may not be prosecuted, or the trial may be halted, or one of two possible defences (where available) may succeed. Finally, if none of these outcomes is possible, a lesser penalty may still be imposed through the sentencing process. As Glazebrook put it, "the most persistent attitude to the problem raised – intellectually unsatisfying though it may be – is that hard cases are best dealt with by the prerogative of mercy."

This chapter has considered the various ways in which a merciful outcome may be attained for defendants who have committed crimes in extreme circumstances of duress, modern slavery, and trafficking. The increased appreciation in recent years of the considerable scale of this problem has generated new substantive laws, new administrative procedures, and has led to a complex jurisprudential area with voluminous case law. As we have seen, Parliament and the courts have been very wary of allowing any defence based upon the defendant's assertion that he or she was compelled into crime by threats. Such claims, it is said, may be spurious, almost impossible to disprove, and are often put forward by those already steeped in criminal activity. To acquit will also simply encourage more intimidation and exploitation. Criminals have always targeted vulnerable people to do their bidding, and to run their risks. The law has therefore adopted a general stance of deterrence – the law must provide an even stiffer threat than that posed by the criminals, otherwise the legitimate rules of the criminal law are seriously undermined. The section 45 defence has been an important liberal counter-development to these prevailing attitudes in English law (new criminal offences are commonplace but new defences extremely rare). Unfortunately, however, the defence is far from perfect, and modelled too closely upon duress. Its terms are too restrictive – there are many offences to which it simply does not apply, and it imposes requirements of rationality and reasonableness on the part of trafficked victims which are unfair and inappropriate.

If no defence is available, or the defence has been rejected by the jury, the matter falls within the remit of the sentencing judge. The sentencing cases considered in this chapter suggest that many of the same sentencing considerations are being applied in relation to trafficking cases as have traditionally been applied in duress. The similarities between the defences perhaps made that tendency inevitable. It is further important for the judge to articulate the findings of fact which will inform the sentencing decision. Namely, was the defence rejected as entirely spurious, or did it fail for a reason which still leaves some room for mitigation? A much wider range of contextual material becomes relevant and available at this sentencing stage than is admissible at trial, including a detailed pre-sentence report, as well as the NRM details and SRA report. In the situation where a defence has failed but the same matters are raised as mitigation, the tight parameters of the defence can be relaxed somewhat.[46] There is more scope for the defence to explain the full circumstances. A background of intimidation can be examined alongside personal mitigation, such as vulnerability and previous good character. Relevant matters for the judge also include the seriousness of the offence (especially if a special deterrent approach is well settled in the case-law), the defendant's age and personal circumstances, and the nature and duration of the defendant's dealings with the traffickers or criminal gang. Always important is whether, or at what stage, the defendant had contact with the police or other authorities. A failure on the defendant's part to seek help when there was a real chance to do so may be fatal to the defence but providing assistance (including co-operation at police interview), naming names, giving a timely frank admission of the offence, and a prompt guilty plea can all provide good mitigation. The extent of the continuing compulsion and threat is also important. The court will consider whether or not the level of compulsion revealed in the defendant's own account and by the reports was such that the defendant's criminality was significantly diminished. Finally, there is also the degree of nexus (including the passage of time) between the criminal exploitation and the offence committed. The defence will not succeed without a clear causal connection. In mitigation the causal link need not be quite so clear. Courts are recognising that the impact of the trauma experienced by some victims will remain with them for a very long time even when the immediate threats have been removed. In *BYA*,[47] the Court of Appeal, reviewing a number of the earlier cases, held that each case was fact-specific, the court could not be prescriptive about the degree of compulsion involved or even the passage of time, but that all questions as to defence or mitigation were to be approached with the greatest sensitivity.

Notes

1. An outmoded defence of "marital coercion" was abolished by statute in 2014.
2. *Hudson and Taylor* [1971] 2 QB 202.
3. *Willer* (1986) 83 Cr App R 225.
4. *Hasan* [2005] UKHL 22. See also *Batchelor* [2013] EWCA Crim 2638.
5. *Johnson* [2022] EWCA Crim 832.
6. *Johnson* [2022] EWCA Crim 832 at para 50.
7. This reversal of the burden of proof in duress was proposed by the Law Commission ("Legislating the Criminal Code: Offences Against the Person and General Defences", Law Com No 218, Cm. 2370 (1993), paras 33-34) and received continuing support from Baroness Hale in *Hasan* [2005] UKHL 22.
8. J Horder, *Ashworth's Principles of Criminal Law* (Oxford University Press: Oxford, 10th edn, 2022), p.89.
9. Indeed, the judge passed sentence immediately after the change of plea, without even waiting for the jury to return a not guilty verdict, a significant procedural error for which he was rebuked by the appeal court.
10. *Taonis* (1974) 59 Cr App R 160.
11. *Robinson* [2004] EWCA Crim 360.
12. *Maloney* [2005] EWCA Crim 2210.
13. For discussion, see M Wasik & A Ashworth, "Issues in sentencing procedure", *Criminal Law Review*, vol. 5 (2020), p.397.
14. *Stallard* [2003] EWCA Crim 1633.

15 *Batt* [1999] 2 Cr App R (S) 223.
16 In accordance with the Criminal Justice Act 1991, s 5, a restriction since removed by the Criminal Justice Act 2003.
17 *Happe* [2010] EWCA Crim 893.
18 *Hynes* [2008] EWCA Crim 1934.
19 *Culpepper* [2013] EWCA Crim 1466.
20 *Greenfield* [2016] EWCA Crim 765.
21 *Ram* [2021] EWCA Crim 2020.
22 It should be noted that at the time of this case, the test for disapplying the minimum sentence was the presence of "particular circumstances" relating to any of the offences or to the offender which would make it unjust do so in all the circumstances. This test has recently been tightened to "exceptional circumstances", bringing it into line with the firearms minimum term provision, Parliament having taken the view that judges were choosing to avoid the minimum sentence provision in too many cases.
23 *N* [2012] EWCA Crim 189.
24 *AAD* [2022] EWCA Crim 106; see further C Gregory, "The modern slavery defence", *Cambridge Law Journal,* vol. 81, no. 3 (2022), p.470.
25 As to which see S Mennim & N Wake, "Does Scotland require a defence equivalent to section 45 Modern Slavery Act 2015 (England and Wales)?", *Journal of Criminal Law,* vol. 82, no. 5 (2018), p.373.
26 K Laird, "Evaluating the relationship between section 45 of the Modern Slavery Act 2015 and the defence of duress: An opportunity missed?", *Criminal Law Review,* no. 6 (2016), pp.395.
27 The term is used to describe the reaction of a victim to chronic and repeated abuse, whereby they feel that whatever they do nothing will change. They have no way of physically or emotionally breaking free from their abuser and the abuse. They cannot extricate themselves from the violent situation no matter how many cries for help they may make: per Hallett LJ in *GAC* (2013) EWCA Crim 1472.
28 SSM Edwards, "Coercion and compulsion – Re-imagining crimes and defences", *Criminal Law Review,* no. 12 (2016), p.876.
29 See *Bowen* [1997] 1 WLR 372.
30 *Joseph* [2017] EWCA Crim 36.
31 Home Office, *Modern Slavery and the National Referral Mechanism* (November 2021).
32 *Brecani* [2021] EWCA Crim 731. See also *AAD* [2022] EWCA Crim 106.
33 *EK* [2018] EWCA Crim 2961.
34 See for these, and other, criticisms: F Gerry KC, R Pagano, & C Hodgetts, "Disorganised crime: Legal and evidential challenges of raising a modern slavery de fence", *Criminal Law Review,* no. 12 (2022), p.961.
35 *van Dao* [2012] EWCA Crim 1717.
36 *AFU* [2023] EWCA Crim 23.
37 *BYA* [2022] EWCA Crim 1326.
38 R Karmy-Jones KC & Sophie Quinton-Carter, "Human trafficking and modern slavery – 'a very particular set of skills'", *Archbold Review,* no. 5 (2022), p.7.
39 *D* [2022] EWCA Crim 603.
40 *HF* [2022] EWCA Crim 1226.
41 *Miller-Cross* [2022] EWCA Crim 346.
42 *Ahmed* [2022] EWCA Crim 1789.
43 *Spence* [2022] EWCA Crim 1623.
44 *AUL* [2022] EWCA Crim 1435.
45 P Glazebrook, "The necessity plea in English criminal law", *Cambridge Law Journal,* vol. 30, no. 1 (1972), p.87.
46 See further A von Hirsch & N Jareborg, "Provocation and culpability", in Ferdinand Schoeman (ed), *Responsibility, Character and the Emotions* (Cambridge University Press: Cambridge, 1987), p.241, and M Wasik, "Excuses at the sentencing stage", *Criminal Law Review* (1983), p.450.
47 *BYA* [2022] EWCA Crim 1326.

References

Legislation

Criminal Justice Act 1991.
Criminal Justice Act 2003.
Modern Slavery Act 2015.

Cases

R v AAD [2022] EWCA Crim 106.
R v AFU [2023] EWCA Crim 23.
R v Ahmed [2022] EWCA Crim 1789.
R v AUL [2022] EWCA Crim 1435.
R v Batchelor [2013] EWCA Crim 2638.
R v Batt [1999] 2 Cr App R (S) 223.
R v Bowen [1997] 1 WLR 372.
R v Brecani [2021] EWCA Crim 731.
R v BYA [2022] EWCA Crim 1326.
R v Culpepper [2013] EWCA Crim 1466.
R v D [2022] EWCA Crim 603.
R v EK [2018] EWCA Crim 2961.
R v GAC (2013) EWCA Crim 1472.
R v Greenfield [2016] EWCA Crim 765.
R v Happe [2010] EWCA Crim 893.
R v Hasan [2005] UKHL 22.
R v HF [2022] EWCA Crim 1226.
R v Hudson and Taylor [1971] 2 QB 202.
R v Hynes [2008] EWCA Crim 1934.
R v Johnson [2022] EWCA Crim 832.
R v Joseph [2017] EWCA Crim 36.
R v Malloney [2005] EWCA Crim 2210.
R v Miller-Cross [2022] EWCA Crim 346.
R v N [2012] EWCA Crim 189.
R v Ram [2021] EWCA Crim 2020.
R v Robinson [2004] EWCA Crim 360.
R v Spence [2022] EWCA Crim 1623.
R v Stallard [2003] EWCA Crim 1633.
R v Taonis (1974) 59 Cr App R 160.
R v van Dao [2012] EWCA Crim 1717.
R v Willer (1986) 83 Cr App R 225.

Books and book chapters

Horder J, *Ashworth's Principles of Criminal Law* (Oxford University Press: Oxford, 10th edn, 2022).
von Hirsch A & Jareborg N, "Provocation and culpability", in Schoeman F (ed), *Responsibility, Character and the Emotions* (Cambridge University Press: Cambridge, 1987).

Journal articles

Edwards SSM, "Coercion and compulsion – Re-imagining crimes and defences", *Criminal Law Review*, no. 12 (2016), pp.876–899.
Gerry F, Pagano R, & Hodgetts C, "Disorganised crime: Legal and evidential challenges of raising a modern slavery de fence", *Criminal Law Review*, no. 12 (2022), pp.961–986.

Glazebrook P, "The necessity plea in English criminal law", *Cambridge Law Journal*, vol. 30, no. 1 (1972), pp.87–119.
Gregory C, "The modern slavery defence", *Cambridge Law Journal*, vol. 81, no. 3 (2022), pp.470–473.
Karmy-Jones R & Quinton-Carter S, "Human trafficking and modern slavery – 'A very particular set of skills'", *Archbold Review*, no. 5 (2022), pp. 7–10.
Laird K, "Evaluating the relationship between section 45 of the Modern Slavery Act 2015 and the defence of duress: An opportunity missed?", *Criminal Law Review*, no. 6 (2016), pp.395–404.
Mennim S & Wake N, "Does Scotland require a defence equivalent to section 45 Modern Slavery Act 2015 (England and Wales)?", *Journal of Criminal Law*, vol. 82, no. 5 (2018), pp.373–377.
Wasik M, "Excuses at the sentencing stage", *Criminal Law Review* (1983), pp.450–465.
Wasik M & Ashworth A, "Issues in sentencing procedure", *Criminal Law Review*, vol. 5 (2020), pp.397–410.

Reports

Home Office, *Modern Slavery and the National Referral Mechanism* (November 2021).
Law Commission, *Legislating the Criminal Code: Offences Against the Person and General Defences*, Law Com. No. 218, Cm. 2370 (1993).

PART III
Domains of Criminal Responsibility

22
CORPORATE ACCOUNTABILITY FOR INTERNATIONAL CRIMES
Towards an International Enforcement Mechanism

Evelyne Owiye Asaala

Introduction

As the debate on corporate accountability for atrocities evolves, its proponents decry three major impediments: the overreaching economic and political influence of corporations,[1] the absence of binding substantive international norms to guide development, and the isolated nature of the corporate accountability movement. Economic and political influence by corporations is often exerted to undermine corporate accountability initiatives, including the adoption of binding international obligations. For instance, this influence has favoured the adoption of voluntary rules like the Corporate Social Responsibility (CSR) in 1970s, and the UN Guiding Principles of 2011, instead of binding obligations. Although the *Legally Binding Instrument to regulate the Activities of Transnational Corporations in International Human Rights Law and other Business Enterprises* (the Human Rights Council Draft Treaty of 2021) and its Protocol seek to regulate corporate behaviour, the two instruments do not create an enforcement mechanism. Instead, article 9 vests jurisdiction over corporate transnational activity "in the courts of the state where such acts or omissions occurred or where the alleged perpetrator is domiciled." Yet, in most cases, enforcement through the host states has proven inadequate, particularly in developing countries because of the dependency syndrome[2] arising from the economic and political influence that corporates wield. The option of international criminal law and its potential impact in closing the impunity gap for corporate atrocities seems to be "a no-go zone".

A recent study has also noted an additional shortcoming in corporate accountability efforts that "transitional justice, business and human rights and corporate accountability movements have operated as largely separate fields",[3] thus necessitating a mechanism with a unifying approach in seeking corporate accountability for atrocities. Therefore, any meaningful debate seeking to advance the discourse on corporate accountability for atrocities must begin by addressing these issues.

The overall objective of this contribution is to advance the debate around these controversial issues and suggest solutions that favor the incorporation of corporate accountability for international crimes within the International Criminal Court (ICC). First, the paper begins with a critique of existing initiatives towards creating binding corporate accountability obligations. This section confirms the absence of such initiatives towards corporate accountability for international crimes in an international forum. The prevailing assumption in this section is that the economic and political influence of corporations compromises the adoption of binding obligations in international law. Second, the paper proposes that corporate criminal accountability be incorporated within the ICC. It argues not only that this initiative has the ability to unify transitional justice, business and human rights and corporate accountability movements, but also that the incorporation of corporate accountability within a permanent international criminal tribunal will overcome the economic and political influence of corporations by making them accountable. However, this section envisages potential corporate opposition towards this initiative. This therefore necessitates sufficient pressure from international/global agents to curtail the corporate veto. Finally, the paper draws some conclusions.

Initiatives for creating binding international norms on corporate accountability in light of the corporate veto

Existing initiatives towards corporate accountability are within the general context of human rights accountability at the national level. Although there exist traces of using international criminal law to address corporate accountability in ad hoc tribunals and in national jurisdictions, this has been greatly limited. Thus, the discussion in this section focuses on human rights based corporate accountability initiatives for national enforcement.

Corporates are bound by the various international human rights treaties as juridical persons inferred within the concept of "legal persons".[4] Thus, when the Preamble to the *Universal Declaration of Human Rights* calls on people to promote and respect the observance and respect for human rights and fundamental freedoms, this includes private sector actors also.[5] And when the *Convention on Economic, Social and Cultural Rights* refers to every individual being "under a responsibility to strive for the promotion and observance of the rights recognised in the present Covenant," this also bestows responsibility upon private sector actors.

Two international treaties expressly create binding obligations for the private sector: the *Convention Against Corruption*[6] and the *Apartheid Convention*[7]. However, these two treaties do not address corporate responsibility for general human rights obligations. Instead, their focus is limited on their respective limited thematic areas.

Despite several initiatives towards adopting binding international rules of corporate accountability for gross human rights violation, there are no binding international norms that regulate corporate accountability for atrocities. Attempts to adopt a binding regulatory framework have, over the years, been frustrated and abandoned. In the 1970s, a UN-led initiative sought to adopt a *Code of Conduct on Transitional Corporations*.[8] During its negotiation, some governments from developed countries favoured a voluntary code:[9] "they were particularly interested in strong investment protection provisions."[10] In its later stages of negotiations, a number of issues concerning investment protection made it difficult to achieve an agreement. Such issues included the legal nature of the Code, definition of terms and their application to state-owned and non-state/private-owned enterprises, national treatment and fair equitable treatment, nationalisation and compensation, settlement of disputes, jurisdiction and respect for national sovereignty. The controversy pitted the position of developed countries against that taken by developing countries. Eventually, these negotiations fizzled out and the initiative was abandoned.[11]

In 2003, the UN Sub-Commission on the Promotion and Protection of Human Rights drafted a document called the *Norms on the Responsibilities of Transnational Corporations and Other Business Enterprises with Regard to Human Rights* (Draft Norms).[12] These norms sought to substantively regulate human rights responsibilities for business. According to Joanna Kyriakakis, these Draft Norms constituted a re-statement of legal principles applicable to corporations drawn from treaty law and customary law.[13] As such, they acquired the characterisation of being soft law[14] of a non-voluntary nature.[15] The pursuit of a potentially binding instrument was vehemently opposed, especially by the business community.[16] This corporate opposition to the norms was later associated with the norms' failure to sufficiently engage businesses in their development process.[17] The UN Human Rights Commission rejected these norms in 2004.[18]

Following the collapse of the Draft Norms, the Human Rights Commission appointed John Ruggie (the then UN Special Representative of the Secretary General on Business and Human Rights) to evaluate the situation and make recommendations on corporate responsibility and accountability for human rights.[19] This initiative created the *Protect, Respect and Remedy: A Framework for Business and Human Rights* in 2008,[20] which is soft law and mainly state-centric in the enforcement of legal obligations with respect to compliance with human rights obligations. As the name suggests, the Framework emphasises three major aspects: (1) the responsibility of the state to protect against corporate human rights abuses; (2) the duty of the private sector to respect human rights through due diligence; and (3) the right of victims of corporate human rights violations to an effective remedy. This Framework was supplemented by the *UN Guiding Principles on Business and Human Rights* endorsed by the Human Rights Council in 2011, to enable further implementation of the framework.[21]

In addition to the Guiding Principles, the *UN Compact Guidance on Responsible Business in Conflict-Affected and High-Risk Areas* seeks to assist companies and other private sector actors to improve their conduct related to human rights.

Notably, there are additional norms which regulate corporate behaviour towards human rights in soft law. International efforts to regulate corporate adherence to human rights standards have been dominated by the concept of Corporate Social Responsibility (CSR). This concept encourages businesses "to take into account social and environmental impacts in their decision making, operations and interaction with stakeholders, rather than being solely guided by immediate economic benefits and costs."[22] CSR was a business-led and voluntary initiative. Essentially, the private sector exercised discretion concerning when and how to exercise this mode of obligation. As a voluntary process undertaken by companies themselves, CSR is inherently limited as an effective tool to guarantee corporate compliance with human rights standards. While most favoured by the business community in lieu of binding treaty obligations, the shortcomings of CSR in enforcing human rights standards within the business community soon led to agitation for binding rules.

Other soft laws have been developed to regulate corporate behaviour, albeit in limited thematic areas of focus. These include, first, the *International Labour Organization Tripartite Declaration of Principles Concerning Multinational Enterprises and Social Policy*.[23] These are social policy guidelines for business actors and their goal is to instil sustainable workplace practices. Second, there is the *UN Global Compact*.[24] Third, there is the Organisation of Economic Co-operation and Development (OECD) *Guidelines for Multinational Enterprises*.[25] These are principles and standards that aim to achieve responsible business conduct in a global context. Finally, there are the *Voluntary Principles on Security and Human Rights*.[26] These are principles that seek to achieve human rights compliance in the manner in which the oil, gas, and mining companies provide security for their operations.

Building upon these soft law guidelines, and in response to critiques about their limitations, efforts towards a binding treaty on business and human rights have re-emerged. In 2014, the HRC appointed an open-ended inter-governmental working group to develop a binding international treaty.[27] The working draft treaty and its protocol were released in 2018. A third draft was published in 2021, and the treaty continued to be negotiated by the Open-Ended Intergovernmental Working Group in October 2022. Notably, the current draft treaty does not create an enforcement mechanism, but article 9 vests jurisdiction in the courts of the state where:

a. the human rights abuse occurred and/or produced effects; or
b. an act or omission contributing to the human rights abuse occurred;
c. the legal or natural persons alleged to have committed an act or omission causing or contributing to such human rights abuse in the context of business activities, including those of a transnational character, are domiciled; or
d. the victim is a national of or is domiciled.[28]

This draft binding treaty follows the footsteps of all the soft laws cited above which interpret the enforcement of corporate obligations towards human rights observance to lie exclusively with respective states.[29] In this regard, the Committee on Economic, Social and Cultural Rights (ESCR) has, thus, observed that states have the primary legal duty under international human rights law to protect its citizens from human rights violations.[30] This duty entails the obligation to respect, protect, and fulfil.[31]

In the context of business and human rights, a state's obligation to respect will require the state to conform its laws and policies on corporate operations to human rights standards.[32] Through legislation, state parties to the Covenant on Social Economic and Cultural Rights have mandatory obligations to guarantee that businesses conduct due diligence to ensure that their activities do not curtail or breach the enjoyment of the various social, economic, and cultural rights.

The obligation to protect requires states to "effectively safeguard rights holders against infringements of their economic, social and cultural rights involving corporate actors, by establishing appropriate laws, regulations, as well as monitoring, investigation and accountability procedures to set and enforce standards for the performance of corporations."[33] Non-compliance with this obligation can either be through action or inaction.[34] In the case of human rights violations by corporates, states are under the responsibility to ensure that victims of corporate abuses of economic, social, and cultural rights can access effective remedies.[35] This can be achieved through judicial, administrative, legislative, or other appropriate means.[36] The duty of states to prevent the violation of social, economic, and cultural rights by corporates is not limited to those corporates that are within a states' jurisdiction. It also extends to contraventions abroad by corporations which have their main seat under the state's jurisdiction.[37]

The UN Guiding Principles also address the duty of states to protect against human rights violations committed by private sector actors. It contains specific provisions that require states to review whether their policies, legislation, and regulations effectively address the heightened risk of business enterprises being involved in human rights violations in conflict-affected areas. Principle 7 of the Guiding Principles specifically requires states to ensure that business enterprises operating in conflict-affected areas are not involved in human rights abuses, including by engaging with private sector actors to identify and mitigate human-rights-related risks of their businesses and activities. Principle 7 also requires states to deny access to public support and services for business enterprises involved in gross human rights violations. It further requires states to ensure that their policies, legislation, regulations, and enforcement measures are effective in addressing the risk of business involvement in gross human rights violations.

State obligations to fulfil the realisation of social economic and cultural rights, as they concern corporate activities, require states to "undertake to obtain the corporate sector's support to the realisation of economic, social and cultural rights".[38] By extension, this obligation also requires states that are home to companies active abroad "to assist, as appropriate, including in situations of armed conflict and natural disaster, host States in building capacities needed to address the corporate responsibility for the observance of economic, social and cultural rights".[39]

Notwithstanding these robust state obligations which envisage corporate criminal accountability, there has been no cohesive state approach at the national, regional, and international level to the active use of international criminal law.

The implementation of these state obligations to safeguard citizens from corporate atrocities is not limited to individual states. States have the freedom to jointly advance the subject of corporate accountability for grave human rights violations at both regional and global levels. Already, regional human rights systems demonstrate some development towards these ends and thus provide a platform to further advance the discourse.

At the regional level, there is no regional human rights court that has jurisdiction over corporate criminal accountability. However, although the Inter-American Court on Human Rights does not have jurisdiction over corporate criminal liability, the court has "issued important decisions on state obligations to investigate corporate-related human rights abuses".[40] In the African region, *General Comment No. 3 on the African Charter on Human and Peoples' Rights: the Right to Life* expressly calls on the African Union (AU) member states to hold to account private individuals and groups involved in violating the right to life.[41] As if to avoid any doubt, *the Protocol on Amendments to the Protocol on the Statute of the African Court of Justice and Human Rights, 2014* (the Malabo Protocol)[42] expressly provides for corporate accountability for transnational and international crimes. Article 46C does not limit the types of incorporated entities that might be prosecuted, which narrows the impunity gap as it allows the Court some flexibility in different circumstances. However, the Malabo Protocol has not yet come to force.

The State Reporting Guidelines and Principles on Articles 21 and 24 of the African Charter Relating to Extractive Industries, Human Rights and the Environment provides that: "states should adopt legislation and put in place measures particularly on restriction of extraction in conflict-affected areas and criminal liability for involvement of companies in human rights abuses in conflict situations".[43]

Notably, the 2019 *African Union's Transitional Justice Policy* is silent on the issue of human rights and businesses. The private sector is only recognised as an entity for resource mobilisation to fund transitional justice processes.[44] However, there is an ongoing AU process of developing a policy framework on business and human rights for Africa. The policy seeks to develop a regional framework for the implementation of the *UN Guidelines on Business and Human Rights* in Africa. The draft is yet to be adopted.

Despite the absence of ad hoc and hybrid courts that exercise jurisdiction over corporates, a few examples of cases involving corporate officials who were prosecuted and, in some instances, convicted do exist.[45]

The exercise of domestic jurisdiction over international crimes has also played a significant role in corporate accountability for human rights abuses by prosecuting officials acting on behalf of corporates in human rights violations. The state practice of domesticating the Rome Statute and the corresponding implication that corporates can be held liable for international crimes within the domestic sphere further reinforce the significance of national jurisdiction over corporate crimes. Indeed, national criminal jurisdictions are courts of first resort under the ICC complementarity principle.[46] Underlying this doctrine is the principle of shared responsibility between the ICC and its member states, where priority is given to member states to prosecute international crimes and the ICC can only be seized of the matter in the manner prescribed under the Statute.[47] Universal jurisdiction also provides an avenue to reinforce ICC initiatives towards corporate accountability. States should be encouraged to legislate on this doctrine in relation to corporate accountability for international crimes.

Despite the significance of the national corporate criminal accountability, there has been no prosecution of corporate agents involved in international crimes that has proceeded to substantial consideration of its merits.[48]. A study has noted that: "no corporation in its own right has yet been found criminally responsible by a national court for crimes under international law."[49] Besides, save for developments under the African Union, most regional initiatives are yet to incorporate the use of international criminal law in holding corporates accountable for gross human rights violations.

International criminal law as an avenue for corporate accountability

The fact that corporates have rights and obligations under international human rights law implies that corporations are already subject to liability under international law. Thus, corporations can be subjected to duties and obligations under international criminal law.[50]

While state obligations towards corporate accountability at the national level is key, it is important to elevate this discourse to an international criminal forum. The analysis in the previous section reinforces the shortcomings of national corporate criminal accountability for international crimes which are mainly informed by the overreaching economic and political influence of corporations and the absence of binding substantive international norms to guide development. Further, the above analysis exemplifies the disparate nature in which corporate accountability efforts in transitional justice, business and human rights and corporate accountability movements have operated. Indeed, the initiatives towards creating binding norms on corporate accountability, as discussed above, underscore the concepts of corporate accountability in business and human rights in stable democracies. They do not take into account the concept of transitional justice whose processes occur in volatile contexts that may not have the ability to enforce corporate accountability for international crimes.

Therefore, international criminal law has the potential to bridge these gaps in two ways. First, it has the ability to admit cases whether arising from transitional justice contexts or general human rights abuses by corporates. Second, an international criminal accountability forum is likely to circumvent the undue political and economic influence exerted by the private sector in developing countries, and thus can address corporate impunity gaps associated with business and human rights. In addition, international criminal law will help to overcome the limitations of human rights accountability initiatives. For instance, international criminal law has the potential to create wider deterrence. It will also broaden reparations for victims. For example, the question of reparations poses one of the greatest challenges to the ICC. In instances where the Court makes the reparation orders against the perpetrator, and the perpetrator is unable to pay for reparations because of indigence, the Trust Fund for Victims of the ICC has to determine how to raise funds that should be used in reparations. Often, this is a heavy task as it purely depends on voluntary contributions from states to this fund. However, making reparative orders against corporate entities is likely to have a positive impact given the massive economic muscles of corporates.

Notably, advocating for international criminal law in addressing corporate accountability is not necessarily a novel idea. A study of this kind must also be willing to learn from the mistakes of the past. During the drafting of the Rome Statute, this was discussed but the idea was shelved as it was perceived to have the potential to lead to "considerable controversy" given most states did not recognise corporate penal responsibility in their domestic legal frameworks.[51] This international disparity, it was argued, would make the principle of complementarity unworkable.[52] Other states argued against the inconsistency of including "one kind of collective legal person (corporations) while simultaneously excluding another (states)".[53] It was also feared that extending the ICC jurisdiction over corporates had the potential of detracting from the ICC's focus on individual criminal responsibility and the concern that the international criminal justice system may be used to punish "groups" rather than individuals, which conflicts with the principle of individual responsibility for criminal offences.[54] Efforts to revisit the proposal in subsequent drafts faced persistent opposition leading to the eventual exclusion of the corporate liability clause from the final draft of 1998, which focused exclusively on individual criminal responsibility.

All these arguments cannot stand today. For example, it is evident that not only have there been numerous domestic jurisdictions legislated on corporate criminal responsibility for international crimes but also, though not successful, there have been several attempts to prosecute corporates for their engagement in international crimes in domestic jurisdictions.[55] Examples where officials acting on behalf of corporates have been prosecuted and, in some instances, convicted in national courts abound.[56] The question as to why corporations should be included as one entity of collective legal person will also not arise. State practice seems to acknowledge the need to focus on corporates as a key facilitator of gross human rights abuses. In addition, current developments disapprove the fear that having jurisdiction over both corporates and individuals will detract from the work of an international court. Although not yet in operation, the legal framework bestowing jurisdiction over international and transnational crimes on the African court demonstrates the possibility of a court focusing its legal mandate over both corporate and individuals.

Notably, while the ICC cannot exercise jurisdiction over corporates, it can exert jurisdiction over individuals acting on behalf of the corporations, as natural persons. For example, the ICC has previously confirmed charges against a corporate executive in the case of Kenya.[57] In addition, the 2016 Office of the Prosecutor (OTP) policy paper on case selection indicated the OTP's intention to give particular consideration to crimes "that are committed by means of, or that result in, *inter alia*, the destruction of the environment, the illegal exploitation of natural resources or the illegal dispossession of land".[58] These crimes involve multinational corporations. Thus, this creates the potential for corporate accountability, albeit limited to officials acting on behalf of these corporates.

However, despite a few communications against businesspeople, none have yielded to prosecution, demonstrating the challenge in fulfilling the threshold required of the Rome Statute Crimes for the individuals involved. For example, victims, human rights lawyers, and civil society organisations in Colombia referred information to the OTP of the ICC and the Colombian situation has been under investigation since 2004. One such instance concerns allegations against Chiquita Brands concerning its involvement in crimes against humanity committed by paramilitary groups using funds from Chiquita banana company.[59]

While corporate complicity does not feature in the OTP's subsequent interim reports on Colombia, this advocacy has positively influenced government responsiveness to matters related to corporate complicity. In its latest update, the OTP reported on specific information shared by the Colombian authorities on active domestic cases against executives and employees of Chiquita Brands.[60] Thus, the existence of an international criminal law tribunal with jurisdiction over corporate crimes may not always prosecute corporates engaged in gross human rights violations. However, it has the potential to positively influence complementarity from national or regional mechanisms.

In conclusion: incorporating corporate criminal liability within the ICC jurisdiction

The current structure of the ICC and international criminal law generally emphasise its focus on an individual's physical integrity. This must be expanded to include redress for environmental and socio-economic violations. Furthermore, the ICC focus on individual criminal responsibility must also be expanded to include the doctrine of corporate criminal responsibility.

In addition to its focus on individual criminal liability, which has the potential to result in prosecutions of individuals for their role in corporate atrocity, the ICC must pursue corporate prosecution of corporates as legal persons. This implies that there might be a need to extend the jurisdiction of the ICC to include corporate criminal liability.

Mechanisms can also be put in place to deal with foreseeable challenges associated with the inclusion of environmental and socio-economic violations as well as prosecution of corporates engaged in international crimes. For example, considering that corporates mainly engage in atrocities through complicity, questions arise relating to the determination of complicity, or how to apportion liability where one's impugned character intersects with legitimate business behaviour; essentially, how to delimit "criminal and permissible business interaction with atrocity".[61] Another foreseeable challenge concerns the extent to which aiding the commission of a crime should render one criminally liable.

This contribution is aware that the ICC alone cannot serve as an adequate tool in enforcing grave human rights violations by corporations. Therefore, it encourages regional human rights court to consider borrowing the example of the Malabo Protocol and incorporate jurisdiction over international crimes for both corporates and individuals in regional human rights courts. Similarly, all states need to work towards expanding their national systems to accommodate corporate accountability for international crimes.

Notes

1. SL Joseph, "An overview of the Human Rights Accountability of Multinational Enterprises", in MT Kamminga and S Zia-Zarifi (eds), *Liability of Multinational Corporations under International Law* (Kluwer Law International: The Hague, 2000); D Rothkopf, *Power, Inc: The Epic Rivalry between Big Business and Government-and the reckoning that lies Ahead* (Farrar, Straus and Giroux: New York, 2012).
2. J Kyriakakis, *Corporations, Accountability and International Criminal Law: Industry and Atrocity* (Edward Elgar Publishing: Cheltenham, 2021), p.16.
3. Global Initiative for Justice Truth and Reconciliation (GIJTR), "The Roles and Responsibilities of Private Sector Actors in Transitional Justice in Africa and Latin America" (2022), available at: https://gijtr.org/wp-content/uploads/2023/01/Private-Sector-Actors-II-Toolkit-6x9-EN-footnotes-final.pdf; I Pietropaoli, *Business, Human Rights and Transitional Justice* (Routledge: New York, 2020), p.79.
4. L Henkin, "The Universal Declaration at 50 and the Challenge of Global Markets", *Brooklyn Journal of International Law*, vol. 25, no. 1 (1999), p.25; Pietropaoli, *Business, Human Rights and Transitional Justice*, p.4.
5. Universal Declaration on Human Rights (UDHR) (10 December 1948) GA Res 217A (III) A/810, Preamble.
6. UN Convention Against Corruption (entered into force 14 December 2005) 2340 UNTS 41.
7. International Convention on the Suppression and Punishment of the Crime of Apartheid (entered into force 18 July 1976) A/2645, art 1(2).
8. Draft United Nations Code of Conduct on Transnational Corporations [1983 version].
9. KP Sauvant, "The Negotiations of the United Nations Code of Conduct on Transnational Corporations: Experience and Lessons Learned", *Journal of World Investment and Trade*, vol. 16 (2015), p.11 at pp.26–27.
10. Sauvant, "The Negotiations of the United Nations", pp.26–27.
11. UN Economic and Social Commission, Development and International Economic Cooperation: Transnational Corporations (1990) E/1990/94.
12. 26 August 2003, UN Doc E/CN/.4/Sub.2/2003/12/Rev.2.
13. Kyriakakis, *Corporations, Accountability and International Criminal Law*, p.28.
14. These are non-legally binding instruments used in international relations by states and international organisations. They are not law per se but they may be evidence of existing law or formative of opinion juris or state practice that generate new customary international law. Soft law can be contrasted with hard law, which is binding law. See: A Boyle, "Soft Law in International Law Making", in MD Evans (ed), *International Law* (Oxford University Press: Oxford, 4th edn, 2010), p.118.
15. Boyle, "Soft Law", p.118.
16. Kyriakakis, *Corporations, Accountability and International Criminal Law*, p.29.
17. K Buhmann, "The development of the 'UN Framework: A Pragmatic Process towards a Pragmatic Output", in R Mares (ed), *The UN Guiding Principles on Business and Human Rights: Foundations and Implementation* (Martinus Nijhoff: Leiden, 2011), p.101.
18. UN Commission on Human Rights (UNCHR), "Responsibilities of Transnational Corporations and Related Business Enterprises with Regard to Human Rights" (22 April 2004) UN Doc E/CN.4/DEC/2004/116.
19. UNCHR, "Human Rights and Transnational Corporations and Other Business Enterprises" (20 April 2005) UN Doc. E/CN.4/RES/2005/69, para 1.

20 UNCHR, *Protect, Respect and Remedy: A Framework for Business and Human Rights*, A/HRC/8/5 (7 April 2008).
21 UNCHR, "Guiding Principles on Business and Human Rights: Implementing the United Nations 'Protect, Respect and Remedy' Framework" (21 March 2011) UN Doc A/HRC/17/31.
22 Kyriakakis, *Corporations, Accountability and International Criminal Law*, pp.25–26, footnote 3.
23 International Labour Organisation (ILO), "Tripartite Declaration of Principles concerning Multinational Enterprises and Social Policy" (ILO, 5th edn, 2017).
24 UN Global Compact (2000) (amended June 2004), available at www.unglobalcompact.org/.
25 Organisation for Economic Co-operation and Development (OECD), *OECD Guidelines for Multinational Enterprises* (OECD Publishing: Paris, 2011).
26 Voluntary Principles Initiative, "Voluntary Principles on Security and Human Rights" (2000), available at www.voluntaryprinciples.org/.
27 UNCHR Res 26/9 (25 June 2014) UN Doc A/HRC/26/L.22/Rev.1.
28 Article 9, OEIGWG Chairmanship Third Revised Draft (2022), available at: www.ohchr.org/sites/default/files/Documents/HRBodies/HRCouncil/WGTransCorp/Session6/LBI3rdDRAFT.pdf.
29 Article 12(3), CAC.
30 International Covenant on Economic Social and Cultural Rights (ICESCR), 16 December 1966, GA Res 2200A (XXI). In the *General Comment No.15 on the Right to Water*, the Committee states that "steps should be taken by States Parties to prevent their own citizens and companies from violating the right to water of individuals and communities in other countries".
31 Committee on Economic, Social and Cultural Rights, "Statement on the obligations of States Parties regarding the corporate sector and economic, social and cultural rights" (20 May 2011) E/C/12/2011/1.
32 CESCR, "Statement on the obligations of States Parties", para 4.
33 CESCR, "Statement on the obligations of States Parties", para 5.
34 CESCR, "Statement on the obligations of States Parties", para 5.
35 CESCR, "Statement on the obligations of States Parties", para 5.
36 CESCR, "Statement on the obligations of States Parties", para 5.
37 CESCR, "Statement on the obligations of States Parties", para 5.
38 CESCR, "Statement on the obligations of States Parties", para 6.
39 CESCR, "Statement on the obligations of States Parties".
40 See Sepur Zarco case; Buzos Miskitos (Honduras) case; LA Payne, G Pereira & L Bernal-Bermúdez, *Transitional Justice and Corporate Accountability From Below: Deploying Archimedes' Lever* (Cambridge University Press: Cambridge, 2020); GIJTR, "*Roles and Responsibilities of the Private Sector in Transitional Justice Processes in Latin America: The Case of Colombia, Guatemala and Argentina*" (2021), pp.39–40, available at: www.dplf.org/sites/default/files/roles_and_responsibilities_of_the_private_sector_in_transitional_justice_processes_in_latin_america_-_the_cases_of_colombia_guatemala_and_argentina_-_dplf_and_gijtr.pdf; GTJR "The Roles and Responsibility of Private Sector actors in Transitional Justice", p.16.
41 Para 2.
42 The Malabo Protocol is not yet in force, with 11 signatories and no ratifications at present.
43 African Commission on Human and People's Rights, "Guidelines and Principles on Articles 21 and 24 of the African Charter Relating to Extractive Industries, Human Rights and Environment", para 45.
44 African Union Transitional Justice Policy, para 131.
45 The International Criminal Tribunal of Rwanda Media cases, which comprised: the prosecution of Ferdinand Nahimana, a director of the *Radio Télévision Libre des Mille Colline* and Jean Bosco Barayagwiza also associated with the station; the prosecution of Hassan Ngeze, the founder and director of Kangura newspaper; the case against Bagaragaza, and the director general of the government office responsible for the Rwandan tea industry who pled guilty for complicity in genocide. The Appeal panels of the Special Tribunal for Lebanon decisions in two cases, *New TV S.A.L* and *Akhbar Beirut S.A.L.*, held that it could assert jurisdiction over corporations for the offence of contempt of court.
46 EO Asaala, "The International Criminal Court Factor on Transitional Justice in Kenya", in K Ambos & OA Maunganidze (eds) *Power and prosecution: Challenges and Opportunities for*

International Criminal Justice in Sub-Saharan Africa, Göttingen Studies in Criminal Law and Justice (Universitätsverlag Göttingen: Göttingen, 2012), p.124.
47 Rome Statute, Preamble, para 10; article 1; article 17 (1) (a).
48 Kyriakakis, *Corporations, Accountability and International Criminal Law*, p.170.
49 Pietropaoli, *Business, Human Rights and Transitional Justice*, p.9.
50 R Slye, "Corporations, Veils, and International Criminal Liability", *Brooklyn Journal of International Law*, vol. 33, no. 3 (2008), p.955.
51 Kyriakakis, *Corporations, Accountability and International Criminal Law*, p.107.
52 Pietropaoli, *Business, Human Rights and Transitional Justice*, p.31.
53 Kyriakakis, *Corporations, Accountability and International Criminal Law*, p.121.
54 Pietropaoli, *Business, Human Rights and Transitional Justice*, p.31.
55 Victims, human rights lawyers, and civil society organisations have innovatively turned to strategic litigation either in host states or in third countries or international courts in search or corporate accountability for atrocities. See for example, the Lundin Energy Case in South Sudan, the Ingegnieros/Techint labour claims of Argentina, the Serpur Zarco gender-based violence Case in Guatemala, La Fronterita's alleged crimes against humanity in Argentina, the Córdoba Livestock Fund of Colombia, and the Drummond coal in Colombia.
56 See the prosecution of Van Anraat in the Netherlands for delivering tons of chemicals to Saddam Hussein; the prosecution of Guus Kouwenhoven in the Netherlands for supplying weapons to Liberian government during the rulership of Charles Taylor; the Swedish indictment of CEO and chairman of the Swedish company Lundin Petroleum.
57 *Prosecutor v William Samoei Ruto, Henry Kiprono Kosgey and Joshua Arap Sang* (Decision on the Confirmation of Charges Pursuant to Article 61(7)(a) and (b) of the Rome Statute), ICC-01/09 01/11-373 (23 January 2012) Pre-Trial Chamber II.
58 International Criminal Court Office of the Prosecutor, "Policy Paper on Case Selection and Prioritisation" (2016), available at: www.icc-cpi.int/sites/default/files/itemsDocuments/20160 915_OTP-Policy_Case-Selection_Eng.pdf.
59 JD Restrepo, "Llevan caso de Chiquita Brands a la Corte Penal Internacional", *Verdad Abierta* (2017), available at: https://verdadabierta.com/especiales-v/2017/chiquita-corte-penal.html.
60 International Criminal Court Office of the Prosecutor, "Report on Preliminary Examination Activities" (2020), available at: www.icc-cpi.int/itemsDocuments/2020-PE/2020-pe-report-col-spa.pdf. Notably, the Colombian Attorney General's Office indicted 13 individuals, in August 2018, for aggravated conspiracy to commit a crime. See Pietropaoli, *Business, Human Rights and Transitional Justice*, p.79. In September 2019, the Office however withdrew the indictment, further placing a permanent stay on any further proceedings against three of the 13 individuals (the general secretary of domestic banana firm C.I. Banacol, and two employees of a second domestic banana trading firm, C.I. Banadex: its director of Labour Relations, and its administrative manager, the latter a US citizen). This is available at: www.fiscalia.gov.co/colombia/noticias/actualizacion-boletin-no-24007-caso-chiquita-brands/.
61 Kyriakakis, *Corporations, Accountability and International Criminal Law*, p.224.

References

Books and book chapters

Asaala EO, "The International Criminal Court Factor on Transitional Justice in Kenya", in Ambos K & Maunganidze OA (eds), *Power and Prosecution: Challenges and Opportunities for International Criminal Justice in Sub-Saharan Africa, Göttingen Studies in Criminal Law and Justice* (Universitätsverlag Göttingen: Göttingen, 2012).
Boyle A, "Soft Law in International Law Making", in Evans M (ed), *International Law* (Oxford University Press: Oxford, 4th edn, 2010).
Buhmann K, "The Development of the 'UN Framework: A Pragmatic Process Towards a Pragmatic Output", in Mares R (ed), *The UN Guiding Principles on Business and Human Rights: Foundations and Implementation* (Martinus Nijhoff: Leiden, 2011).

Joseph SL, "An Overview of the Human Rights Accountability of Multinational Enterprises", in Kamminga MT & Zia-Zarifi S (eds), *Liability of Multinational Corporations Under International Law* (Brill: Leiden, 2000).

Kyriakakis J, *Corporations, Accountability and International Criminal Law: Industry and Atrocity* (Edward Elgar Publishing: Cheltenham, 2021).

Payne LA, Pereira G, & Bernal-Bermúdez L, *Transitional Justice and Corporate Accountability from Below: Deploying Archimedes' Lever* (Cambridge University Press: Cambridge, 2020).

Pietropaoli I, *Business, Human Rights and Transitional Justice* (Routledge: London, 2020).

Rothkopf D, *Power, Inc: The Epic Rivalry Between Big Business and Government – And the Reckoning That Lies Ahead* (Farrar Straus and Giroux: New York, 2012).

Journal articles

Henkin L, "The Universal Declaration at 50 and the Challenge of Global Markets", *Brooklyn Journal of International Law*, vol. 25, no. 1 (1999), pp.17–26.

Sauvant KP, "The Negotiations of the United Nations Code of Conduct on Transnational Corporations: Experience and Lessons Learned", *Journal of World Investment and Trade*, vol. 16 (2015), pp.11–87.

Reports and websites

Committee on Economic, Social and Cultural Rights, *Statement on the Obligations of States Parties Regarding the Corporate Sector and Economic, Social and Cultural Rights* (20 May 2011) E/C/12/2011/1.

Global Initiative for Justice Truth and Reconciliation, *Roles and Responsibilities of the Private Sector in Transitional Justice Processes in Latin America: The Case of Colombia, Guatemal and Argentina*.

Global Initiative for Justice Truth and Reconciliation, *The Roles and Responsibilities of Private Sector Actors in Transitional Justice in Africa and Latin America*, Phase II, Summary Report (November 2022).

International Criminal Court, Office of the Prosecutor, *Report on Preliminary Examination Activities* (2020), available at: www.icc-cpi.int/itemsDocuments/2020-PE/2020-pe-report-col-spa.pdf

International Labour Organisation, *Tripartite Declaration of Principles Concerning Multinational Enterprises and Social Policy* (ILO: Geneva, 5th edn, 2017).

Organisation for Economic Cooperation and Development, *OECD Guidelines for Multinational Enterprises* (OECD Publishing: Paris, 2011).

Restrepo JD, "Llevan caso de Chiquita Brands a la Corte Penal Internacional", *Verdad Abierta* (2017), available at: <https://verdadabierta.com/especiales-v/2017/chiquita-corte-penal.html>

UN Comission on Human Rights, *Responsibilities of Transnational Corporations and Related Business Enterprises with Regard to Human Rights* (22 April 2004) UN Doc E/CN.4/DEC/2004/116.

UN Global Compact (2000) (amended June 2004), available at: <http://www.unglobalcompact.org/>

UN Human Rights Council, *Human Rights and Transnational Corporations and Other Business Enterprises* (20 April 2005) UN Doc. E/CN.4/RES/2005/69.

UN Human Rights Council, *Protect, Respect and Remedy: A Framework for Business and Human Rights* (7 April 2008) A/HRC/8/5.

UN Human Rights Council, *Guiding Principles on Business and Human Rights: Implementing the United Nations 'Protect, Respect and Remedy' Framework* (21 March 2011) UN Doc. A/HRC/17/31.

Voluntary Principles on Security and Human Rights (2000), available at: <http://www.voluntaryprinciples.org/>

23
DISCLOSURE OF CHILDHOOD CRIMINAL RECORDS IN ENGLAND AND WALES

Imposing Enduring Criminal Responsibility for Childhood Behaviours

Raymond Arthur

Introduction

Criminal responsibility is usually "imposed only on persons who are sufficiently aware of what they are doing, and of the consequences it may have, that they can fairly be said to have chosen the behaviour and its consequences".[1] The criminal law's conception of a person as a reasoning and rule-following being who understands the difference between right and wrong underpins both the approach to the imposition of criminal responsibility and the retributivist approach to sentencing, namely that deserving individuals are to blame for their choices and justly deserve their sentence. As Lacey states, conceptions of responsibility legitimate "the calling to account of individuals … in the name of the criminal process (or the state)".[2] In Lacey's analysis of criminal responsibility, she asserted that the focus should not be solely on the formal attributions of responsibility expressed in criminal laws, but critical attention must also be paid to "practices of responsibility–attribution within the context of criminalization overall".[3] Lacey cited the examples of pre-trial remands in custody and "civil preventive hybrid orders" as examples of "risk and character-based patterns of criminal responsibility attribution"[4] which "foster the most dangerous aspects of criminalization and punishment as forms of social power".[5] This chapter will respond to Lacey's call for a holistic analysis of "the patterns of responsibilization [sic] as realised in criminalization practices as a whole"[6] by considering whether the regulation of criminal records disclosure in England and Wales is also an example of the emergence of a dangerous "hybrid pattern and practice of responsibility based on … a new sense of bad character".[7]

    This chapter will examine the excessively and oppressively stigmatising approach to youth criminal records in England and Wales which points to a youth justice system that continues to focus upon the imposition of enduring criminal responsibility. There is a rich body of literature on the "collateral consequences" of criminal records, however the subject of criminal records' disclosure has rarely been considered as a children's rights issue.[8] For example, a 2023 Special Issue of *Criminology & Criminal Justice* devoted to studies of the collateral consequences of criminal records features seven articles on this topic, but none deal specifically with the issue of records of childhood behaviours.[9] This chapter fills this lacuna by investigating the extent to which the approach to criminal record disclosure in England and Wales, with its emphasis on imposing enduring criminal responsibility for offending from childhood throughout the life course, undermines some of the fundamental guiding principles that underpin how criminal responsibility is imposed upon young people, such as the need for proportionate sentencing and the need to have regard to the welfare of the child.[10] The approach to disclosure of records of childhood behaviours also needs to be understood in light of the Youth Justice Board's commitment to the principle of "Child First" as a central guiding principle of the English and Welsh youth justice systems.[11] Child First is a child-focused and developmentally informed approach which aims to provide a holistic, individualistic, tailored response based on a child's needs that focuses on their strengths and future aspirations.[12] This chapter draws on Hollingsworth's theory of foundational rights[13] as a lens through which to critically explore the misalignment between the regulation of the disclosure of childhood offending records and all of the above principles regulating childhood criminal responsibility, as well as international children's rights instruments that require that the best interests of children are unarguably "integrated and consistently applied" in every action taken by public institutions.[14] The chapter will begin by examining the laws which regulate how records of childhood behaviours are disclosed.

Sentencing decisions and criminal records' disclosure in England and Wales

The Rehabilitation of Offenders Act 1974 enables criminal offences to become "spent" after a specified rehabilitation period has elapsed, which means they do not need to be disclosed when applying for employment as the offender is regarded as rehabilitated, unless one of the exceptions which are discussed below applies. For children who were under 18 years at the time of conviction and who have received a custodial sentence of between 30–48 months, their conviction will be considered spent 3.5 years after the end date of the sentence. A custodial sentence (including a Detention and Training Order (DTO)) of between 6–30 months will become spent 2 years after the sentence has been completed by the child, and for sentences of less than 6 months, the rehabilitation period will be 18 months after the end of the sentence, which includes the supervision period of the DTO and not just the period in custody. A Youth Rehabilitation Order (YRO) will become spent 6 months after the order has been completed, or if the YRO has no specified end date, the rehabilitation period is 2 years from the date of conviction. A youth caution is spent immediately upon it being administered and a youth conditional caution is spent 3 months after the date on which it was administered. A referral order is spent once the order is completed, and a compensation order is spent when it is paid.

There are certain exceptions where some convictions and cautions will need to be disclosed even if they are spent. For example, where a child has been sentenced to custody for over 4 years, then this conviction will never become spent. Furthermore, a conviction will need to be disclosed if convicted in the previous 66 months. The Rehabilitation of

Offenders Act 1974 (Exceptions) Order 1975 also identifies certain forms of employment which require a more detailed disclosure of a person's criminal record history, including childhood convictions that are now spent. The current list of professions which requires full disclosure of childhood criminal records include particularly sensitive areas of work such as working with children or in health and social care, law enforcement and the legal system, and high-level financial positions. However, the list also includes professions such as veterinary practitioners, traffic wardens, locksmiths, taxi drivers, dentists, oral hygienists, opticians, chemists, and employment in the private security industry.[15] This list imposes significant restrictions upon the occupations available to people who were convicted as children. In addition to these professions which require full disclosure, there are also some types of cautions and convictions that need to be disclosed even if spent, referred to as "specified offences". The list of "specified offences" comprises approximately 947 offences which include serious offending such as sexual offending, violent offending and offending relevant to safeguarding children and vulnerable adults. The list also includes offences such as the common law offence of affray, common assault, assault with intention to resist arrest and assault occasioning actual bodily harm. New filtering rules were introduced in November 2020[16] which mean that youth cautions for specified offences, or any other offences, will now not be automatically disclosed unless the police consider it is relevant to the work the individual wishes to apply for. The changes have also removed the "multiple conviction rule", which meant that if an individual had more than one conviction, regardless of the type of offence or the time passed between offending, all convictions would be automatically disclosed. Under the updated rules, each conviction is now considered against the filtering rules individually, and therefore provided it is for a minor offence which did not lead to a custodial sentence, it may not be disclosed once the relevant time period has passed, even if there is more than one conviction on the record.

There are also circumstances in which non-conviction intelligence may be disclosed. The Disclosure and Barring Service (DBS) processes requests for criminal record certificates in England and Wales. Part V of the Police Act 1997 provides for different types of criminal record certificates to be issued. A criminal record check at basic disclosure level is the lowest level of disclosure. It only contains details of unspent convictions and conditional cautions. Standard disclosure certificates are issued by the DBS for occupations and activities set out in the 1975 Exceptions Order discussed in the previous paragraph. Standard certificates include all spent and unspent convictions and cautions, subject to the filtering arrangements discussed previously. An enhanced DBS check is a criminal record check at enhanced disclosure level which will disclose both spent and unspent conviction and relevant police intelligence. Police intelligence, including non-conviction information such as reports to the police, is held on the Police National Database for a minimum of 6 years and can be retained until the subject's 100th birthday.[17] Despite the new filtering rules introduced in November 2020, the police still retain the discretion to disclose non-conviction information which they consider to be relevant on enhanced DBS checks, which may include youth cautions and police intelligence even where this has not resulted in an arrest, conviction, or other disposal.

Research conducted with children to ascertain their understanding of the criminal record regime shows that many mistakenly believe that when they reach adulthood their childhood record of offending is "wiped clean".[18] On the contrary, it is clear that there are quite a wide range of circumstances in which records of childhood offending behaviour, including convictions and cautions that are now considered "spent", will need to be disclosed. Such circumstances are not restricted to sensitive occupations which involve working with children and vulnerable adults, and instead include records of behaviour not confined to the most serious violent or sexual behaviour, as well as potentially including disclosure of non-conviction intelligence.

Disclosure of criminal records as a disproportionate and enduring criminal responsibility

Philosophers and criminal law theorists fundamentally agree that criminal punishment must be "proportional" to the offence, and that "disproportionate" or excessive punishment is unjust.[19] However the concept of proportionality remains "one of the most elusive of the central concepts in the theory of punishment".[20] Despite this conceptual obscurity, theorists have sought to understand the meaning of proportionate sentencing. Husak, for example, argues that a "principle of proportionality in censuring" provides that "the amount of reprobation deserved by an offender should be a function of the blameworthiness of his offence"[21] and Hart emphasises that an important element of the principle of proportional punishment is that it "forbid[s] us... to punish the guilty more harshly than they deserve".[22]

In addition to ensuring that sentences are proportionate, every court in England and Wales must also, according to section 125(1) of the Coroners and Justice Act 2009, follow the Sentencing Council's 2017 *Guidelines for Sentencing Children* (the *Guidelines*).[23] The *Guidelines* provide that offence seriousness will be the starting point when considering sentencing options, but the approach to sentencing should not be solely offence focused and should also consider the child and their rehabilitation. When making sentencing decisions, the court should consider the effect the sentence is likely to have on the child and must avoid undue penalisation, stigma, or criminalising the child in a way which would hinder the child's re-integration into society or result in the alienation of the child from society.[24] The *Guidelines* do not make any reference to the issue of criminal records that attach to sentencing decisions.

When determining the appropriate punishment for children convicted of offending behaviour, courts must also consider the statutory requirements enshrined in section 37 of the Crime and Disorder Act 1998 and section 44 of the Children and Young Persons Act 1933, respectively that the principal aim of the youth justice system is to prevent offending and to have regard to the welfare of the child.[25] Therefore, the crime prevention agenda of the 1998 Act must be balanced with the welfare principle. Welfarism is characterised by the pursuit of social justice which reflects a prevailing assumption that the child offender is not a threatening outsider, but is an individual who can be socialised, rehabilitated, and included within society. This approach is based on the view of the child as a future adult in need of guidance and support.[26] Hollingsworth's theory of foundational rights also recognises that the "rights of the child as a future adult are not inseparable from her rights during childhood".[27] In relation to imposing criminal responsibility upon children, Hollingsworth has argued that if a youth justice system is to protect and uphold principles of equality, due process, and justice, then the state must give special status to a class of rights known as "foundational rights".[28] Foundational rights are conceived of as a form of protection of the child's ability to develop into a fully autonomous future adult.[29] Foundational rights are explicitly focused on maximising the child's potential "to become something more"[30] and minimising the long-term stigmatising impact of criminal responsibility on children's potential for autonomy.[31] Hollingsworth's theory of foundational rights means that sentencing decisions should be forward-looking and consider the full impact of the punishment on the adult the child may become.[32] However, the approach to criminal records' disclosure in England clearly runs counter to protecting the child's "foundational rights" and their ability to develop into a future autonomous adult as it is predicated upon a conceptualisation of the child, and the adult they will/have become, as inherently risky and threatening.

In England and Wales, the principle of proportionate responses to imposing criminal responsibility for childhood offending has become secondary to a "hegemonic risk management model"[33] which gives precedence to a preventive and precautionary approach to the disclosure of childhood offending records. Criminal records are effectively serving an additional punitive function which Corda and Lageson have characterised as "disordered punishment".[34] Disordered punishment identifies the largely unpredictable, unevenly imposed, frequently disproportionate and misleading ways criminal records impact people's lives. Disclosing records of childhood offending and other non-offending behaviours impedes rehabilitation, increases future interactions with the criminal justice system and impacts upon job prospects throughout the life course,[35] "… diminish[ing] the individual's social bonds to the community, increasing the likelihood that the individual will engage in offending behaviour".[36] The consequences of criminal record disclosure have also been characterised as: "invisible punishment[s]";[37] akin to bearing a "brand";[38] "amplify[ing] punishment beyond the sanctions imposed by the criminal justice system",[39] allowing for "[a] child's early biography … [to] become a manifested destiny";[40] and as "fail[ing] to take seriously the prospect of offenders' reform".[41] Henley has depicted the stigma of criminal records as a state of "civic purgatory" where records of offending prevent people from enjoying unencumbered access to the same rights and entitlements as full "citizens".[42] Henley has warned that this state of civic purgatory is likely to lead to feelings of injustice and unfairness.[43] Research on legitimacy and the law supports the basic claim, tested under a variety of sampling and measurement conditions, that fair treatment strengthens ties and attachment to the law.[44] It generates obligations to conform to those laws which are considered legitimate and moral.[45] Fair treatment may also reduce feelings of anger that lead to rule breaking[46] and contribute to future law abiding behaviour.[47] Individuals' notions of the fairness and morality of legal rules, including disclosure of childhood offending, may therefore influence their future behaviour.

Despite the changes introduced in 2020, the system for disclosure of youth criminal records in England and Wales continues to reflect a simplistic functionalist perspective which focuses its attention on a policy of risk management and "outcast[s] the subject of the disclosure, blocking his or her access to an avenue of legitimate participation in society".[48] The Youth Justice Board has adopted the principle of "Child First" as a central guiding principle of the English and Welsh youth justice systems.[49] The Youth Justice Board's *Business Plan 2022–23* envisages a youth justice system in England and Wales that supports children to be as successful as they possibly can and make sure that children are not unnecessarily criminalised.[50] There are four key elements, or tenets, of an effective Child First model which include promoting diversion and a pivot away from children being "excessively criminalised" and subjected to "cruel and unusual punishment" in the youth justice system.[51] A Child First approach, similar to a foundational rights approach, questions and challenges constructions of children (when they offend) as "risky" and "threatening" which hinder the development of a pro-social identity for positive child outcomes and sustainable desistance.

The United Nations Convention on the Rights of the Child (UNCRC), which was ratified by the UK in 1991, and associated child-friendly justice instruments, provide the "establishing parameters"[52] of both a Child First and foundational rights approach. Article 3 of the UNCRC requires that the best interests of children is at the heart of the interpretation of children's rights and decision-making processes. The United Nations Committee on the Rights of the Child (CRC) emphasised in General Comment No 24 on *Children's Rights in the Child Justice System* that diversion from criminal proceedings should lead to a definite and final closure of the case, without the child in question being treated as having a criminal record or previous conviction.[53] The Committee also recommended that, in normal circumstances, a child's name should be automatically removed from criminal records when they reach the age of 18.[54] General Comment No 24 explicitly highlights that children differ from adults in their physical and psychological development, and their emotional and educational needs. Neurological research suggests that the process of maturation is a long and complex process that stretches into adulthood. The developmental differences in the brain's biochemistry and anatomy limit adolescents' ability to perceive risks, control impulses, understand consequences and control emotions.[55] The prefrontal lobe is involved in the control of aggression and other behavioural impulses related to criminal responsibility, and yet this lobe is the last area to mature, developing in the twenties rather than the teen years.[56] This evidence highlights that the child's inexperience and under-developed powers of self-control and reasoning make them prone to acting in ways they cannot help, understand, or intend. These insights from neurological research have particular resonance when considering issues of criminal responsibility and punishment. Lacey identified the possession of powers of understanding, self-control, and effective practical reasoning as pre-conditions for being held criminally responsible, specifically that the "core of the idea of criminal responsibility" is "related to the idea of human agency and accountability for conduct".[57] Agency is also an important feature of Hollingsworth's foundational rights. Hollingsworth argues that "[e]quating ... criminal responsibility with agency is beneficial to children" as it "honours the child when it holds her criminally responsible by recognising her status as a rights-holder".[58] However, Hollingsworth cautions that the criminal justice system will lack legitimacy if it "permanently restricts the child's ability to develop the capacities necessary for future (global) full autonomy".[59]

Any understanding of the link between personal agency and criminal responsibility must be read alongside what we know about the "age crime curve", which suggests that the majority of adolescents who engage in criminal activity will simply "grow out of it"[60] given offending behaviour tends to peak at around age 19 and then decline.[61] As McMullen notes, "while young people are more likely than adults to engage in risky behaviour, they are also likely to mature into law-abiding citizens" as children tend to "outgrow" criminal behaviour.[62] Children's identities are more "fluid and changeable"[63] than adults' which creates opportunities for change in the lives of children in conflict with the law. Long-term desistance involves identifiable and measurable changes at the level of personal identity as children who offend "need to develop a coherent, pro-social identity for themselves".[64] Consequently, there is a need to support the child's development, taking into account the Child First imperative of promoting the child assuming a constructive role in society.[65] The current criminal records' regime in England and Wales fails "to take seriously the prospect of offenders' reform"[66] which undermines the utility of criminal record disclosure as a predictive risk management tool because the future risk of offending diminishes over time.[67] The socioeconomic instability generated by criminal records impedes rehabilitation, the freedom to build a legitimate life[68] and ultimately increases future interactions with the criminal justice system.[69] To remedy these adverse effects, much can be learned from practices in other jurisdictions, including in other parts of the United Kingdom.

Comparing England and Wales with other jurisdictions

In 2016, the Standing Committee for Youth Justice, now known as the Alliance for Youth Justice (AYJ), published a study of how childhood criminal records are treated in 16 jurisdictions including England and Wales.[70] This report found that, unlike in England and Wales, most jurisdictions have separate systems for child and adult criminal records with arrangements in place to delete, or restrict access to, records of childhood convictions. For example, in Italy, all non-custodial records are deleted at 18 years; in France, most childhood records are deleted after 3 years; and in Germany, most records must be deleted when the person turns 24. In Spain, it is almost impossible for anyone, even a judge, to access a record once a child turns 18. In the US, 45 states, such as Ohio, Texas and New Mexico, have provisions to ensure that childhood records are "sealed". Sealing records in this way has been found to lower recidivism and enhance employability and earnings.[71] Furthermore, more than 35 US states and 150 cities and counties have adopted some form of "ban the box" policies that require employers to remove questions about criminal records from job applications.[72] The criminal records' systems in the other parts of the United Kingdom – Northern Ireland and Scotland – are very similar to arrangements in England and Wales. However, in both Northern Ireland and Scotland, a far greater proportion of children are diverted to either youth conferences (Northern Ireland) or children's hearings (Scotland), where the criminal records implications are minimised. Furthermore, in Northern Ireland, the role of Independent Reviewer of Criminal Record Certificates was established by the Justice (NI) Act 2015. Where a young person in Northern Ireland is convicted and the conviction becomes spent and there is no further information relating to adult offending, any criminal record information will go to an independent reviewer. Once the reviewer considers all the relevant information, they can expunge the childhood conviction and issue a certificate with none of the criminal record information held if the risk is deemed minimal. Similarly in Scotland, the Disclosure (Scotland) Act 2020 aimed to modernise and improve the proportionality of the criminal record disclosure system by creating the role of an independent reviewer to allow for those with records of childhood behaviour to put these experiences behind them.

Conclusion

This chapter has argued that the regulation of the disclosure of records of childhood behaviours in England and Wales needs to be reconceptualised in a way which embraces the Child First agenda and moves away from imposing enduring and stigmatising criminal responsibility upon children. Specifically, there needs to be a closer alignment between the disclosure of childhood criminal records and the development of a (foundational) rights-based youth justice system which is underpinned by international children's rights instruments, and which acknowledges both the child's rights as a child and also their "foundational right" to develop into a future autonomous adult. There also needs to be a different cultural conception of the implications of the criminal responsibility of children and what proportionate sentencing means for children. Maruna has recognised this more broadly in calling upon society at large to play an active role by accepting people with criminal records[73] and understanding that a record of childhood offending creates a stain that represents the "best-documented roadblock [to reintegration] … [and] employment".[74]

Notes

1. A Ashworth, *Principles of Criminal Law* (Oxford University Press: Oxford, 5th edn, 2003), p.15.
2. N Lacey, *In Search of Criminal Responsibility: Ideas, Interests, and Institutions* (Oxford University Press: Oxford, 2016), p.25.
3. Lacey, *In Search of Criminal Responsibility*, p.151.
4. Lacey, *In Search of Criminal Responsibility*, p.159.
5. Lacey, *In Search of Criminal Responsibility*, p.162.
6. Lacey, *In Search of Criminal Responsibility*, p.62.
7. Lacey, *In Search of Criminal Responsibility*, p.147.
8. Research which has engaged with this topic specifically from a child perspective includes N Carr, C Dwyer and E Larruari, *Young People, Criminal Records and Employment Barriers* (NIACRO: Belfast, 2015); N Carr, "The albatross of juvenile criminal records", in S Meijer, H Annison & A O'Loughlin (eds), *Fundamental rights and legal consequences of criminal conviction* (Hart Publishing: London, 2019); C Sands, *Growing up, Moving on The International Treatment of Childhood Criminal Records* (London: SCYJ, 2016).
9. Currently available at: https://journals.sagepub.com/doi/full/10.1177/17488958231174109.
10. Children and Young Persons Act 1933, s 44.
11. Youth Justice Board, *Strategic Plan 2021-24* (London: YJB, 2020), p.9.
12. AM Day, "'It's a Hard Balance to Find': The Perspectives of Youth Justice Practitioners in England on the Place of 'Risk' in an Emerging 'Child-First' World", *Youth Justice*, vol. 23, no. 1 (2022), p.58.
13. K Hollingsworth, "Theorising children's rights in the youth justice system: the significance of autonomy and foundational rights", *Modern Law Review*, vol. 76, no. 6 (2013), p.1049.
14. United Nations Committee on the Rights of the Child, "General Comment No. 14 on the right of the child to have his or her best interests taken as a primary consideration" (2013), para 13, available at: www2.ohchr.org/English/bodies/crc/docs/GC/CRC_C_GC_14_ENG.pdf.
15. T Thomas, *Criminal Records: A Database for the Criminal Justice System and Beyond* (Palgrave Macmillan: Basingstoke, 2007), pp.98-100. Also, AJ Henley, "Mind the gap: sentencing, rehabilitation and civic purgatory", *Probation Journal*, vol. 63, no. 3 (2018), pp.285.
16. Disclosure and Barring Service, "Guidance: New filtering rules for DBS certificates (from 28 November 2020 onwards)" (2020), available at: www.gov.uk/government/publications/filtering-rules-for-criminal-record-check-certificates/new-filtering-rules-for-dbs-certificates-from-28-november-2020-onwards.
17. The power for police to keep records on the Police National Database is contained in the National Police Records (Recordable Offences) Regulations 2000, SI No 2000/1139.
18. Carr et al, *Young People, Criminal Records and Employment Barriers*; Carr, "The albatross of juvenile criminal records".
19. For example, see MN Berman, "Proportionality, Constraint, and Culpability", *Criminal Law, Philosophy*, vol. 15 (2021), p.373; G Yaffe, *The Age of Culpability: Children and the Nature of Criminal Responsibility* (Oxford University Press: Oxford, 2018), p.61.
20. Yaffe, *The Age of Culpability*, p.61.
21. D Husak, "Strict Liability, Justice, and Proportionality", in AP Simester (ed), *Appraising Strict Liability* (Oxford University Press: Oxford, 2005), pp.95–97.
22. HLA Hart, *Punishment and Responsibility* (Oxford University Press: New York, 1968), pp.3–13.
23. Sentencing Council, "Sentencing children and young people: Overarching principles and offence specific guidelines for sexual offences and robbery. Definitive Guideline" (2017), para 1.2, available at: www.sentencingcouncil.org.uk/overarching-guides/magistrates-court/item/sentencing-children-and-young-people/.

24 Sentencing Council, "Sentencing children and young people", paras 1.4–1.7.
25 Sentencing Act 2020, s 58.
26 R Arthur, "Recognising children's citizenship in the youth justice system", *Journal of Social Welfare & Family Law*, vol. 37, no. 1 (2015), pp.21–37.
27 K Hollingsworth, "The Utility and Futility of International Rights Standards for Children in Conflict with the Law: The Case of England", in L Weber, E Fishwick, & M Marmo (eds), *Routledge International Handbook of Criminology and Human Rights* (Routledge: Abingdon, 2016).
28 Hollingsworth, "Theorising children's rights", p.1049.
29 Hollingsworth, "Theorising children's rights".
30 Hollingsworth, "Theorising children's rights", p.1060.
31 Hollingsworth, "Theorising children's rights", p.1066.
32 Hollingsworth, "Theorising children's rights", p.1066.
33 S Case, CE Sutton, J Greenhalgh, M Monaghan & J Wright, "Searching for context: a review of "what works" revies of interventions to prevent youth offending using the EMMIE Framework", *Safer Communities*, vol. 21, no. 4 (2022), p.272 at p.273.
34 A Corda & SE Lageson, "Disordered Punishment: Workaround Technologies of Criminal Records Disclosure and the Rise of a New Penal Entrepreneurialism", *British Journal of Criminology*, vol. 60, no. 2 (2020), p.245; A Corda, M Rovira, & A Henley, "Collateral consequences of criminal records from the other side of the pond: How exceptional is American penal exceptionalism?", *Criminology & Criminal Justice*, vol. 23, no. 4 (2023), p.528.
35 For example, see P Maurutto, K Hannah-Moffat & M Quirouette, "Punishing the Non-convicted Through Disclosure of Police Records", *British Journal of Criminology* (2023), vol. 63, no. 6, p.3; also AL Burton, VS Burton, F Cullen, JT Pickett & A Thielo, "Beyond the eternal criminal record: Public support for expungement", *Criminology & Public Policy*, vol. 20, no. 123 (2021), p.125.
36 J Purshouse, "Non-conviction disclosure as part of an enhanced criminal record certificate: Assessing the legal framework from a fundamental human rights perspective", *Public Law*, no. 4 (2018), p.668 at p.682.
37 J Travis, *But They All Come Back: Facing the Challenges of Prisoner Re-entry* (The Urban Insitute: Washington, DC, 2005).
38 JB Jacobs & E Larrauri, "Are criminal convictions a public matter? The USA and Spain", *Punishment & Society*, vol. 14, no. 1 (2012), p.3.
39 M Kurlychek, R Brame & S Bushway, "Scarlet letters and recidivism: Does an old criminal record predict future offending?", *Criminology and Public Policy*, vol. 5, no. 3 (2006), p.483 at p.484.
40 S Sacher, "Risking Children: The Implications of Predictive Risk Analytics Across Child Protection and Policing for Vulnerable and Marginalized Children", *Human Rights Law Review*, vol. 22, no.1 (2022), p.1 at p.26.
41 Z Hoskins, *Beyond Punishment? A Normative Account of the Collateral Legal Consequences of Conviction*. (Oxford University Press: New York, 2019), p.168.
42 AJ Henley, "Criminalisation, criminal records and rehabilitation: from supervision to citizenship?", *Probation Journal*, vol. 69, no. 3 (2022), p. 273. Also, Henley, *Mind the gap*.
43 Henley, "Mind the gap".
44 TR Tyler, *Why People Obey the Law* (Yale University Press: New Haven, 1990); TR Tyler & YH Huo, *Trust in the Law* (Russell-Sage: New York, 2002).
45 J Fagan & TR Tyler, "Legal Socialization of Children and Adolescents", *Social Justice Research*, vol. 18 (2005), p.217.
46 R Agnew, "Foundation for a general strain theory of crime and delinquency", *Criminology*, vol. 30, no. 1 (1992), p.47; LW Sherman, "Defiance, deterrence and irrelevance: A theory of the criminal sanction", *Journal of Research in Crime and Delinquency*, vol. 30, no. 4 (1993), p.445.
47 R Paternoster, R Brame, R Bachman & LW Sherman, "Do fair procedures matter? The effect of procedural justice on spouse assault", *Law and Society Review*, vol. 31, no. 1 (1997), p.163.
48 Purshouse, "Non-conviction disclosure", p.682.
49 Youth Justice Board, *Strategic Plan 2021-24*, p.9.
50 Youth Justice Board for England and Wales *Business Plan 2022-23* (YJB: London, 2022), p.9.

51 E Baldry, DB Briggs, B Goldson & S Russell, "'Cruel and unusual punishment': An interjurisdictional study of the criminalisation of young people with complex support needs", *Journal of Youth Studies*, vol. 21, no. 5 (2018), p.636 at p.648; Also S Case & K Haines, "Abolishing Youth Justice Systems: Children First, Offenders Nowhere", *Youth Justice*, vol. 21, no. 1 (2021), p.3.
52 S Case & K Haines, "Transatlantic 'positive youth justice'", *Crime Prevention and Community Safety*, vol. 20 (2018), p.208 at p.215.
53 United Nations Committee on the Rights of the Child, "General Comment No. 24: Children's Rights in child Justice" (2019), para 18, available at: https://tbinternet.ohchr.org/_layouts/15/treatybodyexternal/Download.aspx?symbolno=CRC/C/GC/24&Lang=en
54 UNCRC, "General Comment No. 24", para 24.
55 FJ Lexcen & DN Reppucci, "Effects of Psychopathology on Adolescent medical Decision-Making", *University of Chicago Law School Roundtable*, vol. 5, no. 1 (1998), p.63 at p.77; SB Johnson, M Sudhinaraset & RW Blum, "Neuromaturation and adolescent risk taking: why development is not determinism", *Journal of Adolescent Research*, vol. 25, no. 1 (2010), p.4 at p.10.
56 SJ Blakemore, "Development of the social brain in adolescence", *Journal of the Royal Society of Medicine*, vol. 105, no. 3 (2012), p.111; SJ Blakemore, S Burnett & RE Dahl, "The Role of Puberty in the Developing Adolescent Brain", *Human Brain Mapping*, vol. 31, no. 6 (2010), p.26; P Kelly, "The brain in the jar: a critique of discourses of adolescent brain development", *Journal of Youth Studies*, vol. 15, no. 7 (2012), p.944.
57 Lacey, *In Search of Criminal Responsibility*, p.25.
58 Hollingsworth, "Theorising children's rights", p.1051.
59 Hollingsworth, "Theorising children's rights", p.1052.
60 P Brown, "Reviewing the age of criminal responsibility", *Criminal Law Review*, no. 11 (2018), p.904.
61 DS Bekbolatkyzy, DR Yerenatovna, YA Maratuly, AG Makhatovna & KM. Beaver, "Aging out of adolescent delinquency: Results from a longitudinal sample of youth and young adults", *Journal of Criminal Justice*, vol. 60 (2019), p.108; T Hirschi & M Gottfredson, "Age and the explanation of crime", *American Journal of Sociology*, no. 89, no. 3 (1983), p.553.
62 JG McMullen, "Invisible stripes: the problem of youth criminal records", *Southern California Review of Law & Social Justice*, vol. 27, no. 1 (2018), p.1 at p.39.
63 CLINKS, "Introducing Desistance: A guide for voluntary, community and social enterprise (VCSE) sector organisations" (2013), pp.3–4, available at: www.clinks.org/publication/introducing-desistance.
64 S Maruna, *Making good: How ex-convicts reform and rebuild their lives* (American Psychological Association Books: Washington, DC, 2001), p.6.
65 UNCRC, "General Comment No. 24", paras 12 and 13, 15.
66 Hoskins, *Beyond Punishment*, p.168.
67 See also A Blumstein and K Nakamura, "Redemption in the presence of widespread criminal background checks", *Criminology: An Interdisciplinary Journal*, vol. 47, no. 2 (2009), p.327.
68 Maruna, *Making good*.
69 Maurutto et al, "Punishing the Non-convicted", p.3.
70 Sands, *Growing up, Moving on*.
71 T Wakefiled, S Bialous & DE Appollonio, "Clearing Cannabis Records: A survey of criminal record expungement availability and accessibility among US States", *International Journal of Drug Policy*, no. 114 (2023), p.1. See also T Chiricos, K Barrick, W Bales & S Bontrager, "The labeling of convicted felons and its consequences for recidivism", *Criminology*, vol. 45, no. 3 (2007), p.547.
72 B Avery, *Ban the box: Fair chance guide* (National Employment Law Project: New York, 2019); Burton et al, "Beyond the eternal criminal record".
73 S Maruna, "Reintegration as a right and the rites of reintegration: A comparative review of de-stigmatization practices", in JA Humphry & P Cordella (eds), *Effective Interventions in the Lives of Criminal Offenders* (Springer: New York, 2014), pp.121–138.
74 T LeBel & S Maruna, "Life on the outside: Transitioning from prison to the community", in K Reitz & J Petersilia (eds), *Oxford Handbook of Sentencing and Corrections* (Clarendon Press: Oxford, 2012), p.661.

References

Legislation

Children and Young Persons Act 1933
Coroners and Justice Act 2009
Crime and Disorder Act 1998
Disclosure (Scotland) Act 2020
Justice Act (Northern Ireland) 2015
National Police Records (Recordable Offences) Regulations 2000, SI No 2000/1139
Police Act 1997
Rehabilitation of Offenders Act 1974
Rehabilitation of Offenders Act 1974 (Exceptions) Order 1975

Books and book chapters

Ashworth A, *Principles of Criminal Law* (Oxford University Press: Oxford, 5th edn, 2003).

Carr N, "The albatross of juvenile criminal records", in Meijer S, Annison H, & O'Loughlin A (eds), *Fundamental Rights and Legal Consequences of Criminal Conviction* (Hart Publishing: London, 2019).

Hart HLA, *Punishment and Responsibility: Essays in the Philosophy of Law* (Oxford University Press: New York, 1968).

Hollingsworth K, "The utility and futility of international rights standards for children in conflict with the law: The case of England", in Weber L, Fishwick E, & Marmo M (eds), *Routledge International Handbook of Criminology and Human Rights* (Routledge: Abingdon, 2016).

Hoskins Z, *Beyond Punishment? A Normative Account of the Collateral Legal Consequences of Conviction* (Oxford University Press: New York, 2019).

Husak D, "Strict liability, justice, and proportionality", in Simester AP (ed), *Appraising Strict Liability* (Oxford University Press: Oxford, 2005).

Lacey N, *In Search of Criminal Responsibility: Ideas, Interests, and Institutions* (Oxford University Press: Oxford, 2016).

LeBel T & Maruna S, "Life on the outside: Transitioning from prison to the community", in Reitz K & Petersilia J (eds), *Oxford Handbook of Sentencing and Corrections* (Clarendon: Oxford, 2012).

Maruna S, *Making Good: How Ex-Convicts Reform and Rebuild Their Lives* (American Psychological Association Books: Washington DC, 2001).

Maruna S, "Reintegration as a right and the rites of reintegration: A comparative review of de-stigmatization practices", in Humphry JA & Cordella P (eds), *Effective Interventions in the Lives of Criminal Offenders* (Springer: New York, 2014).

Thomas T, *Criminal Records: A Database for the Criminal Justice System and Beyond* (Palgrave Macmillan: Basingstoke, 2007).

Travis J, *But They All Come Back: Facing the Challenges of Prisoner Re-Entry* (The Urban Insitute: Washington DC, 2005).

Tyler TR, *Why People Obey the Law* (Yale University Press: New Haven, 1990).

Tyler TR & Huo YH, *Trust in the Law: Encouraging Public Cooperation with the Police and Courts* (Russell-Sage: New York, 2002).

Yaffe G, *The Age of Culpability: Children and the Nature of Criminal Responsibility* (Oxford University Press: Oxford, 2018).

Journal articles

Agnew R, "Foundation for a general strain theory of crime and delinquency", *Criminology*, vol. 30, no. 1 (1992), pp.47–87.

Arthur R, "Recognising children's citizenship in the youth justice system", *Journal of Social Welfare & Family Law*, vol. 37, no. 1 (2015), pp.21–37.

Baldry E, Briggs DB, Goldson B, & Russell S, "'Cruel and unusual punishment': An inter-jurisdictional study of the criminalisation of young people with complex support needs", *Journal of Youth Studies*, vol. 21, no. 5 (2018), pp.636–652.

Bekbolatkyzy DS, Yerenatovna DR, Maratuly YA, Makhatovna AG, & Beaver KM, "Aging out of adolescent delinquency: Results from a longitudinal sample of youth and young adults", *Journal of Criminal Justice*, vol. 60 (2019), pp.108–116.

Berman MN, "Proportionality, constraint, and culpability", *Criminal Law and Philosophy*, vol. 15, no. 3 (2021), pp.373–391.

Blakemore SJ, "Development of the social brain in adolescence", *Journal of the Royal Society of Medicine*, vol. 105, no. 3 (2012), pp.111–116.

Blakemore SJ, Burnett S, & Dahl RE, "The role of puberty in the developing adolescent brain", *Human Brain Mapping*, vol. 31, no. 6 (2010), pp.926–933.

Blumstein A & Nakamura K, "Redemption in the presence of widespread criminal background checks", *Criminology: An Interdisciplinary Journal*, vol. 47, no. 2 (2009), pp.327–359.

Brown P, "Reviewing the age of criminal responsibility", *Criminal Law Review*, no. 11 (2018), pp.904–909.

Burton AL, Burton VS, Cullen F, Pickett JT, & Thielo A, "Beyond the eternal criminal record: Public support for expungement", *Criminology & Public Policy*, vol. 20, no. 1 (2021), pp.123–151.

Case S & Haines K, "Transatlantic 'Positive Youth Justice': A distinctive new model for responding to offending by children?", *Crime Prevention and Community Safety*, vol. 20 (2018), pp.208–222.

Case S & Haines K, "Abolishing youth justice systems: Children first, offenders nowhere", *Youth Justice*, vol. 21, no. 1 (2021), pp.3–17.

Case S, Sutton CE, Greenhalgh J, Monaghan M, & Wright J, "Searching for context: A review of 'what works' revies of interventions to prevent youth offending using the EMMIE Framework", *Safer Communities*, vol. 21, no. 4 (2022).

Chiricos T, Barrick K, Bales W, & Bontrager S, "The labeling of convicted felons and its consequences for recidivism", *Criminology*, vol. 45, no. 3 (2007), pp.547–581.

Corda A & Lageson SE, "Disordered punishment: Workaround technologies of criminal records disclosure and the rise of a new penal entrepreneurialism", *British Journal of Criminology*, vol. 60, no. 2 (2020), pp.245–264.

Corda A, Rovira M, & Henley A, "Collateral consequences of criminal records from the other side of the pond: How exceptional is American penal exceptionalism?", *Criminology & Criminal Justice*, vol. 23, no. 4 (2023), pp.528–548.

Corda A, Rovira M, & van't Zand-Kurtovic E, "Collateral consequences of criminal records from a cross-national perspective: An introduction", *Criminology and Criminal Justice*, vol. 23, no.4 (2023), pp.519–527.

Day AM, "'It's a hard balance to find': The perspectives of youth justice practitioners in England on the place of 'Risk' in an emerging 'Child-First' World", *Youth Justice*, vol. 23, no. 1 (2022), pp.58–75.

Fagan J & Tyler TR, "Legal socialization of children and adolescents", *Social Justice Research*, vol. 18 (2005), pp.217–241.

Henley AJ, "Mind the gap: Sentencing, rehabilitation and civic purgatory", *Probation Journal*, vol. 63, no. 3 (2018), pp.285–301.

Henley AJ, "Criminalisation, criminal records and rehabilitation: From supervision to citizenship?", *Probation Journal*, vol. 69, no. 3 (2022), pp.273–277.

Hirschi T & Gottfredson M, "Age and the explanation of crime", *American Journal of Sociology*, vol. 89, no. 3 (1983), pp.552–584.

Hollingsworth K, "Theorising children's rights in the youth justice system: The significance of autonomy and foundational rights", *Modern Law Review*, vol. 76, no. 6 (2013), pp.1046–1069.

Jacobs JB & Larrauri E, "Are criminal convictions a public matter? The USA and Spain", *Punishment & Society*, vol. 14, no. 1 (2012), pp.3–28.

Johnson SB, Sudhinaraset M, & Blum RW, "Neuromaturation and adolescent risk taking: Why development is not determinism", *Journal of Adolescent Research*, vol. 25, no. 1 (2010), pp. 4–23.

Kelly P, "The brain in the jar: A critique of discourses of adolescent brain development", *Journal of Youth Studies*, vol. 15, no. 7 (2012), pp. 944–959.

Kurlychek M, Brame R, & Bushway S, "Scarlet letters and recidivism: Does an old criminal record predict future offending?", *Criminology and Public Policy*, vol. 5, no. 3 (2006), pp. 483–504.

Lexcen FJ & Reppucci DN, "Effects of psychopathology on adolescent medical decision-making", *University of Chicago Law School Roundtable*, vol. 5, no. 1 (1998), pp.63–106.

Maurutto P, Hannah-Moffat K, & Quirouette M, "Punishing the non-convicted through disclosure of police records", *British Journal of Criminology*, vol. 63, no. 6 (2023), pp.1368–1383.

McMullen JG, "Invisible stripes: The problem of youth criminal records", *Southern California Review of Law & Social Justice*, vol. 27, no. 1 (2018), pp.1–44.

Paternoster R, Brame R, Bachman R, & Sherman LW, "Do fair procedures matter? The effect of procedural justice on spouse assault", *Law and Society Review*, vol. 31, no. 1 (1997), pp.163–204.

Purshouse J, "Non-conviction disclosure as part of an enhanced criminal record certificate: Assessing the legal framework from a fundamental human rights perspective", *Public Law*, no. 4 (2018), pp.668–686.

Sacher S, "Risking children: The implications of predictive risk analytics across child protection and policing for vulnerable and marginalized children", *Human Rights Law Review*, vol. 22, no. 1 (2022), pp.1–31.

Sherman LW, "Defiance, deterrence and irrelevance: A theory of the criminal sanction", *Journal of Research in Crime and Delinquency*, vol. 30, no. 4 (1993), pp.445–473.

Wakefiled T, Bialous S, & Appollonio DE, "A survey of criminal record expungement availability and accessibility among US States", *International Journal of Drug Policy*, vol. 114 (2023), 103983.

Reports and websites

Avery B, *Ban the Box: Fair Chance Guide* (National Employment Law Project: New York, 2019).

Carr N, Dwyer C, & Larruari E, *Young People, Criminal Records and Employment Barriers* (NIACRO: Belfast, 2015).

CLINKS, *Introducing Desistance: A Guide for Voluntary, Community and Social Enterprise (VCSE) Sector Organisations* (CLINKS: London, 2013).

Disclosure and Barring Service, *Guidance: New Filtering Rules for DBS Certificates (From 28 November 2020 Onwards)*, available at: www.gov.uk/government/publications/filtering-rules-for-criminal-record-check-certificates/new-filtering-rules-for-dbs-certificates-from-28-november-2020-onwards

Sands C, *Growing up, Moving on: The International Treatment of Childhood Criminal Records* (London: SCYJ, 2016).

Sentencing Council, *Sentencing Children and Young People: Overarching Principles and Offence Specific Guidelines for Sexual Offences and Robbery. Definitive Guideline* (Sentencing Council: London, 2017).

United Nations Committee on the Rights of the Child, *General Comment No. 14 on the Right of the Child to Have His or Her Best Interests Taken as a Primary Consideration* (UNCRC: Geneva, 2013).

United Nations Committee on the Rights of the Child, *General Comment No. 24: Children's Rights in Child Justice* (UNCRC: Geneva, 2019).

Youth Justice Board, *Strategic Plan 2021–24* (YJB: London, 2020).

Youth Justice Board for England and Wales, *Business Plan 2022–23* (YJB: London, 2022).

24
STUCK IN TIME
The Minimum Age of Criminal Responsibility in England and Wales

Tim Bateman

Context: a "Child-first" youth justice that criminalises children of primary school age

Any consideration of the minimum age of criminal responsibility (MACR) in England and Wales, in the context of contemporary youth justice policy within that jurisdiction, lays bare a deep-seated, yet rarely dissected, paradox. In 2018, the Youth Justice Board for England and Wales (YJB), a non-departmental public body sponsored by the Ministry of Justice, with responsibility for the oversight of the youth justice system, formally endorsed a vision that children in conflict with the law should be seen as "children first and offenders second".[1] A year later, in its strategic plan, the YJB elaborated that this newly adopted philosophy entailed a commitment to the development of:

> "A youth justice system that sees children as children, treats them fairly and helps them to build on their strengths so they can make a constructive contribution to society. This will prevent offending and create safer communities with fewer victims".[2]

Drawing on the work of Haines and Case in particular,[3] the key elements of a Child-first approach are described as including, among others:

- prioritising the best interests of children, recognising their particular needs, capacities, rights, and potential;
- promoting a childhood removed from the justice system, using pre-emptive prevention, diversion, and minimal intervention; and
- minimising criminogenic stigma from contact with the system.[4]

These policy developments reflected, and gave further impetus to, ongoing changes in practice, manifested in a dramatic reduction in the number of children entering the youth justice system.[5] Thus, in the decade from 2012, the number of proven offences recorded against children declined by 79%.[6] While there is credible evidence for believing that children's offending has fallen over this period, it would be unrealistic to suppose that changes in youthful behaviour can fully explain the extent of this contraction.[7] Indeed, it is well documented that the decline in the number of children subject to formal criminalisation is, in large part, a reflection of shifts in the way that criminal justice agencies respond to children who come to their attention, demonstrated in particular by a substantial expansion in the use of informal diversionary mechanisms.[8] This expansion was triggered by the introduction of a government target, in 2008, to reduce the number of children entering the youth justice system for the first time (so-called first-time entrants or FTEs), by 20% by 2020.[9] The target was met within 12 months of its adoption[10] and the decline in FTEs has continued in the interim period, falling by a further 78% between 2012 and 2022, from 36,987 to 8,016 children.[11] The adoption of a much less punitive approach to youth crime than that which had dominated youth justice since the early 1990s has been characterised as a pragmatic response to the onset of austerity,[12] but it is also indicative of an acknowledgement on the part of policy makers of the abundant evidence, hitherto largely ignored, of criminalisation's negative consequences for children.[13] This acknowledgement would however appear to be heavily qualified so far as the MACR is concerned.

The MACR in England and Wales was set at ten years in 1963 by the Children and Young Persons Act,[14] extremely low by international standards and by comparison with a range of jurisdictions which do not profess to place the child at the centre of their youth justice arrangements. It has remained unchanged in the intervening 60 years, although, as will be described later in the chapter, other legislative changes have made it easier to prosecute very young children. One would anticipate, in this context, that policy shifts aimed at minimising stigma associated with youth justice processing and promoting non-criminal responses to children's lawbreaking (as well as prioritising children's best interests) would logically entail consideration of the age at which children become criminally liable. In the current instance, such consideration appears to have played no part in the adoption of a Child-first ethos.

It is, by definition, difficult to demonstrate the absence of something, but it is telling that the YJB's guide to Child-first published in 2022, while confirming that such an approach "recognises children according to their age, development and their intrinsic value and potential" and acknowledging that "facilitating their positive development is the responsibility of adults", fails to mention that current provisions allow prosecution of children who are of primary school age.[15] The document extols the benefits of diverting children away from criminal justice processes and recognises that "children make mistakes purely because of lack of experience and knowledge that adults accumulate, as well as biological and cognitive development."[16] But readers are not alerted to the fact that the current MACR would appear to be out of step with such an understanding. Parliament has moreover had ample opportunity to consider the issue. Lord Dholakia, a Liberal Democrat peer, introduced identical private members Bills in 2013, 2015, 2016, 2017, and 2021 aimed at raising the MACR from 10 to 12 years. Most of these attempts at modest reform stalled at first reading and none has progressed beyond second reading; but on each occasion where the matter has been debated, the government has opposed the proposed statutory change.[17]

This paradox, between statutory provisions that determine that children can be held criminally liable from a very young age and policy developments that direct attention to the benefits of attending to children's developmental needs and the criminogenic nature of youth justice involvement, stands in need of explanation, a task attempted in the remainder of this chapter.

The road to paradox: progress stalled

The longstanding common law presumption that children could be held criminally liable at seven years of age was codified in the Children Act 1908.[18] What on its face appears to have been simply a statutory ratification of an existing position was, in fact, a more progressive measure since children above that age would henceforth be liable for prosecution in the newly created juvenile court, established by the same Act as a distinct venue for children, aged 7–16 years, who would previously have appeared in the adult court.[19] The next half century, during which welfarist understandings of child offending, predicated on the assumption that youth crime was primarily a manifestation of underlying welfare need and vulnerability, were in ascendancy, witnessed a number of rises in the MACR.[20] In 1933, the Children and Young Persons Act raised the relevant age to eight years;[21] 30 years later, as noted above, the current MACR of ten years was established in 1963. Although no further increases have been implemented in the period since, the progressive sentiments which had stimulated this trajectory were not fully exhausted. The Children and Young Persons Act 1969 contained provisions to preclude the prosecution of any child below the age of 14 years and a presumption against criminal proceedings for children aged 14–16 years.[22] But a more punitive dynamic emerged in the wake of the legislation's passage and these measures were never implemented, although they remained on the statute book for more than two decades until being repealed in 1991.[23]

As the "punitive turn" became hard wired into discourses around children who broke the law, the direction of legislative travel reversed.[24] The abolition in 1998 of the doctrine of *doli incapax*, a common law presumption, of more than 700 years standing, that children aged below 14 years of age were not criminally liable for offending unless the prosecution could demonstrate that they knew that the behaviour in question was seriously wrong, as opposed to naughty or mischievous, constituted for practical purposes a lowering of the age at which younger children were subject to criminal proceedings.[25] The principle had provided a filter ensuring that issues of maturity, capacity, and culpability were considered before children aged 10–13 years old were criminalised. Removal of that filter, through New Labour's flagship Crime and Disorder Act 1998, rendered children "unequivocally responsible and accountable for choices made and harm caused" from the age of ten.[26] The change had an immediate negative impact: in the year after abolition of *doli incapax*, the number of 10–14 year olds who received a formal youth justice sanction, for an indictable offence, rose by 29% compared with the previous 12 months. Equivalent figures for children aged 15–17 years showed a decline over the same period.[27]

The expansion in diversion from the mid-2000s, described above, and the associated acceptance that responses to youth crime should revolve around Child-first precepts, are testimony to the fact that youth justice policy is no longer in thrall to "punitivism".[28] However, there has been no corresponding relaxation in attitudes towards the MACR. Indeed, in spite of a near unanimity outside of political circles that the current threshold is too low, increasingly out of step with international norms and in tension with Child-first aims,[29] governments of all persuasions have maintained a robust defence of retaining criminalisation at age 10 in England and Wales.[30] This position contrasts with that adopted in other parts of the United Kingdom.

In Northern Ireland, which has developed its own "Children-first" model of youth justice practice,[31] the Department of Justice has acknowledged that the current MACR – also set at 10 years – is:

"counter-productive, it appears at odds with modern norms. While accepting that children need to be held accountable for their actions, this should be achieved through the adoption of a children first approach which supports them to change".[32]

In late 2022, the Department accordingly launched a public consultation on raising the MACR in Northern Ireland to 14 years.[33]

Scotland had, for many years, the lowest MACR in Europe at eight years of age, albeit that prosecution of younger children was "very rare" because children below the age of 16 years are, for the most part, processed within a welfare-based Children's Hearing system rather than the criminal courts.[34] It is sometimes contended that a lower MACR is less problematic where welfare considerations are at the heart of youth justice responses. As the authors of one review put it: "minimum ages of criminal responsibility will vary depending on the kind of youth justice and social care systems in place in different countries".[35] The welfarist foundations of the Scottish system have not however rendered the low MACR immune to criticism. Following extensive public consultation, legislation was passed in 2019 which provided that: "[a] child under the age of 12 years cannot commit an offence".[36] Commencement of the relevant parts of the Act was delayed, but the provisions were fully implemented in December 2021. The legislation moreover requires that Scottish ministers conduct a three-year review, from the date at which the increased age was introduced, to consider whether further changes should be made. The paradoxical refusal of authorities to countenance any reform of the MACR in England and Wales is thus brought into sharper relief when viewed in the context of developments in other UK jurisdictions.

Rationales and irrationalities

Arguments in favour of raising the MACR within England and Wales are well rehearsed.[37] The government's rebuttals, though remarkably consistent over time, are less easily unpicked since they consist largely in unsupported assertion. It is, for instance, frequently contended that criminalisation of children is counterproductive: it may exacerbate the risk of further lawbreaking[38] and stigma associated with youth justice involvement has the potential to hinder children's wellbeing and healthy development.[39] The government has not sought to challenge this evidence; indeed as early as the publication of the *Children's Plan* in 2007, it acknowledged that "the likelihood of re-offending increases the further a young person gets into the criminal justice system" and that children should not receive "a disproportionately harsh response for low-level offences".[40] As outlined earlier, the latter adoption of a Child-first model entails a commitment to avoiding the criminalisation of children wherever possible.[41]

The logical consequences of this position for the MACR are, however, largely ignored. On occasion, government ministers have made reference to the relatively low numbers of children who would be affected by any reform, pointing to the contraction in FTEs and highlighting that the decline for younger children has been sharper than for their older counterparts.[42] It is true that the fall in the number of children cautioned or sentenced has varied with age: between 2012 and 2022, for instance, the reduction for children aged 10–13 years was 83% compared with 79% for children aged 15–17.[43] Nonetheless, 1024 children in the former age range continued to face criminal sanctions in the latter year and while that may constitute a relatively small proportion of the total youth justice population, what happens to upward of 1000 very young, and for the most part extremely vulnerable, children cannot be a matter of indifference, particularly from a Child-first perspective. Where a particular arrangement is demonstrably unjust, arguing that it impacts on relatively small numbers of individuals is clearly not an adequate response. Indeed, in a 2017 Parliamentary debate on the issue, Lord Dholakia suggested that the small numbers involved was a strong argument for *raising* the MACR since it would be relatively easy to make provision for alternative, non-criminal, responses for this cohort.[44] It is furthermore unsatisfactory to base policy on trends which may be contingent. As previous experience attests, a continued decline in the number of children entering the youth justice system is not guaranteed: the decade from 1992, for instance, was characterised by a pronounced expansion in the criminalisation of children. Indeed, the government's own projections anticipate that the number of children in custody will double over the next two years, an unlikely scenario without an equivalent rise in the number of child prosecutions.[45]

Recent advances in developmental science have cast light on the extent of changes to the brain that occur during adolescence, highlighted the impact on teenage emotional regulation and thinking, and clarified that children's behaviour should be understood differently from that of adults.[46] This knowledge, which might be thought to warrant reconsideration of the MACR, has been met by the government with a consistent refrain which simply sidesteps the evidence-base. The assertion that children aged 10 know the difference between right and wrong was first adduced by the Labour administration in 1997 in defence of the abolition of *doli incapax*.[47] It has been routinely replicated by all governments since. In 2017, speaking in terms which mirrored almost exactly those used by Lord Faulkes a year earlier, Baroness Vere set out the government's position as follows:

> "[C]hildren aged 10 and above are able to differentiate between bad behaviour and serious wrongdoing and can therefore be held accountable for their actions. Where a young person commits an offence, it is important they understand that this is a serious matter".[48]

This argument, it has been pointed out, involves a categorical error, in that it represents the acquisition of moral understanding as a once-and-for-all skill, like riding a bike, rather than as a long-term project that takes place over an extended period. Just as one would not expect an infant who had mastered the rudiments of reading to successfully engage with the novels of James Joyce, so too an understanding that stealing from shops is "wrong" is not equivalent to having attained the capacity to contemplate complex ethical dilemmas such as those which might be encountered in a jury trial.[49]

The government's rejoinder to another frequently raised criticism of the current MACR, that it is not compatible with contemporary understandings of children's rights, draws on the same line of defence. The UN Committee on the Rights of the Child, which monitors states' compliance with the Convention on the Rights of the Child, has consistently urged the UK to raise the MACR "in accordance with acceptable international standards",[50] which from 2019, following publication by the Committee of a revised General Comment on youth justice, would entail an increase in the age at which children become criminally liable to at least 14 years.[51] In response, the government has resorted to the familiar proposition that children aged ten are able to differentiate between bad behaviour and serious wrongdoing.[52] Ministers have also referred to a purported benefit of the present arrangements. A low MACR, it is contended, allows children to access the support which they need to help them stop offending, as if criminalisation were a prerequisite of the provision of services to children.[53]

Ironically, maintaining that children's capacities are well developed at age 10 is problematic when considered in the context of another common objection to the current threshold for youth justice involvement, since in other legal contexts, it is apparent that this same standard is not applied. A number of commentators have highlighted a conceptual strain between the age at which children are deemed capable of criminal intent and the age-related thresholds at which other rights and safeguards are crossed.[54] This strain has moreover become more acute over time as conceptions of childhood have developed. Outside of the criminal justice system, it is evident that children are increasingly constructed in terms of their immaturity relative to adults and their right to be safeguarded from the risks, expectations, and pressures to which adults are exposed. One indication of this evolution is given by progressive rises in the school leaving age: from 15 to 16 years in 1972; to 17 years in 2013; and 18 years in 2015;[55] another is the increase in the age at which children can purchase tobacco, from 16 to 18 years in 2007, following an analogous modification in relation to the purchase of alcohol.[56] The absence of corresponding changes to the MACR provides a telling contrast. Other examples of this tension include the fact that while children can be guilty of a sexual offence at age 10, they cannot consent to sex until they are 16; the latter is also the age prior to which a child is precluded from purchasing a pet; before attaining age 18, children are not permitted to apply for a credit card or a mortgage, perform music professionally abroad, buy fireworks, get married without parental permission, vote, or sit on a jury.[57] The government's protestations that the MACR accurately reflects children's developmental maturity is hard to square with expectations outside the justice system.

Concluding thoughts: towards a resolution of paradox

If the government's defence of the MACR is unconvincing, it does at least illuminate the nature of the tension between early criminalisation and Child-first pretensions. The idea that children should be held to account when they infringe the criminal law is fundamental to political understandings of the function of the youth justice system, even though it has no place in Child-first philosophy. The low MACR is a consequence of an imputation to children of responsibility for their behaviour that is analogous to that ascribed to adult defendants. Fionda's observation that the age of criminal responsibility reflects the age at which society chooses to punish children would thus appear apposite.[58] In this context, it is worth recalling that the youth justice system in England and Wales continues to derive its structures and operational frameworks from the criminal justice system for adults, where punishment predominates, rather than being oriented towards, and integrated with, other services for children who require state support.[59] It is thus unsurprising that Child-first aspirations are confronted with, what Raymond Williams calls, "*residual*" culture, embedded assumptions, working practices and traditions that hangover from a more explicitly punitive period.[60]

Such undertones continue to exert a tangible influence on policy, intermittently betrayed even when promoting a Child-first agenda. Thus, the Ministerial foreword to the latest iteration of youth justice National Standards, produced in 2019 to support the introduction of Child-first practice, refers to children as "offenders" and prioritises "breaking the cycle of offending" rather than "the best interests of children, recognising their particular needs, capacities, rights and potential".[61]

The reluctance to abandon punishment is moreover integrally linked with, and reinforced by, another long-term and deeply embedded dynamic whereby children who offend are deemed to have forfeited their childhood status, and lose entitlement to the rights and safeguards associated with that status. Fionda, in an insightful analysis, describes how notions of innocence generally attached to childhood give way where children engage in criminal activity since they have not simply transgressed the law, but have also offended against normative expectations.[62] This transition from "child" to "offender"/ "angel" to "devil" frames how the child's behaviour should be understood and legitimises the imposition of sanctions designed to punish.[63] Because children who offend are denied the protections afforded to those who do not come into contact with the justice system, this reconceptualisation involves a process of "adultification" which requires that the former should bear responsibility for their actions beyond their chronological and developmental stage.[64]

These divergent constructions of childhood can be readily detected in the different policy frameworks that pertain to children who are in trouble and those deemed in need of care and protection. Where punishment is deemed legitimate, legal provision is required to ensure that it is available and a low MACR becomes a standard that enables the attribution of adult forms of responsibility to children whose behaviour has demarcated them as undeserving of considerations that would normally apply to individuals of that age. The adoption of a Child-first model has done little to challenge these fundamental tenets of youth justice in England and Wales; rather it has been grafted onto those foundations.[65] It is accordingly unsurprising that strains are discernible when issues involving holding children responsible for their criminal conduct are subject to scrutiny.

Notes

1 Youth Justice Board, "Strategic Plan 2018-2021" (2018), available at: https://assets.publishing.service.gov.uk/media/5afaa4f8e5274a25e78bbe54/201804_YJB_Strategic_Plan_2018_21_Final.pdf.
2 Youth Justice Board, "YJB Strategic Plan 2019-2022" (2019), p.6, available at: https://assets.publishing.service.gov.uk/media/5cdebf0840f0b652bcff8d7e/YJB_Strategic_Plan_2019_to_2022.pdf.
3 K Haines & S Case, *Positive Youth Justice* (Policy Press: Bristol, 2015).
4 Youth Justice Board, "Strategic Plan 2019-2022".
5 T Bateman, "The State of Youth Justice 2020", *National Association for Youth Justice* (2020), available at: https://thenayj.org.uk/cmsAdmin/uploads/state-of-youth-justice-2020-final-sep20.pdf.
6 Youth Justice Board, "Youth Justice Annual Statistics 2021/2022 England and Wales" (2023), available at: www.gov.uk/government/statistics/youth-justice-statistics-2021-to-2022.
7 T Bateman, "The State of Youth Justice 2020".
8 L McAra & S McVie, "The shrinking youth justice population: a change in behaviour or a change in the system?", *Scottish Justice Matters*, vol. 5, no. 1 (2017), p.38.
9 A Sutherland et al, "An analysis of trends in first time entrants to the youth justice system", *Ministry of Justice* (2017), available at: https://assets.publishing.service.gov.uk/government/uploads/system/uploads/attachment_data/file/653182/trends-in-fte-to-the-youth-justice-system.pdf.
10 T Bateman, "The State of Youth Justice 2020".
11 Youth Justice Board, "Youth Justice Statistics 2021/2022".
12 T Bateman, "Where has all the youth crime gone? Youth justice in an age of austerity", *Children and Society*, vol. 28, no. 5 (2014), p.416.
13 S Case & A Browning, *Child first justice: the research evidence-base* (Loughborough University: Loughborough, 2021).
14 Children and Young Persons Act 1963.

15 Youth Justice Board, "A Guide to Child First" (2022), p.4, available at: https://yjresourcehub.uk/wp-content/uploads/media/Child_First_Overview_and_Guide_April_2022_YJB.pdf.
16 Youth Justice Board, "A Guide to Child First", p.7.
17 House of Lords, "Age of Criminal Responsibility Bill 2017 Library Briefing" (House of Lords: London).
18 Children Act 1908. See also S Bandalli, "Children, Responsibility and the New Youth Justice", in B Goldson (ed), *The New Youth Justice* (Russell House: Lyme Regis, 2000).
19 R Arthur, *Young Offenders and the Law* (Routledge: London, 2010).
20 R Arthur, "Rethinking the Criminal Responsibility of Young People in England", *European Journal of Crime, Criminal Law and Criminal Justice*, vol. 20, no. 1 (2012), p.13.
21 Children and Young Persons Act 1933.
22 Children and Young Persons Act 1969.
23 Sections 4 and 5 of Children and Young Persons Act 1969 were repealed by section 72 of Criminal Justice Act 1991. See also T Bateman, "Criminalising children for no good purpose: the age of criminal responsibility in England and Wales", *National Association for Youth Justice Campaign Paper* (2012), available at: https://thenayj.org.uk/wp-content/uploads/2015/06/2012-The-Age-of-Criminal-responsibility.pdf.
24 See for instance, J Muncie, "The 'punitive' turn in juvenile justice: cultures of control and rights compliance in western Europe and the USA", *Youth Justice*, vol. 8, no. 2 (2008), p.107.
25 S Bandalli, "Children, responsibility and the new youth justice", in B Goldson (ed), *The New Youth Justice* (Russell House: Lyme Regis, 2000), p.81.
26 S Bandalli, "Children, responsibility and the new youth justice", pp. 86–87.
27 T Bateman, "Criminalising children for no good purpose". Figures for children aged 10–13 years, which would give a better reflection of the impact of the changes, are not available.
28 T Bateman, "The State of Youth Justice 2020".
29 From a local government perspective, the Association of Directors of Children's Services, the Association of the Youth Offending Team Managers and the Local Government Association have recently noted the tension between Child first and the low MACR. See Association of Directors of Children's Services, "A youth justice system that works for children: a joint policy position paper by service, strategic and political leaders in local government" (2021), available at: www.local.gov.uk/publications/youth-justice-system-works-children.
30 T Bateman, "Challenging punitive youth justice", in S Case & N Hazel (eds), *Child first: developing a new youth justice system* (Palgrave MacMillan: London, 2023), p.25.
31 Department of Justice, "Strategic Framework for Youth Justice 2022 – 2027" (2022), available at: www.justice-ni.gov.uk/publications/strategic-framework-youth-justice.
32 Department of Justice, "Strategic Framework for Youth Justice 2022 – 2027", p.42.
33 Department of Justice, "Public consultation on increasing the minimum age of criminal responsibility in Northern Ireland from 10 Years to 14 years" (2022), available at: www.justice-ni.gov.uk/consultations/consultation-increasing-minimum-age-criminal-responsibility-ni.
34 T Crofts, "Catching up With Europe: taking the age of criminal responsibility seriously in England", *European Journal of Crime, Criminal Law and Criminal Justice*, vol. 17 (2009), p.267.
35 J Graham, S Perrott, & K Marshall, *A Review of the Youth Justice system in Northern Ireland* (Department of Justice: Belfast, 2011), p.103.
36 The Age of Criminal Responsibility (Scotland) Act 2019, s 1.
37 For a recent summary see S Bunn & P Brown, "Age of criminal responsibility", *Parliamentary Office of Science and Technology* (2018), available at: https://researchbriefings.files.parliament.uk/documents/POST-PN-0577/POST-PN-0577.pdf.
38 L McAra & S McVie, "The case for diversion and minimum necessary intervention", in B Goldson and J Muncie (eds) *Youth Crime and Justice* (Sage: London, 2nd edn, 2015), pp.119–135.
39 J Deakin, C Fox, & R Matos, "Labelled as 'risky' in an era of control: how young people experience and respond to the stigma of criminalized identities", *European Journal of Criminology*, vol. 19, no. 4 (2020), p.653.
40 Department for Children, Schools and Families, *The Children's Plan: building brighter futures* (The Stationery Office: Norwich, 2007), p.139.

41 N Hazel & P Williams, "Developing Child First as the guiding principle for youth justice", in S Case & N Hazel (eds), *Child first: developing a new youth justice system* (Palgrave MacMillan: London, 2023), pp.169–201.
42 For instance, in 2012, Crispin Blunt, then minister with responsibility for youth justice, maintained that for such reasons that the impact of a rise in the MACR would be minimal. Cited in T Bateman, "Criminalising children for no good purpose". In 2020, a similar argument was put by Lucy Frazer, Minister of State for Justice, in evidence to the Justice Committee of the House of Commons. She noted that the "majority of younger children who enter the youth justice system are dealt with by way of an out of court disposal" and pointed to the sharp fall in the cautioning and convictions for children aged 10–11.
43 Youth Justice Board, "Youth justice annual statistics 2021/2022".
44 Lord Dholakia, "Age of Criminal Responsibility Bill, 2nd reading" (Hansard, Volume 783, 8 September 2017).
45 National Audit Office, "Children in custody: secure training centres and secure schools", (2022), available at: www.nao.org.uk/wp-content/uploads/2022/04/Children-in-custody-secure-training-centres-and-secure-schools.pdf.
46 See for instance, J Coleman, *The Teacher and the Teenage Brain* (Routledge: London, 2021); The Royal Society, *Neuroscience and the law* (The Royal Society: London, 2011); E Farmer, "The age of criminal responsibility: developmental science and human rights perspectives", *Journal of Children's Services,* vol. 6, no. 2 (2011), p.86.
47 Home Office, "No more excuses: a new approach to tackling youth crime in England and Wales", *White Paper* (Home Office: London, 1997).
48 Baroness Vere, "Age of Criminal Responsibility Bill, 2nd reading" (Hansard, Volume 783, 8 September 2017). Lord Faulkes' earlier comments are reported in House of Lords, "Age of criminal responsibility Bill 2017 Library Briefing".
49 T Bateman, "Keeping up (tough) appearances: the age of criminal responsibility", *Criminal Justice Matters,* vol. 102, no. 1 (2013), p.35.
50 UN Committee on the Rights of the Child, "Concluding observations on the fifth periodic report of the United Kingdom of Great Britain and Northern Ireland" (2016), paragraph 78, available at: https://digitallibrary.un.org/record/835015.
51 UN Committee on the Rights of the Child, "General Comment No. 24 (2019) on children's rights in the child justice system" (2019), available at: https://tbinternet.ohchr.org/_layouts/15/treatybodyexternal/Download.aspx?symbolno=CRC/C/GC/24&Lang=en.
52 House of Lords, "Age of criminal responsibility Bill 2017 Library Briefing".
53 Baroness Vere, "Age of Criminal Responsibility Bill, 2nd reading".
54 B Goldson, "'Difficult to understand or defend': a reasoned case for raising the age of criminal responsibility", *Howard Journal of Criminal Justice,* vol. 48, no. 5 (2009), p.514.
55 D Gillard, *Education in England: a history* (EducationEngland.org: London, 2018).
56 P Wintour, "Legal age for buying tobacco raised to 18 from October 1", *The Guardian UK* (2007), www.theguardian.com/uk/2007/jan/01/health.smoking.
57 T Bateman, "'Catching them young' – some reflections on the meaning of the age of criminal responsibility in England and Wales", *Safer Communities,* vol. 13, no. 3 (2014), p.133.
58 J Fionda cited in T Crofts, "Catching up with Europe".
59 T Bateman, "Challenging punitive youth justice".
60 R Williams, *Marxism and Literature* (Oxford University Press: Oxford, 1997).
61 Ministry of Justice/Youth Justice Board, "Standards for children in the youth justice system 2019" (2019), p.2, https://assets.publishing.service.gov.uk/media/6363d2328fa8f50570e54222/Standards_for_children_in_youth_justice_services_2019.doc.pdf.
62 J Fionda, *Devils and Angels: Youth Policy and Crime* (Hart: Abingdon, 2005).
63 See for instance S Case and T Bateman, "The punitive transition in youth justice: reconstructing the child as offender", *Children and Society,* vol. 34, no. 6 (2020), p.475.
64 J Davis, "Adultification bias within child protection and safeguarding", *HM Inspectorate of Probation* (2022), available at: www.justiceinspectorates.gov.uk/hmiprobation/wp-content/uploads/sites/5/2022/06/Academic-Insights-Adultification-bias-within-child-protection-and-safeguarding.pdf.
65 T Bateman, "Challenging punitive youth justice".

References

Legislation

Age of Criminal Responsibility (Scotland) Act 2019
Children Act 1908
Children and Young Persons Act 1933
Children and Young Persons Act 1963
Children and Young Persons Act 1969
Crime and Disorder Act 1998
Criminal Justice Act 1991

Books and book chapters

Arthur R, *Young Offenders and the Law* (Routledge: London, 2010).
Bandalli S, "Children, responsibility and the new youth justice", in Goldson B (ed), *The New Youth Justice* (Russell House: Lyme Regis, 2000).
Bateman T, "Challenging punitive youth justice", in Case S & Hazel N (eds), *Child First: Developing a New Youth Justice System* (Palgrave MacMillan: London, 2023).
Coleman J, *The Teacher and the Teenage Brain* (Routledge: London, 2021).
Fionda J, *Devils and Angels: Youth Policy and Crime* (Hart Publishing: Abingndon, 2005).
Gillard D, *Education in England: A History* (EducationEngland.org: London, 2018).
Graham J, Perrott S, & Marshall K, *A Review of the Youth Justice System in Northern Ireland* (Department of Justice: Belfast, 2011).
Haines K & Case S, *Positive Youth Justice* (Policy Press: Bristol, 2015).
Hazel N & Williams P, "Developing Child First as the guiding principle for youth justice", in Case S & Hazel N (eds), *Child First: Developing a New Youth Justice System* (Palgrave MacMillan: London, 2023).
McAra L & McVie S, "The case for diversion and minimum necessary intervention", in Goldson B & Muncie J (eds), *Youth Crime and Justice* (Sage: London, 2nd edn, 2015).
Williams R, *Marxism and Literature* (Oxford University Press: Oxford, 1997).

Journal articles

Arthur R, "Rethinking the criminal responsibility of young people in England", *European Journal of Crime, Criminal Law and Criminal Justice*, vol. 20, no. 1 (2012), pp.13–29.
Bateman T, "Keeping up (tough) appearances: the age of criminal responsibility", *Criminal Justice Matters*, vol. 102, no. 1 (2013), pp.35–36.
Bateman T, "'Catching them young' – some reflections on the meaning of the age of criminal responsibility in England and Wales", *Safer Communities*, vol. 13, no. 3 (2014), pp.133–142.
Bateman T, "Where has all the youth crime gone? Youth justice in an age of austerity", *Children and Society*, vol. 28, no. 5 (2014), pp.416–424.
Case S & Bateman T, "The punitive transition in youth justice: reconstructing the child as offender", *Children and Society*, vol. 34, no. 6 (2020), pp.475–491.
Crofts T, "Catching up with Europe: taking the age of criminal responsibility seriously in England", *European Journal of Crime, Criminal Law and Criminal Justice*, vol. 17, no. 4 (2009), pp.267–292.
Deakin J, Fox C, & Matos R, "Labelled as 'risky' in an era of control: how young people experience and respond to the stigma of criminalized identities", *European Journal of Criminology*, vol. 19, no. 4 (2020), pp.653–673.
Farmer E, "The age of criminal responsibility: developmental science and human rights perspectives", *Journal of Children's Services*, vol. 6, no. 2 (2011), pp.86–95.
Goldson B, "'Difficult to understand or defend': a reasoned case for raising the age of criminal responsibility", *Howard Journal of Criminal Justice*, vol. 48, no. 5 (2009), pp.514–521.
McAra L & McVie S, "The shrinking youth justice population: a change in behaviour or a change in the system?", *Scottish Justice Matters*, vol. 5, no. 1 (2017), pp.38–39.

Muncie J, "The 'punitive' turn in juvenile justice: cultures of control and rights compliance in western Europe and the USA", *Youth Justice*, vol. 8, no. 2 (2008), pp.107–121.

Reports

Association of Directors of Children's Services, *A Youth Justice System That Works for Children: A Joint Policy Position Paper by Service, Strategic and Political Leaders in Local Government* (ADCS: London, 2021).
Bateman T, *Criminalising Children for No Good Purpose: The Age of Criminal Responsibility in England and Wales* (National Association for Youth Justice: London, 2012).
Bateman T, *The State of Youth Justice 2020* (National Association for Youth Justice: London, 2020).
Bunn S & Brown P, *Age of Criminal Responsibility* (Parliamentary Office of Science and Technology: London, 2018).
Case S & Browning A, *Child First Justice: The Research Evidence-Base* (Loughborough University: Loughborough, 2021).
Davis J, *Adultification Bias Within Child Protection and Safeguarding* (HM Inspectorate of Probation, 2022).
Department for Children, Schools and Families, *The Children's Plan: Building Brighter Futures* (The Stationery Office: Norwich, 2007).
Department of Justice, *Public Consultation on Increasing the Minimum Age of Criminal Responsibility in Northern Ireland from 10 Years to 14 years* (Department of Justice: Belfast, 2022).
Department of Justice, *Strategic Framework for Youth Justice 2022–2027* (Department of Justice: Belfast, 2022).
Home Office, *No More Excuses: A New Approach to Tackling Youth Crime in England and Wales* (Home Office: London, 1997).
House of Lords, *Age of Criminal Responsibility Bill 2017 Library Briefing* (House of Lords: London, 2017).
Ministry of Justice /Youth Justice Board, *Standards for Children in the Youth Justice System 2019* (Ministry of Justice: London, 2019).
National Audit Office, *Children in Custody: Secure Training Centres and Secure Schools* (National Audit Office: London, 2022).
Sutherland S, *An Analysis of Trends in First Time Entrants to the Youth Justice System* (Ministry of Justice: London, 2017).
The Royal Society, *Neuroscience and the Law* (The Royal Society: London, 2011).
UN Committee on the Rights of the Child, *Concluding Observations on the Fifth Periodic Report of the United Kingdom of Great Britain and Northern Ireland* (United Nations: Geneva, 2016).
UN Committee on the Rights of the Child, *General Comment No. 24 (2019) on Children's Rights in the Child Justice System* (United Nations, Geneva: 2019).
Wintour P, "Legal age for buying tobacco raised to 18 from October 1", *The Guardian* (1 January 2007).
Youth Justice Board, *Strategic Plan 2018–2021* (Youth Justice Board: London, 2018).
Youth Justice Board, *YJB Strategic Plan 2019–2022* (Youth Justice Board: London, 2019).
Youth Justice Board, *A Guide to Child First* (Youth Justice Board: London, 2022).
Youth Justice Board, *Youth Justice Annual Statistics 2021/2022 England and Wales* (Youth Justice Board: London, 2023).

25
CORPORATE CRIMINAL IR/RESPONSIBILITY

Penny Crofts

Despite innumerable public inquiries and scandals, it is rare for corporations to be prosecuted for the widespread harms that they cause. There is no doubt that corporations are legal subjects – but, despite this, they tend not to be conceptualised and punished as subjects of criminal law. This tendency to disregard corporations as subjects of criminal law is reflected and reinforced in scholarly research and education. Academically, corporate crime is very much a niche topic and has not been subject to the same scrutiny as crimes by individuals, despite the systemic harms caused by corporations.[1] The primary focus of criminal law and criminology is upon individual perpetrators, despite long-term recognition of white-collar and organisational crime,[2] and that the harms caused by corporations greatly exceed those caused by individuals. Meanwhile, corporate law tends to frame corporate malfeasance as a governance problem, focusing on director's duties. This chapter focuses on organisational responsibility, or more accurately, irresponsibility. Key themes of this chapter are the various obstacles to applying criminal law to corporations, and the extent to which law is imbricated in enshrining corporate irresponsibility for harms. This theme draws upon the legal theorist Veitch's insights that law organises not only responsibility, but irresponsibility.[3] Veitch notes that the larger an organisation, the more capable it is of causing systemic harms, and the less likely it is to be held responsible. Given the massive, systemic harms caused by corporations these questions of corporate criminal ir/responsibility are urgent. The criminal law is expressive, it communicates right from wrong. Thus, the failure to criminalise corporate wrongs communicates that the harms caused are acceptable costs of doing business.[4]

This chapter will establish first that corporations are legal subjects and outline the gradual application of criminal law to corporations. The chapter will then argue that much of the criminal legal doctrine has been constructed around the archetypal legal subject – the responsible human being. The remainder of the chapter considers the mechanical difficulties of applying criminal offence elements to corporations and some of the proposals by legislatures and theorists to bypass these obstacles.

Corporations as legal subjects

Corporations have long been recognised and constructed at law as legal subjects – they are right and duty bearing entities.[5] There are different narratives about the history of the development of the corporation, including analysis of early Roman conceptions,[6] medieval corporations in the fifteenth century,[7] the emergence of joint-stock business corporations, the genealogy of corporate ideas, and the development of key legal corporate characteristics.[8] Corporations that resemble the modern corporation emerged in the 1600s and were formed by royal charter or by special Act of Parliament.[9] Legally speaking, a corporation had the following characteristics: "it was a body chartered or recognised by the state; it had the right to hold property for a common purpose; it had the right to sue and be sued in a common name; and its existence extended beyond the life of its members".[10] For example, the East India Company was granted a royal charter in 1600, establishing a monopoly on all English trade in the East Indies as part of the colonial project of exploration and domination, resulting in egregious acts of trading slaves and destroying culture.[11]

The industrial revolution in the eighteenth and nineteenth centuries resulted in the exponential expansion of corporations, accompanied by increasingly wealthy and influential capitalists, who sought (successfully) to evade and disavow responsibility for systemic harms caused by corporations. It was during the nineteenth century, that the modern business corporation emerged with liberalisation.[12] A particularly significant development for the purposes of corporate responsibility was the granting of limited liability to shareholders in 1855, whereby the assets of individuals that invested in a corporation would be protected from harms that a corporation caused.[13] Limited liability protects shareholders from risk – they can only lose the capital that they choose to invest. Thus, if a company incurs losses that are greater than the value of the sum invested, then the shareholders will have no further responsibility for these losses.[14] Limited liability is regarded as a key plank in enabling and requiring the externalisation of harms – shareholders are not responsible for harms caused.[15]

Although corporations have long been recognised as juristic persons,[16] it remains an open question as to what this legal personhood entails. Corporations draw on rights that have been constructed for individuals to protect them against the arbitrary power of the state[17] – such as claims of due process, legal professional privilege,[18] and recently in the USA, human rights such as free speech and religious belief.[19] Theorists such as Glasbeek have argued that given the great wealth and power of corporations, corporations should be treated by law as a menace rather than expanding their rights.[20] Corporations have tended to claim and assert legal protections whilst avoiding, evading, or disavowing responsibility and obligations.

The scope of rights and responsibilities attached to corporations are not identical to the legal rights and obligations of the archetypal legal subject – human beings.[21] One area where this difference is apparent is in relation to criminal responsibility. A recurring question for criminal law is whether and how to ascribe responsibility and blameworthiness to corporations. Should the focus be on the individuals who make up the corporation or on the corporation itself? This question is expressed in corporate law theory in the nominalist versus realist debate. Nominalists accept that corporations are legal entities, but argue that corporations are nothing more than collectives of individuals.[22] Accordingly, corporations can only act and intend through individual human beings.[23] For example, Lord Hoffman in *Meridian Global Funds Management Asia Ltd v Securities Commission*,[24] stated that a company "as such" cannot do anything; it must act by servants or agents – "that may seem an unexceptionable, even banal remark". This belief that corporations can only act and intend through agents continues to be highly influential today. In contrast, realists argue that the corporation is more than the sum of its parts. Corporations can act and be at fault in ways that are different from the ways in which their members can act and be at fault.[25]

This nominalist/realist tension is an ongoing issue in criminal law. A major reason for this is that the bulk of criminal legal doctrine was constructed around the primary legal subject – the responsible, biological, human being.[26] This has led the corporate criminal law theorist Celia Wells to point to an "individualistic bias" in the criminal legal system.[27] I will consider below the difficulties of applying these pre-existing taxonomies to corporations. Second, and relatedly, the bulk of criminal law theorists accept that the criminal law is a system of blaming.[28] This is expressed in the legal requirement that the prosecution prove the *guilt* of the accused, beyond a reasonable doubt.[29] Criminal law is geared towards establishing the blameworthiness of an accused to justify and require imposition of criminal sanctions. A key question for criminal law, is whether a corporation can be at fault, and how this blameworthiness can be established. Is culpability determined through the individual members that make up a corporation, or the corporation in and of itself?[30] As I argue below, this issue is particularly salient for corporate responsibility, because the models of culpability or wickedness (which are necessarily contingent), that are organised and expressed in criminal law, are constructed around the ideal legal subject – the human being. Many of our ideas about fault, crime and punishment enshrine an individualistic bias that fits uneasily to corporations – if at all. This has led to great difficulties in establishing that corporations are (capable of being) at fault, which has long been expressed in the argument that corporations have "no soul" and thus cannot have "wicked intent".[31]

Until the nineteenth century, corporations were regarded as incapable of committing criminal acts, because they did not have the necessary capacity physically, mentally, or morally.[32] Historically, the idea of charging a corporation for a criminal wrong was strictly limited to charges of criminal libel, where the corporation had published the libellous material.[33] Coke summarised the 1612 case of *Sutton's Hospital*, providing an influential definition of the corporation as, "… invisible, immortal, and rests only in the intendment and consideration of the law… cannot commit treason, nor be outlawed, nor excommunicated, for they have no souls, neither can they appear in person, but by attorney".[34] On this basis, the soulless corporation is a fictional creation of the law with a separate legal existence from its members and cannot be subject to the criminal law. Additionally, some offences, such as murder, mandated life imprisonment which meant that corporations could not be found guilty of murder as they could not be imprisoned.[35] Procedural obstacles such as the requirement that a company appear in person or mandated life imprisonment were gradually removed, but the reluctance to hold corporations responsible remained.[36]

In the nineteenth century, with the industrial revolution, corporations became larger and more complex than one-person entrepreneurs. As they grew exponentially, they became more dominant, and their capacity to cause widespread harms to individuals and property likewise increased. The idea of corporations as criminal subjects developed gradually, with no specific point of origin. Courts focused on public nuisance offences that caused widespread harm to the public. Initially, corporations were deemed only able to be criminally liable for inactions, that is, non-feasance (the failure to satisfy a duty required by law).[37] In *R v Birmingham & Gloucester Railway Co*,[38] the corporation was successfully prosecuted for the failure to maintain the railroad that it had been specifically chartered to construct and maintain. In *R v Great North of England Railway Company*,[39] the court held that corporations could be liable for actions as well as omissions. In that case, the corporation had unlawfully laid its rail lines across a public highway which destroyed part of that highway, and then had constructed a bridge over the railway that did not satisfy its specific charter. Lord Denman stated that the earlier distinction between nonfeasance and misfeasance was impossible and illogical, as the unlawful act could often be characterised as both nonfeasance and misfeasance. However, the court also stated that corporations could not be liable for offences such as treason, felony, perjury, offences against the person, or "acts of immorality" as these could only be derived from the "corrupted mind of the person committing them, and are violation of the social duties that belong to men and subjects. A corporation, which, as such, has no such duties, cannot be guilty in these cases".[40] This expressed the belief that corporations could not commit crimes that required criminal intent.

The claim that corporations are fictions and thus could not be liable for criminal offences became less acceptable as the harms that were caused through bribery, stock manipulation, unsafe working conditions, and exploitation of labour became increasingly apparent, whilst investors accumulated vast fortunes.[41] The extension of criminal liability to corporations was aided particularly by the Interpretation Act 1889 (UK) which specified that the expression "person" shall "unless the contrary intention appears, include a body corporate". This meant that corporations could be liable for offences involving *mens rea* – but then raised the issue of *how* a corporation can intend and have knowledge. Various approaches to this issue of fault will be considered below.

Applying criminal law elements to corporations

It is clear that corporations can be a subject of criminal law. In *DPP v Kent & Sussex Contractors*, Justice Hallet stated that it made good sense and good law that a corporation could not escape the consequences that would follow an individual by showing that they are not a natural person.[42] However, this then raises a question of mechanics. Can the corporate legal subject fit into pre-existing categories of law and sanctions expressing an individualistic bias – or if not – can and should new offence elements be created to bypass classic requirements? This section briefly considers criminal legal requirements to highlight the difficulties of applying criminal law to corporations.

Harms and causation – difficulties proving actus reus

There is a tendency in the literature to focus on difficulties in establishing the *mens rea* or fault of the corporation, but problems also arise in applying the *actus reus* elements, and these problems may preclude questions of responsibility arising at all. The *actus reus* may be regarded as a threshold question, and if harms do not fit existing criminal legal categories and/or causation appears too complex – then rather than ascribing criminal responsibility, corporate harms may be reframed as accidents, disasters, or tragedies.

A major obstacle to applying criminal law to corporate wrongs, is that the harms may exceed currently existing categories of criminal law – in terms of offence categories and the apparatus of the criminal legal system to investigate and prosecute. In "The Horror of Corporate Harms", I argued that the harms caused by corporations are "too big, too nasty, too prolific or too much for the criminal law".[43] This is a continuation of the theme that criminal law has an individualistic bias. On a purely pragmatic level, corporations are capable of causing harms on an "industrial scale",[44] that greatly exceeds the capacity of individual perpetrators. The sheer magnitude of harms caused by corporations generate conceptual and practical difficulties for legal systems, and these difficulties are highlighted with a language of estimation and approximation – the harms are too much to calculate accurately. For example, the ILO estimates that more than 2.78 million die annually as a result of occupational illnesses and accidents at work and describes the human cost of occupational health and safety deficits as "vast and unacceptable".[45] The harms inflicted by corporations are "nasty, haunting, insidious and imaginative".[46] The sheer scale and nastiness of corporate harms is shown by the ongoing opioid epidemic in the USA. Initiated by Purdue, pharmaceutical corporations produced, marketed, and sold opioids, falsely representing them as non-addictive. The Centers for Disease Control and Prevention estimated that in 2017 alone, more than 47,000 people died from opioid overdoses and the economic burden of the opioid epidemic that year exceeded $1 trillion:[47]

> "[t]he harms of the opioid crisis are almost unimaginable and uncategorizable in criminal law. Amongst other harms, companies such as Purdue that produce and distribute opioids have caused widespread addiction, ruining countless lives and families, resulting in mass prosecutions and imprisonment of unfortunate addicts. In desperate need, addicts have committed acts that they would never otherwise have done… As shown on the rare occasions where pharmaceutical companies have been prosecuted, there is no clear, existing offence which encapsulates the harms caused by the opioid epidemic".[48]

The harms caused by corporations raise categorical challenges for criminal law because they exceed pre-existing categories of law in terms of size, type, and quality – in terms of the types of harms recognised by the criminal justice system *and* the proliferation of those harms may exceed the apparatus of a criminal legal system which is geared towards individual perpetrators. This results in a perverse outcome whereby the worse the harms in terms of quantity and type, the less likely a corporation is to be subject to criminal law.

Corporations may also escape any responsibility for harms due to complex causal chains. Offences with prohibited results require that the accused caused the prohibited harm. In the bulk of cases, causation is not difficult. For example, where an accused stabs a person and they die from the stab wounds, the accused caused that death. Legal doctrine has developed around more complex causal chains, where there is more than one cause. Even in cases with multiple causes, the focus of the trial is on an individual accused – was that individual "an operating and substantial cause" of the death?[49] Whilst there may be multiple causes, the focus of the court is upon that individual's causal responsibility – legal doctrine requires only that the accused is *a* cause, not *the* cause. However, corporate harms may be due to many actions and omissions, by multiple actors, who may or may not be a part of the corporation.

This argument can be teased out in relation to deaths due to overdoses. Individual drug suppliers have been charged with involuntary manslaughter offences. The common law has long held that a drug supplier will not be liable for the death of a person who dies as a result of the self-administration of those drugs. This is because a voluntary act by the victim has broken the chain of causation.[50] However, hypothetically, what of the production and supply of the medication OxyContin by the corporation Purdue? It is estimated that "one in four patients that receive pro-longed opioid treatment will struggle with addiction. Two out of three drug overdose deaths involve an opioid."[51] No corporation has been charged with manslaughter offences in relation to these deaths (although individual drug dealers have been charged).[52] One reason for not prosecuting Purdue (and other pharmaceutical companies) for involuntary manslaughter due to drug overdoses is that the causal chain has been broken by independent acts by third parties – in the form of doctors who prescribed oxycontin, and patients who took the drug in non-prescribed ways and/or took illicit drugs after they became addicted but were no longer able to get prescriptions. However, this does not recognise the extent to which Purdue misled and manipulated individuals, regulators, and government. Amongst other strategies, Purdue marketed the drug aggressively, holding all-inclusive conferences at vacation resorts, targeting physicians with high prescription rates of opioids. It influenced medical research, emphasising the need for chronic pain relief and manipulating research results to minimise addiction rates.[53] Purdue claimed that the time-release capsule meant that patients would not become addicted, even though as early as 1995 Purdue's own testing showed that crushing the time-release capsule would result in an immediate dose leading to a very strong and euphoric high.[54] One approach to this kind of complex causal chain is to draw upon existing criminal legal doctrine to assert that prescribing practitioners and self-administering drug-takers are not independent third parties, and thus do not break the chain of causation.[55] This builds on Feinberg's argument that the concept of "voluntary act" means that where a person's actions have been manipulated by another to act, then this will not break the chain of causation.[56] As Wells argues, this would also mean that there could be good reason to exonerate individual employees who may have been the immediate causal factor of prohibited results, if their actions or omissions were a consequence of management policies.[57] These arguments suggest that despite the lack of application to corporations, existing causation legal doctrine could be applied to corporations.

Corporate intention and mens rea requirements

The arguments above have considered how and why the question of corporate responsibility may not arise at all, because the harms caused by corporations exceed currently existing criminal law categories, the capacity of the criminal legal apparatus to investigate or prosecute, and/or the causal chain may be perceived as too complex. Despite these arguments, the issue that has attracted most attention in terms of corporate criminal liability is how to establish the *mens rea* of corporations. This question is especially salient because many of our questions of blame revolve around subjective culpability,[58] to the extent that *mens rea* requirements are referred to as "fault elements" in some legislation.[59] How then, do we know what a corporation knows, intends, or recognises as a possibility?

Different approaches have been adopted in different jurisdictions. One approach is vicarious liability. Legg has argued that the application of liability to juristic persons derived from the common law doctrine that masters had vicarious liability for the wrongful acts of their servants.[60] In ancient times, masters were held absolutely liable for the wrongful acts of their servants, but this had eroded by the medieval period.[61] In the USA, vicarious liability is the predominant approach for attributing mental states to corporations, through the doctrine of *respondeat superior*. This approach is consistent with nominalism, and focuses on the mental states of individual corporate employees, expressing the assumption that collective fault must reside with individual members of the collective.[62] One of the many problems with this approach is that it is simultaneously over-inclusive – holding a corporation responsible for rogue employees – and under-inclusive – exculpating corporations for wrongs due to systemic or structural causes, because no single employee has sufficient knowledge.

The common law approach to holding corporations liable for offences is identification doctrine (also called alter ego doctrine). In civil and criminal proceedings brought against a corporation, the identification doctrine equates the corporation with the individuals that are its "directing mind and will".[63] This approach is similar to vicarious liability in terms of sustaining a nominalist approach, that is, it focuses on individual members of the corporation. The difference is that under identification doctrine the requisite conduct and mental elements can only be attributed to a corporation if they could be traced directly to the upper levels of the corporate hierarchy, that is, its "directing mind".[64] This approach has long been recognised as highly restrictive, creating difficulties in terms of first identifying who is the directing mind, then ascertaining what they knew and when, and then attributing those states of mind to the corporation.[65] As companies have become more and more complex, responsibility and knowledge is increasingly diffuse and delegated. The larger a corporation the more difficult it is to identify the directing mind and what they knew, sustaining irresponsibility for those corporations most capable of systemic harms. Identification doctrine "works best in cases where it is needed least and works least in cases where it is needed most".[66]

Identification doctrine and *respondeat superior* have been identified as having perverse incentives that incentivise corporate harms.[67] They encourage corporations to disperse responsibility across employees and discourage oversight.[68] Both approaches increase the likelihood of corporate harms but mitigate corporate liability because individual employees and/or the directing mind are less likely to acquire corporate knowledge.

Jurisdictions have adopted a variety of responses to difficulties in establishing the state of mind of corporations. One approach is to give up on attempting to prove *mens rea* and instead focus on the harm. This has led to many strict and absolute liability offences developed to apply to corporate harms, for example environmental, money laundering, and occupational health and safety offences.[69] However, these offences have been criticised for failing to establish fault and over-criminalisation, diluting the expressive power of the label of criminality.[70] Moreover, evidence suggests that regulators and prosecutors frequently restrict prosecution to only the most egregious cases, where *mens rea* can be established.[71]

More recently, some jurisdictions have introduced failure to prevent offences for corporate crimes.[72] The UK introduced a failure to prevent a bribery offence in 2010,[73] and since then similar failure to prevent offences have been introduced in Australia,[74] New Zealand,[75] and the UK.[76] These are strict liability offences. Under the Bribery Act, a corporation will be liable if a bribery offence is committed by an "associated person" to obtain or retain business or an advantage for the defendant corporation.[77] A corporation may argue a defence to the balance of probabilities, that it had "adequate procedures" in place to prevent associated persons from committing such offences.[78] The failure-to-prevent offences are a pragmatic and principled approach to the types of offences that are ostensibly most likely to be committed by large organisations – those due to omission or failure.[79] These offences focus on the failure by corporations to prevent specific offences. Where a corporation undertakes a business in a specific area, the law will attach legal duties specific to that undertaking, because it recognises that the business comes with risks. For example, there is a legal duty upon those providing childcare to protect children from harm.[80] The failure or absence of practices and procedures to protect against foreseeable risks is culpable, based on a negative model of culpability, of evil as privation, lack, or failure.[81] It thus satisfies the requirement of criminal law as a system of blaming.[82]

Whilst this negative model of culpability is important, it fails to grapple with the extent to which harms are a result of long-term choices and actions by the corporation. Rather than focusing on negative models of culpability, alternative approaches have sought to engage with corporations in accordance with realist conceptions and attribute subjective fault to corporations. Australia introduced a corporate culture model of fault in the 1990s. Corporate culture is defined in the Criminal Code Act as "an attitude, policy, rule, course of conduct or practice existing within the body corporate generally or in the part of the body corporate in which the relevant activities take place".[83] This approach is explicitly realist, attributing fault to a corporation based on its culture, rather than seeking to find fault in relation to specific individuals. Section 12.3 (1) of the Criminal Code specifies that the fault element will be attributed to a corporation where it "expressly, tacitly or impliedly authorised or permitted the commission of the offence." Under section 12.3(2), this can be established by:

"(c) proving that a corporate culture existed within the body corporate that directed, encouraged, tolerated or led to non-compliance with the relevant provision; or
(d) proving that the body corporate failed to create and maintain a corporate culture that required compliance with the relevant provision."

Although the Australian approach has been much lauded,[84] these provisions have rarely been tested in court.[85] There are different explanations for why corporate culture has not been applied, including difficulties in proving the culture of a corporation and how to deal with subcultures – but Comino has persuasively argued that many of these arguments "are exaggerated and that there are possibilities for corporate criminal liability to be pursued under the culture provisions".[86] It is not so difficult to identify the values of a corporation, what it rewards and punishes, especially in relation to behaviour over long periods of time.[87]

A related approach has recently been proposed by the legal theorist Bant, in association with Paterson, called "system intentionality".[88] Rather than focusing on the individuals that make up a corporation, this approach is realist, arguing that a corporation's mental state may be manifested in its "systems of conduct, policies, and practices".[89] Whilst individual staff may leave, including CEOs, "what remains constant are the company's structures, policies, and processes that dictate how the next round of employees should act when engaged in the corporation's activities".[90] Relatedly, I have argued that rather than over-complicating the *mens rea* of a corporation it is possible to draw upon existing legal doctrine applied to human legal subjects.[91] In the absence of confession by an individual offender, intention is not transparent:

"As I said I think when I was directing you originally you cannot take the top of a man's head off and look into his mind and actually see what his intent was at any given moment".[92]

Why, then, do we expect corporate intention to be transparent? Instead of trying to identify the "brain" of a corporation in approaches like identification theory, we can instead rely upon external conduct or results to ascertain the internal conduct of an accused's mind.[93] Rather than accept claims by corporations that prohibited harms were "accidental", instead courts can and should focus on the logical outcome of their choices, culture, and policies. For example, if corporations have chosen over long periods of time to avoid the costs of compliance to existing legal duties, such as safety, anti-money-laundering, etc., then if these prohibited harms result, they can and should be regarded as at a minimum reckless, or even intentional.[94]

Temporal coincidence

Criminal legal doctrine requires that an accused had *mens rea* at the time of the guilty act.[95] Here too, problems may arise in application to corporations. This is because unlike humans, corporations are (potentially) immortal.[96] Harms can be caused in the long-distant past, but it may be difficult to know if and when a corporation knew about the risks. There are many products such as tobacco, asbestos, lead paint, thalidomide – where corporations may initially not have known (or chosen not to know)[97] the dangers associated with their products. It seems that in these cases the corporations did not have the necessary intention or knowledge at the time of acts causing harm and thus do not satisfy the requirement of temporal coincidence. However, in many of these cases, corporations have become aware of the dangers prior to alerting the government and public, and deny these dangers rather than withdrawing products, whilst the products continue harming. I argue elsewhere that the doctrinal idea of a continuing *actus reus* could be applied in these cases, whereby the prosecution need only prove knowledge or intent at one point during the "series of acts" to satisfy the requirement of temporal coincidence. For example, in *Thabo Meli*, the accused thought that they had killed a man (which is when they had the necessary intention), but actually killed him when they threw the body over a cliff to get rid of it (the act causing death).[98] The accused argued that they lacked temporal coincidence, but it was held that this was a "series of acts", and provided that if they had the necessary *mens rea* at some time during the series of acts, they could be charged with murder. I argue that this principle could be applied to corporations. That is, if corporations became aware of the dangers of a product and kept that knowledge to themselves whilst their products or actions continued to cause harms, then the principle from *Thabo Meli* could be applied, so that the requirement of temporal coincidence would be met.

Conclusion

Although corporations have long been recognised as legal subjects and gained many advantages from this status, the law has been much slower to impose responsibilities upon corporations. As corporations have become larger and larger, and more capable of causing systemic harms, the issue of whether and how to attribute criminal responsibility to corporations has become urgent. Much of criminal law was constructed with individuals in mind – in terms of perpetrator and victim. This raises difficulties in terms of all the elements of offences, let alone issues of regulation, investigation, enforcement, and punishment. And yet, as I have argued above, there is a great deal of nuance available in criminal legal doctrine that means that we can and should apply it to corporate malfeasance. There are avenues available in existing legal doctrine to take seriously the idea of corporations as criminal legal subjects. It is important to apply the criminal law to corporations. A major reason for this is the expressive function of criminal law, that is, criminal law communicates right and wrong.[99] The failure to criminalise corporations for the massive, systemic harms that they cause is a message that these harms are just a cost of doing business as opposed to something that is wrong.[100] This encourages corporations to undertake a cost–benefit analysis as to harms, rather than prohibiting the harms. Moreover, this failure to criminalise corporations for harms is inconsistent with the rule of law, a key tenet of which is that we are all subject to the law, it suggests that the powerful can evade the law.[101]

Acknowledgements

This research was funded by the Australian Research Council grant "Rethinking Institutional Culpability: Criminal Law, Horror and Philosophy" (DE180100577).

Notes

1. S Green, "A Normative Approach to White-Collar Crime" in H Pontell & G Geis (eds), *International Handbook of White-Collar and Corporate Crime* (Springer: New York, 2007).
2. Sutherland coined the term "white-collar crime" in 1939 in his address to the American Sociological Society in Philadelphia in an effort to distinguish these types of crimes from street crime. E Sutherland, *White Collar Crime* (Dryden: New York, 1949).
3. S Veitch, *Law and Irresponsibility: On the Legitimation of Human Suffering* (Routledge: London, 2007).
4. G Gilchrist, "The Expressive Cost of Corporate Immunity", *Hastings Law Journal*, vol. 64 (2012), p.1.
5. EW Orts, *Business Persons: A Legal Theory of the Firm* (Oxford University Press: Oxford, 2013). E.g. *Saloman v Saloman & Co Ltd* [1897] AC 22 at 51: "The company is at law a different person altogether from the subscribers..." This is represented in statute, e.g. Corporations Act 2001 (Cth), s 119 provides for a company to "come into existence" on registration, and s 124(1) provides that it has "the legal capacity and powers of an individual". Interpretation Act 1889 (UK), s 2(1) provided that the expression "person" shall "unless the contrary intention appears, include a body corporate".
6. H Hansmann, R Kraakman & R Squire, "Incomplete Organizations: Legal Entities and Asset Partitioning in Roman Commerce" (2014) *European Corporate Government Institute*, available at: http://papers.ssrn.com/sol#/papers.cfm?abstract_id=%"5:##$.
7. The term "corporation" first appears in the medieval Year Books in 1429. JH Baker, *The Oxford History of the Laws of England* (Oxford Univeristy Press: Oxford, 2003).
8. For a summary see DC Smith, "The Beginning of History for Corporate Law: Corporate Government, Social Purpose and the Case of Sutton's Hospital (1612)", *Seattle University Law Review*, vol. 45, no. 1 (2021), p.367.
9. R Harris, *Industrializing English Law* (Cambridge University Press: Cambridge 2000).
10. M Clinard and P Yeager, *Corporate Crime* (Transaction Publishers: New Jersey, 2nd edn, 2011), p.23.
11. W Dalrymple, "The East India Company: The Original Corporate Raiders" *The Guardian UK* (2015), available at: www.theguardian.com/world/2015/mar/04/east-india-company-original-corporate-raiders.
12. E.g. the Joint Stock Companies Act 1844 (UK) established the basic template for laws governing the modern corporation and allowed companies to incorporate by simple registration. Incorporation of a joint stock company was no longer a matter of privilege and became instead a matter of right.
13. Limited Liability Act 1855 (UK). See Corporations Act 2001 (Cth), s 516 which provides for the limited liability of shareholders.
14. S Tombs & D Whyte, *The Corporate Criminal: Why Corporations Must Be Abolished* (Routledge: London, 2015).
15. G Barak, *Unchecked Corporate Power: Why the Crimes of Multinational Corporations Are Routinized Away and What We Can Do about It* (Routledge: London, 2017).
16. This was cemented by the House of Lords in *Saloman v Saloman* [1897] AC 22.
17. P Crofts & H van Rijswijk, *Technology: New Trajectories in Law* (Routledge: London, 2021).
18. L Campbell, "Corporate misuse of legal professional privilege" in Penny Crofts (ed) *Evil Corporations: Law, Culpability and Regulation* (Routledge: London, 2024).

19 *Citizens United v FEC* 558 US 310 (2010). E Pollman, "Corporate Law and Theory in Hobby Lobby" in M Schmartzman, C Flanders, & Z Robinson (eds), *The Rise of Corporate Religious Liberty* (Oxford University Press: Oxford, 2016).
20 HJ Glasbeek, "The Corporation as a Legally Created Site of Irresponsibility" in H Pontell & G Geis (eds), *International Handbook of White-Collar and Corporate Crime* (Springer: New York, 2007); Crofts and van Rijswijk, *Technology*.
21 N Naffine, "Our Legal Lives as Men, Women and Persons", *Legal Studies*, vol. 24, no. 4 (2004), p.621. In contrast, theorists such as Grear have interrogated the paradigmatic legal subject, arguing persuasively that the corporation may well be the epitome of liberal legal personhood, see A Grear, "Deconstructing Anthropos: A Critical Legal Reflection on 'Anthropocentric' Law and Anthropocene 'Humanity'", *Law and Critique*, vol. 26, no. 3 (2015), p.225.
22 PA French, *Corporate Ethics* (Harcourt Brace College Publishers: Fort Worth, 1995).
23 E Colvin, "Corporate Personality and Criminal Liability", *Criminal Law Forum*, vol. 6, no. 1 (1995), p.1.
24 [1995] 2 AC 500 at pp.506-507.
25 E Bant, "The Culpable Corporate Mind: Taxonomy and Synthesis" in E Bant (ed), *The Culpable Corporate Mind* (Hart Publishing: Oxford, 2023); P Crofts, "Crown Resorts and the Im/Moral Corporate Form" in *The Culpable Corporate Mind*; M Diamantis, "How to Read a Corporation's Mind" in *The Culpable Corporate Mind*.
26 SD Smith, *Law's Quandary* (Harvard University Press: Cambridge Massachusetts, 2004), p.8.
27 C Wells, *Corporations and Criminal Responsibility* (Oxford University Press: Oxford, 2nd edn, 2001) p.1.
28 E.g. G Fletcher, *Rethinking Criminal Law* (Little Brown: Boston, 1978); JB White, "Making Sense of Criminal Law", *University of Colorado Law Review*, vol. 50, no. 1 (1978), p.1; P Crofts, *Wickedness and Crime: Laws of Homicide and Malice* (Routledge: London, 2013); Green, "A Normative Approach".
29 *DPP v Woolmington* [1935] AC 462.
30 See for example, C Chapple, *The Moral Responsibilities of Companies* (Palgrave MacMillan: Basingstoke, 2014); Crofts, "Crown Resorts and the Im/Moral Corporate Form".
31 *State v First National Bank* (1872) 2 SD 568 at p.571.
32 KF Brickey, "Corporate Criminal Accountability: A Brief History and Observation", *Washington University Law Quarterly*, vol. 60, no.2 (1982), p.393.
33 *Pharmaceutical Society v London and Provincial Supply Association* (1880) 5 App Cas 859; *Triplex Safety Glass Co v Lancegaye Safety Glass* [1939] 2 KB 395.
34 *Sutton's Hospital Case* (1612) 10 Coke Reports, 1a-35a ER 77 937-976, 32 b, 77 ER 973. This was then quoted by Blackstone, and J Marshall, without identifying his source explicitly made a similar declaration in *Trustees of Dartmouth College v Woodward* 17 US 518 (1819) at p.636.
35 J Coffee Jr, "No Soul to Damn: No Body to Kick: An Unscandalised Inquiry into the Problem of Corporate Punishment", *Michigan Law Review*, vol. 79, no. 3 (1980), p.386.
36 Wells, *Corporations and Criminal Responsibility*, p.93.
37 See for example, *Case of Langforth Bridge* 79 ER 919 (KB 1635) cited in Brickey, "Corporate Criminal Accountability" at p.401.
38 (1842) 114 Eng Rep 492.
39 (1846) 115 Eng Rep 1294.
40 (1846) 115 Eng Rep 1294 at p.1298.
41 M Pieth & R Ivory, "Corporate Criminal Liability" in KB Brown & DV Snyder (eds), *General Reports of the XVIIIth Congress of the International Academy of Comparative Law* (Springer: New York, 2012).
42 [1944] KB 146.
43 P Crofts, "The Horror of Corporate Harms", *Australian Journal of Corporate Law*, vol. 38, no.1 (2022), p.23 at p.24. See also, P Crofts and H van Rijswijk, *Corporate Harms: A Horror Story* (Routledge: London, forthcoming).
44 G Slapper, "Corporate Homicide, Corporate Social Responsibility, and Human Rights" in E Maguire, F Brookman and M Maguire (eds), *The Handbook of Homicide* (Wiley and Sons: Chichester, 2017), p.213.

45 International Labour Organisation, "Quick Guide on Sources and Uses of Statistics in Occupational Safety and Health" (2020), available at: www.ilo.org/wcmsp5/groups/public/---dgreports/---stat/documents/publication/wcms_759401.pdf.5.
46 Crofts, "The Horror of Corporate Harms", p.41.
47 Curtis Florence, Fiejun Luo, Ketra Rice 'The economic burden of opioid use disorder and fatal opioid overdose in the United Staes, 2017' (2018) vol. 218, no. 108350, *Drug and Alcohol Dependence,* pp. 1–7 https://doi.org/10.1016/j.drugalcdep.2020.108350
48 Crofts, "The Horror of Corporate Harms", p.42. Citing Jones, "The Opioid Epidemic".
49 *Royall v R* (1990) 172 CLR 378 (High Court).
50 *Burns v R* [2012] HCA 35. NSW has altered the common law position by creating an offence of supply of drugs causing death, section 25C, Crimes Act 1900 (NSW).
51 Jones, "The Opioid Epidemic", p.33.
52 E.g. US Attorney's Office, California, "New Federal Cases Filed as Law Enforcement Continues Vigorous response to deadly fentanyl epidemic" (2023), available at: www.justice.gov/usao-cdca/pr/12-new-federal-cases-filed-law-enforcement-continues-vigorous-response-deadly-fentanyl.
53 EH Morreim, "Corporations, High-Stakes Biomedical Research, and Research Misconduct: Yes They Can (and Sometimes Do)", *Journal of Law and the Biosciences,* vol. 8, no. 1 (2021), p.1.
54 A van Zee, "The Promotion and Marketing of OxyContin: Commerical Triumph, Public Health Tragedy" (2009) 99 *American Journal of Public Health,* vol. 99, no.2, p.221.
55 For more detailed argument see Crofts, *Evil Corporations.*
56 J Feinberg, *Doing and Deserving: Essays in the Theory of Responsibility* (Princeton University Press: New Jersey, 1970), p.159.
57 Wells, *Corporations and Criminal Responsibility,* p.51.
58 Fletcher, *Rethinking Criminal Law*; C Wells, "Swatting the Subjectivist Bug", *Criminal Law Review,* vol. 20 (1982), p.209; Crofts, *Wickedness and Crime.* For example, Diamantis argues that culpable mental states "are the law's entrenched proxy for fault", see Diamantis, "How to Read a Corporation's Mind", p.211.
59 E.g. Model Criminal Code Act Division 5.
60 M Legg, O Dixon & S Speirs, *Corporate Misconduct and White-Collar Crime in Australia* (Thomson Reuters: New South Wales, 2022), p.16.
61 Legg et al, *Corporate Misconduct,* p.16.
62 Diamantis, "How to Read a Corporation's Mind", p.213.
63 *HL Bolton Engineering Co Ltd v TJ Graham & Sons Ltd* [1957] 1 QB 159, at p.172.
64 *Tesco Supermarkets Ltd v Nattrass* [1972] AC 154.
65 For example in *R v P&O European Ferries (Dover) Ltd* (1991) 93 Cr App R 72 at pp.88–89 (per Turner J), P&O was found not guilty for the manslaughter of 193 passengers and crew, because the Court found no evidence that one sufficiently senior member of management could be said to have been the "embodiment" of the corporation and acting for it in doing the act or omission which caused death.
66 J Gobert, "Corporate Criminality: Four Models of Fault", *Legal Studies,* vol. 14, no. 3 (1994), p.393 at p.401.
67 E Lim, "A Critique of Corporate Attribution: 'Directing Mind and Will' and Corporate Objectives", *Journal of Business Law,* vol. 3 (2013), p.333; SHC Lo, "Context and Purpose in Corporate Attribution: Can the 'Directing Mind' Be Laid to Rest?", *Journal of International and Comparative Law,* vol. 4 (2017), p.349; K Wheelwright, "Goodbye Directing Mind and Will, Hello Management Failure: A Brief Critique of Some New Models of Corporate Criminal Liability", *Australian Journal of Corporate Law,* vol. 19, no. 3 (2006), p.287; M Diamantis, "Functional Corporate Knowledge", *William and Mary Law Review,* vol. 61, no. 2 (2019), p.319.
68 Diamantis, "How to Read a Corporation's Mind", p.214.
69 M Kidd, "The Use of Strict Liability in the Prosecution of Environmental Crimes", *South African Journal of Criminal Justice,* vol. 15, no. 1 (2002), p.23; C Abbott, "The Regulatory Enforcement of Pollution Control Laws: The Australian Experience", *Journal of Environmental Law,* vol. 17, no. 2 (2005), p.161; P Almond, "The Dangers of Hanging Baskets: Regulatory Myths and Media Representations of Health and Safety Regulation", *Journal of Law and Society,* vol. 36, no. 3 (2009), p.352; S Bittle & L Snider, "Law, Regulation, and Safety Crime: Exploring the

Boundaries of Criminalizing Powerful Corporate Actors", *Canadian Journal of Law and Society*, vol. 30, no. 3 (2015), p.445; S Tombs & D Whyte, "Worker Health and Safety" in *Oxford Research Encylopedia: Criminology and Criminal Justice* (Oxford University Press: Oxford, 2017), available at: http://criminology.oxfordre.com/view/10.1093/acrefore/9780190264079.001.0001/acrefore-9780190264079-e-270?rskey=bkTZve&result=8.

70 A Ashworth, "Conceptions of Over-Criminalisation", *Ohio State Journal of Criminal Law*, vol. 5, no.2 (2008), p.407.
71 See for example, P Crofts, "Communicating the Culpability of Illegal Dumping: Bankstown v Hanna (2014)", *Australian Journal of Environmental Law*, vol. II (2015), p.57; Crofts, "Crown Resorts and the Im/Moral Corporate Form".
72 J Clough, "'Failure to Prevent' Offences: The Solution to Transnational Corporate Criminal Liability" in Bant (ed), *The Culpable Corporate Mind*.
73 Section 7, Bribery Act 2010 (UK), s 7.
74 Crimes Legislation Amendment (Combatting Corporate Crime) Bill 2019 (Cth).
75 Crimes Act 1961 (NZ), s 105C(2A).
76 Criminal Finances Act 2017 (UK), Part Three.
77 Bribery Act 2010 (UK), s 7(1).
78 Bribery Act 2010 (UK) s 7(2).
79 P Crofts, "Three Recent Royal Commissions: The Failure to Prevent Harms and Attributions of Organisational Liability", *Sydney Law Review*, vol. 43, no. 4 (2020), p.394 at 418; Clough, "'Failure to Prevent' Offences".
80 Crofts, "Three Recent Royal Commissions".
81 Crofts, "Three Recent Royal Commissions", p.421.
82 HM Hart Jr, "The Aims of Criminal Law", *Law and Contemporary Problems*, vol. 23 (1958), p.401.
83 Criminal Code Act 1995 (Cth), s 12.3(6).
84 S Bronitt, "Rethinking Corporate Prosecution: Reviving the Soul of the Modern Corporation", *Criminal Law Journal*, vol. 42, no. 4 (2018), p.205; J Clough and C Mulhern, *The Prosecution of Corporations* (Oxford University Press: Oxford, 2002); Legg et al, *Corporate Misconduct*.
85 Australian Law Reform Commission, "Corporate Criminal Responsibility" ALRC 136 (2020), available at: www.alrc.gov.au/inquiry/corporate-crime/.
86 V Comino, "Corporate Culture Is the 'new Black' - Its Possibilities and Limits as a Regulatory Mechanism for Corporations and Financial Institutions?", *University of New South Wales Law Journal*, vol. 44, no. 1 (2021), p.295.
87 P Crofts, "Legal Irresponsibility and Institutional Responses to Child Sex Abuse", *Law in Context*, vol. 34 (2016), p.79.
88 Bant, *The Culpable Corporate Mind*.
89 E Bant and J Paterson, "Systems of Misconduct: Corporate Culpability and Statutory Unconscionability", *Journal of Equity*, vol. 15 (2021), p.63 at p.76.
90 E Bant, "Culpable Corporate Minds", *University of Western Australia Law Review*, vol. 48, no. 2 (2021), p.352 at p.371.
91 P Crofts, "Crown Resorts and the Im/Moral Corporate Form", p.72.
92 *R v Moloney* [1985] 1 All ER 1025 at p.1031.
93 P Crofts, "Aliens: Legal Conceptions of the Corporate Invasion", *Law and Literature*, vol. 34, no. 3 (2021), p.387.
94 T Anthony and P Crofts, "The Dreamworld Deaths: Corporate Crime and the Slumber of Law", *Current Issues in Criminal Justice*, vol. 36, no. 2 (2024), p. 197.
95 *Thabo Meli v R* [1954] 1 All ER 373.
96 See Crofts, *Evil Corporations*.
97 J Paterson and HX Chia, "Artificial Aliens: Strict Liability and the State-of-the-Art Defence for Digital Medical Products", in *Evil Corporations*.
98 *Thabo Meli v R* [1954] 1 All ER 373. See Crofts, *Evil Corporations*.
99 D Kahan, "The Secret Ambition of Deterrence", *Harvard Law Review*, vol. 113, no. 2 (1999), p.413.
100 Gilchrist, "The Expressive Cost of Corporate Immunity".
101 Gilchrist, "The Expressive Cost of Corporate Immunity"; Crofts and van Rijswijk, *Technology*.

References

Legislation

Bribery Act 2010 (UK)
Corporations Act 2001 (Cth)
Crimes Act 1900 (NSW)
Crimes Act 1961 (NZ)
Crimes Legislation Amendment (Combatting Corporate Crime) Bill 2019 (Cth)
Criminal Code Act 1995 (Cth)
Criminal Finances Act 2017 (UK)
Interpretation Act 1889 (UK)
Joint Stock Companies Act 1844 (UK)
Limited Liability Act 1855 (UK)

Cases

Burns v R [2012] HCA 35
Citizens United v FEC 558 US 310 [2010]
DPP v Kent & Sussex Contractors [1944] KB 146
DPP v Woolmington [1935] AC 462
HL Bolton Engineering Co Ltd v TJ Graham & Sons Ltd [1957] 1 QB 159
Meridian Global Funds Management Asia Ltd v Securities Commission [1995] 2 AC 500
Pharmaceutical Society v London and Provincial Supply Association [1880] 5 App Cas 859
R v Birmingham & Gloucester Railway Co [1842] 114 Eng Rep 492
R v Great North of England Railway Company [1846] 115 Eng Rep 1294
R v Moloney [1985] 1 All ER 1025
R v P&O European Ferries (Dover) Ltd [1991] 93 Cr App R 72
Royall v R [1990] 172 CLR 378
Saloman v Saloman & Co Ltd [1897] AC 22
State v First National Bank [1872] 2 SD 568
Sutton's Hospital Case [1612] 10 Coke Reports ER 77 937
Tesco Supermarkets Ltd v Nattrass [1972] AC 154
Thabo Meli v R [1954] 1 All ER 373
Triplex Safety Glass Co v Lancegaye Safety Glass [1939] 2 KB 395
Trustees of Dartmouth College v Woodward 17 US 518 [1819]

Books and book chapters

Baker JH, *The Oxford History of the Laws of England* (Oxford University Press: Oxford, 2003).
Bant E, "The Culpable Corporate Mind: Taxonomy and Synthesis" in Bant E (ed), *The Culpable Corporate Mind* (Hart Publishing: Oxford, 2023).
Barak G, *Unchecked Corporate Power: Why the Crimes of Multinational Corporations Are Routinized Away and What We Can Do About It* (Routledge: London, 2017).
Campbell L, "The mis/use of professional privilege" in Penny Crofts (ed) *Evil Corporations* (Routledge: London, 2014).
Chapple C, *The Moral Responsibilities of Companies* (Palgrave MacMillan: London, 2014).
Clinard M & Yeager P, *Corporate Crime* (Transaction Publishers: New Jersey, 2nd edn, 2011).
Clough J, "'Failure to Prevent' Offences: The Solution to Transnational Corporate Criminal Liability" in Bant E (ed), *The Culpable Corporate Mind* (Hart Publishing: Oxford, 2023).
Clough J & Mulhern C, *The Prosecution of Corporations* (Oxford University Press: Oxford, 2002).
Crofts P, *Wickedness and Crime: Laws of Homicide and Malice* (Routledge: London, 2013).
Crofts P, "Crown Resorts and the Im/Moral Corporate Form" in Bant E (ed), *Culpable Corporate Mind* (Hart Publishing: Oxford, 2022).

Crofts P & van Rijswijk H, *Technology: New Trajectories in Law* (Routledge: London, 2021).
Crofts P & van Rijswijk H, *Corporate Harms: A Horror Story* (Routledge: London, forthcoming).
Diamantis M, "How to Read a Corporation's Mind" in Bant E (ed), *The Culpable Corporate Mind* (Hart Publishing: Oxford, 2023).
Feinberg J, *Doing and Deserving: Essays in the Theory of Responsibility* (Princeton University Press: Princeton NJ, 1970).
Fletcher G, *Rethinking Criminal Law* (Little Brown: London, 1978).
French PA, *Corporate Ethics* (Harcourt Brace College Publishers: San Diego CA, 1995).
Glasbeek HJ, "The Corporation as a Legally Created Site of Irresponsibility" in Pontell H & Geis G (eds), *International Handbook of White-Collar and Corporate Crime* (Springer: New York, 2007).
Green S, "A Normative Approach to White-Collar Crime" in Pontell H & Geis G (eds), *International Handbook of White-Collar and Corporate Crime* (Springer: New York, 2007).
Harris R, *Industrializing English Law* (Cambridge University Press: Cambridge, 2000).
Legg M, Dixon O, & Speirs S, *Corporate Misconduct and White-Collar Crime in Australia* (Thomson Reuters: Pyrmont NSW, 2022).
Orts EW, *Business Persons: A Legal Theory of the Firm* (Oxford University Press: Oxford, 2013).
Paterson J & Xian Chia H, "Artificial Aliens: Strict Liability and the State-of-the-Art Defence for Digital Medical Products", *Evil Corporations* (Routledge: London, 2024).
Pieth M & Ivory R, "Emergence and Convergence: Corporate Criminal Liability Principles in Overview" in Pieth M & Ivory R (eds), *Corporate Criminal Liability* (Springer: New York, 2011).
Pieth M & Ivory R, "Corporate Criminal Liability" in Brown KB & Snyder DV (eds), *General Reports of the XVIIIth Congress of the International Academy of Comparative Law* (Springer: New York, 2012).
Pollman E, "Corporate Law and Theory in Hobby Lobby" in Schmartzman M, Flanders C, & Robinson Z (eds), *The Rise of Corporate Religious Liberty* (Oxford University Press: Oxford, 2016).
Slapper G, "Corporate Homicide, Corporate Social Responsibility, and Human Rights" in Maguire E, Brookman F, & Maguire M (eds), *The Handbook of Homicide* (Wiley and Sons: New York, 2017).
Smith SD, *Law's Quandary* (Harvard University Press: Cambridge MA, 2004).
Sutherland E, *White Collar Crime* (Dryden Press: New York, 1949).
Tombs S & Whyte D, *The Corporate Criminal: Why Corporations Must Be Abolished* (Taylor and Francis: Abingdon, 2015).
Tombs S & Whyte D, "Worker Health and Safety", *Oxford Research Encyclopedia: Criminology and Criminal Justice* (Oxford University Press: Oxford, 2017).
Veitch S, *Law and Irresponsibility: On the Legitimation of Human Suffering* (Routledge: London, 2007).
Wells C, *Corporations and Criminal Responsibility* (Oxford University Press: Oxford, 2nd edn, 2001).

Journal articles

Abbott C, "The Regulatory Enforcement of Pollution Control Laws: The Australian Experience", *Journal of Environmental Law*, vol. 17, no. 2 (2005), pp.161–180.
Almond P, "The Dangers of Hanging Baskets: Regulatory Myths and Media Representations of Health and Safety Regulation", *Journal of Law and Society*, vol. 36, no. 3 (2009), pp.352–375.
Anthony T & Crofts P, "The Dreamworld Deaths: Corporate Crime and the Slumber of Law", *Current Issues in Criminal Justice*, vol. 36, no. 2 (2024), pp.197–218.
Ashworth A, "Conceptions of Over-Criminalisation", *Ohio State Journal of Criminal Law*, vol. 5 (2008), pp.407–425.
Bant E, "Culpable Corporate Minds", *University of Western Australia Law Review*, vol. 47, no. 2 (2021), pp.352–388.
Bant E & Paterson J, "Systems of Misconduct: Corporate Culpability and Statutory Unconscionability", *Journal of Equity*, vol. 15, no. 1 (2021), pp.63–91.

Bittle S & Snider L, "Law, Regulation, and Safety Crime: Exploring the Boundaries of Criminalizing Powerful Corporate Actors", *Canadian Journal of Law and Society*, vol. 30, no. 3 (2015), pp.445–464.

Brickey KF, "Corporate Criminal Accountability: A Brief History and Observation", *Washington University Law Quarterly*, vol. 60 (1982), p.393.

Bronitt S, "Rethinking Corporate Prosecution: Reviving the Soul of the Modern Corporation", *Criminal Law Journal*, vol. 42, no. 4, pp.205–207

Chan Smith D, "The Beginning of History for Corporate Law: Corporate Government, Social Purpose and the Case of Sutton's Hospital (1612)", *Seattle University Law Review*, vol. 45, no. 1 (2021), pp.367–412.

Coffee Jr J, "No Soul to Damn: No Body to Kick: An Unscandalised Inquiry into the Problem of Corporate Punishment", *Michigan Law Review*, vol. 79 (1980), pp.386–459.

Colvin E, "Corporate Personality and Criminal Liability", *Criminal Law Forum*, vol. 6, no. 1 (1995), pp.1–44.

Comino V, "Corporate Culture Is the 'new Black' – Its Possibilities and Limits as a Regulatory Mechanism for Corporations and Financial Institutions?", *University of New South Wales Law Journal*, vol. 44, no. 1 (2021), pp.295–325.

Crofts P, "Communicating the Culpability of Illegal Dumping: Bankstown v Hanna (2014)", *Australian Journal of Environmental Law*, vol. 2, no. 1 (2015), pp.57–76.

Crofts P, "Legal Irresponsibility and Institutional Responses to Child Sex Abuse", *Law in Context*, vol. 34 (2016), p.79.

Crofts P, "Three Recent Royal Commissions: The Failure to Prevent Harms and Attributions of Organisational Liability", *Sydney Law Review*, vol. 43, no. 4 (2020), pp.395–423.

Crofts P, "Aliens: Legal Conceptions of the Corporate Invasion", *Law and Literature*, vol. 34, no. 3 (2022), pp.387–415.

Crofts P, "The Horror of Corporate Harms", *Australian Journal of Corporate Law*, vol. 38 (2022), pp.23–45.

Diamantis M, "Functional Corporate Knowledge", *William and Mary Law Review*, vol. 61, no. 2 (2019), pp.319–395.

Gilchrist G, "The Expressive Cost of Corporate Immunity", *Hastings Law Journal*, vol. 64, no. 1 (2012), pp.1–57.

Gobert J, "Corporate Criminality: Four Models of Fault", *Legal Studies*, vol. 14, no. 3 (1994), pp.393–410.

Grear A, "Deconstructing Anthropos: A Critical Legal Reflection on 'Anthropocentric' Law and Anthropocene 'Humanity'", *Law and Critique*, vol. 26, no. 3 (2015), pp.225–249.

Jones KS, "The Opioid Epidemic: Product Liability or One Hell of a Nuisance? Symposium: The Opioid Crisis: An Epidemic Explained", *Mississippi College Law Review*, vol. 39, no. 1 (2021), pp.32–79.

Kahan D, "The Secret Ambition of Deterrence", *Harvard Law Review*, vol. 113, no. 2 (1999), pp.413–500.

Kidd M, "The Use of Strict Liability in the Prosecution of Environmental Crimes", *South African Journal of Criminal Justice*, vol. 15, no. 1 (2002), pp.23–40.

Lim E, "A Critique of Corporate Attribution: 'Directing Mind and Will' and Corporate Objectives", *Journal of Business Law*, vol. 3 (2013), pp.333–353.

Lo SHC, "Context and Purpose in Corporate Attribution: Can the 'Directing Mind' Be Laid to Rest?", *Journal of International and Comparative Law*, vol. 4, no. 2 (2017), pp.349–376.

Morreim EH, "Corporations, High-Stakes Biomedical Research, and Research Misconduct: Yes They Can (and Sometimes Do)", *Journal of Law and the Biosciences*, vol. 8, no. 1 (2021), pp.1–38.

Naffine N, "Our Legal Lives as Men, Women and Persons" *Legal Studies*, vol. 24, vol. 4 (2004), pp.621–642.

van Zee A, "The Promotion and Marketing of OxyContin: Commercial Triumph, Public Health Tragedy", *American Journal of Public Health*, vol. 99, no. 2 (2009), pp.221–227.

Wells C, "Swatting the Subjectivist Bug", *Criminal Law Review* (1982), pp.209–220.

Wheelwright K, "Goodbye Directing Mind and Will, Hello Management Failure: A Brief Critique of Some New Models of Corporate Criminal Liability", *Australian Journal of Corporate Law*, vol. 19, no. 3 (2006), pp.287–303.

White JB, "Making Sense of Criminal Law", *University of Colorado Law Review*, vol. 50, no. 1 (1978), pp.1–27.

Reports and websites

Australian Law Reform Commission, "Corporate Criminal Responsibility" (ALRC 2020) 136, available at: www.alrc.gov.au/inquiry/corporate-crime/

Dalrymple W, "The East India Company: The Original Corporate Raiders", *The Guardian* (United Kingdom, 4 March 2015), available at: www.theguardian.com/world/2015/mar/04/east-india-company-original-corporate-raiders

Hansmann H, Kraakman R, & Squire R, "Incomplete Organizations: Legal Entities and Asset Partitioning in Roman Commerce", *ECGI Working Paper No. 271* (European Corporate Government Institute: 2014), available at: https://papers.ssrn.com/sol3/papers.cfm?abstract_id=2506334

26
RETHINKING THE AGE OF CRIMINAL RESPONSIBILITY

Thomas Crofts

The criminal responsibility of children[1] is a highly charged and tangled issue. It is made all the more confusing by varied understandings of, and approaches to, criminal responsibility in relation to children. These differences are often not clearly acknowledged or articulated but they fundamentally shape debates about age level and legal approaches. To bring greater clarity to debates about the age of criminal responsibility this chapter unravels these differences in understanding and approaches, and examines the implications that they have for how the law deals with the children who transgress the criminal law. The chapter concludes by recommending how the law ought to address the criminal responsibility of children.

Varied understandings of the age of criminal responsibility

Age at which a child should be tried and punished as an adult (procedural-punishment view)

The term age of criminal responsibility can be used in relation to the procedural and punishment aspects of a criminal trial. In a procedural sense, it refers to the age at which it is thought that children should be tried in the same way as adults. For example, the Interstate Commission for Juveniles in the US defines the age of criminal responsibility as the "age which any offense automatically subjects an individual to adult court jurisdiction".[2] Similarly, the Scottish Law Commission notes that the age of criminal responsibility can mean

> the point at which the age of a suspect or offender has no relevance for his treatment or disposal as part of the criminal justice system, most typically the age at which an accused becomes subject to the full or adult system of prosecution and punishment.[3]

This means that until reaching this age the child will generally not be dealt with in the same court or in the same way as adults for infringing the criminal law. Rather, children who transgress the criminal law will be dealt with in child justice proceedings[4] inside the criminal justice system or in non-criminal proceedings, for instance, in the family court or in specialised educational/welfare proceedings (such as the Children's Hearing System in Scotland). The type of criminal behaviour engaged in may also determine the proceedings that apply, with child justice proceedings reserved for more serious criminal behaviour.[5] This age level is usually higher than the age at which a child can be drawn into child justice proceedings or other educational/welfare proceedings designed to address childhood offending, which will be discussed below.

According to this approach, the age of criminal responsibility is set to protect a child from the full force of criminal proceedings and sanctions, recognising that adult proceedings are not appropriate, and indeed can be harmful, for children. This is because children may lack the ability to effectively participate in such proceedings, which may deny them the right to a fair trial.[6] The UN Convention on the Rights of the Child ("UNCRC") acknowledges this and in article 40 requires states to "recognize the right of every child alleged as, accused of, or recognized as having infringed the penal law to be treated in a manner consistent with the promotion of the child's sense of dignity and worth". The UN Committee on the Rights of the Child ("UN Committee") comments that "[t]he child justice system should apply to all children above the minimum age of criminal responsibility but below the age of 18 years at the time of the commission of the offence".[7] It recommends that states that allow children below 18 to be dealt with as adults "change their laws to ensure a non-discriminatory full application of their child justice system to all persons below the age of 18 years at the time of the offence".[8]

Understood in relation to punishment, the age of criminal responsibility may refer to the age at which children can be punished in the same way as adults. The position that children should be protected from certain forms of punishment until adulthood is reflected in the UNCRC article 37, which requires state parties to ensure that certain punishments (e.g. capital punishment or life imprisonment without the possibility of release[9]) are not applied to persons below the age of 18. Furthermore, a child should only be detained as a last resort and for the shortest appropriate period, and not be detained with adults. Many jurisdictions recognise these principles and prohibit the application of adult punishments to children.[10] Instead, diversionary measures and more rehabilitation-oriented disposals will usually be available for responding to offending by children. In this regard, there may be various age levels, which may extend into adulthood, dependent on the offence committed and severity of the disposal available.

Age at which a child should be dealt with in child justice system (policy view)

While the above approach is concerned with when it is appropriate for a child to be dealt with as an adult (i.e. when is it appropriate to end the special protection afforded to children), a related way of thinking about the age of criminal responsibility is when is it appropriate to begin to deal with a child in child justice proceedings. This tends to be more of a policy approach determined by views about from what age it is thought necessary and appropriate to begin to attribute responsibility and address childhood offending in the child justice system. This approach is less concerned with keeping children out of the criminal justice system and more with holding them accountable and ensuring that the procedures and measures for addressing child offending are appropriate to foster their rehabilitation. As Fionda notes: "[T]o some extent the historical and international debates on an appropriate minimum age are more about the age at which we choose to punish children (the policy view)".[11]

Setting an age level according to this approach may be connected to the capacity view of criminal responsibility (discussed below) because arguments about when it is appropriate to deal with children in the child justice system may rely on arguments about when children are thought to have certain capacities. However, as McDiarmid comments, it "is not universally accepted that there is a necessary link" between a child's capacity and when they should be held immune from the child justice system.[12]

Often, with this approach the primary concern is not the child's capacity but the perceived need to deal with children who transgress the criminal law inside the child justice system for their own or society's benefit. Sometimes this approach may simply sidestep the issue of criminal responsibility and point to the non-punitive nature of many child justice systems as an indicator that criminal responsibility should not be the key determinant of whether a child enters that system. The comment of the Independent Commission on Youth Crime and Antisocial Behaviour reflects this approach: "the age of criminal responsibility offers an unreliable guide to the way children and young people are actually treated when they break the law" because even jurisdictions with a low age of criminal responsibility may "apply welfare-oriented principles and can refer children to protective and educative measures, including secure care".[13]

Age at which a child has the capacities to be held responsible in the same way as an adult (legal-capacity view)

Another way of understanding the age of criminal responsibility is from a normative legal-capacity standpoint. This relates to the fundamental nature of criminal law. Criminal law is a harsh and condemnatory tool and "because it burdens interests not implicated by other modes of social control", its imposition on an individual requires justification.[14] A primary justification comes from the idea that criminal law consequences should only be imposed on those who are criminally responsible for their behaviour.[15] As Lacey states

> the idea that criminal liability must involve both conduct and responsibility or fault lies at the heart of contemporary criminal law's idea of itself as not just a system of state power and force, but a legitimate – even in some senses a moral – system.[16]

Criminal responsibility is, according to this conceptualisation, based on the capacities of "understanding, reasoning and control of conduct" which concern "the ability to understand what conduct legal rules or morality require, to deliberate and reach decisions concerning these requirements, and to conform to decisions when made".[17] In order to determine capacity the law may take certain short-cuts, such as legal presumptions, based on likelihood.[18] Most adults have the cognitive and volitional capacities necessary to make a free choice[19] and so the law presumes that an adult is capable of being criminally responsible for what they do. In exceptional cases where an adult lacks these capacities or where these capacities are diminished, due for instance to a mental impairment, the law allows defences to be raised to reduce or negate liability.

In contrast, with children it is common for the law to presume a lack of capacity. This may take the form of a single age level under which it is conclusively presumed that all children lack the capacities necessary to be held criminally responsible (often termed the minimum age of criminal responsibility or "MACR"). Historically, in common law systems (and also in Roman Law) this was fixed at the age of 7.[20] Many common law jurisdictions raised this age level to 10 around the 1960s onwards and in more recent decades there has been a tendency to raise this age level to 12. Even more recently there has been a push for this age level to be raised to at least 14 or higher.[21] In contrast to the common law, civil law countries tend to have a higher age level: for instance, in Germany and Italy it is set at the age of 14.[22]

Another approach is to set an age period during which the child's capacity to be held criminally responsible is assessed individually in each case. This age period may apply alongside a MACR or without a MACR.[23] In evidentiary terms, this tends to take the form of a rebuttable presumption that the child lacks the capacities to be held criminally responsible (often termed the presumption of *doli incapax*). In common law jurisdictions, this age period was historically fixed from the age of 7 until the child's 14th birthday.[24] In recent times there has been a tendency in common law jurisdictions to abolish this upper age period either with[25] or without an increase in the MACR.[26] Again, in civil law countries which operate such a presumption the age level tends to be higher: for instance, in Germany and Italy this is set at the age of 18.[27] Some jurisdictions may also provide different age levels in relation to specific offences[28] or different age levels depending on gender.[29]

This tapestry of age levels and approaches shows that the question of when a child is considered old enough to be held criminally responsible is a complex one. It is made more complicated by the variety of systems for dealing with children who transgress the criminal law. Further complications arise, as evidenced by the wide variations in age levels in different jurisdictions, due to age levels being determined not simply by questions of capacity but also by policy factors relating to when it is thought necessary and appropriate to address childhood offending in the child justice system.

Debates about the age of criminal responsibility

These various ways of understanding and approaching the age of criminal responsibility have implications for the intensity and voracity of arguments in relation to how children who transgress the criminal law should be dealt with. In particular, this impacts on debates around age levels and methods for assessing criminal responsibility. Setting an age of criminal responsibility from a procedural-punishment sense is not terribly controversial. There is wide agreement that this should be set close to the age at which a child reaches adulthood, and sometimes reach into adulthood. More controversial and more intense, and therefore the subject of the following section, are arguments relating to a capacity and/or policy view of the criminal responsibility of children.

Capacity-related arguments

Arguments concerning children's capacity to be held criminally responsibility range from common sense assertions to scientific, evidence-based claims about the age at which a child is thought to have acquired the capacities required to be criminally responsible. The former are generally used to support a low age of criminal responsibility, whereas the latter tend to support a higher age level. Common sense claims tend to state that children are able to understand the difference between right and wrong at an earlier age now than in previous times because, for example, of the benefits of compulsory universal education and access to technological advances, such as the internet. This claim has been made in various cases,[30] and used in the English case, *C v DPP*, as a reason for asserting that the presumption of *doli incapax* should no longer be part of the law.[31] Such common sense arguments even found their way into government rhetoric in the mid-90s, with the Labour Government deciding to abolish the presumption of *doli incapax* for children aged 10 and over on the basis that above this age children "are generally mature enough to be accountable for their actions".[32] And, as Bateman notes, these claims have "been routinely replicated by all governments since".[33] For instance, in debating the Age of Criminal Responsibility Bill in 2017 Baroness Vere argued that "children aged 10 and above are able to differentiate between bad behaviour and serious wrongdoing and can therefore be held accountable for their actions."[34]

One fundamental problem with such claims is that they tend to oversimplify what is and ought to be required to be held criminally responsible. Detail about how capacities can be evidenced is available from scholarly work and caselaw in those jurisdictions which provide for an individual assessment of a child's the required capacities. Where the presumption of *doli incapax* applies it is not sufficient to show that a child can distinguish right from wrong in an abstract sense but rather the child must be able to know, at the time of behaving, that what they were doing was seriously wrong.[35] In Australia this has been interpreted as requiring that the child knows that the behaviour is wrong according to the standards or principles of reasonable people.[36] The High Court of Australia recently reaffirmed that such knowledge of wrong is "a matter of morality" and not a matter of knowing that the behaviour is contrary to law. Furthermore, aside from knowing that the act was wrong in a moral sense, there is "the further dimension ... of knowledge of serious wrongness as distinct from mere naughtiness".[37] An aspect of the required capacity which does not tend to feature as a separate issues in many common law jurisdictions, is whether the child could control their actions according to this understanding.[38] This is recognised in jurisdictions such as South Africa[39] and Germany.[40]

Another issue with such claims is that they tend to be based on generalised assertions about children's capacities. Research particularly from developmental psychology and neuroscience is causing "a reassessment of how recognition of developmental immaturity should affect the way society treats young offenders, particularly in determining the age at which criminal responsibility should be imposed".[41] Childhood is a period of neurodevelopmental immaturity during which different parts of the brain are developing at varied rates. As the United Kingdom's Royal Society note, "the frontal lobes of the brain which are responsible for planning, decision making, and inhibiting impulsivity, develop much later than the amygdala, the part of the brain responsible for reward and emotion-processing".[42] This imbalance in brain development is thought to account for increased arousal, impulsivity, and risk-taking behaviour combined with a limited ability to engage in consequential thinking, evaluate future consequences, empathise, and resist peer influence.[43] However, this is not the only explanation for why children may lack the capacities required to be held criminally responsible. Research is examining how hormones and environmental factors can affect brain development and activation.[44] Negative impact on cognitive and volitional capacities may be caused by a range of factors affecting brain development, including:

> poor prenatal care, a lack of early life access to appropriate physical and mental health support from families (including healthy diets which allow the brain to grow normally), exposure to violence and other traumatic experiences, limited access to other healthcare resources and access to prosocial education experiences, as well as exposure

to things that may damage brain development such as head injuries, drugs and alcohol, and the effect of poor socio-economic conditions.[45]

This brief and incomplete account of recent neuroscientific research is sufficient to show that there is very clear evidence of how children develop the capacities required to be criminally responsible gradually and later than was previous thought. Full capacities may not be gained until into adulthood. Such evidence has been noted by the UN Committee, which comments that, "[d]ocumented evidence in the fields of child development and neuroscience indicates that maturity and the capacity for abstract reasoning is still evolving in children aged 12 to 13."[46] It therefore encourages state parties "to take note of recent scientific findings" and increase their MACR to at least 14 years of age, and it commends state parties that have a higher MACR of 15 or 16 because "the developmental and neuroscience evidence indicates that adolescent brains continue to mature even beyond the teenage years, affecting certain kinds of decision-making".[47]

Despite the overwhelming neuroscientific research and despite repeated calls by the UN Committee for states to ensure that they have a MACR of 14 or higher, many governments have been resistant to calls for change. As Bateman notes in relation to England and Wales, this resistance is particularly paradoxical given that since the mid-2000s there has been an expansion in diversion and an "acceptance that responses to youth crime should revolve around Child-first precepts".[48] Yet, this has not filtered through to any changes to the MACR, with "governments of all persuasions [maintaining] a robust defence of retaining criminalisation at age 10 in England and Wales".[49] Other common law jurisdictions have been a little less resistant to change, with some increasing the MACR to 12.[50] Recently, some Australian jurisdictions have increased the MACR to 12 and some do plan to increase this further to 14 in the near future.[51] However, the slowness of change in light of long-standing and increasing evidence about children's developing capacities suggests that setting the MACR is seen by governments as less about responding to scientific evidence and more of policy issue.[52]

Policy arguments

Policy considerations can be used to support a lower or a higher age level of criminal responsibility and may be based on evidence or generalised assertions. Support for a lower age level of criminal responsibility is often based on a perceived need to respond to childhood offending within the child justice system for the child's own and/or society's benefit. A central feature of such arguments is the assertion that systems for dealing with children are no longer as punitive as they were in earlier times and measures are now much more welfare/education focused, with the aim of preventing offending and reintegrating the child. Accordingly, it is thought that there is less need to protect children from such a system and the chances at rehabilitation may be lost if they are not dealt with in a child justice system.

This line of argument is not new. In the 1960s, the Ingelby Committee found that not bringing prosecutions "results in many children not receiving the treatment they need or not receiving it soon enough".[53] In the 1990s, the tone shifted to responsibilisation and the need to hold children accountable to foster their rehabilitation. Concern was expressed by the Labour Government that an "excuse culture" had developed, where either nothing was done with children or they were given too many warnings.[54] Rather than excuse childhood offending, the policy was that children needed to take responsibility "and to face up to the harm which they have caused to the victim" as "both a valuable moral lesson and a first step to rehabilitation".[55] Such arguments continue to be made in the present day. For example, in

Queensland it was noted that an objection to raising the MACR is that this "could result in the creation of a cohort of undetected, at-risk children".[56]

This leads to a related argument concerning the need to retain a low MACR so that childhood offending can be dealt with in the child justice system in line with community expectations and to protect the community. For instance, while the ACT Government has committed to raising the MACR to 12 with plans for a further increase to 14, exceptions may be made for 12- and 13-year-olds for serious crimes. This is on the basis that "it may be important to include exceptions *to accommodate community expectation* in the rare event that a very serious harmful act is commit [sic] by a 12 or 13 year old child".[57] Similarly, the Queensland Government noted that there was objection to raising the MACR on the basis that "community safety may be threatened, leading to a loss of community confidence" and that "victims of crime will not be adequately protected or supported".[58]

These arguments are only loosely, if at all, related to the capacity of the child to be held criminally responsible and instead focus on policy rationales for setting the MACR, such as, timely intervention, community expectations, community safety, and the need to provide a criminal justice response to childhood offending. However, these arguments downplay, misrepresent, or even ignore the fundamental nature of the child justice system. While it may be true that many modern systems for dealing with children who infringe the criminal law have a more welfare/educational orientation the process of engagement with the apparatus of that system can in itself be stigmatising and traumatising for children. Furthermore, many jurisdictions do provide measures which have a punitive character. The punitive nature of such sanctions was publicly highlighted, for example, in Australia when a TV documentary[59] aired footage showing the treatment of children in detention in the Northern Territory. The Royal Commission into the Protection and Detention of Children in the Northern Territory ("Royal Commission") established to investigate this matter found that: "Children and young people have been subjected to regular, repeated and distressing mistreatment".[60] This included verbal abuse, excessive control (such as withholding necessities like food, water, and the use of toilets), and humiliation (inciting or bribing detainees to engage in degrading and humiliating acts).[61] The Independent Monitoring Boards in the UK have also reported on poor conditions inside young offender institutions, "including limited time out of rooms, lack of purposeful activity and spikes in violence".[62]

There is incontrovertible evidence that: "[e]xposing children and young people to the child justice system can have a significant impact on their neurological and social development and can result in life-long interactions with the justice system".[63] Further evidence about why the child justice system is not the appropriate place to respond to wrongdoing by children, and may very well exacerbate problems they face, can be found in research about the characteristics of children typically involved in that system. A report prepared for the Australian Capital Territory ("ACT") Government found that the major risk factors for criminal behaviours in youth, include "personality or temperament and early environmental conditions, such as harsh and erratic parenting, early behavioural problems or trauma, history of parental offending and the role of adverse childhood experiences".[64] Neurodevelopmental delay and disorders feature significantly more prevalently in children inside the child justice system compared to children outside that system.[65] There is also a clear connection between children who come into contact with child protection services and engagement with the child justice system.[66] A particularly concerning factor in an Australian context is the gross overrepresentation of First Nations children in the child justice system.[67] Taken together the research indicates that a high percentage of children in the child justice system experience complex needs, that are "a combination of: mental health problems; cognitive disability, including intellectual and developmental disability; physical disability; behavioural difficulties; precarious housing; social isolation; family dysfunction; and problematic drug or alcohol use".[68] Such children do need help and support, but the child justice system is not the appropriate place to provide it.

How should criminal law address the criminal responsibility of children?

For jurisdictions adopting a single MACR this should be fixed at the age level at which it can be presumed that all children have the capacities required to be held criminally responsible. In line with the recent neurological and developmental research discussed above this would mean setting that age level close to the age of reaching adulthood, at 16 or 18 years of age. Such an age level would also be appropriate in aligning the MACR with the age at which it is thought that children have the capacities required to make decisions in other areas of law, such as the age at which they can vote, enter a contract, drink in a pub, smoke, and marry without parental consent.

Many common law jurisdictions have a much lower MACR than this, and even where there are plans for an increase these tend to not extend beyond the age of 12 or 14. Even more concerning are approaches, or proposals, whereby a lower MACR applies for certain more serious offences. This is the approach taken, for example, in Ireland, where the MACR is 12 but this age is reduced to 10 for charges of murder, manslaughter, or rape.[69] Similarly, in China, the MACR is 16 but an amendment made in 2021 allows a lower age of 12 to apply for certain offences.[70] This approach is also being considered in the ACT if the MACR is raised to 14.[71] The problem with this approach is that it stems from the view that serious wrongdoing must be dealt with inside the child justice system, regardless of evidence about children's developing capacities or evidence about the negative impacts of early involvement in the child justice system. As the UN Committee comments, this approach is "usually created to respond ... to public pressure and [is] ... not based on a rational understanding of children's development".[72] Such an approach should therefore be avoided.

A MACR of 10, 12, or 14 leaves children who have not yet developed capacities which ought to be required for an ascription of criminal responsibility liable to child justice proceedings. Therefore, recognising that "[t]here is huge individual variability in the timing and patterning of brain development"[73] it would be appropriate for such systems to provide a rebuttable presumption of incapacity starting from the MACR reaching until 16 or 18 years of age.[74]

Such an approach is not without criticism. The UN Committee comments that, while "there is some support for the idea of individualised assessment of criminal responsibility" it "has observed that this leaves much to the discretion of the court and results in discriminatory practices".[75] This concern is not unfounded, as evidenced by research in Australia revealing inconsistencies in the operation of the presumption.[76] However, this does not mean that a presumption of incapacity is unworkable or undesirable. Many of the problems with the presumption of *doli incapax* stem from a lack of clarity over what the presumption requires and how it can be rebutted, as well problematic practices, such as treating the presumption as a mere formality that can be rebutted by inferences about a child's understanding.[77] In countries requiring an expert assessment of a child's capacities there is also the problem of a "lack of specialist resources" which "is a serious issue affecting the outcome of the case, especially because courts may wait months for an expert report".[78]

A number of reforms could address these issues. Better resourcing of clinical services and establishing a "dedicated pool of psychologists or psychiatrists within the criminal justice sector to perform these examinations"[79] would improve the situation. Furthermore, greater clarity over how the presumption operates and what it requires in order to be rebutted would greatly improve the protection offered by the presumption.[80] This is especially important given the challenges facing those who make evaluations about a child's capacities.[81]

Greater clarity could be achieved by anchoring the presumption in legislation with fuller detail on what it requires and upon whom the burden of proof lies. For instance, s11(1) of the South African Criminal Justice Act 2008 requires that the prosecution must prove "beyond reasonable doubt that the capacity of a child who is 12 years or older but under the age of 14 years to appreciate the difference between right and wrong at the time of the commission of an alleged offence and to act in accordance with that appreciation". The latter part of this provision is an important addition to the common law presumption of *doli incapax* by expressly referring to the volitional capacity of the child. Under this provision, an evaluation report of the criminal capacity of the child can be requested by the court, prosecution, or defence, which must include an assessment of the child's cognitive, moral, emotional, psychological, and social development.[82]

The German Youth Court Act 1953, §3 also provides an interesting model. It states that: "a young person is criminally responsible if at the time of the act he was mature enough, due to his moral and mental development, to understand the wrongfulness of the act and to act according to this understanding". The German Association for Youth Courts and Youth Court Services finds the concept of maturity too abstract and has recommended that it be replaced with detail of the factors which indicate a child lacks capacity. The recommended formulation is:

> a young person is only criminally responsible if he, at the time of the act, was able to understand the wrongfulness of the act and behave according to this understanding. The understanding is generally not given if the criminal act damages or harms legally protected interests which are not part of the young person's world of experience or when the act is merely the expression of a playful character. The ability to control actions may not be given where the young person commits the act under the dominating influence of another or in a situation of conflict.[83]

Including such factors may be too prescriptive, lead to debate about what factors should be included, and cause complex and technical argument in practice. Other alternatives would be to include examples in the legislation as illustrations of when capacity will be lacking or detailing such factors in prosecutorial guidelines.

Another approach would be to develop a separate defence of developmental immaturity. McDiarmid argues that this "is indicated because children's understanding of criminal behaviour may be limited in comparison with (or different from) that of their adult counterparts and/or children may be unable, or impaired in their ability, to exercise rational control over their behaviour".[84] Her proposal is based on the Scottish defence of mental disorder[85] and would apply if, due to developmental immaturity, a person aged less than 18 years was unable to sufficiently know the full implications of, to understand and/or to appreciate the

Rethinking the Age of Criminal Responsibility

nature of the conduct, its criminality, its wrongfulness and/or its consequences; and/or was severely restricted in their ability to judge whether to carry out the conduct, exercise rational control over the conduct and/or refrain from commission of the conduct.[86] The advantage of this approach is that it makes the basis for the defence (developmental immaturity) clear and expressly refers to the abilities that lie at the core of criminal responsibility: the cognitive capacity as well as volitional capacity.

Conclusion

Whichever understanding or approach is taken to the age of criminal responsibility children should be protected from the full force of the criminal law until close or into adulthood. From a procedural-punishment perspective, adult procedures and punishments are not appropriate for children. The child justice system is embedded within the criminal justice system and even though procedures and available disposals may be modified until adulthood to reduce the stigmatising and punitive aspects of the child justice system, they do not ameliorate them. Subjecting a child to such proceedings, when they may not understand them or be able to effectively participate can deny them a fair trial. Therefore, from a legal-capacity view it is only just to draw a child into that system when they have the capacities required to be held criminally responsible, which according to recent developmental and neuroscientific research may take until adulthood. From a policy viewpoint in the interests of the child and of the community there may be a need to provide measures to address the causes of the child's offending and support their rehabilitation. However, the demonstrated negative impacts of early contact with the child justice system, and evidence about the characteristics of children typically involved in that system, show that this is not the appropriate place to provide such intervention and support.

Acknowledgements

I would like to thank Andrew Dyer and Normann Witzleb for their insightful and incisive comments on earlier versions of this chapter.

Notes

1. Some jurisdictions use the terms child for younger children and young person for older children in relation to criminal matters, for consistency, the terms children and child are used throughout this chapter to refer to persons under the age of 18.
2. Interstate Commission for Juveniles, *Age Matrix*, (2024), available at: https://juvenilecompact.org/age-matrix.
3. Scottish Law Commission, *Discussion Paper on Age of Criminal Responsibility*, Discussion Paper No 115 (2001), para 1.3.
4. UN Committee on the Rights of the Child (UNCRC), "General Comment No 24 on Children's Rights in the Child Justice System" (CRC/C/GC/24, 2019), refers to child justice proceedings as "the legislation, norms and standards, procedures, mechanisms and provisions specifically applicable to, and institutions and bodies set up to deal with, children considered as offenders", para 8.
5. E.g. in New York a child under 18 (and over 7 years of age) who commits a misdemeanor will be dealt with in the Family Court. If the offence committed is a serious or violent felony the child will be tried in the Youth Part of the Supreme or County Court. See, "Crimes Committed by Children Between 7-18", *New York Courts Website* (2019), available at: www.nycourts.gov/courthelp/criminal/crimesByChildren.shtml\.

6. E.g. *T v UK*, Application No. 24724/94, where it was held that T had been denied the right to a fair trial under art. 6 of the European Convention on Human Rights.
7. UNCRC, "General Comment No 24", para 29.
8. UNCRC, "General Comment No 24", para 30.
9. It should be noted that there is also now wide recognition that these punishments should not be imposed on adults due to their incompatibility with human rights, see e.g. *Vinter v United Kingdom*, Application Nos. 66069/09, 130/10 and 3896/10) (9 July 2013); *R v Bissonnette* 2022 SCC 23.
10. E.g. children will usually not be subjected to imprisonment in the same penal institution as adults, see e.g. Hong Kong ("HK") Criminal Procedure Ordinance (Cap. 221), s 109A, which provides that a child/young adult (16-21) cannot be sentenced to imprisonment (although there are exceptions).
11. J Fionda, "Youth and Justice", in J Fionda (ed), *Legal Concepts of Childhood* (Hart Publishing: Oxford, 2001), pp.85–86.
12. See, C McDiarmid, in this volume.
13. Independent Commission on Youth Crime and Antisocial Behaviour, *Time for a Fresh Start* (2010), p.14.
14. D Husak, "The Criminal Law as a Last Resort", *Oxford Journal of Legal Studies*, vol. 24, no. 2 (2004), p.207 at p.234.
15. HLA Hart, *Punishment and Responsibility: Essays in the Philosophy of Law*, (Oxford University Press: Oxford, 1968), p.181.
16. N Lacey, "In Search of the Responsible Subject: History, Philosophy and Social Sciences in Criminal Law Theory", *Modern Law Review*, vol. 64, no. 3 (2001), p.350 at p.353.
17. Hart, *Punishment and Responsibility*, p.227.
18. D Hamer & T Crofts, "The logic and value of the presumption of doli incapax (failing that, an incapacity defence)", *Oxford Journal of Legal Studies*, vol. 43, no. 3 (2023), p.546.
19. Packer calls the idea of free "a value preference having very little to do with the metaphysics of determinism and free will", H Packer, *The Limits of the Criminal Sanction* (Stanford University Press: Stanford CA, 1968) p.74.
20. For history see T Crofts, *The Criminal Responsibility of Children and Young Persons: A Comparison of English and German Law* (Ashgate Publishing: Surrey UK, 2002), chs.1&4.
21. See e.g. *#Raise the Age*, available at: https://raisetheage.org.au/.
22. E.g. Germany: Criminal Code, §19 and Italy: Penal Code, art.97.
23. E.g. France: Code Penal, article 122-8.
24. See T Crofts, "The Common Law Influence over the Age of Criminal Responsibility — Australia", *Northern Ireland Legal Quarterly*, vol. 67, no. 3 (2016), p.283.
25. E.g. Canada: Criminal Code, s 13.
26. E.g. England and Wales: Crime and Disorder Act 1989, s 34.
27. E.g. Germany: Youth Court Act, §3 and Italy: Penal Code, art.98.
28. E.g. Ireland: Criminal Justice Act 2006 (Irl), s 52(2). For prosecutions of children under 14 the permission of the DPP is required, s 52(4).
29. E.g. Iran, see: J Staines, N Aghtaie & J Roy, "Gendered Justice: Inequalities in the Minimum Age of Criminal Responsibility in Iran", *Youth Justice*, vol. 22, no. 3 (2022), p.290.
30. Forbes J in *JBH and JH v O'Connell* [1981] Crim LR 632.
31. *C v DPP* [1995] 1 Cr App R 118.
32. Home Office, *No More Excuses: A New Approach to Tackling Youth Crime in England and Wales* (HMSO: London, 1997), Introduction.
33. See, T Bateman, in this volume.
34. Baroness Vere, *Age of Criminal Responsibility Bill*, 2nd reading (Hansard, Volume 783, 8 September 2017).
35. See e.g. *RP v The Queen* (2016) HCA 53, [4].
36. *R v M* (1977) 16 SASR 589 at pp.590–591.
37. *RP v the Queen*, [11]; see also *BDO v The Queen* (2023) HCA 16, [13].
38. Although there have been calls for this to be recognised, see for example, C Elliott, "Criminal Responsibility and Children: A New Defence Required to Acknowledge the Absence of Capacity and Choice", *Journal of Criminal Law*, vol. 75, no. 4 (2011), p.289.

39 E.g. South Africa: Criminal Justice Act 2008, s 11.
40 German Youth Court Act 1953, §3.
41 Royal Commission, *The Protection and Detention of Children in the Northern Territory* (2017), vol. 1, p.134.
42 Royal Society, *Neuroscience and the law: Brain Waves Module 4* (2011), available at: https://royalsociety.org/-/media/Royal_Society_Content/policy/projects/brain-waves/Brain-Waves-4.pdf.
43 E Delmage, "The Minimum Age of Criminal Responsibility: A Medico-Legal Perspective", *Youth Justice*, vol. 13, no. 2 (2013), p.102 at p.107.
44 For a summary of such research see T Crofts, E Delmage & L Janes, "Deterring children from crime through sentencing: can it be justified?", *Youth Justice*, vol. 23, no. 2 (2022), p.182 at p.191.
45 Crofts et al, "Deterring Children", p.192.
46 UNCRC, "General Comment no. 24", para 22.
47 UNCRC, "General Comment no. 24", para 22.
48 See, T Bateman, in this volume.
49 T Bateman, "Challenging punitive youth justice", in S Case and N Hazel (eds), *Child first: developing a new youth justice system* (Palgrave MacMillan: London, 2023).
50 See e.g. South Africa, Criminal Justice Act 2008, s 7 as amended by Criminal Justice Amendment Act 2019, s 4.
51 See e.g. Justice (Age of Criminal Responsibility) Legislation Amendment Act 2023 (ACT).
52 For discussion in an Australian context, see T Crofts, "Will Australia Raise the Minimum Age of Criminal Responsibility", *Criminal Law Journal*, vol. 43, no. 1 (2019), p.26.
53 Committee on Children and Young Persons, *Report of the Committee on Children and Young Persons* (chaired by Viscount Ingelby), Cmnd. 1191 (London 1960), para 94.
54 Home Office, *No More Excuses*, Preface.
55 Home Office, *Tackling Youth Crime: A Consultation Paper.* (HMSO: London, 1997).
56 Community Support and Services Committee, *Criminal Law (Raising the Age of Responsibility) Amendment Bill 2021*, Report No. 16, 57th Parliament (2022), available at: https://documents.parliament.qld.gov.au/tableoffice/tabledpapers/2022/5722T275-5736.pdf.
57 Australian Capital Territory Government, *Raising the age of criminal responsibility position paper* (Canberra City, 2022), p.5 [emphasis added].
58 Community Support and Services Committee, *Criminal Law*.
59 August 2016, ABC Four Corners, "Australia's Shame".
60 Royal Commission, *The Protection and Detention of Children in the Northern Territory* (2017), vol. 1, p.9.
61 Royal Commission, *The Protection and Detention of Children*, vol. 2A, ch.12.
62 E Harle, "Prisons watchdog warns of 'heightened' problems in YOIs", *Children & Young People Now* (August 3, 2023), available at: www.cypnow.co.uk/news/article/prisons-watchdog-warns-of-heightened-problems-in-yois.
63 ACT Government, Justice and Community Safety Directorate, *Raising the Age*, available at: www.justice.act.gov.au/safer-communities/raising-the-age#:~:text=Previously%20children%20as%20young%20as,interactions%20with%20the%20justice%20system.
64 M McArthur, A Suomi, & B Kendall, *Review of the service system and implementation requirements for raising the minimum age of criminal responsibility in the Australian Capital Territory: Final Report* (2021), p.17.
65 E Baldry, D Briggs, B Goldson, & S Russell, "'Cruel and unusual punishment': An interjurisdictional study of the criminalisation of young people with complex support needs", *Journal of Youth Studies*, vol. 21, no. 5 (2018), p.636 at p.640; C Cunneen, "Arguments for raising the minimum Age of criminal responsibility", *Jumbunna Institute for Indigenous Education and Research, UTS, Sydney* (2020), p.14, available at: https://ssrn.com/abstract=4183933. (Accessed January 2024); Royal Commission, *The Protection and Detention of Children*, vol. 1, p.135.
66 McArthur et al, *Final Report*, p.20; see also K McFarlane, "Care-Criminalisation: The involvement of children in out-of-home care in the New South Wales criminal justice system", *Australian & New Zealand Journal of Criminology*, vol. 51, no. 3 (2018), p.412.
67 Australian Government, Australian Institute of Health and Welfare *Youth Justice in Australia 2019-20* (2021), p.10; Cunneen, "Arguments for".
68 McArthur et al, *Final Report*, p.18.

69 Criminal Justice Act 2006 (Irl), s 52(2). For prosecutions of children under 14 the permission of the DPP is required, s 52(4).
70 See A Wong, "Can lowering the minimum age of criminal responsibility be justified? A critical review of China's recent amendment", *Howard Journal of Crime and Justice*, vol. 63, no. 1 (2023), p.3.
71 ACT Government, *Position Paper*, p.5.
72 UNCRC, "General Comment No. 24", para 25.
73 Royal Society, *Neuroscience and the Law*, p.13.
74 T Crofts, "Prosecuting child offenders: Factors relevant to rebutting the presumption of doli incapax", *Sydney Law Review*, vol. 40, no. 3 (2018), p.339; W O'Brien & K Fitzgibbon, "The minimum Age of criminal responsibility in Victoria (Australia): examining stakeholders' views and the need for principled reform", *Youth Justice*, vol. 17, no. 2 (2017), p.134; M Tuomi & D Moritz, "Criminal responsibility of older children: The failings of *doli incapax* in Australia", *Children & Society*, vol. 38, no. 2 (2024), p.456.
75 UNCRC, "General Comment No. 24", para 26; see also Australian Law Reform Commission. *Seen and heard: Priority for children in the legal process* (ALCRC Report No. 84, 1997), para 18.19.
76 See for instance, K Fitzgibbon & W O'Brien, "A child's capacity to commit crime: Examining the operation of doli incapax in Victoria (Australia)", *International Journal for Crime, Justice and Social Democracy*, vol. 8, no. 1 (2019), p.18 at p.22; Tuomi & Moritz, "Criminal responsibility".
77 Crofts, "Prosecuting child offenders". This approach was criticised in *RP*.
78 See, A Pillay, in this volume.
79 See, A Pillay, in this volume.
80 See Crofts, "Prosecuting child offenders"; see also comments of Community Support and Services Committee. *Criminal Law*, p.21.
81 For a deeper discussion of the challenges facing those assessing criminal capacity see A Pillay, in this volume.
82 Criminal Justice Act 2008 s 11(3) (South Africa).
83 Deutsche Vereinigung für Jugendgerichte und Jugendgerichtshilfe, 2.Jugendstrafrechtsreform-Kommission. Für ein neues JGG: Die Vorschläge der DVJJ-Kommission. *Zeitschrift für Jugendkriminalrecht und Jugendhilfe EXTRA*, (1992), p.9 at p.12.
84 C McDiarmid, "After the age of criminal responsibility: A defence for children who offend", *Northern Ireland Legal Quarterly*, vol. 67, no. 3 (2016), p.327 at pp.328-9.
85 Criminal Procedure (Scotland) Act 1995, s 51A.
86 McDiarmid, "After the age of criminal responsibility", p.340. For discussion of a similar defence, see Elliot, "Criminal Responsibility". For an alternative defence modelled on s 45 of the Modern Slavery Act 2015 (UK), see N Wake, R Arthur, T Crofts, & S Lambert, "Legislative Approaches to Recognising the Vulnerability of Young People and Preventing their Criminalisation", *Public Law* (2021), p.145 at pp.153-155.

References

Legislation

Code Penal (France)
Crime and Disorder Act 1989 (UK)
Criminal Code (Canada)
Criminal Code (Germany)
Criminal Code (Italy)
Criminal Justice Act 2006 (Irl)
Criminal Justice Act 2008 (South Africa)
Criminal Justice Amendment Act 2019 (South Africa)
Criminal Procedure (Scotland) Act 1995
Criminal Procedure Ordinance (Cap 221) (Hong Kong)
Detention Centre Ordinance (Cap 239) (Hong Kong)
Justice (Age of Criminal Responsibility) Legislation Amendment Act 2023 (Australian Capital Territory)
Modern Slavery Act 2015 (UK)
Youth Court Act 1953 (Germany)

Cases

BDO v The Queen (2023) HCA 16.
C v DPP (1995) 2 All ER 43 at 55 (HL).
R v Bissonnette 2022 SCC 23.
R v M (1977) 16 SASR 589.
RP v The Queen (2016) HCA 53.
T v UK, Application No. 24724/94.
Vinter v United Kingdom, Application Nos. 66069/09, 130/10 and 3896/10) (9 July 2013).

Books and book chapters

Bateman T, "Challenging punitive youth justice", in Case S & Hazel N (eds), *Child First: Developing a New Youth Justice System* (Palgrave MacMillan: London, 2023).

Crofts T, *The Criminal Responsibility of Children and Young Persons: A Comparison of English and German Law* (Ashgate Publishing: Surrey UK, 2002).

Fionda J, "Youth and justice", in Fionda J (ed), *Legal Concepts of Childhood* (Hart Publishing: Oxford 2001).

Hart HLA, *Punishment and Responsibility: Essays in the Philosophy of Law* (Oxford University Press: Oxford, 1968).

Packer H, *The Limits of the Criminal Sanction* (Stanford University Press: Stanford CA, 1968).

Tadros V, *Criminal Responsibility* (Oxford University Press: New York, 2005).

Journal articles

Baldry E, Briggs D, Goldson B, & Russell S, 2018. "'Cruel and unusual punishment': An interjurisdictional study of the criminalisation of young people with complex support needs", *Journal of Youth Studies*, vol. 21, no. 5 (2018), pp.636–652.

Crofts T, "Prosecuting child offenders: Factors relevant to rebutting the presumption of *doli incapax*", *Sydney Law Review*, vol. 40, no. 3 (2018), pp.339–365.

Crofts T, "Will Australia raise the minimum age of criminal responsibility", *Criminal Law Journal*, vol. 43, no. 1 (2019), pp.26–40.

Crofts T, Delmage E, & Janes L, "Deterring children from crime through sentencing: Can it be justified?", *Youth Justice*, vol. 23, no. 2 (2022), pp.182–200.

Delmage E, "The minimum age of criminal responsibility: A medico-legal perspective", *Youth Justice*, vol. 13, no. 2 (2013), pp.102–110.

Elliott C, "Criminal responsibility and children: A new defence required to acknowledge the absence of capacity and choice", *Criminal Law Journal*, vol. 75, no. 4 (2011), pp.289–308.

Fitzgibbon K & O'Brien W, "A child's capacity to commit crime: Examining the operation of *doli incapax* in Victoria (Australia)", *International Journal for Crime, Justice and Social Democracy*, vol. 8, no. 1 (2019), pp.18–33.

Hamer D & Crofts T, "The logic and value of the presumption of *doli incapax* (failing that, an incapacity defence)", *Oxford Journal of Legal Studies*, vol. 43, no. 3 (2023), pp.546–573.

Husak D, "The criminal law as a last resort", *Oxford Journal of Legal Studies*, vol. 24, no. 2 (2004), pp.207–234.

Lacey N, "In search of the responsible subject: History, philosophy and social sciences in criminal law theory", *Modern Law Review*, vol. 64, no. 3 (2001), pp.350–371.

McDiarmid C, "After the age of criminal responsibility: A defence for children who offend", *Northern Ireland Legal Quarterly*, vol. 67, no. 3 (2016), pp.327–341.

McFarlane K, "Care-criminalisation: The involvement of children in out-of-home care in the New South Wales criminal justice system", *Australian & New Zealand Journal of Criminology*, vol. 51, no. 3 (2018), pp.412–433.

Pillay A, "The minimum age of criminal responsibility, international variation, and the dual systems model in neurodevelopment", *Journal of Child & Adolescent Mental Health*, vol. 31, no. 3 (2019), pp.224–234.

Pillay A & Willows C, "Assessing the criminal capacity of children: A challenge to the capacity of mental health professionals", *Journal of Child and Adolescent Mental Health*, vol. 27, no. 2 (2015), pp.91–101.

Staines J, Aghtaie N, & Roy J, "Gendered justice: Inequalities in the minimum age of criminal responsibility in Iran", *Youth Justice*, vol. 22, no. 3 (2022), pp.290–303.

Tuomi M & Moritz D, "Criminal responsibility of older children: The failings of *doli incapax* in Australia", *Children & Society*, vol. 38, no. 2 (2024), pp.456–469.

Wake N, Arthur R, Crofts T, & Lambert S, "Legislative approaches to recognising the vulnerability of young people and preventing their criminalisation", *Public Law* (2021), pp.145–162.

Wong A, 2023, "Can lowering the minimum age of criminal responsibility be justified? A critical review of China's recent amendment", *Howard Journal of Crime and Justice*, vol. 63, no. 1 (2023), pp.3–21.

Reports and websites

Australian Capital Territory Government, *Raising the Age of Criminal Responsibility Position Paper* (Canberra City, 2022), by the authority ACT Government.

Australian Capital Territory Government, Justice and Community Safety Directorate, *Raising the Age*, available at: www.justice.act.gov.au/safer-communities/raising-the-age#:~:text=Previously%20children%20as%20young%20as,interactions%20with%20the%20justice%20system

Australian Law Reform Commission, *Seen and Heard: Priority for Children in the Legal Process* (ALCRC Report No. 84, 1997).

Community Support and Services Committee, *Criminal Law (Raising the Age of Responsibility) Amendment Bill 2021* (Report No. 16, 57th Parliament, 2022), available at: https://documents.parliament.qld.gov.au/tableoffice/tabledpapers/2022/5722T275-5736.pdf

"Crimes Committed by Children Between 7-18", *New York Courts Website* (2019), available at: www.nycourts.gov/courthelp/criminal/crimesByChildren.shtml\

Cunneen C, "Arguments for raising the minimum age of criminal responsibility", *Jumbunna Institute for Indigenous Education and Research, UTS, Sydney* (2020), available at: https://ssrn.com/abstract=4183933

Deutsche Vereinigung für Jugendgerichte und Jugendgerichtshilfe, 2.Jugendstrafrechtsreform-Kommission [German Association for Youth Courts and Youth Court Services, 2nd Juvenile Justice Reform Commission], Für ein neues JGG: Die Vorschläge der DVJJ-Kommission. *Zeitschrift für Jugendkriminalrecht und Jugendhilfe EXTRA* (1999), pp.9–16.

Halpern WD, *Reforming "Raise the Age"* (2023), available at: https://manhattan.institute/article/reforming-raise-the-age#:~:text=In%202018%2C%20New%20York%20State,be%20adjudicated%20as%20juvenile%20delinque

Harle E, "Prisons watchdog warns of 'heightened' problems in YOIs", *Children & Young People Now* (3 August 2023), available at: www.cypnow.co.uk/news/article/prisons-watchdog-warns-of-heightened-problems-in-yois

Home Office, *Report of the Committee on Children and Young Persons*, Cm 1191 (Her Majesty's Stationery Office: London, 1960).

Home Office, *No More Excuses: A New Approach to Tackling Youth Crime in England and Wales*, Cm 3809 (Her Majesty's Stationary Office: London, 1997).

Home Office, *Tackling Youth Crime: A Consultation Paper* (Her Majesty's Stationary Office: London, 1997).

House of Lords, *Age of Criminal Responsibility Bill 2017 Library Briefing* (London, 2017).

Independent Commission on Youth Crime and Antisocial Behaviour, *Time for a Fresh Start* (2010), available at: www.scotlawcom.gov.uk/files/8412/7892/7069/dp115_criminal_response.pdf

Interstate Commission for Juveniles, *Age Matrix* (2024), available at: https://juvenilecompact.org/age-matrix

Law Council of Australia, *Consideration of Raising Minimum Age of Criminal Responsibility Doesn't Go Far Enough* (2021), available at: https://lawcouncil.au/media/media-releases/consideration-of-raising-minimum-age-of-criminal-responsibility-doesn-t-go-far-enough

McArthur M, Suomi A, & Kendall B, *Review of the Service System and Implementation Requirements for Raising the Minimum Age of Criminal Responsibility in the Australian Capital Territory: Final Report* (2021).

Office of the Children's Commissioner (United Kingdom), *Nobody Made the Connection: The Prevalence of Neurodisability in Young People Who Offend* (2012), tendered 12 October 2016, available at: https://assets.childrenscommissioner.gov.uk/wpuploads/2017/07/Nobody-made-the-connection.pdf

"#Raise the Age", available at: https://raisetheage.org.au/

Royal Society, *Neuroscience and the Law: Brain Waves Module* 4 (2011), available at: https://royalsociety.org/-/media/Royal_Society_Content/policy/projects/brain-waves/Brain-Waves-4.pdf

Royal Commission, *The Protection and Detention of Children in the Northern Territory* (2017), available at: www.royalcommission.gov.au/child-detention/final-report

Scottish Law Commission, *Discussion Paper on Age of Criminal Responsibility*, Discussion Paper No. 115 (2001).

UN Committee on the Rights of the Child (UNCRC), *General Comment No. 24 on Children's Rights in the Child Justice System*, CRC/C/GC/24 (2019), available at: www.ohchr.org/en/documents/general-comments-and-recommendations/general-comment-no-24-2019-childrens-rights-child.

Vere Baroness, "Age of Criminal Responsibility Bill", *Hansard*, 2nd Reading (8 September 2017), vol. 783.

27
NEUROTECHNOLOGY AND THE INSANITY DEFENCE

Allan McCay

Introduction

If a person with a brain implant used to treat a neurological condition experiences a device failure causing them to hallucinate and kill someone, might they fall into the scope of the insanity defence as outlined in the common law's *M'Naghten* test[1] or perhaps some statutory implementation of it?

In order to address this question of criminal responsibility, this chapter examines a neurotechnological challenge in the context of the defence of insanity as set out in the *M'Naghten* test and also in the context of an example of a statutory implementation of something approximating it in the law of New South Wales, Australia.

One reason why the *M'Naghten* test is considered is because of its continuing international significance and influence. However, many jurisdictions (including New South Wales) have put *M'Naghten* on a statutory footing. The hope is that this chapter's combined approach will avoid excessive parochiality in addressing only one jurisdiction, but that it will have the virtue of acknowledging that *M'Naghten* often now has a statutory implementation.

A further reason for considering both *M'Naghten* and the statutory reformulation is that the conceptual basis for the insanity defence as set out in the *M'Naghten* test is now very old, dating back to the nineteenth century. It has been said by the New South Wales Attorney General who introduced the legislation that the new law "updates" *M'Naghten*.[2] The statutory formulation has been taken to incorporate "contemporary psychiatric and psychological understandings of incapacity"[3] and we might ask how it addresses the challenges of a future in which neurotechnology becomes more widespread in society.

Whilst some people currently have brain implants that are used to treat neurological conditions there are no reported cases of the kind considered in this paper. In a report on neurotechnology for the Law Society of England and Wales[4] and in a more recent piece for the Law Society Journal[5] I argued for the merits of an anticipatory approach to legal thinking in response to the pace of technological change. Here, I employ such an approach and, after explaining what neurotechology is, and outlining some technological advancements with a view to arguing for the plausibility of a hypothetical situation which raises responsibility issues, I construct a hypothetical scenario in order to consider how doctrine and legislation relating to excusing the mentally ill may address this technologically plausible hypothetical scenario.

The aim is to put some scholarly thinking in place that might inform law reform, should law reform become necessary.[6] In light of the analysis, it is suggested that neurotechnology is an area worthy of attention from scholars and law reform bodies.[7]

Whilst neurotechnology generates other issues for criminal law, one theme that is prominent here is the way that the boundaries of the defendant may be contested in criminal law as humans start to merge with machines such as brain-computer interfaces. Soekadar *et al* have suggested that the law's technological boundary question is likely to become a more significant issue in the coming years.[8] The analysis presented here might be thought of as providing support for their view.

What is neurotechnology?

Neurotechnologies are devices that monitor and/or influence activity in the brain or nervous system. Some devices are implanted in the brain or elsewhere in the nervous system; others are external to the body such as a wearable headsets or wristbands.

The focus in this paper will be on therapeutic neurotechnology, but in order to understand the broader technological context it is worth noting that that there are a variety of non-therapeutic applications. Thus, for example, neurotechnologies are used in scientific research. Researchers have used neurotechnology to decode the mental images of people watching movies and then to create hazy reconstructions of the movies being watched for display on a computer monitor using only the neural activity recorded from the brain.[9] Recent developments in generative artificial intelligence have improved the clarity of images decoded from the brain.[10]

Others have used the technology to control drones by way of mental act (rather than controlling a joystick), giving rise to brain drone racing competitions.[11] Some technologies are used for video gaming, monitoring the brains of employees as they work, or more concerningly to enhance interrogations by gaining neural information during the course of a police or security service interview.[12] It has further been reported that the capacity to interact with forms of generative artificial intelligence, such as ChatGPT, by way of neural device has now been developed.[13]

The therapeutic context includes devices that are currently in clinical use which stimulate the brain to treat Parkinson's disease,[14] obsessive compulsive disorder,[15] epilepsy,[16] depression,[17] and other conditions. Some other devices remain at the clinical trial stage, such as brain-computer interface technologies that monitor activity in the brain allowing a person who cannot use their muscle system to communicate or perform bodily actions to control a cursor or a device such as a wheelchair by having neural activity relating mental actions corresponding with their intentions decoded and converted into commands for the device.[18] There are now signs heralding the possibility of neurotechnology becoming more mainstream as the Belfast company Neurovalens has received FDA approval for a wearable device aimed at treating insomnia.[19]

The neurotech industry more broadly is increasingly becoming an area of economic excitement. Jeff Bezos, Bill Gates, and Elon Musk have all invested in neurotech companies, as has Meta.[20] It seems that these billionaires and companies have formed the view that neurotechnology is likely to become more prevalent in society, which gives reason for legal scholars to consider some of the challenges to law that may emerge if they are right.

Some advances relevant to the hypothetical scenario

In order to lend plausibility to my hypothetical scenario, it is worth understanding a little more about the operation of some existing neurotechnology. This involves the consideration of advances that might be coming, together with the issue of the vulnerability of neurotechnological devices to hacking or other failure. The aim of this section is to understand why a neurotechnogical device might be employed and how it might fail, giving rise to a hallucination and the consequent issue of criminal responsibility.

An example of a neural device that is currently approved for clinical use in the US and currently implanted in the brains of some people to manage their condition is the Neuropace epilepsy device. This device constantly monitors the brain of the person with epilepsy employing a machine learning algorithm to identify the neural precursors to an epileptic fit. When it notices those precursors, it acts to stimulate the brain to avert the fit.[21]

However, there are records of neurotechnological failures. Straw, Ashworth, and Radford describe a case in which the failure of a brain implant aimed at treating Parkinson's disease led to a man presenting at an emergency department with a variety of symptoms including impact on affect (a feeling of intense sadness).[22] After the neurotechnological issue was identified and the problem with the device addressed, the symptoms abated.

But the resolution of this problem was not straightforward. The team had to first identify the device using a Google reverse image search and then after contacting a technical specialist on the phone, they unsuccessfully attempted to address the patient's issues by reconfiguring it. It was not until a programmer was located to correct the brain-stimulation device's settings that the issues were resolved.[23]

The authors note the work of Pycroft *et al* who use the term "brainjacking", referring to the vulnerability of neurotechnological devices to hacking (although there was no suggestion that the patient being discussed in their work had had their device hacked).[24] In connection to this, it is worth noting the emergence of an area known as "cyberneurosecurity". In their discussion of this topic Liv and Greenbaum note that issues include unauthorised neural eavesdropping and neurostimulation, hijacking of prosthetic limbs, and the manipulation of behaviour.[25]

Perhaps the possible involvement of cloud computing in relation to the use of neurotechnology might exacerbate the security risks because of increased interaction between a person's brain and nervous system with external storage devices facilitating the cloud computing. Martins *et al* outline a possible neurotechnological future where a person's brain interacts with the cloud and receives information directly into the nervous system unmediated by the senses.[26] They argue for the desirability of establishing a "a safe, robust, stable, secure, and continuous real-time interface system between the human brain and the data storage and processing systems that reside in the cloud".[27] Presumably, if such a future were to eventuate, then concerns about cyberneurosecurity would become more pressing.

Another technological capacity that may be emerging relating to the hypothetical is that of inducing specific hallucinations in people. It seems that by neurotechnological means it is currently possible to make mice believe they have seen a food stimulus when none is present.[28] Columbia University's Professor Rafael Yuste is both an eminent neuroscientist and a prominent campaigner who draws attention to human rights concerns surrounding the development of neurotechnologies. He notes that the capacity to induce specific hallucinations in animals may expand into a capacity to induce *specific* hallucinations in humans.[29]

As will be seen shortly, the hypothetical draws on some of the features described in this section. It involves a neurotechnological failure, that may have been caused by a hacker, or perhaps by malfunction, which induces a hallucinatory experience that leads a defendant to kill someone.

However, prior to consideration of the insanity defence, I will say something more general about the legal consideration of neurotechnologies for the reader who is new to this topic in order to situate the analysis and demonstrate that various scholars, international bodies, and legislatures are anticipating legal ripples.

The legal and scholarly context for the consideration of insanity

There has been significant discussion of the human rights implications of neurotechnology from advocacy groups,[30] international bodies,[31] and academics.[32] Some domestic legislatures have started to respond to the issues—most notably, Chile, which has changed its Constitution, in part to address the emerging challenges from neurotechnology.[33] As of the end of 2021, section 19 of the Chilean Constitution now reads as follows:

> "Scientific and technological development will be at the service of people and will be carried out with respect for life and physical and mental integrity. The law will regulate the requirements, conditions and restrictions for its use in people, having to protect especially the brain activity, as well as the information coming from it".[34]

In a decision that is in part based on this constitutional change, the country's highest court recently ordered that one of their citizen's brain data held by a neurotech manufacturer be deleted.[35] There are signs that proposals for neurotech-inspired legal change are appearing in other Latin American countries[36] and outside that region some branches of executive government have started to produce work addressing neurotech.[37]

Moving now to criminal law scholarship there is substantial discussion of the implications of science for criminal law,[38] particularly neuroscience,[39] but less in relation to the implications of the integration of technology into the brains and minds of those who are involved in the criminal justice system.[40] I will now briefly mention some examples of criminal law scholarship relating to neurotech.

Brain-computer interfaces enable people to act otherwise than through the body, for example by controlling a cursor by a mental act. Let us suppose that someone commits an offence by a series of mental acts. I have raised the question of what the conduct constituting the *actus reus* might be in these circumstances. Given that the relevant conduct is somewhat non-standard, insofar as it may not be regarded as normal bodily conduct, I have suggested that it might be regarded as a mental act, some neural activity, a form of cyborg action involving inorganic bodily parts, or a combination of these.[41] This *actus reus* consideration raises issues pertaining to the *boundary of the defendant* which will also emerge in the responsibility analysis that is coming.

In the context of sentencing, Gilbert and Dodds have considered the question of whether it would be ethically acceptable for the courts to mandate the use of neurotechnologies to monitor offenders' brains and intervene on them in order prevent angry outbursts leading to recidivism.[42]

But the focus here is on criminal responsibility in the context of a defence. In their recent submission on neurotechnology to the Australian Parliament's Parliamentary

Joint Committee on Human Rights, the law firm advising the Australian Human Rights Commission on neurotechnology noted that defences in the criminal law might require reconsideration as a result of neurotechnological failure (perhaps as a result of hacking).[43] Whilst overseas, Ligthart *et al*[44] have engaged in a brief discussion of the *M'Naghten* rules in the context of a neurotechnological device failure, they do not substantially address hallucination, caselaw related to the test, or the specifics of any subsequent statutory implementation of the test. Globally, there has been little discussion of neurotech/insanity-related issues and none in Australia giving reason to address this gap in the literature.

The hypothetical

The hypothetical asks how the criminal law might address responsibility challenges that are emerging from a world in which brains and nervous systems are increasingly connected to technology in very direct ways. This may be a world in which neural devices manage neurological conditions, are sometimes connected to other external devices or the cloud, and can be hacked or fail in ways that might lead to the neurotech user experiencing a hallucination. It is now time to set out the scenario which runs as follows:

> *When Cassandra was an infant and on the advice of medical professionals, her parents consented to the implantation of a piece of neurotechnology (which had been approved by the medical device regulator) in order to manage a debilitating neurological condition (unrelated to issues of hallucination). They did this knowing there was a small chance that it might malfunction or even be hacked causing her to hallucinate. The device has remained in place and active subject to periodical review and as the technology developed throughout her lifetime new updates were wirelessly delivered to it. However, whilst successful in managing her condition, the risk of technical failure was never entirely eliminated.*
>
> *At no time did Cassandra act in a manner that was contrary to medical advice, but one day, after reaching the age of criminal responsibility, Cassandra was in a kitchen appliance shop and the device malfunctioned, giving rise to a hallucination that a nearby customer was a wild animal.*
>
> *In a confused panic, Cassandra grabbed a knife and stabbed the other customer causing his death. Due to the hallucination, Cassandra believed she was killing an animal and is unable to fully explain why she thought this was the right course of action.*
>
> *It is unclear whether the device simply malfunctioned or whether a hacker had engineered the malfunction.* [45] *If a hacker was involved, it is unclear what their motivation was. Perhaps they were trying to get her to kill someone and had intentionally engineered this specific hallucination, or they might just have been trying to scare her by making her hallucinate, or they just wanted to rise to the challenge of obtaining unauthorised access to a neural device and thereby inadvertently caused the hallucination. However, it is clear that the device malfunctioned giving rise to the hallucination.*

Let us now consider Cassandra's criminal liability. Given that Cassandra thought she was killing an animal, she does not have the *mens rea* for any homicide offence and might well be acquitted. However, as will be demonstrated later, it is possible that she might find herself subject to a special verdict due to a finding of insanity or its New South Wales statutory instantiation—the defence of Mental Health Impairment or Cognitive

Impairment (MHI/CI). Prior to considering the less attractive possibility of a special verdict, I will consider the merits of acquittal.

One reason to think acquittal is preferable is that she lacks prior fault as she was using (if "using" is the right word, given that it might be thought of as now a part of her) a device with a small risk of failure that, on medical advice, was implanted into her brain prior to maturity, in a way that was consistent with medical advice.[46] Like some other drugs that are approved for clinical use, the implanted device had a risk of hallucination and there is nothing therapeutically unique about this being a risk of a therapeutic intervention.[47] Another reason why an acquittal might be desirable is that given the device had a very low risk of failure and there seems to be little merit of detaining her in terms of community protection to prevent recurrence of some similar set of events.

But will she be acquitted? Cassandra might argue that she should simply be acquitted but in New South Wales, judges are permitted to raise the issue of insanity/MHI/CI of their own motion.[48] Let us now assume that the judge in her trial forms the view that the hallucination raises the issue of insanity/MHI/CI and instructs the jury to consider this.

A special verdict of insanity or MHI/CI is a much less attractive option than acquittal for Cassandra given that the judge would then need to decide about some further order. Under the current legislative framework in New South Wales and its predecessors the possibility of indefinite detention in a therapeutic context exists in relation to a special verdict.[49]

It does not seem like other full defences are relevant.[50] This does not seem to be a situation of defective consciousness or of reflex action of the type that might allow a challenge to the voluntariness of what Cassandra did. It seems that she has acted consciously, voluntarily, and intentionally. She is unclear as to why she stabbed what she thought to be an animal and so self-defence does not seem to be available and in any case this defence would seem very strained since it is a defence that applies only to defence against human beings. Similarly, necessity does not seem to be an option because of her lack of clarity on the question of why she did what she did and the unreasonableness of her beliefs about the situation.

Is Cassandra's conduct excused under the M'Naghten rules?

According to the *M'Naghten* test a person is excused from responsibility if they suffer from a defect of reason, resulting from a disease of the mind such that they didn't know the nature and quality of their conduct or they didn't know it was wrong.[51]

It seems that Cassandra did not know the nature and quality of what she was doing as believing she was killing an animal, she didn't know she was killing a human being. However, it seems a bit more difficult to see her mind as being diseased. The device is implanted to address a debilitating condition that does not cause hallucinations and it might be stretching the concept of "disease" to regard a very rare technological device failure affecting her perception, that might have been induced by a hack, as constituting such a condition.

But is there a way of seeing what happened as a manifestation of "disease"? Perhaps the law might view the device as not being an external tool that she was using, but as *part of her*. In this way she is conceived of as a cyborg and the contents of her mind are conceived of as being consequences of the interaction between some biological parts of her (her brain) and the inorganic part of her (the neurotechnological device). To argue for the plausibility of this view, it might be suggested that the device has been in her brain for nearly all of her life, is thus integrated into her, and is indeed part of her rather than a tool that she uses.

Addressing a different form of neurotechnology—a brain-computer interface (BCI) for controlling external objects—the philosopher Kramer Thompson has suggested that "the more well-integrated the function of the BCI is with the agent's agential powers (his ability to engage with and affect the world), the more plausible it is that the BCI counts as part of the agent."[52] This device has a significant role in maintaining Cassandra's capacity to "engage with and affect the world".[53]

Perhaps this kind of functional integration might support the view that she, as a cyborg defendant, has a mind that emerges from the interaction of the biological and non-biological components which are vulnerable to fail in ways that cause her to hallucinate in a way that, although less frequent, is not materially different from the way that a person with schizophrenia has a mind which emerges from fully biological matter which is also liable to fail in a way that causes hallucinations.

However, it might still be hard to shake the idea that what has occurred is just some sort of technical failure especially as it might be that the failure and hallucination was engineered by a hacker.

In *R v Radford* King CJ stated that: "the malfunction of the mental faculties called 'defect of reason' in the *M'Naghten* rules, must result from an underlying pathological infirmity of the mind, be it of long or short duration and be it permanent or temporary, which can be properly termed mental illness, as distinct from the reaction of a healthy mind to extraordinary external stimuli."[54]

As has been suggested earlier, Cassandra's mind might be thought of as not being "healthy" for reasons outlined earlier, and the stimulus might be thought of as being internal (and part of her) rather than external, but it is hard to see that the issue can properly be termed as "mental illness" unless that concept is radically revised to incorporate the non-biological.

In the *Radford* passage mentioned above, the notion of "extraordinary external stimuli" is contrasted with "underlying pathological infirmity".[55] If the device has been hacked, it might be easier to see it as a form of "extraordinary external stimuli" than if the device simply malfunctioned. However, the technology seems to have an ongoing (albeit small) risk of malfunction/hacking and if it is considered to be part of the defendant's brain/mind then the defendant's mind might be regarded as pathologically infirm.

Although the argument that Cassandra had a disease of the mind might seem strained, it is worth noting that the law has been prepared to regard conditions such as epilepsy to be a "disease of the mind" in the context of the insanity defence which might seem rather surprising to those outside the law.[56]

Some uncertainty must be acknowledged as to what the outcome of this kind of debate might be. This uncertainty results from the novel nature of the issues, which raise the question of where the defendant ends and the technology that they employ begins.[57] These issues of cyborgisation are not issues that are normally prominent in debates about criminal responsibility.

Even if there is no hacker, the boundaries of the defendant might be tested if there were to be some external processing in the device's normal function—perhaps in the cloud. Might the defendant's cyborg brain and mind then be thought of as extending into the cloud?

It is not clear that either expert evidence from the psychiatric profession, or legal doctrine is well-placed to address such questions.

A further point is worth noting in relation to the difficulty of seeing Cassandra as having a "disease of the mind" and having a "mental illness". If more and more people start to have brain/minds that are partly constituted by technological devices this may indeed lead to a re-conception of the idea of "mental illness" in the therapeutic professions, society, and perhaps also in law.

So, although *probably* outside its scope, there is some doubt about whether Cassandra's conduct fits into the *M'Naghten* test and the scope question may be contingent on the way that neurotechnology might change notions of what it is to have a "mental illness". But would things be any different under the statutory upgrade to the defence?

Is her conduct excused under the New South Wales defence of Mental Health Impairment or Cognitive Impairment?

Section 28(1) of Mental Health and Cognitive Impairment Forensic Provisions Act 2020 (NSW) states that:

(1) A person is not criminally responsible for an offence if, at the time of carrying out the act constituting the offence, the person had a mental health impairment or a cognitive impairment, or both, that had the effect that the person—
  (a) did not know the nature and quality of the act, or
  (b) did not know that the act was wrong (that is, the person could not reason with a moderate degree of sense and composure about whether the act, as perceived by reasonable people, was wrong).

The issue of "nature and quality" has been discussed in the preceding section and which concluded that she did not know its "nature and quality". There is no suggestion that Cassandra is cognitively impaired as the relevant statutory definition seems unrelated to hallucination[58] and so we need to ask whether she had a "mental health impairment" that led her to fail to know that the nature and quality of her act. In this section, the notion of the "mental health impairment" is playing the role of *M'Naghten*'s "disease of the mind", but did she have such an impairment? Section 4 of the Act states that:

(1) For the purposes of this Act, a person has a mental health impairment if—
  (a) the person has a temporary or ongoing disturbance of thought, mood, volition, perception or memory, and
  (b) the disturbance would be regarded as significant for clinical diagnostic purposes, and
  (c) the disturbance impairs the emotional wellbeing, judgment or behaviour of the person
(2) A mental health impairment may arise from any of the following disorders but may also arise for other reasons—
  (a) an anxiety disorder,
  (b) an affective disorder, including clinical depression and bipolar disorder,
  (c) a psychotic disorder,
  (d) a substance induced mental disorder that is not temporary.[59]

The list of disorders mentioned is *non-exhaustive* and because neurotechnological failure is not on the list does not mean that such a failure is excluded from the definition of "mental health impairment". So, our focus needs to be on section 4(1).

It seems that Cassandra experienced a temporary disorder of perception under section 4(1)(a) and that it impaired her judgment and behaviour under section 4(1)(c)—but is the neurotechnological failure to be regarded as "significant for clinical diagnostic purposes" under s 4(1)(b)? If it is, then it would seem that Cassandra fits into the defence and a special verdict is appropriate. If the neurotechnological failure is not significant for clinical and diagnostic purposes, then she should be acquitted (as discussed earlier).

One reason to think that it might be "significant for diagnostic purposes" is that for a neurologist, knowing that the device had failed in the way that it did, might enable them to form the view that other possible diagnoses were less plausible. However, this could be an overly literal interpretation—it seems reasonably likely that that a New South Wales court might say that the failure would *not* be "significant for diagnostic purposes". In his second reading speech introducing the bill, the then New South Wales Attorney General, Mark Speakman said "[t]he requirement that the disturbance be 'significant for clinical diagnostic purposes' means that the temporary or ongoing disturbance must be serious enough to result in a mental health diagnosis."[60] This seems to suggest that that the categories employed in the mind sciences are of significance to whether or not an issue is significant for the purposes of this section and the device failure may go *beyond* recognised forms of categorisation by the relevant therapeutic professional witnesses and thus not fit easily into the defence.

In the New South Wales Court of Criminal Appeal "sexsomnia" case of *R v DB*, which involved a defendant engaging in sexual activities with an under-age person while asleep, the court had to determine whether he had a "mental health impairment" for the purposes of the legislation under consideration, but found that he did not.[61] Justice Brereton noted the trial judge's comments that suggested that the question of whether there was consensus around the relevant condition being a "true mental health diagnosis", such as those recognised by the psychiatric profession, were significant to the court. Perhaps it might be thought that a neurotechnological failure was not a "true mental health diagnosis" as the boundaries of the psychiatric profession and their categories of diagnosis do not currently extend to the assessment of neurotechnologically induced hallucination.

Assuming this latter interpretation was correct, this would mean that since Cassandra's device failure is *not* "significant for diagnostic purposes" she is excluded from the defence. Again, because the issues are somewhat novel it is hard to be definitive about a court's likely response but again issues of the boundaries of the defendant emerge. It seems the limits of the expertise and approaches to classification from professionals from the mind sciences have a role in the law's conception of the boundaries of the defendant, on the earlier-mentioned analysis of *R v DB*.

But arguably Cassandra is partly *constituted* by a technological device that is unfamiliar to most in the mind sciences. This also seems to raise the more general question of whether Cassandra the cyborg malfunctioned or a device she was using malfunctioned thereby affecting her behaviour?

Reflections and concluding thoughts

It may well be that both *M'Naghten* and MHI/CI would *exclude* Cassandra from the defence leading to an acquittal but there is doubt about this and perhaps the MHI/CI as a test is a little more likely to exclude her and lead to an acquittal than *M'Naghten*. Given that it is hard to see culpability in Cassandra and there is no suggestion that the risk of recurrence is significant, it may be that acquittal is to be welcomed. If so, in this respect perhaps MHI/CI is an improvement on *M'Naghten* at least in relation to the hypothetical under consideration, insofar as it could be a little more likely to acquit in a situation where that result has ethical merit.

However, there is uncertainty about the outcome arising from questions concerning the boundaries of the defendant and the beginning of the technologies they use. Other questions arise as to the role of those in the therapeutic profession in determining the boundaries of the defence and the way it might evolve if neurotechnology starts to change conceptions of what it is to be mentally ill.

A further issue for law might be the nature of relevant expert witnesses. Although the impact was on affect rather than perception, in the case of neurotechnological malfunction described earlier the patient's issues were resolved by a programmer. One can imagine a diverse and for the law, non-standard, group of experts might have something to say about a neurotechnological failure leading to a hallucination in the context of contested criminal responsibility. This group might include a forensic psychiatrist, a neurologist, a biomedical engineer, and a programmer.

Relatedly, in the hypothetical, acquittal was viewed as the most likely outcome but let us assume that here or in respect of some other matter involving neurotechnology the court *did* impose a special verdict. Whereas a mental hospital has been a common destination for those whose responsibility is undermined in such a way that they have received special verdicts thus far, it is worth noting that under the current legislative framework the court can impose "other orders that the court thinks appropriate".[62] Perhaps such orders may require involvement from engineers and programmers and perhaps even cybersecurity professionals.

Maybe one day a superior court will resolve some of these issues but given that the existing legal sources do not easily address questions relating to neurotechnology, and the possible future significance of forms of cyborgisation as humans merge with AI, it might be preferable that law reform engagement begin, and at some point, legislative action be initiated.

In the distant past the law has been concerned with threats to agency from witches who were said to be facilitating demonic possession.[63] Responsible agency might one day need to be protected again but from agents employing means other than witchcraft (i.e. hackers) and the courts might even need to order that measures are taken to ensure that agency receives the protection or restoration it needs, maybe even by way of special verdicts.

Whilst it is clear that a neurotechnological trend is starting to emerge in society, it is unclear how this trend will play out or precisely how the criminal law will be challenged. This chapter has suggested that a consideration of the criminal responsibility of a person with a brain implant used to treat a neurological condition who experiences a device failure causing them to hallucinate and kill someone might present some novel issues for the courts. It is not entirely clear whether the *M'Naghten* test of insanity or its statutory implementation in New South Wales exclude the neurotechnological failure.

Given that that neurotechnology is likely to raise issues for many areas of law, the criminal responsibility questions outlined here could form part of a broader inquiry into the implications of neurotechnology for criminal law more generally, and indeed for other areas of law.

Acknowledgements

I am very grateful to Andrew Dyer, Kramer Thompson, Christopher Ryan, Barri Phatarfod, and Thomas Crofts for their useful comments and to Kevin Zou for research support.

Notes

1. *R v M'Naghten* (1843) 8 ER 718.
2. New South Wales, *Parliamentary Debates*, Legislative Assembly, 3 June 2020, 2350 (Mark Speakman, Attorney-General); Mental Health and Cognitive Impairment Forensic Provisions Bill 2020 (NSW).
3. A Loughnan, "Same but different? Assessing reforms to mental incapacity in criminal law", *Current Issues in Criminal Justice*, vol. 35, no. 1 (2023), p.162.
4. A McCay, "Neurotechnology, law and the legal profession", *Law Society of England and Wales* (2022).
5. A McCay, "Black Mirror lawyering", *Law Society Journal* (2023), available at: https://lsj.com.au/articles/black-mirror-lawyering/.
6. Forward thinking can be found the recent report produced by the Regulatory Horizons Council: Regulatory Horizons Council, "Neurotechnology Regulation" (2022), available at: https://assets.publishing.service.gov.uk/media/63e9e8f88fa8f5050ee37d10/rhc-neurotechnology-regulation.pdf.
7. See A McCay, "Neurotechnology and human rights: developments overseas and the challenge for Australia", *Australian Journal of Human Rights*, vol. 29, no.1 (2023), p.160.
8. S Soekadar et al, "On The Verge of the Hybrid Mind", *Morals & Machines*, vol. 1, no. 1, p.30.
9. S Nishimoto et al, "Reconstructing Visual Experiences from Brain Activity Evoked by Natural Movies", *Current Biology*, vol. 21, no. 19 (2011), p.1641.
10. K Nahas, "AI re-creates what people see by reading their brain scans", *Science* (2023), available at: www.science.org/content/article/ai-re-creates-what-people-see-reading-their-brain-scans.
11. A Hilf, "Mind and Machine: Flying Drones with your Brain", *University of South Florida Magazine* (2018), available at: www.usf.edu/magazine/2018-winter/university/brain-powered-drones.aspx.
12. C Tonkin, "Mind-reading technology raises huge privacy concerns", *Australian Computer Society: Information Age* (2023), available at: https://ia.acs.org.au/article/2023/mind-reading-technology-raises-huge-privacy-concerns.html; McCay, "Neurotechnology, law and the legal profession", pp.11–12.
13. C Rosso, "Breakthrough Interface Enables AI ChatGPT Access Using Thoughts", *Psychology Today* (2023), available at: www.psychologytoday.com/us/blog/the-future-brain/202312/breakthrough-interface-enables-ai-chatgpt-access-using-thoughts.
14. C Spears and A Heston, "Deep Brain Simulators (DBS)", *Parkinson's Foundation*, available at: www.parkinson.org/living-with-parkinsons/treatment/surgical-treatment-options/deep-brain-stimulation.
15. "Deep Brain Stimulation for Obsessive-Compulsive Disorder", *Mount Sinai*, available at: www.mountsinai.org/care/psychiatry/services/ocd-tics/dbs.
16. Neuropace, "Main Page: There's a smarter way to treat epilepsy" *Neuropace*, available at: www.neuropace.com/.
17. "FDA grants approval for brain stimulation technology for depression", *Med-Tech* (2022), available at: www.med-technews.com/news/Medtech-Regulatory-News/fda-grants-approval-for-brain-stimulation-technology/.
18. A Capoot, "Brain implant startup backed by Bezos and Gates is testing mind-controlled computing on humans", *CNBC* (2023), available at: www.cnbc.com/2023/02/18/synchron-backed-by-bezos-and-gates-tests-brain-computer-interface.html.
19. C McConnell, "Neurovalens receives FDA clearance for medical device to treat insomnia", *Neurovalens Blog* (2023), https://neurovalens.com/blogs/news/neurovalens-receives-fda-clearance-for-medical-device-to-treat-insomnia.

20 Capoot, "Brain implant startup"; "Elon Musk's Neuralink to start human trial of brain implant for paralysis patients" (2023), available at: www.abc.net.au/news/2023-09-21/musk-neuralink-chip-human-trial-of-brain-implant-paralysis/102882466; N Statt, "Facebook acquires neural interface startup CTRL-Labs for its mind-reading wristband", *The Verge* (2019), available at: www.theverge.com/2019/9/23/20881032/facebook-ctrl-labs-acquisition-neural-interface-armband-ar-vr-deal.
21 Neuropace, "Main Page".
22 I Straw, C Ashworth, & N Radford, "When brain devices go wrong: a patient with a malfunctioning deep brain stimulator (DBS) presents to the emergency department", *BMJ Case Reports*, vol. 15, no. 12 (2022), e252305, available at: https://casereports.bmj.com/content/15/12/e252305.
23 Straw et al, "When brain devices go wrong".
24 L Pycroft et al, "Brainjacking: Implant Security Issues in Invasive Neuromodulation", *World Neurosurgery*, vol. 92 (2016), p.454.
25 D Greenbaum (ed), *Cyberbiosecurity: A New Field to Deal with Emerging Threats* (Springer Nature: Switzerland, 2023); N Liv & D Greenbaum, "Cyberneurosecurity" in V Dubljević & A Coin (eds), *Policy, Identity, and Neurotechnology: The Neuroethics of Brain-Computer Interfaces* (Springer Nature: Switzerland, 2023).
26 NRB Martins et al, "Human Brain/Cloud Interface", *Frontiers in Neuroscience*, vol. 13, no. 112 (2019), available at: www.frontiersin.org/articles/10.3389/fnins.2019.00112/full.
27 Martins et al, "Human Brain/Cloud Interface", p.18.
28 A McCay, "What does The Matrix have to do with human rights?", *LSJ Online* (2022), available at: https://lsj.com.au/articles/what-does-the-matrix-have-to-do-with-human-rights/.
29 J Dare, "Rafael Yuste: 'Let's act before it's too late'", *UNESCO Courier* (2022), available at: https://courier.unesco.org/en/articles/rafael-yuste-lets-act-its-too-late.
30 See "Main Page: New Human Rights for the Age of Neurotechnology", *The Neurorights Foundation*, available at: https://neurorightsfoundation.org/.
31 See UNESCO, University of Milan-Bicocca, and State University of New York, *The Risks and Challenges of Neurotechnologies for Human Rights* (UNESCO: Paris, Milan and New York, 2023); S O'Sullivan et al, *Neurotechnologies and Human Rights Framework: Do we need Rights?* (CDBIO: Strasbourg, 2022); Advisory Committee, "Call for inputs for the study of the Human Rights Council Advisory Committee on neurotechnology and human rights (HRC resolution 51/3)" *UNHR* (2023), available at: www.ohchr.org/en/calls-for-input/2023/call-inputs-study-human-rights-council-advisory-committee-neurotechnology-and.
32 See S Ligthart et al, "Minding Rights: Mapping Ethical and Legal Foundations of 'Neurorights'", *Cambridge Quarterly of Healthcare Ethics*, vol. 32, no. 4 (2023), p.461; McCay, "Neurotechnology and human rights".
33 A McCay, "Neurorights: the Chilean constitutional change" *AI & Society* (2022), available at: https://link.springer.com/article/10.1007/s00146-022-01396-0.
34 Constitución Política de la República de Chile [C.P.] art. 19; A McCay, "Neurotechnology and human rights in Chile: the Australian implications", *LSJ Online* (2023), available at: https://lsj.com.au/articles/neurotechnology-and-human-rights-in-chile-the-australian-implications/.
35 McCay, "Neurotechnology and human rights in Chile".
36 A Asher-Schapiro & D Baptista, "Hands off my brainwaves: Latin America in race for 'neurorights'" *Reuters* (2023), available at: www.reuters.com/article/tech-privacy-brainwaves-idUSL8N3AH6D6/.
37 See Information Commissioner's Office, *ICO tech futures: neurotechnology* (ICO: Cheshire, 2023); Australian Human Rights Commission, *Protecting Cognition: Human Rights and Neurotechnology* (AHRC: Sydney, 2023).
38 See C Lernestedt & M Matravers (eds), *The Criminal Law's Person* (Hart Publishing: Oxford, 2022).
39 See D Hodgson, "Guilty mind or guilty brain? Criminal responsibility in the age of neuroscience", *Australian Law Journal*, vol. 74, no. 10 (2000), p.661; SJ Morse, "Neuroscience and Law: Conceptual and Practical Issues" in A D'Aloia and MC Errigo (eds), *Neuroscience and Law: Complicated Crossings and New Perspectives* (Springer Nature: Switzerland 2020).

40 For a broader philosophical consideration of neurotechnology that includes ethical and some legal issues, see W Glannon, *Neural Prosthetics Neuroscientific and Philosophical Aspects of Changing the Brain* (Oxford University Press: Oxford, 2021).

41 A McCay, "Neurobionic Revenge Porn and the Criminal Law: Brain–Computer Interfaces and Intimate Image Abuse" in NA Vincent, T Nadelhoffer, & A McCay (eds), *Neurointerventions and the Law: Regulating Human Mental Capacity* (Oxford University Press: Oxford, 2020) cf. K Thompson, "Committing Crimes with BCIs: How Brain-Computer Interface Users can Satisfy Actus Reus and be Criminally Responsible", *Neuroetthics*, vol. 14 (2021), p.311 for a response. See also J Keiler, "Actus Reus", *Elgar Encyclopedia of Crime and Criminal Justice* (Edward Elgar Publishing: Cheltenham, 2024).

42 F Gilbert & S Dodds, "Is There Anything Wrong With Using AI Implantable Brain Devices to Prevent Convicted Offenders from Reoffending?" in NA Vincent et al (eds), *Neurointerventions and the Law*.

43 Wotton + Kearney, Submission No 226 to Parliamentary Joint Committee on Human Rights, *Inquiry into Australia's Human Rights Framework* (21 July 2023), p.4, para 20.

44 S Ligthart et al, "Closed-Loop Brain Devices in Offender Rehabilitation: Autonomy, Human Rights, and Accountability", *Cambridge Quarterly of Healthcare Ethics*, vol. 30, no. 4 (2021), p.669.

45 As the focus is on the insanity defence and one instance of a statutory successor to it, I will not consider any possible liability of the hacker, for example perhaps under the doctrine of innocent agency. For a discussion of possible new forms of criminalisation in response to the possibility of hacking of neural devices, see JC Bublitz & R Merkel, "Crimes Against Minds: On Mental Manipulations, Harms and a Human Right to Mental Self-Determination", *Criminal Law and Philosophy*, vol. 8 (2014), p.51.

46 For a discussion of prior fault in criminal law, see AE Goldberg et al, "Prior-Fault Blame in England and Wales, Germany and the Netherlands", *Journal of International and Comparative Law*, vol. 8, no. 1 (2021), p.53.

47 H Tahir, F Ayyaz, & U Ekwegh, "Visual and Auditory Hallucinations: An Uncommon Side Effect of Levetiracetam in an Elderly Patient" *Cureus*, vol. 14, no. 10, e30668 available at: www.cureus.com/articles/117719-visual-and-auditory-hallucinations-an-uncommon-side-effect-of-levetiracetam-in-an-elderly-patient#!/authors.

48 See *R v Damic* (1982) 2 NSWLR 750; New South Wales Law Reform Commission, "People with cognitive and mental health impairments in the criminal justice system: Criminal responsibility and consequences" *NSWLRC Report*, No. 138 (2013) at pp.71–72.

49 For the current position, see Mental Health and Cognitive Impairment Forensic Provisions Act 2020 (NSW), s 33.

50 As my focus is on insanity and MHI/CI, I will not consider substantial impairment as a partial defence to murder here but it is worth noting that some of the issues raised in relation to the full defence will also be relevant to that partial defence.

51 *R v M'Naghten* (1843) 8 ER 718.

52 Thomson, "Committing Crimes with BCIs", p.319.

53 Thomson, "Committing Crimes with BCIs", p.315.

54 (1985) 42 SASR 266, 274; approved in *R v Falconer* (1990) 171 CLR 30, 54 (Mason CJ, Brennan and McHugh JJ) (although their Honours added that, if the disorder is temporary it must not be prone to recur).

55 *R v Radford* (1985) 42 SASR 266, 274.

56 *Bratty v Attorney-General for Northern Ireland* [1963] AC 386.

57 As foreshadowed earlier, this issue has come up in the discussion of *actus reus*.

58 See Mental Health and Cognitive Impairment Forensic Provisions Act 2020 (NSW), s 4.

59 Mental Health and Cognitive Impairment Forensic Provisions Act 2020 (NSW), s 5.

60 Mark Speakman, *Parliamentary Debates*.

61 *R v DB* [2022] NSWCCA 87.

62 Mental Health and Cognitive Impairment Forensic Provisions Act 2020 (NSW), s 33(1)(d).

63 BP Levack, "Possession, Witchcraft, and the Law in Jacobean England", *Washington and Lee Law Review*, vol. 52, no. 5 (1996), p.1613.

References

Legislation

Constitución Política de la República de Chile [C.P.].
Mental Health and Cognitive Impairment Forensic Provisions Act 2020 (NSW).

Cases

Bratty v Attorney-General for Northern Ireland (1963) AC 386.
R v Damic (1982) 2 NSWLR 750.
R v DB [2022] NSWCCA 87.
R v Falconer (1990) 171 CLR 30.
R v M'Naghten (1843) 8 ER 718.
R v Radford (1985) 42 SASR 266.

Books and book chapters

Gilbert F & Dodds S, "Is There Anything Wrong with Using AI Implantable Brain Devices to Prevent Convicted Offenders from Reoffending?", in Vincent NA, Nadelhoffer T,& McCay A (eds), *Neurointerventions and the Law: Regulating Human Mental Capacity* (Oxford University Press: Oxford, 2020).
Glannon W, *Neural Prosthetics Neuroscientific and Philosophical Aspects of Changing the Brain* (Oxford University Press: Oxford, 2021).
Greenbaum D (ed), *Cyberbiosecurity: A New Field to Deal with Emerging Threats* (Springer: New York, 2023).
Keiler J, "Actus Reus", in Caeiro P, Gless S, Mitsilegas V, Costa MJ, De Snaiger J, & Theodorakakou G, *Elgar Encyclopedia of Crime and Criminal Justice* (Edward Elgar: Cheltenham, 2024).
Lernestedt C & Matravers M (eds), *The Criminal Law's Person* (Bloomsbury Publishing: Oxford, 2022).
Liv N & Greenbaum D, "Cyberneurosecurity", in Dubljević V & Coin A (eds), *Policy, Identity, and Neurotechnology: The Neuroethics of Brain–Computer Interfaces* (Springer: New York, 2023).
McCay M, "Neurobionic Revenge Porn and the Criminal Law: Brain–Computer Interfaces and Intimate Image Abuse", in Vincent NA, Nadelhoffer T, & McCay A (eds), *Neurointerventions and the Law: Regulating Human Mental Capacity* (Oxford University Press: Oxford, 2020).
Morse SJ, "Neuroscience and Law: Conceptual and Practical Issues" in D'Aloia A & Errigo MC (eds), *Neuroscience and Law: Complicated Crossings and New Perspectives* (Springer: New York, 2020).

Journal articles

Bublitz JC & Merkel R, "Crimes Against Minds: On Mental Manipulations, Harms and a Human Right to Mental Self-Determination", *Criminal Law and Philosophy*, vol. 8 (2014), pp.51–77.
Goldberg AE, Child J, Crombag H, & Roef D, "Prior-Fault Blame in England and Wales, Germany and the Netherlands", *Journal of International and Comparative Law*, vol. 8, no. 1 (2021), pp.53–86.
Hodgson D, "Guilty Mind or Guilty Brain? Criminal Responsibility in the Age of Neuroscience", *Australian Law Journal*, vol. 74, no. 10 (2000), pp.661–680.
Levack BP, "Possession, Witchcraft, and the Law in Jacobean England", *Washington and Lee Law Review*, vol. 52, no. 5 (1996), pp.1613–1640.
Ligthart S, Ienca M, Meynen G, Molnar-Gabor F, Andorno R, Bublitz C, Catley P, Claydon L, Douglas T, Farahany N, Fins JJ, Goering S, Haselager P, Jotterand F, Lavazza A, McCay A, Wajnerman Paz A, Rainey S, Ryberg J, & Kellmeyer P, "Minding Rights: Mapping Ethical and Legal Foundations of 'Neurorights'", *Cambridge Quarterly of Healthcare Ethics*, vol. 32, no. 4 (2023), pp.461–481.
Ligthart S, Kooijmans T, Douglas T, & Meynen G, "Closed-Loop Brain Devices in Offender Rehabilitation: Autonomy, Human Rights, and Accountability", *Cambridge Quarterly of Healthcare Ethics*, vol. 30, no. 4 (2021), pp.669–680.

Loughnan A, "Same but Different? Assessing Reforms to Mental Incapacity in Criminal Law", *Current Issues in Criminal Justice*, vol. 35, no. 1 (2023), pp.162–179.

Martins NRB, Angelica A, Chakravarthy K, Svidinenko Y, Boehm FJ, Opris I, Lebedev MA, Swan M, Garan SA, Rosenfeld JV, Hogg T, & Freitas Jr RA, "Human Brain/Cloud Interface", *Frontiers in Neuroscience*, vol. 13, no. 112 (2019), available at: www.frontiersin.org/articles/10.3389/fnins.2019.00112/full

McCay A, "Neurorights: The Chilean Constitutional Change", *AI & Society* (2022), available at: https://doi.org/10.1007/s00146-022-01396-0

McCay A, "What Does the Matrix Have to Do with Human Rights?", *LSJ Online* (22 March 2022), available at: https://lsj.com.au/articles/what-does-the-matrix-have-to-do-with-human-rights/

McCay A, "Black Mirror Lawyering", *Law Society Journal* (24 July 2023), available at: https://lsj.com.au/articles/black-mirror-lawyering/

McCay A, "Neurotechnology and Human Rights in Chile: The Australian Implications", *LSJ Online* (20 September 2023), available at: https://lsj.com.au/articles/neurotechnology-and-human-rights-in-chile-the-australian-implications/

McCay A, "Neurotechnology and Human Rights: Developments Overseas and the Challenge for Australia", *Australian Journal of Human Rights*, vol. 29, no. 1 (2023), pp.160–166.

Nishimoto S, Vu AT, Naselaris T, Benjamini Y, Yu B, Gallant JL et al, "Reconstructing Visual Experiences from Brain Activity Evoked by Natural Movies", *Current Biology*, vol. 21, no. 19 (2011), pp.1641–1646.

Pycroft L, Boccard SG, Owen SLF, Stein JF, Fitzgerald JJ, Green AL, & Aziz TZ, "Brainjacking: Implant Security Issues in Invasive Neuromodulation", *World Neurosurgery*, vol. 92 (2016), pp.454–462.

Soekadar S, Chandler J, Ienca M, & Bublitz C, "On the Verge of the Hybrid Mind", *Morals & Machines*, vol. 1, no. 1 (2021), pp.30–43.

Tahir H, Ayyaz F, & Ekwegh U, "Visual and Auditory Hallucinations: An Uncommon Side Effect of Levetiracetam in an Elderly Patient", *Cureus*, vol. 14, no. 10 (2022), e30668, available at: www.cureus.com/articles/117719-visual-and-auditory-hallucinations-an-uncommon-side-effect-of-levetiracetam-in-an-elderly-patient#!/authors

Thomson K, "Committing Crimes with BCIs: How Brain–Computer Interface Users Can Satisfy Actus Reus and Be Criminally Responsible", *Neuroethics*, vol. 14 (2021), pp.311–322.

Reports and websites

Advisory Committee, "Call for Inputs for the Study of the Human Rights Council Advisory Committee on Neurotechnology and Human Rights (HRC Resolution 51/3)", *UNHR* (2023), available at: www.ohchr.org/en/calls-for-input/2023/call-inputs-study-human-rights-council-advisory-committee-neurotechnology-and

Asher-Schapiro A & Baptista D, "Hands Off My Brainwaves: Latin America in Race for 'Neurorights'", *Reuters* (12 September 2023), available at: www.reuters.com/article/tech-privacy-brainwaves-idUSL8N3AH6D6/

Australian Human Rights Commission, *Protecting Cognition: Human Rights and Neurotechnology* (AHRC 2023).

Capoot A, "Brain Implant Startup Backed by Bezos and Gates is Testing Mind-Controlled Computing on Humans", *CNBC* (18 February 2023), available at: www.cnbc.com/2023/02/18/synchron-backed-by-bezos-and-gates-tests-brain-computer-interface.html

Dare J, "Rafael Yuste: 'Let's Act Before It's Too Late'", *UNESCO Courier* (3 February 2022), available at: https://courier.unesco.org/en/articles/rafael-yuste-lets-act-its-too-late

"Deep Brain Stimulation for Obsessive-Compulsive Disorder", *Mount Sinai*, available at: www.mountsinai.org/care/psychiatry/services/ocd-tics/dbs

"Elon Musk's Neuralink to Start Human Trial of Brain Implant for Paralysis Patients", *ABC* (20 September 2023), available at: www.abc.net.au/news/2023-09-21/musk-neuralink-chip-human-trial-of-brain-implant-paralysis/102882466

"FDA Grants Approval for Brain Stimulation Technology for Depression", *Med-Tech* (13 September 2022), available at: www.med-technews.com/news/Medtech-Regulatory-News/fda-grants-approval-for-brain-stimulation-technology/

Hilf A, "Mind and Machine: Flying Drones with Your Brain", *University of South Florida Magazine* (2018), available at: www.usf.edu/magazine/2018-winter/university/brain-powered-drones.aspx

Information Commissioner's Office, *ICO Tech Futures: Neurotechnology* (ICO 2023).

"Main Page: New Human Rights for the Age of Neurotechnology", *The Neurorights Foundation*, available at: https://neurorightsfoundation.org/

"Main Page: There's a Smarter Way to Treat Epilepsy", *Neuropace*, available at: www.neuropace.com/

McCay A, "Neurotechnology, Law and the Legal Profession", *Law Society of England and Wales* (2022).

McConnell C, "Neurovalens Receives FDA Clearance for Medical Device to Treat Insomnia", *Neurovalens* (31 October 2023), available at: https://neurovalens.com/blogs/news/neurovalens-receives-fda-clearance-for-medical-device-to-treat-insomnia

Nahas K, "AI Re-Creates What People See by Reading Their Brain Scans", *Science* (7 March 2023), available at: www.science.org/content/article/ai-re-creates-what-people-see-reading-their-brain-scans

New South Wales, *Parliamentary Debates*, Legislative Assembly (3 June 2020, p. 2350) (Mark Speakman, Attorney-General).

New South Wales Law Reform Commission, *People with Cognitive and Mental Health Impairments in the Criminal Justice System: Criminal Responsibility and Consequences* (Report No. 138, May 2013).

O'Sullivan S, Chneiweiss H, Pierucci A, & Rommelfanger KS, *Neurotechnologies and Human Rights Framework: Do We Need Rights?* (CDBIO 2022).

Regulatory Horizons Council, *Neurotechnology Regulation* (November 2022).

Rosso C, "Breakthrough Interface Enables AI ChatGPT Access Using Thoughts", *Psychology Today* (7 December 2023), available at: www.psychologytoday.com/us/blog/the-future-brain/202312/breakthrough-interface-enables-ai-chatgpt-access-using-thoughts

Spears C & Heston A, "Deep Brain Simulators (DBS)", *Parkinson's Foundation*, available at: www.parkinson.org/living-with-parkinsons/treatment/surgical-treatment-options/deep-brain-stimulation

Statt N, "Facebook Acquires Neural Interface Startup CTRL-Labs for Its Mind-Reading Wristband", *The Verge* (24 September 2019), available at: www.theverge.com/2019/9/23/20881032/facebook-ctrl-labs-acquisition-neural-interface-armband-ar-vr-deal

Straw I, Ashworth C, & Radford N, "When Brain Devices Go Wrong: A Patient with a Malfunctioning Deep Brain Stimulator (DBS) Presents to the Emergency Department", *BMJ Case Reports*, vol. 15, no. 12 (2022), e252305, available at: https://casereports.bmj.com/content/15/12/e252305

Tonkin C, "Mind-Reading Technology Raises Huge Privacy Concerns", *Australian Computer Society: Information Age* (13 June 2023), available at: https://ia.acs.org.au/article/2023/mind-reading-technology-raises-huge-privacy-concerns.html

UNESCO, University of Milan-Bicocca, & State University of New York, *The Risks and Challenges of Neurotechnologies for Human Rights* (UNESCO 2023).

Wotton + Kearney, Submission No. 226 to Parliamentary Joint Committee on Human Rights, *Inquiry into Australia's Human Rights Framework* (21 July 2023).

28
CRIMINAL CAPACITY AND THE AGE OF CRIMINAL RESPONSIBILITY

Dissecting the Assumptions Underlying a Single Chronological Age

Claire McDiarmid

Introduction

It has been accepted since historical times[1] that criminal responsibility should not be attributed to children. This principle is articulated in the setting of the age of criminal responsibility ("ACR") which draws a bright line, at a specified age, below which no child can be held to be criminally responsible.[2] This chapter will examine the way in which the ACR is drawn in law and some of the underlying assumptions which the ACR brings together. The chapter will firstly consider possible rationales, focussing on the need for anyone – adult or child – to have criminal capacity before they can be convicted.[3] It will examine the complexity of this concept and the bundle of understandings which it comprises. Constraints on the child's ability to acquire and/or act upon such understandings which have been illuminated by developmental psychology and by advances in functional magnetic resonance imaging (fMRI) scanning in neuroscience[4] will be discussed, alongside the child's lived experience. The chapter will then consider more general issues arising from the use of a single chronological age to represent the point in the lifespan at which every child is held to have sufficient understanding and competences to constitute criminal capacity. Mechanisms developed for mitigating the potential *un*fairness of this single age, both to those to whom children have caused harm and to child-accused themselves, will be canvassed. Children's rights will be considered throughout. Overall, the chapter seeks to lay bare the complexity inherent in imputing criminal responsibility to children and to consider issues arising in using an age for this purpose. It concludes that an ACR is essential but not sufficient in this context.

The purpose and function of an ACR

An ACR operates to exclude children aged below it from all aspects of the criminal process. In other words – and categorically – "a child below this age cannot be dealt with in criminal proceedings".[5] The state may still intervene on other grounds in the life of a child aged below the ACR who causes harm. It is only *criminal* interventions which are precluded. Thus, it is not the case that *nothing* can happen where a child engages in behaviour which, but for their age, would constitute a criminal offence.

The ACR is a (possibly deceptively) simply stated legal concept. For example, "[i]t shall be conclusively presumed that no child under the age of ten years can be guilty of any offence".[6] Or, "[a] child under the age of 12 years cannot commit an offence".[7] This simplicity belies the complexity of the factors surrounding the ACR. The Age of Criminal Responsibility (Scotland) Act 2019, for instance, which deals only with the ACR, runs to 85 sections.

In Australia[8] and South Africa,[9] the ACR is supplemented by the *doli incapax* presumption that a child over the ACR but under an upper age, usually 14, also lacks criminal capacity. In other places, the possibility of a defence to recognise developmental immaturity has been opened to discussion.[10] Where it applies, *doli incapax* is a key element of the legal provision on the age of children who offend. Rather than being an absolute, as the ACR should be, *doli incapax* is expressed as a presumption which the prosecution must lead evidence to rebut. While its English common law formulation (which was repealed by the Crime and Disorder Act 1998, s 34) was expressed in terms of knowing that the wrongful act was seriously wrong rather than merely naughty,[11] when set out in legislation, it usually makes overt reference to a lack of capacity.[12] The importance of this link between criminal capacity and the child's criminal responsibility will now be considered.

The importance of criminal capacity

It is not universally accepted that there is a necessary link between the ACR and criminal capacity. In 2002, the Scottish Law Commission argued that:

> "for a variety of reasons there is no need to retain the rule on criminal capacity. Instead, the age of criminal responsibility is better conceptualised as relating to immunity from prosecution".[13]

Of course, it is a corollary of having an ACR that those below it are immune from prosecution, but, without any link to capacity, its justification is lost.[14] A state could as easily decide to make any category of people – firefighters or cyclists say – immune. The link to capacity helps to explain *why* children are to be treated in this way. Having a rationale is important given the frequent politicisation of crime committed by the young.[15]

International treaty obligations also underline the link between the absence of capacity and the ACR.[16] Since 1985, the United Nations Standard Minimum Rules for the Administration of Juvenile Justice ("the Beijing Rules") have explicitly required recognition of the child's developing maturity in setting an age of criminal responsibility. Rule 4.1 states:

> "In those legal systems recognizing the concept of the age of criminal responsibility for juveniles, the beginning of that age shall not be fixed at too low an age level, bearing in mind the facts of emotional, mental and intellectual maturity".

This principle was reiterated, in 1989, by the United Nations Convention on the Rights of the Child ("CRC"). Art. 40(3)(a) requires States Parties to "seek to promote ... [t]he establishment of a minimum age below which children shall be presumed not to have the capacity to infringe the penal law".

Though the obligation imposed is only to "seek to promote", the Committee on the Rights of the Child, in its General Comment 24,[17] has stated that it "Under article 40(3) of the Convention, States parties are *required* to establish a minimum age of criminal responsibility".[18] 14 is identified as the lowest acceptable age.[19] General Comments have been said to "constitute an authoritative interpretation as to what is expected of States parties as they implement the obligations contained in the CRC".[20] Overall, then, there is an obligation to link the ACR with capacity and to set it at 14 or above. It is necessary now to look at the way in which the criminal law does this.

Criminal responsibility in children

To be held to be criminally responsible for a specified offence, the Crown must be able to prove beyond reasonable doubt that the defendant carried out proscribed behaviour (*actus reus*) with the specified mental attitude towards it (*mens rea*).[21] In addition, all defendants must have criminal capacity.[22] According to Pillay and Willows:[23]

> "[c]apacity is usually understood to have a cognitive and a conative component which translates to the need to prove: (i) the presence of an understanding of wrongfulness; and (ii) an ability to control one's behaviour in accordance with such an understanding".

In more legal terms, it can be defined as the understanding of the crime in its context and its consequences as well as having a fair opportunity *not* to commit the crime.[24] It is therefore taken here to be of the essence of the ACR that it should be set at an age at which, at the very least, the likelihood is that all those of that age (and, therefore, above it) can confidently be considered to possess criminal capacity. Otherwise, recognition of the need for such capacity is too weak. As will now be discussed, criminal capacity is a complex concept.

The complexity of criminal capacity

Attaining the ACR, or being deemed by the state to be criminally responsible, is one of a number of indicators of maturity – or social adulthood – which is embodied in law.[25] As will be discussed subsequently, there is an unavoidable element of arbitrariness in the age selected. There is debate as to the level of complexity of the understandings required to constitute criminal capacity. For example, in his dissenting judgment in the US Supreme Court case of *Roper v Simmons*,[26] which abolished the death penalty in all cases where the defendant was aged under 18 at the time of committing the offence, Scalia J stated:

> "As we explained in *Stanford*, 492 U.S., at 374, it is 'absurd to think that one must be mature enough to drive carefully, to drink responsibly, or to vote intelligently, in order to be mature enough to understand that murdering another human being is profoundly wrong, and to conform one's conduct to that most minimal of all civilized standards.' Serving on a jury or entering into marriage also involve decisions far more sophisticated than the simple decision not to take another's life".

These remarks suggest that criminal responsibility is a straightforward, easily comprehensible, concept. This view is underlain by the idea that children ought to take criminal responsibility for their wrongful behaviour, as encapsulated in the mantra "Adult Crime; Adult

Time".[27] This approach, however, fails to analyse the actual understandings required in these instances. The decision to marry is complex because it has lifelong consequences extending beyond the immediate decision to participate in a wedding ceremony.[28] Taking on criminal responsibility also has consequences beyond the commission of the relevant *actus reus* – for example potential loss of liberty and the stigma of conviction.

In addition, Scalia's comment is directed towards crimes of homicide, suggesting that these in particular involve a "simple decision". Determinations about criminal capacity should not, however, differ by reference to the crime committed. Some jurisdictions do lower the ACR for more serious offences such as murder and manslaughter,[29] however General Comment 24 states:

"[s]uch practices are usually created to respond to public pressure and are not based on a rational understanding of children's development. The Committee strongly recommends that States parties abolish such approaches and set one standardized age below which children cannot be held responsible in criminal law, without exception".[30]

Accordingly, it is necessary to examine the concept of criminal capacity.

The component elements of criminal capacity in children

Developmental psychology as a foundation

As noted above, criminal capacity requires both understanding of the criminal act and its consequences *and* a fair opportunity not to commit the offence in the first place. The youngest children (newborns) lack *all* the qualities, skills, and understandings on which capacity rests. From birth onward, children are constantly developing physically, personally, socially, cognitively,[31] mentally, morally, and emotionally. Thus, developmental psychology offers some theoretical foundation for the analysis of capacity. In this regard, Jean Piaget's " 'stage theory' … is prevalent"[32] and will be considered here, alongside his 1932 work[33] on moral development.[34]

Briefly, in relation to cognitive development – the development of thinking – Piaget found that, from infancy, children go through constant processes of assimilation and accommodation as they adapt to novel discoveries.[35] Assimilation involves applying existing understandings into "schemes" to make sense of the new – fitting these new things into that existing knowledge. Accommodation occurs when existing schemes need to be modified to allow for innovations.[36] These come together in "equilibration", the process of seeking to balance understandings of the world.[37]

Piaget then theorised that children develop intellectually through four distinct stages: the sensorimotor stage (from birth to two years); the pre-operational stage (from two to seven years); the concrete operations stage (from seven to eleven or twelve years); and the formal operations stage which starts around age 12. It is only during the last two of these stages that children start to think abstractly and to learn how to reason,[38] both of which are necessary for criminal capacity.

In relation specifically to moral development, Piaget argued that young children understand that they are not to do certain things simply because that is what they are told (i.e. "adult rules are regarded as invariant"),[39] before moving on to an understanding of why certain behaviours are proscribed and beginning to develop their own moral code.[40]

This theoretical approach is significant because it provides a framework within which to start to apply age to the acquisition of capacity.

Difference between right and wrong

The first, and fundamental, element of criminal capacity is that the child-accused must know that the act is wrong – they must have the ability to distinguish between right and wrong. This issue is more nuanced than it may first seem.[41] The requisite understanding will have a moral dimension[42] – that the act is something which should not be done in the society in which the child lives because it is unacceptable. The child must then also know that it is legally wrong, in terms of being contrary to the criminal law.[43] Some recognition of degrees of wrongdoing would also be helpful – that hitting someone with a brick is more seriously wrong than failing to return a borrowed pencil say.

With regard to the moral dimension, the child, on Piaget's model, should have made some move from merely acting on the instructions of others without much independent processing, to some level of moral understanding of their own. Otherwise, without a specific prohibition by an authority figure of the exact behaviour involved in the offence, it is unfair to assume that the child knew it was wrong.[44]

Rationality and causation

Next, it is part of having the requisite understanding of the conduct that the child-defendant is able to offer reasons for the action taken or, in other words, to rationalise it.[45] On Piaget's model, this ability only begins in his final stage of intellectual development, which starts around the age of 12 and is not complete until the mid-teens.

Especially in result crimes, such as homicide offences, children will also require some understanding of causation – that an act may have consequences beyond its initial application. Pillay and Willows note that children may lack "the ability to foresee the possible consequences of [their] actions".[46] Where this is the position, the child-defendant lacks this, arguably essential, element of criminal capacity.[47]

Understanding of criminality and criminal consequences

A further element of capacity requires that the child understands that the act constitutes a criminal offence. Children are subject to many rules, not all of which also apply to adults.[48] They are, for example, required to attend school, but truancy, in the child, is not necessarily a criminal offence. In a classroom context, controls might be placed on behaviours such as talking at specified times, passing notes round the room, and fighting with other children. Only the last, however, is likely also to amount to a criminal offence. The controls and the actions taken in response to all such proscribed childhood behaviours may be relatively similar. For the fair ascription of criminal responsibility, however, it is submitted that the child must understand the distinction between a criminal offence and any other kind of infraction and know that any specified behaviour constitutes a crime.

As Walker states:

"As a result of his or her intellectual immaturity, a child who is quite capable of appreciating that certain types of conduct are considered wrong in general, abstract terms, might nevertheless be incapable of engaging in the complex, abstract reasoning necessary to enable him or her to apply this generalised knowledge to his or her own conduct, at the time and in the particular circumstances in which he or she engaged in that conduct. The danger inherent in applying a vague, generalised right and wrong test is that, in an instance like this, such a child could well be found criminally responsible. This finding would however, be inconsistent with the fundamental principles of criminal law and contrary to all sense of justice".[49]

In this context, it might also be argued that the child's recognition of the particular quality of criminal behaviour, by comparison with other types of wrongful conduct, should extend, at least at a basic level, to cover its possible specific consequences: for example that the state, through the police, may take instant action to incapacitate someone from further such behaviour by arrest; if pursued through the courts, that a criminal conviction can lead to a sentence up to the severity of deprivation of liberty, and that this sentence may continue to be disclosed as part of vetting certain future roles (e.g. working with children) throughout life.

Beyond this, it can perhaps also be accepted that the child needs at least a basic understanding of the criminal law in relation to the charges brought against them. The law on homicide, for example, is complex and draws a series of gradations of seriousness in most jurisdictions, on which there is considerable academic debate. The issue is not so much whether children understand the specific charge against them – though that is, of course, highly significant – but whether they have the capacity to understand the type of complex information of which the criminal law consists.

Ability to avoid committing the criminal act

The second prong of capacity, beyond understanding the criminal behaviour, requires that the child must be able to avoid committing the offence. Criminal theory has addressed, in relation to adult defendants, the question of irresistible impulses – where, for reasons usually of extreme mental disorder, the defence is that the defendant was simply unable to resist that impulse to commit a crime.[50] In children, the question is more fundamental: whether they have, in the first place, developed the intellectual ability *to* conform their actions to their wishes (here not to break the law) and thus to avoid impulses to do just that. As noted above, Piaget theorised that children's cognition constantly develops through processes of assimilation and accommodation to create schemes which are balanced through equilibration. The key point for the child's criminal capacity is that this process must be sufficiently advanced that they are *able* to bring their cognition to bear in rationalising and controlling their acts. If this is not the case, the impulse will be irresistible for them. The importance of this volitional component is recognised by Crofts.[51]

In addition, as will be discussed below, this area has been much advanced by neuroscientific research, facilitated by fMRI,[52] into the actual, physical development of the brain and the implications of this.

Together, the points set out here, can be taken as an argument for the basic formulation of the content of criminal capacity in children. The list is not presented as exhaustive but as at least minimally necessary. Two further issues which can affect and cut across these basic elements also now require consideration: neuroscientific research on the development of the adolescent brain and the child's lived experience.

Cross-cutting issues

Neuroscience

It is now widely accepted that the brain is not fully developed until a young person is in their early 20s.[53] Some of the areas which develop last have particular ramifications in relation to the fair ascription of criminal responsibility. Kramers-Olen states that:

> "[r]esearch has suggested that impulse control, vulnerability to social influences, as well as appraisals of risk-taking and reward interacted with logical reasoning competencies, which sometimes resulted in adolescents making decisions that were less carefully reasoned than those made by adults".[54]

It is recognised that the prefrontal cortex is among the last areas of the brain to reach full maturation[55] and that it "is responsible for goal-directed behaviour which includes planning and response inhibition".[56] Its lack of development means that adolescents are physically less able than their adult counterparts to counter impulses to act in particular ways, including some criminal behaviours. Thus, in capacity terms, their physical brain configuration may deny them a fair opportunity to avoid committing the offence. This would apply particularly to crimes such as those involving recklessness which are committed without pre-planning. Hot cognition ("making decisions in a heightened emotional state") is affected more than cold cognition ("a more deliberative type of decision-making process in less stressful environments").[57]

Additionally, "myelination" is ongoing throughout adolescence. This process coats nerve fibres in the brain in a fatty white substance – myelin – which insulates them and which significantly improves the way in which signals transmit along neural pathways.[58] This goes hand-in-hand with the process of pruning, primarily of grey matter, which also enhances the efficiency of pathways by getting rid of those which are used less.[59] This also affects impulse control.[60]

Finally, there is research evidence that adolescents are significantly more influenced by their peers than adults, sometimes into risky situations.[61] Neuroscience indicates that:

> "compared to children and adults, adolescents' reward centres were activated more in anticipation of a pleasurable reward … [and that] this heightened sensitivity to rewards is greatest when adolescents are with their peers … and the presence of peers increases adolescent risk-taking behaviour, with no such effect in adults".[62]

Again, this suggests that adolescents are less able to avoid risk-taking which constitutes criminal behaviour, in situations where they are accompanied by peers.

These neuroscientific findings have been accepted and relied upon by the US Supreme Court in making its decision in *Roper v Simmons*[63] and they constitute the basis of the Scottish Sentencing Council's *Sentencing Young People: Sentencing Guideline*[64] prior to which the Council commissioned and published a literature review of the area.[65] Thus, their relevance to legal judgments concerning young people is becoming embedded.

Child's lived experience

The second issue which may apply generally to the child's criminal capacity is their lived experience. Catherine Elliott[66] has argued that children are not in a position to make the perceived choice to commit a criminal offence which capacity (and indeed theories of freewill) imply because their autonomy is constrained by those adults (especially parents) who exercise control in their lives. She says:

> "in looking at criminal responsibility we need to be prepared to take into account the social reality of a child's personal experiences, including bad parenting, poverty and violence, rather than trying artificially to ignore these factors".[67]

Children cannot, for example, easily move house away from criminogenic influences – they live where adults live. Similarly, if criminal activity is the norm in their immediate milieu, they lack the fair opportunity to learn and understand its wrongfulness.

Renee Nicole Souris offers an example in the extreme context of the development of child soldiers after abduction. She notes that: "children's moral development does not stop once they enter armed groups, but … it is constructed in problematic ways".[68] After recounting mechanisms by which the Lord's Resistance Army in Uganda actively sought to break children's wills to promote their loyalty through fear,[69] Souris argues that:

> "[o]rdinary moral perception furnished by emotional development [which child soldiers lack due to the extreme cruelty characterising their formative years] is also [alongside practical reason] required for persons to have this ability [i.e. "the capacity to perceive, for example, that killing innocent people is always wrong"]".[70]

Thus, adverse lived experience may affect both the cognitive understanding and the volitional elements of criminal capacity.

It is clear, then, that criminal capacity involves a number of understandings and skills which it cannot be assumed that a child will automatically possess. In this way, the ACR operates partly to prevent criminal responsibility applying to children when they, as a group, can be regarded as lacking capacity. The next question is at what age it should be set.

What is the appropriate age?

The use of an age in law, whether the ACR or the age at which, for example, a child can own a pet, is definitive. It draws a bright line below which the activity is prohibited, or the responsibility not allocated, and above which the child legally acquires the adult attribute. It is clear that the way in which children mature is much more individualised than such bright age lines would suggest. It is inevitable, then, that the ACR will involve an element of arbitrariness.[71] It is important, nonetheless, to have one, otherwise very young children are potentially liable to prosecution for their misdeeds, which would be unwise given their lack of understanding and development in key areas.[72] How then, is an appropriate age to be determined?

International children's rights obligations offer direction in this respect. General Comment 24 states that: "[s]tates parties are encouraged to take note of recent scientific findings, and to increase their minimum age accordingly, to at least 14 years of age".[73]

The Commentary on Rule 4 of the Beijing Rules provides more general guidance. It states that: "[i]n general, there is a close relationship between the notion of responsibility for delinquent or criminal behaviour and other social rights and responsibilities (such as marital status, civil majority, etc.)".

In fact, in the more than 35 years since the promulgation of this Rule, this has largely remained at the level of an aspiration, certainly in the UK. While the specific ages set vary between Scotland and England and Wales, the age of civil majority and the rights to vote, to join the armed forces, to sit on a jury are all postponed until 16 or 18. Indeed, the age of marriage and civil partnership has recently been raised in England and Wales to 18[74] in order to "end child marriage".[75] ACRs of 10 (England and Wales) and 12 (Scotland) demonstrate no "close relationship" between the acquisition of criminal responsibility and these other, more positive, insignia of adult status and responsibility. This would point to a higher age.

Delmage notes that the last two of Piaget's developmental stages "broadly speaking, cover ages 7–16".[76] The neuroscientific evidence on the physical development of the brain indicates that the "frontal lobes … may not be fully developed until halfway through the third decade of life".[77]

In terms of setting the ACR, then, there are rationales for a number of different ages and, even if one seems stronger than another, the nature of the child's development is so individualised that some children younger than any given ACR will, in fact, have criminal capacity already, and some aged above it will not. Given the importance of capacity identified above, the ACR should be drawn to try to ensure that most of those who are deemed to have criminal capacity by being over the age, do *in fact* have much of the bundle of understandings and control over action which it entails. General Comment 24's insistence on 14 provides the requisite starting point.

Mitigating the ACR's arbitrariness and potential unfairness

The single age required thus trails in its wake some unfairness. This can be mitigated in relation to those who lack full capacity by the use of a *doli incapax* presumption or the provision of a defence of developmental immaturity. While *doli incapax* has been criticised, including in General Comment 24,[78] Crofts argues that it "allows the conviction of children, who are developed enough to be held criminally responsible, while protecting those who are not so developed".[79] This ought to be the key aim of any law augmenting the ACR. An alternative to *doli incapax* would be the creation of a defence of developmental immaturity, whether this is conceptualised as a basis for a plea of diminished responsibility[80] or as a defence in its own right.[81] Where the concern is for those who fall below the ACR but do, in fact, possess criminal capacity escaping criminal liability, one of the aims of General Comment 24 is "[s]etting an appropriate minimum age of criminal responsibility and ensuring the appropriate treatment of children *on either side of that age*".[82] For those younger than the ACR, the key aim is prevention of offending behaviour, but intervention is countenanced provided that it is preceded by "a comprehensive and interdisciplinary assessment of the child's need".[83] Individual legal systems will have their own criteria and ways of intervening. For present purposes, it is sufficient to note that young children who carry out seriously harmful behaviour, while excluded from the *criminal* justice system, are not side-stepped altogether by the state.

Conclusion

The ACR has a lengthy history. This chapter has argued that it is – and should be – strongly linked to the question of the child's criminal capacity. This is a matter both of international law and of fairness. In principle, no one who does not understand their crime in its context and its consequences and/or who has lacked a fair opportunity to avoid committing it, is criminally responsible. Children are a special category because they must develop the competencies required. As far as possible, the ACR should be set such that only a minority of children over it will completely lack capacity. The chapter has also set out the nature and complexity of the bundle of understandings and abilities comprised within capacity. An ACR is essential to avoid the spectre of – at an extreme – the prosecution of toddlers. It is not, however, sufficient and the legal provision for children who commit harmful acts must recognise this and provide the additional protection of a *doli incapax* presumption or a defence of developmental immaturity.

Notes

1 W Blackstone, *Commentaries on the Laws of England* (Clarendon Press: Oxford, 1769), vol. 4, pp.22–24.
2 T Crofts, "Act Now: Raise the Minimum Age of Criminal Responsibility", *Current Issues in Criminal Justice*, vol. 35, no. 1 (2023), p.118.
3 N Lacey, *State Punishment: Political Principles and Community Values* (Routledge: London, 1988), p.63.
4 L Steinberg, "A Social Neuroscience Perspective on Adolescent Risk-Taking", *Developmental Review*, vol. 28, no.1 (2008), p.78 at p.81.
5 Crofts, "Act Now", p.118.
6 Children and Young Persons Act 1933, s 50, as amended.
7 Criminal Procedure (Scotland) Act 1995, s 41, as amended.
8 T Drabsch, "Age of Criminal Responsibility", *NSW Parliamentary Research Service E-brief* (Issue 1 / 2022), available at: www.parliament.nsw.gov.au/researchpapers/Documents/Age%20of%20criminal%20responsibility%20-%20Final.pdf.
9 Child Justice Act 2008, ss. 7(2) and 11.
10 Law Commission, *Murder, Manslaughter and Infanticide* (Law Com No 304, 2006), Part 5.
11 *JM (A Minor) v Runeckles* (1984) 79 *Criminal Appeal Reports* 255.
12 See, for example, Tasmania Criminal Code Act 1924, s. 18(2).
13 Scottish Law Commission, *Report on Age of Criminal Responsibility*. (Scot Law Com No 185, 2002), p.2, para. 1.5.
14 C McDiarmid, "Age of Criminal Responsibility: Raise it or Remove it?", *Juridical Review*, vol. 5 (2001), p.245.
15 N Wake, R Arthur, T Crofts, & S Lambert, "Legislative Approaches to Recognising the Vulnerability of Young People and Preventing their Criminalisation", *Public Law* (Jan 2021), p.145 at pp.153–155.
16 EE Sutherland, "The Age of Reason or the Reasons for an Age: The Age of Criminal Responsibility", *Scots Law Times* (2002), pp.1–5.
17 UN Committee on the Rights of the Child (UNCRC) (2019) "General Comment No 24 on Children's Rights in the Child Justice System", (CRC/C/GC/24, 2019), available at: https://documents.un.org/doc/undoc/gen/g19/275/57/pdf/g1927557.pdf.
18 UNCRC, "General Comment No 24", para 21.
19 UNCRC, "General Comment No 24", para 22.
20 Child Rights International Network, "CRC General Comments" (2013), available at: https://archive.crin.org/en/library/publications/crc-general-comments.html#:~:text=General%20comments%20provide%20interpretation%20and,obligations%20contained%20in%20the%20CRC.
21 NA Vincent, "On the Relevance of Neuroscience to Criminal Responsibility", *Criminal Law and Philosophy*, vol. 4 (2010), p.77 at pp.82–83.
22 S Walker, "The Requirements for Criminal Capacity in s 11(1) of the New Child Justice Act, 2008: A Step in the Wrong Direction?", *South African Journal of Criminal Justice*, vol. 24, no. 1 (2011), p.33 at p.36.

23 AL Pillay & C Willows, "Assessing the Criminal Capacity of Children: A Challenge to the Capacity of Mental Health Professionals", *Journal of Child and Adolescent Mental Health*, vol. 27, no. 2 (2015), p.91 at p.92.
24 Lacey, *State Punishment*, p.63; J Mason, "Unfitness to Plead, Insanity and the Law Commission: Do We Need a Diagnostic Threshold?", *Journal of Criminal Law*, vol. 85, no. 4 (2021), p.268 at p.272.
25 J Todres, "Maturity", *Houston Law Review*, vol. 48, no. 5 (2012), p.1107.
26 (2005) 543 U S 551, p.619.
27 RN Miller and BK Applegate, "Adult Crime, Adult Time? Benchmarking Public Views on Punishing Serious Juvenile Felons", *Criminal Justice Review*, vol. 40, no. 2 (2015), p.151 at pp.151–153.
28 See, for example, A Wipat, "When to Say 'I Do'", *Family Law Bulletin*, no. 179 (2022), pp.1–3.
29 For example, New Zealand: Oranga Tamariki Act 1989, s. 272(1)(a), as amended.
30 Para 25.
31 AE Woolfolk, M Hughes, & V Walkup, *Psychology in Education* (Pearson: Harlow, 2nd edn, 2012), p.30.
32 A Daly, "Assessing Children's Capacity: Reconceptualising our Understanding through the UN Convention on the Rights of the Child", *International Journal of Children's Rights* (2020), p.471 at p.486. See also HB Bormanaki & Y Khoshhal, "The Role of Equilibration in Piaget's Theory of Cognitive Development and its Implication for Receptive Skills: A Theoretical Study", *Journal of Language Teaching and Research*, vol. 8, no. 5 (2017), p.996 at p.997.
33 J Piaget, *The Moral Judgment of the Child* (Routledge: Abingdon, 2001 [1932]).
34 For a fuller exposition see C McDiarmid, *Childhood and Crime* (Dundee University Press: Dundee, 2007), Ch.3.
35 Woolfolk et al, *Psychology in Education*, p.39.
36 P Sanghvi, "Piaget's Theory of Cognitive Development: A Review", *Indian Journal of Mental Health*, vol. 7, no. 2 (2020), p.90 at p.91.
37 Bormanaki & Khoshhal, "Equilibration", p.998.
38 Sanghvi, "Piaget's Theory", pp.92–94. Daly, "Assessing", pp.486–488.
39 AL Kramers-Olen, "Neuroscience, Moral Development, Criminal Capacity and the Child Justice Act: Justice or Injustice?", *South African Journal of Psychology*, vol. 45, no. 4 (2015), p.466 at p.467.
40 See Kramers-Olen, "Neuroscience", pp. 467–468; JV Oberstar, EM Anderson, & JB Jensen, "Cognitive and Moral Development, Brain Development, and Mental Illness: Important Considerations for the Juvenile Justice System", *William Mitchell Law Review*, vol. 32, no. 3 (2006), p.1051 at pp.1053–1054.
41 Pillay & Willows, "Assessing", p.92.
42 B Midson, "Risky Business: Developmental Neuroscience and the Culpability of Young Killers", *Psychiatry, Psychology and Law*, vol. 19, no. 5 (2012), p.692.
43 Walker, "Requirements".
44 Walker, "Requirements", p.38.
45 J Gardner, "The Mark of Responsibility", *Oxford Journal of Legal Studies*, vol. 23, no. 2 (2003), p.157.
46 Pillay and Willows, "Assessing", p.92.
47 Midson, "Risky", pp.695–700.
48 UNCRC, "General Comment 24", para 12.
49 Walker, "Requirements", p.38.
50 See, for example, F Santoni de Sio, "Irresistible Desires as an Excuse", *King's Law Journal*, vol. 22, no. 3 (2011), p.289.
51 T Crofts, "Reforming the Age of Criminal Responsibility", *South African Journal of Psychology*, vol. 46, no. 4 (2016), p.436 at p.443.
52 Steinberg, "Social Neuroscience", p.81.
53 See Steinberg, "Social Neuroscience", p.83; Midson, "Risky", p.695; Kramer-Olen, "Neuroscience", p.470.
54 Kramers-Olen, "Neuroscience", p.469.
55 Midson, "Risky", p.700.
56 Pillay and Willows, "Assessing", p.98.
57 Daly, "Assessing", p.494.

58 Midson, "Risky", p. 701. See also M Moreno & ME Trainor, "Adolescence Extended: Implications of New Brain Research on Medicine and Policy", *Acta Paediatrica*, vol. 102, no. 3 (2013), p.226 at p.227.
59 Midson, "Risky", p.701.
60 Kramers-Olen, "Neuroscience", pp.468–469.
61 ES Scott & L Steinberg, "Adolescent Development and the Regulation of Youth Crime", *The Future of Children*, vol. 18, no. 2 (2008), p.15 at p.20, p.21.
62 Kramers-Olen, "Neuroscience", p.470.
63 (2005) 543 U S 551, p.619.
64 2022, available at: www.scottishsentencingcouncil.org.uk/media/2171/sentencing-young-people-guideline-for-publication.pdf.
65 S O'Rourke et al, *The Development of Cognitive and Emotional Maturity in Adolescents and its Relevance in Judicial Contexts: Literature Review* (Scottish Sentencing Council: Edinburgh, 2020), available at: www.scottishsentencingcouncil.org.uk/media/2044/20200219-ssc-cognitive-maturity-literature-review.pdf.
66 C Elliott, "Criminal Responsibility and Children: A New Defence Required to Acknowledge the Absence of Capacity and Choice", *Journal of Criminal Law*, vol. 75, no. 4 (2011), p.289 at pp.296–302.
67 Elliot, "Criminal Responsibility", p.297.
68 RN Souris, "Child Soldiering on Trial: An Interdisciplinary Analysis of Responsibility in the Lord's Resistance Army", *International Journal of the Law in Context*, vol. 13, no. 3 (2017), p.316 at p.323.
69 Souris, "Child Soldiering", pp.319–320.
70 Souris, "Child Soldiering", p.327.
71 Wake et al, "Legislative Approaches", p.156.
72 E Delmage, "The Minimum Age of Criminal Responsibility: A Medico-Legal Perspective", *Youth Justice*, vol. 13, no. 2 (2013), p.102 at p.107.
73 Para 22.
74 Marriage and Civil Partnership (Minimum Age) Act 2022, ss. 1 and 3.
75 Lord Bellamy KC, Parliamentary Under Secretary of State for Justice, Written Statement to the House of Commons, 27 Feburary 2023. Hansard volume 728, Columns 28–30WS.
76 Delmage, "Minimum Age", p.105.
77 SB Johnson, RW Blum, & JN Giedd, "Adolescent Maturity and the Brain: The Promise and Pitfalls of Neuroscience Research in Adolescent Health Policy", *Journal of Adolescent Health*, vol. 45, no. 3 (2009), p.216.
78 Paras 26 and 27.
79 Crofts, "Reforming", p.442.
80 Law Commission, *Murder*, paras 5.125–5.137.
81 See Elliott, "Criminal Responsibility", pp. 301–303; Delmage, "Minimum Age", p. 107; C McDiarmid, "After the Age of Criminal Responsibility: A Defence for Children who Offend", *Northern Ireland Legal Quarterly*, vol. 67, no. 3 (2016), p.327.
82 Para 6(c)(i).
83 UNCRC, "General Comment 24", para. 11.

References

Legislation

Age of Criminal Responsibility (Scotland) Act 2019
Child Justice Act 2008
Marriage and Civil Partnership (Minimum Age) Act 2022
Children and Young Persons Act 1933
Crime and Disorder Act 1998
Criminal Procedure (Scotland) Act 1995
Oranga Tamariki Act 1989
Tasmania Criminal Code Act 1924

Cases

JM (A Minor) v Runeckles (1984) 79 *Criminal Appeal Reports* 255
Roper v Simmons (2005) 543 U S 551

Books and book chapters

Blackstone W, *Commentaries on the Laws of England*, vol. IV (Clarendon Press: Oxford, 1769).
Lacey N, *State Punishment: Political Principles and Community Values* (Routledge: London, 1988).
McDiarmid C, *Childhood and Crime*. (Dundee University Press: Dundee, 2007).
Piaget J, *The Moral Judgment of the Child* (Routledge: Abingdon, 1932 [1999, 2001 reprint]).
Woolfolk AE, Hughes M, & Walkup V, *Psychology in Education* (Pearson: Harlow, 2nd edn, 2012).

Journal articles

Bormanaki HB & Khoshhal Y, "The Role of Equilibration in Piaget's Theory of Cognitive Development and Its Implication for Receptive Skills: A Theoretical Study", *Journal of Language Teaching Research*, vol. 8, no. 5 (2017), pp.996–1005.
Crofts T, "Reforming the Age of Criminal Responsibility", *South African Journal of Psychology*, vol. 46, no. 4 (2016), pp.436–448.
Crofts T, "Act Now: Raise the Minimum Age of Criminal Responsibility," *Current Issues in Criminal Justice*, vol. 35, no. 1 (2023), pp.118–138.
Daly A, "Assessing Children's Capacity: Reconceptualising Our Understanding Through the UN Convention on the Rights of the Child", *International Journal of Children's Rights*, vol. 28 (2020), pp.471–499.
Delmage E, "The Minimum Age of Criminal Responsibility: A Medico-Legal Perspective", *Youth Justice*, vol. 13, no. 2 (2013), pp.102–110.
Elliott C, "Criminal Responsibility and Children: A New Defence Required to Acknowledge the Absence of Capacity and Choice", *Journal of Criminal Law*, vol. 75, no. 4 (2011), pp.289–308.
Gardner J, "The Mark of Responsibility", *Oxford Journal of Legal Studies*, vol. 23, no. 2 (2003), pp.157–171.
Johnson SN, Blum RW, & Giedd JN, "Adolescent Maturity and the Brain: The Promise and Pitfalls of Neuroscience Research in Adolescent Health Policy", *Journal of Adolescent Health*, vol. 45 (2009), pp.216–221.
Kramers-Olen AL, "Neuroscience, Moral Development, Criminal Capacity and the Child Justice Act: Justice or Injustice?", *South African Journal of Psychology*, vol. 45, no. 4 (2015), pp.466–479.
Mason J, "Unfitness to Plead, Insanity and the Law Commission: Do We Need a Diagnostic Threshold?", *Journal of Criminal Law*, vol. 85, no. 4 (2021), pp.268–279.
McDiarmid C, "Age of Criminal Responsibility: Raise It or Remove It?", *Juridical Review*, vol. 5 (2001), pp.243–257.
McDiarmid C, "After the Age of Criminal Responsibility: A Defence for Children Who Offend", *Northern Ireland Legal Quarterly*, vol. 67, no. 3 (2016), pp.327–341.
Midson B, "Risky Business: Developmental Neuroscience and the Culpability of Young Killers", *Psychiatry, Psychology and Law*, vol. 19, no. 5 (2012), pp.692–710.
Miller RN & Applegate BK, "Adult Crime Adult Time? Benchmarking Public Views on Punishing Serious Juvenile Felons", *Criminal Justice Review*, vol. 40, no. 2 (2015), pp.51–168.
Moreno M & Trainor ME, "Adolescence Extended: Implications of New Brain Research on Medicine and Policy", *Acta Paediatrica*, vol. 102 (2013), pp.226–232.
Oberstar JV, Anderson EM, & Jensen JB, "Cognitive and Moral Development, Brain Development and Mental Illness: Important Considerations for the Juvenile Justice System", *William Mitchell Law Review*, vol. 32, no. 3 (2006), pp.1051–1062.
Pillay AL & Willows C, "Assessing the Criminal Capacity of Children: A Challenge to the Capacity of Mental Health Professionals", *Journal of Child and Adolescent Mental Health*, vol. 27, no. 2 (2015), pp.91–101.

Sanghvi P, "Piaget's Theory of Cognitive Development: A Review", *Indian Journal of Mental Health*, vol. 7, no. 2 (2020), pp.90–96.
Santoni de Sio F, "Irresistible Desires as an Excuse", *King's Law Journal*, vol. 22 (2011), pp.289–307.
Scott ES & Steinberg L, "Adolescent Development and the Regulation of Youth Crime", *The Future of Children*, vol. 18, no. 2 (2008), pp.15–33.
Souris RN, "Child Soldiering on Trial: An Interdisciplinary Analysis of Responsibility in the Lord's Resistance Army", *International Journal of the Law in Context*, vol. 13, no. 3 (2017), pp.316–335.
Steinberg L, "A Social Neuroscience Perspective on Adolescent Risk-Taking", *Developmental Review*, vol. 28 (2008), pp.78–106.
Todres J, "Maturity", *Houston Law Review*, vol. 48, no. 5 (2012), pp.1107–1156.
Vincent NA, "On the Relevance of Neuroscience to Criminal Responsibility", *Criminal Law and Philosophy*, vol. 4 (2010), pp.77–98.
Wake N, Arthur R, Crofts T, & Lambert S, "Legislative Approaches to Recognising the Vulnerability of Young People and Preventing Their Criminalisation", *Public Law* (2021), pp.145–162.
Walker S, "The Requirements for Criminal Capacity in Section 11(1) of the New Child Justice Act 2008: A Step in the Wrong Direction?", *South African Journal of Criminal Justice*, vol. 24, no. 1 (2011), pp.33–41.
Wipat A, "When to Say 'I Do'", *Family Law* Bulletin, vol. 179 (2022), pp.1–3.

Reports and websites

Child Rights International Network, *CRC General Comments* (2013), available at: https://archive.crin.org/en/library/publications/crc-general-comments.html#:~:text=General%20comments%20provide%20interpretation%20and,obligations%20contained%20in%20the%20CRC
Drabsch T, *Age of Criminal Responsibility*, NSW Parliamentary Research Service E-Brief (Issue 1/2022), available at: parliament.nsw.gov.au/researchpapers/Documents/Age of criminal responsibility - Final.pdf
Law Commission, *Murder, Manslaughter and Infanticide* (Law Com No. 304) (2006).
O'Rourke S, Whalley H, Janes S, MacSweeney N, Skrenes A, Crowson S, MacLean L, & Schwannauer M. *The Development of Cognitive and Emotional Maturity in Adolescents and Its Relevance in Judicial Contexts: Literature Review* (Scottish Sentencing Council: Edinburgh, 2020), available at: www.scottishsentencingcouncil.org.uk/media/2044/20200219-ssc-cognitive-maturity-literature-review.pdf
Scottish Law Commission, *Report on Age of Criminal Responsibility* (Scot Law Com No. 185) (2002).
Scottish Sentencing Council, *Sentencing Young People: Sentencing Guideline* (Scottish Sentencing Council: Edinburgh, 2022), available at: www.scottishsentencingcouncil.org.uk/media/2171/sentencing-young-people-guideline-for-publication.pdf
Sutherland EE, "The Age of Reason or the Reasons for an Age: The Age of Criminal Responsibility", *Scots Law Times* (2002), pp.1–5.
UN Committee on the Rights of the Child, *General Comment No. 24 on Children's Rights in the Child Justice System*, CRC/C/GC/24 (2019).

29
ORGANISATIONAL CULTURE, INDUSTRY NORMS, AND CORPORATE WRONGDOING

A New Integrated Theory of Crime Prevention

Joe McGrath

Introduction

When corporate wrongdoing occurs, discussions often naturally focus on how these activities were caused and how to punish corporate offenders. Scholarship rarely focuses on how to prevent further wrongdoing. While it is recognised that organisational cultures fuel the generative conditions that give rise to individual criminal acts, research rarely focuses on how organisational cultures may generate positive practices which may reduce the likelihood of wrongdoing. This chapter seeks to address that gap. It does not seek to outline how we punish wrongdoing, or ask why good actors do bad things, but to ask how we can help to promote positive practices that prevent wrongdoing in the workplace. Using the financial services sector as a case study, this chapter identifies a trend in three jurisdictions, the UK, Australia, and Ireland, to further professionalise the banking industry, as a means of generating industry-wide ethical norms that will inform organisational cultures in banks and guide individual behaviours within these organisations. It then constructs a novel, interdisciplinary, theoretical framework which seeks to explain why professionalisation may hold promise as a form of crime prevention. In particular, it employs regulatory theory (meta-regulation), behavioural psychology (groups as moral anchors), and criminological theory (stakes in conformity), to explore how certain types of controls, attachments, and group dynamics, can inform individual decision-making processes and generate more ethical actions to prevent wrongdoing. These theories help to explain: why people resist wrongdoing; the importance of industry's self-regulatory capacities within a pluralistic, compliance-oriented regulatory model of enforcement; and how people internalise ethical standards and good governance norms from the groups to which they belong.

Corporate criminal liability

At various points, there has been an increased interest in corporate criminal liability, stemming, for example, from corporate failings that arose from transport and other disasters that led to a loss of life,[1] and also from more recent corporate failings that led to the recent global financial crisis (GFC).[2] This interest tends to focus on the difficulties of applying the criminal law, which was designed for natural persons, to corporate forms, the various models of attributing criminal liability to corporate persons, and the relative merits and difficulties with those models.[3] The paragraphs below briefly set out an overview of these issues, locating this chapter within the broader concepts and theories of corporate criminal responsibility. The subsequent sections of this chapter analyse the case for professionalisation as a potential form of corporate crime prevention.

It is well established that companies are artificial legal persons with the capacity to buy and sell goods, to sue and be sued, etc.[4] They may also have the capacity to commit crimes.[5] The criminal law, however, was developed to address natural persons, so applying criminal liability – involving fault and conduct elements of offences – presents difficulties, because companies lack a guilty mind or conventional physical presence.[6] In addition, a limited range of penalties may be imposed on companies, usually fines, given that they have "no soul to be damned, and no body to be kicked".[7] Moreover, difficulties securing convictions against companies have implications for imposing derivative or secondary criminal liability on natural persons for offences committed by bodies corporate.[8]

While regulatory offences which impose liability on the basis of absolute or strict liability tend to be less problematic, the law has struggled to attribute a guilty mind to companies. Accordingly, the law has fashioned various doctrines over time to attribute *mens rea* to companies as artificial legal persons.[9] For example, the identification doctrine, the prevailing rule for corporate criminal liability in English and Welsh law, and also Irish law, provides that companies may be criminally liable when the "directing mind and will" of the company is responsible for the crime.[10]

Nevertheless, there are significant difficulties with the operation of the doctrine. In particular, it has been difficult to secure convictions against larger companies with complex organisational structures, where responsibility can be diffuse and fragmented.[11] Prosecutors have, by contrast, found it less difficult to secure the convictions of smaller companies where the actions of the company can be more easily associated with the manager.[12] Consequently, it is thought that the test "works best in cases where it is needed least".[13]

In certain limited circumstances, the courts have been willing to fashion particular rules of attribution to surmount some of the difficulties arising from a strict application of the identification doctrine. This is a more flexible approach which allows the misconduct of an individual, who is not the directing mind and will of the company, to be attributed to the company. This approach may only be taken if it is required on a proper construction of the statute, and to promote the policy of the statute or common law rule.[14] Moreover, the narrower "directing mind and will" test will only be displaced by other rules of attribution when the narrower approach would defeat the intention of the legislature and the aims of the statute.[15]

In 2013, the then Director of the Serious Fraud Office (SFO) in the UK, David Green, stated, "it is extremely difficult to convict a company of an offence because the prosecution has to show that the controlling minds of the company — somebody at the board level — were complicit in the criminality you are trying to prove."[16] Indeed, the prosecution of Barclays Bank for illegal capital raising activities was unsuccessful when the court determined that those executives that were directly involved in these activities could not be considered the directing mind and will of the company, and declined to fashion special rules of attribution that would attribute the intention of these individuals to the bank.[17]

Given the difficulties with the identification doctrine, various law reform bodies, including those in the UK and in Ireland, have explored the merits of other models of corporate criminal liability.[18] Though a detailed consideration of these models is outside the scope of this chapter, the underlying impetus for broadening the scope of corporate criminal liability is significant. In these jurisdictions, law reform bodies are proposing to expand the basis on which corporate criminal liability may be imposed to make it easier to secure convictions for corporate misconduct. This is because the low risk of conviction of companies at present arguably reduces the potential to deter corporate misconduct, inhibiting the ability to prevent further corporate crimes.[19] It is submitted, however, that while an effective regulatory strategy depends on an ability to impose sanctions in appropriate cases, an emphasis on promoting ethical corporate cultures is also an important mechanism for ensuring that companies have adequate policies and practices in place to prevent wrongdoing. The prevailing, contemporary emphasis on criminalisation serves to further demonstrate how the focus on this chapter is different and novel, by focusing on the importance of generating positive corporate cultures and the internalisation of good governance norms, as preventative rather than punitive practices. This is discussed further below in the context of the financial services sector.

"A trajectory towards professionalisation": developments in the UK, Australia, and Ireland

Often, when commentators talk about the need to professionalise banking, they use the phrase quite loosely and without rigour, meaning that there is a need to raise standards in some way. There is, however, very valuable literature which theorises the professions, including functionalist theory which suggests that the professions support the public good and exist because they are instrumental ways of organising activity in economically advanced societies and conflict theory which, by contrast, draws attention to the self-serving aspects of the professions in which they impose educational requirements and restrict supply to enhance their status and earnings.[20] There are also conflicting accounts of how we should characterise a profession. Drawing on literature in law, medicine, and accounting, and also disciplines like teaching and nursing, some scholars theorise that professions are characterised by four indicia: (1) academic training in a body of specialised knowledge to exercise skilled judgements; (2) members commitment to serve a positive social purpose that goes beyond profit maximisation; (3) mechanisms for members to be disciplined by their community for failing to honour those duties, and (4) an underlying code of ethics.[21] The paragraphs below briefly describe the efforts to professionalise banking in the UK, Australia, and Ireland. It is not intended to be an exhaustive description of these developments.[22] Instead, it serves to set up the subsequent discussion on how professionalisation may be an attachment that generates peer pressure to comply with obligations and internalise norms.

Appeals to professionalise banking stretch back at least a century when, in the aftermath of the Great Crash, Americans appealed to a time when a banker "felt he was a quasi-public servant" and when bankers' "code of ethics was on a plane much higher than that of business or industry".[23] These sentiments were also present, to various degrees, in the UK, Australia, and Ireland after the more recent GFC. In the wake of that crisis, the Parliamentary Commission on Banking Standards in the UK examined the extent to which banking could be considered a profession. It concluded that banks did not possess the core indicia of a profession because banking covered too broad an array of activities, lacked a common core of learning, and responsibilities to clients did not trump self-interest. It did recommend, however, that bankers should pursue a "trajectory towards professionalisation" in which the banking sector would establish its own professional body to set expected standards of its members which should, it was suggested, exceed existing regulatory obligations.[24] The Lambert Review also recommended the establishment of a professional body of this nature which led to the creation of the Banking Standards Board in 2015, a membership body that surveys the industry on its "cultural character". It was subsequently expanded to become the Financial Services Cultural Board (FSCB) in 2021 but ceased operations in 2023.[25] Two other self-regulatory bodies, the Chartered Bankers Professional Standards Board (though its work formally transitioned into the Chartered Banker Institute in 2019) and the FICC Market Standards Board, both of which aim to set standards of conduct and influence culture, continue to operate.[26]

In Australia, the Australian Royal Commission Final Report (Hayne Report) documented a wide range of misconduct in the financial services sector, relating to – among other things – overcharging and poorly advising consumers.[27] Having demonstrated a banking culture which was focused on profit at all costs and insufficiently consumer-centred, the Hayne Report concluded that the sector had not transitioned "from an industry dedicated to the sale of financial products to a profession concerned with the provision of financial advice".[28] Noting the efforts to professionalise the financial services sector which predated the Hayne Report, it submitted that further measures were required. It argued that the sector needed to rebuild trust, that conflicts of interest should not be tolerated, and that the industry needed the power to discipline wrongdoing within its ranks.

Australia has taken various steps to professionalise the financial services sector though the thrust of much of these efforts relates to financial advisors specifically. Legislation requires advisors to act in the best interests of retail clients, moved fees to a fee for service model rather than for commission, and increased transparency on the fees which advisors charge.[29] Financial advisors must also meet certain educational requirements, including qualifying degrees, training periods, entrance exams, and ongoing CPD requirements.[30] They must also observe a code of ethics, so that where they "formerly provided a commercial service" they ought now to be "committed to offering a professional service".[31] The Australian Banking Association (ABA) also updated its code which applies to the banking sector more generally,[32] providing hundreds of new or improved consumer rights, and is enforced by an independent committee,[33] the Banking Code Compliance Committee (BCCC).[34]

Various inquiries have also investigated wrongdoing in the banking sector in Ireland since the GFC.[35] The resulting reports have largely focused on identifying the causes of the crisis, how financial regulatory enforcement may be improved, and have sought to generate more ethical, pro-consumer cultures within banks.[36] The conversation on professionalising banking is less advanced in Ireland, though Ireland has set minimum professional standards through various codes.[37] In 2018, the Central Bank of Ireland published a review of the culture of retail banks in Ireland, suggesting that increased individual accountability for senior individuals in banks could improve banking culture, by changing the "tone at the top" which could inform behaviours at the bottom of banks.[38] The Irish government enacted the Central Bank (Individual Accountability Framework) Act 2023 to give effect to this recommendation. The new framework is based on similar regimes in the UK and Australia.[39] The Irish Banking

Culture Board is also working to make banking trustworthy, having developed, for example, its DECIDE model, a decision-making framework, to encourage bankers to think through the ethical dimensions of their behaviours and actions.[40] Moreover, the Institute of Bankers provides a range of programmes that aim to boost educational attainment, raise professional standards, and develop consumer-centred cultures in banks.[41]

Gathering these threads together, the UK and Australia have identified the path to professionalising financial services, and banking in particular, and have taken particular measures to propel banking on a trajectory to professionalisation. Nevertheless, some scholars have argued that more can be done to professionalise banking in each of these jurisdictions. In particular, it has been argued that the banking industry itself should develop professional qualifications and training expectations that go beyond minimum regulatory requirements for all its members; that banks should clearly articulate their social purpose; communicate to their employees the individual and firm-wide impact of their activities on the community and wider society to culturally embed this purpose; and further develop industry-wide codes of conduct to address specific issues in the industry and that go beyond minimum regulatory requirements.[42] Integrating literature from criminology, regulatory theory, and behavioural psychology, the next section of this chapter explains why further professionalisation may help people to internalise ethical standards and resist wrongdoing.

"Why don't we do it?": an integrated model of resistance to wrongdoing

While most criminological theory focuses on the causes of crime, control theory explores how certain types of controls may prevent crime and explains why individuals may resist misconduct. As stated by Hirshi, "The question 'Why do they do it?' is simply not the question the theory is designed to answer. The question is 'Why don't we do it?' ".[43] Control theory does not seek to theorise deviance; it analyses how social order is maintained and how we invest in group norms, constructing "stakes in conformity", which can inhibit departures from existing patterns of behaviour. This theory explains that crime arises from the absence of effective controls.[44]

Resistance to engaging in crime is of two forms: an inner control system and an outer control system. These systems are "elements within the self and within the person's immediate world that enable him [or her] to hold the line against deviancy or to hue to the line of social expectations".[45] Inner controls include "self-concept" or the importance of identifying as a law-abiding person, self-control, feelings or obligations of responsibility, and orientation to legitimate and worthy goals. Outer controls can include an institutional reinforcement of norms and expectations, supervision and discipline, and relationships or a sense of belonging to a group that contains individualistic impulses. When individuals care about how they are perceived by others, they internalise group norms which restrain their own actions. Through this process, external validation becomes an internal control. Over time, as people invest in conventional norms and behaviours, developing a reputation as an honest businessperson, etc., they develop and build greater "stakes in conformity" so that the costs of engaging in wrongdoing are higher.[46] Gottfredson and Hirschi argued that control theory explained all forms of criminality, including white-collar crime.[47]

The literature on control theory is usefully supplemented by the criminological literature on compliance. Bottoms suggested that people will observe the law where compliance is routinised into everyday processes and procedures; made habitual, where individuals alter their way of thinking such that they are inclined to adopt new routines; and normative, in which individuals make decisions because they have actively considered their beliefs, or because of their attachments to others.[48] In addition, compliance is more likely where industry considers that the authority is legitimately requiring compliance in a fair and reasonable way.[49]

As Robinson and McNeill noted, regulators' "best hope arguably rests in encouraging compliance mechanisms that allow for the internalization of controls implied in commitment (via beliefs, attachments, and eventually the development of new habits and routines) rather than the imposition of constraints or appeals to threats or rewards".[50] They observed that when initially non-compliant behaviour is met by a stringent response that is considered unfair, this increases resistance to authority and damages ongoing relationships which precipitates further non-compliance.[51] Accordingly, the ease of obeying a rule, the motivations for observing the duty to comply, and the perceived legitimacy of the enforcement mechanisms all inform a "behavioural code" which supports compliance with the law.[52]

This literature suggests that an over-reliance on sanctioning strategies may disenfranchise and alienate otherwise good market actors who may have engaged in non-compliance but who are generally positively inclined to obey the law. This observation is supported by a much longer line of literature on responsive regulation, developed by Ayres and Braithwaite, which suggested that regulators work best when they adopt compliance-oriented approaches and use sanctions as a last resort when other strategies have failed.[53] According to this model, regulators should be "benign big guns" who "speak softly" and "carry a big stick".[54] They must have very severe sanctions that they are disinclined to use, pulling the trigger on them only in circumstances where there is a high likelihood of success to project a strong image of invincibility. The big stick, when brandished appropriately by the regulator in this way, they suggested, can drive more regulatory activity into the base of the pyramid, obviating the need for sanctions.

Ayres and Braithwaite emphasised that businesses and third parties should also play a critical part in regulatory enforcement. They called this "regulatory tripartism". They argued that industry should be given the chance to regulate itself first. Enforced self-regulation might be necessary where this was unsuccessful. Enforced self-regulation, they stated, was "an arrangement under which firms develop their own set of context-specific conduct rules, which are then publicly ratified and capable of public enforcement".[55] Regulatory tripartism became the basis for "smart" regulatory theory, involving the state as regulator, industry exercising self-regulatory capacities, and third parties like NGOs, business associations, etc., acting as surrogate regulators who can apply pressure on market actors to comply with the law.[56] This is a pluralistic form of regulation in which various actors coalesce to achieve regulatory objectives.[57]

Building on responsive and smart regulatory theory, meta-regulation emphasises that the State does not have a monopoly on regulatory power.[58] Instead, regulatory power is shared and dispersed with a plurality of other actors, including businesses who get to determine their own systems of internal control, albeit with regulatory oversight from government.[59] It recognised that "market forces may themselves be powerful regulatory instruments."[60] These non-state forms of market-driven governance, when supported by compliance-orientated approaches and backed by sanctions, can "institutionalise ethical reflection within firms".[61]

The potential to harness industry itself in the regulatory process is also recognised in the behavioural psychology literature on social identity.[62] This literature suggests that groups may serve as our moral anchors.[63] If individuals in groups regularly see behaviours, if social behaviours in those groups are frequent, they are considered moral. This phenomenon is referred to as the "common is moral" heuristic.[64] These heuristics are intuitive shortcuts to making decisions about what is right and wrong.[65] The stronger the commitment to and identification with the group, the stronger the moral imperative to conform to and observe the group norm; naturally, this may vary among group members.[66]

The way in which groups define morality or ethical conduct can create a shared moral standard that performs a regulatory function when it becomes an aspect of people's identities.[67] Being a good member of a group, subjugating individual impulses in preference to behaviours the group deems positive, earns the individual respect.[68] Individuals are likely to have even stronger attachments to their groups when they believe that their groups are moral or virtuous.[69] The resulting organisational pride is thought to promote positive workplace practices including increased regulatory compliance.[70] Transgressing the group's expectations or standards of morality, however, can operate as a strong form of censure. In short, how people see us affects how we see ourselves which regulates our behaviour by making us "fall in line" because of our need to belong to the group.[71] This kind of social identity, in which our identity is tied to a larger group, team, organisation, or community is called the "group self".[72]

In summation of this section, criminological theory emphasises that particular types of controls, including individual attachments to groups, build "stakes in conformity" which encourage law abiding and responsible behaviours. This research is usefully supplemented by the criminological literature on compliance which argues that meaningful compliance is most likely when controls are internalised through relationships and attachments that routinise ethical behaviours, and through tactics that favour persuasion over sanctions. Responsive, smart, and meta-regulation theory reinforce these findings, favouring a model of enforcement in which industry is required to take more ownership of its activities, albeit with state oversight, and where compliance-oriented approaches are attempted first, and sanctions are a last resort. Much like control theory and social identity theory, the objective is to make corporate actors internalise governance norms. Research in the field of behavioural psychology emphasises that we learn right and wrong from our membership of groups and our interpersonal interactions therein. When people's identity is tied up with the group, the group's standards of ethical behaviour perform a regulatory function because the desire to belong to the group promotes conformity and rule compliance. Moreover, breaking the rules may not only result in group censure, it may also betray one's sense of self. Accordingly, taken together, this literature, when applied to the corporate setting, suggests that industry peer pressure can be an important instrument of control and that condemnation and exclusion from industry groups or professional associations are powerful sanctions. The way in which people view themselves, how they identify with their organisations, and belong to their corporate cultures, can regulate behaviour. This is discussed further in the next section of this chapter.

Discussion and conclusion

While misconduct is an issue for all corporate sectors, the issue has assumed particular significance for the banking sector in the wake of the GFC. The GFC and subsequent scandals suggest that wrongdoing in the financial services sector is often widespread and culturally embedded. For example, the open and pervasive manipulation of the benchmark rates used to calculate the cost of interbank credit, the London Inter-Bank Offered Rate (LIBOR) and the Euro Inter-Bank Offered Rate (EURIBOR), exemplify the problem.[73] Traders stated that the manipulation of LIBOR was so widespread in the industry that it was considered legitimate and that there was a culture in which the manipulation of LIBOR was encouraged by senior managers in the industry.[74] Many of the prosecutions taken for manipulation of LIBOR and EURIBOR were unsuccessful, which raises questions as to whether criminal sanctions are effective ways to punish and deter financial misconduct.[75] While civil sanctions, such as fines, can be easier to secure, it is not clear that they deter misconduct either. As acknowledged by Francis and Ryder, "Currently, financial penalties have done little to alter the future conduct of the offending corporations".[76] Indeed, systemic reviews of the literature and evidence, suggest that while the increased likelihood of detection and punishment can influence the decision to engage in wrongdoing, and therefore deter misconduct,[77] the evidence linking the severity of the sanction to greater deterrence is weak.[78] Van Rooij and Fine vividly describe the belief that sanctions can deter wrongdoing as a "punishment delusion".[79]

Increasingly, this view is also shared by regulators themselves.[80] Punishment is a limited instrument of regulatory enforcement, which is "bound to fail because it promotes a culture of complying with the letter of the law, not its spirit and because authorities will inevitably lag developments in fast-changing markets".[81] If misconduct in the financial services sector can be systematic and widespread, and if sanctions are post-hoc retrospective responses that do little to deter future misconduct, the answer, in part, may be to enlist industry itself in structural and cultural change to make wrongdoing less likely to arise in the first place.

Awrey et al. have argued that both law and markets on their own are inadequate instruments for generating positive cultural change.[82] Acting in concert, however, they are greater than the sum of their parts. Awrey et al. argued that the banking industry must assume a greater role for itself and take more responsibility for meeting regulatory objectives and that this can result in more ethical or "other regarding" behaviours and cultures, though such initiatives must still be backed by the credible threat of sanctions. This form of meta-regulation, in which banks continue to be regulated by the State but also take greater ownership of their activities, may be promoted through further professionalisation.

Professionalisation mandates that the banking industry design and implement internal controls, without significant reliance on the state or financial regulator to do so. This internal steering within the profession does not displace the State from continuing to regulate the financial services sector; regulators also continue to exercise oversight of the sector, administer applicable regulations, and punish misconduct where relevant. In keeping with this model, both the State and the banking sector can act in concert, reinforcing regulatory rules in their respective roles, in a pluralistic process that decentres regulation to make it "smarter".[83]

Research on behavioural psychology supports the argument that professionalisation may help to develop industry-wide norms that may "shape individual choice and action, within an organization, in an endless feedback loop that includes both 'tone from the top' as well as 'echo from the bottom' ".[84] People may learn and replicate positive behaviours by observing and interacting with the group to which they belong.[85] Over time, these patterns and ways of knowing become routine so that "what is common is moral".[86] Professional networks may operate as "webs of influence" that influence the enforcement of norms even with orders backed by sanctions.[87] In this conception, power is not always exercised directly by government enforcement, but instead is anchored in professionalisation, exercised "at a distance" from the state, and woven through relationships in groups within which individuals are positioned.[88]

The literature on "stakes in conformity" may also lend some support for professionalisation as a force for good. This literature suggests that opprobrium from peers is an important sanction for those who build attachments through interpersonal connections, and for those who seek to maintain those relationships and preserve their self-image. They will be less likely to deviate from community norms, provided they have a greater "stake" in that community than the community of wrongdoers.[89] In the corporate context, the research on social control suggests that individuals that form and maintain strong bonds with their managers, colleagues, and firms, who believe in the rules and the purpose of the industry, are less likely to engage in wrongdoing.[90] In the same vein, professionalisation may also operate as a control when it builds stakes in conformity through interpersonal relationships and attachments.

This chapter is not setting out or prescribing in precise detail an enabling structure that might eventually establish a professional framework for banking. Research published elsewhere has provided detail on how the banking industry may play a greater role in improving banking culture, by promoting industry-wide expectations of behaviour that go above and beyond observing regulatory requirements set by a regulator.[91] This research argues that this should involve an increased educational emphasis on banking serving pro-social purposes, through professional associations that more actively steer behaviours, and by developing industry-wide codes of conduct, among other actions.[92] Instead, this chapter sought to construct a novel, interdisciplinary, theoretical framework which seeks to explain why professionalisation may inform individual decision-making processes and generate more ethical actions to prevent wrongdoing. Integrating criminological theory, regulatory theory, and behavioural psychology, it sought to outline how professionalisation may assist people to internalise ethical standards and good governance norms from the groups to which they belong and to resist wrongdoing. It argued that adopting some aspects of the professions, a "trajectory towards professionalisation" could help to normalise good behaviours through creating "stakes in conformity", developing internal controls, and prescribing and regularly emphasising normative standards of behaviour for its membership.

Notes

1 The Law Reform Commission, "Consultation Paper on Corporate Killing" (2003), available at: www.lawreform.ie/_fileupload/consultation%20papers/cpCorporate%20Killing.pdf.
2 The Law Reform Commission, "Report: Regulatory Powers and Corporate Offences" (2018), available at: www.lawreform.ie/_fileupload/Completed%20Projects/LRC%20119-2018%20Regulatory%20Powers%20and%20Corporate%20Offences%20Volume%201.pdf.
3 For an excellent overview in this volume, see: P Crofts, "Corporate Criminal Ir/responsibility".
4 *Salomon v A Salomon & Co Ltd* [1896] UKHL 1, [1897] AC 22.
5 C Wells, *Corporations and Criminal Responsibility* (Oxford University Press: Oxford, 2nd edn, 2001).
6 J Gobert & M Punch, *Rethinking Corporate Crime* (Cambridge University Press: Cambridge, 2003).
7 This quote is attributed to Lord Thurlow. See: JC Coffee, "'No soul to damn: no body to kick': An unscandalized inquiry into the problem of corporate punishment", *Michigan Law Review*, vol. 79, no. 3 (1981), p.386.
8 J McGrath, "Individual Criminal Responsibility for Corporate Managers: Director of Public Prosecutions v TN", *Irish Supreme Court Review*, vol. 3 (2021), p.49.

9. J. Gobert, "Corporate Criminality: four models of fault", *Legal Studies*, vol. 14 no. 3 (1994), p.393.
10. *Tesco Supermarkets v Nattrass* [1972] AC 153.
11. *R v P&O Ferries* [1991] 93 Cr. App. R. 72; *Attorney-General's Reference (No 2 of 1999)* [2000] 2 Cr App R 207; DM Doyle and J McGrath, "Attributing criminal responsibility for workplace fatalities and deaths in custody: Corporate manslaughter in Britain and Ireland", in K Fitzgibbon and S Walklate (eds), *Homicide, Gender and Responsibility: an International Perspective* (Routledge: London, 2016), p.148.
12. *R v Kite and OLL Ltd* [1996] 2 Cr. App. R.(s.) 295; *R v Jackson Transport (Osset) Ltd* (Health and Safety Bulletin, November 1996).
13. J Gobert, "Corporate Criminal Liability: four models of fault", *Legal Studies*, vol. 14, no. 3 (1994), p.393 at p.401.
14. *Meridian Global Funds Management Asia Ltd v Securities Commission* [1995] 2 AC 500.
15. Law Commission, "Corporate Criminal Liability: A Discussion Paper" (2021), para.2.48–2.60.
16. T Harvey, "Man on a Mission an Interview with David Green, CB, QC, Director of U.K.'s Serious Fraud Office" *Fraud Magazine* (2013), available at: www.fraud-magazine.com/article.aspx?id=4294980221.
17. *R v Barclays PLC and Barclays Bank Plc [2018]* (Southwark Crown Court). For more details, see: Law Commission, "Corporate Criminal Liability", paras. 2.48-2.60; Serious Fraud Office, "Former Barclays executives acquitted of conspiracy to commit fraud" (2020), available at: www.sfo.gov.uk/2020/02/28/former-barclays-executives-acquitted-of-conspiracy-to-commit-fraud/#:~:text=Former%20Barclays%20executives%20acquitted%20of%20conspiracy%20to%20commit%20fraud,-28%20February%2C%202020&text=Roger%20Jenkins%2C%20Richard%20Boath%20and,during%20the%202008%20Financial%20Crisis; *R v Varley and others* (2019) EWCA Crim 1074.
18. The Law Reform Commission, "Report: Regulatory Powers"; Law Commission, "Corporate Criminal Liability".
19. D Omerod, "Corporate criminal liability – Lessons from across the Irish Sea", *Law Reform Commission Annual Conference* (2016), available at: www.lawreform.ie/_fileupload/Speeches/Annual%20Conference%202016%20Professor%20David%20Ormerod%20Corporate%20criminal%20liability%20%20Lessons%20from%20across%20the%20Irish%20Sea.pdf.
20. S Ackroyd, "Sociological and organisational theories of professions and professionalism", in M Dent et al (eds), *The Routledge Companion to the Professions and Professionalism* (Routledge: London, 2016), p.15.
21. J McGrath & C Walker, "Regulating ethics in financial services: Engaging industry to achieve regulatory objectives", *Regulation & Governance*, vol. 17, no. 3 (2023), p.791.
22. For a detailed discussion of these developments, see: J McGrath & C Walker, *New Accountability in Financial Services: Changing Individual Behaviour and Culture* (Springer Nature: London, 2021).
23. AM Lamport, "Banking—Business or profession?" *Bankers' Magazine*, vol. 122, no. 3 (1931), p.317, available at: https://archive.org/stream/sim_bankers-magazine_1931-03_122_3/sim_bankers-magazine_1931-03_122_3_djvu.txt.
24. Parliamentary Commission on Banking Standards, "Changing Banking for Good: Vol 1" (2013), para. 94.
25. Financial Services Culture Board, "FCSB Wind-Up-Statement" (2023), available at: https://financialservicescultureboard.org.uk/fscb-wind-up-statement/.
26. E Hickman, "Is the Senior Managers and Certification Regime Changing Banking for Good?", *Modern Law Review*, vol. 85, no. 6 (2022), p.1440.
27. KM Hayne, "Final Report of the Royal Commission into Misconduct in the Banking, Superannuation and Financial Services Industry" (2018), available at: https://treasury.gov.au/publication/p2019-fsrc-final-report.
28. Hayne, "Final Report" p.119.
29. The Corporations Amendment (Future of Financial Advice) Act 2012 and Corporations Amendment (Further Future of Financial Advice Measures) Act 2012, as amended by the Corporations Amendment (Revising Future of Financial Advice) Regulation 2014; Corporations Amendment (Financial Advice) Regulation 2015; and the Corporations Amendment (Financial Advice Measures) Act 2016.

30 The Hon K O'Dwyer MP, Minister for Revenue and Financial Services, "Higher Standards for Financial Advisers to Commence", Media Release (9 February 2017). For an overview of these requirements, see: McGrath and Walker, *New Accountability in Financial Services*.
31 Financial Planners and Advisers Code of Ethics 2019, Introduction, available at: www.legislation.gov.au/F2019L00117/latest/text.
32 Australian Banking Association, "The Banking Code" (2021), available at: www.ausbanking.org.au/banking-code/.
33 Australian Banking Association, "Tougher rules, back to basics and the fixing culture one year on" (2020), available at: www.ausbanking.org.au/wp-content/uploads/2020/01/ABA-Media-Release-One-year-on-from-the-RC.pdf.
34 Australian Banking Association and Banking Code Compliance Committee, "The Banking Code Compliance Committee Charter" (2019), available at: https://bankingcode.org.au/app/uploads/2019/09/BCCC-Charter-1-July-2019-1.pdf.
35 For an overview, see: J McGrath, *Corporate and White-collar Crime in Ireland: A New Architecture of Regulatory Enforcement* (Manchester University Press: Manchester 2015).
36 P Honohan, "The Irish Banking Crisis: Regulatory and Financial Stability Policy 2003-2008", *Central Bank of Ireland* (2010), available at: www.gov.ie/pdf/?file=https://assets.gov.ie/42244/ba5aea41a0c345a1a3767ad036205f93.pdf#page=null; P Nyberg, " Misjudging Risk: Causes of the Systemic Banking Crisis in Ireland, Report of Commission of Investigation into the Banking Sector in Ireland" *Government Publications Office* (2011), available at: www.gov.ie/pdf/?file=https://assets.gov.ie/42234/b40d2827610943fbb78e9120fa70e719.pdf#page=null; K Regling and M Watson, "A Preliminary Report on the Sources of Ireland's Banking Crisis", *Government Publications Office* (2010) available at: https://inquiries.oireachtas.ie/banking/wp-content/uploads/2014/12/Regling-Watson-May-2010.pdf; Central Bank of Ireland, "Behaviour and culture of the Irish Retail Banks" (2018), available at: www.centralbank.ie/docs/default-source/publications/corporate-reports/behaviour-and-culture-of-the-irish-retail-banks.pdf?sfvrsn=2.
37 Central Bank of Ireland, "Consumer Protection Code" (2012), available at: www.centralbank.ie/docs/default-source/regulation/consumer-protection/other-codes-of-conduct/unofficial-consolidation-of-the-consumer-protection-code.pdf?sfvrsn=edd0811d_7; Central Bank of Ireland, "Fitness and Probity Standards" (2014), available at: www.centralbank.ie/docs/default-source/regulation/how-we-regulate/authorisation/fitness-probity/regulated-financial-service-providers/regulatory-requirements/gns-4-1-1-3-1-1-fitness-and-probity-standards.pdf?sfvrsn=6; Central Bank of Ireland, "Minimum Competency Code" (2017), available at: www.centralbank.ie/docs/default-source/regulation/how-we-regulate/authorisation/minimum-competency/minimum-competency-code-2017.pdf?sfvrsn=4. See also, Central Bank (Supervision and Enforcement) Act 2013 (Section 48(1)) Minimum Competency Regulations 2017.
38 Central Bank of Ireland, "Behaviour and Culture of the Irish Retail Banks" (2018), available at: www.centralbank.ie/docs/default-source/publications/corporate-reports/behaviour-and-culture-of-the-irish-retail-banks.pdf?sfvrsn=2.
39 J McGrath, "From Responsive to Meta-regulation: A Critical Review of the Enforcement Powers and Performance of the Central Bank of Ireland", *Irish Jurist*, vol. 66, no. 1 (2021), p.1.
40 Irish Banking Culture Board, "DECIDE" (2020), available at: www.irishbankingcultureboard.ie/wp-content/uploads/2021/02/67621-IBCB-Decide-framework-A5-WEB.pdf.
41 Institute of Bankers in Ireland, "Developing an Effective Consumer Focused Culture in Financial Services", available at: https://iob.ie/areas/culture.
42 McGrath and Walker, "Regulating Ethics".
43 T Hirschi, *Causes of Delinquency* (University of California Press: Berkeley, 1969), p. 33.
44 AK Cohen & J Short, "Juvenile delinquency", in R Merton & R Nisbet (eds), *Contemporary Social Problems* (Harcourt Brace and World: New York, 1961).
45 WC Reckless, "A New Theory of Delinquency and Crime", *Federal Probation*, vol. 25, no. 4 (1961), p.42.
46 J Toby, "Crime in the Schools", in JQ Wilson (ed), *Crime and Public Policy* (Institute for Contemporary Studies: San Francisco, 1983).
47 MR Gottfredson and T Hirschi, *A General Theory of Crime*, (Stanford University Press: Stanford, 1990), p.181.

48 A Bottoms, "Compliance and Community Penalties", in A Bottoms, L Gelsthorpe and S Rex (eds), *Community Penalties: Change and Challenges* (Willan: London, 2013), p.101.
49 TR Tyler, *Why People Obey the Law* (Princeton University Press: Princeton, 1990).
50 G Robinson and F McNeill, "Exploring the Dynamics of Compliance with Community Penalties", *Theoretical Criminology*, vol. 12, no. 4, (2008), p.431.
51 See also: I Ayres & J Braithwaite, *Responsive Regulation: Transcending the Deregulation Debate* (Oxford University Press: Oxford, 1992); K Murphy, "Regulating More Effectively: The Relationship Between Procedural Justice, Legitimacy, and Tax Non-compliance", *Journal of Law and Society*, vol. 32, no. 4 (2005), p.562; LW Sherman, "Defiance, Deterrence and Irrelevance: A Theory of the Criminal Sanction", *Journal of Research in Crime and Delinquency*, vol. 30, no. 4, 1993, p.445; LW Sherman, H Strang, & DJ Woods, "Captains of Restorative Justice: Experience, Legitimacy and Recidivism by Type of Offence", in E Weitkamp & H Kerner (eds), *Restorative Justice in Context: International Practice and Directions*, (Willan: London, 2003).
52 B Van Rooiji & A Fine, *The Behavioral Code: The Hidden Ways the Law Makes us Better or Worse* (Beacon Press: New York, 2021).
53 Ayres and Braithwaite, *Responsive Regulation*; C Parker, "Twenty Years of Responsive Regulation: An Appreciation and Appraisal", *Regulation & Governance*, vol. 7, no. 1 (2013), p.2.
54 Ayres and Braithwaite, *Responsive Regulation*, p. 19.
55 C Ford, "Prospects for Scalability: Relationships and Uncertainty in Responsive Regulation", *Regulation & Governance*, vol. 7, no. 1 (2013), p.14 at p.22.
56 N Gunningham, P Grabosky, & D Sinclair, *Smart Regulation: Designing Environmental Policy* (Oxford University Press: Oxford, 1998); N Gunningham, "Compliance, Enforcement, and Regulatory Excellence", in C Coglianese (ed), *Achieving Regulatory Excellence* (Brookings Institution Press: Washington, DC, 2016).
57 J Van Erp & W Huisman, "Smart regulation and enforcement of illegal disposal of electronic waste", *Criminology & Public Policy*, vol. 9, no. 3 (2010), p.579.
58 J McGrath, "From Responsive to Meta-regulation".
59 C Scott, "The Regulatory State and Beyond", in P Drahos (ed), *Regulatory Theory: Foundations and Applications* (Australian National University Press: Acton, 2017), p.265; C Scott, "Regulation in the Age of Governance: The Rise of the Post-Regulatory State", in J Jordana & D Levi-Faur *The Politics of Regulation: Institutions and Regulatory Reforms for the Age of Governance* (Elgar Publishing: Cheltenham, 2004), p.145; J Black, "Decentring Regulation: Understanding the Role of Regulation and Self-regulation in a 'post-regulatory' World", *Current Legal Problems*, vol. 54, no. 1 (2001), p.103.
60 P Grabowsky, "Meta-Regulation" in Drahos (ed) *Regulatory Theory*.
61 J Braithwaite, "Flipping Markets to Virtue with Qui Tam and Restorative Justice", *Accounting, Organizations and Society*, vol. 38, no. 6-7 (2013), p.458.
62 N Ellemers, R Spears, & B Doosje, "Self and Social Identity", *Annual Review of Psychology*, vol. 53, no.1 (2002), p.161.
63 N Ellemers & J Van der Toorn, "Groups as Moral Anchors", *Current Opinion in Psychology*, vol. 6 (2015), p.189.
64 B Lindström, S Jangard, I Selbing, & A Olsson, "The role of a 'common is moral' heuristic in the stability and change of moral norms", *Journal of Experimental Psychology: General*, vol. 147, no. 2 (2018), p.228.
65 CR Sunstein, "Moral heuristics", *Behavioral and Brain Sciences*, vol. 28 no. 4 (2005), p.531.
66 N Ellemers, R Spears, & B Doosje (eds), *Social Identity: Context, Commitment, Content* (Blackwell: Oxford, 1999).
67 N Ellemers & K van den Bos, "Morality in groups: On the social-regulatory functions of right and wrong", *Social and Personality Psychology Compass*, vol. 6 (2012), p.878.
68 M Barreto & N Ellemers, "You Can't Always do What you Want: Social Identity and Self-presentational Determinants of the Choice to Work for a Low-status Group", *Personality and Social Psychology Bulletin*, vol. 26, no. 8 (2000), p.891.
69 CW Leach, N Ellemers, & M Barreto, "Group virtue: The importance of morality (vs. competence and sociability) in the positive evaluation of in-groups", *Journal of Personality and Social Psychology*, vol. 93, no. 2 (2007), p.234.

70 N Ellemers, S Pagliaro, & M Barreto, "Morality and Behavioural Regulation in Groups: A Social Identity Approach", *European Review of Social Psychology*, vol. 24, no. 1 (2013), p.160.
71 WB Swann, LP Milton, & JT Polzer, "Should we Create a Niche or Fall in Line? Identity Negotiation and Small Group Effectiveness", *Journal Personality and Social Psychology*, vol 79, no. 2 (2000), p.238; RF Baumeister & MR Leary, "The Need to Belong: Desire for Interpersonal Attachments as a Fundamental Human Motivation", *Psychology Bulletin*, vol. 117, no. 3 (1995), p.497.
72 N Ellemers, "The Group Self", *Science*, vol. 336, no. 6083 (2012), p.848; N Ellemers & SA Haslam, "Social Identity Theory", in P van Lange, A Kruglanski, & T Higgins (eds), *Handbook of Theories of Social Psychology*. (Sage Publishing: London, 2011), p.379.
73 A Salz & R Collins, "Salz Review: An Independent review of Barclays' Business Practices", available at: https://online.wsj.com/public/resources/documents/SalzReview04032013.pdf. See also: A Jordanoska & N Lord, "Scripting the Mechanics of the Benchmark Manipulation Corporate Scandals: The 'Guardian' paradox", *European Journal of Criminology*, vol. 17, no. 1 (2020), p.9.
74 *R v Hayes* [2015] EWCA Crim 1944.
75 McGrath & Walker, *New Accountability*, pp.88-95.
76 A Francis & N Ryder, "Preventing and Intervening in White Collar Crimes: The Role of Regulatory Agencies", in ML Rorie (ed) *The Handbook of White-Collar Crime* (Wiley and Sons: New Jersey, 2019), p.262 at p.274.
77 A Bottoms & A Von Hirsch, "The Crime Preventive Impact of Penal Sanctions", in P Cane & HM Kritzer (eds), *The Oxford Handbook of Empirical Legal Research* (Oxford University Press: Oxford, 2010), p.96.
78 S Simpson et al, "Corporate Crime Deterrence: A Systematic Review", *Campbell Systematic Reviews*, vol. 10, no. 1 (2014), p.1.
79 Van Rooij & Fine, *The Behavioral Code*.
80 Z Iscenko et al, "Behaviour and Compliance in Organisations", *FCA Occasional Paper 24* (2016).
81 M Carney, *Value(s): Building a Better World for All* (PublicAffairs: New York, 2021), p.205.
82 D Awrey, W Blair, & D Kershaw, "Between Law and Markets: Is there a Role for Culture and Ethics in Financial Regulation?", *Delaware Journal of Corporate Law*, vol. 38 (2013), p.191.
83 J Black, "Decentring Regulation"; J Braithwaite, "Types of Responsiveness" in Drahos (ed), *Regulatory Theory*, p.117.
84 K Cook & T Malone, "Social Capital & Superminds", in *Starling Compendium: Culture & Conduct Risk in the Banking Sector* (2021), p. 59, available at: https://starlingtrust.com/the-starling-compendium/.
85 N Ellemers, "The Group Self".
86 B Lindström et al, "The role of a 'common is moral'".
87 R Rhodes, *Understanding Governance*, (Open University Press: Buckingham, 1997); N Rose, *Powers of Freedom: Reframing Political Thought* (Cambridge University Press: Cambridge, 1997).
88 M Foucault, *Discipline and Punish* (Penguin: Harmondsworth, 1977); M Foucault (1991) Governmentality, in G Burchell, C Gordon, & P Miller (eds) *The Foucault Effect: Studies in Governmentality* (University of Chicago Press: Chicago, 1991), p.87; N Rose, *Powers of Freedom: Reframing Political Thought* (Cambridge University Press: Cambridge 1999), p.49.
89 For early contributions, see: J Toby, "Social Disorganization and Stake in Conformity: Complementary Factors in the Predatory Behavior of Hoodlums", *Journal of Criminal Law and Criminology*, vol. 48 (1957), p.12; S Briar & I Piliavin, "Delinquency, situational inducements, and commitment to conformity", *Social Problems*, vol. 13 (1965), p.35.
90 JR Lasley, "Toward a Control Theory of White-collar Offending", *Journal of Quantitative Criminology*, vol. 4, no. 4 (1988), p.347. See also: R Agnew, NL Piquero, & FT Cullen, "General strain theory and white-collar crime" in SS Simpson and D Weisburd (eds), *The Criminology of White-collar Crime* (Springer: New York, 2009) p.35; SS Simpson, *Corporate Crime, Law, and Social Control* (Cambridge University Press: Cambridge, 2002).
91 McGrath & Walker, *New Accountability in Financial Services*.
92 McGrath & Walker, "Regulating ethics in financial services".

References

Legislation

Central Bank (Individual Accountability Framework) Act 2023
Corporations Amendment (Further Future of Financial Advice Measures) Act 2012
Corporations Amendment (Future of Financial Advice) Act 2012
Corporations Amendment (Revising Future of Financial Advice) Regulation 2014
Corporations Amendment (Financial Advice) Regulation 2015
Corporations Amendment (Financial Advice Measures) Act 2016

Cases

Attorney-General's Reference (No 2 of 1999) [2000] 2 Cr App R 207.
Meridian Global Funds Management Asia Ltd v Securities Commission [1995] 2 AC 500.
R v Barclays PLC and Barclays Bank Plc [2018] (Southwark Crown Court).
R v Hayes [2015] EWCA Crim 1944.
R v Jackson Transport (Osset) Ltd (Health and Safety Bulletin, November 1996).
R v Kite and OLL Ltd [1996] 2 Cr. App. R.(s.) 295.
R v P&O Ferries [1991] 93 Cr. App. R. 72.
R v Varley and others [2019] EWCA Crim 1074.
Salomon v A Salomon & Co Ltd [1896] UKHL 1 [1897] AC 22.
Tesco Supermarkets v Nattrass [1972] AC 153.

Books and book chapters

Ackroyd S, "Sociological and Organisational Theories of Professions and Professionalism", in Dent M, Bourgeault IL, Denis L, & Kuhlmann E (eds), *The Routledge Companion to the Professions and Professionalism* (Routledge: London, 2016).
Agnew R, Piquero NL, & Cullen FT, "General Strain Theory and White-Collar Crime", in Simpson SS & Weisburd D (eds), *The Criminology of White-Collar Crime* (Springer: New York, 2009).
Ayres I & Braithwaite J, *Responsive Regulation: Transcending the Deregulation Debate* (Oxford University Press: Oxford, 1992).
Bottoms A & Von Hirsch A, "The Crime Preventive Impact of Penal Sanctions", in Cane P & Kritzer HM (eds), *The Oxford Handbook of Empirical Legal Research* (Oxford University Press: Oxford, 2010).
Carney M, *Value(s): Building a Better World for All* (PublicAffairs: New York, 2021).
Cohen AK & Short J, "Juvenile Delinquency", in Merton R & Nisbet R (eds), *Contemporary Social Problems* (Harcourt Brace and World: New York, 1961).
Doyle DM & McGrath J, "Attributing Criminal Responsibility for Workplace Fatalities and Deaths in Custody: Corporate Manslaughter in Britain and Ireland", in Fitzgibbon K & Walklate S (eds), *Homicide, Gender and Responsibility: An International Perspective* (Routledge: London, 2016).
Ellemers N & Haslam SA, "Social Identity Theory", in van Lange P, Kruglanski A, & Higgins T (eds), *Handbook of Theories of Social Psychology* (Sage Publishing: London, 2011).
Ellemers N, Spears R, & Doosje, B (eds), *Social Identity: Context, Commitment, Content* (Blackwell: Oxford, 1999).
Foucault M, *Discipline and Punish* (Penguin: Harmondsworth, 1977).
Foucault M, "Governmentality", in Burchell G, Gordon C, & Miller P (eds), *The Foucault Effect: Studies in Governmentality* (University of Chicago Press: Chicago, 1991).
Francis A & Ryder N, "Preventing and Intervening in White Collar Crimes: The Role of Regulatory Agencies", in Rorie ML (ed), *The Handbook of White-Collar Crime* (Wiley and Sons: New Jersey, 2019).
Gobert J & Punch M, *Rethinking Corporate Crime* (Cambridge University Press: Cambridge, 2003).
Gottfredson MR & Hirschi T, *A General Theory of Crime* (Stanford University Press: Stanford, 1990).
Grabowsky P, "Meta-Regulation", in Drahos P (ed), *Regulatory Theory: Foundations and Applications* (Australian National University Press: Acton, 2017).

Gunningham N, "Compliance, Enforcement, and Regulatory Excellence", in Coglianese C (ed), *Achieving Regulatory Excellence* (Brookings Institution Press: Washington, DC, 2016).
Gunningham N, Grabosky P, & Sinclair D, *Smart Regulation: Designing Environmental Policy* (Oxford University Press: Oxford, 1998).
Hirschi T, *Causes of Delinquency* (University of California Press: Berkeley, 1969).
McGrath J, *Corporate and White-Collar Crime in Ireland: A New Architecture of Regulatory Enforcement* (Manchester University Press: Manchester 2015).
McGrath J & Walker C, *New Accountability in Financial Services: Changing Individual Behaviour and Culture* (Springer Nature: London, 2021).
Rhodes R, *Understanding Governance* (Open University Press: Buckingham, 1997).
Rose N, *Powers of Freedom: Reframing Political Thought* (Cambridge University Press: Cambridge 1999).
Scott C, "Regulation in the Age of Governance: The Rise of the Post-Regulatory State", in Jordana J & Levi-Faur D (eds), *The Politics of Regulation: Institutions and Regulatory Reforms for the Age of Governance* (Elgar Publishing: Cheltenham, 2004).
Scott C, "The Regulatory State and Beyond", in Drahos P (ed), *Regulatory Theory: Foundations and Applications* (Australian National University Press: Acton, 2017).
Sherman LW, Strang H, & Woods DJ, "Captains of Restorative Justice: Experience, Legitimacy and Recidivism by Type of Offence", in Weitkamp E & Kerner H (eds), *Restorative Justice in Context: International Practice and Directions* (Willan: London, 2003).
Simpson SS, *Corporate Crime, Law, and Social Control* (Cambridge University Press: Cambridge, 2002).
Toby J, "Crime in the Schools", in Wilson JQ (ed), *Crime and Public Policy* (Institute for Contemporary Studies: San Francisco, 1983).
Tyler TR, *Why People Obey the Law* (Princeton University Press: Princeton, 1990).
Van Rooiji B & Fine A, *The Behavioral Code: The Hidden Ways the Law Makes Us Better or Worse* (Beacon Press: New York, 2021).
Wells C, *Corporations and Criminal Responsibility* (Oxford University Press: Oxford, 2nd edn, 2001).

Journal articles

Awrey D, Blair W, & Kershaw D, "Between Law and Markets: Is There a Role for Culture and Ethics in Financial Regulation?", *Delaware Journal of Corporate Law*, vol. 38 (2013), pp.191–245.
Barreto M & Ellemers N, "You Can't Always Do What You Want: Social Identity and Self-Presentational Determinants of the Choice to Work for a Low-status Group", *Personality and Social Psychology Bulletin*, vol. 26, no. 8 (2000), pp.891–906.
Baumeister RF & Leary MR, "The Need to Belong: Desire for Interpersonal Attachments as a Fundamental Human Motivation", *Psychology Bulletin*, vol. 117, no. 3 (1995), pp.497–529.
Black J, "Decentring Regulation: Understanding the Role of Regulation and Self-Regulation in a 'Post-Regulatory' World", *Current Legal Problems*, vol. 54, no. 1 (2001), pp.103–146.
Braithwaite J, "Flipping Markets to Virtue with Qui Tam and Restorative Justice", *Accounting, Organizations and Society*, vol. 38, no. 6–7 (2013), pp.458–468.
Briar S & Piliavin I, "Delinquency, Situational Inducements, and Commitment to Conformity", *Social Problems*, vol. 13 (1965), pp.35–45.
Coffee JC, "'No Soul to Damn: No Body to Kick': An Unscandalized Inquiry into the Problem of Corporate Punishment", *Michigan Law Review*, vol. 79, no. 3 (1981), pp.386–459.
Ellemers N, "The Group Self", *Science*, vol. 336, no. 6083 (2012), pp.848–852.
Ellemers N, Pagliaro S, & Barreto M, "Morality and Behavioural Regulation in Groups: A Social Identity Approach", *European Review of Social Psychology*, vol. 24, no. 1 (2013), pp.160–193.
Ellemers N, Spears R, & Doosje B, "Self and Social Identity", *Annual Review of Psychology*, vol. 53, no.1 (2002), pp.161–186.
Ellemers N & van den Bos K, "Morality in Groups: On the Social-Regulatory Functions of Right and Wrong", *Social and Personality Psychology Compass*, vol. 6 (2012), pp.878–889.
Ford C, "Prospects for Scalability: Relationships and Uncertainty in Responsive Regulation", *Regulation & Governance*, vol. 7, no. 1 (2013), pp.14–29.
Gobert J, "Corporate Criminality: Four Models of Fault", *Legal Studies*, vol. 14, no. 3 (1994), pp.393–410.

Hickman E, "Is the Senior Managers and Certification Regime Changing Banking for Good?", *Modern Law Review*, vol. 85, no. 6 (2022), pp.1440–1462.

Jordanoska A & Lord N, "Scripting the Mechanics of the Benchmark Manipulation Corporate Scandals: The 'Guardian' Paradox", *European Journal of Criminology*, vol. 17, no. 1 (2020), pp.9–30.

Lasley JR, "Toward a Control Theory of White-Collar Offending", *Journal of Quantitative Criminology*, vol. 4, no. 4 (1988), pp.347–362.

Leach CW, Ellemers N, & Barreto M, "Group Virtue: The Importance of Morality (vs. Competence and Sociability) in the Positive Evaluation of In-Groups", *Journal of Personality and Social Psychology*, vol. 93, no. 2 (2007), pp.234–249.

Lindström B, Jangard S, Selbing I, & Olsson A, "The Role of a 'Common is Moral' Heuristic in the Stability and Change of Moral Norms", *Journal of Experimental Psychology: General*, vol. 147, no. 2 (2018), pp.228–242.

McGrath J, "From Responsive to Meta-Regulation: A Critical Review of the Enforcement Powers and Performance of the Central Bank of Ireland", *Irish Jurist*, vol. 66, no. 1 (2021), p.101–133.

McGrath J, "Individual Criminal Responsibility for Corporate Managers: Director of Public Prosecutions v TN", *Irish Supreme Court Review*, vol. 3 (2021), pp.1–16.

McGrath J & Walker C, "Regulating Ethics in Financial Services: Engaging Industry to Achieve Regulatory Objectives", *Regulation & Governance*, vol. 17, no. 3 (2023), pp.791–809.

Murphy K, "Regulating More Effectively: The Relationship Between Procedural Justice, Legitimacy, and Tax Non-compliance", *Journal of Law and Society*, vol. 32, no. 4 (2005), pp.562–589.

Parker C, "Twenty Years of Responsive Regulation: An Appreciation and Appraisal", *Regulation & Governance*, vol. 7, no. 1 (2013), pp.2–13.

Robinson G & McNeill F, "Exploring the Dynamics of Compliance with Community Penalties", *Theoretical Criminology*, vol. 12, no. 4, (2008), pp.431–449.

Reckless WC, "A New Theory of Delinquency and Crime", *Federal Probation*, vol. 25, no. 4 (1961), pp.42–46.

Sherman LW, "Defiance, Deterrence and Irrelevance: A Theory of the Criminal Sanction", *Journal of Research in Crime and Delinquency*, vol. 30, no. 4 (1993), pp.445–473.

Simpson S, Rorie M, Alper M, Schell-Busey N, Laufer WS, & Craig Smith N, "Corporate Crime Deterrence: A Systematic Review", *Campbell Systematic Reviews*, vol. 10, no. 1 (2014), pp.1–105.

Sunstein CR, "Moral heuristics", *Behavioral and Brain Sciences*, vol. 28 no. 4 (2005), pp.531–542.

Swann WB, Milton LP, & Polzer JT, "Should We Create a Niche or Fall in Line? Identity Negotiation and Small Group Effectiveness", *Journal Personality and Social Psychology*, vol. 79, no. 2 (2000), pp.238–250.

Toby J, "Social Disorganization and Stake in Conformity: Complementary Factors in the Predatory Behavior of Hoodlums", *Journal of Criminal Law and Criminology*, vol. 48 (1957), pp.12–17.

Van Erp J & Huisman W, "Smart Regulation and Enforcement of Illegal Disposal of Electronic Waste", *Criminology & Public Policy*, vol. 9, no. 3 (2010), pp.579–590.

Reports and websites

Australian Banking Association, "The Banking Code" (2021), available at: www.ausbanking.org.au/banking-code/

Australian Banking Association, "Tougher Rules, Back to Basics and the Fixing Culture One Year On" (2020), available at: www.ausbanking.org.au/wp-content/uploads/2020/01/ABA-Media-Release-One-year-on-from-the-RC.pdf

Australian Banking Association and Banking Code Compliance Committee, "The Banking Code Compliance Committee Charter" (2019), available at: https://bankingcode.org.au/app/uploads/2019/09/BCCC-Charter-1-July-2019-1.pdf

Central Bank of Ireland, "Behaviour and Culture of the Irish Retail Banks" (2018), available at: www.centralbank.ie/docs/default-source/publications/corporate-reports/behaviour-and-culture-of-the-irish-retail-banks.pdf?sfvrsn=2

Central Bank of Ireland, "Consumer Protection Code" (2012), available at: www.centralbank.ie/docs/default-source/regulation/consumer-protection/other-codes-of-conduct/unofficial-consolidation-of-the-consumer-protection-code.pdf?sfvrsn=edd0811d_7

Central Bank of Ireland, "Fitness and Probity Standards" (2014), available at: www.centralbank.ie/docs/default-source/regulation/how-we-regulate/authorisation/fitness-probity/regulated-financial-service-providers/regulatory-requirements/gns-4-1-1-3-1-1-fitness-and-probity-standards.pdf?sfvrsn=6

Central Bank of Ireland, "Minimum Competency Code" (2017), available at: www.centralbank.ie/docs/default-source/regulation/how-we-regulate/authorisation/minimum-competency/minimum-competency-code-2017.pdf?sfvrsn=4

Cook K & Malone T, "Social Capital & Superminds", in *Starling Compendium: Culture & Conduct Risk in the Banking Sector* (2021), available at: https://starlingtrust.com/the-starling-compendium/

Financial Planners and Advisers Code of Ethics (2019), available at: www.legislation.gov.au/F2019L00117/latest/text

Financial Services Culture Board, "FCSB Wind-Up-Statement" (2023), available at: https://financialservicescultureboard.org.uk/fscb-wind-up-statement/

Harvey T, "Man on a Mission an Interview with David Green, CB, QC, Director of U.K.'s Serious Fraud Office", *Fraud Magazine* (2013), available at: www.fraud-magazine.com/article.aspx?id=4294980221

Hayne KM, "Final Report of the Royal Commission into Misconduct in the Banking, Superannuation and Financial Services Industry" (2018), available at: https://treasury.gov.au/publication/p2019-fsrc-final-report

Honohan P, "The Irish Banking Crisis: Regulatory and Financial Stability Policy 2003–2008", *Central Bank of Ireland* (2010), available at: www.gov.ie/pdf/?file=https://assets.gov.ie/42244/ba5aea41a0c345a1a3767ad036205f93.pdf#page=null

Institute of Bankers in Ireland, "Developing an Effective Consumer Focused Culture in Financial Services", available at: https://iob.ie/areas/culture

Irish Banking Culture Board, "DECIDE" (2020), available at: www.irishbankingcultureboard.ie/wp-content/uploads/2021/02/67621-IBCB-Decide-framework-A5-WEB.pdf

Iscenko Z, Pickard C, Smart L & Vasas Z, "Behaviour and Compliance in Organisations", *FCA Occasional Paper 24* (2016).

Lamport AM, "Banking – Business or Profession?", *Bankers' Magazine*, vol. 122, no. 3 (1931), p.317, available at: https://archive.org/stream/sim_bankers-magazine_1931-03_122_3/sim_bankers-magazine_1931-03_122_3_djvu.txt

Nyberg P, "Misjudging Risk: Causes of the Systemic Banking Crisis in Ireland, Report of Commission of Investigation into the Banking Sector in Ireland", *Government Publications Office* (2011), available at: www.gov.ie/pdf/?file=https://assets.gov.ie/42234/b40d2827610943fbb78e9120fa70e719.pdf#page=null

O'Dwyer K, "Higher Standards for Financial Advisers to Commence", Media Release (9 February 2017).

Omerod D, "Corporate Criminal Liability – Lessons from Across the Irish Sea", *Law Reform Commission Annual Conference* (2016), available at: www.lawreform.ie/_fileupload/Speeches/Annual%20Conference%202016%20Professor%20David%20Ormerod%20Corporate%20criminal%20liability%20%20Lessons%20from%20across%20the%20Irish%20Sea.pdf.

Parliamentary Commission on Banking Standards, "Changing Banking for Good: Vol. 1" (2013).

Regling K & Watson M, "A Preliminary Report on the Sources of Ireland's Banking Crisis", *Government Publications Office* (2010) available at: https://inquiries.oireachtas.ie/banking/wp-content/uploads/2014/12/Regling-Watson-May-2010.pdf

Salz A & Collins R, "Salz Review: An Independent Review of Barclays' Business Practices", available at: https://online.wsj.com/public/resources/documents/SalzReview04032013.pdf

Serious Fraud Office, "Former Barclays Executives Acquitted of Conspiracy to Commit Fraud" (2020), available at: www.sfo.gov.uk/2020/02/28/former-barclays-executives-acquitted-of-conspiracy-to-commit-fraud/#:~:text=Former%20Barclays%20executives%20acquitted%20of%20conspiracy%20to%20commit%20fraud,-28%20February%2C%202020&text=Roger%20Jenkins%2C%20Richard%20Boath%20and,during%20the%202008%20Financial%20Crisis

The Law Reform Commission, "Consultation Paper on Corporate Killing" (2003), available at: www.lawreform.ie/_fileupload/consultation%20papers/cpCorporate%20Killing.pdf

The Law Reform Commission, "Report: Regulatory Powers and Corporate Offences" (2018), available at: www.lawreform.ie/_fileupload/Completed%20Projects/LRC%20119-2018%20Regulatory%20Powers%20and%20Corporate%20Offences%20Volume%201.pdf

30
ECOCIDE, ECOJUSTICE, AND CRIMINAL RESPONSIBILITY IN INTERNATIONAL LAW

Liana Georgieva Minkova

Introduction

Amidst the environmental devastation caused during the Vietnam War, in the 1970s legal scholars began advocating for the prohibition of "ecocide" in international law.[1] Following the establishment of the International Criminal Court (ICC) in 1998,[2] that campaign embraced the prospect of making ecocide the "fifth international crime", alongside genocide, crimes against humanity, war crimes, and aggression.[3] Advocates for the criminalisation of ecocide at the ICC consider individual criminal responsibility a potent tool for addressing environmental harm. On this account, unlike fining corporations, which may not significantly disrupt their operation, criminalising ecocide would make the individuals who authorise environmentally harmful conducts personally accountable for their actions.[4] That campaign culminated in 2021 when the Independent Expert Panel (IEP) convened by the Stop Ecocide Foundation presented a new draft definition of ecocide, which received significant attention within the international criminal justice community.[5]

This chapter, first, situates the efforts to criminalise ecocide within the political and normative context of international criminal justice. While previous work has focused on evaluating different elements of the IEP's definition,[6] this chapter will discuss that and earlier definitions of ecocide by view of the degree to which they conform to both state expectations and the principled foundations of international criminal law (ICL). From that perspective, the IEP's ecocide definition appears pragmatic and with more realistic chances of being adopted into the ICC Statute compared to some previous definitions. Second, this chapter contributes to the critical scholarship on the implications of pursuing socio-ecological justice through ICL.[7] Specifically, the chapter discusses whether individual criminal responsibility could be an effective tool for delivering ecojustice, considering the difficulty of addressing the structural dimensions of environmental violence in ICL.

Criminalising ecocide

The concept

The term ecocide, coined in 1970 by biologist Arthur Galston, originates from the Greek word "oikos" (home) combined with the suffix "cide" (to kill).[8] Barrister and international environmental lawyer Polly Higgins, the best-known advocate of criminalising ecocide, defined it as:

> "...the extensive damage to, destruction of or loss of ecosystem(s) of a given territory, whether by human agency or by other causes, to such an extent that peaceful enjoyment by the inhabitants of that territory has been severely diminished".[9]

Other scholars and civil society initiatives soon joined the anti-ecocide campaign by proposing their own definitions.[10] Examples include the work of Neyret and colleagues[11] and of the international citizens' movement End Ecocide on Earth (End Ecocide).[12]

Even though none of those definitions has been incorporated into the ICC Statute, they have been used by "opinion tribunals" – civil society initiatives seeking to publicise criminal conducts that have not been addressed by "real" domestic and international courts.[13] In 2017, the International Monsanto Tribunal, a civil society project based at The Hague, delivered its advisory opinion which called for the criminalisation of ecocide in the ICC Statute[14] and in 2018, the Permanent Peoples' Tribunal included the term "ecocide" in its statute under the rubric of "ecological crimes".[15] End Ecocide has also worked with the International Rights of Nature Tribunal, which employs earth jurisprudence to address environmental injustices.[16] While the decisions of opinion tribunals carry only symbolic value, they nevertheless indicate a growing interest among international lawyers and non-governmental organisations (NGOs) in pursuing the criminalisation of ecocide in a *real* court, such as the ICC.[17]

The challenges

Yet, those efforts face important challenges. First, as definitions of ecocide proliferate, commentators have started expressing concerns that the lack of consensus on the precise requirements could reduce the "effectiveness" of the term ecocide.[18] Apart from the shared understanding that ecocide referred to significant instances of environmental harm,[19] there has been little agreement on the elements of that crime. Even the degree of significance of environmental harm has remained uncertain, with proposals including terms such as "massiv[e]",[20] "extensive",[21] and "severe".[22] The lack of a uniform definition has been a major obstacle to its criminalisation. As observed at the Monsanto Tribunal, making progress on a "precise legal definition" of ecocide would be the necessary first step towards the incorporation of that crime into the ICC Statute.[23]

The second challenge was framing the definition in a way that would gain support from ICC state parties. The criminalisation of ecocide in ICL would require government officials and business managers to give up on lucrative but ecologically harmful practices. The general hesitancy among states to pay those costs in exchange for offering environmental protection[24] was displayed in 1996, when efforts to criminalise peacetime environmental destruction in the Draft Code of Crimes Against the Peace and Security of Mankind failed.[25] Yet, that does not suggest that any effort to criminalise ecocide at the ICC would remain unsuccessful.

International organisation theory has shown that the lack of *unanimous* support among states is not an obstacle to the promotion of new norms.[26] In ICL, a well-known example is the successful lobbying of NGOs, supported by a group of "like-minded" states, to grant more freedoms to the ICC prosecutor and judges, despite the opposition of powerful states to those ideas.[27] It is possible that a similar like-minded group of states could support the criminalisation of ecocide at the ICC. Since 2019 the Republic of Vanuatu has publicly expressed support for that idea.[28] More recently, in 2022, Belgium proposed the criminalisation of ecocide in domestic law.[29] Efforts have also been made at the European Union (EU) to recognise ecocide as a crime in the revised version of the Directive on Protection of the Environment Through Criminal Law.[30] In fact, in March 2023 the European Parliament agreed on a text for the new directive[31] which proposes that:

"Member States shall ensure that any conduct causing severe and widespread, or severe and long-term, or severe and irreversible damage is treated as an offence of particular gravity and sanctioned as such in accordance with the legal systems of the Member States".[32]

Stop Ecocide have welcomed this development as a historic step forward to the criminalisation of ecocide.[33]

Yet, there are still challenges to overcome. As observed by Heller, the ecocide definitions under consideration in Belgium and at the EU[34] both restrict ecocide to acts that are unlawful under domestic or EU legislation *and* cause severe environmental damage.[35] Specifically, according to the proposal for a revised EU Directive on Protection of the Environment Through Criminal Law, "unlawful" acts are those that breach "Union law protecting the environment or national laws, administrative regulations or decisions giving effect to that Union law".[36] But severe environmental destruction could also result from acts that have not yet been prohibited by law. While restricting the definition of ecocide to "unlawful" conducts "makes sense" in the context of harmonising EU legislation on the matter[37] it might prove inadequate in ICL, considering the scarcity of absolute prohibitions in international environmental law.[38] To offer greater protection to the environment, an ecocide definition in ICL should address both unlawful and lawful conducts resulting in severe ecological harm.[39] However, it appears that anti-ecocide activists would need to convince even "like-minded" states, which have otherwise expressed interest in accountability for ecocide, that the criminalisation of lawful ecocidal conducts would not significantly disrupt the economic activities of their nationals.

The third challenge to the criminalisation of ecocide in ICL concerns what Robinson calls "the deontic constraints" of international criminal justice,[40] namely, the normative significance of constructing the definitions of criminal conducts in a clear and restrained manner. The understandings of ecojustice behind much of the ecocide law proposals resemble the idea that has animated much of the 1990s ICL jurisprudence – namely, that legal rules should be tailored in such a fashion as to prevent the perpetrators of international crimes from escaping responsibility by hiding behind "the fog of collective criminality".[41] In the case of ecocide, "the fog of collective criminality" comprises the complex bureaucratic structures of governments and big corporations, which make it difficult to attribute the crime to a specific individual.[42] A notable obstacle is determining the degree of the individual's intent or knowledge concerning the environmental consequences of their actions,[43] especially in big corporations and government bureaucracies, where individual officers could claim ignorance of the overall effect of their decisions.[44] To prevent those persons from escaping criminal responsibility, many anti-ecocide campaigners have proposed a strict liability approach where "simply establishing that the act was committed", without inquiring into the accused's intent or knowledge of the crime, "would be sufficient to secure a conviction".[45]

However, despite the commitment to piercing the fog of collective criminality, the ambitious proposals to criminalise ecocide as a strict liability offence would likely meet significant obstacles.[46] The principle that criminal responsibility requires both a culpable act (*actus reus*) and a culpable state of mind (*mens rea*) has been central to international criminal justice, even before its official codification into the 1998 ICC Statute. For instance, while the 1945 Charter of the International Military Tribunal (IMT) for Nuremberg criminalised participation in a "criminal organisation" as such, the IMT judges decided to restrict the scope of that provision by instituting a further requirement: that only those members of the organisation who had *known* of its criminal acts could be held criminally responsible for participating in that organisation.[47]

Possibly with such considerations in mind, some ecocide definitions have proposed an alternative approach – to criminalise negligent conducts resulting in ecocide.[48] The negligence standard provides an objective test for establishing the mental element of liability: it asks whether under the same circumstances a prudent person should have known better and refrained from engaging in the prohibited conduct.[49] For instance, the Monsanto Tribunal concluded that the mental element of liability was satisfied where the perpetrator "knew, or *should have known*" that their conduct could result in ecocide.[50]

But a negligence standard would still likely prove controversial in international criminal justice. Even though Article 28(a) ICC Statute, by exception, allows for the punishment of negligent conduct, that provision applies only to the failure of *military* commanders to control the actions of their subordinates.[51] The ICC Statute's drafters were reluctant to extend the negligence standard to civilian superiors, such as corporate and government officials (the likely perpetrators of ecocide). Unlike military commanders, civilian superiors are neither in charge of "an inherently lethal force", nor equipped with a strict disciplinary system of punishing misbehaviour.[52] Consequently, the drafters concluded that a negligence standard applied in a civilian context was "basically contrary to the usual principles of criminal law responsibility".[53]

A new opportunity

The IEP's definition of ecocide

In 2020 Stop Ecocide International embarked upon a new effort to criminalise ecocide in the ICC. The organisation set out to produce a "legally robust" definition of ecocide by convening an independent expert panel of lawyers and academics.[54] Considering the long history of unsuccessful attempts to criminalise ecocide in ICL, it is perhaps unsurprising that pragmatism, in terms of taking both state interests and the normative principle of international criminal justice into consideration, was a guiding factor behind the IEP's definition.[55] Philippe Sands, the IEP's co-chair, noted:

"If we come up with a definition that doesn't have a reasonable prospect of being considered by governments as a possible basis for inclusion in the [ICC] Statute, I consider we would have failed".[56]

To draft a definition with realistic chances of being adopted into the ICC Statute, the IEP first conducted a public consultation with "legal, economic, political, youth, faith and indigenous perspectives"[57] in the form of a survey, which received 402 responses.[58] Following several months of deliberation, in June 2021, the IEP delivered a definition of ecocide, accompanied by a commentary.[59] The panel defined ecocide as:

> "...unlawful or wanton acts committed with knowledge that there is a substantial likelihood of severe and either widespread or long-term damage to the environment being caused by those acts".[60]

Thus, the IEP produced a definition of ecocide which departed from most previous ecocide definitions in important ways.

First, unlike earlier proposals concerning strict and negligence liability, the IEP defines ecocide as a conscious conduct (committed with "knowledge" of a "substantial likelihood"), thus, strengthening its mental element. The survey which preceded the IEP's deliberations shows that only 35 out of 280 recorded responses proposed "no [mental element]"/"strict liability".[61] Intriguingly, the mental element which received the highest support was the most challenging one to establish with respect to environmental harm, namely, "intent" (62 responses). As the survey data does not indicate the professional background of the respondents supporting each option, it remains unclear whether the "intent" proposals were made by government and business representatives, by legal experts who considered that as a more realistic option to convince states to adopt ecocide into the ICC Statute, or by respondents who simply used the term "intent" to refer to the existence of *a* mental element, as opposed to strict liability.[62] In any case, the survey results clearly showed a preference for including a mental element and the rejection of strict liability for ecocide, as well as a preference for demonstrating that the accused had been, at least to some degree, conscious of the environmental risks of their actions.[63] This approach concurs with the position that, while lower standards such as negligence and strict liability might be employed within domestic criminal systems, they are inappropriate in *international* criminal law, which deals with the gravest instances of criminality.[64]

The second way in which pragmatism seems to have influenced the IEP's definition is exemplified by their approach to criminalising otherwise *lawful* conducts that nevertheless lead to environmental destruction. As discussed above, including lawful conducts in the definition of ecocide is crucial for offering meaningful protection to the environment, but it might prove difficult to convince states to support such a definition. The IEP's solution to that dilemma was to strengthen the criminalising threshold that would turn otherwise lawful conducts into ecocide. In many earlier definitions of ecocide, the criminalising threshold had concerned the gravity of the ensuing environmental destruction – only very serious instances of environmental harm could be criminalised as ecocide.[65] By contrast, the IEP decided to add a *second* threshold, in addition to the one concerning the degree of environmental harm, namely, that of "wantonness". According to the IEP's definition, lawful activities constitute ecocide if they are (1) "wanton" and (2) produce a "substantial likelihood of severe and either widespread or long-term damage to the environment", where "wanton" is understood as: acting "with reckless disregard for damage which would be clearly excessive in relation to the social and economic benefits anticipated".[66] The addition of the wantonness requirement reflected the view that socially beneficial industries, such as air transport and the production of computers and smartphones, could, over time, produce severe environmental impact.[67] To avoid obstructing the operation of those industries, the IEP has decided that only "wanton" instances of otherwise lawful severe environmental destruction could be criminalised as ecocide.[68]

The idea of ecocide as a wanton conduct is not new. It is reminiscent of Mark Allan Gray's 1996 definition which included the element of "wastefulness", understood as acts that, in addition to causing serious environmental damage, "produc[e] nothing of benefit *to society*" even if it "greatly benefits a profiteering minority" among government officials and business executives.[69] Similarly, one of the recurring themes in the responses to the IEP's survey was the proposition that the ecocide definition should reflect the notion of "corporate greed/selfishness/profiteering".[70] These suggestions follow the common intuition that severe environmental harm often results from deeply unethical conducts committed by opportunistic individuals at the expense of both society and nature.

What is new, however, is the way in which the IEP has framed the idea of wantonness. The IEP does not propose to criminalise wanton conducts as such, but rather wanton conducts that have been committed with "reckless disregard" for their environmental costs. Consequently, it would not be enough to show that the environmental costs of a particular conduct have exceeded its benefits to prosecute it as ecocide. It must further be shown that the perpetrator had been *conscious* of that fact. The reference to "social and economic benefits anticipated" coupled with the "recklessness" element provides certain leeway to state agencies and corporations.[71] However, members of the IEP have defended that approach as "realistic". According to Voigt, an ecocide definition that excluded any considerations for socio-economic benefits "could perhaps have given a stronger environmental signal but might have been detrimental to the likelihood for being adopted".[72] By contrast, the definition of wantonness which the IEP chose would be a familiar one to states, as it followed the principle of "sustainable development", which, as the IEP insisted, has been adopted in "[m]uch national and international environmental law".[73]

Critical assessment of the IEP's definition

The IEP's definition has been welcomed as the "culmination of years of progress".[74] Stop Ecocide has described it as "the consensus international definition of ecocide".[75] But despite the efforts of the IEP to produce a robust legal definition of ecocide with realistic chances of being incorporated into the ICC Statute, their work has not escaped criticism. Some have called the mental element of liability in the definition "deeply confusing".[76] The "wantonness" element has proven even more contentious as scholars have expressed concern that it would significantly lower the chances of establishing the accused's criminal responsibility for ecocide.[77] A few commentators have further lamented the "missed opportunity" for incorporating corporate liability into the definition of ecocide.[78]

These lines of critique result from the challenges of reconciling the high expectations of environmental advocacy concerning the degree of protection that international trials could offer to the natural environment with the political and normative reality of international criminal justice. As observed by Robinson, there is no "simple" solution when trying to align environmental principles with those of ICL. Rather, international lawyers are left which choosing "which imperfect, criticisable option is the least problematic".[79] While there is still (and would likely continue to be) disagreement among legal experts on the precise nature of that compromise, any definition of ecocide that has a realistic chance of being accepted *into the ICC Statute* has to take into consideration the political and normative reality of ICL.

In fact, many environmental advocates seem to share this view. Proponents of the criminalisation of ecocide have emphasised that the proposed new crime of ecocide is neither "a radical expansion of the foundations of western law, ... nor does it threaten to undermine these foundations". Rather, it is simply "a natural progression" towards addressing environmental harm *through* the existing system of international law.[80] Thus, to obtain state support, ecocide law has been presented not as a challenge to, but as a new development in international law. The same rules which have already been employed to protect human rights are now simply being extended to nature.

Ecocide and ecojustice

These observations, however, do not exhaust the debate on criminalising ecocide in international law. To conclude with the proposition that the IEP's definition of ecocide might be a realistic compromise within the current framework of ICL, precludes bigger questions about the appropriateness of that framework for delivering ecojustice in the first place.[81] While the IEP and many legal commentaries have taken the ICL regime as a given, as observed by Cusato and Jones, the nature of that regime poses challenges to delivering ecojustice.[82]

The argument for individual criminal responsibility

Advocates of the criminalisation of ecocide in international law have argued that individual criminal responsibility is the most effective mechanism for protecting the environment against severe destruction. While some proposals include the idea of corporate liability, it is generally discussed as a complementary mechanism, in addition to that of individual criminal responsibility.[83] The most ardent supporter of criminalising ecocide, Polly Higgins, perceived the attempts to hold accountable "fictional persons", such as corporations, as an opportunity for the real persons – the true authors of corporate conducts – to escape responsibility by "hiding" behind the myth of corporate liability.[84] This line of reasoning echoes older justifications for adopting individual criminal responsibility for crimes against humanity and genocide, namely, that individual criminal responsibility would help end impunity for those persons, who "normally hiding behind the shield of state sovereignty, grossly breach human rights".[85] This argument, once evoked with respect to human rights and now – environmental rights – suggests that individual criminal responsibility would have a significant deterrent impact. As Higgins notes, while a fictional person cannot be imprisoned and could only incur financial sanctions, a natural person risks being deprived of their freedom.[86] Facing that threat, CEOs and government officials are likely to be much more careful in avoiding ecocide prosecutions. Consequently, for Higgins, Short, and South, the criminalisation of ecocide would stop the "flow of [environmental] destruction *at source*".[87] While that is a compelling possibility, the concept of individual criminal responsibility also bears important limitations, which could end up obstructing the process of delivering ecojustice.

The limits of individual criminal responsibility

Studies drawing on insights from political economy and political ecology have elucidated the role of *structural* factors, such as the international capitalist economy, as contributors to ecocide. According to Crook and Short, the capitalist economic model, whose international expansion they call "ecological imperialism",[88] is "structurally compelled to transgress ... the natural limits of production" and, consequently, inevitably leads to significant environmental crises.[89] Understanding the structural dimension of environmental violence is also important for appreciating the link between ecocide and other forms of harm. A proliferating set of publications have explored the nexus between ecocide and genocide.[90] A major theme of those studies is the long history of extraction and exploitation which spans from colonialism to the modern neoliberal economy, simultaneously facilitating ecocidal and genocidal processes.[91]

Another system-level factor which has been identified as a contributor to ecocide is the dominance of Western systems of environmental knowledge production, which present a reductive and misleading picture of environmental harm and the appropriate means to address it.[92] In its quest to rationalise and quantify reality, Western environmentalism has normalised the logic of "offsetting" environmental harm, namely, the idea that environmentally harmful acts (e.g. producing carbon emissions) taking place in one part of the world could be offset by green activities (e.g. planting trees) in another part of the world.[93] But mechanisms such as carbon offsets have triggered significant criticism among environmentalists for failing to challenge "business as usual"[94] and perpetuating the "delusion" that increasing consumption and economic growth could be environmentally sustainable.[95] As observed by Higgins herself, stopping ecocide requires more than greening the economy. Rather, it requires "a shift in thinking, one that does not subject the world to market measurements".[96]

However, instead of inspiring a shift in thinking, international trials might end up perpetuating unsustainable modes of thinking among the ICC's global audience.[97] As observed by Rauxloh, if only individual persons were to be held accountable for ecocide, "it would be too easy" for global corporations "to use them as scapegoats or single them out as 'a few bad apples'", with little disruption to corporate activities.[98] Indeed, international criminal law has often been criticised for its inability to account for structural violence.[99] The *Ongwen* case, which concerned crimes committed by the Lord's Resistance Army (LRA) in Northern Uganda provides an apt example. By singling out Dominic Ongwen's actions as the causal factor behind the crimes, the prosecution's narrative left out other factors that had contributed to the suffering of the people of Northern Uganda, including the government policy of displacing civilians into camps, leaving them vulnerable to both LRA attacks and diseases.[100]

Notably, the inability of ICL to provide an accountability mechanism for structural violence is not a deficiency that could be "fixed" over time. Rather, it results from the fundamental principles of criminal law. The remarks of the ICC prosecution in *Gbagbo and Blé Goudé*, a case which concerned the 2010–2011 post-electoral violence in Côte d'Ivoire, illustrate this point. According to the prosecution, "to establish the history of Ivory Coast ... is not the purpose of this trial". Rather, the purpose of the trial was limited to establishing the criminal acts of the individual accused and their "intent and knowledge" concerning those acts.[101]

Some supporters of the criminalisation of ecocide have recognised the important limitations of individual criminal responsibility. According to Robinson:

"After all, criminal law is a blunt instrument with many negative side-effects. Curbing humanity's self-destructive frenzy of environmental degradation will require systemic societal reforms ... Criminal law is not a viable tool to achieve most of these aims".[102]

Nevertheless, from this perspective, ICL could still be a useful tool for combatting ecocide. While individual criminal responsibility in international law cannot by itself deliver ecojustice, the argument goes, it could deliver more modest results, such as communicating the wrongfulness of ecocide to the ICC's global audience and potentially enforcing that symbolic act with some prosecutions of specific ecocidal conducts in the future.[103] This line of argument suggests that, at worst, the individualisation of criminal responsibility for ecocide would simply not be able to facilitate ecojustice *to the extent* to which environmental advocates aspire.

A more concerning possibility, however, is that the individualisation of criminal responsibility for ecocide could also have an obstructive impact on ecojustice efforts by fostering problematic ways of thinking about environmental harm, namely, in terms of the opportunistic acts of a few greedy individuals rather than as a systemic problem that produces the conditions for such actions.[104] Individual criminal responsibility for ecocide would communicate to the ICC's global audience that the specific actions of a few individuals that have resulted in (or risked resulting in) severe environmental destruction in a particular place and time are wrongful. However, it would not delegitimise the structure of the international political economy which enables such actions by those opportunistic individuals.[105]

Conclusion

While the IEP's definition has been designed to address the political and normative challenges of being accepted as a *legal rule* within the current system of international criminal justice, it might still face significant obstacles to its broader goal, namely, to deliver *justice* for environmental harm. Those obstacles become evident once the focus of discussion shifts away from the elements of the definition and onto the implications of relying on individual criminal responsibility and international trials as tools to address environmental harm. While individual criminal responsibility has been argued to prevent individual persons from "hiding" behind their governments and corporations, it could equally enable major polluters to hide behind the popular image of individual greed and selfishness. Notably, those obstacles could not be easily resolved by simply redrafting the definition of ecocide because they result from the very nature of individual criminal responsibility as a legal tool. While reforming international criminal law at the system level might be significantly more challenging than introducing a new crime to the ICC Statute, it is an important question to start considering in the international legal discussions on ecojustice.

Notes

1 See R Falk, "Environmental Warfare and Ecocide – Facts, Appraisal and Proposal", *Bulletin of Peace Proposals*, vol. 4, no. 1 (1974), p.80.
2 The year of adopting the Rome Statute of the ICC, the ICC began operation in 2002. Rome Statute of the International Criminal Court 1998, in force on 1 July 2002, *United Nations Treaty Series*, vol. 2187, No. 38544, available at: www.icc-cpi.int/sites/default/files/RS-Eng.pdf.

3 A Gauger, MP Rabatel-Fernel, L Kulbicki, D Short, & P Higgins, "The Ecocide project: Ecocide is the missing 5th Crime Against Peace", *Human Rights Consortium* (2013), available at: https://sas-space.sas.ac.uk/4830/1/Ecocide_research_report_19_July_13.pdf.
4 P Higgins, "Seed-Idea: Seeding Intrinsic Values: How a Law of Ecocide will Shift our Consciousness", *Cadmus*, vol. 1, no.5 (2012), p.9 at p.10.
5 See K Heller, "Skeptical Thoughts on the Proposed Crime of 'Ecocide' (That Isn't)" *OpinioJuris* (2021), available at: https://opiniojuris.org/2021/06/23/skeptical-thoughts-on-the-proposed-crime-of-ecocide-that-isnt/; K Ambos, "Protecting the Environment through International Criminal Law?" *EJIL:Talk!* (2021), available at: www.ejiltalk.org/protecting-the-environment-through-international-criminal-law/https://www.ejiltalk.org/protecting-the-environment-through-international-criminal-law/; D Minha, "The Proposed Definition of the Crime of Ecocide: An Important Step Forward, but Can Our Planet Wait?" *EJIL:Talk!* (2021), available at: www.ejiltalk.org/the-proposed-definition-of-the-crime-of-ecocide-an-important-step-forward-but-can-our-planet-wait/?utm_source=mailpoet&utm_medium=email&utm_campaign=ejil-talk-newsletter-post-title_2; D Robinson, "Ecocide – Puzzles and Possibilities", *Journal of International Criminal Justice*, vol. 20, no. 2 (2022), p.1; J Aparac, "A Missed Opportunity for Accountability? Corporate Responsibility and the Draft Definition of Ecocide", *Völkerrechtsblog* (2021), available at: https://voelkerrechtsblog.org/a-missed-opportunity-for-accountability/.
6 Heller, "Skeptical Thoughts"; Robinson, "Ecocide – Puzzles and Possibilities"; Aparac, "A Missed Opportunity".
7 A Branch & L Minkova, "Ecocide, the Anthropocene, and the International Criminal Court", *Ethics & International Affairs*, vol. 37, no. 1 (2023), p.51; E Cusato, *The Ecology of War and Peace: Marginalising Slow and Structural Violence in International Law* (Cambridge University Press: Cambridge, 2021); E Cusato & E Jones, "The 'Imbroglio' of Ecocide: A Political Economic Analysis", *Leiden Journal of International Law*, vol. 37, no. 1 (2024), p. 42.
8 Independent Expert Panel for the Legal Definition of Ecocide, "Commentary and Core Text", *Stop Ecocide Foundation* (2021), available at: https://static1.squarespace.com/static/5ca2608ab9144 93c64ef1f6d/t/60d7479cf8e7e5461534dd07/1624721314430/SE+Foundation+Commentary+and+core+text+revised+%281%29.pdf, p.6.
9 Higgins, "Seed-idea", p.10.
10 See for instance R Rauxloh, "The Role of International Criminal Law in Environmental Protection" in FN Botchway (ed.) *Natural Resource Investment and Africa's Development* (Edward Elgar: Cheltenham, 2011), pp.423–461. For an earlier work on ecocide see MA Gray, "The International Crime of Ecocide", *California Western International Law Journal*, vol. 26, no. 2 (1996), p.215.
11 L Neyret et al, Draft Convention against Ecocide 2015, translated and cited in The Promise Institute for Human Rights, UCLA School of Law, "Report of the Expert Workshop on International Criminal Law & The Protection of the Environment" (2020), available at: https://law.ucla.edu/sites/default/files/PDFs/Academics/Report%20of%20the%20Expert%20Workshop%20%20ICL%20and%20environment%20v2.pdf, p.14.
12 End Ecocide on Earth, "Ecocide Amendment Proposal" (2016), available at: www.endecocide.org/wp-content/uploads/2016/10/ICC-Amendements-Ecocide-ENG-Sept-2016.pdf.
13 International Monsanto Tribunal, "Advisory Opinion" (2017), available at: www.monsanto-tribunal.org/upload/asset_cache/189791450.pdf, p.9.
14 International Monsanto Tribunal, "Advisory Opinion", p.46.
15 Permanent Peoples' Tribunal, "New Statute of the Permanent Peoples' Tribunal" (2018), available at: http://permanentpeoplestribunal.org/wp-content/uploads/2019/05/Statute-of-the-PPT_ENG_FINAL.pdf, Article 1(d) and Article 5(1).
16 Third International Rights of Nature Tribunal (2015), available at: www.rightsofnaturetribunal.org/tribunals/paris-tribunal-2015/.
17 G MacCarrick & J Maogoto, "The Significance of the International Monsanto Tribunal's Findings with Respect to the Nascent Crime of Ecocide", *Texas Environmental Law Journal*, vol. 48, no. 2 (2018), p.217 at p.226.
18 A Greene, "The Campaign to Make Ecocide an International Crime: Quixotic Quest or Moral Imperative?", *Fordham Environmental Law Review*, vol. 30, no. 3 (2019), p.1 at p.31.

19 A Bustami & M Hecken, "Perspectives for a New International Crime Against the Environment: International Criminal Responsibility for Environmental Degradation under the Rome Statute", *Goettingen Journal of International Law*, vol. 11, no.1 (2021), p.145 at p.171.
20 LA Teclaff, "Beyond Restoration—The Case of Ecocide", *Natural Resources Journal*, vol. 34, no. 4 (1994), p.933 at p.953.
21 Higgins, "Seed-idea", p.10.
22 End Ecocide on Earth, "Ecocide Amendment Proposal", p.4.
23 Judge Françoise Tulkens, cited in European Civic Forum and Foundation Monsanto Tribunal, "Ecocide: Corporations on Trial, International Monsanto Tribunal, The Hague 2016", *European Civil Forum (EBF) Association* (2018), p.67.
24 For an analysis of this problem see S Malhotra, "The International Crime That Could Have Been but Never Was: An English School Perspective on the Ecocide Law", *Amsterdam Law Forum*, vol. 9, no. 3 (2017), p.49.
25 Gauger et al, "Ecocide Project".
26 See M Finnemore and K Sikkink, "International Norm Dynamics and Political Change", *International Organization*, vol. 52, no. 4 (1998), p.887.
27 N Deitelhoff, "The Discursive Process of Legalization: Charting Islands of Persuasion in the ICC Case", *International Organization*, vol. 63, no.1 (2009), p.33.
28 ICC, Statement by HE JH Licht, General Debate of the 18th Session of the Assembly of State Parties to the Rome Statute of the International Criminal Court (2019), available at: https://asp.icc-cpi.int/iccdocs/asp_docs/ASP18/GD.VAN.2.12.pdf.
29 Stop Ecocide International, "Belgium and the Recognition of Ecocide as a Crime" (2022), available at: www.stopecocide.earth/belgium-and-the-recognition-of-ecocide-as-a-crime.
30 Stop Ecocide, "Support EU Recognition of a Crime of Ecocide" (2023), available at: www.stopecocide.earth/eu-crime-directive-position-paper.
31 In November 2023, Stop Ecocide reported that the EU had reached a political agreement on this proposal. Stop Ecocide, "Agreement Reached! EU to Criminalise Severe Environmental Harms" (2023), available at: www.stopecocide.earth/breaking-news-2023/agreement-reached-eu-to-criminalise-severe-environmental-harms-comparable-to-ecocide.
32 Draft European Parliament Legislative Resolution on the proposal for a directive of the European Parliament and of the Council on the protection of the environment through criminal law and replacing Directive 2008/99/EC (COM(2021)0851 – C9-0466/2021 – 2021/0422(COD) (COD)), available at: www.europarl.europa.eu/doceo/document/A-9-2023-0087_EN.html#_section1, Article 3, paragraph 1a (new), Amendment text.
33 Stop Ecocide, "European Parliament Proposes Including 'Ecocide' in EU Law" (2023), available at: www.stopecocide.earth/breaking-news-2023/european-parliament-proposes-including-ecocide-in-eu-law.
34 European Law Institute, "ELI Report on Ecocide, Model Rules for an EU Directive" (2023), available at: www.europeanlawinstitute.eu/fileadmin/user_upload/p_eli/Publications/ELI_Report_on_Ecocide.pdf.
35 K Heller, "Belgium Set to Criminalise Ecocide (Kinda Sorta)", *OpinioJuris* (2022), available at: http://opiniojuris.org/2022/11/08/belgium-set-to-criminalise-ecocide-kinda-sorta/; K Heller, "ELI's Overly Narrow Definition of Ecocide", *OpinioJuris* (2023), available at: http://opiniojuris.org/2023/02/23/elis-overly-narrow-definition-of-ecocide/.
36 Proposal for a Directive of the European Parliament and of the Council on the protection of the environment through criminal law and replacing Directive 2008/00/EC (2021) 851 final, 2021/0422 (COD), available at: https://eur-lex.europa.eu/legal-content/EN/TXT/PDF/?uri=CELEX:52021PC0851, p.22.
37 Kate Mackintosh, 'European Parliament Votes Unanimously for Ecocide', *OpinioJuris* (2023), available at: http://opiniojuris.org/2023/04/10/european-parliament-votes-unanimously-for-ecocide/.
38 Independent Expert Panel, "Commentary", p.10.
39 Heller, "Belgium Set to Criminalise"; "ELI's Overly Narrow Definition".
40 Robinson, "Ecocide – Puzzles and Possibilities", p.12.

41 A Cassese and Members of the Journal of International Criminal Justice, "Amicus Curiae Brief of Professor Antonio Cassese and Members of the Journal of International Criminal Justice on Joint Criminal Enterprise Doctrine", *Criminal Law Forum*, vol. 20, no. 2–3 (2009), p.289 at p.294.
42 Similarly observed by V Singhania, "The Proposed Crime of Ecocide – Ignoring the Question of Liability", *OpinioJuris* (2022), available at: http://opiniojuris.org/2022/02/16/the-proposed-crime-of-ecocide-ignoring-the-question-of-liability/.
43 P Higgins, D Short, & N South, "Protecting the Planet: A Proposal for a Law of Ecocide", *Crime Law and Social Change*, vol. 59, no. 3 (2013), p.251 at p.262.
44 Greene, "Campaign to Make Ecocide an International Crime", p.27.
45 Eradicating Ecocide, "Closing the Door to Dangerous Industrial Activity: A Concept Paper for Governments to Implement Emergency Measures" (2012), available at: http://eradicatingecocide.com/wp-content/uploads/2012/06/Concept-Paper.pdf, p.13. See also P Higgins, *Eradicating Ecocide: Laws and Governance to Prevent the Destruction of Our Planet* (Shepheard-Walwyn Publishers Ltd: London, 2nd edn, 2015), p.68. End Ecocide on Earth, "Ecocide Amendment Proposal", p.8.
46 Greene, "Campaign to Make Ecocide an International Crime", p.33.
47 Trial of the Major War Criminals before the International Military Tribunal, Nuremburg (1945–1946), Vol. 22, available at: www.loc.gov/rr/frd/Military_Law/pdf/NT_Vol-XXII.pdf, p.500.
48 See Neyret et al.'s Draft Convention cited in The Promise Institute of Human Rights, "Report of the Expert Workshop", p.14. International Monsanto Tribunal, "Advisory Opinion", p.47. Gray, "International Crime of Ecocide", p.218.
49 E Van Sliedregt, *Individual Criminal Responsibility in International Law* (Oxford University Press: Oxford, 2012), p.44.
50 International Monsanto Tribunal, "Advisory Opinion", p.47, emphasis added.
51 Greene, "Campaign to Make Ecocide an International Crime", p.41.
52 United Nations Diplomatic Conference of Plenipotentiaries on the Establishment of an International Criminal Court, "Summary Records of the Plenary Meetings and of the Meetings of the Committee of the Whole", vol. II (1998), available at: https://legal.un.org/icc/rome/proceedings/E/Rome%20Proceedings_v2_e.pdf, p.136.
53 United Nations Diplomatic Conference of Plenipotentiaries on the Establishment of an International Criminal Court, p.137.
54 The Promise Institute for Human Rights, "Ecocide Public Consultation February 2021" (2021), available at: https://docs.google.com/presentation/d/10x7yameO1v_uhM8pW6GfMHTEabms2Bs2Adel_-L6fF4/present?slide=id.p, p.2.
55 C Voigt, "«Ecocide» as an International Crime: Personal Reflections on Options and Choices" *EJIL:Talk!*, (2021), available at: www.ejiltalk.org/ecocide-as-an-international-crime-personal-reflections-on-options-and-choices/?utm_source=mailpoet&utm_medium=email&utm_campaign=ejil-talk-newsletter-post-title_2.
56 P Sands, J Batura, P Eschenhagen, & R Oidtmann, "Defining Ecocide: An interview with Philippe Sands", *Völkerrechtsblog* (2021), available at: https://voelkerrechtsblog.org/defining-ecocide/.
57 Independent Expert Panel, "Commentary", p.2.
58 The Promise Institute for Human Rights, "Ecocide Public Consultation", p.3.
59 Independent Expert Panel, "Commentary".
60 Independent Expert Panel, "Commentary", p.5.
61 The Promise Institute for Human Rights, "Ecocide Public Consultation", p.10.
62 Another 39 respondents supported the inclusion of a mental element without specifying what, The Promise Institute for Human Rights, "Ecocide Public Consultation", p.10.
63 In addition to "intent" (62 responses), "knowledge" received 41 responses and "recklessness" – 57 responses. "Negligence" received only 46 responses, The Promise Institute for Human Rights, "Ecocide Public Consultation", p.10.
64 Bustami & Hecken, "Perspectives for a New International Crime", pp.184–185.
65 See, for instance, Higgins, "Seed-idea". End Ecocide on Earth, "Ecocide Amendment Proposal", p.4. Neyret et al.'s Draft Convention cited in The Promise Institute of Human Rights, "Report of the Expert Workshop", p.14.
66 Independent Expert Panel, "Commentary", p.5.
67 Robinson, "Ecocide – Puzzles and Possibilities", p.22.

68 Independent Expert Panel, "Commentary", p.5.
69 Gray, "International Crime of Ecocide", p.218, emphasis added.
70 The Promise Institute for Human Rights, "Ecocide Public Consultation", p.10.
71 See Kevin Heller, "The Crime of Ecocide in Action", *OpinioJuris* (2021), available at: http://opiniojuris.org/2021/06/28/the-crime-of-ecocide-in-action/.
72 Voigt, "«Ecocide»".
73 Independent Expert Panel, "Commentary", p.10.
74 M Shinde, "Opinion: The New Legal Definition of 'Ecocide' Could Be a Gamechanger for the Environmental Movement", *Climatetracker.org* (2021), available at: https://climatetracker.org/new-legal-definition-ecocide-gamechanger-environment/.
75 Stop Ecocide, "European Parliament Proposes".
76 Heller, "Skeptical Thoughts". See also Ambos, "Protecting the Environment".
77 Heller, "Crime of Ecocide in Action".
78 Aparac, "A Missed Opportunity". See also Singhania, "Proposed Crime".
79 Robinson, "Ecocide - Puzzles and Possibilities", p.3.
80 B Lay, L Neyret, D Short, MU Maumgartner, & AA Oposa Jr, "Timely and Necessary: Ecocide Law as Urgent and Emerging", *The Journal Jurisprudence*, vol. 28 (2015), p.431 at p.438.
81 Branch & Minkova, "Ecocide, the Anthropocene".
82 Cusato & Jones, "'Imbroglio' of Ecocide".
83 See End Ecocide on Earth, "Ecocide Amendment Proposal"; International Monsanto Tribunal, "Advisory Opinion".
84 Higgins, *Eradicating Ecocide*, p.112.
85 A Cassese, "Reflections on International Criminal Justice", *Journal of International Criminal Justice*, vol. 9, no. 1 (2011), p.271 at p.272.
86 Higgins, *Eradicating Ecocide*, p.111.
87 Higgins et al, "Protecting the Planet", p.262, emphasis added.
88 M Crook & D Short, "Marx, Lemkin and the Genocide–Ecocide Nexus", *The International Journal of Human Rights*, vol. 18, no. 3 (2014), p.298 at p.311, emphasis omitted.
89 Crook & Short, "Marx, Lemkin", p.301
90 Crook & Short, "Marx, Lemkin". See also the 2021 special issue "Genocide-Ecocide Nexus" in the *Journal of Genocide Nexus*, vol 23, no. 2.
91 MJ Lynch, A Fegadel, & MA Long, "Green Criminology and State-Corporate Crime: The Ecocide-Genocide Nexus with Examples from Nigeria" *Journal of Genocide Research*, vol. 23, no. 2 (2021), p.236 at p.243.
92 J Dehm, "Reconfiguring Environmental Governance in the Green Economy", in U Natarajan & J Dehm (eds), *Locating Nature: Making and Unmaking International Law* (Cambridge University Press: New York, 2022), p.102.
93 Dehm, "Reconfiguring Environmental Governance", pp.83–85.
94 V De Lucia, "Towards an Ecological Philosophy of Law: A Comparative Discussion", *Journal of Human Rights and the Environment*, vol. 4, no. 2 (2013), p.167 at p.169.
95 RB Norgaard, "Ecosystem Services: From an Eye-opening Metaphor to Complexity Blinder", *Ecological Economics*, vol. 69, no. 6 (2010), p.1219.
96 Higgins, *Eradicating Ecocide*, p.66.
97 Cusato and Jones, "'Imbroglio' of Ecocide".
98 Rauxloh, "Role of International Criminal Law", p.449. See also Singhania, "Proposed Crime"; Cusato & Jones, "'Imbroglio' of Ecocide", p.19.
99 R DeFalco, *Invisible Atrocities: The Aesthetic Biases of International Criminal Justice* (Cambridge University Press: Cambridge, 2022); Cusato, *Ecology of War*, pp.114–116.
100 LG Minkova, "Expressing What? The Stigmatization of the Defendant and the ICC's Institutional Interests in the Ongwen Case", *Leiden Journal of International Law*, vol. 34, no. 1 (2021), p.223 at p.240.
101 ICC, *Gbagbo and Blé Goudé*, Trial Hearing, Transcript ICC-02/11-01/15-T-9-ENG, Trial Chamber I (2016), available at: www.icc-cpi.int/Transcripts/0CR2016_00664.PDF, p.70, lines 6–9.
102 Robinson, "Ecocide – Puzzles and Possibilities", pp.4–5.

103 Robinson "Ecocide – Puzzles and Possibilities", pp.5–6. N Kersting, "On Symbolism and Beyond: Defining Ecocide", *Völkerrechtsblog* (2021), available at: https://voelkerrechtsblog.org/on-symbolism-and-beyond/.
104 For a thorough discussion see Cusato & Jones, "'Imbroglio' of Ecocide".
105 Cusato & Jones, "'Imbroglio' of Ecocide", p.8.

References

Books and book chapters

Cusato E, *The Ecology of War and Peace: Marginalising Slow and Structural Violence in International Law* (Cambridge University Press: Cambridge, 2021).

DeFalco R, *Invisible Atrocities: The Aesthetic Biases of International Criminal Justice* (Cambridge University Press: Cambridge, 2022).

Dehm J, "Reconfiguring Environmental Governance in the Green Economy", in Natarajan U & Dehm J (eds) *Locating Nature: Making and Unmaking International Law* (Cambridge University Press: New York, 2022).

Higgins P, *Eradicating Ecocide: Laws and Governance to Prevent the Destruction of Our Planet* (Shepheard-Walwyn Publishers Ltd: London, 2nd edn, 2015).

Rauxloh R, "The Role of International Criminal Law in Environmental Protection" in Botchway FN (ed.) *Natural Resource Investment and Africa's Development* (Edward Elgar: Cheltenham, 2011).

Van Sliedregt E, *Individual Criminal Responsibility in International Law* (Oxford University Press: Oxford 2012).

Journal articles

Branch A & Minkova L, "Ecocide, the Anthropocene, and the International Criminal Court", *Ethics & International Affairs*, vol. 37, no. 1 (2023), pp.51–79.

Bustami A & Hecken MC, "Perspectives for a New International Crime Against the Environment: International Criminal Responsibility for Environmental Degradation Under the Rome Statute", *Goettingen Journal of International Law*, vol. 11, no. 1 (2021), pp.145–189.

Cassese A, "Reflections on International Criminal Justice", *Journal of International Criminal Justice*, vol. 9, no. 1 (2011), pp.271–275.

Cassese A & Members of the Journal of International Criminal Justice, "Amicus Curiae Brief of Professor Antonio Cassese and Members of the Journal of International Criminal Justice on Joint Criminal Enterprise Doctrine", *Criminal Law Forum*, vol. 20, nos. 2–3 (2009), pp.289–330.

Crook M & Short D, "Marx, Lemkin and the Genocide–Ecocide Nexus", *The International Journal of Human Rights*, vol. 18, no. 3 (2014), pp.298–319.

Cusato E & Jones E, "The 'Imbroglio' of Ecocide: A Political Economic Analysis", *Leiden Journal of International Law*, vol. 37, no. 1 (2023), pp.42–61.

De Lucia V, "Towards an Ecological Philosophy of Law: A Comparative Discussion", *Journal of Human Rights and the Environment*, vol. 4, no. 2 (2013), pp.167–190.

Deitelhoff N, "The Discursive Process of Legalization: Charting Islands of Persuasion in the ICC Case", *International Organization*, vol. 63, no. 1 (2009), pp.33–65.

Falk R, "Environmental Warfare and Ecocide – Facts, Appraisal and Proposal", *Bulletin of Peace Proposals*, vol. 4, no. 1 (1973), pp.80–96.

Finnemore M & Sikkink K, "International Norm Dynamics and Political Change", *International Organization*, vol. 52, no. 4 (1998), pp.887–917.

Gray MA, "The International Crime of Ecocide", *California Western International Law Journal*, vol. 26, no. 2 (1996), pp.215–271.

Greene A, "The Campaign to Make Ecocide an International Crime: Quixotic Quest or Moral Imperative?", *Fordham Environmental Law Review*, vol. 30, no. 3 (2019), pp.1–48.

Higgins P, "Seed-Idea: Seeding Intrinsic Values: How a Law of Ecocide will Shift Our Consciousness", *Cadmus*, vol. 1, no. 5 (2012), pp.9–10.

Higgins P, Short D, & South N, "Protecting the Planet: A Proposal for a Law of Ecocide", *Crime Law and Social Change*, vol. 59, no. 3 (2013), pp.251–266.

Lay B, Neyret L, Short D, Maumgartner MU, & Oposa Jr AA, "Timely and Necessary: Ecocide Law as Urgent and Emerging", *The Journal Jurisprudence*, vol. 28 (2015), pp.431–452.

Lynch MJ, Fegadel A, & Long MA, "Green Criminology and State-Corporate Crime: The Ecocide-Genocide Nexus with Examples from Nigeria", *Journal of Genocide Research*, vol. 23, no. 2 (2021), pp.236–256.

MacCarrick G & Jackson M, "The Significance of the International Monsanto Tribunal's Findings with Respect to the Nascent Crime of Ecocide", *Texas Environmental Law Journal*, vol. 48, no. 2 (2018), pp.217–237.

Malhotra S, "The International Crime That Could Have Been but Never Was: An English School Perspective on the Ecocide Law", *Amsterdam Law Forum*, vol. 9, no. 3 (2017), pp.49–70.

Minkova LG, "Expressing What? The Stigmatization of the Defendant and the ICC's Institutional Interests in the Ongwen Case", *Leiden Journal of International Law*, vol. 34, no. 1 (2021), pp.223–245.

Norgaard RB, "Ecosystem Services: From an Eye-opening Metaphor to Complexity Blinder", *Ecological Economics*, vol. 69, no. 6 (2010), pp.1219–1227.

Robinson D, "Ecocide – Puzzles and Possibilities", *Journal of International Criminal Justice*, vol. 20, no. 2 (2022), pp.1–35.

Teclaff LA, "Beyond Restoration – The Case of Ecocide", *Natural Resources Journal*, vol. 34, no. 4 (1994), pp.933–956.

Reports and websites

Ambos K, "Protecting the Environment Through International Criminal Law?", *EJIL:Talk!* (29 June 2021), available at: www.ejiltalk.org/protecting-the-environment-through-international-criminal-law/

Aparac J, " 'A Missed Opportunity for Accountability' Corporate Responsibility and the Draft Definition of Ecocide", *Völkerrechtsblog* (9 June 2021), available at: https://voelkerrechtsblog.org/a-missed-opportunity-for-accountability/

End Ecocide on Earth, "Ecocide Amendment Proposal" (2016), available at: www.endecocide.org/wp-content/uploads/2016/10/ICC-Amendements-Ecocide-ENG-Sept-2016.pdf

Eradicating Ecocide, "Closing the Door to Dangerous Industrial Activity: A Concept Paper for Governments to Implement Emergency Measures" (2012), available at: http://eradicatingecocide.com/wp-content/uploads/2012/06/Concept-Paper.pdf

European Civic Forum and Foundation Monsanto Tribunal, "Ecocide: Corporations on Trial, International Monsanto Tribunal, The Hague 2016", *European Civil Forum* (EBF Association: Basel, 2018).

European Law Institute, "ELI Report on Ecocide, Model Rules for an EU Directive" (19 January 2023), available at: www.europeanlawinstitute.eu/fileadmin/user_upload/p_eli/Publications/ELI_Report_on_Ecocide.pdf

Gauger A, Pouye Rabatel-Fernel M, Kulbicki L, Short D, & Higgins P, "The Ecocide Project: Ecocide is the Missing 5th Crime Against Peace" (Human Rights Consortium, 2013), available at: https://sas-space.sas.ac.uk/4830/1/Ecocide_research_report_19_July_13.pdf

Heller K, "Skeptical Thoughts on the Proposed Crime of 'Ecocide' (That Isn't)", *OpinioJuris* (23 June 2021), available at: https://opiniojuris.org/2021/06/23/skeptical-thoughts-on-the-proposed-crime-of-ecocide-that-isnt/

Heller K, "The Crime of Ecocide in Action", *OpinioJuris* (28 June 2021), available at: http://opiniojuris.org/2021/06/28/the-crime-of-ecocide-in-action/

Heller K, "Belgium Set to Criminalise Ecocide (Kinda Sorta)", *OpinioJuris* (8 November 2022), available at: http://opiniojuris.org/2022/11/08/belgium-set-to-criminalise-ecocide-kinda-sorta/

Heller K, "ELI's Overly Narrow Definition of Ecocide", *OpinioJuris* (23 February 2023), available at: http://opiniojuris.org/2023/02/23/elis-overly-narrow-definition-of-ecocide/

ICC, *Gbagbo and Blé Goudé*, Trial Hearing, Transcript ICC-02/11-01/15-T-9-ENG, Trial Chamber I (28 January 2016), available at: www.icc-cpi.int/Transcripts/0CR2016_00664.PDF

ICC, "Statement by H. E. John H. Licht, General Debate of the 18th Session of the Assembly of State Parties to the Rome Statute of the International Criminal Court" (2 to 7 December 2019), available at: https://asp.icc-cpi.int/iccdocs/asp_docs/ASP18/GD.VAN.2.12.pdf

Independent Expert Panel for the Legal Definition of Ecocide, "Commentary and Core Text" (June 2021), available at: https://static1.squarespace.com/static/5ca2608ab914493c64ef1f6d/t/60d7479cf8e7e5461534dd07/1624721314430/SE+Foundation+Commentary+and+core+text+revised+%281%29.pdf

International Monsanto Tribunal, "Advisory Opinion", *The Hague* (18 April 2017), available at: www.monsanto-tribunal.org/upload/asset_cache/189791450.pdf

Kersting N, "On Symbolism and Beyond: Defining Ecocide", *Völkerrechtsblog* (8 July 2021), available at: https://voelkerrechtsblog.org/on-symbolism-and-beyond/

Minha D, "The Proposed Definition of the Crime of Ecocide: An Important Step Forward, but Can Our Planet Wait?" *EJIL:Talk!* (1 July 2021), available at: www.ejiltalk.org/the-proposed-definition-of-the-crime-of-ecocide-an-important-step-forward-but-can-our-planet-wait/?utm_source=mailpoet&utm_medium=email&utm_campaign=ejil-talk-newsletter-post-title_2

Neyret L et al, "Draft Convention Against Ecocide" (2015), translated and cited in The Promise Institute for Human Rights, UCLA School of Law, "Report of the Expert Workshop on International Criminal Law & The Protection of the Environment" (April 2020), available at: https://law.ucla.edu/sites/default/files/PDFs/Academics/Report%20of%20the%20Expert%20Workshop%20%20ICL%20and%20environment%20v2.pdf

Permanent Peoples' Tribunal, "New Statute of the Permanent Peoples' Tribunal", Rome (27 December 2018), available at: http://permanentpeoplestribunal.org/wp-content/uploads/2019/05/Statute-of-the-PPT_ENG_FINAL.pdf

Rome Statute of the International Criminal Court, Done at Rome on 17 July 1998, in Force on 1 July 2002, United Nations, Treaty Series, vol. 2187, No. 38544, available at: www.icc-cpi.int/sites/default/files/RS-Eng.pdf

Sands P, Batura J, Eschenhagen P, & Oidtmann R, "Defining Ecocide: An interview with Philippe Sands", *Völkerrechtsblog* (24 April 2021), available at: https://voelkerrechtsblog.org/defining-ecocide/

Shinde M, "Opinion: The New Legal Definition of 'Ecocide' Could Be a Gamechanger for the Environmental Movement", *Climatetracker.org* (25 June 2021), available at: https://climatetracker.org/new-legal-definition-ecocide-gamechanger-environment/

Singhania V, "The Proposed Crime of Ecocide – Ignoring the Question of Liability", *OpinioJuris* (16 February 2022), http://opiniojuris.org/2022/02/16/the-proposed-crime-of-ecocide-ignoring-the-question-of-liability/Stop Ecocide "Support EU Recognition of a Crime of Ecocide" (2022), available at: www.stopecocide.earth/eu-crime-directive-position-paper

Stop Ecocide, "Agreement Reached! EU to Criminalise Severe Environmental Harms 'Comparable to Ecocide'" (2023), available at: www.stopecocide.earth/breaking-news-2023/agreement-reached-eu-to-criminalise-severe-environmental-harms-comparable-to-ecocide

Stop Ecocide International, "Belgium and the Recognition of Ecocide as a Crime" (2022), available at: www.stopecocide.earth/belgium-and-the-recognition-of-ecocide-as-a-crime

The Promise Institute for Human Rights, UCLA School of Law "Report of the Expert Workshop on International Criminal Law & The Protection of the Environment" (April 2020), available at: https://law.ucla.edu/sites/default/files/PDFs/Academics/Report%20of%20the%20Expert%20Workshop%20%20ICL%20and%20environment%20v2.pdf

The Promise Institute for Human Rights, "Ecocide Public Consultation February 2021" (2021), available at: https://docs.google.com/presentation/d/10x7yameO1v_uhM8pW6GfMHTEabms2Bs2Adel_-L6fF4/present?slide=id.p

Third International Rights of Nature Tribunal, Maison des Métallos, Paris, France, (4 and 5 December 2015), available at: www.rightsofnaturetribunal.org/tribunals/paris-tribunal-2015/

Trial of the Major War Criminals Before the International Military Tribunal, Nuremberg (14 November 1945 – 1 October 1946), vol. 22, available at: www.loc.gov/rr/frd/Military_Law/pdf/NT_Vol-XXII.pdf

United Nations Diplomatic Conference of Plenipotentiaries on the Establishment of an International Criminal Court Rome, "Vol. II: Summary Records of the Plenary Meetings and of the Meetings of the Committee of the Whole" (15 June–17 July 1998), available at: https://legal.un.org/icc/rome/proceedings/E/Rome%20Proceedings_v2_e.pdf

Voigt C, "«Ecocide» as an International Crime: Personal Reflections on Options and Choices" *EJIL:Talk!* (3 July 2021), available at: www.ejiltalk.org/ecocide-as-an-international-crime-personal-reflections-on-options-and-choices/?utm_source=mailpoet&utm_medium=email&utm_campaign=ejil-talk-newsletter-post-title_2

31
CRIMINAL RESPONSIBILITY IN CHILDREN

Anthony Pillay

The extent to which children's involvement in criminal behaviour is changing or increasing, is not well known, largely due to under-reporting, inadequate data collection, and the ways in which nations define and record youth transgressions. However, data on arrests from the United States Department of Justice, for example, revealed that 424,300 children under the age of 18 years old were arrested for criminal acts in 2020, with the figure being 38% lower than the previous year and 71% lower than in 2011.[1] Of course, the number of arrests is not necessarily an indication of the number of children actually involved in criminal behaviour. Data from South Africa, for the year ending March 2020, indicated that 15,706 children (10–17 years old) were in conflict with the law, including 779 murders and 2569 rapes.[2] Nevertheless, despite the data availability and interpretation of the numbers of children convicted or suspected of criminal involvement, their developmental level raises concern.

In particular, the consequences for children in conflict with the law, how their cases are dealt with in the criminal justice system, and the extent to which they are deemed to have criminal responsibility or criminal capacity,[3] are matters of concern. There are several sides to this issue that warrant consideration, including (1) ensuring that children learn that their actions have consequences, (2) developing systems to prevent future criminal tendencies in children, and (3) assuring society that actions are being taken against children in conflict with the law. The latter is a significant concern for governments and politicians, who are likely to find themselves straddling the line between upholding children's rights while also trying to satisfy the voting public. In the face of serious crimes, especially those involving sexual assault and other forms of extreme violence, societal responses are understandably severe, usually calling for harsh punishments. However, the science favours an approach that is more social service and education-based, that is geared towards rehabilitation and maturation for children under 15 years old, rather than one carrying specifically punishment-oriented consequences based in the criminal justice system.[4]

There is, of course, an over-riding ethical requirement in the development of laws regarding the age at which children can or should be held criminally responsible, the most appropriate ways to respond to suspected child offenders, and the appropriate consequences for offenders. It is critical that punishments or other consequences imposed on child offenders are consistent with their developmental level, and that they are not inhumane. For example, in *Roper v Simmons*, the American Medical Association, the American Psychological Association and other professional bodies successfully argued against the imposition of the death penalty on a defendant who was under the age of 18 years at the time of the offence, based on the neurocognitive development of adolescents.[5] The court ruled that it was unconstitutional to impose capital punishment for a crime committed while the defendant was under the age of 18 years. For countries with capital punishment systems, there is an imperative to ensure that children are not subjected to such sentences. However, even in the case of sentences involving incarceration, there needs to be consideration of the child's developmental level, appropriateness of the response, and the long-term outcomes of institutionalised sentences, especially considering that there is minimal evidence that extended incarceration reduces recidivism.[6]

In this chapter, the situation in South Africa will be used to illustrate the various issues and challenges affecting child justice, in view of the author's work in that context. However, reference will also be made to legislation and practice issues elsewhere in the world.

Global discrepancies in the minimum age of criminal responsibility

Interestingly, within national contexts there are a host of age thresholds governing the different civil liberties and responsibilities accorded to citizens, but the extent to which they synchronise and work meaningfully together is a concern. These include the ages at which a young person can obtain a driver's licence, consume alcohol, own a firearm, or attain the right to vote. These age requirements vary depending on the specific liberty or responsibility, and there is also no global uniformity.

The minimum age of criminal responsibility (MACR) is one of the legal age thresholds that affects the lives of young people, and perhaps carries greater consequences than the others. Having been a consideration for decades in all parts of the world, the MACR has been cited as one of the most controversial and contested issues that confront contemporary youth justice.[7] Among the reasons for the debates and arguments are the matter of determining the precise age at which a child assumes responsibility for unlawful actions and the achieving of consensus nationally and globally for this civil responsibility. There is no agreement about the age at which a child develops the ability to think and behave in a way that can enable courts to hold them criminally responsible. This, in itself, points to the difficulty in developing laws and policies on ways to deal with children in conflict with the law. The result is that there are considerable variations in the MACR and the way that children in conflict with the law are dealt with across nations.

On the one hand, it is strange that there is not a uniform MACR across the world, but given the differences in socio-political thinking and ideologies it is not surprising. Currently, children as young as seven years may be held criminally responsible in parts of the United States, India, the United Arab Emirates, and others.[8] On the other extreme, a number of South American countries set their MACR between 16–18 years. However, across Europe the average MACR is around 14 years.[9] On the African continent, a few countries have an absolute minimum age of seven years or higher, with a rebuttable presumption (see below), while many set the MACR or upper limit of the rebuttable presumption at around 13 or 14 years. The net effect is that, globally, the MACR varies from around seven to 18 years, which reflects a considerable discrepancy in (1) how nations are conceptualising their children's cognitive and behavioural development, and (2) the extent of legislators' awareness and willingness to incorporate neurodevelopmental evidence into law reform.

There are no logical reasons for such a wide variation in the MACR internationally, which serves only to illustrate the lack of a common understanding of what constitutes criminal responsibility as well as the fundamental characteristics of child development. In particular, governments may be paying less heed to the science regarding children's thinking, decision-making, and restraint capacity, among other neurodevelopmental abilities (discussed below), than they should. While cultural variations in child development must be acknowledged, there is no reason to believe that such variations are so large as to completely account for the extent of the MACR disparity around the world. In this respect, it is worth noting that (1) there is little to no evidence that governments have taken specific note of cultural make-up in determining their MACR, and (2) there are several countries with multicultural societies but have only one MACR that is supposed to apply to all its cultural groups.

The upshot of the global variation in the MACR is that children are being treated differently for the same offence, depending on where they live.[10] This is a concern given the ramifications such as conviction and sentencing consequences like deprivation of liberty and even the death penalty, more so for children accused of serious violations. International guiding principles have spoken to this issue, with the United Nations recommending an MACR not lower than 14 or 16 years.[11] In its recommendation, the African Union (2003) noted that "The age of criminal responsibility should not be fixed below 15 years of age. No child below the age of 15 shall be arrested or detained on allegations of having committed a crime".[12] However, there are several countries on the African continent that do not subscribe to this MACR, as there are also many UN member countries that do not adhere to its recommendations.

The MACR disparities around the world also include the provision of "socio-educative measures" in some countries, especially in South America. This stipulation refers to non-custodial options available to courts, such as warning or reprimanding the child, limits on freedom, community service or even undertaking reparation to the victim, but evidence shows that custodial sentences are still fairly widely used.[13] The rebuttable presumption of *doli incapax* (discussed below) is also a complication in the MACR because, although this usually provides a higher age band (than the absolute MACR) in which the child is deemed not criminally responsible, it also allows the argument that they do have criminal responsibility.

The rebuttable presumption of *doli incapax*

The laws of several countries include two minimum ages, one being an absolute minimum below which a child is deemed indisputably not criminally responsible, and a higher age band where a child is presumed to lack criminal responsibility, unless proven otherwise. The latter age bracket constitutes the rebuttable presumption of *doli incapax*. In South Africa, for example, the MACR is 12 years, with the rebuttable presumption set at 12–14 years.[14] Children in this age group are referred to a psychologist or psychiatrist for evaluation to assist the court in its determination of the child's criminal capacity, and thus whether a criminal case should be pursued within the justice system. Generally, the intention with this rebuttable presumption, is to call for expert evidence to assist the court in answering the criminal responsibility question. However, this is not the case in all countries, and the United Nations Committee on the Rights of the Child raised concern over the procedural issues, noting as follows:

"The assessment of this maturity is left to the court/judge, often without the requirement of involving a psychological expert, and results in practice in the use of the lower minimum age in cases of serious crimes. The system of two minimum ages is often not only confusing but leaves much to the discretion of the court/judge and may result in discriminatory practices".[15]

In addition to concerns over the discretionary powers of the court, there is also the problem of the lack of specialist resources in many countries, which limits expert evidence options. Of course, this situation may reflect political-economic factors and how seriously governments view youth crime and the criminal responsibility issue in the context of resource allocation. Unfortunately, this seems insufficiently considered when laws, like the rebuttable presumption, are developed. The South African situation is a case in point, even though it may be relatively better resourced than some other countries in the global South. The lack or shortage of expert witnesses to perform the required evaluations is a serious issue affecting the outcome of the case, especially because courts may wait months for an expert report depending on the availability of psychologists or psychiatrists. The system in South Africa, and likely in other countries incorporating this legal provision, is that the party challenging the criminal incapacity presumption (usually the state) has the onus of bringing forward the disputing evidence. Since there is no dedicated pool of psychologists or psychiatrists within the criminal justice sector to perform these examinations, the work is allocated to the Department of Health. However, the state employed clinicians on whom this assessment work falls have a clinical case load, meaning they are primarily employed to treat patients with mental health problems, but the court order for a criminal capacity assessment requires the assessment to be conducted and reported on within 30 days of the date of the order. This results in clinicians having to give priority to the forensic examinations, while putting their clinical cases on the back-burner, and is one of the ethical issues involved in such court-ordered examinations in a country with limited resources.

While a number of regions (e.g. England and Wales) have abolished the rebuttable presumption of *doli incapax* from their statutes, the arguments for retaining it centre around it being an instrument to protect the rights of children. This concern pertains especially to those children above the minimum age who lack the capacity to appreciate the wrongfulness of their actions or to regulate their behaviour in accordance with societal laws.[16] The rebuttable presumption offers the opportunity for the individual assessment of children, to determine, on a case-by-case basis, the extent to which the child's developmental and behavioural history together with the nature of the offence warrants criminal prosecution. In effect, it speaks to the concept of individual variation in human development,[17] and against the idea that a single age can be used as a universal (or national) benchmark to determine criminal capacity. Commenting on the High Court judgment of *RP v The Queen*, Crofts noted the court's position that the acceptability of the rebutting evidence will vary depending on the nature of the offence as well as the child in question.[18] The rebuttable presumption, where included, is an indication of the legislators' awareness that the concept of criminal capacity in children is a fluid one, which requires leeway above the minimum prescribed age, especially where that age is set relatively low. This consideration may account for the decision in many South American countries, to set the MACR much higher (at around 16–18 years) with the absence of the rebuttable presumption, although younger children involved in infractions of the law may be subject to "socio-educative measures".[19]

Interestingly the rebuttable presumption appears to be more prevalent in countries previously under colonial rule, a large proportion of which were colonised by Britain. For countries that have not included a rebuttable presumption or abolished it from their law, opting instead for a single minimum age threshold, one has to wonder about the rationale. Do they know something that the others do not, or *vice versa*? This inclusion (or exclusion) in national laws has been a source of debate in the broader area of child justice,[20] and where recent changes have been made to the disadvantage of the child, the extent to which public pressure on governments has contributed, is a concern. The abolition of the presumption in England and Wales a few decades ago, as part of a response to rising criticism of government's approach to crime, left children over 10 years old open to the full might of the criminal justice system.[21]

The inclusion of this presumption has significant, though very different implications for the legislators and the clinicians who form the body of expert witnesses. For the lawmakers, the aforementioned protective effects appear to be the main motivating factor, but there may be a lack of consideration regarding the mechanics and reliability of the processes to establish the required evidence to rebut the presumption. For clinicians having to conduct the assessments to establish criminal capacity, the challenges are significant.[22] Therefore, if the rebuttable presumption is to be included, the requirement of expert evidence may need reconsideration. Moreover, the disjuncture between law and disciplines like psychology needs revisiting to enable a more meaningful collaboration in the interests of child justice.

Challenges in assessing criminal capacity/rebutting the presumption

In countries where the rebuttable presumption is included and mental health professionals are required to conduct examinations to determine criminal responsibility, there are multiple inherent difficulties that impact the process, as well as its reliability. Perhaps one of the primary concerns is the need for a better understanding of criminal responsibility, what it entails, and what is required to prove it. In this regard, Crofts argued that

> "Rethinking exactly what criminal responsibility requires, formulating that requirement in an appropriate test of criminal responsibility alongside greater clarity on what proof may establish such understanding might go some way in ensuring that the presumption is more rigorously applied".[23]

To rebut the presumption of *doli incapax*, South African law requires the State to prove that the child between 12 and 14 years old could appreciate the difference between right and wrong and act in accordance with that appreciation, at the time of the alleged offence.[24] Included in the legislation is the requirement that the child be examined by a psychologist or psychiatrist to evaluate the child's criminal capacity. For a child to be found to have criminal responsibility, both the cognitive and conative aspects of the child's functioning at the time, usually need to be satisfied. This means that, in addition to the understanding of the wrongfulness of the act, there should be proof of the child's ability to act in accordance with that understanding. These two abilities constitute the basis of the individual's criminal capacity and hence, responsibility.[25]

However, there are several challenges facing evaluators which are inherent to the process and the legal requirements, including (1) the fact that there are no psychometrically validated instruments with proven reliability to assess the criminal responsibility of youth, (2) the fundamental challenges in retrospectively forming an impression of an individual's developmental and mental state, (3) the difficulty in assessing the child's conative capacity, i.e. the ability to act in accordance with their understanding of right and wrong, and (4) the extensive periods that often lapse between the offence and the time of examination.

Given the courts' preference for objective evidence by expert witnesses, the burden on psychologists or psychiatrists to provide unequivocal proof that a child does or does not have criminal capacity is far too weighty for the available toolkits. Current psychological assessment techniques are considerably less reliable in making such absolute, irrefutable determinations of criminal capacity, than the criminal justice system may assume.[26] This is especially true for those children/adolescents falling into the rebuttable presumption age band (12–14 years old in South Africa), and thus in the borderline range in terms of the cognitive, emotional, social, and moral development dimensions that characterise criminal capacity. It is also critical to recognise that there are contextual variables relating to a child's understanding of wrongfulness that increase the difficulty in making such assessments. This includes determining whether the child's understanding that an act is "seriously wrong", as opposed to simply being "naughty", which is a legal distinction made in Australia, for example.[27] Retrospectively evaluating and calibrating behaviour to inform such a distinction is a difficult task, the reliability of which is subject to question. Courts have also accepted that the concept "seriously wrong", on its own, may lack the level of clarity required in criminal justice.[28] Another contextual variable relates to the child's understanding of the wrongfulness of a specific behaviour, as opposed to distinguishing right from wrong in general terms, or in relation to another behaviour. This means that a child's understanding of a specific act being seriously wrong may not necessarily coincide with an understanding of wrongfulness in the case of another act. In principle, a child found to have criminal responsibility in one offence could simultaneously be deemed not to have criminal responsibility in another matter.

A significant concern for clinicians conducting this type of assessment is the retrospective component of the examination. By their nature, psychological assessment techniques are not geared towards reliably assessing human functioning at developmental points that have passed. The mere fact that the child's thinking and behaviour during a past timeframe is being assessed, means that much of the examination has to rely on information provided by the child, their caregivers, and other relevant parties. In other words, there is little or no objective evidence that can be brought forward, nor are there psychological tests that can provide such evidence. Unlike expert witnesses presenting findings based on medical or biochemical samples (e.g. blood alcohol level), psychological expert evidence is always vulnerable in terms of its relatively subjective findings.

A further challenge relates to giving an expert opinion on whether the child had the ability to act in accordance with their understanding of right and wrong (i.e. the conative test). Answering this question is, of course, more relevant when the first leg of the test (i.e. the ability to distinguish right and wrong, namely the cognitive component) reveals that child possessed that competency. The conative component, according to Snyman, rests on the idea of self-control, and involves the individual's ability to "resist impulses or desires to act contrary to what his insights into right and wrong reveal to him".[29] Providing psychological evidence to either prove or refute this capacity is a tall order. To the author's knowledge, there are no psychological tests with acceptable validity and reliability properties that can conclude with certainty, that the child could resist the urge to commit the offence in question, more so at a specific point in history. In this context, research has revealed that adolescents are not as "self-controlled" as adults and that the absence of this ability lies in the development and maturation of the brain.[30] It is also vital to remember that the child's future rests on the decisions made by the court after considering the expert evidence. Therefore, it is incumbent on expert witnesses to ensure that they provide a firm answer to this question only if they are absolutely certain, because if there is doubt, the benefit should be given to the child.

The time that elapses from the alleged offence to the psychological examination is another serious, though under-recognised, challenge in the assessment of the child's functioning and developmental status at the time of the offence. There are several reasons why there could be significant delays, including investigative challenges, court backlogs, and resource constraints impeding the scheduling of appointments for the forensic psychological examinations. The latter is a more severe problem in low- and middle-income countries that include the rebuttable presumption in their legislation, which could easily result in courts reaching decisions without expert evidence, raising much concern.[31] The consequence of conducting the examination much later than the alleged offence lies in the intervening development and the environmental learning that the child is exposed to, which inevitably contaminate the assessment findings. For example, if the examination is conducted six months (or longer) after the event, that is a substantial period in terms of cognitive and related development in the life of a 12-year-old, meaning that it is not possible to know, with accuracy, what the child's competencies were at the earlier developmental level. In the author's experience, children have been referred for examinations up to one year after the event. Even more significant, is the effect of the input the child receives from caregivers upon hearing of the accusation. A common response from caregivers is one of reprimand and admonishment relating to such an offence, in other words, the wrongfulness of such behaviour. The effect is that the child, inadvertently, receives teaching about the wrongfulness of the specific behaviour, and the new information forms part of the child's responses in the psychological examination. It is almost impossible to tease out what level of knowledge and understanding the child possessed at the time of the offence, versus what was subsequently acquired knowledge.

The aforementioned challenges are formidable in the sense that they greatly reduce the clinician's ability to provide absolute, unequivocal answers to the criminal capacity question. The result is that the evidence needed to rebut the presumption, especially for children aged close to the threshold for capacity, is likely to lack the precision desired by the court. This again raises the issue of the overall benefit of the rebuttable presumption of criminal incapacity and the extent to which it actually works, more so in resource-constrained countries.

Neurodevelopmental considerations in criminal capacity

Cognitive neuroscience and brain research have seen remarkable developments over the latter half of the twentieth century, but it is largely around the turn of the century that the neurodevelopmental evidence began to emerge that would steer the thinking around criminal responsibility in children and adolescents.[32] Drawing from the cognitive neuroscience research, Steinberg and Scott noted,

> "Thus, there is good reason to believe that adolescents, as compared with adults, are more susceptible to influence, less future oriented, less risk averse, and less able to

manage their impulses and behavior, and that these differences likely have a neurobiological basis".[33]

The field of cognitive neuroscience has contributed a significant body of work to date, demonstrating the need for legislators, courts and expert witnesses to take heed of these developments in cases involving children in conflict with the law. There is generally insufficient acknowledgement in criminal law and regulations regarding children's lesser-developed cognitive and conative capacities in relation to that of adults. The child justice legislation in South Africa, and in many other countries, do not include a "lesser" standard by which the offending actions of youth are to be judged. This speaks to the diminished culpability model and its usefulness in child justice.[34] While it may be difficult to conceptualise or establish a "lesser" standard for judgement of culpability, in the absence of another standard, children's actions are being judged using criteria benchmarked for adult ways of thinking, decision-making, and responding. This is troubling, considering the evidence showing that neurocognitive development is a continuing process with brain maturation not yet complete until the mid-twenties.[35] In this respect it has been pointed out that adolescents and even young adults are still developing in aspects of their cognitive and conative functioning that influence culpability in criminal justice contexts.[36]

Holding youth criminally responsible means providing convincing evidence that their offending behaviour was committed while fully cognisant of the wrongfulness of their action, and that they had the capacity to restrain themselves from engaging in the behaviour. Noting these two psychological capacities, and that both need to be present, the concern is whether adolescents possess them and whether they emerge at the same time in the developing individual. Cauffman et al. cautioned that although adolescents may be capable of reasoning and making mature decisions, their ability to give effect to such decisions is highly vulnerable to contextual influences, meaning their responses are easily influenced by the emotional arousal of the situation or by others in the environment, such as peers.[37] Neurodevelopment research has also shown that the capacity to exercise restraint and control, particularly in situations of high emotional arousal, lags behind the capacity to reason and consider alternatives by as much as five years.[38] This is highly significant in the context of the two-legged test of cognitive and conative capacities used to prove criminal responsibility.

A further issue in the neurocognitive development of youth, relates to their susceptibility to reward-seeking and risk-taking behaviours. In their amicus brief in *Roper v Simmons*, the American Psychological Association, noted that adolescence is characterised by heightened risk-taking, which is not an enduring trait, but a developmental one that usually diminishes with adult maturity.[39] Supporting Simmons' argument against the death penalty, they pointed out that an individual prone to risky (or even offending) behaviour during adolescence may abstain from such behaviour as an adult, and linked this to neurobiological development. In their study of brain development across developmental stages, using functional magnetic resonance imaging techniques, Padmanabhan et al. concluded,

"Our results support current models regarding adolescent immaturities in reward processing and cognitive control, suggesting that an overall over-reactive reward response may enhance engaging in behaviors that result in immediate rewards. Taken together, these findings indicate immaturities in the developing brain that could be especially vulnerable to risk taking and other suboptimal behaviors during adolescence".[40]

Essentially, the neurodevelopmental research suggests that at no other time in human development are reward-seeking and risk-taking propensities so strong. Studies of the brain's limbic system, which is involved in controlling emotions, revealed that adolescent decision-making is more influenced by emotion than evident in adults.[41] There is also evidence that adolescents over-value rewards that can be immediately attained over those that are delayed, which speaks to their limited capacity to delay gratification, and brain development and maturation in this respect continues until at least the age of 21 years.[42]

In summary, the current brain development science does not confirm that adolescents are fully capable of making and executing rational decisions in situations of high emotion, which is the context of most offending behaviours. This is compounded by the fact that adolescence is a period of heightened tendencies toward reward-seeking and risk-taking. These neurodevelopmental characteristics raise questions about the extent to which adolescents can be held criminally responsible, considering their cognitive and conative controls. Given their less mature decision-making and restraint capacity, compared to adults, adolescents should perhaps be considered less culpable than adults, and receive less severe punishments.[43] However, the diminished culpability model carries with it several complexities of measurement and scale relating to the offence, the adolescent's maturity, and the level of responsibility that should be accorded.[44]

Conclusion

With the numbers of children in conflict with the law, and the increasing body of knowledge regarding brain development, there is an urgent need for close collaboration between legal and child development experts to figure out a more appropriate, rights-based approach to dealing with affected children. While public concern and outcries over the rate and severity of offending behaviour by children need to be acknowledged, it is vital that responses take cognisance of the neurodevelopment science, while also ensuring that offending youth learn the error of their ways and understand that there are consequences to their actions. However, whether such consequences should occur within the criminal justice system is a matter of concern that warrants serious deliberation. This includes careful thought about the extent to which criminal conviction and incarceration of adolescents necessarily serve the desired outcome of rehabilitation. In addition, the multiple concerns regarding the variations in the MACR globally, the difficulties inherent in the rebuttable presumption and the assessment of criminal responsibility in youth, warrant re-examination of the policy and procedural components relating to children in conflict with the law.

Notes

1 US Department of Justice, "Law Enforcement and Juvenile Crime" (2022), available at: www.ojjdp.gov/ojstatbb/crime/qa05101.asp.
2 South African Police Services, "Crime Statistics" (2020), available at: www.saps.gov.za/services/april_to_march_2019_20_presentation.pdf.
3 While it is acknowledged that the terms criminal responsibility and criminal capacity have distinct, nuanced meanings, they are used interchangeably in this work, with the latter favoured by the South African child justice legislation.

4. ME Lamb & MPY Sim, "Developmental Factors Affecting Children in Legal Contexts", *Youth Justice*, vol. 13, no. 2 (2013), p.131.
5. See: American Psychological Association, "Roper v. Simons" (2014), available at: www.apa.org/about/offices/ogc/amicus/roper.aspx.
6. ES Scott & L Steinberg, *Rethinking Juvenile Justice* (Harvard University Press: Cambridge, MA, 2008), p.20.
7. R Church, B Goldson, & N Hindley, "The Minimum Age of Criminal Responsibility: Clinical, Criminological/Sociological, Developmental and Legal Perspectives", *Youth Justice*, vol. 13, no. 2 (2013), p.99.
8. Child Rights International Network, "Minimum Ages of Criminal Responsibility Around the World" (2018), available at: https://archive.crin.org/en/home/ages.html.
9. L Haysom, "Raising the Minimum Age of Criminal Responsibility to 14 Years", *Journal of Paediatrics and Child Health*, vol. 58 (2022), p.1504.
10. AL Pillay, "The Minimum Age of Criminal Responsibility, International Variation, and the Dual Systems Model in Neurodevelopment", *Journal of Child and Adolescent Mental Health*, vol. 31, no. 3 (2019), p.224 at p.226.
11. United Nations Committee on the Rights of the Child, "General Comment No. 10: Children's Rights in Juvenile Justice" (2007), para 17, available at: www2.ohchr.org/english/bodies/crc/docs/AdvanceVersions/GeneralComment10-02feb07.pdf.
12. African Commission on Human and People's Rights, "Principles and Guidelines on the Right to a Fair Trial and Legal Assistance in Africa" (2003), p.18, available at: https://archives.au.int/bitstream/handle/123456789/2065/Right%20to%20a%20Fair%20Trial_E.pdf?sequence=1&isAllowed=y.
13. N Espejo, "Specialised Child Justice Systems in Latin America", in W O'Brien & C Foussard (eds), *Violence Against Children in the Criminal Justice System: Global Perspectives on Prevention* (Routledge: London, 2019), p.94.
14. Child Justice Amendment Act 2019 (SA), s 11.
15. UNCRC, "General Comment No. 10", para 16.
16. S Bandalli, "Abolition of the Presumption of *Doli Incapax* and the Criminalisation of Children", *Howard Journal of Criminal Justice*, vol. 37, no. 2 (1998), p.114 at p.115; T Crofts, "Reforming the Age of Criminal Responsibility", *South African Journal of Psychology*, vol. 46, no. 4 (2016), p.436 at p.441.
17. RN Turner, G Hodson, & K Dhont "The Role of Individual Differences in Understanding and Enhancing Intergroup Contact", *Social and Personality Psychology Compass*, vol. 14, no. 6 (2020), p.1 at p.2.
18. T Crofts, "*RP v The Queen*: Rebutting the Presumption of *Doli Incapax*", *LSJ Online* (2017), available at: https://lsj.com.au/articles/rp-v-the-queen-rebutting-the-presumption-of-doli-incapax/.
19. CRIN, "Minimum Ages of Criminal Responsibility".
20. Crofts, "Reforming the Age", p.441.
21. K Fitz-Gibbon, "Protections for Children Before the Law: an empirical analysis of the age of criminal responsibility, the abolition of *doli incapax* and the merits of a developmental immaturity defence in England and Wales", *Criminology & Criminal Justice*, vol. 16, no. 4 (2016), p.391 at p.392.
22. AL Pillay & C Willows, "Assessing the Criminal Capacity of Children: a challenge to the capacity of mental health professionals", *Journal of Child & Adolescent Mental Health*, vol. 27, no. 2 (2015), p.91 at p.93.
23. Crofts, "Reforming the Age", p.443.
24. Child Justice Amendment Act 2019 (SA), s 11.
25. CR Snyman, *Criminal Law* (LexisNexis: Durban, 2008), p.162.
26. Pillay & Willows, "Assessing the Criminal Capacity", p.99.
27. N Wortley, "Merely Naughty or Seriously Wrong? 'Childish Sexual Experimentation' and the Presumption of *Doli Incapax*: R v PF [2017] EWCA Crim 983", *Journal of Criminal Law*, vol. 81, no. 5 (2017), p.346 at p.347.
28. I Freckelton, "Children's Responsibility for Criminal Conduct: The Principle of *Doli Incapax* under Contemporary Australian Law: *RP v The Queen* [2016] HCA 53", *Psychiatry, Psychology, and Law*, vol. 24, no. 6 (2017), p.793 at p.794.

29 Snyman, *Criminal Law*, p.162.
30 L Steinberg & ES Scott, "Less Guilty by Reason of Adolescence: Developmental Immaturity, Diminished Responsibility and the Juvenile Death Penalty", *American Psychologist*, vol. 58, no. 12 (2003), p.1009 at p.1016; A Padmanabhan et al, "Developmental Changes in Brain Function underlying the Influence of Reward Processing on Inhibitory Control", *Developmental Cognitive Neuroscience*, vol. 1, no. 4 (2011), p.517 at p.527.
31 UNCRC, "General Comment No. 10", para 16.
32 E Sowell et al, "In Vivo Evidence for Post-adolescent Brain Maturation in Frontal and Striatal Regions", *Nature Neuroscience*, vol. 2 (1999), p.859.
33 Steinberg & Scott, "Less Guilty by Reason of Adolescence", p.1013.
34 J Ryberg, "Punishing Adolescents – on immaturity and diminished responsibility", *Neuroethics*, vol. 7 (2014), p.327 at p.328.
35 SB Johnson, RW Blum, & JN Giedd, "Adolescent Maturity and the Brain: The promise and pitfalls of neuroscience research in adolescent health policy", *Journal of Adolescent Health*, vol. 45, no. 3 (2009), p.216.
36 G Icenogle et al, "Adolescents' cognitive capacity reaches adult levels prior to their psychosocial maturity: Evidence for a 'maturity gap' in a multinational, cross-sectional sample", *Law and Human Behavior*, vol. 43, no. 1 (2019), p.69 at p.88.
37 Cauffman et al, "How Developmental Science Influences Juvenile Justice Reform", *UC Irvine Law Review*, vol. 8, no. 1 (2018), p.21 at p.28.
38 L Steinburg and G Icenogle, "Using Developmental Science to Distinguish Adolescents and Adults under the Law", *Annual Review of Developmental Psychology*, (2019), p.21.
39 APA, "*Roper v Simmons*", p.5.
40 Padmanabhan et al, "Developmental Changes", p.527.
41 M Arain et al, "Maturation of the Adolescent Brain", *Neuropsychiatric Disease and Treatment*, vol. 9 (2013), p.449 at p.453.
42 Steinberg and Icenogle, "Using Developmental Science", p.29.
43 Cauffman et al, "How Developmental Science Influences", p.29.
44 Ryberg, "Punishing Adolescents", pp.333–335.

References

Legislation

Child Justice Amendment Act 2019 (SA)

Books and book chapters

Espejo N, "Specialised child justice systems in Latin America", in O'Brien W & Foussard C (eds), *Violence Against Children in the Criminal Justice System. Global Perspectives on Prevention* (Routledge: London, 2019).
Scott ES & Steinberg L, *Rethinking Juvenile Justice* (Harvard University Press: Cambridge MA, 2008).
Snyman CR, *Criminal Law* (LexisNexis: Durban, 2008).

Journal articles

Arain M, Haque M, Johal L, Mathur P, Nel W, Rais A, Sandhu R, & Sharma S, "Maturation of the adolescent brain", *Neuropsychiatric Disease and Treatment*, vol. 9 (2013), pp.449–461.
Bandalli S, "Abolition of the presumption of *doli incapax* and the criminalisation of children", *Howard Journal of Criminal Justice*, vol. 37, no. 2 (1998), pp.114–123.
Cauffman E, Fine A, Mahler A, & Simmons C, "How developmental science influences juvenile justice reform", *UC Irvine Law Review*, vol. 8, no. 1 (2018), pp.21–40.
Church R, Goldson B, & Hindley N, "The minimum age of criminal responsibility: Clinical, criminological/sociological, developmental and legal perspectives", *Youth Justice*, vol. 13, no. 2 (2013), pp.99–101.

Crofts T, "Reforming the age of criminal responsibility", *South African Journal of Psychology*, vol. 46, no. 4 (2016), pp.436–448.

Fitz-Gibbon K, "Protections for children before the law: An empirical analysis of the age of criminal responsibility, the abolition of *doli incapax* and the merits of a developmental immaturity defence in England and Wales", *Criminology & Criminal Justice*, vol. 16, no. 4 (2016), pp.391–409.

Freckelton I, "Children's responsibility for criminal conduct: The principle of *doli incapax* under contemporary Australian law: RP v The Queen [2016] HCA 53", *Psychiatry, Psychology, and Law*, vol. 24, no. 6 (2017), pp.793–801.

Giedd J, Blumenthal J, Jeffries N, Castllanos F, Liu H, Zijdenbos A, Paus T, Evans AC, & Rapoport JL, "Brain development during childhood and adolescence", *Nature Neuroscience*, vol. 2 (1999), pp.861–863.

Haysom L, "Raising the minimum age of criminal responsibility to 14 years", *Journal of Paediatrics and Child Health*, vol. 58 (2022), pp.1504–1507.

Icenogle G, Steinberg L, Duell N, Chein J, Chang L, Chaudhary N, Di Giunta L, Dodge KA, Fanti KA, Lansford JE, Oburu P, Pastorelli C, Skinner AT, Sorbring E, Tapanya S, Uribe Tirado LM, Alampay LP, Al-Hassan SM, Takash HMS, & Bacchini D, "Adolescents' cognitive capacity reaches adult levels prior to their psychosocial maturity: Evidence for a 'maturity gap' in a multinational, cross-sectional sample", *Law and Human Behavior*, vol. 43, no. 1 (2019), pp.69–85.

Johnson SB, Blum RW, & Giedd JN, "Adolescent maturity and the brain: The promise and pitfalls of neuroscience research in adolescent health policy", *Journal of Adolescent Health*, vol. 45, no. 3 (2009), pp.216–221.

Lamb ME & Sim MPY, "Developmental factors affecting children in legal context", *Youth Justice*, vol. 13, no. 2 (2013), pp.131–144.

Padmanabhan A, Geier CF, Ordaz SJ, Teslovich T, & Luna B, "Developmental changes in brain function underlying the influence of reward processing on inhibitory control", *Developmental Cognitive Neuroscience*, vol. 1, no. 4 (2011), pp.517–529.

Pillay AL, "The minimum age of criminal responsibility, international variation, and the Dual Systems Model in neurodevelopment", *Journal of Child and Adolescent Mental Health*, vol. 31, no. 3 (2019), pp.224–235.

Ryberg J, "Punishing adolescents – On immaturity and diminished responsibility", *Neuroethics*, vol. 7 (2014), pp.327–336.

Sowell E, Thompson P, Holmes C, Jernigan T, & Toga A, "In vivo evidence for post-adolescent brain maturation in frontal and striatal regions", *Nature Neuroscience*, vol. 2 (1999), pp.859–861.

Steinberg L & Icenogle G, "Using developmental science to distinguish adolescents and adults under the law", *Annual Review of Developmental Psychology*, vol. 1 (2019), pp.21–40.

Steinberg L & Scott ES, "Less guilty by reason of adolescence: Developmental immaturity, diminished responsibility, and the juvenile death penalty", *American Psychologist*, vol. 58, no. 12 (2003), pp.1009–1018.

Turner RN, Hodson G, & Dhont K, "The role of individual differences in understanding and enhancing intergroup contact", *Social and Personality Psychology Compass*, vol. 14, no. 6 (2020), e12533, pp.1–17.

Wortley N, "Merely naughty or seriously wrong? 'Childish sexual experimentation' and the presumption of *doli incapax*: R v PF [2017] EWCA Crim 983", *Journal of Criminal Law*, vol. 81, no. 5 (2017), pp.346–349.

Reports and websites

African Union, "Principles and guidelines on the right to a fair trial and legal assistance in Africa" (2003), available at: https://archives.au.int/bitstream/handle/123456789/2065/Right%20to%20a%20Fair%20Trial_E.pdf?sequence=1&isAllowed=y

American Psychological Association, "Roper v. Simons" (2014), available at www.apa.org/about/offices/ogc/amicus/roper.aspx

Child Rights International Network, "Minimum ages of criminal responsibility around the world" (2018), available at: https://archive.crin.org/en/home/ages.html

Crofts T, "RP v The Queen: rebutting the presumption of doli incapax", *LSJ Online* (2017), available at: https://lsj.com.au/articles/rp-v-the-queen-rebutting-the-presumption-of-doli-incapax/

South African Police Services, *Crime Statistics* (2020), available at: www.saps.gov.za/services/april_to_march_2019_20_presentation.pdf

United Nations Committee on the Rights of the Child, "General Comment No. 10. Children's rights in Juvenile Justice" (2007), available at: www2.ohchr.org/english/bodies/crc/docs/AdvanceVersions/GeneralComment10-02feb07.pdf

US Department of Justice, "Law enforcement and juvenile crime" (2022), available at: www.ojjdp.gov/ojstatbb/crime/qa05101.asp.

INDEX

Note: Endnotes are indicated by the page number followed by "n" and the note number e.g., 177n20 refers to note 20 on page 177.

accountability 37–38 *see also* corporate accountability; answerability and liability 37–38; and reciprocal responsibility 41–45; and responsibility as relational 37–41; and socio-economic factors 40–41, 44–45

age of criminal responsibility 360–61, 392–93; arbitrariness and unfairness of 400; appropriate age, and measurement of 399–400; Beijing Rules (UN) 393, 399–400; brain development, and impact on child behaviour 324, 336, 364–65, 398; child criminal actions, and avoidance of the impulse to commit 397–98; child criminalisation, and impact of 335–36; child development and psychological foundations of 395–96; child justice system, and age considerations 361–62, 366–67; child maturity, and measurement of 324, 336, 368–69; childhood status, and safeguarding rights 337; debates relating to 363–65; international rules and regulations relating to 393–94; introduction of, and changes to 333, 334–35, 365; juvenile court, and development of 334; policy arguments, and challenges to 365–67; purpose and function of 392–93; right and wrong, and understanding of criminality 396–97; rules and regulations governing children 337, 367, 399–400, 441; social and environmental influences, and consideration of 364–65, 398–99; trial and punishments, and age-related process and procedures 360–61, 443; UN Committee on the Rights of a Child 336, 361, 442–43; variations on and international views of 393, 441–42; young offender institutions, and child detention 366

Alexander, Larry 175

Antill, Gregory 65

banking Australian banking sector, culture and standards 409; corporate wrongdoing, and civil sanctions for 412–13; Irish Banking sector, professional standards for 409–10; Lambert Review 409; misconduct in financial services sector, and regulatory standards to address 409–10; professional bodies for, and formation of 409; professionalisation of, and need for 408–10, 413–14; regulatory standards and obligations 409

Becker, Gary 222–23

blameworthiness concepts 3–4, 82–84, 232–33; basic elements of 233; blame, and didactic function of 62–63; capacity and agency, considerations of 87, 89; cognates, and agency of 84–87; corporate accountability, and approach to 7, 344–45; criminal culpability, and framework of 14, 19, 20, 21, 144; culpability and wrongness, and relation between 236–38, 239–40; cultural conditioning, and patterns of blaming 13–14; danger formations, and concept of 19–20; definition and functions 82–83; emotions and emotional factors 161; formalism, and

453

Index

'legal guilt' 65, 89; harmfulness, and harm to others 233–34; harmfulness, culpability and wrongness, and relation between 238–40; joint enterprise law, and parasitic accessional liability doctrine 21–22; moral and political considerations 14, 19; and motive 237; non-human 'agents,' and blame 85–87; responsibility attribution, and measurement of 62–63; and retributive theory 5; 'sifting' of blame and blameworthiness 88–89; socio-contextual factors, and approach to blame 31; tort law, and blameworthy conduct 211; worthiness of blame, and concept of 85; wrongness, and wrongful acts 234–36

capacity *see also* criminal insanity and mental disorder; and age of criminal responsibility 7, 8, 443; and agency of children 7, 8, 17, 319, 337, 362–65, 367–69, 392–94; assessments for, and challenges of 444–46; and character attributes 17

Carrara, Francesco 113

casuistic reasoning 138–39; malice and negligence, and consideration of 142–43; Medieval period, and description of criminal responsibility 139–41; offender's intention, and degrees of volition 139–41, 142–43; sin and salvation, and considerations of punishments 139–40

childhood criminal records criminal law, and responsibility of children 367–69; Disclosure and Barring Service (DBS), and criminal record checks 321–22; disclosure of, and long-term impact 7, 319–20, 323; employment implications, and disclosure of 321; multiple conviction rule 321; personal agency and age of offending behaviour 324; Police intelligence, and retention of 321–22; proportionality of punishment 322–23; Rehabilitation of Offenders Act (1974), rules for and exceptions to 320–21; sentencing decisions, and impact of 320–21, 322, 324–25; welfare principles, and foundational rights 322–23

children 7, 440–41 *see also* age of criminal responsibility, *also* childhood criminal records; capacity and age of criminal responsibility 7, 8, 319, 337, 362–65, 366, 367–69, 392–94, 441–42; 'Child First' vision 7, 323–24, 332–33, 334–35, 337; criminal behaviour, involvement in and changes to 440; cultural variations in child development 442; foundational rights for children and theory of 320, 324; maturation, and complexities of 324, 336, 368–69; mental health problems, and childhood offending 366; school-leaving age, and changes to 337; UN Convention on the Rights of the Child (UNCRC) 324; Youth Justice Board, and role of 332, 333

civil responsibility aims and effects of 262–64; attributing responsibility, and process for 261–62; compensation for injuries claims, and issues with 226–62; criminal responsibility, and distinctions between 258–59; and definition of 258; dignitarian or emotional harm, and damages for 263–64; rape cases and sexual offences, and treatment of 260, 263–65

civility and civil society 18–19

Claro, Giulio 140–41

Classical School of Law, Positivist School, and challenge to 112–13

codification Model Penal Code (MPC) 5, 169–70, 172, 177n20, 236, 243n26; Zandarelli Code 112, 113–14

colonialism *see also* imperialism; African colonisation 111–12; colonial criminal law, and principles of 111–12; criminal law debate (19th century) 112; Horn of Africa, and colonial developments in 113; Italy and Italian colonisation 111–12; Positivist School, and development of 112–13; Zandarelli Code 112, 113–14

corporate accountability 6–7, 307–08, 343 *see also* corporate wrongdoing; banking professionalisation, and development of 408–10; blameworthiness concepts, and approach to 7, 344–45; causal chains, and complexities of 347–48; codes of conduct initiatives 308–09; corporate criminality, and prosecution challenges 343; corporate intention and *mens rea* requirements 348–51; and corporation identity, development of and legal status 344–46; and criminal libel charges 345; elements of law, and application of 346–51; enforcement mechanisms, and development of 7; environmental and socio-economic violations 314; failure to prevent crime offences 349–50; fault attribution, and corporate culture 350; harms and causation, and proof of guilt 346–47; human rights accountability, and legal obligations 308–10; identification doctrine, and corporate liability 349, 407–08; individualistic nature of criminal law, and limitations of 344–45, 347; international crimes, and domestic jurisdiction over 312; International Criminal Court, shared responsibility principles and jurisdiction of 312, 313–14; international criminal law, and avenues for 312–14; international rules and obligations, and transnational corporations 307, 309–12; large-scale harms 7; and legal personhood 344; legally binding

454

accountability initiatives, and development of 308–12; opioid crisis (USA), and corporate responsibility for 347–48; and prevention of corporate crimes 8; public nuisance charges and non-feasance 345–46; reparations, and reparation orders 313; shareholder liability, and limitations of 344; temporal coincidence requirement, and application of 351

Corporate Social Responsibility (CSR) 309

corporate wrongdoing 406; banking sector 412–13; control theory, and maintenance of social order 410–11; criminal liability, designation of and challenges with 406–08; fines and civil sanctions 413; group morality and promotion of ethical conduct 411; misconduct in financial services sector, and regulatory standards to address 409–10, 412–13; professionalisation, and need for 408–10; regulatory offences 407; resistance to, and integrated model for 410–12; self-regulation, and enforcement of 411

crime and punishment 144; criminal culpability, and codification process 2, 13, 143–44; knowledge conditions, changes to and impact on 273–74; legal definitions and purpose 62; neuroscientific developments, and legal impact of 274; Scottish legal doctrine, and concepts of self-defence 160–61; theorisation of (XVI century) 141–43; and tort law 5, 206–07

Criminal Injuries Compensation Scheme (CICS) 258; aims of 263; award of claims, and restrictions of 261–62; compensatory criteria 260–61

criminal insanity 6, 246–47; criterion for and evaluation of 249–50, 251–52; imbecility, and moral insanity 54–55; impaired reality understanding, and definition of 252; legal and psychiatric constructs, and challenging associations of 251–52; legal definition for 48; legal doctrine relating to, and need for clarification on 247, 252–53; 'mixed model' doctrines 246; neurological conditions, and neurotechnological interventions 376–77, 379–81; Norwegian legal approach to 248–49; personality disorders, and consideration of 252; psychiatry, and academic developments in 250; psychosis, and mental state of 248–49; status excuse approach 250–51

cultural theory cultural apparatus of criminal law 15–16; cultural conditioning, and patterns of blaming 13–14; hegemony, and common sense 15–16

d'Almeida, Duarte L. 182, 191n3
d'Amelio, Mariano 116, 118

danger formations and conception of 19–20; social and political construction of 20–21; and social change 20–21; structures of feeling, and concept of 20–22

defences theory 5 *see also* duress of circumstances; duress of circumstances 289–91; emotions and emotional factors 60, 155–56; and excuse doctrine 60, 69–70; and incorporationalist position on 180–83; and justification theory 180, 185–86; medical applications of 5; modern slavery defence 6, 294–96; necessity defence 6, 158–59, 196, 298; offence/defence dichotomy, and developments in knowledge conditions 277–78; personalised responsibility, and future developments in 278; practical reasoning considerations 183–85; Raz, Joseph, and view of 183–85; Scottish self-defence doctrine 160–61; self-defence justifications 94, 156, 157–58, 159–60; situational partial excuse defence (SPE) 31–32; tort law 212

desistance theory 3, 59–60; community-oriented benefits of 70; doctrinal reform, and offender-oriented benefits 69–70; excuse doctrine, and neutralisation 69–70; objectives of 67; relational nature of 68; responsibility attribution, and significance of 67–69; social cohesion, and promotion of 66, 70–71

dispositional-relational responsibility 4, 123–24, 128–29, 133; actions, and motivation considerations 125; agency and character relations 124–25; character/disposition, and responsibility for 130–31; dreams, and responsibility for 131–32; hierarchical account of responsibility 124–25; human identity, and relations of 129; 'mesh theory,' and human moral psychology 124, 134n2; objections to 131–32; psychological foundations of 132; sociological implications 132–33; unconscious motivation, and challenges of 126–27; and value alienation 125–26, 127–28

doli incapax, and abolition of 8, 334, 336, 363, 364, 393, 442–44

Douglas, Mary 14, 19

duress of circumstances 6, 289–91; challenges to 290–91; coercion 94; and cognitive theories of emotion 157, 158–59; compulsion and modern slavery 294–96; drug offences, and guidelines on 292–94; and duress by threats 289; limitations, and application of 290; sentencing considerations as a result of 291–94, 299–300; and socio-contextual factors 30; wrongness, and consideration of 234

ecocide 423 *see also* environmental wrongs; carbon offsetting, and criticisms of 430;

concept definition, and development of 424; criminalisation of, and challenges to 424–26; ecojustice, and ecocide law proposals 425–26, 429–31; environmental knowledge production systems, Western dominance of 430; Independent Expert Panel, definition of 423, 426–29; individual criminal responsibility, and limitations of 429–31; lawful conducts causing environmental damage, and criminalisation of 427–28; and legal definition of 424–25; negligent conduct, and criminalisation of 426; wanton conduct, and criminalisation of 427–28

Elliot, Catherine 398–99

emotion theory 4, 155; and cognitive theory 156; culpability, and reactive defence 155–58; and duress defence 60, 157, 158–59; and legal processes relating to 155; self-defence, and legal doctrine for 156, 157–58, 159–61

environmental wrongs 8; and corporate accountability 314; 'ecocide,' and criminalisation of 423

Feinberg, Joel 233
Ferri, Enrico 113
Ferzan, Kimberly 175
Filangieri, Gaetano 144
Frankfurt, Harry 124
Freud, Sigmund 131

Gambiglioni, Angelo 140
Gardner, John 180; justification theory, and view of 185–86
Garofalo, Raffaele 116
Gramsci, Antonio 15
Green, David 407

Hall, Stuart 15
Hart, H.L.A. 207
hegemony civility and civil society, and maintenance of 18–19; historical and institutional factors 16; and legal rationality 19; state ideologies, and common vision 15–16
Higgins, Polly 424, 429, 430
Hollingsworth, K. 322, 323
Holmes, Oliver Wendell (Jr.) 83, 87–88
homicide 232–33; and culpability 236
Hörnle, Tatjana 195–96
human identity character/disposition, and responsibility for 130–31; human experience and life cycle 129; influences on 129; and relations 129
human rights African region, the Malabo Protocol and initiatives relating to 311–12; Inter-American Court on Human Rights 311; international rules and obligations, and transnational corporations 309–11; UN Human Rights Commission, and initiatives developed by 309–11

Husak, Douglas 66, 172–75; recklessness and negligence, and view of 178n26

imperialism 3, 47; Italian Colonialism; and Anglicisation 3, 47; and civilisation of society 48–49, 51–52; colonial criminal law, and 'two speed' application 111–12, 114–16; cultural and racial superiority 113–14; exploitative and imperialistic policies 113; positivist theory, and principles of 111; primitivism, and view of mental capacity 49–50, 53, 114–15, 116; race and racial hierarchies 49–50; and the 'rule of colonial difference' 53; subjecthood, and imperial governance 51–52, 53

incorporationism challenges, and implications of 182–83, 190–91; denials/defences and offences/defences, and differences of 180–83, 190

Indigenous laws in settler colonial contexts and developments in knowledge conditions 276; Indigenous populations, and the rule of law 52–53, 114–16

intimate partner violence, and criminal justice developments in 275–76

ius commune doctrine 143; development of 138–39

joint enterprise and accomplice liability 22; parasitic accessorial liability doctrine (PAL) 21–22

justification theory 180; collision of duties defence 194, 195–96, 197; explanatory reasons 185, 187; guiding reasons 185–87; and hierarchy of rationality 187–88; necessity defence 196; permission view 188–89; reasonableness, and rehabilitation 189–90

knowledge conditions changes to, and challenges of 6, 272–73, 277, 281–82; cognitive sciences and social scientific knowledges, and developments in 272, 274, 275; criminal law practices, and impact of 273–74; genetics and epigenetics, and developments in 274; intimate partner violence, and criminal justice developments 275–76; lived experience knowledge, and legitimation of 276; mental capacity and brain disorders, and advancements in 279; offence/defence dichotomy, and challenges of 277–78; perpetrator and victim dichotomy, and changes to 279–80; responsibility and non- or partial responsibility dichotomy, and outcomes of criminal process 280–82; technical knowledges, and advancements in 272, 274–75; trauma and victims of violence, and developments in 279–80; trust, reduction in and rise of 276–77; victims' movements, and rise of 276

Kräpelin, Emil 116

Lacey, Nicola 14, 16–17, 362
Lippke, Richard 30–31
Loewald, Hans 132
Lombroso, Cesare 112–13, 117–18; 'median occipital fossa' discovery, and born-criminal theory 112

market misconduct 5, 219–21, 223; deterrence, and economic theory of 222–23; economic models, and market competition 225–26; economic theory and criminal law 220–21, 224–25; fault, criminal or moral and issues of 220; *homo economics* theoretic model, and economic rationality 221–23; *homo juridicus* theoretic model 223–25; market function and regulation 225; market relations and transactions 225; risk factors, and excessive recklessness 226–27

Maudsley, Henry 50, 53–54

medical triage justification defence 193–94; collision of duties defence 194, 195–96, 197; and criminal liability considerations 194; *ex ante pre-emptive* triage scenarios 197, 199; *ex ante* triage scenarios 193, 195–96, 198; *ex post* triage scenarios 196–97; human life, equality and imponderability of 198–99; necessity defence 196; rights-centred system, and impact of 197–98; survival expectations, and consolidation of 199–201; utility-maximising killing 194, 197, 202n4

mens rea principles 5, 13, 17, 62, 94, 143; corporate intention and *mens rea* requirements 348–51; definition of 170–72; intent and conscious planning 13; mental disorder, and negation of 95–96; negligence and recklessness considerations 5, 170–72

mental disorder 4, 93, 246–47 *see also* criminal insanity; behavioural neuroscience, and view of 93, 383–84; capacity, and child responsibility 7, 8, 319, 337, 362–65, 367–69; insanity, and legal definition for 48–49, 94–95, 383–84; and intellectual disability 4; *mens rea* principles, and negation of 95–96; personality disorders 252; rules for and responses to 94–96; self-regulating tests for 95

Mill, John Stuart 221–22, 223

M'Naghten test 7–8, 48, 50, 54, 95, 376, 381–84

modern slavery defence 6, 294–95; exploitation, and evidence of 297–98; human trafficking, victims of 297; Modern Slavery Act (2015), and application of 294–96; procedures, and problems with 296–97

Moore, Michael 248, 250
Morris, Herbert 132

negligence and recklessness 169–70; and difference between 172–75; and misperception or misestimation 175–76; Model Penal Code (MPC) definitions 169–70, 172, 177n20; risk awareness, and issues of 173–76

neurotechnology and behavioural neuroscience 93, 376–77; agency, and questions of 99–101; and biological variables 101–02; brain development, and impact on child behaviour 324, 336, 364–65, 398, 446–48; brain implants and surgical procedures, and impact of 376–77, 379–80; brain-computer interface device 382; and compatibilism theory 100; determinism, and challenge of 99–100; development of and advances in 377–79; and epiphenomenalism 100–01; future technologies, hypothetical responses to and legal position of 380–85; insanity and mental integrity, and criminal law scholarship 379–80; law, and challenges of 99–101; legal applications of 96; limitations of 96–99; mental capacity, and impact of neurotechnical intervention 378–79; neuroimaging and fMRI techniques 97; neurological and genetic disorders 97; neuroscientific data, and legal relevance of 101–03; neurotechnological failure, and risk of 378–79; scans and imaging, and value of 102–03; scientific developments in 96–97, 446–48; studies and research analysis 98–99

Nicholson, David, Dr 54

Ongwen, Dominic 430

personhood agency, and understanding of 60–61; and the 'norm of reasoning' 60

Positivist School of Law 4, 117–18; Classical School of Law, and challenge to 112–13; colonialism, and principles of 111; development of 112–13; free will debate 113

practical reasoning and defence theory 183–85; first-order and second-order reasons 183–84; and reason assessment types 184

rational agency paradigm blame, and didactic function of 62–63; individualism, in relation to 64–65, 67–68; moralism and formalism 65–66; punitive credentials of 63–64,

70–71; reason-responsiveness theory 65–66; responsibility attribution, and measurement of 62–63
Ravizza, Adelgiso 111
Raymond of Peñafort 140
Raz, Joseph 180; defences theory, and view of 183–85
reactive defences 155–56 *see also* defences theory; culpability, and paradigms of 156–58; legal landscape relating to 158–60; provocations and motivating factors 158–60; self-defence justifications, and reasonable response 159–60
reciprocal responsibility and accountability 41–45
Reeves, Craig 60
relational and reciprocal accountability 3, 61; public blaming, and impact of 61
retributive theory 5
Roman law, *Corpus Iuris Civilis* 139
Ruggie, John 309

Sands, Philippe 426–27
sentencing determinations 32–33; child sentencing decisions, and impact of 320–21, 322, 324–25; duress of circumstances, and considerations as a result of 291–94, 299–300; mental disorder, punishment and sentencing models for 116–17
sexual wrongs 6; civil and criminal responsibility, and boundaries of 6
Smith, Adam 221
socio-contextual factors 3, 26–27; accountability, and injustice of 40–41, 44–45; age of criminal responsibility, and influence of 364–65; blameworthiness concepts, and approach to 31; 'chronic temptations,' and capacity for self-control 30–31; and duress of circumstances 30; fairness, and consideration of 31; human conduct, and impact of 28; intimate partner violence, and criminal justice developments in 275–76; legal doctrine, and lack of consideration for 27–28; negative social environments, and criminogenic effects of 28–29; neurobiological impacts of 29; rationality and autonomy, and capacity for 29–30; sentencing determinations, and consideration of 32–33; situational partial excuse defence (SPE) 31–32; social and environmental influences, and consideration of 27–28; and social injustice 26; social scientific knowledge conditions, and impact on criminal law 272, 274, 275; voluntarist model, and impact of 3, 27–28
Souris, Renee Nicole 399
Stephen, James Fitzjames 51
Strawson, Peter 89

Tadros, Victor 124–25, 126
Thomson, Judith 234
tort law blameworthiness and blameworthy conduct 211; causation 211–12; civil liability, and criminal procedures 209–10, 213; criminal and civil fault, and integration of 210; criminal law, and differences of 5, 206–07; damage and fault 210–11; defences 212; and definition of responsibility 207; prescription, and limitation periods 213–14; principles of 209–10; remedies and outcomes 208; standards of proof, and procedural expressions of responsibility 212–13; tort and criminal proceedings, timing and binding rules 214; vehicles for responsibility 208–09
Tractatus criminalis (Deciani, Tiberio) 142–43, 147n38
Tsai, George 62–63
Tuke, Daniel Hack 47, 50, 54

UN Human Rights Commission 309–11

voluntarist model 34n19; free-will, and concepts of 156–57; and socio-economic factors 3, 27–28

Walker, S., 396–97
Watson, Gary 124
Williams, Raymond 14, 15; structures of feeling concept 20–22